T5-AEU-288

WESTERN PERSPECTIVES

A CONCISE HISTORY OF CIVILIZATION

This book may be kept

FOURTEEN DAYS

A fine will be charged for each day the book is kept overtime.

GAYLORD 142			PRINTED IN U.S.A.

WESTERN PERSPECTIVES

A CONCISE HISTORY OF CIVILIZATION

T. WALTER WALLBANK

Emeritus Professor of History, University of Southern California

ALASTAIR M. TAYLOR

Professor of Political Studies and Geography, Queen's University

NELS M. BAILKEY

Professor of History, Tulane University

Southern Baptist College
FELIX GOODSON
LIBRARY
Walnut Ridge, Ark.

SCOTT, FORESMAN AND COMPANY

Glenview, Illinois   Brighton, England

Cover art adapted from the Bayeux Tapestry by Karyn Kozak

Library of Congress Catalog Card Number: 72-92340
ISBN: 0-673-07855-8

Copyright © 1962, 1967, 1971, 1973 by Scott, Foresman and Company,
Glenview, Illinois 60025.
Philippines Copyright 1973 by Scott, Foresman and Company.
All Rights Reserved.

Printed in United States of America.
Regional offices of Scott Foresman and Company are located in Dallas, Texas; Glenview, Illinois;
Oakland, New Jersey; Palo Alto, California; Tucker, Georgia; and Brighton, England.

37,867

910.031
W155w

PREFACE

Western Perspectives answers a long-felt need on the part of many history instructors for a western history which would incorporate many of the proven characteristics of *Civilization Past and Present*. This book has borrowed from its parent volume the breadth of coverage—not only political, but economic, social, intellectual, artistic, religious, and scientific events—which is a hallmark of the previous texts. Without oversimplifying, political and cultural events are described in a vocabulary that is readily understood by college freshmen not only in four-year institutions, but in community or junior colleges as well. The approach of *Civilization Past and Present* has been successfully tested on thousands of students, and those same characteristics have been incorporated into *Western Perspectives*.

Designed for two kinds of western history courses, this book is particularly useful as a core text around which the instructor can build with supplementary lectures and readings. Secondly, the book is especially fitted to situations where a formidable text—either in length or coverage—would be inappropriate. The authors have stressed brevity, a lucid writing style, and a concise approach to the complexities of the past. Believing that good organization and a clear presentation help the student to grasp more easily the fundamentals of western history, the authors have paid close attention to these areas.

In response to students' demands for relevance, a consistent effort has been made throughout the text to point out parallels between earlier events and current situations. The seven Part Openings particularly emphasize these comparisons. Confronted by massive problems, many people tend to view the present as unique, discarding the past as mainly irrelevant. Impatient as one may be to solve present-day difficulties, such an objective is not well served by viewing them without understanding how we got where we are. Historical perspective alone can give the background indispensable for understanding—and coping with—the contemporary world.

In keeping with the objective of providing essential background for contemporary problems, special attention has been paid to the coverage of the decades since World War II. The most recent happenings have been thoroughly incorporated not only in the political sphere, but the cultural as well. Every attempt has been made to present the latest scholarship so that the narrative will support the reader's search for significance in his own time and experience.

The authors have emphasized the fundamental forces which are speeding up change as we move toward the final quarter of the twentieth century. Throughout the book special attention has been paid to technology and its impact on the social environment as well as to explain how the processes of change have increased, especially during the last hundred years. Consequently the text prepares the student for the widespread shifts occurring now and in the years immediately ahead. Evidence of change is all about us—in ideological and political regroupings, in new relationships among the superpowers, and in the unleashings of powerful economic and social forces. The need is greater than ever to understand these seismic changes in their historical perspective.

T.W.W.
A.M.T.
N.M.B.

CONTENTS

PART FOUR 240

CHARTING THE PRESENT

PART FIVE 302

EUROPE'S CENTURY

PROLOGUE
PERSPECTIVE ON MAN

If the time span of our planet—now estimated at some five billion years—were telescoped into a single year, the first eight months would be devoid of any life. The next two months would be taken up with plant and very primitive animal forms, and not until well into December would any mammals appear. In this "year" members of *Homo erectus*, the best known species of "near men," would mount the global stage only between 10 and 11 P.M. on December 31. And how has man spent that brief allotment? He has given over most of it—the equivalent of half a million years or more—to making tools and weapons out of stone. His revolutionary changeover from a food-hunting nomad to a farmer who raised grain and domesticated animals would occur in the last sixty seconds. And into that final minute would be crowded all of his other accomplishments: the use of metal, the creation of civilizations, the mastery of the oceans, the harnessing of steam, then gas, electricity, oil, and, finally, in our own lifetime, atomic energy. But brief though it may have been, man's time on the planet reveals a rich tapestry of religion, art, science and industry. This accumulated experience, the memory of the race, is available for study. We call it *history*.

THE "USE" OF HISTORY

Definition of history. History is the record of the past actions of mankind, based upon surviving evidence. The historian uses this evidence to reach conclusions which he believes are valid. In this way, he becomes an interpreter of the development of mankind. History shows that all patterns and problems in human affairs are the products of a complex process of growth. By throwing light on that process, history provides a means for profiting from human experience. There would be no landmarks, no points of reference, no foundations on which to build if the individual were bereft of the knowledge of his past. The system of

1

government under which he lives, the frontiers of his country, and its economy—
such factors are meaningful because of history. In our age of global interdependence and atomic propulsion, the neglect of history would be more than
folly—it could prove suicidal.

In this connection it is salutary to recall the words of the philosopher George
Santayana when he declared, "Those who cannot remember the past are
condemned to repeat it." Actually, history is itself a way of looking at reality, and
many cultures, particularly food-collecting societies, which tend to exist on a
day-to-day basis, appear to be little aware of their own past, content to live more
or less in the present. As economic, social, and political activities grow more
complex, however, it becomes necessary to keep records—of the grain sown, or
of battles waged over disputed land. A knowledge of the past then becomes
indispensable to decisions that are relevant to contemporary needs and future
prospects. In such literate societies, where knowledge can be written down and
preserved for future use, we find the birth and development of history and the
historical method.

THE "HOW" OF HISTORY

Is history a science?   There is more than one way of treating the past. In dealing
with the American Revolution, for example, the historian may describe its events
in narrative form. Again, he may prefer to analyze its general causes or perhaps
compare its stages of revolution with the patterns of revolutions in other
countries. Because of these descriptive and analytical functions, historical writing
has sometimes been regarded as a science. But the historian does not aim for or
attain the same kind of results as the scientist. The latter can verify his
conclusions by repeating his experiment under controlled conditions in his
laboratory, and he also attempts to classify the phenomenon in a general group or
category. The historian, on the other hand, has to pay much greater attention to
the *uniqueness* of his data, because each event takes place at a particular time and
in a particular place. And since that time is now past, he cannot verify his
conclusions by duplicating the circumstances in which the event occurred.
Moreover, since history is concerned fundamentally with the lives and actions of
men, the search for causes is bound to be relatively subjective.

Nevertheless, historians insist that history be written as scientifically as
possible and that evidence be analyzed with the same objective attitude employed
by the scientist when he examines natural phenomena. This scientific spirit
requires the historian to handle his evidence according to established rules of
historical analysis, to recognize his own biases and attempt to eliminate their
effects from his work, and to draw only such conclusions as the evidence seems to
warrant.

Historical method.   To meet these requirements, historians have evolved the
"historical method." The first step is the search for what is called *sources*, without
which there can be no history. These sources may consist of material remains
such as bones, tools, weapons, and pottery; oral traditions such as myths, legends,
and songs; pictorial data such as drawings and maps; and, of course, written

records ranging from ancient manuscripts to treaties, diaries, books, and yesterday's newspaper.

Having acquired his sources, the historian must next infer from them the facts. This process has two parts. *External criticism* tests the genuineness of the source. The importance of external criticism was demonstrated dramatically in recent years by the unmasking of a hoax—Piltdown man—which had long duped scientists. Generally, however, the historian has to deal with less spectacular problems, such as checking ancient documents for errors that have crept into the text through faulty copying or translating.

The second step in the analytical process is called *internal criticism*. In evaluating written materials, the historian must ascertain the author's meaning and the accuracy of his work. To do so may require study of the language of the era or of the circumstances in which the author's statement was made. A politician's memoirs may be highly suspect because of an almost universal human tendency to present oneself in the most favorable light. Official documents must also be examined for what they may conceal as well as reveal—especially if they are documents released by governments to explain or justify a change in foreign policy or their involvement in a war.

The final step in historical method is *synthesis*. Here the historian must determine which factors in a given situation are most relevant to his purpose, since obviously he cannot include everything that occurred in the period under review. This delicate process of selection underscores the role that subjectivity plays in the writing of history. "The more complex the events dealt with, the wider their spread in time and space, the greater are the calls made upon the historian's judgment."[1]

The problem of periodization. Can we really categorize history as "ancient," "medieval," and "modern"? When we reflect upon this question, it becomes obvious that what is "modern" in the twentieth century could conceivably be considered "medieval" in the twenty-fifth century, and ultimately "ancient" in the thirty-fifth or fortieth century A.D. Yet not to break up the account would be akin to reading this book (or any other) without the benefit of parts, chapters, paragraphs, or even separate sentences. Like time itself, history would then become a ceaseless flow of consciousness and events. To simplify his task and to manage his materials more easily, the historian divides time into periods. The divisions he chooses, the lines he draws, reveal the distinctive way the historian regards the past—namely, in terms of patterns which appear to him logical and meaningful. Needless to say, no two historians see the past in an identical pattern; thus the division of the past into periods is necessarily arbitrary and, like railway or airline timetables, subject to change without prior notice.

THE "WHY" OF HISTORY

Historical analysis. The historian seeks to describe not only *what* has happened in the past and *how* it happened but also *why* society undergoes change. Any search of this kind raises a number of fundamental questions: the roles of Providence, the individual, and the group in history; the extent to which historical events are unique and the extent to which they fit into patterns; and the problem of progress in human affairs. The answers vary with the different philosophical views of mankind.

Providence or the individual. Those who hold the teleological view see in history the guidance of a Divine Will, directing human destinies according to a cosmic purpose. This concept was accepted as self-evident in ancient theocratic societies and remained prevalent in medieval thought, but it lost ground after the Renaissance, when the spread of rationalistic doctrines and scientific triumphs seemed to forecast unlimited progress in human affairs. Yet in our own day there has been a reaction against the nineteenth century's comfortable assumption that man is a completely free agent. One distinguished historian, for example, has asserted that the only tenable interpretation of the human drama is the religious one.[2]

Others have minimized the role of Providence while exalting the role of the individual in the historical process. The nineteenth-century historian Thomas Carlyle maintained that the Alexanders, Muhammads, and Cromwells were the "Great Men" whose leadership chiefly determined the course of human events.

"Laws" and "forces" in history. The opponents of Carlyle's approach often contend that history is determined by "forces" and "laws" and by the actions of entire societies. One geographer, for example, has even argued that a people's genius and progress are decided principally by climate. We can reject such an extreme claim but—as we shall see when we take up the earliest, or fluvial, civilizations—physical environment does play a significant part in the development of human societies.

Sociologists approach history primarily by analyzing the origins, institutions, and functions of groups. Some attach special importance to population factors as criteria for judging the evolution of a given society, while others analyze societies in terms of their division of labor.

Like the sociologist, the economist tends to look at the historical record from the standpoint of group action and especially the impact of economic forces such as that of, say, supply and demand or diminishing returns. Whereas historians have traditionally emphasized political and military events, sociologists and economists have brought a new dimension of interpretation to the study of history, since they are concerned with such areas as the interaction of various classes in a society, the ethics and political consequences of economic philosophies, and the impact of technology upon the living standard and economic well-being of a given society.

Karl Marx's theory of history. The most explosive interpretation of history in modern times was made by Karl Marx. To him, irresistible economic forces governed men and determined the trend of events. Marx contended that the shift from one economic stage to another—such as from feudalism to capitalism—is attained by sporadic upheavals, or revolutions, occurring because the class controlling the methods of production eventually resists further progress in order to maintain its vested interests. Marx predicted that the proletariat would overthrow the exploiting capitalists and that the end result would be a classless society, followed by a gradual withering away of the state itself.

Contrary to his prediction, however, social legislation and higher productivity have enabled the living standards of the "exploited" masses in capitalist countries to become higher than ever before. And instead of the development of a classless society in the Soviet Union, the state controls all aspects of a stratified society in which a wage and privilege differential exists between the administrative and military elites on one hand and the masses of workers and peasants on the other. In short, many of Marx's assumptions have been disproved by events—although a number of later theorists have, in their own ways, attempted to adapt Marxism to the insights of the twentieth century.

Theories of civilization. Numerous other attempts have been made to explain the rise and fall of civilizations according to a set of principles. Oswald Spengler, a disillusioned German, maintained that civilizations were like organisms; each grew with the "superb aimlessness" of a flower and passed through a cycle of spring, summer, autumn, and winter. He declared that western civilization was in its winter period and had already entered a state of rapid decline.

Spengler influenced the English historian Arnold J. Toynbee, whose works became best sellers after World War II. To Toynbee, "challenge and response" explain the rise and fall of civilizations. Man achieves civilization "as a response to a challenge in a situation of special difficulty which rouses him to make a hitherto unprecedented effort."[3] The ancient Egyptians, for example, built their civilization by learning to control the Nile River. Toynbee holds that a civilization continues to grow as long as it is motivated by creative individuals; when they can no longer inspire the majority, social disunity brings about decline and disintegration.

Spengler was not unique in likening societies to organisms. Other thinkers have also sought to explain the life and behavior of human society in terms of biological growth and decay. In particular, the evolutionary hypothesis developed by Charles Darwin had a strong impact upon nineteenth-century intellectuals and gave rise to the concept that the principle of "survival of the fittest" must equally apply to human societies. This line of thought—known as social Darwinism— raises social and ethical questions of major importance (see Chapter 15).

Is the course of history inevitable? Many eminent historians profess to find no recurring pattern in past events, seeing only, as one of them has put it, "the only safe rule for the historian [is] that he should recognize in the development of human destinies the play of the contingent and unforeseen."[4] These differences of view all lead to the question: Are men really free to choose or does history obey impersonal laws and forces—in short, is the course of history inevitable? We seem to have to accept either inevitable laws—which appear to leave no room for significant freedom of action—or the equally extreme alternative that makes every event a unique act and history merely the record of unrelated episodes.

Can this dilemma be avoided? We believe it can. Even though all events are in various respects unique, they also contain elements which invite comparison—as in the case of the origin and course of revolutions in different countries. The comparative approach permits us to seek relationships between historical phenomena and to group them into movements, or patterns, or civilizations.

The authors of this book eschew any single "theory" of history. They are eclectic in their approach because they see merit in a number of basic concepts. These include the important effects of physical environment on social organization and institutions; the powerful roles played not only by economic but also by political and religious factors; and the impact exerted upon events by various outstanding personalities occupying key positions in history.

The question of progress. Somewhere along the line, the student is likely to ask: "Are we making any progress? Is mankind getting better?" Nineteenth-century optimists confidently answered "Yes!" but our crisis-ridden century is by no means so sure. In any case, such questions are difficult to answer because of the difficulty of defining such terms as *progress* or *better.* (Better than what, for example?) Those who equate progress with material advancement might remember that the Athens of Socrates and Aristotle produced an unsurpassed galaxy of thinkers and artists without the benefit of electricity, television, or the Madison Avenue ad-man. Conversely, the advanced literacy and technology boasted by Nazi Germany did not prevent it from wallowing in the moral depravity which created concentration camps and gas chambers.

Nevertheless, our lawmakers, educators, and scientists do assume that progress can be both defined and defended on rational grounds. Various factors might be applied to test this proposition. *Material advancement* calls for improved living and health standards, increased economic production, and a distribution of goods so as to benefit the greatest number of people. *Intellectual and spiritual progress* includes educational opportunities for all and is measured in terms of creative achievements in science, the humanities, and arts. For example, Einstein's theory constitutes an advance over Newton's theory of gravitation because it can solve not only the same problems as the earlier theory but also problems that hitherto defied solution. *Social progress* covers the "pursuit of happiness" and includes such essentials as equal status for women, abolition of conditions of servitude, and enlightened treatment of prisoners and the insane.

Yet another significant factor is *political participation.* In a democracy progress can be tested by the opportunities for the individual to assume public responsibilities and by the protection of his right to hold views at variance with those held by others, especially in the case of minorities. Finally, the growth of *international cooperation* becomes basic in any meaningful discussion of progress. This growth depends on and contributes to the maintenance of peace and security, the peaceful settlement of international disputes, and world-wide improvement in economic and social standards.

THE CULTURAL APPROACH TO HISTORY

The universal culture pattern.   In the interplay of man with his environment and with his fellowmen, of which history is the written record, men have always expressed certain fundamental needs. These form the basis of a "universal culture pattern" and deserve to be enumerated.

1. *The need to make a living.* Man must have food, shelter, clothing, and the means to provide for his offspring's survival.

2. *The need for law and order.* From the earliest times communities have had to keep peace among their members, defend themselves against external attack, and protect property.

3. *The need for social organization.* In order that people may make a living, raise families, and maintain law and order, a social structure is necessary. Ideologies may differ in their concepts of the relative importance of the group and the individual within any such social organization.

4. *The need for knowledge and learning.* Since earliest times mankind has transmitted the knowledge painfully acquired from experience, first orally and then by means of language and writing systems. As societies grow more complex, there is an increasing need to preserve knowledge and to make it available through education to as many people as possible.

5. *The need for self-expression.* Man has responded creatively to his environment even before the days when he decorated the walls of Paleolithic caves with paintings of the animals he hunted. The arts appear to have a lineage as old as man himself.

6. *The need for religious expression.* Equally as old is man's attempt to answer the "why" of his existence. What primitive peoples considered supernatural in their environment could at a later date often be explained by science in terms of natural phenomena. Yet today, no less than in prehistoric times, men continue to search for answers to the ultimate questions of existence.

These six briefly described needs have been common to men at all times and in all places. Taken together, they form the basis of a universal culture pattern. To carry this concept one step further: when a group of people behave similarly and share the same institutions and ways of life, they can be said to have a common culture. Each person born into that group will in turn derive from it his basic way of life. It follows that the basic differences between the farmers of ancient China and those of present-day Nebraska are due mainly to the fact that their culture traits are at different stages of development or that they have worked out different methods of solving the same problems of existence. In the succeeding chapters we shall be looking at a large number of different cultures, some of which are designated as *civilizations* (for a definition of this term see p. 15).

Diffusion as a factor in culture change. Cultures are never static or wholly isolated. A particular culture may have an individuality which sets it off sharply from other cultures, but invariably it has been influenced by external contacts. Such contacts may be either peaceful or warlike, and they meet with varying degrees of resistance. The early American colonists took from the Indians the use of corn and tobacco, while the latter obtained the horse and firearms from the newcomers. On the other hand, the Second World War saw the Nazis and Japanese force their cultures upon subjugated peoples with no permanent results.

Environment and invention in culture change. While geography has profoundly influenced the development of cultures, we should not exaggerate its importance. Although riverine civilizations evolved along the Nile and the Tigris-Euphrates, for example, none emerged in the physically comparable valleys of the Jordan and the Rio Grande.[5] Moreover, environmental influences tend to become less marked as man gains increasing mastery over nature, as shown by the transformation of deserts in southwestern United States into rich citrus belts and the extension of the grain-growing belt in the Canadian prairies further north through the development of frost- and rust-resistant types of wheat.

Invention is therefore another important source of culture change. The automobile—which has revolutionized transportation, the growth of cities, and even home life—was made possible only by a host of earlier inventions, such as the internal-combustion engine and that most ancient and indispensable tool, the wheel. The study of the origins of certain basic inventions again underscores the fact that historical change is a continuous process at once dynamic and often unpredictable. The domestication of animals and grain, for example, took place in both the old and new worlds, albeit the animals and cereals were different because of the dissimilar ecological factors involved; yet so far as we know, there was no physical contact at the time between the two cultural heartlands. To what extent, then, is physical contact required in the process of invention? Or, is it possible for men in different times and places to hit upon similar solutions to the challenges posed by their respective environments—resulting in the phenomenon known as "parallel invention"?

Is race a factor in culture change?   Just as no pure culture was ever developed in isolation by one group, so there is no pure race of people. Ethnic types have intermingled along with the diffusion of cultures. *Race*, a much misused term, has value only in denoting the major human divisions, each with its own distinctive physical characteristics: Caucasian (white), Mongoloid (yellow), and Negroid (black). No race has ever monopolized culture, though for a specific period one race may produce an impressive record of cultural creativity.

Unfortunately, just as ignorance has all too often led to unscientific generalizations about the differences between the "races" of *Homo sapiens*—which in turn have been employed to justify discriminatory, and even brutal, behavior toward one people by another—so the factor of race has also been employed at different times and places to "explain" the superiority which groups perceive in their own cultures as compared with those of others. Thus Caucasian peoples have been all too guilty of assuming that their particular cultural patterns and activities must be superior to the cultures which they associate with Asian and African peoples. To hold such arrogant, and demonstrably fallacious, views was more understandable, if not pardonable, in the era of western colonialism. In today's world, however, to retain such stereotyped concepts of nonwestern peoples can be dangerously explosive. New and scientifically valid images of the nonwestern world are required, and a study of history can do much to get rid of western cultural myopia.

Culture lag.   Some parts of a culture pattern change more rapidly than others, so that one institution sometimes becomes outmoded in relation to others in a society. When different parts of a society fail to mesh harmoniously, the condition is often called *culture lag*. Numerous examples of this lag could be cited: the failure to enfranchise women until this century, the tragedy of hunger in the midst of plenty during the 1930's, or, in our own day, the repeated inability of the United Nations to limit atomic energy to peaceful use because of the insistence by national states to arm themselves as they wish.

In the view of some observers, culture lag has assumed its most dangerous form in the apparently widening gap in communications and outlook between science and the accelerating technological sector on the one hand and our traditional humanistic culture and values system on the other. These two major segments of our culture pattern appear to be advancing, and changing, at the speeds of a supersonic jet and of a horse and buggy respectively. Just what dynamic factors are at work which bring about different rates of speed in the processes of change? Because our modern age owes its particular world outlook in ever growing measure to the discoveries and philosophy of science, and because the processes of change are today most apparent in our contemporary technological order, we have need to understand much more clearly than ever before the nature of the scientific revolution—not only in the way that it began in the sixteenth century, but also how it operates today and is already shaping the pattern of our culture for the decades ahead.

The role of history today. Among man's greatest achievements on earth has been his development of tools, machines, and controlled power—in short, technology. Yet even this planet earth no longer satisfies man's technological ambitions, for he has at last succeeded in escaping his age-old bondage to the earth and is about to propel himself into the interplanetary age.

While human technology is at present moving ahead at supersonic speed, there has been no corresponding increase in man's own mental or physical capacity. He probably has no more native intelligence than his Stone Age ancestors—and undoubtedly less muscle. So we come to a fundamental question: how is twentieth-century man to cope with the ever widening disparity between what he *is* and what he *has*? How can he control and utilize his tremendous technological powers for happiness and not for nuclear self-annihilation? Today he seeks to conquer other planets before he has learned to govern his own.

Surely an indispensable step toward solving contemporary man's dilemma—technology without the requisite control and power without adequate wisdom—must be a better understanding of how man and all his works became what they are today. Only by understanding the past can mankind assess both the perils and the opportunities of the present.

PART ONE
THE ANCIENT WORLD

"Students today are interested in the living present, not in the dead past." How many times have we heard this view expressed on the campus! It reveals a laudable concern with the crisis through which our civilization is passing, but it denies the past any relevancy for the present. Why, then, study history? Even more to the point, why devote the first three chapters of this volume to an account of the ancient and long-dead civilizations of the Near East, Greece, and Rome?

One answer is that the question of relevancy is itself irrelevant; ancient history exists in its own right, because it tells an interesting story. Furthermore, the study of ancient history, like all history, helps train the student in ways of thinking that we associate with a liberally educated person—a concern for origins and relationships, a respect for both sides of a case, and an awareness of dynamic forces in society. Another answer stresses the heritage left to us by the ancient past—the cultivation of cereals, metallurgy, the calendar, the alphabet, our religions, and the foundations of our philosophies—to list a few.

Perhaps the most engrossing relevancy of all comes from the insights and illumination derived from studying civilizations comparatively. Even a quick reading of Greek history, for example, will reveal a periodization that parallels that of later Europe. Both histories begin after the collapse of an earlier advanced civilization and develop through "medieval," "renaissance," and "modern" phases. Closer attention to the political, economic, social, cultural, and religious institutions and ideas that emerge during the course of Greek history will reveal that many are strikingly similar to those found in the analogous periods of European history.

It is because men in different civilizations tend to devise similar solutions to similar problems that broad patterns of parallel development are discernible. The political pattern is best seen in the history of the ancient Greeks, who experienced and gave enduring names to virtually every major type of government: an early form of monarchy in which the ruler, who is hardly more than a war leader, can take no important action without the approval of an aristocratic council of his fellow nobles and a popular assembly of arms-bearing warriors; oligarchy—called feudalism in later Europe—the exercise of political power by the nobility after the actual or virtual elimination of both the early monarch and the popular assembly; tyranny—absolute monarchy in Europe—the rule of a despot who is supported by the non-noble classes; democracy, the direct "rule of the people" that replaces tyranny. The dissatisfaction of a specific social class with the existing type of government is the cause of these constitutional changes, and in time democracy, too, comes under attack. It is often replaced by types of oligarchy or tyranny— fascist and Communist dictatorships being modern forms of the latter.

The broad pattern of economic development moves from an early collectivistic economy, like that of the medieval manor, to an economic individualism, which the ancient Mesopotamians were the first to call capitalism. Like all institutions, capitalism is fragile and flourishes only when conditions are favorable. In time it is modified or replaced by some new form of economic collectivism, among which socialism is the most notable.

The religious pattern consists of a movement from lower to higher forms of belief and practice. The outstanding feature of the lower religions, which exist at the beginning of every civilization, is its premoral nature—the rewards men receive from the gods are based on material rather than moral considerations. The gods are viewed as a hungry lot who, as described in the Babylonian *Epic of Gilgamesh,* "gather like flies" around a sacrificed ox and reward the sacrificer. The higher religions are born out of deep suffering which leads to a new view of the gods as rewarders of good character rather than material gifts. "More acceptable [to the gods] is the character of one upright of heart than the ox of the evildoer," states an Egyptian text. "Give the love of thyself to the whole world. . . . "[1] This emphasis on love, a self-sacrificing love for God and all His creatures, is the essence of all higher religion. St. Paul said it best in the course of describing his own religious development from childhood to maturity, and he said it in words that have a strong appeal to today's youth:

> When I was a child, my speech, feelings, and thinking were all those of a child; now that I am a man, I have no more use for childish ways. . . . Meanwhile these three remain: faith, hope, and love; and the greatest of these is love. (I Corinthians 13:11–13)[2]

Patterns in the development of thought, art, and the changing relationship of social classes also become evident when civilizations are viewed comparatively. Some evidence for them will be found in the following chapters.

There is nothing inevitable about the patterns of development that have been described. History never repeats itself in exact detail, and only in Greek and European history do we find what deserve to be called complete patterns in the development of the major aspects of civilization. But wherever any aspect of the general pattern is absent, the reason is usually apparent. The civilizations of the ancient Near East did not advance beyond the political stage of tyranny. We must not conclude from this that these peoples were political failures because they did not achieve what the Greeks, the Romans, and the Europeans achieved. Apparently despots of the stamp of Hammurabi, who was, as he claimed (see p. 19), "a real father to his people," satisfied their major needs. Another significant deviation from the general pattern occurred at Sparta and Rome where the nobility succeeded in avoiding tyranny by granting democratic concessions to the lower-class citizens. Furthermore, collectivistic economies remained the rule in the Near East, with the notable exception of a short period of capitalistic individualism under the dynasty of Sargon of Akkad. Here, too, as during the Middle Ages in Europe, thought and art remained the handmaidens of religion, lacking the full freedom to develop that characterized the culture of Greece, Rome, and Renaissance Europe.

11

SOUTHERN BAPTIST COLLEGE LIBRARY

CHAPTER 1

ALONG THE BANKS
OF RIVERS

The Civilizations of the Ancient Near East

Perhaps as early as two million years ago, man's ancestors first appeared on earth, naked in a world of enemies. The story of man's journey out of the darkness of ignorance and fear covers a period of hundreds of thousands of years during which he mastered the skills necessary for survival. Early man's most important achievements concern agriculture and the ways of life it engendered. Wild beasts were domesticated and kept for their meat and hides. The first farmers scattered kernels of grain on the earth and waited patiently for harvest time. With fields and flocks to supply most of their wants, men were no longer compelled to move on endlessly in search of food, as their food-gathering ancestors had done for countless generations. Where conditions were favorable, these ancient farmers were able to acquire more food than they needed for survival—surpluses to tide them over seasons of cold and drought. Thus, on fertile plateaus and in green oases farming villages sprang up.

It was along the banks of great rivers that simple farming villages first grew into complex cities. In early Egyptian picture writing a city is shown as a cross within a circle— —the intersection of two roads enclosed by a wall. The symbol is an appropriate one, for in the history of mankind the city marks the spot where civilization began.

Within the cities the majority still farmed. But now there were more craftsmen turning out specialized wares, merchants trading for metals and other needed raw materials, priests conducting religious ceremonies, and administrators planning and supervising the necessary cooperative effort for the common good. And there was also time for intellectual and artistic pursuits and the development of a cultural heritage.

A culture can endure only if the knowledge necessary for its survival is passed on from generation to generation. Early peoples relied on information transmitted by word of mouth. But as cities emerged, and cultures became increasingly complex, methods for keeping records were devised and systems of writing were created. To most authorities, the development of writing is a prerequisite to civilization.

SOUTHERN BAPTIST COLLEGE LIBRARY

The four earliest civilizations—the Sumerian, the Egyptian, the Indian, and the Chinese—arose between c. 3500 B.C. and c. 1500 B.C. in each case in the valley of a great river system. In this chapter we shall trace the progress of civilization in Mesopotamia and Egypt.

TOOLS AND ART OF EARLY MAN

Africa: birthplace of man? Benjamin Franklin is credited with defining man as a "tool-making animal." This ability to fashion and use tools is the first evidence of man's unique faculty of reasoning out solutions to the problems of life. Since the use of stone implements, made by striking pieces of rock with other stones, was the distinctive feature of early man's culture, the first stage in man's cultural development is known as the Paleolithic or Old Stone Age. (Paleolithic culture survives among a few primitive peoples today.) Who were the ancestors of early man and when and where tools were first fashioned are much debated questions in scholarly circles.

Until recently Asia was thought to have been the home of the earliest tool-making *hominids* ("near men"). Here much evidence of a group called *Homo erectus* has come to light, beginning with Java man in 1890 and Peking man in 1927. *Homo erectus* fossils, which date back at least half a million years, have also been found in Europe and Africa. Because of *Homo erectus'* brain size (c. 1000 cc.; that of modern man averages c. 1500 cc.), it is thought probable that he knew how to speak. He was about five feet tall, had a fully erect posture, but retained heavy brow ridges and a receding forehead. *Homo erectus* was clearly a tool-maker, fashioning hand-axes by chipping hard rocks to form cutting and scraping edges. He often lived in caves and knew how to use fire.

Most anthropologists give priority to Africa as the birthplace of man and of human culture. Recent discoveries indicate that about 750,000 years ago hominids began to make tools in East Africa. The earliest tools were only small pebbles shaped in a crude way, but they were gradually displaced by the "hand-ax," a more sophisticated general purpose implement and chopper. The center of this hand-ax culture was Africa, and from here this refined stone culture spread to Europe and western Asia, carried perhaps by various waves of immigrants. The discovery of these earliest tools has forced a basic reconsideration of the theory that "in the history of mankind Africa had always been the recipient, never the donor."[1]

Middle and late Paleolithic cultures. From about 70,000 to 35,000 B.C.—that is, during the last half of the middle Paleolithic period—the European and western Asian landscape was inhabited by Neanderthal man, the favorite "cave man" of contemporary cartoonists. He was about five feet tall with a thick-set body (reconstructions showing him stooped are now known to be in error), and he used more specialized flake tools made from large flakes broken off a stone block. His stone-tipped spears made him a powerful hunter.

About 35,000 B.C. the middle Paleolithic era in Europe gave way to late Paleolithic cultures, a development accompanied by the displacement of Neanderthal man by modern *Homo sapiens*. By 20,000 B.C. *Homo sapiens* inhabited Europe, Asia, Africa, and Australia—and had begun to move across the Bering

Strait from Asia to America. A new technique of pressure-flaking produced long, slender, sharp-edged blades which made excellent projectile points and a most useful chisel, the burin. The invention of the spear-thrower made hunting much more efficient.

To withstand the cold weather, late Paleolithic peoples sewed garments from skins and erected buildings where natural caves did not exist. The reindeer and mammoth hunters of present-day Czechoslovakia and Russia lived in tents and huts made of hides and brush or in communal houses partially sunk into the ground with mammoth's ribs for roof supports. There is also evidence that they used coal for fuel.

The first artists.   Man was an artist long before he could write or fashion a metal knife. Animated, realistic paintings of bison, reindeer, primitive horses, and other animals, colored in shades of black, red, yellow, and brown, have been found in more than a hundred caves in Spain and France. Cave art rivals that of civilized man not only stylistically but also as an expression of significant human experience. It represents Paleolithic man's response to his complete dependence on an abundance of game animals and success in hunting them. By drawing pictures of food animals he may have believed that he could wield a mystical power over their spirits, thus assuring their multiplication and his mastery over them in hunting. Like the religious art of civilized man, the magico-religious basis of Paleolithic art in no way detracts from its esthetic qualities as true art. Paleolithic man also modeled in clay and chiseled pictures on rock and bone.

Mesolithic or Transitional cultures.   With the final retreat of the glaciers that had intermittently covered large portions of Europe, Asia, and North America during the million or so years before 10,000 B.C., Europe became covered with dense forests. Because of their highly specialized adaptation to cold weather, the reindeer moved north and the hairy mammoth and other animals hunted by late Paleolithic peoples became extinct.

Man himself, however, proved able to adjust to postglacial conditions by developing new cultures called Mesolithic or Transitional. Our Mesolithic forebears fished and gathered shellfish, made bows and arrows for hunting, and devised such forms of transport as skis, sleds, and dugout canoes. They also domesticated the dog—the first of many animals brought into this special relationship with man.

The Neolithic revolution.   While the Mesolithic peoples of Europe were adjusting to the postglacial environment by developing new food-gathering techniques, something of far greater consequence—a shift from food gathering to food producing—was taking place in the Near East. Here, on the hilly flanks of the mountains bordering what is called the Fertile Crescent (see map, p. 16), there was sufficient rainfall to nourish wild forms of wheat and barley and to provide grass for wild sheep, goats, and pigs. By 7000 B.C. men in this region had domesticated these grains and animals and were living in village communities near their herds and fields. This momentous change, the most far-reaching breakthrough in the relationship of man to his environment, ushered in the Neolithic or New Stone Age.

Between 7000 and 6000 B.C. hundreds of peasant villages arose in the foothills of northern Iraq and adjacent parts of Turkey, Syria, Iran, and Palestine. The best preserved early village so far uncovered is Çatal Hüyük in southern Turkey, excavated in 1961. The large, 32-acre site, first occupied shortly before 6500 B.C., contains some of the most advanced features of Neolithic culture: pottery, woven textiles, mud-brick houses, shrines honoring a mother goddess, and plastered walls decorated with murals and carved reliefs.

In time the Neolithic revolution spread out from its original center in the Near East, reaching the Balkan peninsula of Europe by 5000 B.C., central Europe by 4000 B.C., and the British Isles by 3000 B.C.

MESOPOTAMIA: THE FIRST CIVILIZATION

Prelude to civilization. About 5000 B.C., after the agricultural revolution had begun to spread from its place of origin on the fringes of the Fertile Crescent, Neolithic farmers started filtering into the Fertile Crescent itself. Although this broad plain received insufficient rainfall to support agriculture, it was watered by the Tigris and Euphrates rivers. Known in ancient days as Mesopotamia (Greek for "between the rivers"), the lower reaches of this plain, beginning near the point where the two rivers nearly converge, was called Babylonia. Babylonia in turn encompassed two geographical areas—Akkad in the north and Sumer, the delta of this river system, in the south.

Broken by river channels teeming with fish and refertilized every year by alluvial silt laid down by uncontrolled floods, Babylonia had a splendid agricultural potential—provided the floods were controlled, the swamps drained, and irrigation canals dug and maintained. In the course of the several successive cultural phases that followed the arrival of the first Neolithic farmers, these and other related problems were solved by large-scale cooperative effort. By 3500 B.C. the foundations had been laid for a type of economy and social order markedly different from anything previously known. This far more complex culture, based on urban centers rather than simple villages, is what we associate with the term *civilization.*

Authorities do not all agree about the definition of *civilization*. Most would accept the view that "a civilization is a culture which has attained a degree of complexity usually characterized by urban life"[2]—that it is capable, in other words, of sustaining a substantial number of specialists to cope with the economic, social, political, and religious needs of a populous society. Other characteristics usually present in a civilization include a system of writing to keep records, monumental architecture in place of simple buildings, and an art that is no longer merely decorative but representational of man and his activities.

During the millennium preceding 3500 B.C. some of the most significant discoveries and inventions in human history were achieved. By discovering how to use metals to make tools and weapons, Neolithic man effected a revolution nearly as far-reaching as that wrought in agriculture. By 4500 B.C. Neolithic artisans had discovered how to extract copper from oxide ores by heating them with charcoal. Unlike those made of stone or bone, copper implements could be formed into any desired shape, and they were less likely to break. Soon after 3000 B.C. metalworkers discovered that copper was improved by the addition of tin. The resulting alloy, bronze, was more fusible than copper and therefore could be cast more easily; also, bronze was harder and provided a sharper cutting edge.

The farmer's first plow was probably a stick which he pulled through the soil with a rope. In time, however, the cattle that his forebears had domesticated for

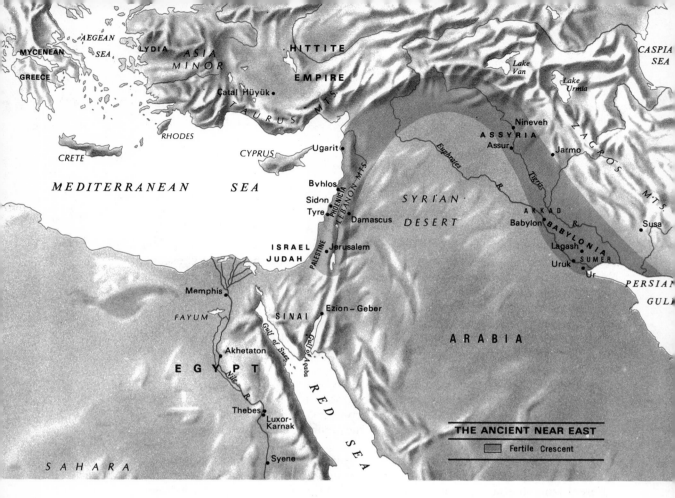

The following labels appear on the map:

AEGEAN SEA · LYDIA · ASIA MINOR · HITTITE EMPIRE · CASPIAN SEA · MYCENEAN GREECE · Çatal Hüyük · TAURUS MTS. · Lake Van · Lake Urmia · ZAGROS MTS. · Nineveh · ASSYRIA · Assur · Jarmo · RHODES · CYPRUS · Ugarit · EUPHRATES R. · Tigris R. · Susa · CRETE · MEDITERRANEAN SEA · Byblos · PHOENICIA · LEBANON MTS. · Sidon · Tyre · Damascus · SYRIAN DESERT · AKKAD · BABYLON · BABYLONIA · Lagash · SUMER · Uruk · Ur · ISRAEL · JUDAH · PALESTINE · Jerusalem · PERSIAN GULF · Memphis · FAYUM · SINAI · Ezion-Geber · ARABIA · Gulf of Suez · Gulf of Aqaba · EGYPT · Akhetaton · Nile R. · RED SEA · Thebes · Luxor-Karnak · Syene · SAHARA

THE ANCIENT NEAR EAST

▨ Fertile Crescent

food and milk were harnessed to drag the hoe in place of his mate or himself. Yoked, harnessed animals pulled plows in the Mesopotamian soil by 3000 B.C. As a result, farming advanced from the cultivation of small plots to the tilling of extensive fields.

Since the Mesopotamian plain had no stone, no metals, and no timber except its soft and inadequate palm trees, there was great need of an economical means of transporting these materials from Syria and Asia Minor. Water transport down the Tigris and Euphrates solved the problem. The oldest sailing boat known is represented by a model found in a Sumerian grave of about 3500 B.C. Soon after this date wheeled vehicles appear in the form of ass-drawn war chariots. For the transport of goods overland, however, men continued to rely on the pack ass.

Another important invention was the potter's wheel, first used in Sumer soon after 3300 B.C. Earlier, men had fashioned pots by molding or coiling clay by hand, but now a symmetrical product could be produced in a much shorter time. A pivoted clay disk heavy enough to revolve of its own momentum, the potter's wheel has been called "the first really mechanical device."

The emergence of civilization in Sumer. Scholars cannot agree on when the Sumerians appeared in Babylonia, or from where they came; the Sumerian language is not related to those major language families of mankind that later appear in the Near East—Semites and Indo-Europeans. (The original home of the Semitic-speaking peoples is thought to have been the Arabian peninsula, while the Indo-Europeans migrated from the region north of the Black and Caspian seas. A third, much smaller language family is the Hamitic, which included the Egyptians and other peoples of northeastern Africa.) Regardless of their origins by 3100 B.C. the population of Sumer had increased to the point where people were living in cities and had developed those elements previously noted as constituting civilization. Since these included the first evidence of writing, this phase of Sumerian civilization, to about 2800 B.C., is called the Protoliterate period.

How would life in Protoliterate Sumer have appeared to a visitor seeing it for the first time? As he approached Ur, one of about a dozen Sumerian cities, he would pass farmers working in their fields with ox-drawn plows. He might see some of the workers using bronze sickles. The river would be dotted by boats carrying produce to and from the city. Dominating the flat countryside would be a ziggurat, a platform (later a lofty terrace, built in the shape of a pyramid) crowned by a sanctuary. This was the "holy of holies," sacred to the local god. Upon entering the city, the visitor would see a large number of specialists—craftsmen casting bronze tools and weapons or fashioning their wares on the potter's wheel, and merchants arranging to trade grain and manufactured goods for the metals, stone, lumber, and other essentials not available in Sumer. Scribes would be at work incising thin tablets of clay with picture signs. Some tablets might bear the impressions of cylinder seals, small stone cylinders engraved with a design; these tablets were memoranda used in administering the temple, which was at once the warehouse and workshop of the entire community. Some of the scribes might be making an inventory of the goats and sheep received that day for sacrificial use; others might be drawing up wage lists. They would be using a system of counting based on the unit 60, still used today, over five thousand years later, in computing divisions of time and angles.

The symbols on the oldest Sumerian clay tablets were primarily pictures. However, many matters, including thought processes, cannot be depicted conveniently by pictures. Sumerian scribes overcame this problem by arbitrarily adding marks to the picture signs to denote new meanings. During the Protoliterate period some two thousand signs were in use. Fortunately, the Sumerians later developed a system whereby the signs represented sounds rather than objects or ideas. By giving the signs a phonetic value, the Sumerians could spell out names and compound words instead of inventing new signs. By 2800 B.C. they had reduced the number of signs to some six hundred.

In writing, a scribe used a reed stylus to make impressions in soft clay tablets. The impressions took on a wedge shape, hence the term *cuneiform* (Latin *cuneus*, "wedge"), which was adopted by many other peoples of the Near East, including the Babylonians, Assyrians, Hittites, and Persians.

The Old Sumerian period. By 2800 B.C. the Sumerian city-states had emerged into the full light of history. This first historical age, called the Old Sumerian (or Early Dynastic) period, was characterized by incessant warfare as each city sought to protect or enlarge its land and water rights. Each city-state was a theocracy, for the local god was believed to be the real sovereign. His earthly representative was the *ensi*, the high priest and city governor, who acted as the god's steward in both religious and secular functions. Though endowed with divine right by virtue of being the human agent of the god, the *ensi* was not considered divine.

Like life on a medieval manor, early Sumerian society was highly collectivized, with the temples of the city god and subordinate deities assuming the central role. "Each temple owned lands which formed the estate of its divine owners. Each citizen belonged to one of the temples, and the whole of a temple community—the officials and priests, herdsmen and fishermen, gardeners, craftsmen, stonecutters, merchants, and even slaves—was referred to as 'the people of the god X.' "[3] That part of the temple land called "common" was worked by all members of the community, while the remaining land was divided among the citizens for their support at a rental of from one sixth to one third of the crop. Priests and temple administrators, however, held rent-free lands.

In time, priests, temple administrators, and *ensis* became venal, usurping temple property and oppressing the common people. This development, together with reverses in war, led to the rise of despots, called *lugals*, who rode to power on a wave of popular discontent. These secular rulers made the general welfare their major domestic concern. Best known is Urukagina, who usurped power at Lagash at the end of the Old Sumerian period. His reform inscriptions state that when he "had received the lugalship . . . he removed from the inhabitants of Lagash usury, forestalling, famine, robbery, attacks; he established their freedom . . . [and] protected the widow and the orphan from the powerful man."[4]

Akkadian dominance.   Immediately north of Sumer lay the narrow region of Akkad, inhabited by Semites who had absorbed Sumerian culture. The Akkadians were the earliest of the Semitic peoples who filtered into Mesopotamia from Arabia. A generation after Urukagina, Sargon I (2370–2315 B.C.), an energetic Akkadian ruler, conquered Sumer and went on to establish the world's first empire, which extended from the Persian Gulf to the Mediterranean Sea.

Very proud of his lower-class origins, Sargon boasted that his humble, unwed mother had been forced to abandon him: "She set me in a basket of rushes . . . [and] cast me into the river."[5] Rescued and brought up by a gardener, Sargon rose to power through the army. As *lugal*, Sargon looked after the welfare of the lower classes and aided the rising class of private merchants. At the latter's request he once sent his army to far-off Asia Minor to protect a colony of merchants from interference by a local ruler. We are told that Sargon "did not sleep" in his efforts to promote prosperity; trade moved as freely "as the Tigris where it flows into the sea, . . . all lands lie in peace, their inhabitants prosperous and contented."[6]

Sargon's successors, however, were unable either to withstand the attacks of semibarbaric highlanders or to overcome the desire for independence of the priest-dominated Sumerian cities. As a result, the house of Sargon collapsed about 2230 B.C.

The Neo-Sumerian period.   Order and prosperity were restored a century later by the *lugals* of the Third Dynasty of Ur (c. 2113-2006 B.C.). By creating a highly centralized administration in Sumer and Akkad, these rulers solved the problem of internal rebellion that had plagued Sargon and his successors. The formerly temple-dominated cities became provinces administered by governors who were watched closely by a corps of "messengers." The "church" became an arm of the state; the high priests were state appointees, and the temple economic organization was used as the state's agent in rigidly controlling the economy.

At the head of this bureaucratic state stood the now-deified ruler, celebrated in hymns as a heaven-sent messiah who "brings splendor to the land, . . . savior of orphans whose misery he relieves, . . . the vigilant shepherd who conducts the people unto cooling shade."[7] Much of what we now call social legislation was passed by these "vigilant shepherds." Such new laws were called "rightings," since their object was the righting of wrongs that were not covered by the old customary law. The prologue to the law code of Ur-Nammu, founder of the dynasty, declared that it was the king's purpose to see that "the orphan did not fall a prey to the wealthy" and that "the man of one shekel did not fall a prey to the man of one mina (sixty shekels)."[8]

Disaster struck Ur about 2006 B.C., when Elamites from the highlands to the east destroyed the city. The Sumerians were never again a dominant element politically, but their culture persisted as the foundation for all subsequent civilizations in the Tigris-Euphrates valley.

For more than two centuries following the destruction of Ur, disunity and warfare again plagued Mesopotamia, along with depression, inflation, and acute hardship for the lower classes. Merchants, however, utilized the lack of state controls to become full-fledged capitalists who amassed fortunes which they invested in banking operations and in land. (These merchants used a form of double-entry bookkeeping which they called "balanced accounts.") The stronger local rulers of the period freed the poor from debt slavery and issued a variety of reform laws which are best illustrated by the legislation of Hammurabi.

Hammurabi and the Babylonian empire.   Semitic Amorites (from *Amurru*, the "West"), under the rule of their capable king, Hammurabi of Babylon (c. 1792–1750 B.C.), again brought most of Mesopotamia under one rule by 1760 B.C.

Hammurabi is best known for his code of nearly three hundred laws whose stated objective was "to cause justice to prevail in the land, to destroy the wicked and the evil, to prevent the strong from oppressing the weak . . . and to further the welfare of the people."[9] Hammurabi's legislation reestablished a state-controlled economy in which merchants were required to obtain a royal permit; interest was limited to 20 percent, and prices were set for basic commodities and for fees charged by physicians, veterinarians, and builders. Minimum wages were established, and debt slavery was limited to three years. Other laws protected wives and children, although a wife who had "set her face to go out and play the part of a fool, neglect her house, belittle her husband"[10] could be divorced without alimony, or the husband could take another wife and compel the first to remain as a servant.

In the epilogue to the code, Hammurabi eloquently summed up his efforts to provide social justice for his people:

> Let any oppressed man, who has a cause, come before my image as king of righteousness! Let him read the inscription on my monument! Let him give heed to my weighty words! And may my monument enlighten him as to his cause and may he understand his case! May he set his heart at ease! (and he will exclaim): "Hammurabi indeed is a ruler who is like a real father to his people . . . ."[11]

Mathematics and science.   Carrying on the work of the Sumerians, the Babylonians made advances in arithmetic, geometry, and algebra. For ease of computation with both whole numbers and fractions, they compiled tables for multiplication and division and for square and cube roots. They knew how to solve linear and quadratic equations, and their knowledge of geometry included the theorem later made famous by the Greek philosopher Pythagoras: the square of the hypotenuse of a right-angled triangle is equal to the sum of the squares of the other two sides. Perhaps their greatest achievement was the principle of place-value notation which gave numbers a value according to their position in a series.

The Babylonians achieved little that today deserves to be called science. They did observe nature and collect data, which is the first requirement of science; but in seeking intelligible explanations of natural phenomena, they did not go beyond the formulation of myths which explained things in terms of the unpredictable whims of the gods. The sun, the moon, and the five visible planets were thought to be gods who were able to influence men's lives; accordingly, their movements were watched, recorded, and interpreted.

Babylonian literature. The Babylonians took over from the Sumerians a body of literature ranging from heroic epics that compare favorably with the *Illiad* and the *Odyssey* to writings that have their counterparts in the Old Testament books of Job, Proverbs, and Ecclesiastes. Longest and most famous is the *Epic of Gilgamesh*, which recounts the exploits of a heroic ruler of Uruk who lived about 2700 B.C. The central theme of the epic is Gilgamesh's hope of immortality. This leads him to seek out and question Ut-napishtim, the Babylonian Noah who was granted eternal life because he saved all living creatures from the flood. Ut-napishtim's story has many remarkable similarities with the Hebrew account of the flood. But Gilgamesh's quest is hopeless, and he is so informed on several occasions:

> Gilgamesh, whither rovest thou?
> The life thou pursuest thou shalt not find.
> When the gods created mankind,
> Death for mankind they set aside,
> Life in their own hands retaining.
> Thou, Gilgamesh, let full be thy belly,
> Make thou merry by day and by night.
> Of each day make thou a feast of rejoicing,
> Day and night dance thou and play! . . .
> Pay heed to the little one that holds on to thy hand,
> Let thy spouse delight in thy bosom!
> For this is the task of mankind![12]

And here are a few lines from the lamentation of the Babylonian Job:

> I look about me: evil upon evil!
> My affliction grows, I cannot find justice . . .
> Yet I thought only of prayer and supplication,
> Invocation was my care, sacrifice my rule;
> The day of the worship of the gods was my delight.. . . .
> Who can comprehend the counsel of the gods in heaven?
> The plan of a god is deep waters, who can fathom it?
> Where has befuddled mankind ever learned what is a god's conduct?[13]

Fall of the Babylonian empire. The pattern of disunity and warfare, all too familiar in Mesopotamia, reasserted itself following Hammurabi's death. In 1595 B.C. the Hittites, an Indo-European people who had established themselves in Asia Minor by 2000 B.C. (see map, p. 16), mounted a daring raid down the Euphrates, capturing and plundering Babylon. The next five centuries is a dark age about which little is known; yet it did preserve the cultural heritage left by the Sumerians and Babylonians. Meanwhile, in a neighboring river valley, another civilization had emerged.

Predynastic Egypt. Egypt is literally "the gift of the Nile," as the ancient Greek historian Herodotus observed. The Nile valley, extending 750 miles from the first cataract to the Mediterranean, is a fertile oasis cut out of a limestone plateau. Its soil is renewed annually by the rich silt deposited by the flood water of the river, which rises and falls with unusual precision. The rise begins early in July and continues until the banks are overrun, reaching its crest in September. By the end of October the river is once more contained within its banks.

By 4000 B.C. Neolithic villagers had begun to build dikes to catch and hold the Nile flood and to construct ditches and wells for irrigation. Population grew and social organization advanced, leading to the formation of two distinct kingdoms late in the fourth millennium: Lower Egypt comprised the broad Nile delta north of Memphis, while Upper Egypt extended southward along the narrow ten- to twenty-mile-wide valley as far as the first cataract at Syene (now called Aswan). Each kingdom contained about a score of districts, or *nomes*, which had formerly been ruled by independent chieftans.

The Predynastic period ended about 3000 B.C. when Menes, ruler of Upper Egypt, united the two kingdoms and founded the First Dynasty with its capital at Memphis. Because little is known of the first two dynasties, the period is called Egypt's Archaic Age.

The Old Kingdom (c. 2700–2200 B.C.). The pharaohs of the Third through the Sixth Dynasties—the period called the Old Kingdom or Pyramid Age—firmly established order and stability and the essential elements of Egyptian civilization. The nobility lost its independence, and all power was centered in the pharaoh (*Per-ao,* "Great House"). The pharaoh was considered a god rather than the human agent of a god, as was the rule in Mesopotamia. As the god of Egypt, the pharaoh owned all the land (although frequent grants were made to temples and private persons), controlled the irrigation system, decided when the fields should be sown, and received the surplus from the crops produced on the huge royal estates. This surplus supported a large corps of specialists—administrators, priests, scribes, artists, artisans, and merchants—who worked for the pharaoh. The people's welfare was thought to rest on absolute fidelity to the god-king. As a consequence, the Egyptian felt a sense of security that was rare in Mesopotamia.

The belief that the pharaoh was a god led to the practice of mummification and the construction of colossal tombs—the pyramids—to preserve the pharaoh's mummy for eternity. The pyramid tombs, in particular those of the Fourth Dynasty at Gizeh near Memphis which are the most celebrated of all ancient monuments, reflect the great power and wealth of the Old Kingdom pharaohs. Their construction provided employment during the months when the land was inundated by the Nile.

Toward the end of the Sixth Dynasty the centralized authority of the pharaohs was undermined when the nobles assumed the prerogatives of the pharaohs, including the claim to immortality, and the *nomes* again became independent. For about a century and a half, known as the First Intermediate Period (c. 2200–2050 B.C.), civil war raged, and outsiders raided and infiltrated the land. The lot of the common people became unbearable as they faced famine, robbery, and oppression by petty tyrants.

The Middle Kingdom (c. 2050–1800 B.C.). Egypt was rescued from anarchy by the pharaohs of the Eleventh and Twelfth Dynasties, which reunited the country and ruled from Thebes. Stressing their role as watchful shepherds of the people, the Middle Kingdom pharaohs promoted the welfare of the downtrodden. One of them claimed: "I gave to the destitute and brought up the orphan. I caused him who was nothing to reach [his goal], like him who was [somebody]."[14] No longer was the nation's wealth expended on huge pyramids, but on public works. The largest of these, a drainage and irrigation project in the marshy Fayum district south of Memphis, resulted in the reclamation of 27,000 acres of arable land. Moreover, a concession that has been called "the democratization of the hereafter" gave the lower classes the right to have their bodies mummified and thereby to enjoy immortality.

Following the Twelfth Dynasty, Egypt again was racked by civil war as provincial governors fought for the pharaoh's throne. During this Second Intermediate Period (c. 1800–1570 B.C.), the Hyksos, a mixed but preponderantly Semitic people, invaded Egypt from Palestine about 1700 B.C. They easily conquered the delta and made the rest of Egypt tributary. It was probably at this time that the Hebrews entered Egypt, led by the patriarch Joseph, who rose to high position under a friendly Hyksos king.

The New Kingdom or Empire (c. 1570–1090 B.C.). The Egyptians viewed the Hyksos conquest as a great humiliation imposed on them by detestable barbarians. An aggressive nationalism emerged, promoted by the native prince of Thebes. Adopting the new weapons introduced by their conquerors—horse-drawn chariots, the composite bow, and weapons of bronze rather than copper—the Egyptians expelled the Hyksos and pursued them into Palestine. The pharaohs of the Eighteenth Dynasty, who reunited Egypt and founded the New Kingdom, made Palestine the nucleus of an Egyptian empire in western Asia.

The outstanding pharaoh of the aggressive state that Egypt now became was Thutmose III (c. 1490–1436 B.C.). This "Napoleon of Egypt" led his professional standing army on seventeen campaigns into Syria, where he set up his boundary markers on the banks of the Euphrates. Nubia and northern Sudan were also brought under his sway. The native princes of Palestine, Phoenicia, and Syria were left on their thrones, but their sons were taken to Egypt as hostages. Here they were brought up and, thoroughly Egyptianized, eventually sent home to rule as loyal vassals.

The Empire now reached its peak. Tribute flowed in from conquered lands; and Thebes, with its temples built for the sun-god Amon across the Nile at Luxor and Karnak, became the most magnificent city in the world. The Hittites of Asia Minor and the rulers of Babylonia and Crete, among others, sent gifts, including princesses for the pharaoh's harem. In return, they asked the pharaoh for gold, "for gold is as common as dust in your land."

During the reign of Amenhotep IV (c. 1369–1353 B.C.), however, the Empire went into sharp decline as the result of an internal struggle between the pharaoh and the powerful and wealthy priests of Amon. The pharaoh undertook to revolutionize Egypt's religion by proclaiming the worship of the sun's disk, Aton, in place of Amon and all the other deities. Often called the first monotheist (although, as Aton's son, the pharaoh was also a god), Amenhotep changed his name to Akhenaton ("Devoted to Aton"), left Amon's city to found a new capital (Akhetaton), and concentrated upon religious reform. Most of Egypt's vassal princes in Asia defected when their appeals for aid against invaders went unheeded. Prominent among these invaders were groups of people called the

The temple at Luxor, dedicated to Amon, was built by several New Kingdom pharaohs over a period of about two hundred years and testifies to the characteristic Egyptian love of grandiose monuments. The obelisk and massive statues were built by Ramses II, who was responsible for numerous other huge testimonials to his own power and grandeur.

Habiru, whose possible identification with the Hebrews of the Old Testament has interested modern scholars. At home the army leaders joined with the wealthy and powerful Amon priesthood to encourage dissension. When Akhenaton died, his weak successor, Tutankhamen—famed for his small but richly furnished tomb discovered in 1922—returned to Thebes and the worship of Amon.

One of the army leaders who succeeded Tutankhamen founded the Nineteenth Dynasty (c. 1305–1200 B.C.), which sought to reestablish Egyptian control over Palestine and Syria. The result was a long struggle with the Hittites, who in the meantime had pushed south from Asia Minor into Syria. This struggle reached a climax in the reign of Ramses II (c. 1290–1224 B.C.), the pharaoh of the Hebrew Exodus from Egypt. Ramses II regained Palestine, but when he failed to dislodge the Hittites from Syria, he agreed to a treaty. Its strikingly modern character is revealed in clauses providing for nonaggression, mutual assistance, and extradition of fugitives.

The long reign of Ramses II was ancient Egypt's last period of national grandeur. Outstanding among his monuments are the great Hypostyle Hall, built for Amon at Karnak, and the temple at Abu Simbel, with its four colossal statues of Ramses, which has recently been raised to save it from inundation by the waters of the new High Dam at Aswan (Syene). After Ramses II, royal authority gradually declined as the power of the priests of Amon rose.

Period of Decadence (1090–332 B.C.). During the early part of the Period of Decadence the Amon priesthood at Thebes became so strong that the high priest was able to found his own dynasty and to rule over Upper Egypt. Civil war and invasion grew increasingly common, and Egypt became, in the words of the Old Testament, a "broken reed." After passing under Assyrian and Persian rule, Egypt came within the domain of Alexander the Great. Alexander's conquest in 332 B.C. marked the end of thirty-one dynasties which had ruled Egypt for nearly three thousand years.

Egyptian society and economy. Although most Egyptians were serfs and subject to forced labor, class stratification was not rigid, and people of merit could rise to a higher rank in the service of the pharaoh. The best avenue of advancement was education. The pharaoh's administration needed many scribes, and young men were urged to attend a scribal school: "Be a scribe, who is freed from forced labor, and protected from all work. . . . he directeth every work that is in this land." Yet then as now the education of a young man was beset with pitfalls: "I am told thou forsakest writing, that thou givest thyself up to pleasures; thou goest from street to street, where it smelleth of beer, to destruction. Beer, it scareth men from thee, it sendeth thy soul to perdition."[15]

The economy of Egypt has been called "theocratic socialism" because the state, in the person of the divine pharaoh, owned the land and monopolized commerce and industry. Because of the Nile and the proximity to the Mediterranean and Red seas, most of Egypt's trade was carried on by ships. Boats plied regularly up and down the Nile, which, unlike the Tigris and the Euphrates, is easily navigable in both directions up to the first cataract at Aswan (Syene). Egypt's indispensable imports were lumber, copper, tin, and olive oil, paid for with gold from its rich mines, linens, wheat, and papyrus rolls for writing.

Mathematics and science. The Egyptians were much less skilled in mathematics than were the Mesopotamians. Their arithmetic was limited to addition and subtraction, which also served them when they needed to multiply and divide. They could cope with only simple algebra, but they did have considerable knowledge of practical geometry. The obliteration of field boundaries by the annual flooding of the Nile made land measurement a necessity. Similarly, a knowledge of geometry was essential in computing the dimensions of ramps for raising stones during the construction of pyramids. In these and other engineering projects the Egyptians were superior to their Mesopotamian contemporaries. Like the Mesopotamians, the Egyptians had acquired a "necessary" technology without effecting a conceptual breakthrough to a truly scientific method.

What has been called the oldest known scientific treatise was composed during the Old Kingdom. Its author described forty-eight cases requiring surgery, drawing conclusions solely from observation and rejecting supernatural causes and treatments. In advising the physician to "measure for the heart" which "speaks" in various parts of the body, he recognized the importance of the pulse and approached the concept of the circulation of the blood. This text remained unique, however, for in Egypt as elsewhere in the ancient Near East, thought failed to free itself permanently from bondage to religion.

The Old Kingdom produced the world's first known solar calendar, the direct ancestor of our own. In order to plan their farming operations in accordance with the annual flooding of the Nile, the Egyptians kept records and discovered that the average period between inundations was 365 days. They also noted that the Nile flood coincided with the annual appearance of the Dog Star (Sirius) on the eastern horizon at dawn, and they soon associated the two phenomena. (Since the Egyptian year was six hours short of the true year, Julius Caesar in Roman times corrected the error by adding an extra day every four years.)

Egyptian religion. Early Egyptian religion had no strong ethical character. Relations between men and gods were based largely on material considerations, and the gods were thought to reward those who brought them gifts of sacrifice. But widespread suffering during the First Intermediate Period led to a revolution in religious thought. It was now believed that instead of propitiatory offerings the gods were interested in good character and love for one's fellow man: "More acceptable [to the gods] is the character of one upright of heart than the ox of the evildoer. . . . Give the love of thyself to the whole world; a good character is a remembrance."[16]

The cult of the god Osiris, judge of the dead, became very popular when it combined the new emphasis on moral character with the supreme reward of an attractive afterlife. "Do justice whilst thou endurest upon earth," men were told. "A man remains over after death, and his deeds are placed beside him in heaps. However, existence yonder is for eternity. . . . He who reaches it without wrongdoing shall exist yonder like a god."[17] Osiris, according to an ancient myth, was the god of the Nile, and the rise and fall of the river symbolized his death and resurrection. The myth recounted that Osiris had been murdered by Seth, his evil brother, who cut the victim's body into many pieces. When Isis, the bereaved widow, collected all the pieces and put them together, Osiris was resurrected and became king of the dead. Osiris was thus the first mummy, and every mummified Egyptian was another Osiris.

But only a soul free of sin could survive the judgment of Osiris and live forever in what was described as the "Field of the Blessed, an ideal land where there is no wailing and nothing evil; where barley grows four cubits high, and emmer wheat seven ells high; where, even better, one has to do no work in the field oneself, but can let others take care of it."[18] At the time of soul testing, Osiris weighed the candidate's heart against the Feather of Truth. If the ordeal was not passed, a horrible creature devoured the rejected heart. During the Empire the priesthood of Osiris became corrupt and claimed that it knew clever methods of surviving the soul testing, even though a man's heart were heavy with sin. Charms and magical prayers and formulas were sold to the living as insurance policies guaranteeing them a happy outcome in the judgment before Osiris. They constitute much of what is known as the Book of the Dead, which was placed in the tomb.

Akhenaton's religious reformation was directed against the venal priests of Osiris as well as those of the supreme god Amon. As we have seen, Akhenaton failed to uproot Amon and the multiplicity of lesser gods; his monotheism was too cold and intellectual to attract the masses who yearned for a blessed hereafter.

Monumentalism in architecture. Because of their impressive and enduring tombs and temples, the Egyptians have been called the greatest builders in history. The earliest tomb was the mud-brick mastaba, so called because of its resemblance to a low bench. By the beginning of the Third Dynasty stone began to replace brick, and an architectural genius named Imhotep constructed the first pyramid by piling six huge stone mastabas one on top of the other. Adjoining this Step Pyramid was a temple complex whose stone columns were not freestanding but attached to a wall, as though the architect was still feeling his way in the use of the new medium.

The most celebrated of the true pyramids were built for the Fourth Dynasty pharaohs Khufu, Khafre, and Menkaure. Khufu's pyramid, the largest of the three, covers thirteen acres and originally rose 481 feet. It is composed of 2,300,000 limestone blocks, some weighing fifteen tons, and all pushed and pulled into place by human muscle. This stupendous monument was built without mortar, yet some of the stones were so perfectly fitted that a knife cannot be inserted in the joint. The Old Kingdom's pyramids are a striking expression of Egyptian civilization. In their dignity, massiveness, and repose, they reflect the religion-motivated character of Egyptian society.

As the glory and serenity of the Old Kingdom can be seen in its pyramids, constructed as an act of faith by its subjects, so the power and wealth of the Empire survives in the temples at Thebes, made possible by the booty and tribute of conquest. On the east side of the Nile stand the ruins of the magnificent temples of Karnak and Luxor. The Hypostyle Hall of the temple of Karnak, built by Ramses II, is larger than the cathedral of Notre Dame. Its forest of 134 columns is arranged in sixteen rows, with the roof over the two broader central aisles (the nave) raised to allow the entry of light. This technique of providing a clerestory over a central nave was later used in Roman basilicas and Christian churches.

Sculpture and painting. Egyptian art was essentially religious. Tomb paintings and relief sculpture depict the everyday activities that the deceased wished to continue enjoying in the afterlife, and statues glorify the god-kings in all their serenity and eternity. Since religious art is inherently conservative, Egyptian art seldom departed from the traditions established during the vigorous and self-assured Old Kingdom. Sculptors idealized and standardized their subjects, and the human figure is shown looking directly ahead.

Yet on two occasions an unprecedented naturalism appeared in Egyptian sculpture. The faces of some of the Middle Kingdom rulers appear drawn and weary, as though they were weighed down by the burden of reconstructing Egypt after the collapse of the Old Kingdom. An even greater naturalism is seen in the portraits of Akhenaton and his beautiful queen, Nefertete. The pharaoh's brooding countenance is realistically portrayed, as in his ungainly paunch and his

In contrast to conventional Egyptian art, this representation of Akhenaton is so naturalistic that it borders on caricature.

happy but far from god-like family life as he holds one of his young daughters on his knee or munches on a bone. The "heretic" pharaoh, who insisted on what he called "truth" in religion, seems also to have insisted on truth in art.

Painting in Egypt shows the same precision and mastery of technique that are evident in sculpture. However, no attempt was made to show objects in perspective, and the scenes give an appearance of flatness. The effect of distance was conveyed by making objects in a series or by putting one object above another.

Writing and literature. In Egypt, as in Sumer, writing began with pictures. But unlike the Mesopotamian signs, Egyptian hieroglyphs ("sacred signs") remained primarily pictorial. At first the hieroglyphs represented only objects, but later they came to stand for ideas and syllables. Early in the Old Kingdom the Egyptians began to use alphabetic characters for twenty-four consonant sounds. Although they also continued to use the old pictographic and syllabic signs, this discovery was of far-reaching consequence. It led to the development of the Semitic alphabet, from which our present alphabet is derived.

Egypt's oldest literature is the Pyramid Texts, a body of religious writing found inscribed on the walls of the burial chambers of Old Kingdom pharaohs. Their recurrent theme is a monotonous insistence that the dead pharaoh is really a god.

The troubled life that followed the collapse of the Old Kingdom produced the highly personal literature of the First Intermediate Period and Middle Kingdom. It contains protests against the ills of the day, demands for social justice, and praise for the romantic excitements of wine, women, and song. The following lines are from a love poem, in which the beloved is called "sister":

> I behold how my sister cometh, and my heart is in gladness.
> Mine arms open wide to embrace her; my heart exulteth within me: for my
>   lady has come to me. . . .
> She kisseth me, she openeth her lips to me: then am I joyful even without
>   beer.[19]

A classic of Egyptian literature is Akhenaton's *Hymn to the Sun*, which is similar in spirit to Psalm 104. A few lines will indicate its lyric beauty and its conception of one omnipotent and beneficent Creator.

> How manifold are thy works!
> They are hidden before men,
> O sole god, beside whom there is no other.
> Thou didst create the earth according to thy heart
> While thou wast alone.[20]

THE ERA OF SMALL STATES

The Phoenicians. After 1200 B.C., with Egypt in decline and the Hittite empire destroyed by new Indo-European invaders, the Semitic peoples of Syria and Palestine ceased being pawns in a struggle between rival imperialisms (see p. 30). For nearly five hundred years, until the rise of new empires, these peoples—

Phoenicians and Hebrews in particular—were to play an independent and significant role in history.

Phoenician is the name the Greeks gave to those Canaanites who dwelt along the Mediterranean coast of Syria, an area that is today the state of Lebanon. Hemmed in by the Lebanon Mountains to the east, the Phoenicians turned to the sea and by the eleventh century B.C. had become the greatest traders, shipbuilders, navigators, and colonizers before the Greeks. To obtain silver and copper from Spain and tin from Britain, Gades (Cadiz) was founded on the Atlantic coast of Spain. Carthage, one of a number of Phoenician trading posts around the shores of the Mediterranean, was destined to become Rome's chief rival in the third century B.C.

Although the Phoenicians were essentially traders, their home cities—notably Tyre, Sidon, and Byblos—also produced manufactured goods. Their most famous export was woolen cloth dyed with the purple dye obtained from shellfish found along their coast. They were also skilled makers of furniture (made from the famous cedars of Lebanon), metalware, glassware, and jewelry.

Culturally the Phoenicians were not creative. They left behind no literature and little art. Yet they made one of the greatest contributions to human progress, the perfection of the alphabet, which they carried westward. The origin of the alphabet is still a moot question. Between 1800 and 1600 B.C. various Canaanite peoples, influenced by Egypt's semialphabetical writing, started to evolve a simplified method of writing. The Phoenician alphabet of twenty-two consonant symbols (the Greeks later added the vowel signs) is derived from the thirty-character alphabet of Ugarit, a Canaanite city on the Syrian coast opposite Cyprus.

The half-dozen Phoenician cities never united to form a strong state, and in the last half of the eighth century B.C. all but Tyre were conquered by the Assyrians. When Tyre finally fell to the Chaldeans in 571 B.C., the Hebrew prophet Ezekiel spoke what reads like an epitaph to the once great role played by the Phoenicians:

> When your wares came from the seas, you satisfied many peoples; with your abundant wealth and merchandise you enriched the kings of the earth. Now you are wrecked by the seas, in the depths of the waters; your merchandise and all your crew have sunk with you.[21]

The Hebrew kingdoms. In war, diplomacy, inventions, and art, the Hebrews made little splash in the stream of history. In religion and ethics, however, their contribution to world civilization was tremendous. Out of their experience grew three great religions: Judaism, Christianity, and Islam.

Hebrew experience is recorded in the Holy Writ of Israel, the Old Testament of the Christian Bible, whose present content was approved about 90 A.D. by a council of rabbis. All of us are familiar with the power and beauty of some of its many great passages. As a work of literature it remains unsurpassed; but it is more than that. "It is Israel's life story—a story that cannot be told adequately apart from the conviction that God had called this people in his grace, separated them from the nations for a special responsibility, and commissioned them with the task of being his servant in the accomplishment of his purpose."[22]

The Biblical account of the history of the Hebrews (later called Israelites and then Jews) begins with the patriarchal clan leader Abraham. About 1800 B.C. Abraham led his people out of Ur in Sumer, where they had settled for a time in their wanderings, and eventually they arrived in the land of Canaan, later called Palestine.

About 1700 B.C., driven by famine, some Hebrews followed Abraham's great-grandson Joseph into Egypt. Joseph's rise to power in Egypt, and the hospitable reception of his people there, is attributed to the presence of the largely Semitic Hyksos, who had conquered Egypt about 1700 B.C. (see p. 22). Following the expulsion of the Hyksos by the pharaohs of the Eighteenth Dynasty, the Hebrews were enslaved by the Egyptians. Shortly after 1300 B.C. Moses led them out of bondage and into the wilderness of Sinai, where they entered into a pact or covenant with their God, Yahweh. The Sinai Covenant bound the people as a whole—the nation of Israel, as they now called themselves—to worship Yahweh before all other gods and to obey his Law. In return, Yahweh made the Israelites his chosen people whom he would protect and to whom he granted Canaan, "a land flowing with milk and honey." The history of Israel from this time on is the story of the working out of this covenant.

The Israelites had to contend for Palestine against the Canaanites, whose Semitic ancestors had migrated from Arabia early in the third millennium B.C. Joined by other Hebrew tribes already in Palestine, the Israelites formed a confederacy of twelve tribes and, led by war leaders called judges, in time succeeded in subjugating the Canaanites. In the meantime, however, a far more formidable foe had appeared. The Philistines, from whom we get the word *Palestine*, settled along the coast about 1175 B.C., having been uprooted from Asia Minor by the invasions that destroyed the Hittite empire. Aided by the use of iron weapons, which were new to Palestine, the Philistines were well on their way to dominating the entire land by the middle of the eleventh century.

It became apparent that the loose twelve-tribe confederacy could not cope with the Philistine danger. "Give us a king to govern us," the people demanded, "that we also may be like all the nations, and that our king may govern us and go before us and fight our battles."[23] Saul, the first king of Israel (1020–1000 B.C.), died while fighting the Philistines, but his successor David (1000–961 B.C.) not only restricted the Philistines to a narrow coastal strip but became the ruler of the largest state in the ancient history of the area, stretching from the Euphrates to the Gulf of Aqaba.

The work of David was completed by his son Solomon, in whose long reign (961–922 B.C.) Israel reached a pinnacle of worldly power and splendor as an oriental-style monarchy. In the words of the Bible:

> Now the weight of gold that came to Solomon in one year was six hundred and sixty-six talents of gold, besides that which came from the traders and from the traffic of the merchants, and from all the kings of Arabia and from the governors of the land. . . . The king also made a great ivory throne, and overlaid it with the finest gold. . . . [24]

But the price of Solomon's vast bureaucracy, building projects (especially the palace complex and the Temple at Jerusalem), standing army (1400 chariots and 12,000 horses), and harem (700 wives and 300 concubines) was great. High taxes, forced labor, and the loss of tribal independence led to dissension, and on the death of Solomon in 922 B.C. the realm was split into two kingdoms—Israel in the north and Judah in the south. These two weak kingdoms were in no position to defend themselves when new, powerful empires rose again in Mesopotamia. In

721 B.C. the Assyrians captured Samaria, the capital of the northern kingdom, taking 27,900 Israelites into captivity and settling foreign peoples in their place.

The southern kingdom of Judah held out until 586 B.C. when Nebuchadnezzar, the Chaldean ruler of Babylonia, destroyed Jerusalem and carried away ten thousand captives; "none remained, except the poorest people of the land."[25] Thus began the famous Babylonian Exile of the Jews (Judeans), which lasted until 538 B.C. when Cyrus the Persian, having conquered Babylon, allowed them to return to Jerusalem where they rebuilt the Temple destroyed by Nebuchadnezzar.

Persian rule was followed by that of the Hellenistic Greeks and Romans. In 66–70 A.D. the Jews rebelled against Rome, and Jerusalem was totally destroyed in the savage fighting that ensued. Many Jews were again driven into exile, and the Diaspora—the "scattering"—was at its height.

Hebrew religion. From the time of Abraham the Hebrews worshipped one god, a stern, warlike tribal deity whose name, Yahweh (Jehovah), was first revealed to Moses. Yahweh differed from the many Near Eastern nature gods in being completely separate from the physical universe which He had created. This view of Yahweh as the Creator of all things everywhere was inevitably to lead to the monotheistic belief that He was the sole God in the universe.

After their entrance into Palestine, many Hebrews adopted the fertility deities of the Canaanites as well as the luxurious Canaanite manner of living. As a result prophets arose who "spoke for" Yahweh in insisting on strict adherence to the Sinai Covenant and in condemning the "whoring" after other gods, the selfish pursuit of wealth, and the growth of social injustice.

Between roughly 750 and 550 B.C. appeared a series of great prophets who wrote down their messages. They sought to purge the religion of Israel of all corrupting influences and to elevate and dignify the concept of Yahweh. As summed up by Micah in a statement often cited as the essence of all higher religion, "He has shown you, O man, what is good; and what does the Lord require of you but to do justice, and to love kindness, and to walk humbly with your God?"[26] The prophets viewed the course of Hebrew history as being governed by the sovereign will of Yahweh, seeing the Assyrians and the Chaldeans as "the rod of Yahweh's anger" to chastise His stubborn, wayward people. They also developed the idea of a coming Messiah, the "anointed one" from the family of King David, who would inaugurate a reign of peace and justice.

Considered the greatest of the prophets are Jeremiah and the anonymous Second Isaiah, so-called because his message was incorporated in the Book of Isaiah (chapters 40–55). Jeremiah witnessed the events that led to Nebuchadnez-zar's destruction of Jerusalem and the Temple and to the Babylonian Captivity of the Jews. He prepared the people for these calamities by affirming that Yahweh would forgive their sins and restore "a remnant" of his people and by proclaiming a "new covenant." The old covenant had been between Yahweh and the nation, which no longer existed, and it had become overlaid with ritual and ceremony and centered in the Temple, which had been destroyed. The new covenant was between Yahweh and each individual; religion was now a matter of a man's own heart and conscience, and both the nation and the Temple were considered superfluous. The Second Isaiah, who lived at the end of the Babylonian Captivity, capped the work of his predecessors by proclaiming Israel to be Yahweh's "righteous servant," purified and enlightened by suffering and ready to guide the world to the worship of the one, eternal, supreme God. Thus were the Jews who returned from the Exile provided with a renewed faith in their destiny and a new

comprehension of their religion which would sustain them through the centuries
to come.

LATER EMPIRES OF WESTERN ASIA

Assyrian expansion. By 700 B.C. the era of small states was at an end. For two
hundred years the Assyrians had been bidding to translate the growing economic
unity of the Near East—evidenced by Solomon's trading operations—into political unity. The Assyrian push toward the Mediterranean began in the ninth century
and, after a lapse, was resumed in the eighth century, during which Babylon was
also subdued. By 721 B.C. the Assyrians were the masters of the Fertile Crescent,
and in 671 B.C. they conquered Egypt.

A Semitic people long established in the hilly region of the upper Tigris, the
Assyrians had been schooled for a thousand years by constant warfare. But their
matchless army was only one of several factors that explain the success of
Assyrian imperialism: a policy of calculated terrorization, an efficient system of
political administration, and the support of the commercial classes that wanted
political stability and unrestricted trade over large areas.

The Assyrian army, with its chariots, mounted cavalry, and sophisticated siege
engines, was the most powerful yet seen in the ancient world. Neither troops or
walls could long resist the Assyrians who, in Byron's well-known phrase, "came
down like a wolf on the fold." Conquered peoples were held firmly in control by
systematic terrorization: "From some I cut off their noses, their ears and their
fingers, of many I put out the eyes. . . . I bound their heads to tree trunks round
about the city."[27] In addition mass deportations effectively destroyed national
feeling.

The well-coordinated Assyrian system of political administration was another
factor in the success of the empire. Conquered lands became provinces ruled by
governors who exercised extensive military, judicial, and financial powers. Their
chief tasks were to ensure the regular collection of tribute and the raising of
troops for the permanent army that eventually replaced the native militia of sturdy
Assyrian peasants. An efficient system of communications carried the "king's
word" to the governors as well as the latter's reports to the royal court—including
one prophetic dispatch reading: "The king knows that all lands hate us. . . . "[28]
Nevertheless, the Assyrians must be credited with laying the foundations for the
later more humane administrative systems of the Persians and Alexander the
Great and his successors.

Downfall of the Assyrian empire. Revolt against Assyrian terror and tribute
was inevitable when Assyria's strength waned and effective opposition arose. By
the middle of the seventh century B.C. the sturdy Assyrian stock had been
decimated by wars, and the Assyrian kings had to rely on unreliable mercenary
troops and subject levies. Egypt regained its independence, and the Medes
refused further tribute. Then the Chaldeans, a new group of Semites who had
filtered into Babylonia, revolted. In 612 they joined the Medes in destroying
Nineveh, the Assyrian capital. From one end of the Fertile Crescent to the other
people rejoiced: "Nineveh is laid waste: who will bemoan her?"[29]

The Median and Chaldean empires. The Medes were an Indo-European people
who by 1000 B.C. had established themselves on the Iranian plateau east of

Assyria. In the seventh century B.C. they had created a strong kingdom with Ecbatana as capital and with the Persians, their kinsmen to the south, as vassals. Following the collapse of Assyria, the Medes expanded into Armenia and eastern Asia Minor, but their short-lived empire ended in 550 B.C. when they were absorbed by the Persians.

While the Medes controlled the highland region, the Chaldeans, with their capital at Babylon, were masters of the Fertile Crescent. Nebuchadnezzar, becoming king of the Chaldeans in 604 B.C., raised Babylonia to another epoch of brilliance after more than a thousand years of eclipse. The tremendous city walls of his rebuilt Babylon were wide enough at the top to have rows of small houses on either side with a road between. The immense palace of Nebuchadnezzar towered terrace upon terrace, each resplendent with masses of ferns, flowers, and trees. These roof gardens, the famous Hanging Gardens of Babylon, were so beautiful that they were regarded by the Greeks as one of the seven wonders of the ancient world. The king also rebuilt the great temple-tower or ziggurat, the famed Biblical "Tower of Babel."

Nebuchadnezzar was the last great Mesopotamian ruler, and Chaldean power quickly crumbled after his death in 562 B.C. The Chaldean priests—whose interest in astrology greatly added to the fund of Babylonian astronomical knowledge—continually undermined the monarchy. Finally, in 539 B.C., they opened the gates of Babylon to Cyrus the Persian, thus fulfilling Daniel's message of doom upon the notorious Belshazzar, the last Chaldean ruler: "You have been weighed in the balances and found wanting."

The Persian empire. Cyrus the Persian was the greatest conqueror in the history of the ancient Near East. In 550 B.C. he had ended Persian vassalage to the Medes by capturing Ecbatana and ousting the Median dynasty. The Medes readily accepted their vigorous new ruler, who soon demonstrated that he deserved to be called "the Great." When King Croesus of Lydia advanced in 547 B.C. to pick up some of the pieces of the Median empire, Cyrus defeated him and annexed Lydia, including those Greek cities on the coast of Asia Minor which were under the nominal control of Lydia. Then he turned east, establishing his power as far as the frontier of India. Babylon and its empire, as we have seen, was next on his list. Following the death of Cyrus, his son Cambyses conquered Egypt. The next ruler, Darius I (522–486 B.C.), began a conflict with the Greeks that continued intermittently for more than 150 years until the Persians were conquered by Alexander the Great. Long before this event the Persian nobles had forgotten Cyrus the Great's answer to their suggestion that they "leave this small and barren country of ours" and migrate to Babylonia, a pleasanter land:

> Do so if you wish, but if you do, be ready to find yourselves no longer governors but governed; for soft lands breed soft men; it does not happen that the same land brings forth wonderful crops and good fighting men.[30]

Although built upon the Assyrian model, the Persian administrative system was far more efficient and humane. The empire was divided into twenty provinces, or satrapies, each ruled by a governor called a satrap. To check the satraps, a secretary and a military official representing the "Great King, King of Kings" were installed in every province. Also, special inspectors, "the Eyes and Ears of the King," traveled throughout the realm.

Imperial post roads connected the important cities of the empire. Along the

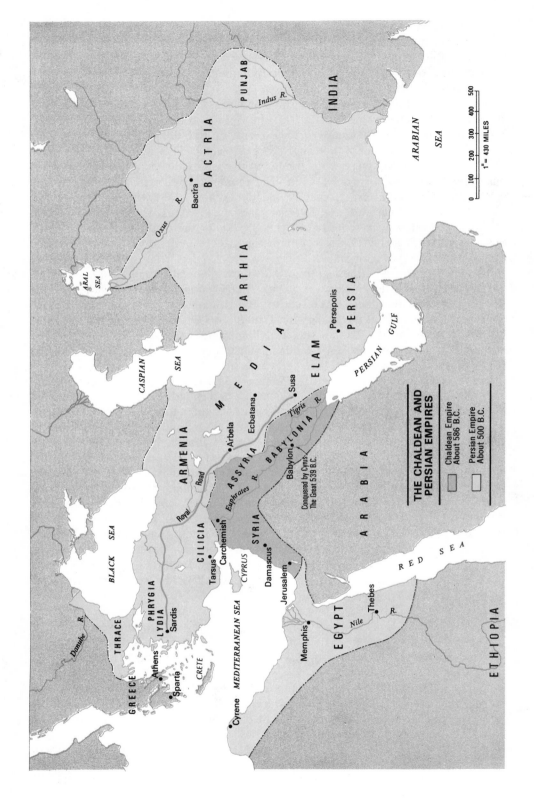

THE CHALDEAN AND PERSIAN EMPIRES

Chaldean Empire
About 586 B.C.

Persian Empire
About 500 B.C.

500
400
300
200
100
1" = 430 MILES
0

PUNJAB

INDIA

Indus R.

BACTRIA

Bactra

ARABIAN
SEA

Oxus R.

PARTHIA

ARAL
SEA

PERSIA

Persepolis

MEDIA

ELAM

CASPIAN SEA

Susa

Tigris R.

Ecbatana

ARMENIA

ASSYRIA

Arbela

BABYLONIA

Royal Road

Babylon

Euphrates R.

Conquered by Cyrus
The Great 539 B.C.

PERSIAN GULF

ARABIA

CILICIA

Carchemish

SYRIA

Tarsus

CYPRUS

Damascus

BLACK SEA

Jerusalem

PHRYGIA

Sardis

LYDIA

Danube R.

THRACE

RED SEA

GREECE

Athens

Sparta

CRETE

MEDITERRANEAN SEA

EGYPT

Thebes

Memphis

Nile R.

Cyrene

ETHIOPIA

Royal Road between Sardis and Susa there was a post station every fourteen miles, where the king's couriers could obtain fresh horses, enabling them to cover the 1600 miles in a week. "Nothing mortal travels so fast as these Persian messengers," wrote the Greek historian Herodotus. "These men will not be hindered . . . , either by snow, or rain, or heat, or by the darkness of night."[31]

The Persian empire was the first to attempt governing many different racial groups on the principle of equal responsibilities and rights for all peoples. So long as his subjects paid their taxes and kept the peace, the king did not interfere with local religion, customs, or trade. Indeed, Darius was called the "shopkeeper" because he stimulated trade by introducing a uniform system of gold and silver coinage, an invention of the Lydians about 675 B.C.

Persian religion. The humaneness of the Persian rulers may have stemmed from the ethical religion founded by the prophet Zoroaster, who lived in the early sixth century B.C. Zoroaster sought to replace what he called "the lie"—ritualistic, idol-worshiping cults and their Magi priests—with a religion centered on the sole god Ahura-Mazda ("Wise Lord"), who demanded "good thoughts of the mind, good deeds of the hand, and good words of the tongue" from those who would attain paradise (a Persian word). The new religion made little progress until first Darius and then the Magi adopted it. The Magi revived many old gods as lesser deities, added much ritual, and replaced monotheism with dualism by transforming what Zoroaster had called the principle or spirit of evil into the powerful god Ahriman, rival of Ahura-Mazda. The complicated evolution of Zoroastrianism is revealed in its holy writ, the *Avesta* ("The Law"), assembled in its present form between the fourth and the sixth centuries A.D. Zoroastrian doctrines of the resurrection of the dead and the last judgment influenced Judaism. Following the Muslim conquest of Persia in the seventh century A.D., Zoroastrianism gradually died out in its homeland. It exists today among the Parsees in India.

Although the Persian kings exercised a generally benevolent and tolerant rule, their diverse subjects received no share in government. Let us now turn to Greece, in whose city-states very different ideas about the individual's rights in society were emerging.

CHAPTER 2
THE GLORY
THAT WAS GREECE

Aegean, Hellenic, and Hellenistic Civilizations

Scarred by time and weather, the ruins of the Athenian Acropolis stand against a vivid blue sky and overlook the trees and buildings of a modern city sprawled beneath. These ruins are striking symbols of the departed civilization of ancient Greece.

In the fifth century B.C. the temples and statuary of the Acropolis were gleaming and new, fresh from the hands of builders and sculptors. Five hundred years later Plutarch wrote:

[The Acropolis looks] at this day as if it were but newly done and finished, there is such a certain kind of flourishing freshness in it . . . that the injury of time cannot impair the sight thereof. As if every one of those . . . works had some living spirit in it, to make it seem young and fresh: and a soul that lived ever, which kept them in their good continuing state.[1]

Today the Acropolis bears the heavy "injury of time"; yet for us no less than for Plutarch, ancient Athens has retained a "flourishing freshness." This quality, together with a refined sense of symmetry and proportion, is characteristic of the Greek spirit and the dazzling achievements of Greek civilization. The ancient Greeks repeatedly demonstrated an ability to regard the world about them from a "young and fresh" perspective and to inject a love of proportion not only into their architecture but into almost everything they attempted. Yet in the crucial sphere of politics, their sense of proportion failed them. Instead of compromising their differences, the city-states quarreled continually, and that fervid individualism which moved them to brilliant creative efforts blinded them to the necessity of cooperation. Thus the political life of the Greeks was marked by conflicts between the city-states until they were at last subjugated by King Philip of Macedonia and his son, Alexander the Great.

Yet Greece's accomplishment has proved so enduring that its magnificent legacy of knowledge and art has provided much of the cultural heritage of the West and, to a lesser extent, of the East. Thus the English poet Shelley could say with justification, "We are all Greeks."

Aegean civilization. The Greek achievement was preceded by an advanced civilization that flourished in Greece and in other areas surrounding the Aegean Sea. This Aegean civilization, as it is called, which came into full flower about 2000 B.C. and collapsed suddenly following 1200 B.C., developed through two major periods. The first and longer period, which ended about 1450 B.C., is called "Minoan" after the legendary Cretan King Minos. Crete was the center of Minoan civilization, which spread to the Aegean Islands, to Troy in Asia Minor, and to Greece. The last period of Aegean civilization, which extended from 1450 to 1200 B.C., when the center of Aegean political power and culture lay on the Greek mainland, is called "Mycenaean" after its most important site at Mycenae.

The Minoans. The narrow, 160-mile-long island of Crete was a stepping stone between Europe, Asia, and Africa. Stimulated by contacts with Mesopotamia and Egypt, a brilliant and prosperous civilization emerged here. Minoan trade ranged from Troy to Egypt and from Sicily to Syria and employed the first ships capable of long voyages over the open sea. Chief exports were olive oil, wine, metalware, and magnificent pottery. This trade was the monopoly of an efficient bureaucratic government whose records were written on clay tablets, first in a form of picture writing and later in two scripts, which the English archaeologist Sir Arthur Evans labeled Linear A and B. For years these forms of writing were not translated, but a lecture by Evans on the scripts fascinated an English schoolboy, Michael Ventris. In 1952 Ventris, who by this time was a young architect, startled the scholarly world by deciphering Linear B. The script turned out to be an early form of Greek, written in syllabic characters. This feat of an amateur had upset academic ideas of Greek history, proving that the earliest antecedents of the Greeks, the Minoans, were literate. not semibarbarian, as had been believed.

It was Evans who first uncovered this civilization, whose existence had previously only been hinted at in Greek legends and the epics of Homer. Between 1900 and 1905 Evans unearthed the ruins of a great palace at Knossos, the dominant city in Crete after 1700 B.C. Rising at least three stories high and sprawling over nearly six acres, this Palace of Minos was a maze of royal apartments, storerooms, corridors, open courtyards, and broad stairways. Walls were painted with elaborate frescoes in which the Minoans appear as a gay, peaceful people with a pronounced liking for dancing, festivals, and athletic contests. Women are shown enjoying a freedom and dignity unknown elsewhere in the ancient Near East or classical Greece. Furnished with running water, the palace had a sanitation system surpassing anything constructed in Europe until Roman times. The palace was linked to other parts of Crete by well-paved roads lined with the luxurious dwellings of the nobility.

The glory of Minoan culture was its art—gay, spontaneous, and full of rhythmic motion. Art was an essential part of everyday life and not, as in the ancient Orient, an adjunct to religion and the state. What little is known of Minoan religion also contrasts sharply with conditions in the Near East: there were no great temples, powerful priesthoods, or large cult statues of the gods. The principal deity seems to have been the Mother Goddess, and a number of recovered statuettes show her dressed like a fashionable Cretan lady with flounced skirts, a tightly laced, low-cut bodice, and an elaborate coiffure.

The Mycenaeans. About 2000 B.C., or shortly thereafter, the first Indo-

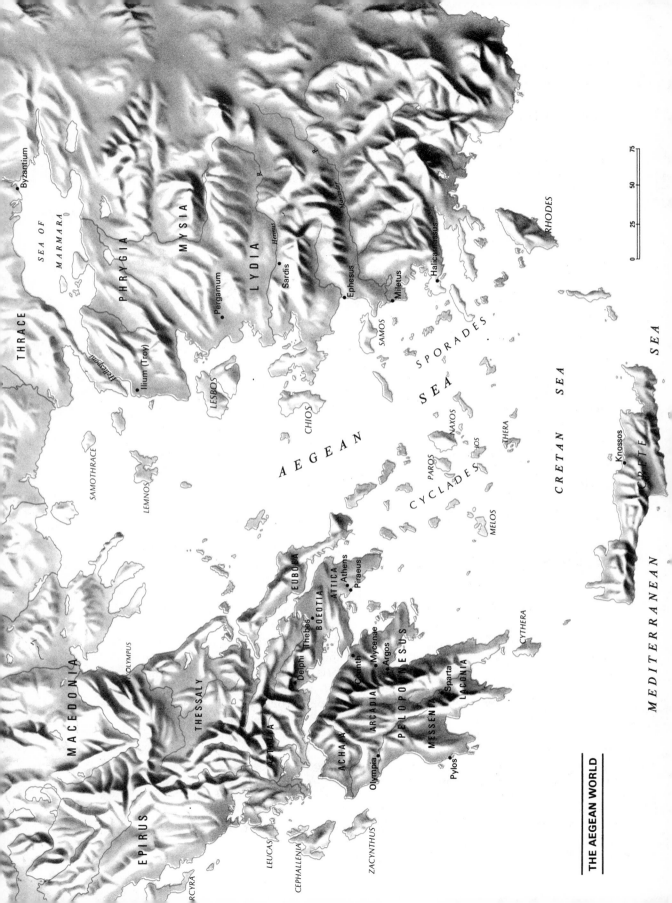

THE AEGEAN WORLD

European Greek tribes, collectively called Achaeans, entered Greece, where they absorbed the earlier settlers and ruled from strongly fortified citadels at Mycenae, Pylos, Thebes, and other sites. By 1600 B.C. the Achaeans—or Mycenaeans, as they are usually called—had evolved their own civilization, based largely on borrowings from the Minoans, and were plying the seas both as pirates and as traders.

The expansive force of this Mycenaean civilization led to the planting of colonies in the eastern Mediterranean (Hittite sources refer to Mycenaeans in Asia Minor) and to the conquest of Knossos about 1450 B.C. This latter event was made possible by the destruction of the labyrinthian palace at Knossos by fire—the aftereffect, it is now conjectured, of a great tidal wave caused by the eruption of the small volcanic island of Thera (Santorini) eighty miles north of Crete. The palace at Knossos was rebuilt by the Mycenaeans, but it was permanently destroyed about 1380 B.C. by earthquake and fire. At that point the center of Aegean civilization shifted from Crete to the Greek mainland. The Mycenaean conquest of the Minoans and their cultural debt to them was clearly spelled out when the Linear B translations indicated that the rulers of Knossos after 1450 B.C. must have been the Mycenaeans who had adopted the Cretan script to write their own language.

From the many Linear B tablets found on the mainland, scholars have added greatly to our knowledge of Mycenaean life. The Mycenaean centers were fortified palaces and administrative centers and not, as in Crete, true cities. The bulk of the population lived in scattered villages where they worked either communal land or land held by nobles or the king. The nobles were under the close control of the monarchs, whose administrative records were kept daily by a large number of scribes. The most important item of income was olive oil, the major article in the wide-ranging Mycenaean trade, which operated as a royal monopoly.

The commercial success of Mycenaean trade was apparent in the hoard of gold, silver, and ivory objects unearthed by Heinrich Schleimann, who came to Mycenae fresh from even more sensational discoveries at Troy (see below). The royal palace on the acropolis, or citadel, of Mycenae had well-proportioned audience rooms and apartments, fresco-lined walls, floors of painted stucco, and large storerooms. Noteworthy also were the royal "beehive" tombs, constructed of cut stone and covered with earth.

Troy, site of the Homeric epics. Perhaps it was their role as traders that led the Mycenaean kings late in the 13th century B.C. to launch their famous expedition against Troy in an attempt to eliminate a commercial rival. The city of Troy occupied a strategic position on the Hellespont (the straits between the Black and Aegean seas now known as the Dardanelles). From there, Troy could command both the sea traffic through the straits and the land caravans between Asia and Europe. For many years scholars thought this city existed only in the epic poems of Homer. Heinrich Schliemann (1822-1890), a German amateur archaeologist, believed otherwise. As a boy, he had read Homer's *Iliad*, and thereafter he remained firmly convinced that Troy had actually existed. At the age of forty-eight, having amassed a fortune in world trade and in the California gold rush, Schliemann put his persistent dream of ancient Troy to the test.

In 1870 Schliemann excavated at the legendary site of Troy, where he unearthed several cities, built one on top of the other. He discovered a treasure of golden earrings, hairpins, and bracelets in the second city, which led him to believe that this was the city of Homer's epics. Excavations in the 1930's, however, showed that the seventh city, over a thousand years more recent than the second, was the one made famous by Homer. Twice in his lifetime Heinrich Schliemann uncovered the real remains of legendary cities—Mycenae, which opened up a whole new link in Aegean history, and Troy, which had previously been thought to exist only in Homer's epics.

The fall of Mycenaean civilization.   Shortly after the fall of Troy, a new wave of Indo-Europeans, the Dorian Greeks, materially aided by weapons made of iron instead of bronze, burst upon Greece about 1200 B.C. First of the Mycenaean strongholds to fall was Pylos, whose Linear B archives contain numerous references to hastily undertaken preparations to repel the invaders. We find orders directing women and children to places of safety; instructions to armorers, "rowers," and food suppliers; and a report entitled "how the watchers are guarding the coastal regions." The preparations were in vain, however. Pylos was sacked and burned, and the destruction of the other major Mycenaean citadels soon followed. Mycenaean refugees found a haven at Athens and in Ionia on the western coast of Asia Minor. The next four centuries, often called the Greek Middle Ages, were marked by the disappearance of the major characteristics of Mycenaean civilization—political centralization, wide-ranging commerce, sophisticated art forms, and writing. Yet while the Dorian invasion was a catastrophe at the time, it allowed the ultimate rise of a unique Hellenic civilization that was not largely an offshoot of the Near East, as was the Aegean civilization. (The Greeks called their land *Hellas* and themselves *Hellenes*, hence the term "Hellenic" civilization.)

THE RISE OF HELLENIC CIVILIZATION

The Homeric Age.   Most of our information about the Greek Dark Ages (c. 1150–750 B.C.), which followed the Dorian invasion is derived from the epics, the *Iliad* and the *Odyssey*, composed during the last century of this period and attributed to the blind Ionian poet Homer. The epics describe the political, economic, and social life, the religious beliefs and practices, and the ideals of Homer's day, even though the events described took place earlier. The values of the Homeric Age were predominantly heroic—the strength, skill, and valor of the preeminent warrior. Such was the earliest meaning of *aretē*, "excellence" or "virtue," a key term throughout the course of Greek culture. To obtain *aretē*—defined by one Homeric hero as "to fight ever in the forefront and outvie my peers"—and the imperishable fame that was its reward, men welcomed hardship, struggle, and even death. Honor, like fame, was a measure of *aretē*, and the greatest of human tragedies was the denial of honor due to a great warrior.

To the Homeric Greeks, the gods were plainly human: Zeus, the king of the gods, was often the undignified victim of the plots of his wife Hera and other deities, and he asserted his authority through threats of violence. Hades, the abode of the dead, was a subterranean land of dust and darkness; Achilles, as Homer tells us in the *Odyssey*, would have preferred to be a slave on earth than a king in Hades.

Society was clearly aristocratic—only the *aristoi* ("aristocrats") possessed *aretē*. The king was hardly more than a chief among his peers, his fellow nobles,

The Persian invasion made Athens a heap of ruins, but the withdrawal of the invaders left the Athenians free to reconstruct the Acropolis into a treasury of temples and statues. In the Parthenon, which housed Phidias' huge gold and ivory statue of Athena, great care was taken to design a structurally and visually perfect building. The tops of the Doric columns lean toward the center of each colonnade, the steps curve upward at the center, and the columns are more widely spaced in the middle of each row than at the ends—all these refinements create an illusion of perfect regularity which would be lacking if the parts were actually perfectly proportioned. The Parthenon was originally brightly painted, and painted sculpture adorned the gables and parts of the frieze, while another sculptured and painted frieze ran around the walls inside the colonnade.

who sat in his council to advise him and to check any attempt he might make to act on his own. The common people were reviled and beaten when they dared to question their betters. Yet they had certain political rights as members of the assembly that was summoned whenever a crisis such as war required their participation. Economic conditions were those of a simple, self-sufficient agricultural system much like that of the early Middle Ages in western Europe.

The city-states: origin and political growth.   About the time that the Homeric Age came to a close, the famed Greek political unit, the city-state (*polis*), consisting of a city and its surrounding plains and valleys, began to take form. The nucleus of the city-state was the elevated, fortified site—the acropolis—where people could take refuge from attack. With the revival of commerce in the eighth and seventh centuries B.C., a trading center developed below the acropolis. The two parts combined, forming the city-state.

The political development of the city-state was so rich and varied that it is difficult to think of a form of government not experienced—and given a lasting name—by the Greeks. Four major types of government evolved: (1) monarchy, limited by an aristocratic council and a popular assembly, as described in the Homeric epics; (2) oligarchy ("rule of the few"), arising when the aristocratic council ousted the king and abolished or restricted the popular assembly; (3) tyranny, imposed by one man who rode to power on the discontent of the lower classes; (4) democracy ("rule of the people"), the outstanding political achievement of the Greeks, which emerged after the tyrant was deposed and the popular assembly revived and made the chief organ of government. After dissatisfaction with democratic government became widespread in the fourth century B.C., many of the city-states returned either to oligarchy or to one-man rule.

The Age of Oligarchy.   By the middle of the eighth century B.C., the nobles, who resented the power wielded by the tribal kings, had taken over the government, ushering in the Age of Oligarchy. Ruthlessly exercising their superior power, the nobles acquired a monopoly of the best land, reducing many commoners to virtual serfdom and forcing others to seek a living on rocky, barren soil.

The hard lot of the common man under oligarchy produced the anguished protest of Hesiod's *Works and Days* (c. 700 B.C.). A commoner who had been cheated out of his parcel of land by his evil brother in league with "bribe-swallowing" aristocratic judges, Hesiod was the prophet of a more exalted conception of the gods and a new age of social justice. To establish a just society, Hesiod argued, men must learn to pursue moderation (*sophrosynē*) in all things—apparently the first expression of this famous Greek ideal—and realize that "far-seeing" Zeus and the other gods punish evildoers and reward the righteous. He redefined human excellence, or *aretē*, in a way to make it attainable for the common man. Its essential ingredients were righteousness and work—honest work in competition with one's fellows being a form of strife in moderation. "Gods and men hate him who lives without work," Hesiod insisted. "His nature is like the drones who sit idle and eat the labor of the bees." Furthermore, "work is no shame, but idleness is a shame," and "esteem," "glory," and "riches" follow work.[2]

Hesiod's new ideals of moderation and justice took root slowly, and the poor found relief only by emigrating to new lands overseas. As Plato later noted, the wealthy promoted colonization as a safety valve to ward off a threatened political and economic explosion:

When men who have nothing, and are in want of food, show a disposition to follow their leaders in an attack on the property of the rich—these, who are the natural plague of the state, are sent away by the legislator in a friendly spirit as far as he is able; and this dismissal of them is euphemistically termed a colony.[3]

From 750 to 550 B.C. the Greeks planted colonies throughout much of the Mediterranean world, a development often compared with the expansion of Europe in modern times. Settlements sprang up along the northern coast of the Aegean and around the Black Sea. So many Greeks migrated to southern Italy and eastern Sicily that the region became known as *Magna Graecia*, or Great Greece. Colonies were also founded as far west as present-day France—at Massilia, modern Marseilles—and Spain and on parts of the African coast.

In time colonization ameliorated Greece's economic and social problems. By 600 B.C. the use of coined money, learned from the Lydians, had created the beginnings of a middle class. The Greek home states gradually became "industrialized" by producing specialized wares—vases, metal goods, textiles, olive oil, and wine—for export in exchange for foodstuffs and raw materials. But before this economic revolution was completed, the continuing land hunger of the peasants contributed to a political revolution. After 650 B.C. tyrants arose in many Greek states and, supported by the aggrieved peasantry and the rising merchant class, seized the reins of government from the nobility. These tyrants (the word meant simply "master" and did not at first have the unfavorable meaning it now possesses) not only distributed land to the peasants but, by promoting further colonization, trade, and industry, accelerated the rise of a mercantile class and the completion of the Greek economic revolution.

Athens to 500 B.C. Athens' political, economic, and social evolution was typical of most other Greek states. During the course of the seventh century B.C. at Athens, the council of nobles became supreme. The popular assembly no longer met, and the king was replaced by nine aristocratic magistrates, called archons, chosen annually by the council to exercise the king's civil, military, and religious powers. The nobility acquired the good land on the plain; the peasants either stayed on as sharecroppers, who were often reduced to debt slavery, or took to the hills.

When the Athenian nobles finally realized that their failure to heed the cry for reform would result in the rise of a tyrant, they agreed to the policy of compromise advocated by the liberal aristocrat Solon. In 594 B.C. Solon was made sole archon with broad authority to reconcile the lower classes. Inspired by the new ideals of moderation and justice, Solon instituted middle-of-the-road reforms that have made his name a byword for wise statesmanship.

Solon provided a new start for the lower classes by canceling all debts and forbidding future debt bondage, but he rejected as too radical their demand for the redivision of the land. His long-range solution to the economic problem was to seek full employment by stimulating trade and industry.

Moderation also characterized Solon's political reforms—the common people were granted important political rights, but not equality. While laws continued to originate in the new aristocratic Council of Four Hundred, they now had to be ratified by the popular assembly, which Solon revived. Furthermore, the assembly could now act as a court to hear appeals from the decisions of the archons and to try them for misdeeds in office.

Unfortunately, Solon's moderate reforms satisfied neither party. The poor had received neither land nor political equality, while the nobles thought Solon a radical who had betrayed his class. In 560 B.C., after a period of civil strife, Pisistratus, a military hero and champion of the commoners, usurped power as tyrant. He solved the economic problem by banishing many nobles, whose lands he distributed among the poor, and by promoting commerce and industry.

Pisistratus was succeeded by his two sons, one of whom was assassinated and the other exiled. When the nobles, aided by a Spartan army, took this opportunity to restore oligarchy, Cleisthenes temporarily seized power in 508 B.C. and put through constitutional reforms that destroyed the remaining power of the nobility. The popular assembly acquired the right to initiate legislation, while a new and democratic Council of Five Hundred, selected by lot, advised the assembly and supervised the administrative actions of the archons. A final reform was the peculiar institution of *ostracism*, an annual referendum in which a quorum of six thousand citizens could vote to exile for ten years any individual thought to be a threat to the new Athenian democracy.

Sparta to 500 B.C. In sharp contrast to Athens was the rival city-state Sparta. Sparta had not joined the other Greek cities in trade and colonization but had expanded instead by conquering and enslaving its neighbors. To guard against revolts by the state slaves (helots), who worked the land for their conquerors, Sparta was forced to deviate from the normal course of Greek political development and transform itself into a militaristic totalitarian state. Aristotle called the government of Sparta a "mixed constitution"; for the small minority of ruling Spartans, it was a democracy, but for the great mass of subjected people it was an oligarchy. The government included two kings, a small Council of Elders, and a popular assembly. True power resided in five overseers, the ephors, who were elected by the assembly and wielded more influence than the dual monarchs.

The Spartan was subordinated to his state. Every male Spartan was first of all a soldier. Sickly infants were left to die on lonely mountaintops; boys over seven lived under rigorous military discipline for the rest of their lives; girls were trained to become healthy mothers of warrior sons. As their men marched off to war, Spartan women bid them a laconic farewell: "Come back with your shield or on it."

While Sparta developed the finest military machine in Greece, it remained backward culturally and economically. Trade and travel were prohibited because the city fathers feared that alien ideas might disturb the status quo. The result was cultural stagnation.

To provide additional assurance that its helots remain uncontaminated by democratic ideas, Sparta allied itself with oligarchic parties in other Peloponnesian states and aided them in suppressing their democratic opponents. The resulting Spartan League of oligarchic states, in operation by the end of the sixth century B.C., was shortly to be faced by an Athenian-led union of democratic states.

UNITY AND STRIFE IN THE HELLENIC WORLD

The Persian Wars. The leaders of the Greek economic and cultural revival after 750 B.C. were the Ionian Greeks, descendants of the Mycenaeans who had fled to the Aegean coast of Asia Minor and its offshore islands. Influenced by contacts with Phoenician traders (from whom they borrowed the alphabet in the eighth century), neighboring Lydia, and Egypt, the Ionians "first kindled the torch of Hellenism."

We have seen in Chapter 1 that when the Persians conquered Lydia in 547 B.C. they also annexed Ionia, which had been under nominal Lydian rule. Chafing under Persian-appointed tyrants, the Ionian cities revolted in 499 B.C., established democratic regimes, and appealed to the Athenians, who were also Ionians, for aid. Athens sent twenty ships, but to no avail. By 494 B.C. Darius I had crushed the revolt.

To punish Athens, in 490 B.C. a Persian force of about twenty thousand men sailed across the Aegean and debarked on the plain of Marathon, northeast of Athens. The Athenian army, half the size of the Persian, won an overwhelming victory and demonstrated, in the words of the Greek historian Herodotus, that "free men fight better than slaves." The victory gave the Athenians the self-confidence that would soon make their city the leading Greek state.

Ten years later the Greeks faced a new Persian invasion under Xerxes, Darius' successor, whose objective was the subjection of all of Greece. Athens now had two hundred ships, the largest fleet in Greece, and Sparta had agreed to head a defensive alliance of thirty-one states.

The Persian army—probably 150,000 strong—was too huge to be transported by ship. Crossing the swift-flowing, mile-wide Hellespont on two pontoon bridges—a notable feat of engineering—the Persians advanced along the Aegean coast accompanied by a great fleet carrying provisions. The Spartans wanted to abandon all of Greece except the Peloponnesus to the invaders but finally agreed to a holding action at the narrow pass of Thermopylae. Here three hundred Spartans and a few thousand other Greeks held back the Persians for three days, until a Greek traitor led them over a mountain path to the rear of the Greek position.

The Persians then burned Athens, whose inhabitants had fled, for they placed their faith in "wooden walls"—their fleet. Their faith was not misplaced; in the Bay of Salamis the Greek fleet, largely Athenian, turned the tide of victory with the shout: "On, sons of the Greeks! Set free your country, set your children free, your wives, the temples of your country's gods, your fathers' tombs; now they are all at stake."[4] With 200 of his 350 ships destroyed and his lines of communication cut, Xerxes had no alternative but to retreat. The following summer (479 B.C.) the Greek army, with the Spartan contingent in the van, routed the Persian force at Plataea, and Greece was for the time being safe from invasion.

Culmination of Athenian democracy. Following the expulsion of the Persians, the Athenians "felt themselves suddenly to be 'on top of the world,' and from this in a large measure sprang the reckless confidence and boundless energy which now carried them forward to the greatest phase of their history. Athens' heyday lasted less than eighty years, and the number of her adult male citizens scarcely exceeded fifty thousand. Yet this handful of men attempted more and achieved more in a wider variety of fields than any nation great or small has ever attempted or achieved in a similar space of time."[5]

For more than thirty years (461–429 B.C.) during this Golden Age of Greece, the great statesman Pericles guided Athenian policy. In Pericles' time the actual executive power resided in a board of ten elected generals, which operated much like a modern-day governmental cabinet. The generals urged the popular assembly to adopt specific measures, and the success or failure of their policies determined whether or not they would be reelected at the end of their annual term. Pericles failed of reelection only once, and so great was his influence on the Athenians that, in the words of the contemporary historian Thucydides, "what was in name a democracy was virtually a government by its greatest citizen."[6]

To enable even the poorest citizen to participate in government, Pericles extended payment to jurors (a panel of six thousand citizens chosen annually by lot) and to members of the Council. The majority of Athenians, however, were not citizens. Womens, slaves, and resident aliens had no voice in the government, and no standing in the law courts.

Athenian imperialism. Following the victory over Persia, Sparta, fearful of helot rebellion at home, recalled its troops and resumed its policy of isolation. Because the Persians still ruled the Ionian cities and another invasion of Greece seemed probable, Athens in 478 B.C. invited the city-states bordering on the Aegean to form a defensive alliance called the Delian League. To maintain a navy to police the seas, each state was assessed ships or money in proportion to its wealth. From the beginning, Athens dominated the League. Since almost all of the 173 member states paid their assessments in money, which Athens was empowered to collect, the Athenians furnished the necessary ships.

By 468 B.C., the Ionian cities had been liberated and the Persian fleet destroyed, so various League members thought it unnecessary to continue the confederacy. In suppressing all attempts to secede, the Athenians were motivated by the fear that the Persian danger still existed and by the need to maintain and protect the large free-trade area so necessary for Greek—and especially Athenian—commerce and industry. The Athenians created an empire because they dared not unmake a confederation. By aiding in the suppression of local aristocratic factions within its subject states, Athens both eased the task of controlling its empire and emerged as the leader of a union of democratic states. To many Greeks—above all to the members of the oligarchic Spartan League and the suppressed aristocratic factions within the Athenian empire—Athens was a "tyrant city" and an "enslaver of Greek liberties." Pericles, on the other hand, justified Athenian imperialism on the ground that it brought "freedom" from fear and want to the Greek world:

> We are alone among mankind in doing men benefits, not on calculations of self-interest, but in the fearless confidence of freedom.[7]

The Peloponnesian War. In 431 B.C. the Peloponnesian War broke out between the Spartan League and the Athenian empire. While commercial rivalry between Athens and Sparta's ally Corinth was an important factor, the conflict is a classic example of how fear can generate a war unwanted by either side. Several incidents served to ignite the underlying tension, and Sparta declared war on the "aggressors."

Sparta's hope for victory lay in its army's ability to besiege Athens and lay waste its fields. Pericles, on the other hand, relied on Athen's unrivaled navy to import foodstuffs and to harass its enemies' coasts. Fate took a hand in this game, however. In the second year of the war a plague killed a third of the Athenian population, including Pericles. His death was a great blow to Athens, for leadership of the government passed to demagogues, who, in the words of Thucydides, "ended by committing even the conduct of state affairs to the whims of the multitude. This, as might have been expected in a great imperial state, produced a host of blunders. . . . "⁸ Eight more years of indecisive warfare ended in 421 B.C. with a compromise peace.

The war was resumed in 415 B.C. with an Athenian expedition against Syracuse in Sicily. Acting on the invitation of states that feared Syracusan expansion, the Athenians hoped to add Sicily to their empire and so become powerful enough to rule the whole of the Greek world. But ill luck and incompetent leadership resulted in two great Athenian fleets and a large army being destroyed by the Syracusans, who were supported by Sparta. The war dragged on until 404 B.C., when Athens capitulated after its last fleet was destroyed by a Spartan fleet built with money received from Persia in exchange for possession of the Greek cities in Ionia. At home Athens had been weakened by the plots of oligarchic elements to whom Sparta now turned over the government. The once great city was also stripped of its possessions and demilitarized.

Aftermath of the war.   Anarchy and depression were the political and economic legacies of the Peloponnesian War. The Spartan rule which supplanted Athens' "tyranny" over Greece was harsh indeed. Everywhere democracies were replaced by oligarchies, supported by Spartan troops, whose bloody excess led to revolutions. As one of their generals admitted, the Spartans did not know how to govern free men. Incessant war filled the early fourth century as a bewildering series of shifting alliances kept Greece disunited and weak. Persia often encouraged this instability by financing the alliances.

Political disintegration in turn contributed to the economic and social ills that plagued Greece during the fourth century B.C. Commerce and industry languished, and the unemployed who did not go abroad as soldiers of fortune supported demagogues and their radical schemes for the redivision of wealth. The wealthy, for their part, became increasingly reactionary and uncompromising. Even the intellectuals lost faith in democracy and joined with the wealthy in looking for "a champion powerful in action" who would bring order to Greece. They found him, finally, in the person of the king of Macedonia.

The Macedonian unification of Greece.   To the north of Greece lay Macedonia, inhabited by hardy peasants and nobles who were related to the Greeks but were culturally inferior to them. Macedonia became a centralized, powerful state under the able and crafty Philip II (359–336 B.C.), who created the most formidable army yet known by joining the crack Macedonian cavalry of nobles with the infantry phalanx used by the Greeks.

After unifying Macedonia—including a string of Greek colonies that had been established along its coast during the earlier centuries of Macedonia's weakness—Philip turned to the Greek city-states, whose wars afforded him the opportunity first to intervene, then to dominate. In vain did Demosthenes, the great Athenian orator and democratic leader, warn that "democracies and dictators cannot exist together" and urge the Athenians and other Greeks to stop Philip before it was too late. Belatedly, Athens and Thebes acted, but their combined forces were shattered at Chaeronea in 338 B.C. Philip then forced the Greeks into a federal league in which each state, while retaining self-government, swore to "make war upon him who violates the general peace" and to furnish Philip with men and supplies for a campaign against Persia. On the eve of setting out for Asia Minor, Philip was assassinated by a noble with a personal grudge, leaving the war against Persia as a legacy for his brilliant son Alexander.

Incapable of finding a solution to the anarchy that tore their world to shreds, the

Greeks ended as political failures and at the mercy of outside powers, first Macedonia and then Rome. They retained their cultural leadership, however, and the culture of the new Hellenistic Age and its successor, the world of Rome, was to be largely Greek.

THE GREEK GENIUS

The Greek character. The Greeks were the first to formulate many of the western world's fundamental concepts in philosophy, science, and art. How was it that a relative handful of people could bequeath such a legacy to civilization? A good part of the explanation lies in environmental and social factors.

Unlike the Near Eastern monarchies, the city-state was not governed by a "divine" ruler, nor were its citizens dominated by a powerful priesthood. The Greeks relished debate and argument. The nature of the universe and of man, man's duty to the state and to his fellow citizens, law and freedom, the purpose of art and poetry, the standards of a good life—these were a few of the numerous problems they discussed brilliantly. They also believed that an ideal life should include a healthy balance between action and thought.

Greek religion. Early Greek religion abounded in gods and goddesses who personified physical elements. Thus Demeter was the earth and giver of grain, Apollo, the sun and giver of light, and Dionysus was the god of fertility and wine. The Greeks of Homeric times believed in manlike deities, capable of malice, favoritism, and jealousy, and differing from ordinary men only in their immortality and their possession of supernatural powers. Zeus, the king of the gods, ruled the world from Mount Olympus with the aid of lesser deities.

By the time of Hesiod, as we have seen (p. 42), a religious reformation had begun which changed the vengeful and capricious gods of Homer into austere arbiters of justice who rewarded the good and punished the wicked. Demeter and Dionysus gained prominence as the central figures of "mystery" cults whose initiates were promised an afterlife of bliss in Elysium—formerly the abode of heroes only. And from the famous oracle at Delphi the voice of Zeus' son Apollo urged all Greeks to follow the ideals of moderation and reasonableness: "Nothing in excess."

Early Greek philosophy and science. Philosophy arose from the insatiable Greek curiosity about nature. The early Greek philosophers, beginning with Thales of Miletus (c. 636–546 B.C.), changed the course of human knowledge by insisting that the phenomena of the universe can be explained by natural causes. This rejection of the supernatural and the application of reason to discern universal principles in nature has been called the "Greek miracle." It led men to the threshold of today's world of science and technology.

Thales speculated on the nature of the basic substance from which all else in the universe is composed. He concluded that it was water, which exists in different states or forms and is indispensable to the maintenance and growth of organisms. Thales' successors in Ionia proposed elements other than water as the primal substance in the universe. This search for a material substance as the first principle or cause of all things culminated two centuries after Thales in the atomic theory of Democritus (c. 460–370 B.C.). To Democritus, reality was the mechanical motion of indivisible atoms, which differed in shape, size, position, and arrangement but not in quality. Moving about continuously, atoms combined to create objects. Scientists have used this theory to the present day, although we are now aware that the atom is neither indivisible nor indestructible.

While these and other early Greek philosophers were proposing some form of matter as the basic element in nature, Pythagoras of Samos (c. 582–500 B.C.) countered with the profoundly significant notion that the "nature of things" was something nonmaterial—numbers. By experimenting with a vibrating cord, Pythagoras discovered that musical harmony is based on arithmetical proportions, and he intuitively concluded that the universe was constructed of numbers and their relationships. His mathematical interpretation of nature greatly influenced Plato.

An important consequence of early Greek philosophical speculation was the undermining of conventional beliefs and traditions. The eroding of traditional views caused Greek inquiry to turn away from nature to man—to a consideration of human values and institutions. During the last half of the fifth century B.C., the Sophists—"men of wisdom" who taught public speaking and prepared men for public life—submitted all conventional beliefs to the test of rational criticism. Concluding that truth was relative, they denied the existence of universal standards to guide human actions.

Socrates and Plato. The outstanding opponent of the Sophists was the Athenian Socrates (c. 470–399 B.C.). Like the Sophists, Socrates turned from cosmic to human affairs; but unlike the Sophists, Socrates believed that by asking salient questions and by subjecting the answers to logical analysis, agreement could be reached about ethical standards and rules of conduct. Taking as his motto the famous inscription on the temple of Apollo at Delphi, "Know thyself," he insisted that "the unexamined life is not worth living." To Socrates, human excellence or virtue (*aretē*) is knowledge; and evil and error are the result of ignorance. In time Socrates' quest for truth led to his undoing, for his forthright questioning of important public figures often made them look ridiculous. The Athenians, unnerved by the Peloponnesian War, charged him with impiety and corrupting youth, and condemned Socrates to die.

Socrates' disciple, Plato (427–347 B.C.), also believed that truth exists, but only in the realm of thought, the spiritual world of Ideas or Forms. Such universals as Beauty, Good, and Justice exist apart from the material world, and the beauty, good, and justice that we encounter in the world of the senses are only imperfect reflections of eternal and changeless Ideas. Man's task is to come to know the True Reality—the eternal Ideas—behind these imperfect reflections. Only the soul, and the "soul's pilot," reason, can accomplish this.

Disillusioned with democracy, Plato expounded his concept of an ideal state, founded on the Idea of Justice, in the *Republic*. Plato described a kind of "spiritualized Sparta" in which the state regulated every aspect of life, including thought. The family and private property, for example, were abolished on the grounds that both bred selfishness, and marriage was controlled in order to produce strong, healthy children. Individuals were grouped into three classes and found happiness through their contribution to the community: workers by producing the necessities of life, warriors by guarding the state, and philosophers by ruling in the best interests of all the people. Plato later founded the Academy in Athens to train an intellectual elite that would go forth and reform society.

Aristotle. Plato's greatest pupil was Aristotle (384–322 B.C.), who set up his own school, the Lyceum, at Athens. Reacting against the other-worldly tendencies of Plato's thought, Aristotle insisted that Ideas have no separate existence apart from the material world; knowledge of universal Ideas is the result of the painstaking collection and organization of particular facts. Aristotle's Lyceum, accordingly, became a center for the analysis of data from many branches of learning.

To us today Aristotle's most significant treatises are the *Ethics* and the *Politics*. They deal with what he called the "philosophy of human affairs," whose object is the acquisition and maintenance of human happiness. Two kinds of virtue (*aretē*), intellectual and moral, which produce two types of happiness, are described in the *Ethics*. Intellectual virtue is the product of reason, and only such men as philosophers and scientists ever attain it. Much more important for the good of society is moral virtue—for example, liberality and temperance—which is the product less of reason than of habit and thus can be acquired by all.

In the *Politics* Aristotle viewed the state as necessary "for the sake of the good life," because its laws and educational system provide the most effective training needed for the attainment of moral virtue and hence happiness. Thus to Aristotle the viewpoint that the state stands in opposition to the individual would be unthinkable. Aristotle also investigated such diverse fields as biology, mathematics, astronomy, physics, psychology, rhetoric, logic, and metaphysics.

Medicine. Preconceived and false ideas about the human body blocked the development of medical science until 420 B.C., when Hippocrates, the "father of medicine," founded a school in which he emphasized the value of observation and the careful interpretation of symptoms. The members of this school were firmly convinced that disease resulted from natural, not supernatural, causes. Despite their empirical approach, the Hippocratic school adopted the theory that the body contained four liquids or humors—blood, phlegm, black bile, and yellow bile— whose proper balance was the basis of health. This doctrine was to impede medical progress until modern times.

The writing of history. If history be defined as an "honest attempt first to find out what happened, then to explain why it happened," Herodotus of Halicarnassus (484?–425? B.C.) deserves to be called the "father of history." In his highly entertaining history of the Persian Wars he discerned the clash of two distinct civilizations, the Hellenic and the Near Eastern. His portrayal of both the Greeks and the Persians was eminently impartial, but his fondness for a good story often led him to include tall tales in his work.

The first truly scientific historian was Thucydides (460–400? B.C.), who wrote a notably objective chronicle of the Peloponnesian War. Although he was a contemporary of the events and a loyal Athenian, a reader can scarcely detect whether he favored Athens or Sparta. In describing the character and purpose of his work, Thucydides probably had Herodotus in mind:

> With reference to the narrative of events, far from permitting myself to derive it from the first source that came to hand, I did not even trust my own impressions, but it rests partly on what I saw myself, partly on what others saw for me, the accuracy of the report being always tried by the most severe and detailed tests possible. . . . The absence of romance in my history will, I fear, detract somewhat from its interest; but I shall be content if it is judged useful by those inquirers who desire an exact knowledge of the past as an aid to the interpretation of the future. . . . [9]

Hellenic poetry and drama.   Sometime during the eighth century B.C. in Ionia, the *Iliad* and the *Odyssey*, the two great epics attributed to Homer, were set down in their present form. The *Iliad,* describing the clash of arms between the Greeks and the Trojans, glorifies heroic valor and physical prowess against a background of divine intervention in human affairs. The *Odyssey*, relating the adventure-filled wanderings of Odysseus on his return to Greece after Troy's fall, places less stress on divine intervention and more on the cool resourcefulness of the hero in escaping from danger and in regaining his kingdom.

As Greek society became more sophisticated, a new type of poetry, written to be sung to the accompaniment of the lyre, arose among the Ionian Greeks. Its authors sang not of legendary events but of present delights and sorrows. This new note, personal and passionate, can be seen in the following examples, in which the contrast between the new values and those of Homer's heroic age is sharply clear. Unlike Homer's heroes, Archilochus of Paros (seventh century B.C.) unashamedly throws away his shield and runs from the battlefield:

> My trusty shield adorns some Thracian foe;
> I left it in a bush—not as I would!
> But I have saved my life; so let it go.
> Soon I will get another just as good.[10]

And in contrast to the older view of an unromantic, purely physical attraction between Paris and Helen, Sappho of Lesbos (sixth century B.C.), a great lyric poet, saw Helen as the helpless victim of romantic love:

> She, who the beauty of mankind
> Excelled, fair Helen, all for love
> The noblest husband left behind;
> Afar, to Troy she sailed away,
> Her child, her parents, clean forgot;
> The Cyprian [Aphrodite] led her far astray
> Out of the way, resisting not.[11]

Drama, which developed from the religious rites of the Dionysian mystery cult, filled a civic-religious function in Greek society. In Athens, by the fifth century B.C., two distinct forms—tragedy and comedy—had evolved. Borrowing the old familiar legends of gods and heroes for their plots, the tragedians reinterpreted them in the light of the changing spirit of the times.

By depicting man in conflict with destiny, Aeschylus (525–456 B.C.) expressed the new concern for achieving harmony and avoiding the excesses which led to suffering. In his trilogy, the *Oresteia*, for example, he concerned himself with pride, as applied to the murder of the hero Agamemnon by his false queen, and then proceeded to work out its ramifications—murder piled on murder until men through suffering learn to substitute the moral law of Zeus for the primitive law of the blood feud. Like the prophets of Israel, Aeschylus taught that while "sin brings misery," misery in turn leads to wisdom:

> Zeus the Guide, who made man turn
> Thought-ward, Zeus, who did ordain
> Man by Suffering shall Learn.

So the heart of him, again
Aching with remembered pain,
Bleeds and sleepeth not, until
Wisdom comes against his will.[12]

A generation later, Sophocles (c. 496–406 B.C.) largely abandoned the problem of how to justify the ways of god to man and concentrated upon character. To Sophocles, a certain amount of suffering was inevitable in life. No man was perfect; there was a tragic flaw in the character of the best of men which caused them to make mistakes. Sophocles dwelled mainly on the way in which men react to suffering. Like his contemporary, the sculptor Phidias, Sophocles viewed man as an ideal creature—"Many are the wonders of the world, and none so wonderful as Man"—and he displayed man's greatness by depicting him experiencing great tragedy without whimpering.

Euripides (c. 480–406 B.C.), the last of the great Athenian tragedians, reflects the rationalism and critical spirit of the late fifth century. To him, the life of man was

Between the sixth and fourth centuries B.C. Greek sculpture showed the rigid stylization evident in this *Kourai* figure. This manner of portraying a person is reminiscent of Egyptian art.

pathetic, the ways of the gods ridiculous. His recurrent theme was "Since life began, hath there in God's eye stood one happy man?" Euripides has been called the first psychologist, for he looked deep into the human soul and described what he saw with intense realism. Far more than Aeschylus or even Sophocles, Euripides strikes home to modern man.

Comedies were bawdy and spirited. There were no libel laws in Athens, and Aristophanes (c. 445–385 B.C.), the famous comic dramatist and a conservative in outlook, brilliantly satirized Athenian democracy as a mob led by demagogues, the Sophists (among whom he included Socrates) as subversive, and Euripides as an underminer of civic spirit and traditional faith.

Architecture and sculpture. Hellenic architecture reached its zenith in fifth-century Athens, then at the height of its power and wealth. The Parthenon, the Erechtheum, and the other temples on the Acropolis exhibit the highly developed features that make Greek structure so pleasing to the eye. All relationships, such as column spacing and height and the curvature of floor and roof lines, were calculated and executed with remarkable precision to achieve a perfect balance,

In sharp contrast to the earlier *Kourai* statues, this figure of Hermes, the messenger of the gods, holding the young Dionysus is more complex, realistic, and yet idealized.

both structurally and visually. The three orders, or styles, usually identified by the characteristics of the columns, were the Doric, which was used in the Parthenon; the Ionic, seen in the Erechtheum; and the later and more ornate Corinthian.

Other types of buildings, notably the theaters, stadiums, and gymnasiums, also express the Greek spirit and way of life. In the open-air theaters the circular shape of the spectators' sections and the plan of the orchestra section set a style which has survived in principle to the present day.

Greek sculpture of the archaic period (c. 625–480 B.C.), although crude in its representation of human anatomy, has the freshness and vigor of youth. Influenced partly by Egyptian models, the statues of nude young men and draped maidens usually stand stiffly with clenched fists and with one foot thrust awkwardly forward. The fixed smile and formalized treatment of hair and drapery also reveal how the sculptor is struggling to master the technique of his art.

The achievement of mastery of technique by 480 B.C. ushered in the classical period of fifth-century Greek sculpture whose principles of harmony and proportion have shaped the course of western art. Sculpture from this period displays both the end of technical immaturity and the beginning of idealization of the human form which reached its culmination in the dignity and poise of Phidias' figures in the Parthenon frieze and pediments.

The more relaxed character of fourth-century B.C. Hellenic sculpture contrasts with the grandeur and dignity of fifth-century art. Charm, grace, and individuality characterize the work of Praxiteles, the most famous sculptor of the century. These qualities can be seen in his supple statue of the god Hermes holding the young Dionysus.

THE HELLENISTIC AGE

Alexander the Great. When Philip of Macedonia was assassinated in 336 B.C., his crown fell to his gifted twenty-year-old son, Alexander, who was alive to the glories of Hellenic culture, having as a youth been tutored by Aristotle. Alexander quickly proved himself a resolute, ambitious king, and began by crushing a rebellion in Greece. Two years after Philip's death, he set out with an army of 35,000 soldiers recruited from Macedonia and the Greek League that his father had organized (see p. 47). In quick succession he subdued Asia Minor, Syria, Palestine, and Egypt. Then the young leader marched into Mesopotamia and there, in 331 B.C., defeated the last powerful army of Darius III, the Persian monarch. Alexander was now master of Persia, the proud empire that had controlled the Near East. He ventured as far east as the rich river valleys of India, where his weary soldiers forced him to turn back. In 323 B.C., while he was planning the circumnavigation of Arabia, Alexander died at the age of thirty-two, the victim of malaria. With the Greeks now masters of the ancient Near East, a new and distinctly cosmopolitan period in their history and culture began—the Hellenistic Age.

Alexander's legacy to political thought was the vision of a unified world and the brotherhood of mankind. He sought to unify the lands he conquered and to promote what he himself called "concord and partnership in the empire" between East and West. He blended orientals with Greeks and Macedonians in his army

Before Alexander the expansionist tendency of the Persian Empire had inaugurated a movement toward the political unification of the Near East. Following the route shown by arrows on
the map, Alexander conquered Asia Minor, Egypt, and Mesopotamia, destroyed the Persian Empire, and advanced as far as
northern India, where his army rebelled against further advance into Asia. It is probable that Alexander wanted to create
a vast world state in which Greek and Oriental would share a
common citizenship and the two cultures of West and East
would be blended. To achieve this end, he established new
cities with mixed populations. The most important of these was
Alexandria in Egypt, which became a great center of both
commerce and learning and where Greek and Oriental systems of thought were indeed blended in various philosophies
and religions.

and administration; he founded numerous cities—seventy, according to tradition—in the East and settled many of his veterans in them; and he married two
oriental princesses and encouraged his officers and men to take foreign wives.
Finally, for reasons that remain unclear, Alexander ordered the Greek city-states
to accord him "divine honors."

The division of Alexander's empire.   For several decades following Alexander's
sudden death, his generals vied for the spoils of empire. Three major Hellenistic
kingdoms emerged and maintained a precarious balance of power until the Roman
conquests of the second and first centuries B.C.: Egypt, ruled by Ptolemy and his
successors; Asia, comprising most of the remaining provinces of the Persian
empire and held together with great difficulty by the dynasty founded by Seleucus;
and Macedonia and Greece, ruled by the descendants of Antigonus the One-Eyed.

While the Antigonids in Macedonia followed the model of Alexander's father

Philip in posing as national kings chosen by the army, the Ptolemies ruled Egypt as divine pharaohs, and some of the Seleucids became deified "saviors" and "benefactors." Ptolemaic and Seleucid administrations were centralized in bureaucracies staffed by Greeks, an arrangement which created a vast gulf between a ruler and his native subjects.

Plagued by native revolts, dynastic troubles, and civil war, the Hellenistic kingdoms soon began to crumble. Macedonia lost effective control of Greece when Athens asserted its independence and most of the other Greek states formed two federal leagues, the Aetolian in the north and the Achaean in the Peloponnesus, which successfully resisted Macedonian domination. The eastern reaches of Alexander's empire—India, Bactria, and Parthia—gradually drifted out of the Seleucid sphere of influence. Pergamum, in northwestern Asia Minor, renounced its allegiance to the Seleucids and became an independent kingdom famous for its artists and scholars. In the year 200 B.C. the new power of Rome entered upon the scene, and by 30 B.C. Rome had annexed the last remaining Hellenistic state, Egypt.

Hellenistic economy and society. The Hellenistic Age was a time of economic expansion and social change. In the wake of Alexander's conquests, thousands of Greeks flocked eastward to begin a new era of Greek colonization. An economic union between East and West permitted the free flow of trade, and prosperity was stimulated further when Alexander put into circulation huge hoards of Persian gold and silver and introduced a uniform coinage. The result was a much larger and more affluent middle class than had hitherto existed.

By the third century B.C. the center of trade had shifted from Greece to the Near East. Largest of the Hellenistic cities, and much larger than any cities in Greece itself, were Antioch in northern Syria and Alexandria in Egypt. The riches of India, Persia, Arabia, and the Fertile Crescent were brought by sea and land to these Mediterranean ports.

Hellenistic philosophy. Developments in philosophy reflected the changed environment of the Hellenistic Age. With the growing loss of political freedom and the prevalence of internal disorder, philosophers concerned themselves less with the reform of society and more with the attainment of happiness for the individual. This emphasis on peace of mind in an insecure world led to the rise of four principal schools of thought.

The Skeptics and Cynics reflected most clearly the doubts and misgivings of the times. The Skeptics denied the possibility of finding truth. The wise man, they argued, will suspend his judgment and not dogmatize. The Cynics carried negativism further; their ideal was nonattachment to the values and conventions of society. Cynic philosophers wandered from city to city, preaching a concept of virtue that is echoed by today's hippies: "Look at me, I am without house or city, property or slave. I sleep on the ground. I have no wife, no children. What do I lack? Am I not without distress or fear? Am I not free?"[13]

More practical and popular were Epicureanism and Stoicism. The Athenian Epicurus (342–270 B.C.) taught that the wise man could achieve happiness simply by freeing his body from pain and his mind from fear—particularly the fear of death. To reach this goal, men must avoid bodily excesses, including those of pleasure, and accept the scientific teaching of Democritus that both body and soul are composed of atoms which fall apart at death. Thus, beyond death there is no existence and nothing to fear. Epicurus maintained that the finest pleasures were intellectual, but many of his followers later distorted his teachings so that

Epicureanism appeared to be concerned only with sensual gratification.

The Stoics, followers of Zeno (c. 336–c. 264 B.C.), a Semite from Cyprus, argued in contrast to Epicureanism that the universe is controlled by some power—variously called Reason, World Soul, Fortune, or God—which determines everything that happens. Fortified by this knowledge, the Stoic wise man conforms his will to the World Will and "stoically" accepts whatever part fortune allots him in the drama of life. With its insistence on duty and on the brotherhood of man in One Great City, Stoicism was particularly attractive to the Romans.

Science and mathematics. The Greek concern for rational, disinterested inquiry reached a zenith in the Hellenistic period, particularly at Alexandria where the Ptolemies subsidized a great research institute, the Museum, and a library of more than half a million books. Emphasizing specialization and experimentation, and enriched by Near Eastern astronomy and mathematics, Greek science in the third century B.C. achieved results unmatched until early modern times.

The expansion of geographical knowledge incited scientists to make accurate maps and to estimate the size of the earth, which had been identified as a globe through observation of its shadow in a lunar eclipse. Eratosthenes, the outstanding geographer of the century, calculated the circumference of the globe with only 1 percent error by measuring the difference in the angles of the noonday sun at Aswan and Alexandria.

In astronomy, Aristarchus put forward the radical theory that the earth rotates on its axis and moves in an orbit around the sun. Most of his contemporaries were convinced that the earth was stationary and the sun revolved around it. This view not only was supported by the powerful authority of Aristotle, but it also seemed to explain all the known facts of celestial motion. Aristarchus' heliocentric theory was not revived until the sixteenth century A.D.

Mathematics also made great advances. Euclid systematized the theorems of plane and solid geometry, and Archimedes of Syracuse, who had studied at Alexandria, calculated the value of π, invented a terminology for expressing numbers up to any magnitude, and laid the foundations of calculus. Archimedes also discovered specific gravity by noticing the water he displaced in his bath. And despite his disdain for making practical use of his knowledge, he invented the compound pulley, the windlass, and the endless screw for raising water.

The Hellenistic Greeks extended the advances in medicine made earlier by Hippocrates and his school. By dissecting bodies of dead criminals, they were able to trace the outlines of the nervous system, to understand the principle of the circulation of the blood, and to ascertain that the brain, not the heart, was the true center of consciousness.

Art and literature. Hellenistic sculptors continued and intensified the realistic, dramatic, and emotional approach that began to appear in Hellenic sculpture during the fourth century B.C. Supported by rulers and other rich patrons in Alexandria, Antioch, Rhodes, and Pergamum, they displayed their technical virtuosity by depicting violent scenes, writhing forms, and dramatic poses—all with a realism which could make stone simulate flesh. Little evidence remained of the balance and restraint of classical Greek sculpture. The famous Laocoön group with its twisted poses, contorted faces, and swollen muscles reminds one of the Baroque sculpture of seventeenth-century Europe which replaced the classical art of the Italian Renaissance. "Baroque" grandeur and ornamentation also characterized Hellenistic architecture; the more ornate Corinthian was preferred to the simple Doric and Ionic orders.

The quality of literature from the Hellenistic Age was generally inferior to that of the Hellenic Age. Scholarship flourished, and we are indebted for the preservation of much of Greek classical literature to the subsidized scholars at the Alexandrine library. Yet, paradoxically, these sophisticated scholars produced superb pastoral poetry extolling the simple life of shepherds. The best of this escapist poetry was written by Theocritus at Alexandria in the third century B.C.

The Hellenistic contribution. The greatest contribution of the Hellenistic Age was the diffusion of Greek culture throughout the ancient East and the newly rising Roman West. In the East the cities that Alexander and his successors built were the agents for spreading Hellenistic culture from the Aegean Sea to India. Literate Asians learned Greek to facilitate trade, become members of the ruling circles of the Hellenistic states, and read Hellenic classics.

In the history of western civilization there is little of greater significance than Rome's absorption of Greek civilization and its transference of that heritage to modern Europe. The stage on which this story began was the cosmopolitan Hellenistic Age, which "longed and strove for *Homonoia*, Concord, between man and man . . . [and] proclaimed a conception of the world as One Great City."[14] The process by which the Roman West was Hellenized will be described in the following chapter.

The trend toward realism and increased complexity in sculpture begun in the fourth century B.C. culminated in the art of the Hellenistic period, which produced such intricate sculptures as the contorted Laocoön group.

CHAPTER 3

THE GRANDEUR THAT WAS ROME

The Roman World and Early
Christianity: to 475 A.D.

As the Athenian saw the symbol of his city-state's democracy and culture in the rock-jutting Acropolis, so the Roman viewed the Forum as the symbol of imperial grandeur. While the Acropolis was crowned with statues to Athena, the Forum gloried in triumphal arches and columns commemorating military conquests. Rome was the capital of a world-state, extending from the Rhine to the Euphrates, and its citizens were proud of their imperial mission.

Rome was the great intermediary—the bridge over which passed the rich contributions of the Fertile Crescent, Egypt, and especially Greece to form the basis of modern western civilization. The Romans replaced the anarchy of the Hellenistic Age with law and order and embraced the intellectual and artistic legacy of the conquered Greeks. As Rome's empire expanded, this legacy was spread westward throughout Europe.

Yet Rome was more than an intermediary, for it made many important and original contributions to our western culture. In the shadows of its marching legions went engineers and architects, so that today, scattered throughout the lands that once were part of the Roman world, the remains of roads, walls, baths, basilicas, amphitheaters, and aqueducts offer convincing evidence of the Romans' technical prowess. Most lasting and far-reaching of all, is Roman law, whose principles have influenced in varying degree the legal opinion of mankind.

ROME TO 509 B.C.

Early settlers of Italy. Between 2000 and 1000 B.C., when Indo-European peoples invaded the Aegean world, a western wing of this nomadic migration filtered into the Italian peninsula, then inhabited by indigenous Neolithic tribes. The first invaders, skilled in the use of copper and bronze, settled in the Po valley. Another wave of Indo-Europeans, equipped with iron weapons and tools,

59

followed; and in time the newer and older settlers intermingled and spread throughout the peninsula. One group, the Latins, settled in the lower valley of the Tiber River, a region that became known as the plain of Latium.

During the ninth century B.C. the Etruscans, a non-Indo-European people who probably came from Asia Minor, brought the first city-state civilization to Italy. Expanding from the west coast north to the Po valley and south to the Bay of Naples, the Etruscans organized the backward Italic peoples into a loose confederation of Etruscan-dominated city-states. After 750 B.C. Greek colonists migrated to southern Italy and Sicily, where they served as a protective buffer against powerful and prosperous Carthage, a Phoenician colony established in North Africa about 800 B.C. Yet the future was not to belong to these advanced peoples, but to an insignificant settlement on the Tiber River—Rome.

Rome's origins.   According to ancient legend, Rome was founded in 753 B.C. by the twin brothers Romulus and Remus. A different tradition held that the founder of the Roman race was Aeneas, a Trojan who after the fall of Troy founded a settlement in Latium. Modern scholars believe that in the eighth century B.C. the inhabitants of some Latin villages on hills beside the Tiber united and established a common meeting place, the Forum. Situated at a convenient place for fording the river and protected by the hills and marshes from invaders, Rome was strategically located. Nevertheless, the expanding Etruscans conquered Rome about 600 B.C., and under their tutelage Rome first became an important city-state.

Some aspects of Etruscan culture were borrowed from the Greek colonies in southern Italy, and much of this, including the alphabet, was passed on to the conquered Romans. Even the name *Roma* appears to be an Etruscan word.

The Roman monarchy.   Rome's constitutional development was similar to most Greek city-states: limited monarchy of the sort described by Homer, oligarchy, democracy, and, finally, the permanent dictatorship of the Roman emperors. We shall see that in moving from oligarchy to democracy, the Romans, unlike the Greeks, succeeded in avoiding the intermediate stage of tyranny.

According to tradition, early Rome was ruled by kings elected by the people. After the Etruscan conquest, this elective system continued, although the kings chosen were usually of Etruscan origin. The king's executive power, both civil and military, was called the *imperium*, which was symbolized by an eagle-headed scepter and an ax bound in a bundle of rods. Although the *imperium* was conferred by a popular assembly made up of all arms-bearing citizens, the king turned for advice to a council of nobles called the Senate. Each senator had lifelong tenure, and the members of this group and their families constituted the patrician class. The other class of Romans, the plebeians, or commoners, included small farmers, artisans, and many clients, or dependents, of patrician landowners. In return for a livelihood, the clients gave their patrician patrons political support in the assembly.

The fundamental unit of early Roman society was the family. The father's power was absolute, and strict discipline was imposed to instill in children those virtues to which the Romans attached particular importance—loyalty, courage, self-control, and respect for laws and ancestral customs. The early Romans were stern, hard-working, and practical. Man's relationship to the universe and the possibilities of immortal life did not concern them unduly, and religious practices were confined to placating the spirits of the family and the state. Under Etruscan influence the major spirits were personified. Thus the sky-spirit Jupiter became god of the universe; Mars, spirit of vegetation, became god of war; and Janus, whose temple doors remained open when the army was away at war, was originally the spirit of the city gate.

THE EARLY REPUBLIC, 509–133 B.C.

Establishment of the Republic.   In 509 B.C., according to tradition, the patricians expelled the last Etruscan king, claiming that he had acted despotically, and established what they called a republic, in which they held the reins of power. The King's civil and military powers were transferred to two new officials, called consuls, elected annually from the patrician class. In the event of war or serious domestic emergency, a dictator could be substituted for the two consuls, but he was given absolute power for six months only.

Struggle for equal rights.   For more than two centuries following the establishment of the Republic, the plebeians struggled for social and political equality. As in Greece, civil war and the emergence of tyrants were averted by the willingness, however reluctant, of the patricians to compromise.

In 494 B.C. the plebeians refused all army service until the patricians agreed to recognize their right to organize as the *concilium plebis* ("gathering of the plebeians") with their own officials, called tribunes. The latter also obtained the right to veto any action of the state considered injurious to the plebeians. Another landmark concession was the publication about 450 B.C. of the Law of the Twelve Tables, the unwritten customary law of Rome. Hitherto the patricians, who alone knew what the law was, had used this knowledge for their own advantage. The Law of the Twelve Tables was the first turning point in the long history of Roman law. Other noteworthy plebeian gains were the right of intermarriage with patricians and the abolition of debt slavery.

Gradually, too, the plebeians acquired political equality. In 367 B.C. the consulship was opened to the plebeians, and before the end of the century they were eligible to hold other important magistracies which the patricians had in the meantime created. The right to hold political office became a stepping stone to the Senate for rich plebeians.

The long struggle for equality ended in 287 B.C. when the *concilium plebis* was recognized as a constitutional body, henceforth known as the Tribal Assembly, with the right to pass laws that were binding on all citizens, patricians as well as plebeians. The Roman Republic was now technically a democracy, although in actual practice a senatorial aristocracy of patricians and rich plebeians continued to control the state. Having gained political and social equality, the plebeians were willing to allow the more experienced Senate to run the government during the remainder of this period of almost constant warfare down to 133 B.C.

Roman conquest of Italy.   The growth of Rome from a small city-state to the dominant power in the Mediterranean world in less than four hundred years (509–133 B.C.) is a remarkable success story. By 270 B.C. the first phase of Roman expansion was over. Ringed about by hostile peoples—Etruscans in the north, predatory hill tribes in central Italy, and Greeks in the south—Rome had subdued them all after long, agonizing effort and found itself master of all Italy south of the Po valley. Roman expansion was not deliberately planned; rather, it was the result of dealing with successive crises, caused by unsettled conditions in Italy, which the Romans considered to be threats to their security.

Soon after ousting their Etruscan overlords in 509 B.C., Rome and the Latin League, composed of Latin peoples in the vicinity of Rome, entered into an alliance against the Etruscans. In time this combination became the chief power in central Italy. But the members of the Latin League grew alarmed at Rome's increasing strength, and war broke out between the former allies. Victorious Rome in 338 B.C. dissolved the League, and the Latin cities were forced to sign individual treaties as allies of Rome. Thus the same year which saw the rise of Macedonia over Greece (see p. 47) also saw the rise of a new power in Italy.

Border clashes with aggressive highland Samnite tribes led to three fiercely fought Samnite wars and the extension of Rome's frontiers southward to the Greek colonies in Great Greece. Fearing Roman conquest, the Greeks prepared for war and called in the Hellenistic Greek king, Pyrrhus of Epirus, who dreamed of becoming a second Alexander the Great. Pyrrhus twice routed the Romans, but at so heavy a cost that such a triumph is still called a "Pyrrhic victory." When a third battle failed to induce the Romans to make peace, Pyrrhus is reported to have remarked, "We are waging a war against a hydra," and returned to his homeland. The Roman army then moved into southern Italy and by 270 B.C. had subdued the Greek cities there.

The Romans treated their defeated foes fairly, in time creating a strong loyalty to Rome throughout the peninsula. Defeated states were required to sign a treaty of alliance which bound them to adhere to Rome's foreign policy and to supply troops for the Roman army. No tribute was required, and each state retained local self-government. Rome did, however, actually annex about one third of the conquered lands.

The First and Second Punic Wars. After 270 B.C. only Carthage remained as Rome's rival in the West. Much more wealthy and populous than Rome, with a magnificent navy that controlled the western Mediterranean and with a domain that included the northern coast of Africa, Sardinia, western Sicily, and parts of Spain and Corsica, Carthage seemed more than a match for Rome.

The First Punic War (from *punicus*, Latin for "Phoenician") broke out in 264 B.C. when Rome sought to oust a Carthaginian force that had occupied Messina on the northeastern tip of Sicily just across from Roman Italy. The war dragged on for twenty years before Carthage sued for peace in 241 B.C. In contrast to their treatment of the Italians, the Romans now annexed Sicily, Sardinia, and Corsica as the first provinces of an overseas empire, governed and taxed by Roman proconsuls.

Thwarted Carthage then concentrated upon enlarging its empire in Spain, and Rome's counter measures led to the greatest and most difficult war in Roman history. While both powers jockeyed for position, a young Carthaginian general, Hannibal, precipitated the Second Punic War by attacking a Spanish town claimed by Rome as an ally. Rome declared war, and Hannibal, seizing the initiative, in 218 B.C. led an army across the Alps into Italy. Although Hannibal defeated the Romans three times within three years, Rome doggedly refused to surrender, and most of its allies remained loyal—a testimony to Rome's generous and statesman-like treatment of its Italian subjects.

After fifteeen years of sweeping back and forth across Italy, Hannibal was forced to return to Carthage when the Romans invaded Africa. The war ended in 201 B.C. with a Roman victory at Zama and the imposition of a harsh peace treaty that forced Carthage to pay a huge indemnity, disarm its forces, and turn Spain over to the Romans.

Roman intervention in the East. The defeat of Carthage left Rome free to turn eastward and settle a score with Philip V of Macedonia, who, fearing Roman expansion, had allied himself with Hannibal during the darkest days of the war. The heavy Macedonian phalanxes were no match for the mobile Roman legions, and in 197 B.C. Philip was soundly defeated and deprived of his warships and military bases in Greece. The Romans then proclaimed the independence of Greece and were eulogized by the grateful Greeks as the "one people in the world which would fight for others' liberties at its own cost, to its own peril, and with its own toil, . . . ready to cross the sea that there might be no unjust empire anywhere. . . ."[1]

A few years later Rome declared war on the Seleucid emperor who had moved into Greece, urged on by a few greedy Greek states that resented Rome's refusal to dismember Macedonia. The Romans forced him to vacate Greece and Asia Minor, pay a huge indemnity, and give up his warships and war elephants. The Seleucids were checked again in 168 B.C. when a Roman ultimatum halted their invasion of Egypt, which became a Roman protectorate, and a year later Rome supported the Jews in their successful revolt against the Seleucids.

Most of the East was now a Roman protectorate, the result of a policy in which Roman self-interest was mingled with idealism. But Roman idealism turned sour when anti-Romanism became widespread in Greece, particularly among the radical masses who resented Rome's support of conservative governments and the status quo in general. The new policy was revealed in 146 B.C. when, after many Greeks had supported an attempted Macedonian revival, Rome destroyed Corinth as an object lesson, supported oligarchic factions in all Greek states, and placed Greece under the watchful eye of the governor of Macedonia, which was made a Roman province.

Rome, supreme in the ancient world. In the same year Rome's hardening policy led to suspicion of Carthage's reviving prosperity and to a demand by extremists for war—*Carthago delenda est* ("Carthage must be destroyed"). Treacherously provoking the Third Punic War, the Romans destroyed Carthage and annexed the territory as a province.

Rome acquired its first province in Asia in 133 B.C. when the king of Pergamum, dying without heir, bequeathed his kingdom to Rome. Apparently he feared that the discontented masses would revolt after his death unless Rome, with its reputation for maintaining law and order in the interest of the propertied classes, took over. Rome accepted the bequest and then spent the next three years suppressing a proletarian revolution in the new province.

With provinces on three continents—Europe, Africa, and Asia (see map p. 64)—the once obscure Roman Republic was now supreme in the ancient world. But the next century, during which Rome's frontiers reached the Euphrates and the Rhine, would witness the failure of the Republic to solve the problems that were the by-products of the acquisition of an empire.

LATE REPUBLIC, 133–30 B.C.

Effects of Roman expansion. One of the most pressing problems resulting from Roman expansion was the disappearance of the small landowner, whose energy and spirit had made Rome great. Burdened by frequent military service, his farm

THE ROMAN WORLD 133 B.C.

Roman Territories
Allies Of Rome By Treaty

buildings destroyed by Hannibal, and unable to compete with the cheap grain imported from the new Roman province of Sicily, the small farmer sold out and moved to Rome. Here he joined the unemployed, discontented proletariat, so called because their only contribution was *proles*, "children." On the other hand, rich aristocrats bought more and more land and, abandoning the cultivation of grain, introduced large-scale scientific production of olive oil and wine, or of sheep and cattle. These large estates were especially profitable because an abundance of cheap slaves from the conquered areas was available to work on them.

Corruption in the government was another mark of the growing degeneracy of the Roman Republic. Provincial officials seized opportunities for lucrative graft, and a new class of Roman businessmen scrambled selfishly for the profitable state contracts to supply the armies, collect taxes in the provinces, and lease mines and forests. The tribunes, once guardians of the people's rights, became mere yes-men of the Senate.

Thus by the middle of the second century B.C., the government was in the hands of the wealthy, self-seeking Senate, while Rome swarmed with fortune hunters, imported slaves, unemployed farmers, and discontented war veterans. The poverty of the many, coupled with the opulence of the few, hastened the decay of the old Roman traits of discipline, simplicity, and respect for authority. The next century (133–30 B.C.) revealed the Senate's inability to solve the economic and social problems following in the wake of Rome's conquests. This led to the establishment of a dictatorship and the end of the Republic.

Reform movement of the Gracchi. An awareness of Rome's profound social and economic problems led to the reform program of an idealistic young aristocrat named Tiberius Gracchus. Supported by a few liberal Senators, Tiberius was elected tribune for the year 133 B.C. at the age of twenty-nine. He sought to arrest Roman decline by restoring the backbone of the old Roman society—the small landowner. A large quantity of public land, acquired in the conquest of the Italian peninsula, had been leased to patricians and wealthy plebeians who in time viewed it as their own property. Tiberius proposed a limit of 320 acres of public land per person, with the remainder being allotted to landless citizens. In his address to the assembly Tiberius declared:

> it is with lying lips that their commanders exhort the soldiers in their battles to defend sepulchres and shrines from the enemy; . . . they fight and die to support others in wealth and luxury, and though they are styled masters of the world, they have not a single clod of earth that is their own.[2]

When the Tribal Assembly adopted Tiberius' proposal, the Senate induced one of the other tribunes to veto the measure. On the ground that a tribune who opposed the will of the people thereby forfeited his office, Tiberius took what the Senate claimed was the unconstitutional step of having the assembly depose the tribune in question. The agrarian bill was then passed. Soon thereafter Tiberius

The Colosseum, built by the Flavian emperors, uses arch construction both to light the interior and to disperse weight. Largest of the Roman amphitheaters, it was used for gladiatorial combats, animal fights, and even for naval exhibitions—water pipes for flooding still exist in some arenas.

again violated custom by standing for reelection after completing his one-year term. On the pretext that he sought to make himself king, partisans of the Senate murdered him and three hundred of his followers.

Tiberius' work was taken up by his younger brother, Gaius Gracchus, who was elected tribune for 123 B.C. In addition to the reallocation of public land, Gaius proposed establishing Roman colonies in southern Italy and on the site of Carthage. To protect the poor against speculation in the grain market, Gaius committed the government to the purchase and storage of wheat and to its subsequent distribution to the urban masses at about half the former market price. Unfortunately, what Gaius intended as a relief measure later became a dole, used all too often for the advancement of astute politicians.

Another of Gaius' proposals would have granted citizenship to Rome's Italian allies, who were now being mistreated by Roman officials. This proposal cost Gaius the support of the Roman proletariat, which did not wish to share the privileges of citizenship or endanger its control of the Tribal Assembly. Consequently, in 121 B.C. Gaius failed to be reelected to a third term and the Senate was emboldened to resort to force again. Martial law was declared and three thousand of Gaius' followers were arrested and executed, a fate Gaius avoided by committing suicide. The Gracchi's deaths were ominous portents of the manner in which the Republic was henceforth to decide its internal disputes.

In foreign affairs, too, the Senate soon demonstrated its incompetence. Rome was forced to grant citizenship to its Italian allies after the Senate's failure to deal with their grievances goaded them into revolt (99–88 B.C.). Other blunders led to the first of the civil wars that destroyed the Republic.

Three civil wars. Between 111 and 105 B.C. Roman armies, dispatched by the Senate and commanded by senators, failed to protect Roman capitalists in North Africa and to prevent Germanic tribes from overrunning southern Gaul and from threatening Italy itself. Accusing the Senate of lethargy and incompetence, the Tribal Assembly elected Gaius Marius to the consulship in 107 B.C. and commissioned him to raise an army and deal with the foreign dangers. Marius first pacified North Africa and then crushed the first German threat to Rome. In the process he created a new-style Roman army that was destined to play a major role in the turbulent history of the late Republic.

In contrast to the old Roman army, which was composed of conscripts who owned their own land and who thought of themselves as loyal citizens of the Republic, the new army created by Marius was recruited from landless citizens for long terms of service. These professional soldiers identified their own interests with those of their commanders, to whom they looked for bonuses of land or money, and were ready to follow them in any undertaking. Thus the character of the army changed from a militia to a career service in which loyalty to the state was no longer paramount. Aspiring generals would soon use their military power to seize the government.

In 88 B.C. the ambitious king of Pontus in Asia Minor, encouraged by the growing anti-Roman sentiment in Asia Minor and Greece caused by corrupt governors and tax collectors, declared war on Rome. When the Senate chose Sulla for the eastern command, the Tribal Assembly countered by granting the command to Marius. The result was Rome's first civil war, out of which Sulla emerged victorious to be appointed dictator by the Senate for an unlimited period to "reorganize the Republic." Sulla drastically curtailed the powers of the tribunes and the Tribal Assembly, giving the Senate the control of legislation which it had enjoyed two hundred years before. He then resigned his dictatorship (79 B.C.), but his reactionary constitutional changes were not to last.

Popular discontent with Sulla's reforms nursed the ambitions of individuals eager for personal power. The first to come forward was Pompey. In 70 B.C. he was elected consul, and courted the populace by repealing Sulla's laws against the tribunes and the Tribal Assembly. Pompey then put an end to anarchy in the East caused by piracy, the protracted ambitions of the king of Pontus, and the death throes of the Seleucid empire. New Roman provinces and client states brought order eastward to the Euphrates and southward through Palestine.

Still another strong man made his appearance in 59 B.C., when Julius Caesar allied himself politically with Pompey and was elected consul. Following his consulship, Caesar spent nine years conquering Gaul, where he accumulated a fortune in plunder and trained a loyal army of peerless veterans. His conquest of Gaul was to have tremendous consequences for the course of western civilization, for Romanized Gaul—or France—emerged later as the center of medieval civilization.

Fearful of Caesar's growing power, Pompey conspired with the Senate to ruin him. When the Senate demanded in 49 B.C. that Caesar disband his army, he crossed the Rubicon, the river in northern Italy which formed the boundary of Caesar's province, and marched on Rome. After Pompey was defeated, Caesar assumed the office of dictator for life, for he was convinced that only benevolent despotism could save Rome from continued anarchy. But Caesar incurred the enmity of those who viewed him as a tyrant who had destroyed the Republic. On the Ides (the fifteenth) of March, 44 B.C., a group of conspirators, led by ex-Pompeians whom Caesar had pardoned, stabbed him to death in the Senate, and Rome was once more plunged into conflict.

Following Caesar's death, his eighteen-year-old nephew and heir, Octavian, joined forces with Caesar's lieutenant, Mark Antony, to defeat the armies of the conspirators and the Senate. Then for more than a decade Octavian and Antony exercised dictatorial power and divided the Roman world between them. Antony, in the eastern half of the empire, became infatuated with Cleopatra, the last of the Egyptian Ptolemies. He even went so far as to transfer Roman territories to her dominions. Octavian took advantage of this high-handedness to arouse Rome against Antony and his oriental queen. The showdown came at the naval battle of Actium off Greece—a fiasco for Antony, after which he and Cleopatra committed suicide. In 30 B.C. Octavian annexed Egypt, the last of the major Hellenistic states. Then he proceeded to remodel the Roman constitution, and the Roman Republic gave way to the Roman Empire.

THE EARLY EMPIRE: 30 B.C. TO 180 A.D.

Reconstruction under Augustus. Octavian announced that he would "restore the Republic," but he did so only outwardly by blending republican institutions with strong personal leadership. He consulted the Senate on important issues, allowed it to retain control over Italy and half of the provinces, and gave it the legislative functions of the nearly defunct Tribal Assembly. The Senate in return bestowed upon Octavian the title *Augustus* ("The Revered," a title previously used for gods), by which he was known thereafter.

Augustus never again held the office of dictator but he kept the power of a tribune (which gave him the right to initiate and to veto legislation) and the governorship of the frontier provinces, where the armies were stationed. Augustus' control of the army meant that his power could not be successfully challenged. Augustus preferred the modest title of *princeps,* "first citizen" or "leader," which he felt best described his position, and his form of disguised monarchy is therefore known as the Principate.

Augustus faced the problems of curing a sick society and removing the scars resulting from a century of civil strife. The aristocracy was too decadent to be patriotic, and in the cities an unemployed mob satiated with free bread and circuses had long since lost interest in hard work. Accordingly, Augustus concentrated on internal reform, although he did extend the Roman frontier to the Danube as a defense against barbarian invasions. By means of legislation and propaganda, he sought with some success to check moral and social decline and to revive the old Roman ideals and traditions. Augustus' reforms engendered a new optimism and patriotism which were reflected in the art and literature of the Augustan Age (see p. 72). His thorough reconstruction of government and society laid the foundation for two centuries of order and prosperity known as the *Pax Romana* (the Roman peace).

Augustus' successors. Augustus was followed by four descendants of his family, the line of the Julio-Claudians. Nero, last of the line, committed suicide in 68 A.D. when faced by army revolts. In the following year four emperors were proclaimed by rival armies, with Vespasian the final victor. From 69 to 96 A.D. the Flavian dynasty (Vespasian and his two sons) provided the Empire with effective, if autocratic, rule.

An end to autocracy and a return to the Augustan principle of an administration of equals—*princeps* and Senate—characterized the rule of the Antonine emperors (96–180 A.D.), under whom the Empire reached the height of its prosperity and power. Selected on the basis of proven ability, these "five good emperors" succeeded, according to the Roman historian Tacitus, in "reconciling things long incompatible, supreme power and liberty."

The last Antonine emperor, Marcus Aurelius, approached Plato's ideal of the "philosopher king" and preferred the quiet contemplation of his books to the blood and brutality of the battlefield. Yet, ironically, he was repeatedly troubled by the invasions of Germanic tribes across the Danube. While engaged in his Germanic campaigns, he wrote his *Meditations,* a philosophical work notable for its lofty Stoic idealism and love of humanity.

The Pax Romana. Under the Principate a vast area stretching from Britain to the Euphrates and from the North Sea to the Sahara and containing upwards of 100 million people was welded together into what Pliny the Elder, in the first century A.D., termed the "immense majesty of the Roman peace." At the head of this huge world-state stood the emperor, its defender and symbol of unity as well as an object of veneration. The major theme of the many tributes written to celebrate the enlightened, beneficent government of the Principate was that liberty had been exchanged for order and prosperity. The Empire was said to represent a new kind of democracy—"a democracy under the one man that can rule and govern best." "The whole world speaks in unison, more distinctly than a chorus; and so well does it harmonize under this director-in-chief that it joins in praying this Empire may last for all time."[3]

Rome's unification of the ancient world had far-reaching economic conse-

THE GROWTH OF THE ROMAN EMPIRE
44 B.C. TO 180 A.D.

Acquired before the Death of Caesar, 44 B.C.
Acquired before the Death of Augustus, 14 A.D.
Acquired before the Death of Marcus Aurelius,
180 A.D.

0   250   500

quences. The *Pax Romana* was responsible for the elimination of tolls and other
artificial barriers, the suppression of piracy and brigandage, and the establishment
of a reliable coinage. Such factors, in addition to the longest period of peace the
West has ever enjoyed, explain in large measure the great expansion of commerce
that occurred in the first and second centuries A.D. Industry also was stimulated,
but its expansion was hindered since wealth remained concentrated and no mass
market for industrial goods arose.

Although the cities were the centers of political and cultural life, most of them,
particularly in the West, were of secondary importance economically. They
consumed much more than they produced and flourished only because the
economy of the Empire remained prosperous enough to support them. Most were
like Rome itself, into which so much revenue poured from the provinces that its
citizens had the necessary purchasing power to buy great quantities of goods from
other parts of the Empire and even from regions far beyond the imperial
frontiers—amber from the Baltic region, aromatics from Arabia, ivory and
rhinoceros horn from East Africa, and spices, cotton, Chinese silk, and numerous
other luxuries from India.

The economy of the Empire remained basically agrarian, and the huge estates,
or *latifundia*, prospered. On these tracts, usually belonging to absentee owners,
large numbers of *coloni*, free tenants, tilled the soil as sharecroppers. The *coloni*
were gradually replacing slave labor, which was becoming increasingly hard to
secure with the disappearance of the flow of captives from major wars.

Once the Empire had ceased to expand geographically, its economy in turn became progressively more static. Late in the first century A.D. Italian agriculture began to suffer from the loss of its markets in the western provinces, which were becoming self-sufficient in the production of wine and olive oil. To aid the wine producers the Flavian emperor Domitian created an artificial scarcity by forbidding the planting of new vineyards in Italy and ordering the plowing under of half the existing vineyards in the provinces. This was followed by a program of state subsidies, inaugurated by the Antonine emperors. Loans at 5 percent interest were made to ailing landowners, with the interest to be paid into the treasuries of declining Italian municipalities and earmarked "for girls and boys of needy parents to be supported at public expense." This system of state subsidies to both producers and consumers was soon extended to the provinces. Also contributing to Roman economic stagnation was the continuing drain of money into the oriental luxury trade.

THE ROMAN CONTRIBUTION

The Graeco-Roman cultural synthesis.   Writing during the rule of Augustus, the Roman poet Virgil was the spokesman for what enlightened Romans felt to be the mission of the Empire:

> Others, doubtless, will mould lifelike bronze with greater delicacy, will win from marble the look of life, will plead cases better, chart the motions of the sky with the rod and foretell the risings of the stars. You, O Roman, remember to rule the nations with might. This will be your genius—to impose the way of peace, to spare the conquered and crush the proud.[4]

By "others," Virgil was referring to the Greeks, to whom the Romans willingly acknowledged a cultural debt. Although Greek ways of life introduced sophisticated habits which were often corrupting to the Roman virtues of self-reliance, personal integrity, family cohesion, and discipline, Greek influences made the Romans on the whole less harsh and insensitive. Largely because of their admiration for Greek culture, the Romans helped perpetuate the legacy of Greece. The *Pax Romana* was the acme of Graeco-Roman civilization.

Roman engineering and art.   The Empire's needs, together with the practical nature of the Romans and their skill in engineering, resulted in the construction of a system of paved roads and bridges as well as huge public buildings and aqueducts. Constructed of layers of stone according to sound engineering principles, their roads were planned for the use of armies and messengers and were kept in constant repair. It has been said that the speed of travel possible on Roman highways was not surpassed until the early nineteenth century. In designing their bridges and aqueducts, the Romans placed a series of stone arches next to one another to provide mutual support. At times several tiers of arches were used, one above the other. Fourteen aqueducts supplied some fifty gallons of water daily for each inhabitant of Rome.

Roman buildings were built to last, and their size, grandeur, and decorative richness aptly symbolized Rome's proud imperial spirit. At first the Romans copied Etruscan architectural models, but later they combined basic Greek elements with distinctly Roman innovations. The structural simplicity of Hellenic buildings was too restrained for the Romans who, by utilizing brick and concrete, developed new methods for enclosing space. The static post and lintel system of the Greeks was replaced with the more dynamic techniques of vaulting—barrel vaults, cross vaults, and domes. The standard type of Roman public building was the basilica, a colonnaded structure that became a model for early Christian churches. Rows of columns divided the interior into a central nave and side aisles, with the roof over the nave raised to admit light, creating a clerestory like those found in Egyptian temples.

Although strongly influenced by Etruscan and Greek models, the Romans developed a distinctive sculpture of their own which was remarkably realistic, secular, and individualistic. Their lifelike portraiture probably originated in the early practice of making and preserving wax images of the heads of important families. What little Roman painting has been preserved clearly reflects the influence of Hellenistic Greek models. The Romans were particularly skilled in producing floor mosaics—often copies of some Hellenistic painting—and in painting frescoes which show objects in clear though imperfect perspective.

Literary Rome.   In literature as in art the Romans turned to the Greeks for their

Roman skill at portraiture is illustrated by the individuality of these busts of various emperors and their families. Augustus, crowned with laurel and somewhat idealized, appears in the foreground.

models. Roman epic, dramatic, and lyric poetry forms were usually written in conscious imitation of Greek masterpieces. Hence Latin writing was less creative than Greek, but it remains one of the world's great literatures largely because of its influence upon medieval, Renaissance, and modern culture.

The oldest examples of Latin literature to survive intact are the twenty-one comedies of Plautus (c. 254–184 B.C.), which were adapted from Hellenistic Greek originals but with many Roman allusions, colloquialisms, and customs added. Plautus' comedies are bawdy and vigorously humorous, and their rollicking plots of illicit love and stock characters of the shrewish wife, henpecked husband, lovelorn youth, clever slave, and swashbuckling soldier reveal the level of culture and taste in early Rome.

Latin literature entered its first great period of creative activity during the last years of the Republic. This period marks the first half of the Golden Age of Latin literature, known as the Ciceronian period because of the stature of Marcus Tullius Cicero (106–43 B.C.), the greatest master of Latin prose and perhaps the outstanding intellectual influence in Roman history. Cicero made a rich contribution to knowledge by passing on to later ages much of Greek thought and at the same time interpreting it from the standpoint of a Roman intellectual and practical man of affairs.

The philosophical poet Lucretius found in the philosophy of Epicurus an antidote to his profound disillusionment with his fellow citizens who, he wrote, "in their greed of gain . . . amass a fortune out of civil bloodshed: piling wealth on wealth, they heap carnage on carnage. With heartless glee they welcome a brother's tragic death."[5] (His long philosophical poem, *On the Nature of Things*, is discussed on p. 73).

Augustus provided the Roman world with a stability that was conducive to a further outpouring of literary creativeness. The second phase of the Golden Age of Latin literature, the Augustan Age, was notable particularly for its excellent poetry. Virgil (70–19 B.C.) was probably the greatest of all Roman poets. His *Aeneid*, modeled on Homer's *Iliad* and *Odyssey*, recounts the fortunes of Aeneas, the legendary founder of the Latin people, who came from his home in Troy to Italy. The *Aeneid* eloquently asserts Rome's destiny to conquer and rule the world (see quotation, p. 70).

Horace (65–8 B.C.) was famous for both lyrical odes and satirical verse. Succeeding generations have turned to Horace because of his urbane viewpoint and polished style:

> Happy the man, and happy he alone,
> He, who can call to-day his own:
> He who secure within, can say,
> To-morrow do thy worst, for I have lived to-day.[6]

Quite a different sort was Ovid (43 B.C.–17 A.D.), a poet who combined a predilection for themes of sensual love (*The Art of Love*) with first-rate storytelling. It is largely through his *Metamorphoses*, a collection of Greek stories about the life of the gods, that classical mythology was transmitted to the modern world.

The literature of the so called "Silver Age," the century following the death of Augustus, substituted a more critical and negative spirit for the patriotism and optimism of the Augustan Age. Despite a great emphasis upon artificial stylistic devices, the Silver Age was memorable for its moral emphasis and its brilliant satirical poetry which reached its peak in Juvenal (55?–130 A.D.). This master of poetic invective flayed the short-comings of contemporary Roman society:

> Whatever mankind does, their hope, fear, rage, and pleasure,
> Their business and their sport, are the hotch-potch of my book.
> And when was there a richer crop of vices?[7]

The writing of history. Two Roman historians produced notable works during the Golden and Silver Ages. In his *History of Rome*, Livy (59 B.C.–17 A.D.) assembled the legends and traditions of early Rome and welded them into a continuous narrative. He glorified the virtues of the ancient Romans—their heroism, patriotism, and piety—and sought to draw moral lessons from an idealized past.

Tacitus (55–117 A.D.), like his contemporary Juvenal, was concerned with improving society. His *Germania* contrasts the life of the idealized, simple Germanic tribes with the corrupt and immoral existence of the Roman upper classes, and his *Annals* and *Histories* depict the shortcomings of the emperors and their courts from the death of Augustus to 96 A.D. Tacitus suffered from the bias of his own senatorial class; he looked upon the emperors as tyrants and thus could not do justice to the positive contributions of imperial government.

The most famous Greek author in the Empire was Plutarch (46?–120? A.D.), who composed one of the eminently readable classics of Greek literature. His *Parallel Lives*, containing forty-six biographies of famous Greeks and Romans, delineates the qualities that make men great or ignoble.

Stoicism and Epicureanism. The Romans contributed no original philosophical theories, preferring to adapt existing Greek systems of thought to suit their needs. Epicureanism made its greatest impact during the last days of the Republic, since men found its tenets comforting in a period of political upheaval when no one knew what the morrow would bring. As young men, Virgil and Horace embraced Epicureanism, but Lucretius was its most important Roman interpreter. In his *On the Nature of Things*, Lucretius followed Epicurus (see p. 56) in basing his explanation of the "nature of things" on materialism and atomism. He exhorted his readers to seek pleasure in philosophical serenity, rather than in sensuous gratification, and to have no fear of death since souls, like bodies, are composed of atoms that fall apart when death comes.

More enduring, especially in the days of the Empire, was the appeal of Stoicism to the Roman ruling classes. Roman Stoicism not only emphasized constancy to duty, courage in adversity, and service to humanity, but it also became a kind of religious creed by stressing an all-wise Providence, or fatherly God, and the immortality of the soul.

Science in the Roman Empire. The Romans had a utilitarian approach to science. By putting the findings of Hellenistic science to practical use, they became masters in engineering and applied medicine. They also produced encyclopedias, the most important being the *Natural History* compiled by Pliny the Elder (23–79 A.D.), an intriguing mixture of fact and fable thrown together with scarcely any method of classification. Nevertheless, it was the most widely read work on science during the Empire and the early Middle Ages.

The last great scientific minds of the ancient world were two Greeks, Claudius Ptolemy and Galen, both of whom lived in the second century A.D. Ptolemy resided at Alexandria, where he became celebrated as geographer, astronomer, and mathematician. Although his maps show a comparatively accurate knowledge of the Old World, he exaggerated the size of Asia, an error which influenced Columbus to underestimate the width of the Atlantic. His work on astronomy, usually called the *Almagest* ("the great work") from the title of the Arabic translation, summed up the geocentric, or earth-centered, view of the universe that was to rule men's minds until the sixteenth century. In mathematics, Ptolemy's work in improving and developing trigonometry became the basis for modern knowledge of the subject.

Galen, born in Pergamum in Asia Minor, was called to Rome where he became physician to Marcus Aurelius. Forbidden by the Roman government to dissect human bodies, Galen experimented with animals and demonstrated that an excised heart can continue to beat outside the body and that injuries to one side of the brain produce disorders in the opposite side of the body. He was also the first to explain the mechanism of respiration. Galen's medical encyclopedia, in which he summarized the medical knowledge of antiquity, remained the standard authority until the sixteenth century.

Roman law. Of the Roman contributions to later ages, Roman law is preeminent. It is the basis for the law codes of Italy, Spain, France, Scotland, and the Latin American countries. And where English common law is used, as in the United States, there is also a basic heritage of great legal principles originated by ancient Roman jurists. In addition, Roman law has strongly affected the canon law of the Roman Catholic Church, international law, and commercial law.

Roman law evolved slowly over a period of about a thousand years. At first unwritten, mixed with religious custom, and harsh in its judgments, in the fifth century B.C. it was written down as the Law of the Twelve Tables (see p. 61). During the remainder of the Republic the body of Roman law was enlarged by legislation passed by the Senate and the assembly and, equally important, by judicial interpretation of existing law to meet new conditions. By the second century A.D. the emperor had become the sole source of law, a responsibility he entrusted to scholars "skilled in the law" (*jurisprudentes*). Holding to the idea of equity and influenced by the Stoic concept of a law common to all men and ascertainable by human reason, these jurists humanized and rationalized Roman law to meet the needs of a world-state. Finally, in the sixth century A.D., the enormous bulk of Roman law from all sources was codified (see p. 94) and thus preserved for posterity.

THE RISE AND TRIUMPH OF CHRISTIANITY

Romans and Jews. At the very time when the Principate of Augustus was laying the foundations of Rome's imperial greatness, events were taking place in the distant Roman province of Judea that would one day alter the course of western history. Soon after the death of King Herod the Great, a Roman appointee, Judea became in 6 A.D. a minor Roman province, governed by procurators. The Jews had detested Herod, who was half Arab, and they remained unhappy under direct Roman rule.

During earlier centuries of tribulation the prophets had taught that God would one day create a new Israel when righteousness prevailed under a God-anointed leader, the Messiah. By the time of Augustus many Jews had lost hope in a political Messiah and an earthly kingdom and instead conceived of a spiritual Messiah who would lead all the righteous, including the resurrected dead, to a spiritual kingdom. But a group of ardent Jewish nationalists, called Zealots, favoring the use of force to drive the hated foreigner out of God's land, in 66 A.D. precipitated a fatal clash with Rome. After a five-year siege, Jerusalem was laid waste and the Temple destroyed (70 A.D.). The Jewish dream of an independent homeland was to remain unrealized for almost nineteen centuries, until the republic of Israel was proclaimed in 1948.

Jewish religious thought. In the centuries just preceding and following the birth of Christ, Judaism exhibited vigor and strength. While the aristocratic Sadducees, who controlled the office of high priest, stood for strict adherence to the written Law or Torah, the more numerous Pharisees believed that, with divine guidance, men could modify and amend the Law. For example, they accepted the belief in personal immortality and the Kingdom of Heaven. From their ranks came the rabbis, scholars who expounded the Law and applied it to existing conditions. Moreover, following the destruction of the Temple and the end of the high priesthood, the rabbinical schools of the Pharisees did much to ensure that Judaism would endure.

Since 1947 the discovery of the Dead Sea Scrolls has added greatly to our knowledge of another Jewish sect, the Essenes. Near the caves in which the scrolls were hidden are the ruins of an Essene monastery, destroyed by the Romans during the great Jewish revolt of 66–70 A.D. Some scrolls are portions of the Old Testament dating from the first century B.C. and thus are centuries older than the earliest text previously known.

Other scrolls describe the Essene sect and are said to constitute "a whole missing chapter of the history of the growth of religious ideas between Judaism and Christianity."[8] Some scholars have attached much significance to common elements in the beliefs and practices of the Essenes and early Christians. The Essenes' founder, a shadowy figure known as the Teacher of Righteousness, suffered persecution and perhaps martyrdom late in the second century B.C. The sect considered itself the true remnant of God's people, preached a "new covenant," and waited patiently for the time when God would destroy the powers of evil and inaugurate His Kingdom. Similar views concerning the transition from an "Old Age" to a "New Age" were held by Christians. For the Christians, however, the gap had been bridged. The Messiah had come, and his resurrection was proof that the New Age had arrived.

The life of Jesus. Whatever its parallels with the Essene sect—including baptism and a communal meal—Christianity bears the unmistakable imprint of the personality of its founder, Jesus of Nazareth. According to the Biblical account, he was born in Bethlehem during the reign of Herod. After spending the first years of his life as a carpenter in the village of Nazareth, Jesus began his brief mission, preaching a gospel of love for one's fellow man and urging people to "Repent, for the kingdom of heaven is at hand" (Matthew 4:17).

The fame of Jesus' teaching and holiness spread among the Jews as he and his twelve disciples traveled from village to village in Palestine. When he came to Jerusalem to observe the feast of the Passover, he was welcomed triumphantly by huge crowds as the promised Messiah. But Jesus was concerned with a spiritual, not an earthly, kingdom, and when the people saw that he had no intention of leading a nationalistic movement against the Romans, they turned against him. His enemies then came forward—the moneylenders whom he had denounced, the Pharisees who resented his repudiation of their minute regulations of daily behavior, the people who considered him a disturber of the status quo, and those who saw him as a blasphemer of Yahweh. Betrayed by Judas, one of his disciples, Jesus was condemned by the Jews for blasphemy "because he claimed to be the Son of God" (John 19:7). Before the procurator Pontius Pilate, however, Jesus was charged with treason for claiming to be the king of Jews. He was condemned to the death that Rome inflicted on criminals—crucifixion. With Jesus' death it seemed as though his cause had been exterminated. Yet in the wake of his martyrdom the Christian cause took on new impetus. Reports soon spread that Jesus had risen from the dead and had spoken to his disciples, giving them solace and inspiration.

Paul's missionary work. As long as the followers of Jesus regarded him exclusively as a Messiah in the traditional Jewish sense, requiring his followers to observe the Jewish Law, the new religion could have no universal appeal. Largely through the missionary efforts of Paul, this obstacle was removed.

Paul, whose original Jewish name was Saul, began as a strict Pharisee who considered Christians to be blasphemers against the Law and took an active part in their persecution. One day, on the road to Damascus—in Paul's own words—"a bright light suddenly flashed from the sky around me. I fell to the ground and heard a voice saying to me, 'Saul, Saul! Why do you persecute me?' 'Who are you, Lord?' I asked. 'I am Jesus of Nazareth, whom you persecute,' he said to me."[9] This mystical experience turned Paul from a persecutor into the greatest of Christian missionaries.

Paul taught that Jesus was the Christ (from *Christos*, Greek for "Messiah"), the Son of God, and that He had died to atone for the sins of mankind. Acceptance of this belief guaranteed salvation to Jews and gentiles alike. The Law, with its strict dietary regulations and other requirements that discouraged the conversion of gentiles, was unnecessary. After covering eight thousand miles teaching and preaching, Paul was beheaded in Rome about 65 A.D. (as was also Peter, founder of the church at Rome) during the reign of Nero.

From persecution to triumph. To the Roman government, notably tolerant of all religions, Christianity appeared to be a subversive danger to society and the state. The Christians refused to participate in the worship of the emperor which, although not an official state religion, was considered an essential patriotic rite uniting all Roman subjects in common loyalty to the imperial government. To Christians there was only one God; no other could share their loyalty to Him. In the eyes of the Roman officials this attitude branded them as traitors. In addition, the Christians seemed a secret, unsociable group forming a state within a state. Many were pacifists who refused to serve in the army, and all were intolerant of other religious sects and refused to associate with pagans or take part in social functions that they considered sinful or degrading.

During the first two centuries A.D. persecution was only sporadic and local, but during the late third and early fourth centuries, when, as we shall see, the Empire was in danger of collapse, three organized empirewide efforts were made to suppress Christianity. By far the longest and most systematic persecution was instigated by the emperor Diocletian from 303 to 311. But the inspired defiance of the Christian martyrs, who seemed to welcome death, could not be overcome.

In 311 the emperor Galerius recognized that persecution had failed and issued an edict of toleration making Christianity a legal religion in the East. In the following year the emperor Constantine was swayed toward Christianity during a desperate battle with the army of a rival for the throne. At the height of the conflict, tradition has it that he saw emblazoned across the sky a cross with the words *In hoc signo vinces* ("By this sign thou shalt conquer"). Constantine won the battle, and in 313 he issued the Edict of Milan, which legalized Christianity throughout the Empire and put it on a par with all the pagan cults. Constantine favored Christianity by granting many privileges to the Church, but he waited until he was on his deathbed before receiving baptism. Near the end of the century Theodosius I (379–395) made Christianity the official religion of the Empire. Henceforth paganism was persecuted, and even the Olympic games were suppressed.

Reasons for the spread of Christianity. In its rise to preeminence Christianity competed with the philosophies and religions of the day. The philosophies were becoming more religious and other-worldly, however, which made it easy for their adherents to accept a Christianity whose doctrines, as we shall see, were becoming more philosophical. Roman Stoics believed in God and the immortality of the soul (see p. 73), and the dominant philosophy of the third century, Neo-Platonism, rejected human reason and taught that the only reality is spirit and that the soul's principal objective is to escape from the material world and, by union with God, return to its spiritual home.

There were also the popular mystery religions such as the worship of the Phrygian Great Mother (Cybele), the Egyptian Isis, the Greek Dionysus, and the Persian Mithras, god of light who fought against darkness. All of these cults presented the comforting idea of a divine savior and the promise of everlasting life. Their followers found Christian beliefs and practices sufficiently familiar so as to make conversion easy.

But Christianity had far more to offer than did the mystery religions. Its founder was not a creature of myth, like the gods and goddesses of the mystery cults, but a real historic personality whose lofty ethical teachings and whose death and resurrection as the divine incarnation of God were preserved in detail in a unique record—the New Testament. Moreover, Christianity was a dynamic, aggressive faith. It upheld the equality of all men—Jesus' ministry was chiefly to the poor and downtrodden—taught that a loving Father had sent His only Son to atone for men's sins, and offered a vision of immortality and an opportunity to be "born again" cleansed of sin. In time, also, a Church organization was created that was far more united and efficient than any possessed by its competitors.

Church organization. At first there was little or no distinction in the Christian movement between laity and clergy. But the steady growth in the number of Christians made special Church officials necessary. The earliest were called presbyters (elders) or bishops (overseers). By the second century the offices of bishop and presbyter had become distinct. Churches in the villages adjacent to the mother Church, which was usually located in a city, were administered by priests (a corruption of *presbyter*) responsible to a bishop. Thus evolved the bishop's diocese. Furthermore, the bishops were recognized as the successors of the apostles and, like them, the guardians of Christian teaching and tradition.

A number of dioceses made up a province; the bishop of the most important city in each province enjoyed more prestige than his fellows and was known as an archbishop or metropolitan. The provinces were grouped into larger administrative divisions called patriarchates. The title of patriarch was applied to the bishop of such great cities as Rome, Constantinople, and Alexandria.

A development of outstanding importance was the rise of the bishop of Rome to a position of preeminence in the West with the title of pope—from the Greek word meaning "father." As the largest city in the West and the capital of the Empire, Rome had an aura of prestige that was transferred to its bishop. Thus when the Empire in the West collapsed in the fifth century, the bishop of Rome emerged as a stable and dominant figure looked up to by all. The primacy of Rome was fully evident during the pontificate of Leo I, called the Great (440–461), who provided both the leadership that saved Italy from invasion by the Huns (see p. 83) and the major theoretical support for papal headship of the Church—the Petrine theory. This doctrine held that since Peter, whom Christ had made leader of the apostles, was the first bishop of Rome, his authority over all Christians was handed on to his successors at Rome. The Church in the East, insisting on the equality of all the apostles, has never accepted the Petrine theory.

Origins of Christian doctrine and worship. Meanwhile, Christian belief, or dogma, was being defined and systematized, often amid much controversy. An outstanding example concerned the relative position of the three persons of the Trinity—God the Father, God the Son, and God the Holy Spirit. The view that the Father and the Son were equal was vigorously denied by Arius, a priest of Alexandria, who believed that Christ was not fully God because he was not of a substance identical with God and, as a created being, was not coeternal with Him. The controversy became so serious that in 325 the emperor Constantine convened the first ecumenical Church council, the Council of Nicaea, to resolve the problem. With Constantine presiding, the council branded the Arian belief a heresy—an opinion or doctrine contrary to the official teachings of the Church—and Christ was declared to be of the same substance as God, uncreated, and coeternal with Him. This mystical concept of the Trinity, without which the central Christian doctrine of the incarnation would be undermined, received official formulation in the Nicene Creed.

The development of the Church's dogma owed much to the Church Fathers of the second through fifth centuries. Since most of them were intellectuals who came to Christianity by way of Neo-Platonism and Stoicism, they maintained that Greek philosophy and Christianity were compatible. Because reason and truth come from God, "philosophy was a preparation," wrote Clement of Alexandria (d. 215), "paving the way towards perfection in Christ,"[10] the latest and most perfect manifestation of God's reason. Thus Christianity was viewed as a superior philosophy which could supersede all pagan philosophies and religions.

In the West three Church Fathers stand out. The scholarship of St. Jerome (340–420) made possible the famous Vulgate translation of the Bible into Latin, which in a revised form is still the official translation of the Roman Catholic Church. St. Ambrose (340–397) resigned his government post to become bishop of Milan, where he employed his great administrative skills to establish a model bishopric. By reproving the actions of the strong emperor Theodosius I and forcing him to do public penance, St. Ambrose was the first to assert the Church's superiority over the state in spiritual matters. St. Augustine (354–430) was probably the most important of all the Church Fathers. At the age of thirty-two, as he relates in his *Confessions*, he found in Christianity the answer to his long search for meaning in life. As bishop of Hippo in North Africa, he wrote more than a hundred religious works which became the foundation of much of the

Church's theology. The early Christian had worshipped God and sought salvation largely through his own efforts. With the growth of its organization and dogma, however, the Church was now believed to be the indispensable intermediary between God and man.

The regular clergy. So far we have discussed the secular clergy, who moved through the world administering the Church's services and communicating its teachings to the laity. But another type of churchmen also arose—the regular clergy, so called because they lived by a rule (*regula*) within monasteries. These monks sought seclusion from the distractions of this world in order to prepare themselves for the next.

The monastic way of life was older than Christianity, having existed in Judaism, for example, among the Essenes (see p. 75). Christian ascetics, who had abandoned the worldly life and become hermits, could be found in the East as early as the third century A.D. Some went so far as to denounce even beauty as evil and, in pursuit of spiritual perfection by subordinating their flesh, tortured themselves and fasted to excess. In Syria, for example, St. Simeon Stylites lived for thirty-seven years on top of a pillar sixty feet high. St. Basil, a Greek bishop in Asia Minor, in the fourth century drew up a rule based on work, charity, and a communal life in which, however, each monk retained most of his independence. The Rule of St. Basil became the standard system in the eastern Church.

About 529 in Italy, St. Benedict composed a rule which gave order and discipline to western monasticism. Benedictine monks took the three basic vows of poverty, chastity, and obedience to the abbot, the head of the monastery. Unlike eastern monks, the daily activities of the Benedictine monks were closely regulated: they participated in eight divine services, labored in field or workshop for six or seven hours, and spent about two hours studying and preserving the writings of Latin antiquity at a time when chaos and illiteracy had overtaken the western half of the Roman Empire. Benedictine monasticism was to be the most dynamic civilizing force in western Europe between the sixth and the twelfth centuries.

DECLINE AND DIVISION IN THE ROMAN WORLD

The crisis of the third century. In the third century A.D., while Christianity was spreading throughout the Roman world, internal anarchy and foreign invasion drastically transformed the nature of the Empire. What can be called the constitutional monarchy of the first and second centuries changed to a despotic absolute monarchy. By the late third century the emperor was no longer addressed as *princeps*, meaning first among equals, but as *dominus et deus*, "lord and god." The Principate had been replaced by absolute rule known as the Dominate.

The decline of the Roman Empire began with the reign of Commodus (180–192), who hated his austere father, Marcus Aurelius. Commodus was an incompetent voluptuary whose dissipations, cruelties, and neglect of affairs of state motivated a group of conspirators to have him strangled. Civil war followed as rival armies fought for the imperial throne—on one occasion troops holding Rome sold the throne to the highest bidder—until Septimius Severus established a dynasty that provided some measure of order from 193 to 235. But the price was high—although the size and pay of the army were doubled, the last member of the dynasty was murdered by his mutinous troops. During the next fifty years the Empire was rent from within by the bloody civil wars of rival army-made emperors and lashed from without by German tribes to the north and a reinvigorated Persia, under the rule of the Sassanid dynasty, to the east.

As deadly to the wellbeing of the Empire as military anarchy and foreign invasions was prolonged economic decline. The Empire was no longer expanding, and its economy had become static. In the past military expansion had paid off in rich booty, and the tapping of new sources of wealth had justified a large army. Now, however, wars were defensive, and the army had become a financial liability rather than an asset. Gold and silver were also being drained away because of the one-sided trade with India and China.

The trend toward the concentration of land ownership in a few hands was greatly accelerated by the turbulent conditions of the third century. Small farmers abandoned their lands, which were then bought up cheaply by large landowners, and the emperors added to their vast estates through confiscation. The number of tenant farmers, or *coloni* (see p. 69), increased as small farming decreased, and men fled the insecurity of city life to find jobs and protection on the large estates with their fortified villas. There they cultivated patches of land, paying rent to the landowner and providing him with free labor at sowing and reaping time. The condition of the *coloni* worsened as they fell behind in their rents and taxes and, by imperial order, were bound to their tenancies until they had discharged their debts. This was a first step toward serfdom and the social and economic pattern of the Middle Ages.

Matters were made worse when the emperors, in order to meet their increasing military expenses, repeatedly devalued the coinage by reducing its silver content. Prices soared as people gradually lost confidence in the debased currency. Even the government eventually refused to accept its own money for taxes and required payment in goods and services. Civil war also disturbed trade and thus helped undermine the prosperity of the cities, whose population decreased correspondingly.

Diocletian. A much-needed reconstruction of the Empire was accomplished by Diocletian (284–305), a rough-hewn soldier and administrative genius who completed the trend toward an undisguised despotism. The Senate was relegated to the status of a mere city council, while the person of the emperor was exalted. Adorned in robes laden with jewels, the emperor surrounded himself with all the splendor of an oriental despot.

Realizing that the Empire's problems had become too great for one man, Diocletian divided it, retaining the eastern half for himself. In the West he created a coemperor who, like himself, was designated an Augustus. Each Augustus in turn was to entrust the direct rule of half his realm to an assistant, termed Caesar. Since each Caesar would succeed his Augustus when the senior official died or retired, the problem of succession was supposedly solved. Next, Diocletian greatly increased the number and variety of administrative units within the four divisions of the Empire. The provinces were reduced in size and more than doubled in number. Paralleling this civil administration was a separate hierarchy of military officials. Finally, a large secret service was created to keep close watch over this vast bureaucracy. Even the Christian Church did not escape the

spreading tentacles of the new regimented state, as Diocletian's ruthless persecution of Christianity demonstrates.

Diocletian also made strenuous efforts to arrest economic decay in the Empire.
He gradually restored confidence in the debased currency by issuing new standard
silver and gold coins. In the meantime his effort to stem the runaway inflation by
decreeing maximum prices for all essential goods and services proved unwork-
able.

Constantine. After Diocletian and his fellow Augustus retired in 305, his
scheme for the succession collapsed, and civil war broke out once again. Within a
few years Constantine (306–337), the only one of five rival emperors who favored
Christianity (see p. 77), forged to the front, and after sharing the Empire for a
few years with an eastern rival, became sole emperor in 324.

Constantine carried on Diocletian's work of reconstructing and stabilizing the
Empire. We have already noted his solution of the Christian problem. To stabilize
the manpower situation, necessary for the production of essential goods and
services as well as the collection of taxes, Constantine issued a series of decrees
which foze people to their occupations and places of origin. Henceforth no
colonus could leave the soil, and the children of a *colonus* had to accept the same
status as that of their father. In the cities the same restrictions were applied to
members of those guilds whose activities were essential to the state, such as
baking and transportation. Born into and bound to their occupations, members
had to marry within the guild and train their sons to carry on the same line of
work. Thus, to serve the interests of the state and to arrest further economic
decline, a veritable caste system was established.

Division of the Empire. The Roman world's center of gravity shifted eastward
during the age of Diocletian and Constantine. Diocletian chose to govern the
eastern half of the Empire and set up his court at Nicomedia in northwestern Asia
Minor. His was a logical choice; the East had declined less than the West, and the
greatest dangers to the Empire came from beyond the Danube River and from
Persia. But even more strategic than Nicomedia was the old Greek colony of
Byzantium, across the straits, selected by Constantine for a new capital. Reached
only through a narrow, easily defended channel, Byzantium possessed a splendid
harbor at the crossroads of Europe and Asia. Constantine dubbed his capital New
Rome, but it soon became known as Constantinople.

The establishment of an eastern capital foreshadowed the impending division of
the Empire into two completely separate states, the East and the West. For about
fifty years following the death of Constantine in 337, the unity of the Empire was
preserved, but after Theodosius I divided it between his two sons in 395, the
Empire was never again governed as a single unit. Henceforth we can speak of a
western Roman empire, which soon fell, and of an eastern Roman—or Byzantine—empire, which endured for another thousand years during which it adhered
to the paternalistic and authoritarian pattern laid down by Diocletian and
Constantine.

UPHEAVAL IN THE WEST

The Germans. The internal crisis of the Roman Empire in the third century
was compounded by mounting external pressures that threatened to stave in its

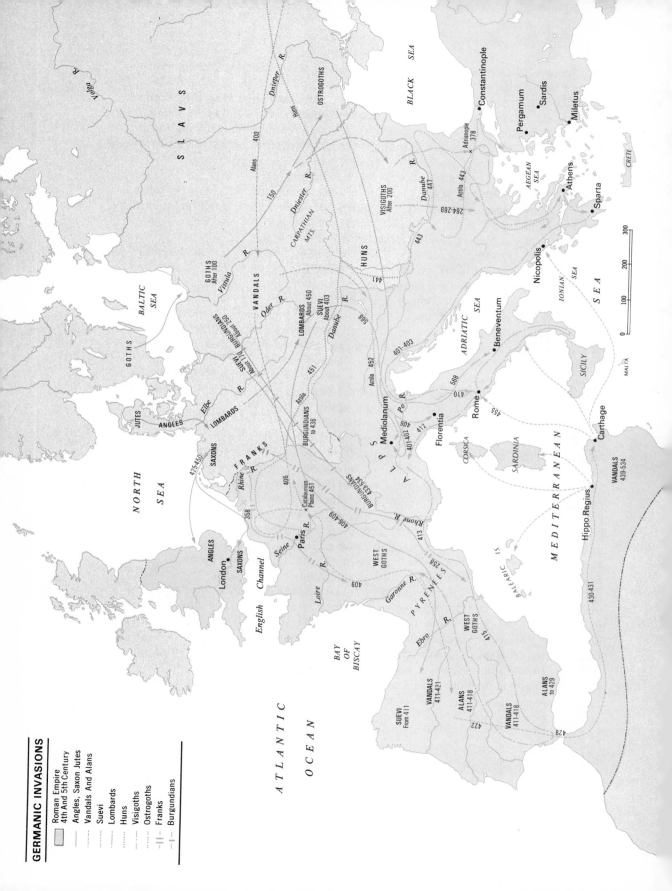

GERMANIC INVASIONS

Roman Empire
4th And 5th Century

Angles, Saxon Jutes

Vandals And Alans

Suevi

Lombards

Huns

Visigoths

Ostrogoths

Franks

Burgundians

ATLANTIC OCEAN

NORTH SEA

BALTIC SEA

BAY OF BISCAY

English Channel

MEDITERRANEAN SEA

ADRIATIC SEA

IONIAN SEA

AEGEAN SEA

BLACK SEA

SLAVS

GOTHS

JUTES

ANGLES

SAXONS

FRANKS

LOMBARDS

BURGUNDIANS to 436

VANDALS

SUEVI About 403

LOMBARDS About 450

GOTHS After 100

OSTROGOTHS

VISIGOTHS After 200

HUNS

WEST GOTHS

ITALY

GAUL

SPAIN

London

Paris

Mediolanum

Florentia

Rome

Beneventum

Carthage

Hippo Regius

Nicopolis

Constantinople

Pergamum

Sardis

Miletus

Athens

Sparta

Adrianople 378

CORSICA

SARDINIA

SICILY

MALTA

CRETE

BALEARIC IS.

Volga R.

Dnieper R.

Dniester R.

Vistula R.

Oder R.

Elbe R.

Rhine R.

Seine R.

Loire R.

Garonne R.

Ebro R.

Rhone R.

Danube R.

Po R.

CARPATHIAN MTS.

PYRENEES

SUEVI Old BURGUNDIANS About 250

VANDALS 439-534

SUEVI From 411

VANDALS 411-421

ALANS 411-418

VANDALS 411-418

ALANS to 429

WEST GOTHS

BURGUNDIANS 433-534

Catalaunian Plains 451

400

150

Alans

264-269

443

447

441

452

401-403

401-402

406

412

410

413

406-409

409

406

455

430-431

429

422

358

415-450

451

Attila

Attila 443

Attila 452

0 100 200 300

far-flung frontiers. The greatest danger lay to the north, the home of restless bands of fierce barbarians—the Germans.

The Roman historian Tacitus described the Germans as heavy drinkers and gamblers, but he also praised their courage, respect for women, and freedom from many Roman vices. A favorite amusement was listening to the tribal bards recite ancient tales of heroes and gods. Each warrior leader had a retinue of followers, who were linked to him by personal loyalty. According to Tacitus:

> it is a disgrace to the chief to be surpassed in valour by his companions, to the companions not to come up to the valour of their chief. As for leaving a battle alive after your chief has fallen, *that* means lifelong infamy and shame.[11]

This war band—called *comitatus* in Latin—had an important bearing on the origin of medieval feudalism, which was based on the personal bond between knights and their feudal lords. The heroic virtues associated with the *comitatus* also continued into the Middle Ages where they formed the basis of the value system of the feudal nobility.

In an effort to eliminate blood feuds, the Germanic system of justice was based on the principle of compensation, the amount of compensation varying according to the severity of the crime and the social position of the victim. To prove his innocence, a person charged with a crime either had to produce oath-helpers who would swear to his innocence or had to be subjected to various kinds of trial by ordeal.

The Germanic invasions. During the troubled third century many Germans were invited to settle on vacated lands within the Empire or to serve in the Roman legions. The Germans beyond the frontiers were kept in check by force of arms, by gifts, and by playing off one tribe against another. In the last decades of the fourth century, however, these methods proved insufficient to prevent a series of great invasions. Land hunger long had caused the Germans to be restless, but the impetus that now thrust entire tribes across the frontier came from the Huns, the first of a series of Asian nomads that would periodically threaten western Europe until the seventeenth century. In 372 these fierce horsemen crossed the Volga and soon subjugated the easternmost Germanic tribe, the Ostrogoths. Terrified at the prospect of being conquered in turn, the neighboring Visigoths successfully petitioned the Romans to allow them to settle as allies inside the Empire. But when corrupt Roman officials cheated and mistreated the Visigoths, they defeated and killed the East Roman emperor at Adrianople in 378, a battle that ushered in a century and a half of chaos. After pillaging the Balkans, the Visigoths invaded Italy and in 410 sacked Rome. The weak West Roman emperor ceded southern Gaul to the Visigoths, who soon expanded into Spain.

To counter the Visigothic threat to Italy, the Romans had withdrawn most of their troops from the Rhine frontier and from Britain. The momentous consequence of this action was a flood of Germanic tribes across the defenseless frontiers. The Vandals pushed their way through Gaul to Spain and, after pressure from the Visigoths, moved on to Africa, the granary of the Empire. Meanwhile the Burgundians settled in the Rhone valley, the Franks gradually spread across northern Gaul, and the Angles and Saxons invaded Britain. Although each of these several tribes set up a German-ruled kingdom within the confines of the Empire, only the Franks in Gaul and the Angles and Saxons in Britain managed to perpetuate their kingdoms longer than a few centuries.

The Huns also pushed farther into Europe. Led by Attila, the "scourge of God," they crossed the Rhine in 451. The remaining Roman forces in Gaul, joined by the Visigoths, defeated the Huns near Troyes. Attila then plundered northern Italy and planned to take Rome, but disease, lack of supplies, and the dramatic appeal of Pope Leo I—which was to give the papacy great prestige—caused him to return to the plains of Hungary. The Hunnic hordes disintegrated after 453, when Attila died on the night of his marriage to a Germanic princess.

Meanwhile Roman rule in the West had grown increasingly impotent under a series of incompetent emperors. The leaders of the mercenary soldiers, whose ranks were now mainly German, wielded the real power. In 475 the Germanic army commander forced the Senate to elect his young son Romulus Augustulus ("Little Augustus") as emperor in the West. In the following year another Germanic commander, Odovacar, seeing no reason for continuing the sham of an imperial line, deposed Romulus Augustulus and proclaimed himself head of the government. The deposition of the boy, who by a strange irony bore the names of the legendary founder of Rome and the founder of the Empire, marks the traditional "fall" of the Roman Empire. Actually, no single date is accurate, for the fall of Rome was a long and complicated process. Yet 476 at least symbolizes the end of the Roman Empire in the West.

The disintegration of the Hunnic empire following the death of Attila freed the Ostrogoths to migrate under their energetic king, Theodoric (c. 454–526), who accepted a commission from the emperor in the East to reimpose imperial authority over Italy. In 488 he led his people into the Italian peninsula where he established a strong Ostrogothic kingdom with its capital at Ravenna. Because he appreciated Roman culture, Theodoric pursued a successful policy of maintaining classical culture on a high level. His death without a male heir in 526 paved the way for a twenty-year war of reconquest (535–555) by the armies of the East Roman emperor Justinian. Italy was ravaged from end to end by the fighting, and the classical civilization that Theodoric had carefully preserved was in large part destroyed.

In 568 the last wave of Germanic invaders, the fierce Lombards, poured into Italy. The Eastern emperor held on to southern Italy, as well as Ravenna and Venice, and the pope now became the virtual ruler of Rome. Not until the late

POLITICAL DIVISIONS
OF EUROPE
ABOUT 526 A.D.

nineteenth century would Italy again be united under one government. The Lombard kingdom in Italy, weakened by the independent actions of many strong dukes, did not last long. In 774 it was conquered by the Franks, who, as we shall see in Chapter 5, had in the meantime established the most powerful and longest lasting of all the Germanic kingdoms that arose on the territory of the western empire.

The problem of the fall of Rome. The shock and dismay felt by contemporaries throughout the Roman world on learning of the sack of the Eternal City in 410 were to echo down the centuries. Pagan writers attributed the disaster to the abandonment of the ancient gods. In *The City of God* St. Augustine argued against this charge and put forth the theory that history unfolds according to God's design. Thus Rome's fall was part of the divine plan—"the necessary and fortunate preparation for the triumph of the heavenly city where man's destiny was to be attained."[12]

Most historians today account for Rome's decline in terms of a variety of interacting forces. On the political side, the failure of civil power to control the army following the death of Marcus Aurelius resulted in military anarchy, the disintegration of central authority, and the weakening of Rome's ability to withstand external pressures. On the economic side, the small farmer class disappeared, and more and more land was consolidated into huge estates; civil war and barbarian attacks disturbed trade relations; a debased currency and a crushing tax burden undermined the confidence of the people. Eventually the rigid economic and social decrees of Diocletian and Constantine created a vast bureaucracy which only aggravated the existing ills in the western half of the Empire, already far gone along the road to decline. The stronger eastern half of the Empire managed to ride out the storm of the Germanic invasions; in the following chapter we shall see how it maintained the Roman imperial tradition and administrative structure for another thousand years, together with an advanced culture that was a synthesis of Greek, Roman, and Near Eastern elements.

PART TWO

THE MIDDLE AGES

In the West by the sixth century the Roman Empire was no more than a memory. In its place were new states that foreshadowed most of the major political divisions of modern Europe: Visigothic Spain, Anglo-Saxon England, Frankish Gaul, and a divided Italy ruled by Lombard dukes, the Eastern emperor, and the pope.

Vast tracts of formerly cultivated land were left untilled, and the failure of communications and transportation, coupled with the flight of the labor force from the cities to the country, had brought on a progressive disruption and decentralization of the economy. With much industry transferred from cities to large country estates, scores of once flourishing towns near the frontiers ceased to exist, while those closer to the Mediterranean shrank in size and importance. "Roman civilization had been essentially urban; medieval civilization was to be essentially rural. With the decline of the towns the general level of civilization was lowered and western Europe began to assume its medieval aspect."[1]

Yet the Germanic invasions were not as cataclysmic as was once thought. The Germans seized a great deal of land, but most of it was either vacant or belonged to the emperors. In most areas the invaders still represented a minority of the population, and a gradual blending and fusing of the cultures and the blood of the two peoples began. Thus the barbarians in time lost their Germanic customs, religion, and speech. The Church, under the dual leadership of Benedictine monasticism and the papacy, assisted the fusion between German and Roman.

By the sixth century, then, the three elements that were to create the pattern of western civilization in the Middle Ages were being interwoven: Graeco-Roman culture, the Christian Church, and the Germanic peoples and their institutions. Here, in a sense, were the mind, spirit, and muscle that were to work together in western man during the following centuries.

This thousand-year span between the fall of Rome and the Renaissance was first termed the "Middle Ages" by the humanists of the Renaissance at the end of the period. They emphasized the links between their "modern" Renaissance world and the ancient world of Rome and Greece, and they saw the intervening centuries as a time of deterioration characterized by barbarism, ignorance, and superstition. Although modern historians have retained the term Middle Ages for this long period, they have revalued its importance by viewing it not as a halting place in the story of civilization but as the first phase, during which the foundations were laid, of a new European civilization.

Many changes occurred during the ten centuries encompassed by the Middle Ages; and we shall find, for example, that the institutions and ideas of the thirteenth century differ greatly from those of the ninth. In other words, there is really no "typical medieval man," because men's ideas and outlook did not remain static during the course of the Middle Ages. For this reason subdividing the Middle Ages into three distinct periods—the Early Middle Ages, the High Middle Ages, and the Late Middle Ages—both unifies and clarifies medieval civilization.

The Early Middle Ages, which lasted until about 1050, was a turbulent era which witnessed the disintegration of the Mediterranean world and the collapse of its political and economic unity. Roman emperors were replaced first by Germanic tribal war leaders similar to the primitive monarchs of ancient Greece, then by Charlemagne's temporary and frail reincarnation of the Roman Empire, and finally by the complex and fragile stability of oligarchic feudalism. As for the thought, religion, and art of the period, perhaps the best descriptive term is immaturity. We shall see that the achievements of this first period of medieval civilization—the so-called "Dark Ages"—contrast sharply with those of the bordering civilizations of Byzantium and Islam in the East. In the West many people were aware of the fact that they lived in an age of decline; a good example is the anonymous Anglo-Saxon poet who in the eighth century viewed the ruins of the Roman town now called Bath, and wrote:

> There were giants once. This was the wonder
> They fashioned out of stone. Now it has fallen
> To rack and ruin. . . . Where are the builders now?
> Gone, all gone, held in the clasp of earth. . . .
> And where they looked were rich stuffs, gems and silver,
> Lands and good living, all the broad domains
> Of a splendid city. . . . It was a good life, then.[2]

But in the High Middle Ages, roughly 1050 to 1300, the recognition of failure gave way to the realization of success. New kingdoms arose; population increased; revived cities spawned revolutionary economic and social changes; and thought, art, and religion reached greater maturity. Most of the institutions and ideas that are commonly called medieval are the products of the short but extremely fruitful High Middle Ages.

Finally, there are the Late Middle Ages—the fourteenth and fifteenth centuries—which began with a sense of anxiety as population declined, the economy stagnated, and war and plague stalked the land before recovery came and Europe with renewed vigor launched into the Renaissance and the transition to modern times.

CHAPTER 4

CITADEL AND CONQUEROR

The Byzantine Empire, Early Russia,
and Muslim Expansion

When we speak of the fall of the Roman Empire, we sometimes forget that in fact only the western portion of that empire succumbed to the German invaders and entered into what is often described as its "Dark Ages." In the East, despite many vicissitudes, the east Roman or Byzantine empire stood for a thousand years as a citadel protecting an unappreciative West slowly emerging from semibarbarism.

Furthermore, the Byzantine empire made great contributions to civilization: Greek language and learning were preserved for posterity; the Roman imperial system was continued and Roman law codified; the Greek Orthodox Church converted the Slavic peoples and fostered the development of a splendid new Graeco-oriental art. Situated at the crossroads of East and West, Constantinople acted as the disseminator of culture for all peoples who came in contact with the empire. This rich and turbulent metropolis, called with justification "The City," was to the early Middle Ages what Athens and Rome had been to classical times. By the time the empire collapsed in 1453, its religious mission and political concepts had borne fruit among the Slavic peoples of eastern Europe and especially among the Russians. The latter were to lay claim to the Byzantine tradition and to dub Moscow the "Third Rome."

The only rival of Byzantine civilization close at hand was the culture developed by followers of the Prophet Muhammad, who united the Arabian peninsula under the banner of his new religion, Islam. The dynamic faith of Muhammad spread so rapidly that within a hundred years after the Prophet's death his followers had established a vast empire stretching from the Pyrenees to the Indus. This breathtaking religious and political expansion was followed by a flowering of Islamic culture that rivaled the achievements of the Byzantine empire and far surpassed those of western Europe at this time. The Muslims share with the Byzantines chief credit for preserving and disseminating learning in the centuries following the fall of Rome.

Constantine's city. At the southern extremity of the Bosporus stands a promontory that juts out from Europe toward Asia, with the Sea of Marmora to the south and a long harbor known as the Golden Horn to the north. On this peninsula stood the ancient Greek city of Byzantium, which Constantine enlarged considerably and formally christened "New Rome" in 330 A.D.

Constantine had chosen his site carefully. The city commanded the waterway connecting the Mediterranean and the Black seas and separating Europe and Asia. Moreover, the site favored defense; it enabled Constantinople not only to become a great warehouse for commerce but above all to be a buffer protecting Europe from attack.

In Chapter 3 we saw how both the eastern and western provinces of the Roman Empire were beset by dangers from beyond the northern frontier. Although Visigoths, Huns, and Ostrogoths pillaged the Balkans and threatened Constantinople, the more populous eastern provinces, with their greater military and economic strength, managed to escape the fate that befell Rome. After the western half of the Empire crumbled, Constantinople turned eastward and became gradually less Roman and western and more Greek and oriental. The last truly "Roman" emperor was Justinian, who came to the throne in 527.

Justinian's reconquests. The overriding ambition of Justinian (527-565) was to restore the Roman Empire to its ancient scope and grandeur. He owed much to his wife, Theodora, who had been a dancer and was said to be the daughter of a circus animal trainer. She proved to be a brave empress and wise counselor. Early in Justinian's reign occurred the Nike rebellion (named after the victory cry of the rioters), the most famous of many popular revolts that have led historians to characterize Byzantine history as a despotism tempered by revolution. Theodora's coolness and bravery inspired her hard-pressed husband to remain in the capital and crush the rebellion: "If, now, it is your wish to save yourself, O Emperor, there is no difficulty. . . . as for myself, I approve a certain ancient saying that royalty is a good burial-shroud."[1]

To carry out his plan for recovering the West from the Germans, Justinian first bought off the Persian Sassanid kings, who threatened Syria and Asia Minor (see p. 80). Then he quickly seized North Africa and the islands of the western Mediterranean from the Vandals. But it took twenty years of exhausting warfare for his generals to regain Italy from the Ostrogoths, with the result that Rome and other great Italian cities lay in ruins. Justinian also wrested the southeastern portion of Spain from the Visigoths. But his protracted wars had overextended and exhausted the empire's resources; three years after his death most of devastated Italy fell to the Germanic Lombards, and the Persians made inroads into Syria.

In domestic affairs as in warfare, Justinian sought to restore the dignity and splendor of the Roman Empire. In this area are found his greatest accomplishments—the codification of Roman law and the erection of the great Church of Hagia Sophia, both described later in this chapter.

Nine centuries of peril. With Justinian's death, the greatest period of Byzantine history ended. For nine hundred years thereafter, until Constantinople fell in 1453, the empire faced almost constant attacks. Slavic Serbs and Bulgars filtered in to the Balkans from the north, and Persians attacked from the east. No sooner

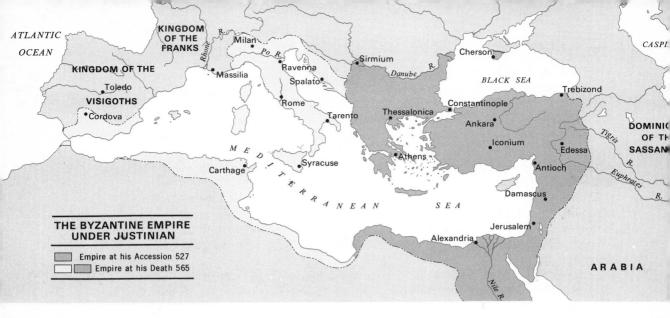

ATLANTIC

OCEAN

KINGDOM OF THE

VISIGOTHS

Toledo

Cordova

KINGDOM
OF THE
FRANKS

Milan

Massilia

Ravenna

Spalato

Rome

Tarento

Carthage

Syracuse

Sirmium

Danube R.

Thessalonica

Athens

M E D I T E R R A N E A N   S E A

Alexandria

Nile R.

Cherson

BLACK SEA

Constantinople

Ankara

Iconium

Antioch

Damascus

Jerusalem

Trebizond

Edessa

Tigris

Euphrates R.

R.

ARABIA

CASPI

DOMINIC
OF TH
SASSAN

THE BYZANTINE EMPIRE
UNDER JUSTINIAN

Empire at his Accession 527
Empire at his Death 565

had the formidable Persians been crushed than the empire faced the threat of the Arabs, united and unified by a new faith, Islam. By the middle of the seventh century the Persian and Byzantine east, except for Asia Minor, was in Arab hands (see map, p. 99). Asia Minor was the main source of Byzantine manpower, and after it fell to the Seljuk Turks in the eleventh century the West responded to Byzantine appeals for aid by sending the First Crusade. But the crusades turned into an unqualified disaster for Byzantium when the Fourth Crusade in 1204 was diverted from its goal, the Holy Land, to capture and sack Constantinople. Sixty years later the Byzantine emperor regained his capital, but only a pitiable remnant of the empire remained. The final blow was struck by the Ottoman Turks. In the late thirteenth century these Turkish adventurers had received from the Seljuk sultan a military fief along the Byzantine border in western Asia Minor. The prospect of booty from raids across the border attracted swarms of recruits, with the result that in 1356 the Ottomans crossed over to Europe and overran Bulgaria and Serbia. Following an interval during which they expanded eastward in Asia Minor, the Ottomans in 1453 besieged and captured Constantinople, which had defended itself heroically for seven weeks. Thus fell New Rome, the eastern bulwark of Christian civilization and the last direct link with the classical era.

Why the Byzantine empire endured. The empire's internal history was as stormy as its external affairs. During its thousand years of existence it experienced some sixty-five revolutions and the abdications or murders of more than sixty emperors. How did the empire manage to survive for such a long period?

One reason lay in its continuous use of a money economy, in contrast to the primitive barter economy then prevailing in the West. The use of money facilitated trade and the payment of taxes and enabled the empire to maintain standing military and naval forces. Until the latter days of the empire Byzantine military science was relatively advanced and the armed forces effective. Surviving military manuals indicate the efficiency of army organization, which included engineering and medical units. Also, the Byzantines had a secret weapon called "Greek fire," an inflammable chemical mixture whose main ingredient, saltpeter, made it a forerunner of gunpowder. Much like a modern flamethrower, Greek fire was catapulted out of tubes onto the decks of enemy ships.

Another reason for the empire's endurance was its centralized system of administration. Where the West was broken up into numerous feudal principalities, the Byzantines were governed by a strong monarchy, aided by a well-trained bureaucracy. The emperor's authority rested on the claim that he was chosen by God to rule the Christian empire entrusted to him by God. So absolute was the emperor's control that his title *Autokrator* has been carried over into the English word *autocracy*, meaning "absolute supremacy." Only a successful revolution could depose him.

The Orthodox Church was another factor in the endurance of the empire. Linked closely to the state, the Church usually was the staunchest ally of the throne.

THE ORTHODOX CHURCH

Collaboration between Church and state. The Byzantine, or Orthodox, Church not only dominated religious and cultural life in the empire but was also interwoven with the political fabric. Whereas the Roman Church did not identify itself with the Roman Empire or any other state in the West but became an international body, the Orthodox Church was a state church ruled by God's vicar on earth—the king-priest who, surrounded by splendid pomp and ceremony, ruled the Byzantine empire. The patriarch of Constantinople, who headed the Orthodox Church, was the emperor's nominee. In essence, the Church was a department of the state, and the emperor at times even intervened in spiritual matters. Such blending of authority over Church and state in the office of emperor has been termed *Caesaropapism* (combining the functions of Caesar and pope).

Separation of the churches. Relations between the eastern and western branches of the Church, continually undermined by what Constantinople viewed as Rome's excessive claims of primacy (see p. 78), deteriorated sharply in the eighth century as a result of the policies of the emperor Leo III. Although Leo had no use for Islam as a religion, he agreed with its contention that the employment of images and pictures in worship eventually led to idolatry. Therefore, in 726 Leo issued an edict forbidding the use of religious images (icons). Statues were removed from churches and church walls were whitewashed to cover all pictures. Rioting in protest against iconoclasm, or image breaking, followed. At Rome, the pope read out of the Church all those who accepted iconoclasm. This caused an open breach between the papacy and the Eastern emperor.

In 843 the iconoclastic controversy was finally settled by the restoration of images, but other sources of friction made permanent reunion of the Byzantine and Roman churches impossible. The final break came in 1054, when doctrinal and liturgical disputes (the use of leavened vs. unleavened bread in the communion service, for example) caused the pope and the patriarch of Constantinople to excommunicate each other, thus creating a schism that has yet to be healed.

Missionary activity of the Church. The credit for converting many Slavic tribes to Christianity goes to the Orthodox Church. About 863 two monks who were also brothers, Cyril and Methodius, set out from Constantinople to bring the gospel to the pagan Moravians, a Slavic group living in what is now Czechoslovakia. They took with them translations of the Bible and the divine service written in an alphabet of modified Greek characters adapted to the Slavic languages. (The Cyrillic alphabet, used even now in Bulgaria, Serbia, and Russia, is named after Cyril, who invented it.) Although the Moravians and others of the westernmost Slavs eventually came under the sway of the Roman Church, the work begun by the two brothers triumphed among the Slavs to the east and south, so that ultimately the Orthodox Church extended throughout eastern Europe.

BYZANTINE ECONOMY, SOCIETY, AND CULTURE

Byzantine prosperity.   During the early Middle Ages, visitors to Constantinople were fascinated by the pomp and pageantry of its court and Church and by its wealth, which far surpassed anything to be found in the West. The complex urban civilization of the Byzantine world rested upon a foundation of strong and well-diversified economic activities.

Constantinople stood at the crossroads of Europe and Asia, and its site ensured its being a port of transit for a great marine trading basin extending from the Adriatic to southern Russia. Metalwork, leather goods, and other products manufactured in the empire went to India and China, while back to Constantinople came spices, precious stones, costly woods, and perfumes, some of which were transported on to the few western Europeans who could afford the luxuries of the Orient. Trade supported, and was in turn stimulated by, the existence of a sound gold currency. In the West a decline in commerce had been attended by a shrinkage in the supply and use of money. The Byzantine empire, on the other hand, retained a currency of such excellence that its gold bezant was a medium of international exchange, remaining free of debasement until the eleventh century—far longer than any other coinage in history.

Constantinople's industries supplied Christendom with many products. The city specialized in luxury goods, and was famous for the manufacture of armor, weapons, hardware, and textiles. After silkworms were smuggled out of China about 550 A.D., silk production began to flourish within the empire as a profitable state monopoly. Byzantine silks embroidered with gold and silver thread and fashioned into costly vestments for Church services or court attire were eagerly sought all over Europe. The state controlled the economy through a system of guilds to which all tradesmen and members of the professions belonged. Wages, profits, hours of labor, and the price of foodstuffs—all were controlled.

Constantinople, city of contrasts.   The colorful social life of the empire was concentrated at three centers in Constantinople: the imperial palace, the giant Hippodrome, and the Church of Hagia Sophia.

Court ceremonial was arranged to impress both foreigners and Byzantines with the emperor's exalted nature. An envoy to the palace was escorted through great lines of uniformed guards and dignitaries into a resplendent hall. At the appointed time a curtain was raised, disclosing the emperor clad in his imperial robes on his throne. Golden lions flanked the throne and golden birds perched in pomegranate trees. While the envoy prostrated himself, the throne would be raised aloft, symbolizing the unapproachability of the heir of the Caesars. During the audience the emperor remained motionless, silent, and aloof, while a court official spoke in his name.

Seating perhaps eighty thousand spectators, the Hippodrome was the scene of hotly disputed chariot races between the two major factions, the Blues and the Greens, each of which acquired large popular followings and political overtones. The emperor and the people came face to face at the Hippodrome, and one faction or the other often used the occasion to voice their displeasure with government policy. In the Nike rebellion (see p. 89), the Blues and Greens united in opposition to Justinian's costly wars.

The Byzantine synthesis in art and architecture. While Byzantine art was basically Roman in character during the reigns of the first Constantine and his immediate successors, the new capital's eastern location could not fail to bring additional artistic forces into play. Greek and Persian traditions were fused with the strong Christian spirit that had motivated New Rome since its inception; the result was a new style of a uniquely Byzantine character. The Greek tradition provided a graceful and idealistic approach; but oriental influences—a more abstract and formalized style, vivid coloring, and ornamentation—eventually predominated.

The first great age of Byzantine art was associated with Justinian, who commissioned the magnificent Church of Hagia Sophia (Holy Wisdom). According to Procopius, the historian of Justinian's reign, it was "a church, the like of which has never been seen since Adam, nor ever will be."

The dome is the crowning glory of Hagia Sophia both because of its beauty and because it represents a major advance in architecture. The Romans had been able to construct a huge dome in the Pantheon but had erected it upon massive circular walls which limited the shape of the building. The dome of Hagia Sophia was supported by pendentives, four triangular segments which received the weight of the dome and distributed it to four supporting piers. The use of pendentives made it possible to place a dome over a square area.

In the decoration of churches, Byzantine artists made extensive use of mosaics—small pieces of multicolored glass or stone cemented into patterns to form brilliant decorations. Not only did the rich colors of the mosaics increase the splendor of the church interiors and heighten the emotional appeal of the rituals, but the representations also served as useful teaching devices by presenting the viewer with scenes from the Bible and with images of Christ, the Virgin, and the saints. Byzantine wall paintings also decorated churches, and icons—panel paintings of sacred personages—were used in daily worship. As in mosaics, the subject matter of Byzantine painting was treated symbolically rather than realistically: "Like much of the art of today, which is not easy to understand at first glance, its significance lies below the surface; it is an art of the spirit rather than of the flesh, and must be approached from that point of view."[2]

The preservation of classical learning. The official adoption of the Greek language by the time of Justinian proved a stimulus to the preservation of classical works in philosophy, literature, and science. The scholars who perpetuated the Greek tradition were not clerics, as in the West, but members of the civil service. Byzantine scholars, concerned chiefly with recovering and classifying Hellenic and Hellenistic learning, were imitative rather than creative, and their own contributions tended to be a rehash of classical works. Yet when in the twelfth century the West began absorbing Greek science and Aristotelian philosophy from Islamic Spain, it was to Byzantine scholarship that the latter was indebted. Moreover, most of the West's knowledge of Greek literature and Platonic philosophy came directly from Constantinople in the fourteenth and fifteenth centuries.

One of the great achievements of Byzantine scholarship was the codification of Roman law. In 528 Justinian convoked a commission of scholars to gather and classify the vast, disorganized, and often contradictory mass of law that had accumulated during centuries of Roman government. The result was a great legal work popularly known as the Justinian Code and formally titled the *Corpus Juris Civilis*. It organized the imperial decrees of the last four centuries into the *Codex* and included as well the *Digest* of the writings of republican and imperial jurists, and the *Institutes*, a commentary on the principles underlying the laws. By this codification, Rome's priceless legal heritage was preserved and passed on to posterity. In holding that the will of the emperor is the source of law, that the judge is the emperor's representative in interpreting law, and that equity is the

Hagia Sophia was erected in the sixth century, a crucial transitional era between the end of the Roman Empire and the beginning of the Middle Ages. An immense stone symbol, Hagia Sophia linked the past and future. The grandeur of its construction—it is one of the greatest domed vaults of all time—recalls the glory of Rome, while its almost mystical interior prefigures the coming dominance of Christianity. After Constantinople was captured by the Turks in 1453, Hagia Sophia became an Islamic mosque, serving in this capacity until recently, when it was converted into a museum.

basic principle of law, Justinian's Code stands in sharp contrast to Germanic folk law. The Code was unknown in the West during the Early Middle Ages, but in the twelfth century it slowly began to have a notable influence on the improvement of medieval justice and the emergence of strong monarchs, who borrowed for their own use the Roman doctrine of imperial autocracy.

EARLY RUSSIA

The Slavs. While the fortunes of the Byzantine empire had been ebbing and flowing, its culture had exercised continuous and substantial influence upon the development of Russia in its formative centuries. The Russians were an eastern branch of the Slavic peoples whose original home is thought to have been the forests of western Russia. The Slavs moved into the lands vacated by the migrating Germans, and in time three main groups developed. The Western Slavs—Poles and Bohemians—reached the Elbe and came under Latin Christian influences. Both the Southern Slavs, who moved into the Balkans, and the Eastern Slavs, the ancestors of the Russians, were subjected to Greek Christian influences.

Founding of a Russian state. During the ninth century, Swedish Norseman, called Varangians by the Byzantines, combined piracy with trade and began to venture along the waterways from the eastern Baltic to the Black and Caspian seas. The Slavic settlements along the rivers often hired the fierce Varangians as protectors. In 862 the people of Novgorod employed one such warrior, the half-legendary Rurik, who became prince of the city. His brothers and companions established themselves in other cities, one being Kiev (see map, p. 144).

By the late ninth century Kiev had succeeded in establishing its supremacy over a large area which gradually became known as Russia, a name derived from *Rus* (meaning "rowers"), by which the Slavs knew the Norse. By the end of the tenth century the Norse minority had been absorbed by the Slavic population.

The Kievan state operated as a loose confederation, with the prince of Kiev recognized as senior among his kinsmen who ruled the other Russian city-states. Their common interest was in maintaining trade along the river routes. Every spring after the ice had melted on the Dnieper, cargoes of furs, wax, honey, and slaves were floated down to Kiev. From there a great flotilla would descend the Dnieper and proceed along the Black Sea shore to Constantinople. Returning with silks, spices, jewelry, wines, and metalwares, the Kievans would pass these goods on to northeastern Europe via Novgorod and the Baltic.

Christianity in Kievan Russia. The official conversion of the Russians to Christianity took place about 989 under Prince Vladimir of Kiev. According to an early Russian chronicle, Vladimir shopped around before making his choice of religions. He rejected Islam because of its injunctions against the use of strong drink, Judaism because the God of the Jews could not be considered very powerful since He had allowed them to be ejected from their Holy Land, and Roman Christianity because the pope entertained dangerous ideas about his superiority to all secular rulers. There remained the Orthodox Church of the Byzantines, which was presented to Vladimir's subjects as his choice.

From the outset the Kievan princes followed the Byzantine example and kept the Church dependent on them, even for its revenues, so that the Russian Church and state were always closely linked. The Russians also copied the Byzantines in Church ritual, theology, and such practices as monasticism.

Apogee and decline of Kiev.   Kievan Russia reached its height in the reign of Yaroslav the Wise (1019-1054 A.D.), who issued Russia's first law code (based on the customary law of the Eastern Slavs) and was a patron of art and learning. Byzantine architects and artists were brought to Kiev to build and decorate the cathedral of Hagia Sophia, named after its prototype in Constantinople.

Following the death of Yaroslav, the princes of the various cities fought increasingly among themselves for possession of the Kievan state; and to these disruptions was added the devastation of the nomads who roamed uncomfortably close to the capital and cut the trade route to Constantinople. The trading and farming population around Kiev could not sustain such hardships, and they sought refuge in flight. Many fled northeastward to city-states in the neighborhood of present-day Moscow. When the Asiatic Mongols destroyed Kiev in 1240 (see p. 145), it had already lost much of its power, wealth, and population.

At its height, however, Kievan Russia could boast of a culture and an economy that were superior to what then existed in western Europe; for these achievements Kiev was primarily obligated to Byzantium. In the wake of the fall of Constantinople in 1453, the Russians would appropriate even more of the Byzantine tradition, calling Moscow the "Third Rome."

MUHAMMAD AND HIS FAITH

Pre-Islamic Arabia.   The Ottoman Turks, who conquered Byzantium in 1453, belonged to a rival religion, Islam. The term *Islam,* meaning "submission to God," is derived from the Muslim holy book, the Koran. The followers of Muhammad, the founder of the faith, are known as Muslims. (This faith is often referred to as Muhammadanism, but Muslims frown on this term, which implies the worship and deification of Muhammad.)

The story of Islam begins in Arabia where nomads, or Bedouins, lived according to a tribal pattern. At the head of the tribe was the sheik, elected and advised by the heads of the related families comprising the tribe. Aside from their flocks, the Bedouins relied on booty from raids on settlements, on passing caravans, and on one another. They worshiped a large number of gods and spirits, many of whom were believed to inhabit trees, wells, and stones.

One of the few cities in Arabia was Mecca, located on the caravan route that ran from Yemen and Abyssinia in the south to the Byzantine and Persian empires in the north. Merchants of the Quraysh tribe, which controlled Mecca, were also concerned with protecting a source of income derived from the annual pilgrimage of tribes to a famous religious sanctuary at Mecca. Known as the Kaaba (cube), this square temple contained a sacred black stone and the images of some 360 local deities and fetishes.

Muhammad, founder of Islam.   Into this environment at Mecca was born a man destined to transform completely the religious, political, and social organization of his people. Muhammad (570-632) came from a family belonging to the Quraysh tribe. Left an orphan in early life, he was brought up by an uncle and later engaged in the caravan trade. When he was about twenty years old, Muhammad entered the service of a wealthy widow, whose caravans traded with Syria. He soon married his employer, who was some fifteen years his senior. Despite the difference in their ages, the marriage was a happy one, and they had four daughters.

According to tradition, Muhammad frequently went into the foothills near Mecca to meditate. One night he dreamed that the archangel Gabriel appeared with the command, "Recite!" When Muhammad asked, "What shall I recite?" he was told:

> Recite in the name of thy Lord who created
> Man from blood coagulated.
> Recite! Thy Lord is wondrous kind
> Who by the pen has taught mankind
> Things they knew not (being blind).[3]

This was the first of a series of visions and revelations. After a period of doubt and anguish, Muhammad became certain that he was a divinely appointed prophet of Allah, *"The* God"—the same God worshiped by the Jews and Christians—who had chosen him to perfect the religion revealed earlier to Abraham, Moses, the Hebrew prophets, and Jesus.

At first Muhammad had little success in attracting followers. His first converts were his wife, his cousin Ali, and Abu Bakr, a respected merchant. Opposition came from the leading citizens ("Shall we forsake our gods for a mad poet?"), who ridiculed Muhammad's doctrine of resurrection (pre-Islamic Arabs had only vague notions concerning the afterlife) and feared that his monotheistic teaching would harm the city's lucrative pilgrimage trade to the Kaaba.

The Hijra and triumphal return to Mecca. The first encouraging development occurred when a group of pilgrims from neighboring Medina accepted the Prophet's teachings. This event, plus increased persecution in Mecca, encouraged the Prophet to migrate with his band to Medina. This move took place in 622 and is known as the *Hijra,* which means "flight" or, in this context, "the breaking of old ties." The Hijra was such a turning point in Muhammad's career that the year in which it occurred is counted as the first in the Muslim calendar.

In the year 630 Muhammad marched on Mecca with an army. His old enemies were forced to surrender to the Prophet, who acted with magnanimity toward them. His first act was to cast out of the Kaaba its multitude of idols and fetishes; but the temple itself, together with the black stone, was preserved as the supreme center of Islam. In the two remaining years of Muhammad's life tribe after tribe of Bedouins throughout Arabia offered him their loyalty. Upon his death in 632 the Prophet left behind a faith which had united Arabia and which was to astound the world with its militant expansion.

Islamic theology. Muslims believe that the Koran contains the actual word of God as revealed to Muhammad over a period of more than twenty years. Because the Koran must never be used in translation for worship, the spread of Islam created a great deal of linguistic unity. Arabic supplanted many local languages as the language of daily use, and that part of the Muslim world which stretches from Morocco to Iraq is still Arabic-speaking. Furthermore, this seventh-century book remains the last word on Muslim theology, law, and social institutions and is therefore still the most important textbook in Muslim universities.

Within the Koran one finds the central tenet of Islam—monotheism. There is only one God, Allah; this is proclaimed five times daily from the minaret of the mosque as the faithful are called to prayer: "God is most great. I testify that there is no God but Allah. I testify that Muhammad is God's Apostle. Come to prayer, come to security. God is most great."

Belief in one God and in Muhammad as His Prophet is the first of five obligations, known to Muslims as the "Pillars of Faith;" the others are prayer, almsgiving, fasting, and a pilgrimage to Mecca. Prayers are said five times a day, either alone or, preferably, in a mosque. The Muslim is required to give alms, a practice regarded as expressing piety and contributing to one's salvation. During the month of Ramadan, the ninth month of the lunar year, Muslims fast. Finally, the Koran commands Muslims to make a pilgrimage to Mecca, where they go through traditional ceremonies, such as kissing the Kaaba stone, which is thought to have been white originally but blackened by the sins of those touching it. Each Muslim should make the pilgrimage to Mecca at least once during his lifetime if he has the means.

The Koran also provides Muslims with a body of ethical teachings. Idolatry, infanticide, usury, gambling, the drinking of wine, and the eating of pork are all prohibited. Muslim men were allowed four wives and an unspecified number of concubines. After death those who have submitted to Allah's rule—the charitable, humble, and forgiving—and those who have fought for His faith, shall dwell in a Garden of Paradise, reposing in cool shades, eating delectable foods, attended by "fair ones with wide, lovely eyes like unto hidden pearls," and hearing no vain speech or recrimination but only "Peace! Peace!" This veritable oasis is far different from the agonies of the desert hell that awaits the unbelievers, the covetous, and the erring. Cast into hell with its "scorching wind and shadow of black smoke," they will drink of boiling water.

Pervading Islam is the principle of religious equality. There is no priesthood—no intermediaries between man and God. There are leaders of worship in the mosques as well as the *ulema*, a class of learned experts in the interpretation of the Koran; but they are all laymen.

THE SPREAD OF ISLAM

Expansion under the first four caliphs. The Prophet's death in 632 was a dangerous moment. Muhammad left no son to succeed him; and, even if he had, neither his unique position as the Prophet nor Arab custom permitted any such automatic succession. Acting swiftly, Muhammad's associates selected the Prophet's most trusted friend and advisor, Abu Bakr, as his official successor, the caliph (from *khalifa*, meaning "deputy"). The second caliph was also one of Muhammad's companions, while the fourth was his cousin and son-in-law, Ali.

During the reigns of the first four caliphs (632-661) Islam spread rapidly over much of the Near East (see map), aided by the long struggle between the Byzantine and Persian empires, which had left both exhausted and open to conquest. Also an aid to conquest was the Prophet's belief that any Muslim dying in battle for the faith was assured entrance into paradise. This concept of holy war bred fanatical courage in the Arabs. Moreover, the prospect of rich and fertile

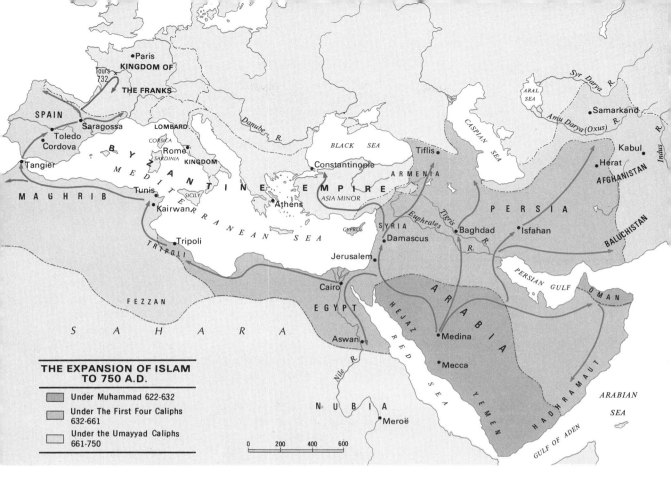

THE EXPANSION OF ISLAM
TO 750 A.D.

Under Muhammad 622-632

Under The First Four Caliphs
632-661

Under the Umayyad Caliphs
661-750

territory, as well as plunder, proved a strong incentive to a people who had been eking out a bare existence from the desert.

The new religion converted and embraced peoples of many colors and cultures. This egalitarian feature of Islam undoubtedly aided its expansion. Contrary to exaggerated accounts in the West of the forceful infliction of Islam upon conquered peoples, Jews and Christians enjoyed toleration because they worshiped the same God as the Muslims. In time, however, the imposition of a head tax on all non-Muslims encouraged many to become converts to Islam.

Arab domination under the Umayyads.   The expansion of Islam under the first four caliphs produced a new type of claimant to the caliphate—powerful generals and governors of provinces. In 661 the governor of Syria proclaimed himself caliph, made Damascus his capital, and founded the Umayyad dynasty which lasted until 750. Thus the caliphate became in fact, although never in law, a hereditary office, not, as previously, a position filled by election.

The Umayyad navy held Cyprus, Rhodes, and a string of Aegean islands, which served as a base for annual sea-borne attacks on Constantinople from 674 to 678. With the aid of Greek fire, Constantinople was saved, and the Arab advance was checked for the first time. Westward across North Africa, however, the Umayyad armies had great success. The Berbers, a warlike Hamitic-speaking people inhabiting the land between the Mediterranean and the Sahara, resisted stubbornly until converted to Islam. A Muslim army crossed the Strait of Gibraltar into

Spain in 711, and seven years later the kingdom of the Visigoths had completely crumbled. The Muslims then swept across the Pyrenees in a major raid to explore the possibility of a further northward advance. However, they were defeated by the Franks near Tours in 732, a battle which, together with their defeat by the Byzantine emperor in 718, proved decisive in halting their westward expansion. Meanwhile the Muslims had been expanding eastward into Central Asia, and by the eighth century they could claim lands as far as Turkestan and the Indus valley.

The mainstay of Umayyad power was the ruling class of Arabs, who formed a privileged aristocracy, even though greatly outnumbered by non-Arabic converts to Islam. Many of the latter possessed cultures much more advanced than that of the Arabs, but because they were not Arab by birth they were treated as second-class Muslims. Resentment grew and eventually helped bring about the downfall of the Umayyads.

This resentment also found expression in the religious sphere, where large numbers of the non-Arabic Muslims joined the sect known as the Shia, formed when Ali, Muhammad's son-in-law and fourth caliph, was deposed by the Umayyads. The Shia continued to regard Ali and his descendants as the rightful rulers of the Islamic community. The Shia rejected the Sunna, the body of traditions concerning Muhammad, and insisted on the Koran as the sole authority for the life and teachings of the Prophet. Though originally an Arab party, the Shia over a period of time became a general Islamic movement that stood for opposition to the ruling dynasty. The Shia evolved into one of the two major groups in Islam. Their opponents, named the Sunnites because they were the "orthodox" perpetuators of Muhammad's Sunna, upheld the principle that the caliph owed his position to the consent of the Islamic community.

The Abbasids, high tide of Islamic civilization. In 750 the Umayyad dynasty was overthrown, and a new dynasty, the Abbasid, ruled most of the Muslim world until 1258. The Abbasids owed their success to the discontent of the non-Arabic Muslims. The fall of the Umayyad dynasty marked the end of Arab predominance; henceforth all Muslims were treated as equals. The Arabs had dominated Islam during the great period of its expansion, but with the advent of more stable political conditions, the important status thus far held by the Arab soldier fell to non-Arab administrators and merchants.

The location of a new capital at Baghdad resulted in a shift of Islam's center of gravity to the province of Iraq, whose soil, watered by the Tigris and Euphrates, had nurtured man's earliest civilization. Here the Abbasid caliphs set themselves up as potentates in the traditional style of the ancient East—and more particularly of Persia—so that they were surrounded by a lavish court that contrasted sharply with the simplicity of the Prophet. Their empire, which was greater in size than that of the Roman Caesars, marked the high tide of Islamic power and civilization.

Trade and industry. From the eighth to the twelfth centuries the Muslim world enjoyed a prosperity such as post-Roman Europe did not experience until early modern times. In close contact with three continents, the Muslims could shuttle goods back and forth from China to western Europe and from Russia to central Africa. Trade was facilitated also by the absence of tariff barriers within the empire and by the tolerance of the caliphs, who allowed non-Muslim merchants and craftsmen to reside in their territories and carry on commerce with their home countries. Joint-stock companies flourished along with a system of branch banking, and checks drawn on a bank in one city could be cashed elsewhere in the empire. Muslim textile industries turned out excellent muslins, silks, and linens.

The steel of Damascus and Toledo, the leather of Cordova, and the glass of Syria became world famous. Notable also was the art of papermaking, learned from China, which eventually would be of great importance.

Disintegration of the Abbasid empire. The political unity of Islam began to disappear soon after the accession of the Abbasid dynasty. In 756 a member of the deposed Umayyad family founded his own dynasty at Cordova in Spain; and in the tenth century the Fatimids—Shiites who claimed descent from Muhammad's daughter Fatima who had married Ali, the fourth caliph—proclaimed themselves the true caliphs of all Islam. Centered at Cairo, Fatimid rule eventually extended from Morocco to northern Mesopotamia.

Meanwhile, in the latter part of the tenth century Turkish nomads, called Seljuks, had migrated from Central Asia into the Abbasid lands, where they accepted Islam. After annexing most of Persia, the Seljuks gained control of Baghdad in 1055 and absorbed Iraq. Subsequently they conquered Syria and Palestine at the expense of the Fatimids and proceeded to annex most of Asia Minor from the Byzantines. It was the Seljuk's great advance that prompted the First Crusade in 1095. The Seljuks permitted the Abbasids to retain nominal rule, but a new and terrible enemy was now to appear and change everything.

Early in the thirteenth century Genghis Khan succeeded in uniting the nomads of Mongolia; he and his successors conquered eastern and central Asia and swept into Persia and Iraq. In 1258 a grandson of Genghis Khan captured Baghdad and had the caliph put in a sack and trampled to death. Not only did the Abbasid dynasty come to an end, but so did most of the vast irrigation system that had supported the land since the beginning of civilization. Iraq did not recover until modern times. The dynasty established by the Mongols survived for only a short time, and the Mongol ruling class was eventually absorbed into the native population of Persia and Iraq.

Muslim Egypt had been saved from the Mongol advance by the Mamluks, an army of foreign-born slaves. The Mamluks also took over Palestine and Syria, ejecting the last of the crusaders in 1291. Ultimately they fell before the onslaught of another offshoot of the once great Seljuk empire, the Ottoman Turks.

Having settled in northwestern Asia Minor in the thirteenth century as vassals of the Seljuks, the Ottoman Turks had organized their own aggressive state of Muslim frontier fighters by the end of the century (see p. 90). The Ottomans pitted their strength against the crumbling power of the Byzantines, and after capturing Constantinople in 1453 they pressed on into southeastern Europe. Driving as far as Vienna, they were turned back with difficulty in 1529 and again in 1683. Meanwhile the Ottomans had conquered the Mamluk territories, and they soon added Iraq, much of Arabia, and all of the North African coastal belt to the borders of Morocco.

ISLAMIC CULTURE

Borrowing the best from other cultures. The high attainment of the Muslims in the intellectual and artistic fields can be primarily attributed not to the Arabs, who as a group remained concerned with religion, politics, and commerce, but rather to those peoples who had embraced Islam in Persia, Mesopotamia, Syria, Egypt,

North Africa, and Spain. The cosmopolitan spirit permeating the Abbasid dynasty supplied the tolerance necessary for a diversity of ideas, so that the science and philosophy of ancient Greece and India found a welcome in Baghdad. The writings of Aristotle, Euclid, Ptolemy, Archimedes, Galen, and other great Greek scientific writers were translated into Arabic. This material was later transmitted to scholars in western Europe (see p. 159). In addition to being invaluable transmitters of learning, the Muslims also made some original contributions of their own to science.

Science. The two hundred years between 900 and 1100, called the golden age of Muslim learning, were particularly significant for advances made in medicine. In spite of a ban against the study of anatomy and a few other limitations imposed on Muslims by their religion, their medical men were in most ways far superior to their European contemporaries. Muslim cities had excellent pharmacies and hospitals, and both pharmacists and physicians had to pass state examinations to

Muslim scholars devoted themselves to the study of science and medicine. In an observatory in Constantinople some astronomers make mathematical computations with the assistance of a variety of instruments, while others gather around a globe showing Asia, Africa, and Europe.

be licensed. Physicians received instruction in medical schools and hospitals. The most influential Muslim medical treatise is the vast *Canon of Medicine* of the Persian scholar Avicenna (d. 1037), in which all Greek and Muslim medical learning is systematically organized. In the twelfth century the *Canon* was translated into Latin and was much in demand until the seventeenth century.

Although astronomy remained astrology's handmaiden, Muslim astronomers built observatories, recorded their observations over long periods, and achieved greater accuracy than the Greeks in measuring the length of the solar year and in calculating eclipses. Interest in alchemy—the attempt to transmute base metals into precious ones and to find the magic elixir for the preservation of human life—produced the first chemical laboratories in history and an emphasis on the value of experimentation. Muslim alchemists prepared many chemical substances (sulphuric acid, for example) and developed methods for evaporation, filtration, sublimation, crystallization, and distillation. The process of distillation, invented around 800, produced what was called *alkuhl*, a new liquor that has made Geber, its inventor, an honored name in some circles.

In mathematics the Muslims were indebted to the Hindus as well as to the Greeks. From the Greeks came the geometry of Euclid and the fundamentals of trigonometry which Ptolemy had worked out. From the Hindus came arithmetic and algebra and the nine signs, known as Arabic numerals. The Muslims invented the all-important zero, although some scholars credit the Indians with first using it.

Literature and scholarship. To westerners, whose literary tastes have been largely formed by classical traditions, Arabic literature may seem strange and alien. It abounds in elegant expression, subtle combinations of words, fanciful and even extravagant imagery, and witty conceits.

Westerners' knowledge of Islamic literature tends to be limited to the *Arabian Nights* and to the hedonistic poetry of the Persian Omar Khayyám (d. 1123?). The former is a collection of often erotic tales told with a wealth of local color; although it professedly covers different facets of life at the Abbasid capital, it is in fact often based on life in medieval Cairo. The fame of Omar Khayyám's *Rubáiyát* is partly due to the lyrical (though not overaccurate) translation of Edward Fitzgerald. The following stanzas indicate the poem's beautiful imagery and gentle pessimism:

A Book of Verses underneath the Bough,
A Jug of Wine, a Loaf of Bread—and Thou
   Beside me singing in the Wilderness—
Ah, Wilderness were Paradise enow! . . .

The Moving Finger writes; and, having writ,
Moves on: nor all your Piety nor Wit
   Shall lure it back to cancel half a Line,
Nor all your Tears wash out a Word of it.[4]

Muslim philosophy, essentially Greek in origin, was developed by laymen and not, as in the West, by churchmen. Like the medieval Christian philosophers (see Chapter 7), Muslim thinkers were largely concerned with reconciling Aristotelian rationalism and religion. The earlier Muslim thinkers, including Avicenna, the physician with many talents, sought to harmonize Platonism, Aristotelianism, and Islam. Avicenna's work was widely read in the West, where it was translated in the twelfth century. The last great Islamic philosopher, Averroës (d. 1198), lived in

Spain where he was the caliph's personal doctor. His commentaries on Aristotle's works gave the Christian West its knowledge of Aristotle long before the original Greek texts were obtained from Constantinople. Averroës rejected the belief in the ultimate harmony between faith and reason along with all earlier attempts to reconcile Aristotle and Plato. Faith and reason, he argued, operate on different levels; a proposition can be true philosophically but false theologically. On the other hand, Moses Maimonides, Averroës' contemporary who was also born in Muslim Spain, sought, in his still influential *Guide to the Perplexed*, to harmonize Judaism and Aristotelian philosophy.

Islamic historiography found its finest expression in the work of ibn-Khaldun of Tunis (d. 1406), who conceived of history as an evolutionary process in which societies and institutions change continually. Because his large general history deals particularly with man's social development, which he held to be the result of the interaction of society and the physical environment, ibn-Khaldun has been called "a father of sociology."

Art and architecture. Muslim art, like Muslim learning, borrowed from many sources. Islamic artists and craftsmen followed chiefly Byzantine and Persian models and eventually integrated what they had learned into a distinctive and original style.

The Muslims excelled in two fields—architecture and the decorative arts. That Islamic architecture can boast of many large and imposing structures is not surprising, because it drew much of its inspiration from the Byzantines and Persians, who were monumental builders. In time an original style of building evolved, embodying such typical features as domes, arcades, horseshoe arches and minarets, the slender towers from which the faithful are summoned to prayer. The Spanish interpretation of the Muslim tradition was particularly delicate and elegant. In India the Taj Mahal, based largely on Persian motifs, is another notable example.

Religious attitudes played an important part in Muslim art. Because the Prophet inveighed strongly against idols and their worship, there was a prejudice against pictorial representation of human and animal figures. Thus restricted in their subject matter, Muslim craftsmen conceived beautiful patterns from flowers and geometric figures. Even the Arabic script, the most beautiful ever devised, was used as a decorative motif. Muslim decorative skill also found expression in such fields as carpet and rug weaving, brass work, and the making of steel products inlaid with precious metals.

Today the religious solidarity and cultural heritage of the Muslim peoples, who compose about one-seventh of the world's population, provide the basis for a program of political resurgence.

CHAPTER 5
EUROPE'S SEARCH FOR STABILITY

The Franks, the Carolingian Empire, and Feudalism (500-1050); Trade, Towns, and a New Society (1050-1450)

We last surveyed the fortunes of Europe at a crucial turning point in civilization—the fifth and sixth centuries (see Chapter 3). The mighty Roman Empire in the West had broken apart under the pressure of incoming Germanic tribes, and unity and stability had given way to fragmentation and disorder. What was the future of western Europe to be?

The Germanic Franks, in alliance with the Church, took the lead in forming the new Europe. In the single century from 714 to 814, the Carolingian House of the Franks fashioned a great empire and gave Europe an interim of stability. This accomplishment was premature, however, partly because the new empire lacked the economic basis that had supported the empire of the Romans. By the ninth century Muslim conquests had cut off what remained of European trade in the Mediterranean, and inland trade and urban life almost disappeared. In addition, there existed no strong administrative machinery to compensate for the weak Carolingian rulers who followed the dominating figure of Charlemagne on the throne.

Out of the ruins of the Carolingian empire emerged a new form of government known as feudalism. Based on local authority, feudalism was a poor and primitive substitute for a centralized government; but it was better than no authority at all. Also appropriate to the times was the rural, self-sufficient economy known as the manorial system. In sum, the poverty and localism of western Europe in the tenth century contrasted sharply with the contemporary societies of Byzantium and Islam.

But not for long. Between 1050 and 1300, a period known as the High Middle Ages, Europe experienced a veritable economic revolution marked by the revival of trade, towns, industry, and a money economy. Although this initial burst of vigor collapsed after 1300, a second period of sustained economic expansion that would complete the trend toward modern capitalism was underway by 1450.

NEW EMPIRE IN THE WEST

The Franks under Clovis. In the blending of the Roman and Germanic peoples and cultures, the Franks played an especially significant part. The kingdom of the Franks was not only the most enduring of all the Germanic states established in the West, but it became, with the active support of the Church, the center of the new Europe that arose upon the ruins of the western Roman empire.

Before the Germanic invasions the several tribes that made up the Franks lived along the east bank of the Rhine close to the North Sea. Late in the fourth century the Franks began a slow movement south and west across the Rhine into Gaul. By 481 they occupied the northern part of Gaul as far as the old Roman city of Paris, and in this year Clovis I of the Merovingian House became ruler of one of the petty Frankish kingdoms. By the time of his death in 511, Clovis had united the Franks into a single kingdom that stretched southward to the Pyrenees.

As a first step in achieving this goal, Clovis allied himself with other petty Frankish kings to dispose of Syagrius, the last Roman general in Gaul. The victor then turned against his Frankish allies and subdued them. Next, Clovis was converted to Christianity as the result of a successful battle in which he called upon Christ for aid. Thus Clovis became the only orthodox Christian ruler in the West, for the other Germanic tribes were either pagan or embraced the heretical form of Christianity known as Arianism (see pp. 78 and 148).

The conversion of the Franks ultimately led to an alliance of the Franks and the papacy, and immediately it assured Clovis the loyalty of the Gallo-Roman bishops, the leaders of the native Christian population of Gaul. This was a political advantage not open to the heretical Arian Visigothic and Burgundian kings who ruled southern Gaul (see map, p. 82). Thus with the help of the native population of Gaul, Clovis was able to expand his realm at the expense of the Visigoths in the name of Christian orthodoxy. Soon thereafter, in 511, Clovis died at the age of forty-five—a ripe old age for a barbarian. Although hardly more than a Germanic chieftain, he had created what came to be called France.

Decline of the Merovingians. Clovis' sons and grandsons conquered the Burgundian kingdom and extended the Frankish domain to the Mediterranean and further into Germany. At the same time, however, the Merovingian House began to decay from inner weaknesses. The Germanic practice of treating the kingdom as personal property and dividing it among all the king's sons resulted in constant and bitter civil war. The Merovingian princes also engaged in all manner of debaucheries, the least unpleasant of which was excessive drinking. Soon the Frankish state broke up into three separate kingdoms; in each, power was concentrated in the hands of the chief official of the royal household, the mayor of the palace, a powerful noble who kept the king weak and ineffectual.

A dark age. By the middle of the seventh century western Europe had lost most of the essential characteristics of Roman civilization. The Roman system of administration and taxation had completely collapsed, and the dukes and counts who represented the Merovingian king received no salary and usually acted on their own initiative in commanding the fighting men and presiding over the courts in their districts. International commerce had ceased except for a small-scale trade in luxury items carried on by adventurous Greek, Syrian, and Jewish traders, and the old Roman cities served mainly to house the local bishop and his retinue. The virtual absence of a middle class meant that society was composed of the nobility, a fusion through intermarriage of aristocratic Gallo-Roman and German families who owned and exercised authority over vast estates, and, at the other end of the social scale, the semi-servile *coloni*, who were bound to the land. These serfs included large numbers of formerly free German farmers. Only about 10 percent of the peasant population of Gaul maintained a free status.

Coinciding with Merovingian decay, new waves of invaders threatened. A great movement of Slavic people from the area that is now Russia had begun about 500 A.D. (see p. 95). From this nucleus the Slavs fanned out, filling the vacuum left by the Germanic tribes when they pushed into the Roman Empire. By 650 the western Slavs had reached the Elbe River, across which they raided German territory. Another danger threatened western Europe from the south; in the late seventh century the Muslim Moors prepared to invade Spain from North Africa.

Charles Martel and the rise of the Carolingians. A new period dawned when Charles Martel became mayor of the palace in 714. His father, one of the greatest Frankish landowners, had eliminated all rival mayors, and Charles ruled a united Frankish kingdom in all but name. For the time being, however, the Merovingian kings were kept as harmless figureheads at the court.

Charles is best remembered for his victory over the Muslim invaders of Europe (see p. 100), which earned him the surname Martel, "The Hammer." In 732 Charles Martel met the Muslims near Tours, deep within the Frankish kingdom. Muslim losses were heavy, and during the night they retreated toward Spain.

A major military reform coincided with the battle of Tours. For some time before this conflict, the effectiveness of mounted soldiers had been growing, aided by the introduction of the stirrup, which gave the mounted warrior a firm seat while wielding his weapons. To counteract the effectiveness of the quick-striking Muslim cavalry, Charles recruited a force of professional mounted soldiers whom he rewarded with sufficient land to enable each knight to maintain himself, his equipment, and a number of war horses. Such grants of land later became an important element in feudalism.

Pepin the Short. Charles Martel's son, Pepin the Short, ruled from 741 to 768. To legalize the regal power already being exercised by the mayors of the palace, he requested and received from the pope a ruling which stipulated that whoever had the actual power should be the legal ruler. After the last Merovingian king was quietly shelved in a secluded monastery in 751, the pope reaffirmed the usurpation by crossing the Alps and personally anointing Pepin, in the Old Testament manner, as the Chosen of the Lord.

Behind the pope's action lay his need for a powerful protector. In 751 the Lombards had conquered the exarchate of Ravenna, the seat of Byzantine government in Italy, and were demanding tribute from the pope and threatening to take Rome. Following Pepin's coronation, the pope secured his promise of armed intervention in Italy and his pledge to give the papacy the exarchate of Ravenna. A Frankish army forced the Lombard king to relinquish his conquests, and Pepin officially conferred the exarchate upon the pope. Known as the "Donation of Pepin," the gift made the pope a temporal ruler over the Papal States (see map, p. 108).

The alliance between the Franks and the papacy affected the course of politics and of religion for centuries. It accelerated the separation of Latin from Greek Christendom by providing the papacy with a dependable western ally in place of the Byzantines, hitherto its only protector against the Lombards; it created the Papal States which played a major role in Italian politics until the late nineteenth

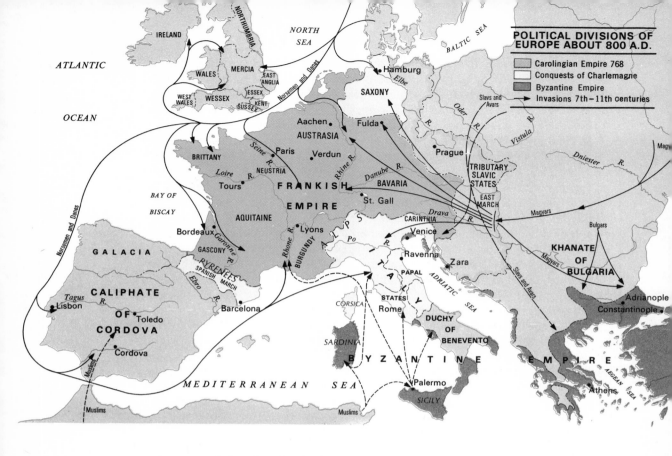

POLITICAL DIVISIONS OF
EUROPE ABOUT 800 A.D.

Carolingian Empire 768
Conquests of Charlemagne
Byzantine Empire
→ Invasions 7th–11th centuries

century; and, by the ritual of anointment, it provided western kingship with a religious sanction that would in time contribute to the rise of monarchs strong enough to pose a threat to the papacy.

Charlemagne's conquests. Under Pepin's son, Charlemagne (Charles the Great), who ruled from 768 to 814, the Frankish state and the Carolingian House reached the summit of their power. Charlemagne was preeminently a successful warrior-king, leading his armies on yearly campaigns. Taking advantage of feuds among the Muslims in Spain, he sought to extend Christendom southward into that land but without much success. As the Frankish army headed back north, it aroused the antagonism of the Christian Basques, who attacked its rear guard. In the melee the Frankish leader, a gallant count named Roland, was killed. The memory of his heroism was later enshrined in the great medieval epic, the *Song of Roland*. On later expeditions the Franks drove the Muslims back to the Ebro River and established a frontier area known as the Spanish March, or Mark, centered around Barcelona.

Charlemagne also conquered the Bavarians and the Saxons, the last of the independent Germanic tribes. To protect Bavaria from the Avars, who were Asiatic nomads related to the Huns, and the Slavs, Charlemagne established the East Mark, a frontier territory later to become Austria. It took thirty-two campaigns to subdue the pagan Saxons, who lived between the Rhine and Elbe rivers. Charlemagne divided Saxony into bishoprics, built monasteries, and proclaimed harsh laws against paganism. Eating meat during Lent, cremating the dead (an old pagan practice), and pretending to be baptized were offenses punishable by death.

Like his father before him, Charlemagne intervened in Italian politics. When the Lombard king again invaded the territories of the papacy, Charlemagne defeated the Lombards and proclaimed himself their king. While in Italy, he cemented his father's alliance with the Church by confirming the Donation of Pepin.

Charlemagne's coronation in Rome. One of the most important single events in Charlemagne's reign took place on Christmas Day in the year 800. The previous year the unruly Roman nobility had ousted the pope, charging him with moral laxity. Charlemagne came to Rome and restored the pope to his office. Then, at the Christmas service while Charlemagne knelt before the altar at St. Peter's, the pope unexpectedly placed a crown on his head amid the cries of the assembled congregation: "To Charles Augustus crowned of God, great and pacific Emperor of the Romans, long life and victory!"

This ceremony demonstrated that the memory of the Roman Empire still survived; in fact, Charlemagne had already named his capital at Aix-la-Chapelle (Aachen) "New Rome" and was about to take the title of emperor. By seizing the initiative and crowning Charlemagne by the Grace of God, the pope had assumed a position of superiority as the maker of emperors. The collapse of both the empire and the papacy in the ninth and tenth centuries postponed the inevitable clash between the imperial and papal powers.

Charlemagne's administration. Charlemagne's empire was divided into some three hundred administrative divisions, each under a count (*graf*) or, in the marks along the border, a margrave (*mark graf*). In addition, there were local military officials, the dukes. In an effort to solve the problem of supervising the counts and dukes, Charlemagne created the *missi dominici*, the king's envoys. Pairs of these itinerant officials, usually a bishop and a lay noble, traveled throughout the realm to check on the local administration. To make the *missi* immune to bribes, they were chosen from men of high rank, were frequently transferred from one region to another, and no two of them were teamed for more than one year.

Charlemagne's territories were too vast and the nobility too powerful, however, to be held together under existing conditions after the dominating personality of their creator had passed from the scene. Charlemagne had no standing army; his foot soldiers were essentially the old Germanic war band summoned to fight by its leader, and his mounted warriors served him, as they had Charles Martel, in return for grants of land. Nor did Charlemagne—even with his local officials and the *missi dominici*—have a bureaucratic administrative machine comparable to that of Roman times. The Frankish economy was agricultural and localized, and there was no system of taxation adequate to maintain an effective and permanent administration. Under Charlemagne's weak successors the empire disintegrated amid the confusion of civil wars and devastating new invasions. Progress toward an advanced civilization in the new Europe founded by Charlemagne, whose center was in the north rather than on the Mediterranean, was delayed for two centuries.

The Carolingian Renaissance. Charlemagne fostered a revival of learning and the arts which was destined to be far more lasting than his revival of the Roman Empire in the West. Concerned over the spread of illiteracy even among the clergy, Charlemagne decreed that every monastery must have a school for the education of boys in "singing, arithmetic, and grammar." At Aix-la-Chapelle, his capital, the emperor also sponsored a palace school for the education of the royal household and the stimulation of learning throughout the realm. Alcuin, an Anglo-Saxon scholar in charge of the school, began the arduous task by writing

NORTH SEA

THE DANELAW

ENGLISH KINGDOMS

ENGLISH CHANNEL

Aix-la-Chapelle (Aachen)•

•Paris

Verdun

Strasbourg•

W E S T

F R A N K S

Loire R.

KINGDOM OF CHARLES

Elbe R.

Vistula R.

E A S T

KINGDOM OF LOUIS

F R A N K S

Rhine R.

TRIBUTARY

SLAVIC

Danube R.

STATES

Rhone R.

KINGDOM OF LOTHAIR

Ebro R.

UMAYYAD EMIRATE OF CORDOVA

CORSICA

BYZANTINE EMPIRE

MEDITERRANEAN SEA

Since primogeniture was still rare, Charlemagne's son, Louis the Pious, divided his kingdom among his three sons. The western portion, which went to Charles, became the nucleus of later France; East Frankland evolved centuries later into Germany; but the central portion, which was Lothair's inheritance lacked any unifying element and rapidly disintegrated into a series of smaller domains which were beset by invaders until modern times.

textbooks on grammar, spelling, rhetoric, and logic. In time, copyists were laboring in monasteries to preserve the classics of pagan and Christian thought with the result that the oldest manuscripts of most of the Latin classics that have come down to us date from the age of Charlemagne. Thus Charlemagne's patronage of learning left a heritage that later generations would build upon.

Charlemagne also strove to recapture something of the grandeur of ancient Rome by building at Aix-la-Chapelle a stone palace church modeled after a sixth-century church in Ravenna. Its mosaics were probably the work of Byzantine artisans, and its marble columns were taken from ancient buildings in Rome and Ravenna.

The division of the empire.   Before his death in 814, Charlemagne himself, ignoring the pope, placed the imperial crown on the head of his only surviving son, Louis the Pious. After Louis died in 840, strife erupted among his three sons. Lothair, the elder, was opposed by the two younger—Louis the German and Charles the Bald. In 842 the younger brothers joined forces in the famous Strasbourg Oaths. The text of these oaths is significant in that one part was in an early form of French, the other in German. Here is evidence that the Carolingian empire was splitting into two linguistic parts—East Frankland, the forerunner of modern Germany, and West Frankland, or France.

In 843 the brothers met at Verdun, where they agreed to split the Carolingian lands three ways. Charles the Bald obtained the western part and Louis the

German the eastern; Lothair, who retained the title of emperor, obtained an elongated middle kingdom which stretched a thousand miles from the North Sea to central Italy (see map). The Treaty of Verdun began the shaping of modern France and Germany by giving political recognition to the cultural and linguistic division shown in the Strasbourg Oaths. Lothair's middle kingdom soon collapsed into three major parts, Lorraine in the north and Burgundy and Italy in the south. Lorraine was divided in 870 between Charles and Louis, but the area was to be drenched with the blood of French and German armies for centuries to come.

The rival Carolingian houses produced no strong leaders worthy of being called "Hammer" (Martel) or "Great"; instead, we find kings with such revealing names as Charles the Fat, Charles the Simple, Louis the Child, and Louis the Sluggard. Both lines of weak Carolingian rulers—German and French—died out in the tenth century.

New invasions. During the ninth and tenth centuries the remnants of Charlemagne's empire were battered by new waves of invaders. Scandinavians attacked from the north, Muslims from the south, and a new wave of Asiatic nomads, the Magyars, struck from the east. These plundering raiders did far more damage to life and property than the Germanic invaders of the fifth century.

From bases in North Africa, Muslim corsairs in full command of the sea plundered the coasts of Italy and France. In 827 they began the conquest of Byzantine Sicily and southern Italy. From forts erected in southern France they penetrated far inland to attack the caravans of merchants in the Alpine passes. What trade still existed between Byzantium and western Europe, except for that of Venice and one or two other Italian towns, was now almost totally cut off, and the great inland sea became a Muslim lake.

The most widespread and destructive raiders came from Scandinavia. During the ninth and tenth centuries Swedes, Danes, and Norwegians—collectively known as Vikings—stormed out of their remote forests and fiords. Viking sailors had developed expert sailing techniques; without benefit of the compass, they were able to navigate by means of the stars at night and the sun during the day. Three main routes of Viking expansion can be identified. The outer path, which was followed principally by the Norwegians, swung westward to Ireland and the coast of Scotland. Between 800 and 850 Ireland was ravaged severely. Monasteries, the centers of a flourishing culture attained by the Irish Celts, were destroyed. By 875 the Norwegians were beginning to occupy remote Iceland, and it was here rather than in their homeland that the magnificent Norse sagas were preserved, little affected by either classical or Christian influences. During the tenth century the Icelandic Norsemen ventured on to Greenland and, later, to North America (see Chapter 11).

Another route, the eastern line, was followed chiefly by the Swedes, who went down the rivers of Russia as merchants and soldiers of fortune and, as has been described in Chapter 4, forged the nucleus of a Russian state.

The Danes took the middle passage, raiding England and the shores of Germany, France, and Spain. By the 870's they had occupied most of England north of the Thames. On the Continent their long boats sailed up the Rhine, Scheldt, Seine, and Loire. Unable to fend off the Viking attacks, the West Frankish king Charles the Simple arranged an epoch-making treaty with a Norse chieftain named Rollo in 911. This agreement created a Viking buffer state, later called Normandy, and recognized Rollo as duke and vassal of the French king. Like Viking settlers elsewhere, these Northmen, or Normans, soon adopted

Christian civilization. By the eleventh century, Normandy was a powerful duchy, and the Viking spirit of the Normans was producing the most vigorous crusaders, conquerors, and administrators in Europe.

Europe in 900. Europe's response to the invasions of the ninth and tenth centuries was not uniform. In England by 900 Viking occupation initiated a strong national reaction which soon led to the creation of a united English kingdom. Similarly, Germany in 919 reacted to the Magyar danger by installing the first of a new and able line of kings who went on to become the most powerful European monarchs since Charlemagne. In France, however, the Viking attacks had the effect of accelerating the trend toward political fragmentation that began under the Merovingians but was temporarily halted by the strong personal leadership provided by the early Carolingians.

When Charlemagne's weak successors were unable to cope with the incessant Viking assaults, people in France increasingly surrendered both their lands and their persons to the many counts, dukes, and other local lords in return for protection. The decline of trade further strengthened the aristocracy, whose large estates, or manors, became economically self-sufficient. In addition, the old Germanic levy of foot soldiers, who provided their own arms when called to battle, was dying out in favor of a professional force of heavily armed mounted knights, who received land grants from the king in return for military service.

Out of all these elements—the disintegration of central power, the need for protection, the decrease in the class of freemen, the rise of a largely independent landed aristocracy, and the creation of the mounted knight—new patterns of society took shape in the form of feudalism and the manorial system. Reaching their height in France during the tenth and eleventh centuries, feudalism and manorialism were the culmination of earlier trends that had been accelerated by the Viking attacks.

FEUDALISM AND MANORIALISM

Nature and origins of feudalism. Feudalism can be defined as a type of government in which political power is exercised locally by private individuals rather than by the agents of a centralized state. It is often a transitional stage which follows the collapse of a unified political system and serves as a stopgap until conditions permit the emergence of a centralized government.

Fully developed feudalism was a fusion of three basic elements: (1) the personal element, called lordship or vassalage, by which one nobleman, the vassal, became the loyal follower of a stronger nobleman, the lord or suzerain; (2) the property element, called the fief (usually land), which the vassal received from his lord in order to enable him to fulfill the obligations of vassalage; and (3) the governmental element, meaning the private exercise of governmental functions over vassals and fiefs. The roots of these three elements run back to late Roman and early Germanic times.

By the fifth century the ability of the Roman emperor to protect his subjects had disappeared, and citizens had to depend on the patronage system, by which a Roman noble organized a group of less fortunate citizens as a personal bodyguard and in return looked after their wants and interests. A similar arrangement existed among the Germans—the war band or *comitatus*, described by Tacitus (see p. 82). Vassalage, the personal element in feudalism, arose from the combination of patronage and the *comitatus*.

The roots of the property element in feudalism, the fief, go back to Roman practices mainly. In the late Roman Empire the owners of great estates were steadily adding to their already extensive holdings. Unable to manage their tracts, the nobles granted the temporary use of portions to other people in exchange for dues and services. Such land was called a *beneficium*, or benefice (literally, a "benefit"). During the civil wars and foreign invasions of late Carolingian times, the competition among Charlemagne's successors for the available supply of mounted knights led not only to the wholesale granting of benefices but also to making the benefice hereditary. On the death of the vassal, the benefice now passed to his heir instead of reverting to the king. Hereditary benefices were commonly called fiefs.

The third basic element in feudalism, the exercise of governmental power by private individuals, also had antecedents in late Roman times. As the imperial government weakened, the powerful Roman landowners organized their own private armies to police their estates and fend off governmental agents, particularly tax collectors. The emperors also favored certain estates with grants of immunity from their authority, a practice which the Germanic kings often followed and which became the rule with Charlemagne's successors in their competitive efforts to fill their armies with mounted fief-holding vassals. And where immunity from the king's authority was not freely granted, it was often usurped.

With the coalescing of these three elements, feudalism can be said to have emerged as a definable—although highly complex and variable—governmental system in France by the end of the ninth century. To a greater or less degree the feudal system spread throughout most of western Europe, but our description of it applies particularly to the form it took in northern France.

The feudal hierarchy. In theory feudalism was a vast hierarchy. At the top stood the king, and theoretically all the land in his kingdom belonged to him. He kept large areas for his personal use (royal or crown lands) and, in return for the military service of a specified number of mounted knights, invested the highest nobles—such as dukes and counts (in England, earls)—with the remainder. Those nobles holding lands directly from the king were called tenants-in-chief. They in turn, in order to obtain the services of the required number of mounted warriors (including themselves) owed to the king, parceled out large portions of their fiefs to lesser nobles. This process, called *subinfeudation*, was continued until, finally, the lowest in the scale of vassals was reached—the single knight whose fief was just sufficient to support one mounted warrior. By maintaining a king at the head of the hierarchy, feudalism kept intact the vestiges of monarchy, which would in time reassert itself and restore centralized government.

Relation of lord and vassal: the feudal contract. Basic to feudalism was the personal bond between lord and vassal. In the ceremony known as the act of *homage*, the vassal knelt before his lord, or suzerain, and swore to be his loyal "man." Next, in the ritual of *investiture*, a lance, glove, or even a bit of straw was handed the vassal to signify his jurisdiction (not ownership) over the fief.

The feudal contract thus entered into by lord and vassal was considered sacred and binding upon both parties. The lord for his part was obliged to give his vassal protection and justice. The vassal's primary duty was military service. He was expected to devote forty days' service each year to the lord without payment. In addition, the vassal was obliged to assist the lord in rendering justice in the lord's court. At certain times, such as when he was captured and had to be ransomed, the lord also had the right to demand money payments, called *aids*. Unusual aids, such as defraying the expense of going on a crusade, could not be levied without the vassal's consent. The lord had other rights, called feudal *incidents*, regarding the administration of the fief. These included *wardship*—the right to administer the fief during the minority of a vassal's heir—and *forfeiture* of the fief if a vassal failed to honor his feudal obligations. Despite these mutual obligations, the final authority in the feudal age was force, and the general atmosphere of the era was one of violence as recalcitrant vassals frequently defied their suzerains.

The Church and feudalism. Another unhappy result of feudalism was the inclusion of the Church in the system. The unsettled conditions caused by the Viking and Magyar invasions forced Church prelates to enter into close relations with the only power able to offer them protection—the feudal barons in France and the kings in Germany. Bishops and abbots thus became vassals, receiving fiefs for which they were obligated to provide the usual feudal services. The papacy fared even worse; during much of the tenth and early eleventh centuries the papacy fell into decay after becoming a prize sought after by local Roman nobles.

On the positive side, however, the Church in time sought to influence for the better the behavior of the feudal warrior nobility. In addition to attempting to add Christian virtues to the code of knightly conduct called chivalry, which will be described later in this chapter, the Church sought to impose limitations on feudal warfare. In the eleventh century bishops inaugurated the Peace of God and Truce of God movements. The Peace of God banned from the sacraments all persons who pillaged sacred places or refused to spare noncombatants. The Truce of God established "closed seasons" on fighting: from sunset on Wednesday to sunrise on Monday and certain longer periods, such as Lent. These peace movements were generally ineffective, however.

Feudal society. Nobles, peasants, and clergy constituted the classes of society in the feudal age, and each had its own task to perform. The nobles were primarily fighters, belonging to an honored society distinct from the peasant workers— freemen and serfs. In an age of physical violence, society obviously would accord first place to the knight with the sword rather than to the peasant with the hoe. The Church drew on both the noble and the peasant classes for the clergy. Although most higher churchmen were sons of nobles and held land as vassals under the feudal system, the clergy formed a class that was considered separate from the nobility and peasantry.

One of the most interesting legacies of the Middle Ages is its concept of chivalry, a code which governed the behavior of all truly perfect and gentle knights. Such a paragon was Sir Galahad—"the gentlest man that ever ate in hall among the ladies." Early chivalry, however, which emerged during the heyday of feudalism in the eleventh century, was rough and masculine. It stressed the warrior virtues that were essential in a feudal society: prowess in combat, courage, and loyalty to one's lord and fellow warriors. The virtues of early chivalry are best expressed in early medieval epics, such as the eleventh-century *Song of Roland*, where they are summed up in the words of the hero who, surrounded by foes, cries: "Better be dead than a coward be called."

The later chivalry of the twelfth and thirteenth centuries contained new virtues which the Church and the ladies sought to impose upon the generally violent and uncouth behavior of feudal warriors. The chivalric romances that began to be written in the twelfth century mirror these new influences. In Chrétien de Troyes' *Perceval*, for example, the hero's mother sends him off to be dubbed a knight with these words of advice:

> Serve ladies and maidens if you would be honored by all. If you capture a lady, do not annoy her. Do nothing to displease her. He has much from a maiden who kisses her if she agrees to give a kiss. You will avoid greater intimacy if you wish to be guided by me. . . . Above all I wish to beg you to go to churches and abbeys and pray to our Lord so that the world may do you honor and you may come to a good end.[1]

In sum, fully developed chivalry was a combination of three elements: warfare, religion, and reverence toward women. It required the knight to fight faithfully for his lord, champion the Church and aid the humble, and honor womankind. Unfortunately, practice often differed from theory. The average knight was more superstitious than religious, and he continued to fight, plunder, and abuse women, especially those of the lower class. The ideals of chivalry, however, have affected manners in later eras, and even today they color our concept of a gentleman.

Women in general shared the characteristics of the menfolk. They lived in a crude and often brutal age devoid of many of our modern refinements. Like their husbands, medieval women were heavy drinkers and eaters. It is said that a common compliment to a member of the fair sex was that she was "the fairest woman who ever drained a bottle."

The manorial system. While the feudal system was the means whereby protection was obtained for society, the manor was the agency that provided food and other necessities for society's members. In their origins these self-sufficient manors go back to the Roman estates with their *coloni* workers (see p. 80). In Gaul, in particular, these estates survived the Germanic invasions and were held either by the descendants of their Roman owners or by Frankish kings, nobles, and the Church. The medieval serf was like the late Roman *colonus* who worked the land, paid rent in kind, and could not leave the estate without the owner's permission.

Each tenant was really a shareholder in the manorial community, not only in the open fields but also in the meadow, pasture, wood, and wastelands. His rights in these common lands were determined by the number of acres he held in the open fields. The center of the manor was the village of thatched cottages. Around each peasant cottage was a space large enough for a vegetable patch, chicken yard, haystack, and stable. An important feature of the landscape was the village church, together with the priest's house and the burial ground. The lord's dwelling might be a castle or a more modest manor house.

Every manor contained two types of land, arable and nonarable. The nonarable land, consisting of meadow, wood, and wasteland, was used in common by the villagers and the lord. Part of the arable land, called the *demesne*, was reserved for the lord and was cultivated for him by his serfs. The remainder of the arable land was allotted among the villagers under the open-field system, whereby the fields were subdivided into strips. The strips, each containing about an acre, were separated by narrow paths of uncultivated turf. The serf's holding, usually about thirty acres, was not all in one plot, for all soil throughout the manor was not equally fertile, and a serious attempt was made to give each of the villagers land of the same quality.

The implements used by the peasants were extremely crude. The plow was a cumbersome instrument with heavy wheels, often requiring as many as eight oxen to pull it. (By the twelfth century plow horses were common.) There were also crude harrows, sickles, beetles for breaking up clods, and flails for threshing. Inadequate methods of farming soon exhausted the soil.

In ancient times farmers had learned that soil planted continually with one crop rapidly deteriorated. To counteract this, they employed a two-field system, whereby half of the arable land was planted while the other half lay fallow to recover its fertility. Medieval farmers learned that wheat or rye could be planted in the autumn as well as in the spring. As a result, by the ninth century they were

Into this medieval print the artist has crowded the whole life of the manorial village. A hunting party is shown in the foreground, the ladies riding behind the knights. The castle, with its moat and drawbridge, dominates the countryside. In the midst of the village houses, which are surrounded by a fence, stands the church. Note also the mill and the millrace at the left and what appears to be a wine or cider press to the right of the mill. In the upper right corner a serf is using the heavy plow common to northwestern Europe (the artist has shown only two draft animals). The nets were apparently set to catch hares, and below them stands a wayside shrine. Visible on the horizon is a gibbet with buzzards wheeling over it.

dividing the land into three fields, with one planted in the fall, another in the spring, and the third left lying fallow. This system not only kept more land in production but also required less plowing in any given year.

There often were a few freemen on the manor who were not subject to the same demands as the semifree peasants, or serfs. The freeman did not have to work in the lord's fields himself but could send substitutes. He paid rent for his holding and he could leave the manor if he located a new tenant for the land. Aside from these privileges, however, the freeman was little different from the serf. His strips were in the same open fields and he lived in the same village.

Serfdom was a hereditary status; the children of a serf were attached to the soil as their parents were. Serfs did have security, however, for it was established manorial custom that so long as they paid their dues and services they could not be evicted from their hereditary holdings.

The most important service was *week-work*. The peasant had to work two or three days each week on his lord's fields, with extra *boon-work* required during planting and harvesting. Various dues or payments—usually in produce, in money if it was available—were made to the lord. The *taille* (or tallage), a tax on whatever property a peasant managed to accumulate, was the most common. It was levied on all peasants one or more times a year. Another burdensome tax was imposed when a peasant died; before a son could inherit his father's cottage and strips, the lord claimed the best beast or movable possession as inheritance tax. The lord also profited from certain monopolies; he operated the only grain mill, oven for baking bread, and wine and cider press on the manor, and he collected a toll each time these services were needed.

The margin between starvation and survival was narrow, and the life of the peasant was not easy. Famines were common; warfare and wolves were a constant threat; grasshoppers, locusts, caterpillars, and rats repeatedly destroyed the crops. Men and women alike had to toil long hours in the fields. A medieval poem vividly describes the life of a peasant family:

> I saw a poor man o'er the plough bending. . . .
> All befouled with mud, as he the plough followed. . . .
> His wife walked by him with a long goad, . . .
> Barefoot on the bare ice, so that the blood followed.
> And at the field's end lay a little bowl,
> And therein lay a little child wrapped in rags,
> And twain of two years old upon another side;
> And all of them sang a song that sorrow was to hear,
> They cried all a cry, a sorrowful note,
> And the poor man sighed sore, and said 'Children, be still.'[2]

THE RISE OF TRADE, TOWNS, AND A NEW SOCIETY

The economic revolution of the High Middle Ages. The period from 1050 to 1300, often called the High Middle Ages, witnessed remarkable progress in every aspect of medieval civilization. Underlying all the major developments of the era was an economic boom marked by improvements in agricultural techniques, growth in population, clearing of more land for food production, expansion of trade, and revival of town life.

An important catalyst of this medieval economic revolution was increased food production, the cumulative result of such technological improvements as the three-field system, heavy wheeled plows capable of turning over the heavy soils of northern Europe, improved horseshoes and horse collars along with tandem harnesses that utilized the strength of several horses or oxen, and water mills and windmills that provided power for grinding grain and draining marshlands. Greater food production in turn led to a very large increase in population; in England, for example, the population nearly tripled between 1066 and 1300.

Revitalized trade routes. The increase in food production and population was accompanied by—and contributed to—a revival of trade. Although scholars have long debated the extent of trade and urban life that existed during the Early Middle Ages, there is general agreement that fresh trade activity was evident by 1050. With the ending of Viking and Magyar attacks in the tenth century, a northern trading area developed which extended from the British Isles through the Baltic Sea and southward along the Varangian trade route in Russia to the Black Sea and Constantinople (see p. 95). The center of this northern trade system was the county of Flanders. By 1050 Flemish artisans were producing a surplus of woolen cloth of such fine quality that it was in great demand. Baltic furs, honey and forest products, and British tin and raw wool were exchanged for Flemish cloth. Oriental goods—silks, sugar, and spices—came to Flanders by way of the Varangian route and from the south by way of Venice, which never completely lost its connections with Constantinople.

Equally important in the revival of European commerce was the opening up of the Mediterranean trading area after 1095 by the crusades (see p. 151). With the Muslim hold on the Mediterranean broken, the merchants of Venice, joined by others from Genoa and Pisa, lost no time in expanding their trade in oriental goods. From Crusader-held ports such as Acre and Sidon, and even from Arab Alexandria, these western merchants transported oriental luxury items to Italy and on to the markets of northern Europe. The easiest route north from the Mediterranean was via Marseilles, up the Rhone valley.

Along this and other European trade routes, astute lords set up fairs, where merchants and goods from Italy and northern Europe met. During the twelfth and thirteenth centuries the fairs of Champagne in France functioned as the major clearing house for this international trade. The feudal law of the region was set aside during a fair, and in its place was substituted a new commercial code called the "law merchant." Special courts, with merchants acting as judges, settled all disputes which arose.

Factors in the rise of towns. The resurgence of trade in Europe was the prime cause of the revival of towns. Trade and towns had an interacting effect on each other; the towns arose because of trade, but they also stimulated trade by providing greater markets and by producing goods for the merchants to sell.

In the revival of towns, geography played a significant role. Rivers were natural highways on which articles of commerce could be easily transported, and many towns developed at the confluence of two important streams. Other towns arose where a river might be easily crossed by a ford or bridge, "Ox-ford" or "Cam-bridge," for example.

Often at a strategic geographic location a feudal noble had already erected a fortified castle, or *burg* (*bourg* in French, *borough* in English). Such a stronghold offered the merchants a good stopping place, and in time a permanent merchant settlement, called a *faubourg*, grew up outside the walls of the burg. Frequently, too, merchants settled at an old Roman episcopal city like Cologne or a fortified abbey or cathedral. Munich grew up around a monastery, and Durham was "half cathedral and half fortress against the Scot."

The decline of serfdom. Interacting with the growth of towns was the decline of serfdom. Many serfs escaped from the manors and made their way to the towns where, after living there a year and a day, they were considered freemen. As a result the remaining serfs became unreliable. Sometimes they secured enough money to buy their freedom by selling food surpluses in the towns, but often the lords freed their serfs and induced them to remain on the manor as tenants or hired laborers. As a first step in the emancipation of the serfs, the lords accepted a money payment from them as a substitute for their old obligations of labor and produce. The final step was for the lord to become a landlord in the modern sense, renting the arable land of the manor to free tenants. Thus former serfs became satisfied tenants or, on occasion, members of the yeoman class who owned their small farms. Serfdom had largely died out in England and France by 1500, although in the latter country many of the old and vexatious obligations, such as payment for the use of the lord's mill and oven, were retained. In eastern Europe serfdom persisted until the nineteenth century.

Merchant and craft guilds. The economy of medieval towns was strictly controlled in order to protect the interests of both producers and consumers. The controlling agency was the guild, of which there were two types: merchant and craft. The merchant guild ensured a monopoly of trade within a given locality. All alien merchants were supervised closely and made to pay tolls. Disputes among merchants were settled at the guild court according to its own legal code. The guilds also tried to make sure that the customers were not cheated: they checked weights and measures and insisted upon a standard quality for goods. To allow only a legitimate profit, the guild fixed a "just price," which was fair to both producer and consumer.

The increase of commerce brought a quickening of industrial life in the towns so that, as early as the eleventh century, the artisans began to organize. Craftsmen in each of the medieval trades—weaving, cobbling, tanning, and so on—joined forces. The result was the craft guild, which differed from the merchant guild in that membership was limited to artisans in one particular craft.

The general aims of the craft guilds were the same as those of the merchant guilds—the creation of a monopoly and the enforcement of a set of trade rules. Each guild had a monopoly of a certain article in a particular town, and every effort was made to prevent competition between members of the same guild. The guild restricted the number of its members, regulated the quantity and quality of the goods produced, and set prices. It also enforced regulations to protect the consumer from bad workmanship and inferior materials.

The craft guild also differed from the merchant guild in its recognition of three distinct classes of workers—apprentices, journeymen, and master craftsmen. The apprentice was a youth who lived at the master's house and was taught the trade thoroughly. Although he received no wages, all his physical needs were supplied. His apprenticeship commonly lasted seven years. When his schooling was finished, the youth became a journeyman (from the French *journée*, meaning "day's work"). He was then eligible to receive wages and to be hired by a master. When about twenty-three, the journeyman sought admission into the guild as a master. To be accepted he had to prove his ability. Some crafts demanded the making of a "master piece"—for example, a pair of shoes that the master shoemakers would find acceptable in every way.

The guild's functions stretched beyond business into charitable and social activities. If a guildsman fell into poverty, he was aided. The guild also provided financial assistance for the burial expenses of its members and looked after their dependents. Members attended social meetings in the guildhall and periodically held processions in honor of their patron saints.

Self-government for the towns. The guilds played an important role in town government. Both artisans and merchants, even though freemen, were at first subject to the feudal lord or bishop upon whose domain the city stood. The townsmen demanded the right to govern themselves—to make their own laws, administer their own justice, levy their own taxes, and issue their own coinage— and they acquired it in various ways.

The earliest self-governing towns, called communes, won their independence through community effort under the leadership of the merchant guilds. Charters of self-government were acquired either through force or, more often, through purchase—feudal lords were always in need of money. By 1200 the Lombard towns of northern Italy, as well as many French and Flemish towns, had become self-governing communes. Where royal authority was strong, we find kings granting charters of self-government to what were called "privileged towns." The king was glad to grant such a charter, for it weakened the power of his nobles and won him the support of the townsmen.

Founding new towns was still another way in which feudal restrictions were broken down. Shrewd lords and kings, who recognized the economic value of having towns in their territories, founded carefully planned centers with well-laid-out streets and open squares. As a means of obtaining inhabitants, they offered many inducements in the form of personal privileges and tax limitations. Among such new towns were Newcastle, Freiburg, and Berlin.

The Hanseatic League. Sometimes a group of towns joined forces for mutual protection and to win special privileges. This was particularly true in Germany where by the thirteenth century a strong state capable of maintaining order ceased to exist. Most famous was the Hanseatic League, whose nucleus was Lübeck, Hamburg, and Danzig, but which by the fourteenth century comprised more than seventy cities. The League built up a lucrative monopoly on Baltic and North Sea trade. Its wealth came primarily from its control of the Baltic herring fisheries, its corner on Russian trade, and its rich business with England and Flanders. It established permanent trading stations in such leading European centers as London, Bruges, and Novgorod. Until the fifteenth century, when it began to lose its privileges and monopolies, the Hanseatic League remained the great distributor of goods to northern Europe. Its navy safeguarded its commerce from pirates and even waged a successful war with the king of Denmark when he threatened its Baltic monopoly.

The use of money, banking, and credit. Europe's economic expansion had far-reaching effects on the financial structure. The first big change came with the reappearance of money as a medium of exchange. Coins were made from silver dug from old and new mines throughout Europe, but during the whole of the Middle Ages silver bullion was in short supply. In the thirteenth century silver coins were superseded in international trade by gold, especially the Venetian ducat and the florin of Florence.

When the English king Henry III invaded France in 1242, he carried with him thirty barrels of money, each containing 160,000 coins, to defray the expenses of the expedition. This incident graphically illustrates the need for instruments of credit and other forms of banking. All-important was the technique of "symbolic transfer." By this system a man deposited his money in a bank and received in return a letter of credit which, like a modern check, could later be cashed at any of the offices of the same bank. Letters of credit were common at fairs and very useful during the crusades, when the Knights Templar arranged a system whereby crusaders could deposit money in the Paris office and withdraw it from the office in the Holy Land.

Banking also sprang from the activities of moneychangers at fairs and other trading centers. In addition to exchanging the coin of one region for another, these moneychangers would also accept money on deposit for safekeeping. The most important bankers, however, were Italian merchants from Florence and the Lombard cities, who by the middle of the thirteenth century were loaning their accumulated capital to kings and prelates. They found various ways of circumventing the Church's disapproval of all interest as usury. For example, if a sum was not repaid by a certain date, a penalty charge was levied.

The bourgeoisie. The triumph of the townsmen in their struggle for greater self-government meant that a new class had evolved in Europe, a powerful, independent, and self-assured group that was to exert great impact on social, economic, and political history. The members of this class were called burghers or the bourgeoisie. Kings came to rely more and more on them in combating the power of the feudal lords, and their economic interests gradually gave rise to a nascent capitalism.

A medieval townsman's rank was based on money and goods rather than birth and land. At the top of the urban social scale were the great merchant and banking families, the princes of trade, bearing such names as Medici, Fugger, and Coeur. Then came the moderately wealthy merchants and below them the artisans and small shopkeepers. In the lowest slot was the unskilled laborer.

The depression of the Late Middle Ages. While the twelfth and thirteenth centuries had been a boom period, during the Late Middle Ages—the fourteenth and fifteenth centuries—the economy leveled off and then stagnated. By 1350 a great economic depression, which lasted approximately a century, was underway. Its causes are difficult to ascertain, but one of its symptoms, population decline, was probably also a major cause.

By 1300 the population of western Europe had ceased increasing, probably because it had expanded up to the limits of the available food supply. Famines had once again become common by the time of the Black Death. A bubonic plague from Asia carried by fleas on rats, the Black Death struck western Europe in 1347, decimating and demoralizing society. It is estimated that about one third of the population was wiped out. Hardest hit were the towns; the population of Florence, for example, fell from 114,000 to about 50,000 in five years. Coupled with this blow was the destruction and death caused by the Hundred Years' War between France and England (1337-1453).

Another symptom of economic stagnation was social unrest and tension. Individual folk heroes such as Robin Hood robbed the rich to benefit the poor, but more important was concerted group action. For the first time since the fall of Rome the common people organized themselves into pressure groups. Organized textile workers in the Flemish cities and in Florence waged class war against guild masters and rich merchants, while peasant unrest flamed into revolt in France and England. A famous example of the latter was the Wat Tyler uprising in England in 1381. The decimation of the peasant population by the Black Death caused a rise in the wages of the day laborers and an increased demand for the abolition of serfdom. Parliament tried to legislate against the pay raise but succeeded only in incurring the anger of the peasants. This resentment was fanned by the sermons of a priest, John Ball, known as the first English socialist:

> Ah, ye good people, the matter goeth not well to pass in England, nor shall not do so till everything be common, and that there be no villains [serfs] or gentlemen, but that we may be all united together and that the lords be no greater masters than we be. What have we deserved or why should we be thus kept in serfdom; we be all come from one father and one mother, Adam and Eve.[3]

As in the case of all other lower-class revolts, this uprising was crushed amid a welter of blood and broken promises.

Depression and economic stagnation began to be eased by the middle of the fifteenth century. A new period of economic expansion was at hand, encouraged by a new breed of strong and efficient monarchs and greatly stimulated by geographical discovery and expansion over the face of the globe (see Chapter 11).

CHAPTER 6
NATIONS IN THE MAKING

Medieval Political History: 1050-1500

During the High Middle Ages (1050-1300), not only did trade revive, cities grow, and a new bourgeois social class emerge, but kings developed their power at the expense of the feudal nobility. Inadequate to meet the demands of a new and progressive society in the making, feudalism was on the wane.

Perhaps the greatest weakness of feudalism was its inability to guarantee law and order. Too often feudalism meant anarchy in which robber barons, in the words of a twelfth-century observer, "levied taxes on the villages every so often, and called it 'protection money' " (see p. 000). Feudalism provided no consistently effective agency to deal with such ruffians.

The anarchy inherent in the feudal system also hindered economic progress. Trade and commerce spread over ever larger areas, but the boundaries of the many tiny feudal principalities acted as barriers to this expansion. Along the Seine River, for example, there were tolls every six or seven miles. Only by welding the confusing multiplicity of fiefs and principalities into a large territorial unit—the nation—could the irritating tolls and tariffs imposed by local barons be removed, trade advanced, and such lacks as a uniform currency and justice be remedied. In other words, the ills of feudalism could be cured only by the creation of unified and centralized national states. By 1300, the end of the High Middle Ages, monarchs in England and France had expanded their power and improved the machinery of government, thus laying the foundations for such states. In Germany and Italy, however, efforts to create a national state had ended in failure; and in Spain unification had been retarded by the formidable task of ousting the Muslims.

During the fourteenth and fifteenth centuries—the Late Middle Ages—the process of nation-making continued despite formidable crises and setbacks. In western Europe the contrasting political trends clearly evident at the end of the thirteenth century—unification in England, France, and Spain, and fragmentation in Germany and Italy—reached their culmination. And in Slavic Europe significant progress in nation-making occurred in Russia. In much of Europe by the end of the fifteenth century, the conflicting aims of what are called the "new monarchs" had superseded the quarrels of feudal barons.

THE GENESIS OF MODERN ENGLAND

The Anglo-Saxon kingdom. When the Roman legions withdrew from Britain at the beginning of the fifth century, they left the Romanized Celtic natives at the mercy of the Anglo-Saxon invaders. These Germanic tribes devastated Britain so thoroughly that little remained of Roman civilization other than a splendid system of roads. Not only did the Anglo-Saxons push most of the Celts out of Britain, but they also fought among themselves. Eventually there were more than a dozen little tribal kingdoms, all jealous and hostile, on the island. In the ninth century the kingdom of Wessex (see map, p. 84) held the dominant position. The famous Wessex king, Alfred the Great (871-899), was confronted with the task of turning back the Viking Danes, who overran all the other English kingdoms. Alfred defeated the Danes and forced them into a treaty whereby they settled in what came to be called the Danelaw (see map, p. 110) and accepted Christianity.

Alfred's successors were able rulers who conquered the Danelaw and unified England. Danes and Saxons intermarried, and soon all differences between the two people disappeared. After 975, however, a decline set in. The power of the central government lagged and with it the ability to keep order at home and repel outside attacks. The impotence of the kingdom is well illustrated in the unhappy reign of Ethelred the Unready (978-1016), who was unable to keep a firm hand on the great nobles, the earls, who were the king's deputies in their districts, or to cope with a new attack by the Danes. Ethelred's son, Edward the Confessor, was so pious that he remained a virgin all his life and so weak that he had little control over the powerful earls. This decline in government was reversed after the Normans conquered the island in 1066.

The Norman Conquest. When Edward the Confessor died without an heir in 1066, the *Witan*—the council of the kingdom—selected Harold Godwinson, a powerful English earl, as the new ruler. Immediately William, duke of Normandy, claimed the English throne, basing his demand on a flimsy hereditary right and on the assertion that Edward had promised him the crown. William's well-equipped army of hard-fighting Norman knights and landless nobles from Brittany and Flanders looked upon the conquest of England as an investment that would pay them rich dividends in the form of lands and serfs. After a hazardous crossing of the Channel in open boats, William's mounted knights broke the famed shield-wall of the English infantry, and resistance ceased when King Harold was slain. The defeat ended Anglo-Saxon rule and brought a new pattern of government to England.

William the Conqueror's centralized feudal monarchy. As king of England, William directed all his energies toward a single goal—the increase of his own power within the context of a highly centralized form of feudalism which he introduced into England. As owner of all England by right of conquest, William retained some land as his royal domain and granted the remainder as fiefs to royal vassals called tenants-in-chief, among whom were bishops and abbots. In return for their fiefs, the tenants-in-chief provided William with a stipulated number of knights to serve in the royal army. To furnish the required number of knights, the great vassals—most of whom were French-speaking Normans—subinfeudated parts of their fiefs among their own vassals. But from all the landholders in England, regardless of whether or not they were his immediate vassals, William exacted homage and an oath that they would "be faithful to him against all other men." Furthermore, private feudal warfare was forbidden, and no castle could be built without royal permission.

The Domesday Survey is another example of the energetic and methodical manner in which William took over full control of England. Because William, like all medieval kings, constantly needed money, he ordered an accurate census of the property and property holders in his realm as a basis for collecting all the feudal "aids" (see p. 114) owed to him. Royal commissioners gathered this information from local groups of older men who were put under oath and questioned. He also retained the Anglo-Saxon shires as administrative divisions, along with the system of shire courts and shire reeves, or sheriffs. The sheriffs became the effective local agents of the king in collecting feudal dues and in presiding over the shire courts. The long arm of royal power also reached the local level through the king's commissioners, who occasionally toured the shires.

William also utilized some other existing English institutions. He retained the old Anglo-Saxon militia, in which every freeman was required by custom to serve. The old Anglo-Saxon *Witan*, which had elected and advised the kings, was revamped, too. The new Norman ruler changed its title to the Great Council—also called *curia regis*, the king's council or court—and converted it into a feudal body

The Bayeux tapestry, actually a woolen embroidery on linen, dates from the eleventh century. Over 230 feet long and 20 inches wide, it both depicts and narrates (in Latin) the events of the Norman Conquest of England in 1066. This section shows the English shield wall being attacked by the mounted French knights.

composed of his tenants-in-chief. The Great Council met at least three times a year as a court of justice for the great barons and as an advisory body in important matters. At other times a small permanent council of barons advised the king.

William also dominated the English Church. He appointed bishops and abbots and required them to provide military service for their lands. Although he permitted the Church to retain its courts, he denied them the right to appeal cases to the pope without his consent. Nor could the decrees of popes and Church councils circulate in England without royal approval.

Thus William formed the conquered island into one of Europe's most advanced states. The nobility and the Church were burdened with feudal services, and the Anglo-Saxon freemen, oppressed by the exactions of their Norman lords, were in time reduced to serfdom. William advanced political feudalism and the manorial system and fused the two into a highly centralized feudal structure.

William's sons and feudal reaction. Utilizing his father's methods, but without his ability, William II stirred up several baronial revolts before being shot in the back—accidentally, it was said—while hunting. Succeeding him was his brother, Henry I (1100-1135), a more able and conciliatory monarch who met with only one baronial revolt.

While the Great Council, made up of the chief nobles, occasionally met to advise the king, the small permanent council of barons grew in importance. From it now appeared the first vague outlines of a few specialized organs of government. The exchequer, or treasury, supervised the collection of royal revenue, now greatly increased with the revival of a money economy. Notable was *scutage* or "shield money," a fee which the king encouraged his vassals to pay in lieu of personal military service. At times members of the small council were sent throughout the realm to judge serious crimes which endangered what was called the King's Peace.

Henry I's achievements in strengthening the monarchy were largely undone by the nineteen years of chaos that followed his death. Ignoring their promise to recognize Henry's only surviving child, Matilda, wife of Geoffrey Plantagenet, count of Anjou in France, many barons supported Henry's weak nephew Stephen. During the resulting civil war the nobility became practically independent of the crown and, secure in their strong castles, freely pillaged the land. According to a contemporary account:

> They levied taxes on the villages every so often, and called it "protection money." . . . If two or three men came riding to a village, all the villagers fled, because they expected they would be robbers. The bishops and learned men were always excommunicating them, but they thought nothing of it. . . .[1]

Henry II. Anarchy ceased with the accession of Matilda's son, Henry II (1154-1189), the founder of the Plantagenet, or Angevin, House in England. As a result of his inheritance (Normandy and Anjou) and his marriage to Eleanor of Aquitaine, the richest heiress in France, Henry's possessions stretched from Scotland to the Pyrenees. The English holdings in France far exceeded the land directly ruled by the French kings, who eyed their vassal with jealousy and fear. Henry's reign marks the outbreak of strife between England and France, which runs like a red thread throughout the tapestry of medieval and modern history.

Henry's chief contribution to the development of the English monarchy was to

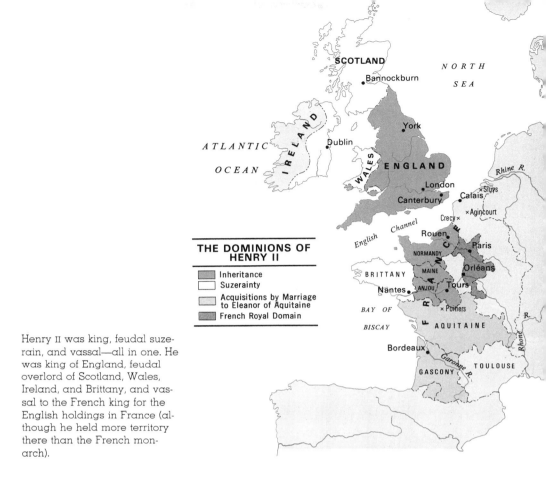

THE DOMINIONS OF
HENRY II

- ▨ Inheritance
- ☐ Suzerainty
- ▨ Acquisitions by Marriage
  to Eleanor of Aquitaine
- ▨ French Royal Domain

Henry II was king, feudal suzerain, and vassal—all in one. He was king of England, feudal overlord of Scotland, Wales, Ireland, and Brittany, and vassal to the French king for the English holdings in France (although he held more territory there than the French monarch).

increase the jurisdiction of the royal courts at the expense of the feudal courts of the nobility. This produced three major results: a permanent system of circuit courts presided over by itinerant justices, the jury system, and a body of law common to all England.

Itinerant justices on regular circuits were sent out once each year to try breaches of the King's Peace. To make this system of royal criminal justice more effective, Henry employed the method of inquest used by William the Conqueror in the Domesday Survey. In each shire a body of important men were sworn (*juré*) to report to the sheriff all crimes committed since the last session of the king's circuit court. Thus originated the modern-day grand jury which presents information for an indictment.

Henry's courts also used the jury system as a means of settling private lawsuits. Instead of deciding such civil cases by means of oath-helpers or trial by ordeal, the circuit judges handed down decisions based upon evidence sworn to by a jury of men selected because they were acquainted with the facts of the case. This more attractive and efficient system caused litigants to flock to the royal courts, a procedure facilitated by the sale of "writs," which ordered a sheriff to bring the case to a royal court. Not only was the king's income greatly increased by fees from the sale of writs, but the feudal courts were greatly weakened.

This petit or trial jury eventually evolved into the modern trial jury whose members, no longer witnesses, determine guilt or innocence. Trial by jury became the most characteristic feature of the judicial system of all English-speaking nations and was carried to the far corners of the earth as a hallmark of justice.

Henry's judicial reforms promoted the growth of the common law—one of the most important factors in welding the English people into a nation. The decisions of the royal justices became the basis for future decisions made in the king's courts, superseded the many diverse systems of local justice in the shires, and became the law common to all Englishmen.

Thomas à Becket, victim of Church-state rivalry. While Henry skillfully diminished the activities of the feudal courts, he was not so successful against his other legal rival—the Church courts. His appointee as archbishop of Canterbury, Thomas à Becket, proved to be stubbornly independent, stoutly upholding the authority of the Church. When Henry stipulated that clergymen found guilty by a Church court of committing heinous crimes, such as murder and grand larceny, were to be unfrocked and handed over to a royal court where punishments were more severe than in the Church courts, Becket refused to yield on the grounds that clergymen would suffer unjust "double punishment" for a crime—unfrocked by the Church and punished by the state.

Receiving no support from the English clergy, Becket fled to France and appealed to the pope for aid. After a few years the pope patched up the quarrel, and the archbishop returned to England. His first act, however, was to excommunicate the bishops who, in his absence, had crowned the eldest prince heir to the throne. When this news reached Henry, in a fit of passion he roared: "What a pack of fools and cowards I have nourished in my house, that not one of them will avenge me of this turbulent priest."[2] Responding to this tirade, four knights went to Canterbury and murdered Becket before the high altar of the cathedral. The resulting uproar destroyed all chance of reforming the Church courts. Becket became a martyr and, after miracles were reported to have occurred at his tomb, was canonized a saint. Legend soon made him the symbol of English resistance to the yoke of Norman tyranny.

Richard and John. As was the case after William the Conqueror's reign, the good beginning made by Henry II was marred by the mistakes of his immediate successors. Having no taste for the prosaic tasks of government, Richard the Lion-Hearted wasted his country's wealth in winning a great reputation as a crusader (see p. 152) and in fighting the king of France. Richard spent only five months of his ten-year reign (1189-1199) in England, which he regarded as a source of money for his overseas adventures.

Richard's successor, his brother John (reigned 1199-1216), worked hard to promote his father's governmental system but his cruelty and unscrupulousness cost him the support of his barons at the very time he needed them most in his struggles with the two ablest men of the age, Philip II of France and Pope Innocent III. As feudal overlord for John's possessions in France, Philip found the occasion to declare John an unfaithful vassal and his fiefs forfeit. John put up only feeble resistance, and after losing more than half his possessions in France he became involved in a struggle with Innocent III in which he was forced to make abject surrender (see p. 153). In the meantime, John had completely alienated the English barons by attempting to collect illegal feudal dues and committing other infractions of feudal law. The exasperated barons rebelled and in 1215 forced John to affix his seal to Magna Carta, which bound the king to observe all their feudal rights and privileges.

The importance of Magna Carta, however, does not lie in its original purpose but rather in the subsequent use made of it. Two great principles were potential in the charter: (1) the law is above the king; and (2) the king can be compelled by force to obey the law of the land. This concept of the rule of law and the limited power of the crown was to play an important role in the seventeenth-century movement toward constitutional monarchy and representative government.

Edward I and the beginnings of Parliament. The French-speaking Normans commonly used the word *Parlement* (from *parler,* "to speak") for the Great Council, or *curia regis,* composed of the king's feudal tenants-in-chief. Anglicized as *Parliament,* the term was used interchangeably with Great Council and *curia regis.* Modern historians, however, generally apply the term to the Great Council only after 1265, when its membership was radically enlarged.

The first meeting of Parliament—the enlarged Great Council—took place in the midst of a baronial rebellion against Henry III, the son of King John. In an effort to gain the widest possible popular support, Simon de Montfort, the leader of the rebellion, summoned not only the barons but also two knights from every shire and two burghers from every borough to the Great Council in 1265.

Henry III's son, Edward I (1272-1307), one of England's half-dozen outstanding monarchs, followed the pattern set by Simon de Montfort in summoning representatives of shires and towns to meetings of the Great Council. In calling Parliaments, Edward had no idea of making any concession to popular government. In recognition of the growing wealth and influence of the bourgeoisie and as a means of obtaining another source of revenue, Edward began the practice of including representatives of the bourgeoisie in his feudal council.

Early in the fourteenth century the representatives of the knights and the burghers, called the "Commons," adopted the practice of meeting separately from the lords spiritual and temporal. Thus arose the divisions of Parliament that came to be called the House of Commons and the House of Lords.

Parliament, particularly the Commons, soon discovered its power as a major source of money for the king. It gradually became the custom for Parliament to exercise this "power of the purse" by withholding its financial grants until the king had redressed grievances, made known by petitions. Parliament also presented petitions to the king with the request that they be promulgated as statutes, as the laws drawn up by the king and his council and confirmed in Parliament were called. Gradually the right to initiate legislation through petition was obtained. Again, Parliament's "power of the purse" turned the trick.

Edward issued through Parliament a series of great statutes, many aimed at curtailing the power of the nobility that had greatly increased during the baronial revolts of his father's reign. For example, the statute known as *Quo Warranto,* which demanded of a lord that he prove "by what warrant" he exercised certain rights and privileges, led to the recovery of lost royal rights.

Edward I was the first English king who was determined to be master of the whole island of Britain—Wales, Scotland, and England. In 1284, after a five-year struggle, English law and administration were imposed on Wales. As a concession to the Welsh, Edward gave his oldest son the title of Prince of Wales.

A dispute over the succession to the Scottish throne in the 1290's gave Edward his opportunity to intervene and be accepted as overlord. But the fires of Scottish nationalism continued to burn despite numerous attempts to put out the flames. When Edward II, the next English king, was defeated at Bannockburn (1314), the Scots, led by Robert Bruce, won their independence. Not until 1603 were the two kingdoms united under a common monarch.

THE BEGINNINGS OF THE FRENCH NATIONAL STATE

The early Capetians. At the time William the Conqueror set sail, the monarchy in France barely existed. As we saw in Chapter 5, the later Carolingian rulers were generally weak and unable to defend the realm from Viking incursions. This task fell to the local counts and dukes, who built castles to protect the countryside and exercised the powers of the king in their territories. In France by the beginning of the tenth century there were more than thirty great feudal princes who were nominally vassals of the king but who gave him little or no support. When the last French Carolingian, Louis the Sluggard, died in 987, the nobles elected as his successor Hugh Capet, count of Paris. Hugh's tiny royal domain, called the Ile de France, was surrounded by many independent duchies and counties, such as Flanders, Normandy, Anjou, and Champagne, which were a law unto themselves.

The major accomplishment of the first four Capetian kings was their success in keeping the French crown within their own family. The nobles who elected Hugh Capet to the kingship had no thought of giving the Capetian family a monopoly on the royal office. But the Capetian kings, with the support of the Church, which nurtured the tradition of kingship as a sacred office, cleverly arranged for the election and coronation of their heirs.

Louis the Fat, Philip Augustus, and St. Louis. The reign of the fifth Capetian king, Louis VI (1108-1137), also known as Louis the Fat, heralded the end of Capetian weakness. Supported by the Church (which supplied him with able advisers), Louis crushed the lawless barons who were defying royal authority in the Ile de France, an achievement which paralleled on a smaller scale the work of William the Conqueror in England. Louis thus established a solid base from which royal power could be extended, and he so increased the prestige of the monarchy that the great duke of Aquitaine deigned to marry his daughter Eleanor to Louis' son. Unfortunately, Eleanor's behavior so scandalized Louis' pious son ("I thought I married a king," Eleanor once exclaimed, "but instead I am the wife of a monk") that he had the marriage annulled, and Aquitaine passed to Eleanor's second husband, Henry II of England.

The first great expansion of the royal domain was the work of the next Capetian, Philip II, Augustus (1180-1223), during whose reign the French king for the first time became more powerful than any of his vassals and France became the strongest monarchy in continental Europe. Philip Augustus' great ambition was to wrest from the English Plantagenets the vast territory they held in France. He took Normandy, Maine, Anjou, and Touraine from King John, thereby tripling the size of the royal domain.

Late in Philip Augustus' reign the groundwork was laid for the extension of the royal domain to the Mediterranean. In southern France, particularly in Toulouse, the heretical Albigensian sect flourished. Determined to stamp out this sect, Pope Innocent III in 1208 called the Albigensian Crusade, discussed in Chapter 7. Philip, faced with the enmity of King John and the German emperor, did not take part, but he allowed his vassals to do so. After Philip's death his son Louis VIII led a new crusade to exterminate the remnants of Albigensian resistance. Later in the century Toulouse escheated to the French crown when its count died without heir. The royal domain now stretched from the chilly coast of the English Channel to the warm shores of the Mediterranean.

Philip Augustus also greatly strengthened the royal administrative system by devising new agencies for centralized government and tapping new sources of revenue, including a money payment from his vassals in lieu of military service. New salaried officials, called bailiffs, performed duties similar to those carried out in England by itinerant justices and sheriffs. A corps of loyal officials, like the bailiffs recruited not from the feudal nobility but from the ranks of the bourgeoisie, was collected around the king. As in England, special administrative departments were created: the *parlement*, a supreme court of justice (not to be confused with the English Parliament, which became primarily a legislative body); the chamber of accounts, or royal treasury; and the royal or privy council, a group of advisers who assisted the king in the conduct of the daily business of the state.

After the brief reign of Louis VIII, France came under the rule of Louis IX (1226-1270), better known as St. Louis because of his piety and noble character. Just, sympathetic, and peace-loving, St. Louis convinced his subjects that the monarchy was the most important agency for assuring their happiness and well-being. His belief that he was responsible only to God, who had put him on the throne to lead his people out of a life of sin, did much to advance the concept of absolute monarchy ruling by divine right. Accordingly, St. Louis was the first French king to issue edicts for the whole kingdom without the prior consent of his council of great vassals. He also ordered an end to trial by battle and the time-honored feudal right of private warfare. Certain matters, such as treason and crimes on the highways, were declared to be the exclusive jurisdiction of the royal courts. Furthermore, St. Louis insisted on the right of appeal from the feudal courts of his vassals to the high royal court of *parlement* at Paris.

When Hugh Capet was elected king, he could actually claim control over only the Ile de France, the small district around Paris. By centralizing and streamlining the government of their gradually expanding domain, the Capetian kings made themselves the most powerful feudal lords in France. By 1300 they ruled all of France.

Climax of Capetian rule under Philip IV. The reign of Philip IV, the Fair (1285-1314), climaxed three centuries of Capetian rule. The antithesis of his saintly grandfather, Philip was a man of craft, violence, and deceit. He took advantage of the growing anti-Semitism that had appeared in Europe with the crusades to expel the Jews from France and confiscate their possessions. (Philip's English contemporary, Edward I, had done the same.) Furthermore, heavily in debt to the Knights Templars, who had turned to banking after the crusades, Philip had the order suppressed on trumped-up charges of heresy.

Philip's need of money also caused him to clash with the last great medieval pope. Pope Boniface VIII refused to allow Philip to tax the French clergy and made sweeping claims to supremacy over secular powers. But the national state had reached the point where such leaders as Philip IV would not brook interference with their authority no matter what the source. The result of this controversy was the humiliation of Boniface, a blow from which the medieval papacy never recovered.

In domestic affairs the real importance of Philip's reign lies in the increased power and improved organization of the royal government. Philip's astute civil servants, recruited mainly from the middle class, concentrated their efforts on exalting the power of the monarch. Trained in Roman law, and inspired by its maxim that "whatever pleases the prince has the force of law," they sought to make the power of the monarch absolute.

Like Edward I in England, Philip enlarged his feudal council to include representatives of the third "estate" or class—the townsmen. This Estates-General of nobles, clergy, and burghers was used as a means of obtaining popular support for Philip's policies, including the announcement of new taxes. Significantly, Philip did not need to ask the Estates-General's consent for his tax measures, and it did not acquire the power of the purse that characterized the English Parliament. Philip had sown the seeds of absolutism in France, but their growth was to be interrupted by the Hundred Years' War between France and England, which broke out twenty-three years after his death.

CRISIS IN ENGLAND AND FRANCE

The Hundred Years' War. Nation-making in both France and England was greatly affected by the long conflict that colored much of their history during the Late Middle Ages. In both lands the crisis of war led to a resurgence of feudalism and a temporary increase in the power of the representative assemblies, Parliament and the Estates-General. Nevertheless, in the long run the anarchy and misery of the times stimulated nationalistic feelings and a demand for strong rulers who could guarantee law and order. Thus by the late fifteenth century the French and English kings were able to resume the task of establishing the institutions of the modern nation-state.

The Hundred Years' War sprang from the desire of the English kings to regain the large holdings in France that had been theirs in the days of Henry II. The French kings, on the other hand, were determined to expel the English from their last French possession, Aquitaine. Another source of friction was prosperous Flanders, whose count was a French vassal. This region was coming more and more under French control, to the chagrin of the English wool growers who supplied the great Flemish woolen industry, and of the English king whose income came in great part from duties on wool.

The immediate excuse for the Anglo-French conflict was a dispute over the succession to the French throne. In 1328, after the direct line of the Capetians became extinct, Philip VI of the House of Valois assumed the throne. The English king, Edward III, maintained that he was the legitimate heir to the French throne because his mother was a sister of the late French king. The French denied this claim, which became a pretext for war. Interrupted by several peace treaties and a number of truces, the conflict stretched from 1337 to 1453. The English won a series of great victories—at Crécy (1346), Poitiers (1356), and Agincourt (1415), where the French lost some 7000 knights, including many great nobles, and the English only 500. Their secret weapon was the longbow, apparently taken over from the Welsh. Six feet long and made of special wood, the longbow shot steel-tipped arrows which were dangerous at four hundred yards and deadly at one hundred. English military triumphs caused a patriotic stirring among the French, or what we now think of as nationalism—love of country and a sense of difference from, and usually superiority to, other peoples. The revival of French spirit is associated with Joan of Arc, a peasant girl who initiated a series of French victories. Impelled by inward voices which she believed divine, and clad in white armor and riding a white horse, Joan inspired confidence and a feeling of invincibility in the French. But Joan met a tragic end. Captured by the enemy, she was found guilty of bewitching the English soldiers and was burned at the stake.

The martyrdom of Joan of Arc was a turning point in the long struggle. English resistance crumbled as military superiority now turned full circle; the English longbow was outmatched by French artillery. Of the vast territories they had once controlled in France, the English retained only Calais when the war ended in 1453.

Aftermath of war in England. The Hundred Years' War exhausted England, and discontent was rife in Parliament. Richard II (1377-1399), the last Plantagenet king, was unstable, cruel, and power hungry; he foreshadowed modern absolute monarchs in believing that the king should control the lives and property of his subjects. His seizure of the properties of Henry, the duke of Lancaster, led to a revolt in which Henry was victorious.

Henry IV established the House of Lancaster, which ruled England from 1399 to 1461. He had the support of Parliament, which had deeply resented Richard's autocratic reign and was determined that its authority should not again be slighted. Hard-pressed for money to suppress revolts at home and carry on the war in France, the Lancastrian kings became more and more financially dependent upon Parliament. In return for money grants, Parliament acquired the guarantee of freedom of debate, the right to approve the appointment of the king's chief officials and members of his council, the stipulation that money bills must originate in the House of Commons, and the rule that the king's statutes should duplicate exactly petitions presented by the Commons. Not until 1689, when England became a constitutional monarchy, would Parliament again exercise such powers.

Baronial rivalry to control both Parliament and the crown flared up during the reign of the third Lancastrian king, and when he went completely insane in 1453, the duke of York, the strongest man in the kingdom, became regent. Two years later full-scale civil war, known as the Wars of the Roses, broke out between the partisans of York and Lancaster. In 1461 the Yorkists managed to have their

THE RECONQUISTA 910

The main thrust of Spanish unification centered on ejecting the Muslims from the peninsula. As can be seen in the first map, the Christian areas were restricted to Leon, Navarre, and the county of Barcelona. Gradually the invaders were pushed south by the efforts of Castile and Aragon, leaving only Granada in Muslim hands. The marriage of Ferdinand and Isabella united the thrones of Aragon and Castile, and together they conquered Granada, completing Christian control of the Iberian peninsula and the unification of Spain.

leader, Edward IV, crowned king. Ten years later Edward had succeeded in cowing the nobles and in winning the support of the middle class, who saw a strong monarchy as the only alternative to anarchy. Edward's power became practically absolute, foreshadowing the strong rule of the Tudors that soon followed.

The promise of the House of York ended in 1483 when Edward IV died, leaving two young sons as his heirs. Their uncle bribed and intimidated Parliament to declare his nephews illegitimate and took the throne as Richard III. The two boys were imprisoned in the Tower of London, where they were secretly murdered. The double murder was too much for the nation, and support was thrown to the cause of Henry Tudor, who, in his lineage and later marriage to Edward IV's daughter, united the Houses of Lancaster and York. At Bosworth Field in 1485 Richard died fighting as his army deserted him. According to tradition, his crown was found in a bush on the battlefield and placed on the head of Henry VII, the first of the Tudor line, which ruled England from 1485 to 1603.

Beginning of Tudor rule. During the reigns of the shrewd Henry VII (1485-1509) and his successor, Henry VIII (1509-1547), strong, almost absolute government was reintroduced into England, with the people supporting the monarchy because it held the nobility in check. The Court of Star Chamber was the most effective royal instrument in suppressing the unruly barons; it bypassed the established common law courts, whose judges and juries were too often intimidated and bribed by powerful nobles, and operated secretly and swiftly without benefit of juries. Because the Tudor rulers restored order and promoted trade at home and abroad, they won the support of the middle class—the burghers and landed gentry—and upon this support their power was primarily built. Though often high-handed, Tudor kings always worked through Parliament.

France after the Hundred Years' War: Louis XI. The Hundred Years' War left France with a new national consciousness and a royal power that was stronger than ever before. In 1438 the king had become the virtual head of the church in France by decreeing that it be run by a council of French bishops whose appointment was controlled by the monarch. Furthermore, the *taille*, a land tax

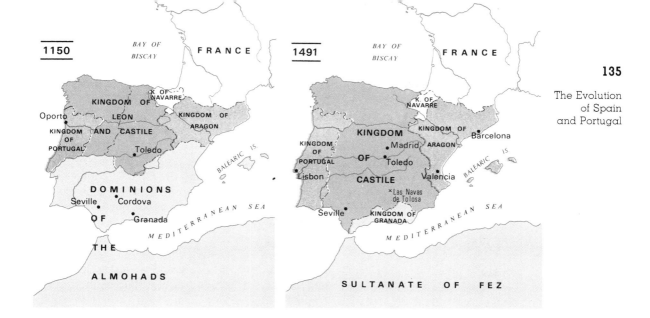

voted during the war to support a standing army, became permanent, making the king financially independent of the Estates-General. Thus the purse strings, which the English Parliament used to gain concessions from the king, were kept firmly under royal control in France.

After the war the process of consolidating royal power was continued by Louis XI (1461-1483). Physically unattractive and completely lacking in scruples, Louis earned himself the epithet, the "Spider King." In his pursuit of power he used any weapon—violence, bribery, and treachery—to obtain his ends. When the French nobles rose in revolt, dignifying themselves as the League for the Public Welfare, Louis outfoxed them by agreeing to their Magna Carta-like demands and then ignoring his pledged word.

Louis XI's most powerful antagonist was the duke of Burgundy, Charles the Bold, whose possession of Flanders and the other Low Countries or Netherlands (modern Holland, Belgium, and Luxemburg) made him one of Europe's richest rulers. After Charles' death in 1477, Louis seized most of Burgundy, while the remainder of the duke's possessions passed to his daughter Mary. When she married the German emperor Maximilian I, the Netherlands came into the hands of the House of Hapsburg (see map, p. 211). Like Henry VII of England, Louis XI was one of the "new monarchs" who created the absolute states which were to dominate Europe in the early modern period. In the meantime, another "new monarch" had emerged in Spain.

THE EVOLUTION OF SPAIN AND PORTUGAL

The Reconquista.   Nation-making in Spain was a more complex process than in either France or England. The customary rivalry between the feudal aristocracy and the royal authority was complicated by another significant element—a religious crusade to eject the Muslims from the peninsula. Unity also called for the integration of several distinct Christian states. During the period of Muslim dominance the following Christian states survived in the north of Spain: the county of Barcelona, nucleus of later Aragon, in the east; Leon in the west; and in between, Navarre, peopled by the fiercely independent Basques whom neither the Romans nor the Visigoths had wholly subdued. An offshoot of Leon was the county of Castile, named after the many castles built to defend it. In the mid-tenth century Castile became strong enough to throw off the rule of the king of Leon.

Slowly these Christian states expanded south through the hills. The disintegration of the Caliphate of Cordova into small Muslim states after 1031 opened the way for further Christian advances. In 1063, a generation before the first crusade to the Holy Land, the pope proclaimed the *Reconquista* to be a holy crusade, and the first of many northern knights flocked to Spain to fight the Muslims. In 1085 the mighty bastion of Toledo fell to the king of Castile, and early in the thirteenth century his successors captured first Cordova, whose great mosque was reconsecrated as a cathedral, and then Seville. By the end of the thirteenth century Muslim political control was confined to Granada, which was conquered two centuries later by Ferdinand and Isabella.

Ferdinand and Isabella.   Spain emerged as one of Europe's "new monarchies" in 1479 when Isabella of Castile and Ferdinand of Aragon, who had married ten years earlier, began a joint rule that united the Iberian peninsula except for Granada, Navarre, and Portugal. The "Catholic Sovereigns," to use the title the pope conferred on Ferdinand and Isabella, set out to establish an effective royal despotism in Spain. The Holy Brotherhood, a league of cities which had long existed for mutual protection against unruly nobles, was taken over by the crown, and its militia was used as a standing army and police force. The powerful and virtually independent military orders of knights, which had emerged during the *Reconquista*, were also brought under royal control.

Ferdinand and Isabella believed that the Church should be subordinate to royal government—a belief they shared with the other "new monarchs" of Europe. By tactful negotiations, the Spanish sovereigns induced the pope to give them the right to make Church appointments in Spain and to establish a Court of Inquisition, largely free of papal control. The Spanish Inquisition confiscated the property of most Jews and Muslims and terrified the Christian clergy and laymen into accepting royal absolutism as well as religious orthodoxy. Although the Inquisition greatly enhanced the power of the Spanish crown, it also caused many talented people to flee the land of persecution. About 150,000 Spanish Jews, mainly merchants and professional people, fled to Holland, England, North Africa, and the Ottoman empire. Calling themselves Sephardim, these exiles retained their Spanish language and customs into the twentieth century.

A final manifestation of Spanish absolutism, defined by Isabella herself as "one king, one law, one faith," was the virtual ignoring of the Cortes of Castile and Aragon. These representative assemblies had emerged in the twelfth century and were thus older than the English Parliament.

The most dramatic act of the Catholic Sovereigns was the conquest of Granada in 1492, the same year that Columbus claimed the New World for Spain. Before Ferdinand died in 1516, twelve years after Isabella, he seized that part of Navarre which lay south of the Pyrenees Mountains. This acquisition, together with the conquest of Granada, completed the national unification of Spain. Royal absolutism and unification, coupled with the acquisition of territory in the New and Old Worlds, would make Spain the strongest power in sixteenth-century Europe.

Portugal. The nucleus of the area which eventually became Portugal was a part of Castile until 1095. In that year the king of Castile gave his daughter to Count Henry of Burgundy, one of many French knights who had helped take Toledo. Her dowry was the county of Portugal, named after its chief town Oporto ("The Port") at the mouth of the Duero River. The son of this marriage organized a revolt against his overlord, the king of Castile, and in 1139 proclaimed himself king of Portugal.

Attempts by Castile to regain Portugal ended in 1385 when John I, aided by English archers, decisively defeated the invader. The following year John signed an alliance with England which has been reaffirmed down the centuries and remains the oldest alliance in existence. In 1415 John took Ceuta in North Africa, thus initiating Portuguese overseas expansion. Carried on by his son, Henry the Navigator, this policy eventually led to the creation of a great overseas empire (see Chapter 11).

FAILURES OF THE NATIONAL STATE: GERMANY AND ITALY

German tribal duchies. Following the collapse of the Carolingian empire, the tribal consciousness of its people kept Germany from falling into the extreme political fragmentation that characterized feudal France. When the successors of Louis the German, who received East Frankland in the Treaty of Verdun in 843 (see p. 110), proved incapable of coping with the attacks of savage Magyar horsemen in the late ninth and early tenth centuries, the task was taken over by the tribal leaders of the Saxons, Bavarians, Swabians, and Franconians who assumed the title of duke. The dukes of the five German duchies—including Lorraine, which Louis the German had acquired on the breakup of Lothair's middle kingdom—usurped the royal power and crown lands in their duchies and also took control over the Church.

When the last Carolingian, Louis the Child, died in 911, the dukes elected the weakest among them, Conrad of Franconia, to be their king. The new monarch ruled just eight years and proved himself incapable of meeting the menace of the Magyar raids. On his deathbed he recommended that the most powerful of the dukes, Henry the Fowler, duke of Saxony, be chosen as his successor. Henry founded the illustrious Saxon dynasty, which ruled until 1024 and made Germany the most powerful state in western Europe.

Henry the Fowler. After some initial opposition, Henry I (919-936) obtained recognition of his kingship from the other dukes. He exercised little authority outside of his own duchy, however, and his kingdom was hardly more than a confederation of independent duchies.

Against Germany's border enemies, Henry was more successful. He pushed back the Danes and established the Dane Mark as a protective buffer. Inroads were also made against the Slavs across the Elbe, where in 928 Brandenburg was set up as another defensive mark. Thus began the *Drang nach Osten* ("push to the East"), which became a permanent feature of German history. Further to the southeast, in Bohemia, Henry forced the Slavic Czechs to recognize his overlordship.

More spectacular was Henry's great victory over the Magyars in 933, following his refusal to pay the annual tribute demanded by these marauders. By this victory Henry earned the gratitude of the German people, and when he died no one disputed the election of his son Otto to succeed him.

Otto the Great.   Realizing that the great hindrance to German unity was the truculence of the dukes, Otto I, the Great (936-973), initiated a policy of gaining control of the unruly duchies by setting up his own relatives and favorites as their rulers. As an extra precaution he appointed, as supervising officials, counts who were directly responsible to the king. However, both the counts and Otto's relatives and favorites proved unreliable.

In the long run it was by means of an alliance with the Church that Otto constructed a strong German monarchy. Otto appointed the bishops and abbots, and since their offices were not hereditary, he could be sure that their first obedience was to his royal person. These prelates replaced the counts as the chief agents of the king in the duchies and furnished as much as three quarters of his military forces.

This alliance of crown and Church was a natural one at the time. At his coronation at Aachen, Otto had insisted on being anointed *rex et sacerdos* ("king and priest"), thus reviving the Carolingian concept of the theocratic ruler and the alliance between crown and Church. Furthermore, both partners feared the unruly and arrogant dukes whose usurpations included the right to appoint bishops and abbots in their duchies.

In 955, at a great battle at Lechfeld, Otto put an end to the Magyar menace, thereby enhancing his claim that the king, and not the dukes, was the true defender of the German people. The remaining Magyars settled quietly in Hungary, and by the year 1000 they had accepted Christianity.

Otto continued German expansion eastward against the Slavs, and the region between the Elbe and the Oder became more and more Germanized. Perhaps the most significant accomplishment of the medieval Germans was this movement toward the east. It has been estimated that 60 percent of German territory before the First World War had been taken from the Slavs. On the other hand, because the borders between the German colonists and the Slav natives were never clearly defined, pockets of Slavs and Germans intermingled. This ethnic admixture has caused serious disputes and conflicts in modern times.

The German empire.   Fragmented Italy in the tenth century was a tempting field for an invader. In the north the old Lombard realm, which had been a part of Lothair's middle kingdom, was the object of various rival contenders. In central Italy were the Papal States, ruled by the pope. During this century, however, the popes were appointed and controlled by the Roman nobility, and the power and prestige of the papacy was at its lowest ebb. In southern Italy, Lombard dukes and the Byzantine emperor disputed for power.

In deciding to invade Italy, Otto the Great was influenced not only by politics but, as chivalrous contemporary accounts explained it, by romance also. Queen Adelaide, the widow of the former king of Lombardy, had been imprisoned by a usurper. Her plight suited Otto's political ambitions. In 951 he crossed the Alps, rescued and married Adelaide, and proclaimed himself king of Italy. On his second expedition to Italy in 962, Otto was crowned emperor by the pope, whose Papal States were threatened by an Italian duke. Otto thought of himself as the successor of the imperial Caesars and Charlemagne; he also needed the imperial title to legitimatize his claim to Lombardy, Burgundy, and Lorraine, which had belonged to the middle kingdom of Lothair, the last man to hold the imperial title.

Otto's coronation was a momentous event that brought Italy and Germany, pope and emperor, into a forced and unnatural union.

The distracting, even malevolent, effect of the German pursuit of empire in Italy is demonstrated by the reign of Otto III (938-1002), who eagerly promoted his grandiose scheme for "the renewal of the Roman Empire." Ignoring Germany, the real source of his power, he made Rome his capital, built a palace there, and styled himself "emperor of the Romans." As the "servant of Jesus Christ," another of his titles, Otto installed non-Italian popes in Rome and conceived of the papacy as a partner in ruling an empire of Germans, Italians, and Slavs.

Despite the distractions in Italy, the Saxon rulers were the most powerful in Europe. They had permanently halted Magyar pillaging and, by utilizing the German Church as an ally, had curbed the divisive tendencies toward feudalism. Economically, too, there was progress. German eastward expansion had begun, and the Alpine passes had been freed of Muslim raiders and made safe for the Italian merchants who by the year 1000 were ready to act as middlemen linking western Europe with the eastern Mediterranean.

Henry IV vs. the papacy. The Saxon kings were succeeded by a new royal line, the Salian House (1024-1125), whose members set about with increased vigor to strengthen the centralized monarchy. To the dismay of many nobles, a body of lowborn royal officials was recruited; and the power of the dukes was weakened further when the crown won the allegiance of the lesser nobles.

The reign of Henry IV (1056-1125) was a watershed in German history. The monarchy reached the height of its power, but it also experienced a major

The breadth of the Holy Roman Empire at this date derived largely from the energetic reign of Otto the Great. A successful warrior, Otto was also a match for the Church, which provided him with an additional source of power.

reversal. For a century the Ottonian system, by which the king had governed his kingdom through the clergy, whom he appointed, had functioned smoothly. Under Henry IV, however, the revival of a powerful papacy led to a bitter conflict, centering on the king's right to appoint Church officials who were at the same time his most loyal supporters. This conflict, known as the Investiture Struggle (see p. 150), resulted in the loss of the monarchy's major sources of strength: the loyalty of the German Church, now transferred to the papacy; and the chief material base of royal power, the king's lands, which were dissipated by grants to loyal nobles.

The real victors in the Investiture Struggle were the German nobles, many of whom allied themselves with the papacy and continued to wage war against the monarchy long after the reign of Henry IV. From the time of Henry's death in 1106 until the accession of Frederick Barbarossa in 1152, the Welfs of Bavaria and the Hohenstaufens of Swabia, along with other noble factions, fought over the throne, which they made elective rather than hereditary. The outcome was that the structure of a strong national state was wrecked and Germany became extensively feudalized. The great nobles usurped royal rights, built strong castles, and forced lesser nobles to become their vassals. On the other hand, the great nobles acknowledged no feudal relationship to the king. Many free peasants, in turn, lost their freedom and became serfs. The evil effects of this period were to hinder the development of a unified Germany until modern times.

The Welf-Hohenstaufen rivalry in Germany was reflected in Italy, where the rival factions were known as Guelphs and Ghibellines. The former were usually pro-papal; the latter strongly favored the German monarchy's imperial claims in Italy. Yet, amidst the turmoil, the vitality, wealth, and culture of the northern Italian cities increased.

Frederick Barbarossa.   Frederick I Barbarossa ("Red-beard"), a member of the Hohenstaufen family who reigned from 1152 to 1190, realistically accepted the fact that during the preceding half century Germany had become thoroughly feudalized; his goal was to make himself the apex of the feudal pyramid by forcing the great nobles to acknowledge his overlordship. He was largely successful, and Germany became a centralized feudal monarchy not unlike England in the days of William the Conqueror.

To maintain his hold over his German tenants-in-chief, Frederick needed the resources of Italy—particularly the income from taxes levied on wealthy north Italian cities, which, encouraged by the papacy, joined together in the Lombard League to resist him. Frederick spent about twenty-five years fighting intermittently in Italy, but although some of the cities submitted to his authority, the final result was failure. The opposition from the popes and the Lombard League was too strong. Frederick did score a diplomatic triumph, however, by marrying his son to the heiress of the Kingdom of Naples and Sicily, which had been founded in 1127 by land-hungry adventurers from Normandy. The threat of encirclement by the empire—called the "Holy Roman Empire" by the anti-papal Frederick Barbarossa in claiming that he, too, was God's agent—made it vital to the papacy that the Hohenstaufens be destroyed.

Frederick Barbarossa died in Asia Minor while en route with the Third Crusade, and in time he became a folk hero in Germany. It was believed that he still lived, asleep in a cave in the mountains near Berchtesgaden in Bavaria. Some day, awakened by a flight of ravens, he would emerge and bring unity and strength back to Germany.

Frederick II, a brilliant failure. It fell to the lot of Frederick Barbarossa's grandson, Frederick II (1194-1250), to meet the pope's challenge to the threat of Hohenstaufen encirclement. Orphaned at an early age, Frederick was brought up as the ward of the most powerful medieval pope, Innocent III. During Frederick's minority the empire fell on evil days; the Welf and Hohenstaufen factions resumed their struggle over the throne, and the strong feudal monarchy created by Frederick Barbarossa collapsed. In 1215, one year before Innocent died and with his support, Frederick was elected emperor. Faced by a resurgent nobility in Germany, he soon turned his attention to wealthy Italy. But there he experienced the same opposition and the same failure as had Frederick Barbarossa.

Meanwhile, Frederick II had sacrificed Germany. He transferred crown lands and royal rights to the German princes in order to keep them quiet and to win their support for his inconclusive Italian wars. Born in Sicily, he remained at heart a Mediterranean monarch. He shaped his kingdom of Sicily into a modern state, the most centralized and bureaucratic in Europe, administered by paid officials who were trained at the University of Naples, which he founded for that purpose.

End of an era. Following Frederick II's death in 1250, his empire quickly collapsed. In Germany his son ruled ineffectively for four years before dying. Soon afterward Frederick's descendants in Sicily were killed when the count of Anjou, brother of St. Louis of France, was invited by the pope to lead a crusade against the "viper breed of the Hohenstaufen" and take over Naples and Sicily. After the fall of the Hohenstaufens, German emperors seldom interfered in Italian affairs, and they ceased going to Rome to receive the imperial crown from the pope. In German affairs the emperors no longer even attempted to assert their authority over the increasingly powerful nobles. Germany lapsed more and more into the political disunity and ineffectual elective monarchy that remained characteristic of its history until the late nineteenth century.

The early Hapsburgs and the Golden Bull. Between 1254 and 1273 the German monarchy was made virtually nonexistent by the election of two rival foreign princes, neither of whom received wide recognition. Then in 1273 the imperial crown was bestowed upon the obscure Count Rudolf (1273-1291) of the House of Hapsburg—from Habichtsburg (Castle of the Hawk), their home in northern Switzerland. Rudolph acquired Austria through marriage and thereafter the Hapsburgs ruled their holdings from Vienna.

For the time being, however, the Hapsburg hold on the imperial crown proved to be brief. After Rudolf's reign it was passed from one family to another. Then in 1356 the nobility won another significant victory. The Golden Bull, a document which served as the political constitution of Germany until early in the nineteenth century, laid down the procedure for election of the emperor by seven German dignitaries—three archbishops and four lay princes. The electors and other important princes were given rights that made them virtually independent rulers, and the emperor could take no important action without the consent of the imperial feudal assembly, the Diet, which met infrequently. It has been said that the Golden Bull "legalized anarchy and called it a constitution"; in reality it stabilized the political situation in Germany by recognizing the independence of the princes, hereby encouraging them to emulate the new national monarchs and create stable governments in their principalities. It also ended disputed elections and civil wars over the succession.

The imperial crown of Germany was returned to the Hapsburg family in 1438. From this time until 1806, when the Holy Roman Empire disappeared, the

Hapsburgs held the imperial crown almost without a break. In the early sixteenth century they obtained Bohemia and Hungary. Maximilian I (1493-1519) helped make the Hapsburgs the most potent force in sixteenth-century Europe by taking as his wife Mary of Burgundy (see p. 135), heiress of the rich Low Countries, and by marrying his son to the heiress of Spain, the daughter of Ferdinand and Isabella. But in Germany itself the emperor continued to be limited in power, without an imperial treasury, an efficient central administration, or a standing army. And so the phantom Holy Roman Empire lived on as Voltaire later characterized it: "Neither Holy, nor Roman, nor an Empire."

Italy: Wealthy but Divided.   The virtual ending of German imperial influence after 1250 left the three major divisions of Italy—the city-states of northern Italy, the Papal States, and the Kingdom of Naples—free to follow their own devices. Such city-states as Venice, Florence, Milan, Genoa, and Pisa had grown wealthy from their thriving industries, lucrative trade, and banking houses that handled papal revenues and made loans to European monarchs. Unlike the situation in northern Europe, where the bourgeoisie inhabited the towns and the nobles lived on country manors, the Italian nobility had city houses as well as country villas. Within each city-state there were intense rivalries and feuds.

In both the intracity rivalries and the struggles between city-states, mercenary soldiers under the command of leaders called *condottieri* were employed. Coming from all over Europe, these adventurers sold their swords to the highest bidder, but, in order to live and fight another day, they carried on their fighting with a minimum of bloodshed. These petty conflicts did not hinder the spectacular progress in art and learning called the Italian Renaissance (see Chapter 8).

By the twelfth century the prosperous burghers had succeeded in ousting the restless feudal aristocrats from positions of power. Ingenious city charters and civic constitutions were drafted, and there was much trial and error in the art of government. Until the end of the thirteenth century the prevailing political trend in the cities was toward republicanism and representative government.

Two city-state republics were of unusual interest. Venice controlled an empire of ports and islands in the eastern Mediterranean and carried much of Europe's maritime trade in its great fleets. The government of this rich republic had been in the hands of a doge (duke), together with a popular assembly, but beginning in the thirteenth century the rich merchants gradually took over the reins of power. They alone sat in the Great Council, which replaced the popular assembly. This oligarchic council appointed the doge and the members of smaller councils which administered the government. Most famous among the smaller councils was the secret Council of Ten, which dealt swiftly with suspected enemies of the government. The merchant oligarchy of Venice provided good government and, unlike other city-states, resolutely squashed internal strife.

Florence—the center of flourishing wool, leather, and silk industries—boasted merchants and bankers who were among the most prosperous in Europe, and its gold florin circulated in many lands as a standard coin. With its many checks and counterchecks of power, the Florentine constitution was bewilderingly complex. In theory Florence was a democracy but, as in Venice, real political power was wielded by wealthy businessmen.

During the fourteenth century republicanism declined and most Italian city-states came under the rule of despots. Conspiracy, confusion, and incompetence caused many citizens to welcome a strong leader as political boss or despot. Although Venice maintained the benevolent oligarchy of its merchants with the doge as a figurehead, Florence went under the thumb of the Medici family, and its republican institutions became largely empty forms.

The Papal States, extending from fifty miles south of the mouth of the Tiber to the northeast across Italy as far as the mouth of the Po River, were poorly organized. The popes found it difficult to force their will upon various petty despots who defied their political authority, and the long struggle between popes and emperors had lost the papacy much of its prestige. Men had seen popes using spiritual means to achieve earthly ambitions—preaching crusades against Frederick II and his descendants, for example. More and more, popes acted like Italian princes, playing the game of diplomacy amid shifting rivalries. This involvement in worldly concerns and the accompanying decay in ideals helps explain the revolt against papal authority—one of the themes of Chapter 9.

The Kingdom of Naples covered the southern half of the Italian peninsula as well as Sicily. After 1250 the kingdom was disputed between Spaniards from Aragon, who had married into the Hohenstaufen family, and Frenchmen representing Anjou. Impoverished by the warfare of foreign armies, with its powerful nobles rebellious, and with brigandage rampant, southern Italy and Sicily sank into a backwardness that was to continue into the twentieth century.

EASTERN EUROPE

Teutonic Knights, Poles, and Lithuanians. Since the early tenth century German barons and churchmen had been founding bishoprics and colonizing the land east of the Elbe. The German settlements, however, remained precariously isolated in the midst of large Slavic populations. Then, shortly after 1200, a new development occurred. The Teutonic Knights, a military-religious order founded at the time of the Third Crusade, transferred their operations from the Holy Land to eastern Europe. Within fifty years the Knights had conquered the pagan Slavs in Prussia, and by 1350 they ruled the Baltic coastlands as far north as the Gulf of Finland. Assuming the role of a colonial aristocracy, the Knights built castles and towns, and a steady stream of German settlers moved into the conquered lands.

To the south of Prussia lived the Slavic Poles. They were first united into a state late in the tenth century, but the Polish nobility seldom allowed their monarch to exercise much power. Also in the late tenth century the Poles were converted to Roman Christianity, thus linking Poland to western European culture.

The continued threat of the aggressive Teutonic Knights caused the Polish nobles in 1386 to offer the Polish crown to the king of the neighboring Lithuanians, a pagan people who had expanded into a Russia weakened and fragmented by the Mongol conquest (see p. 144). Converted to Latin Christianity, the Lithuanians joined with the Poles in defeating the Teutonic Knights in the great battle of Tannenberg in 1410. The Knights never regained their former power, and in 1466 they turned West Prussia over to the Poles, retaining East Prussia as a fief of the Polish crown (see map, p. 144). This settlement was a great blow to German expansion, for the Poles obtained control of the Vistula River and a corridor north to the Baltic Sea, including the important port of Danzig. East Prussia was now cut off from the rest of Germany. In the history of modern Europe, the Polish Corridor and Danzig have played an important role.

The Polish-Lithuanian state was the largest in Europe, but its promise was never realized. The nobility succeeded in keeping the monarchy elective and weak, and the middle class, composed largely of German settlers and Jewish refugees from persecution in western Europe, remained small and powerless. Above all, Poland faced the hostility of the ambitious tsars of Moscow who sought to rule over all Russians, including those in Poland-Lithuania.

Bohemians and Magyars. Two other peoples appeared in the east European family in the Middle Ages. During the ninth and tenth centuries the Slavic Czechs established a kingdom on the Bohemian plain. German influence became strong in Bohemia, which was a part of the Holy Roman Empire, and the Golden Bull of 1356 made the Bohemian king one of the seven imperial electors. Living southeast of Bohemia in the wide and fertile plain known as Hungary were the Magyars. Originally the terror of eastern Europe because of their brutal raids, they settled down and about 1000 their first king, St. Stephen, accepted Christianity and a golden crown from the pope. In Chapter 10 we shall see how these two emerging nations were acquired by the Hapsburgs in 1526 when the king of Hungary, who happened also to be king of Bohemia, met his death fighting the Turks.

The Mongol conquest of Russia. Toward the middle of the thirteenth century Europe was menaced by a new invasion of Asiatic nomads, the Mongols. Genghis Khan ("Universal Ruler") had united the unruly tribesmen of Mongolia and then launched them like a thunderbolt on a campaign of world conquest. By 1240 the Mongols, or Tatars, had conquered the various Russian principalities, and in 1242 they penetrated to the outskirts of Vienna. Western Europe seemed theirs for the taking, but the death of the great Khan in far-off Mongolia caused the Mongol

CENTRAL AND EASTERN
EUROPE 1526

Hungary

The fortunes of both Hungary and Bohemia shifted drastically in 1526 when their king was killed trying to hold back the tide of Turkish expansion. The Hungarians offered their throne to the Hapsburg ruler, who was able to claim only a small strip along the east, since the Turks had overrun the rest of the country.

armies to return to the lower Volga pending the election of a new khan. Central Europe was not molested again, but the Mongols continued to dominate Russia from their capital at Sarai on the Volga. The various Russian principalities were allowed to govern themselves as long as they paid tribute to the Golden Horde, as the Mongols in Russia were called.

Mongol domination completed the break between Russia and western European civilization initiated by the decline of Kiev (see p. 96). Asian cultural influences were strong—the status of women was lowered as they accepted the veil and oriental seclusion. Mongols and Russians intermarried freely; hence the saying, "Scratch a Russian and you will find a Tatar." Russia was cut off from Europe, and a new Russia north and east of Kiev began to develop. Its nucleus was the grand duchy of Moscow.

Moscow, challenge to Tatar rule. Well situated in the central river system of Russia and surrounded by protective forests and marshes, Moscow would eventually expel the Tatars from Russia. A major factor in the ascendency of Moscow was the cooperation of its rulers with their Mongol overlords, who granted them the title of Grand Prince of Russia and made them agents for collecting the Tatar tribute from the Russian principalities. Moscow's prestige was further enhanced when the metropolitan of Kiev, head of the Russian Orthodox Church, settled there soon after 1300.

By the middle of the fourteenth century the power of the Tatars was declining, and the Grand Princes felt capable of openly opposing the Mongol yoke. In 1380, at Kulikovo on the Don, the khan was defeated, and although this hard-fought victory did not end Tatar rule of Russia, it did bring great fame to the Grand Prince. Moscow's leadership in Russia was now firmly based, and by the middle of the fifteenth century its territory had greatly expanded through purchase, war, and marriage (see map).

Ivan the Great. The Muscovite prince who laid the foundations for a Russian national state was Ivan III, the Great (1462-1505), a contemporary of the Tudors and other "new monarchs" in western Europe. Ivan more than doubled his territories by placing most of north Russia under the rule of Moscow, and he proclaimed his absolute sovereignty over all Russian princes and nobles by taking the title of "Great Prince and Autocrat of All Russia." Refusing further tribute to the Tatars, Ivan initiated a series of attacks that opened the way for the complete defeat of the declining Golden Horde, now divided into several khanates.

Ivan married the niece of the last Byzantine emperor, and she brought with her to Moscow a number of gifted Italians. Among them were architects who designed an enormous walled palace complex called the Kremlin. Ivan not only adopted the double-headed eagle and court ceremonies of the Byzantine emperors but also claimed to be their legitimate successor. Thus Ivan sometimes used the title of *tsar*, derived from "Caesar," and he viewed Moscow as the Third Rome, the successor of New Rome (Constantinople).

The doctrine that the Russian tsar was the successor of the Byzantine emperors was expressed by the monk Philotheos of Pskov late in the fifteenth century. "Two Romes have fallen," he wrote, "and the third stands, and a fourth one there shall not be." On the basis of the conviction that they were heirs of the Byzantine tradition, Russian rulers were later to press claims to the Dardanelles and parts of southeastern Europe. Moreover, as in the idea expressed by Philotheos when he said, "you are the only tsar for Christians in the whole world,"[3] the Russian tradition would henceforth encompass a great imperial mission.

Ivan the Terrible. The next great ruler of Moscow was Ivan III's grandson, Ivan IV (1547-1584), called "the Terrible." Russia became more despotic as Ivan ruthlessly subordinated the great nobles to his will, exiling or executing many on the slightest pretext. With no consideration for human life, Ivan ordered the destruction of Novgorod, Russia's second city, on suspicion of treason. Another time, in a rage, he struck and killed his gifted eldest son. Yet Ivan was also a farseeing statesman who promulgated a new code of laws and established a representative assembly of nobles, clergy and townsmen called the *zemskii sobor.* He also built the fabulous St. Basil's Cathedral that still stands in Moscow's Red Square.

During Ivan's reign eastern Russia was conquered from the Tatars, and Cossack pioneers then crossed the Ural Mountains in their push to the Pacific—a movement which can be compared with the simultaneous expansion of western Europe across the Atlantic. Ivan's efforts to reach the Baltic and establish trade relations with western Europe were forcibly stopped by Sweden and Poland. Later, however, he was able to inaugurate direct trade with the West by granting English merchants trading privileges at the White Sea port of Archangel (Arkhangelsk) in the far north.

Ivan's death in 1584 was followed by the Time of Troubles, a period of civil wars over the succession and resurgence of the power of the nobility. Both Poland and Sweden intervened in Russian affairs, and their invasions across an indistinct frontier which contains no major natural barriers demonstrated again the danger from the West and contributed to Russia's growing tendency to withdraw into her own distinctive heritage. Order was restored in 1613 when Michael Romanov, the grandnephew of Ivan the Terrible, was elected to the throne by the *zemskii sobor.* Although the *zemskii sobor* never became a true parliament but faded out of existence during the seventeenth century, the Romanov dynasty continued to rule Russia until 1917.

CHAPTER 7
TO THE GLORY OF GOD

Faith, Thought, and Art in Medieval Europe (400-1300)

In Paris, on a small island in the Seine, stands an edifice of weather-beaten stone, the Cathedral of Notre Dame. Dedicated to the glory of God and the veneration of Our Lady, this cathedral offers a fascinating glimpse into the life and spirit of medieval Europe. Notre Dame de Paris was built by cooperative community action between 1163 and 1235, during the epoch-making years of the High Middle Ages. While workmen were supporting the cathedral's vault with flying buttresses and carefully fitting the multicolored windows into place, churchmen and students lolled on the Petit Pont, a bridge that led to the Left Bank. The students wrangled over theology, accused one another of heresy, and occasionally composed blasphemous poems that parodied the sacred liturgy.

The underlying difference between our medieval ancestors and ourselves would appear to be one of perspective. To them theology was the "science of sciences," whereas today there are those who say that we have made science our theology. Yet this difference is not due exclusively to the extension of knowledge during the intervening centuries. It also lies in the fundamental premise governing the lives of our medieval forefathers. They believed in world order, divinely created and maintained. For them, the universe possessed an inner coherence and harmony, which it was the function of the theologian and the scientist alike to discover. Revelation and knowledge, faith and reason, Church and state, spirit and matter—these dualities could be reconciled in a great spiritual and social synthesis.

In this chapter we will examine the methods by which medieval men sought to realize this synthesis and the measure of their success. As a first step, we shall trace the institutional growth of the one universal organization of medieval Europe, the Church. Next we shall watch its progressive assumption of secular powers, culminating in the triumphs of Pope Innocent III. Finally, we shall see how, under the sponsorship of the Church, scholars and philosophers, scientists and inventors, and artists and artisans labored for the glory of God and the salvation of man.

Gregory the Great and the early medieval papacy. While Europe gradually recovered from the shock of the Roman Empire's demise, the Church—the papacy and Benedictine monasticism in particular—became the mainstay of European civilization. During the pontificate of Gregory I, the Great (590-604), the medieval papacy began to take form. Gregory's achievement was to go beyond the claim of papal primacy in the Church (see p. 78) to establish the actual machinery of papal rule, temporal as well as spiritual.

A Roman aristocrat by birth, Gregory witnessed and commented on the devastation of Rome as the city changed hands three times during Justinian's long struggle to retake Italy from the Ostrogoths:

> Ruins on ruins. . . . Where is the senate? Where the people? All the pomp of secular dignities has been destroyed. . . . And we, the few that we are who remain, every day we are menaced by scourges and innumerable trials.[1]

Concluding that the world was coming to an end, Gregory withdrew from it to become a Benedictine monk. In 579 the pope drafted him to undertake a fruitless mission seeking Byzantine aid against the Lombards, who had invaded Italy a few years before. After the people of Rome elected Gregory pope in 590, he assumed the task of protecting Rome and its surrounding territory from the Lombard threat. Thus Gregory was the first pope to act as temporal ruler of a part of what later became the Papal States.

Gregory the Great also laid the foundations for the later elaborate papal machinery of Church government. He took the first step toward papal control of the Church outside of Italy by sending a mission of Benedictine monks to convert the heathen Anglo-Saxons. The pattern of Church government Gregory established in England—bishops supervised by archbishops, and archbishops by the pope—became standard in the Church.

Gregory's work was continued by his successors. In the eighth century English missionaries transferred to Germany and France the pattern of papal government they had known in England; and the Donation of Pepin (see p. 107), by creating the Papal States, greatly increased the pope's temporal power. The papacy's spiritual and temporal power suffered a severe setback, however, with the onset of feudalism. Beginning in the late ninth century, the Church, including the papacy, fell more and more under the under the control of feudal lords and kings.

Missionary activity. Long before Gregory the Great missionaries had been proselytizing in Germany and Ireland. By disseminating Christianity, the missionaries aided in the fusion of Germanic and classical cultures. And in an age of feeble or nonexistent secular government, monasteries took over much of the burden of caring for society. They provided the only schools and hospitals, and they served as havens for those seeking a contemplative life, as repositories of learning, and as progressive farming centers.

The earliest Christian missionary to the Germans was Ulfilas (c. 311-383), who left Constantinople to spend forty years among the Visigoths, where he translated most of the Bible into Gothic. Ulfilas was a follower of Arius, and thus the heretical creed of Arianism (see p. 78) came to be adopted by all the Germanic tribes in the Empire except the Franks and Anglo-Saxons.

Another great missionary, St. Patrick, was born in Britain about 389 and later fled to Ireland to escape the Anglo-Saxon invaders. Monasteries were founded in Ireland and Christianity became dominant. Irish monks eagerly pursued scholarship, and their monasteries were repositories for priceless manuscripts. From these monasteries in the late sixth and seventh centuries a stream of missionaries went to Scotland, northern England, the kingdom of the Franks, and even to Italy.

Beginning with the pontificate of Gregory the Great, the papacy joined forces with Benedictine monasticism to become very active in the missionary movement. Gregory, as we saw, sent a Benedictine mission to England in 596. Starting in Kent, where an archbishopric was founded at Canterbury, Roman Christianity spread through England, and finally even the Irish Church founded by St. Patrick acknowledged the primacy of Rome.

The English Church in turn significantly widened the area of papal control over Christianity on the Continent. St. Boniface, England's greatest missionary, in the eighth century spent thirty-five years among the Germans. He established several important monasteries, bishoprics, and an archbishopric at Mainz before he turned to the task of reforming the Church in France. There he revitalized the monasteries and organized a system of local parishes to bring Christianity to the countryside.

The monks as custodians of knowledge. One of the great contributions of the monasteries was the preservation of learning. The man who first inspired the monks to assume this task was Cassiodorus, a sixth-century scholar and administrator under Theodoric, the Ostrogothic king of Italy. Cassiodorus founded two monasteries and instructed the monks to collect and copy classical manuscripts. Following this example, many monasteries established scriptoria, departments concerned exclusively with this task of preserving classical knowledge.

Boethius, a contemporary of Cassiodorus who also served Theodoric, noting that the ability to read Greek was fast disappearing in western Europe, determined to preserve Greek learning by translating all of Plato and Aristotle into Latin. Only Aristotle's treatises on logic were translated, and these remained the sole works of that philosopher available in the West until the twelfth century. Unjustly accused of treachery by Theodoric, Boethius was thrown into prison, where he wrote *The Consolation of Philosophy* while awaiting execution. This little classic later became a medieval textbook on philosophy.

During the Early Middle Ages most education took place in the monasteries, and it was the Irish monasteries that took the early lead in providing a safe haven for learning. There men studied Greek and Latin, copied and preserved manuscripts, and in illuminating them produced masterpieces of art. The outstanding scholar of the Early Middle Ages, the Venerable Bede (d. 735), followed the Irish tradition of learning in a monastery in northern England. Bede's many writings, which included textbooks and commentaries on the Scriptures, summed up much of the knowledge available in his age.

THE CHURCH MILITANT AND TRIUMPHANT

Church and state. Medieval political theory begins with the concept of a universal community divided into two spheres, the spiritual and the temporal—a view based upon Christ's injunction to "Render therefore to Caesar the things that are Caesar's, and to God the things that are God's" (Matthew 22:21). As Pope Gelasius I declared in the fifth century, God had entrusted spiritual and temporal powers to two authorities—the Church and the state—each supreme in its own sphere. At first the question of ultimate superiority between these authorities did not arise, although Gelasius had implied that the Church was superior to the state in the same way that the soul was superior to the body. The issue could not be permanently shelved, however; a fight for supremacy was in the long run inevitable.

When the German king Otto the Great revived the Roman empire in the West in 962 (see p. 138), his act reemphasized the concept of the dual leadership of pope and emperor. Otto claimed to be the successor of Charlemagne, although his actual power was confined to Germany and Italy. At first the popes looked to the German king for protection against the unruly Italian nobles who for a century had been making a prize of the papacy. This arrangement had its drawbacks, however, for the German kings continued to interfere in ecclesiastical affairs— even in the election of popes.

By the eleventh century secular interference in the election of Church officials had become a problem—the problem of lay investiture. Theoretically, on assuming office a bishop or abbot was subject to two investitures; his spiritual authority was bestowed by an ecclesiastical official and his feudal or civil authority by the king or a noble. In actual fact, however, feudal lords and kings came to control both the appointment and the installation of church prelates. As noted earlier (p. 138), this practice was most pronounced in Germany, where control of the Church was the foundation of the king's power. The German Church was in essence a state Church.

Cluniac reform. A religious revival—often called the medieval reformation— was well underway in the eleventh century at the beginning of the High Middle Ages. The first far-reaching force of the revival was the reformed Benedictine order of Cluny, founded in Burgundy. The Cluniac program began as a movement for a stricter monastic life, but by the eleventh century a more radical element in the movement was seeking to free the entire Church from secular control and subject it to papal authority. All Cluniac monasteries were freed from lay control, and in 1059 the papacy itself was removed from secular interference by the creation of the College of Cardinals, which henceforth elected the popes.

The most ambitious proponent of Church reform was Pope Gregory VII (1073-1085), who claimed unprecedented power for the papacy. Gregory held as his ideal the creation of a Christian commonwealth under papal control. Instead of conceding equality between the Church and the state, he claimed that the papal authority was supreme over that of lay rulers; in Gregory's own words, "the Roman pontiff alone can with right be called universal."

The Investiture Struggle. In 1075 Gregory VII formally prohibited lay investitures and threatened to excommunicate any layman who performed it and any ecclesiastic who submitted to it. This drastic act virtually declared war against Europe's rulers, since most of them practiced lay investiture. The climax to the struggle occurred in Gregory's clash with the emperor Henry IV. The latter was accused of simony (the purchase or sale of a Church office) and lay investiture in appointing his own choice to the archbishopric of Milan. Henry's answer was to convene a synod of German bishops which declared Gregory unfit to occupy the Roman See:

Wherefore henceforth we renounce, now and for the future, all obedience unto thee—which indeed we never promised to thee. And since, as thou didst publicly proclaim, none of us has been to thee a bishop, so thou henceforth wilt be Pope to none of us.[2]

In retaliation Gregory excommunicated Henry and deposed him, absolving his subjects from their oaths of allegiance.

At last, driven to make peace with the pontiff by a revolt among the German nobles, Henry appeared before Gregory in January 1077 at Canossa, a castle in the Apennines. Garbed as a penitent, the emperor is said to have stood barefoot in the snow for three days before the pope exercised his priestly duty to forgive a repentant sinner.

This dramatic humiliation of the emperor did not resolve the quarrel, nor do contemporary accounts attach much significance to the incident—public penance was not uncommon in those days even for kings. Yet the pope had made progress toward freeing the Church from interference by laymen and toward increasing the power and prestige of the papacy. The problem of lay investiture was settled in 1122 by the compromise known as the Concordat of Worms. The Church maintained the right to elect the holder of an ecclesiastical office, but only in the presence of the king or his representative. The candidate, such as a bishop or an abbot, was invested by the king with the scepter, the symbol of his administrative jurisdiction, after which he performed the act of homage and swore allegiance as the king's vassal. Only after this ceremony had taken place was the candidate consecrated by the archbishop, who invested him with the symbols of his spiritual functions. Since the kings of England and France had earlier accepted this compromise, the problem of lay investiture waned. The struggle between popes and emperors continued for more than a century, however, sparked by the papacy's resentment at the emperors' continued interference in Italian affairs (see Chapter 6).

In the meantime not only had progress been made toward freeing the Church from interference by laymen, but the moral authority of the emperor as the leader of Christendom—an ideal first expressed by Charlemagne—had been irreparably damaged. During the course of the Investiture Struggle the papalists had propounded the theory that royal power was not of divine origin and that the temporal power of lay rulers was subordinate to the spiritual authority of the papacy. The fact that the pope had indeed become the effective leader of Christendom both temporally and spiritually was to be demonstrated a few years after Gregory VII's death by the First Crusade and was to be confirmed a century later by the pontificate of Innocent III.

The crusades: "God wills it!"   During the eleventh century the Seljuk Turks, new and fanatical converts to Islam from central Asia, seized Jerusalem from their fellow Muslims and most of Asia Minor from the Byzantine empire. When Pope Urban II in 1095 responded to the Byzantine emperor's appeal for aid by summoning the European nobility to take up the cross and reconquer the Holy Land, he was assuming a duty first announced by Charlemagne: "to defend the holy Church of Christ with arms against the attack of pagans and devastation by infidels from without." The response of the feudal nobility—"God wills it!"—to Urban's proclamation of the First Crusade dramatically acknowledged the fact that the pope had replaced the emperor as the temporal leader of the Christian people. No one challenged Urban's right to lead the crusading army, delegating a papal legate to command it in the field.

From the end of the eleventh century to the end of the thirteenth, there were seven major crusades, as well as various small expeditions which from time to time tried their hands against the infidel. The First Crusade was the most successful of the seven; with not more than five thousand knights and infantry, it conquered Jerusalem and a long strip of territory along the eastern coast of the Mediterranean. The conquests were organized according to feudal principles into four states, with the kingdom of Jerusalem dominant. To protect these crusader states, new semi-monastic military orders were created: the Templars, or Knights of the Temple, so called because their first headquarters was on the site of the old Temple of Jerusalem; the Hospitalers, or Knights of St. John of Jerusalem, who were founded originally to care for the sick and wounded; and the Teutonic Knights, exclusively a German order.

When the kingdom of Jerusalem became endangered in 1147, the Second Crusade met with disaster when its forces were routed at Damascus. The fall of Jerusalem in 1187 to the Muslims, reinvigorated under the leadership of Saladin, the sultan of Egypt and Syria, served to provoke the Third Crusade (1189). Its leaders were three of the most famous medieval kings—Frederick Barbarossa of Germany, Richard the Lion-Hearted of England, and Philip Augustus of France. Frederick was drowned in Asia Minor; and, after many quarrels with Richard, Philip returned home. To keep the Muslims united against Richard, Saladin proclaimed a holy war, but he remained a patient statesman and chivalrous warrior. "Abstain from the shedding of blood," he once said, "for blood that is spilt never slumbers."[3] Richard and Saladin finally agreed to a three-year truce and free access to Jerusalem for Christian pilgrims.

The Fourth Crusade (1202-1204) is an example of the degradation of a religious ideal. The few knights who answered Pope Innocent III's call were unable to meet the outrageous shipping charges demanded by the Venetians, who persuaded them to pay off the sum by capturing the Christian town of Zara, a Venetian trading rival on the Adriatic coast. Then, in order to absorb all Byzantine commerce, the Venetians pressured the crusaders into attacking Constantinople. After conquering and sacking the greatest city in Europe, the crusaders set up the Latin empire of Constantinople, which included Greece and other Byzantine territory in Europe, and forgot about recovering the Holy Land. The Byzantine empire never recovered from this mortal blow.

The thirteenth century saw other crusades. The youngsters of the ill-fated Children's Crusade in 1212 hoped to succeed where their fathers had failed. They fully expected the waters of the Mediterranean to part and make a path to the Holy Land, which they would take without fighting, but they never got beyond Marseilles where thousands of them were tricked and sold into slavery by a merchant named William the Pig. The Fifth Crusade in 1219 failed in its attack on Egypt, the center of Muslim power in the Near East. The unique Sixth Crusade in 1228 was organized and led by the excommunicated enemy of the pope, the emperor Frederick II, who by skillful diplomacy succeeded in acquiring Jerusalem, Bethlehem, and Nazareth from the sultan of Egypt without striking a blow. This arrangement ended in 1244 with the Muslim reconquest of the Holy City. The loss inspired the saintly Louis IX of France to organize the Seventh Crusade in 1248, but despite his zeal it ended in a fiasco when Louis was captured in Egypt and forced to pay an enormous ransom. This was the last major attempt to regain Jerusalem, and the era of the crusades ended in 1291 when Acre, the last stronghold of the Christians in the Holy Land, fell to the Muslims.

Even though the crusades failed to achieve their specific objective permanently, they cannot entirely be written off as mere adventures. The contact with the East widened the scope of the Europeans, ended their isolation, and exposed them to a vastly superior civilization. Although it is easy to exaggerate the economic effects of the crusades, they did complete the reopening of the eastern Mediterranean to western commerce, which in turn stimulated the rise of cities and the emergence of a money economy in the West. The crusades as a movement were a manifestation of the dynamic vitality and expansive spirit of Europe, evident in many fields by the end of the eleventh century.

The papacy's zenith: Innocent III.   As demonstrated by Urban II's leadership of the First Crusade, the papacy emerged from the Investiture Struggle as the most powerful office in Europe. A century later the zenith of papal power was reached under Innocent III (1198-1216), a new type of administrator-pope. Unlike Gregory VII and other earlier reform popes, who were monks, Innocent and other great popes of the later twelfth and thirteenth centuries were trained as canon lawyers.

Innocent III told the princes of Europe that the papacy was as the sun, whereas the kings were as the moon. As the moon derives its light from the sun, so the kings derived their powers from the pope. So successful was the pontiff in asserting his temporal as well as spiritual supremacy that many states, both large and small, formally acknowledged vassalage to the pope. In the case of King John of England, a struggle developed over the election of the archbishop of Canterbury, and Innocent placed England under interdict and excommunicated John. Under attack from his barons, John capitulated to Innocent by becoming his vassal, receiving England back as a fief, and paying him an annual monetary tribute. Innocent forced Philip Augustus of France to comply with the Church's moral code by taking back as his queen the woman he had divorced with the consent of the French bishops. As for the Holy Roman Empire, Innocent intervened in a civil war between rival candidates for the throne, supporting first one, then the other. In the end Innocent secured the election of his ward, the young Hohenstaufen heir Frederick II, who promised to respect papal rights and to go on a crusade.

Within the Church itself, nothing better illustrates the power of the papal monarchy under Innocent III than the Fourth Lateran Council, which he called in 1215 to confirm his acts and policies. More than four hundred bishops, some eight hundred abbots and priors, and representatives of all leading secular rulers answered Innocent's call. The Council dealt with a wide range of subjects; for example, it outlawed trial by ordeal, required Jews to wear distinctive yellow badges, declared clergymen exempt from state taxation, and formally defined the Christian sacraments, setting their number at seven: baptism, confirmation, matrimony, holy orders, penance, extreme unction, and the Eucharist or Lord's Supper. The significance of the Eucharist can be fully appreciated only when the doctrine of transubstantiation is understood. According to this doctrine—a subject of dispute until formally defined by the Fourth Lateran Council—when the priest performing the mass pronounces over the bread and wine the words Christ used at the Last Supper, "This is My Body. . . . This is the chalice of My Blood . . . ," a miracle takes place. To all outward appearances, the bread and wine remain unchanged, but in "substance" they have been transformed into the very body and blood of the Savior.

Church administration. The universality and power of the Church rested not only upon a systematized, uniform creed but also upon the most highly organized administrative system in the West. At the head was the pope, or bishop of Rome. He was assisted by the Curia, the papal council or court, which in the twelfth and thirteenth centuries developed an intricate administrative system. Judicial and secretarial problems were handled by the papal Chancery, financial matters by the Camera, and disciplinary questions by the Penitentiary. Special emissaries called legates, whose powers were superior to those of local prelates, carried the pope's orders throughout Europe.

The Church was ahead of secular states in developing a system of courts and a body of law. Church or canon law was based on the Scriptures, the writings of the Church Fathers, and the decrees of Church councils and popes. In the twelfth century the Church issued its official body of canon law, which guided the Church courts in judging perjury, blasphemy, sorcery, usury (the medieval Church denounced the taking of interest), and heresy. Heresy was the most horrible of all crimes in medieval eyes. A murder was a crime against society, but the heretic's disbelief in the teachings of Christ or His Church was considered a crime against God Himself.

The papacy's chief weapons in support of its authority were spiritual penalties. The most powerful of these was excommunication, by which people became anathema, "set apart" from the Church and all the faithful. "They could not act as judge, juror, notary, witness, or attorney. They could not be guardians, executors, or parties to contracts. After death, they received no Christian burial, and if, by chance, they were buried in consecrated ground, their bodies were to be

At the bottom of this detail of the "Last Judgment" scene at Autun Cathedral the dead rise from their graves in fear; at the top their souls are weighed in the balance. While the saved cling to the angels, the damned are seized by grinning devils and thrown into hell.

disinterred and cast away. If they entered a church during Mass, they were to be expelled, or the Mass discontinued. After the reading of a sentence of excommunication, a bell was rung as for a funeral, a book closed, and a candle extinguished, to symbolize the cutting off of the guilty man."[3]

Interdict, which has been termed "an ecclesiastical lockout," was likewise a powerful instrument. Whereas excommunication was directed against individuals, interdict suspended all public worship and withheld all sacraments other than Baptism and Extreme Unction in the realm of a disobedient ruler. Pope Innocent III successfully applied or threatened the interdict eighty-five times against refractory princes.

THE MEDIEVAL REFORMATION

Reform and heresy. From the reign of Innocent III until the end of the thirteenth century, the Church radiated power and splendor. It possessed perhaps one third of the land of Europe, and all secular rulers and Church prelates acknowledged the power of Christ's vicar who, as Innocent III claimed, could and did "judge all and be judged by no one." Yet while the Church's wealth enabled it to perform educational and charitable functions that the states were too poor and weak to provide, this wealth also encouraged abuses and worldliness among the clergy. Cracks were appearing in the foundation even while the medieval religious structure received its final embellishments. Weaknesses were evident in the demand for internal reform and in the growth of heresy.

The medieval reformation gained momentum late in the eleventh century with a second movement of monastic reform brought on by the failure of the Cluniac reform to end laxity in monastic life. Among the new orders were the severely ascetic and hermit-like Carthusians and the very popular Cistercians. The latter received their greatest impetus from the zealous efforts of St. Bernard of Clairvaux in the twelfth century. Cistercian abbeys were situated in solitary places, and their strict discipline emphasized fasts and vigils, manual labor, and a vegetarian diet. Their churches contained neither stained glass nor statues, and the puritanical Bernard denounced the beautification of churches in general: "Oh! vanity of vanities! . . . What has all this imagery to do with monks, with professors of poverty, with men of spiritual minds?"[4]

Spurred on by this militant denouncer of wealth and luxury in any form, the Cistercian order had founded 343 abbeys in western Europe by the time of St. Bernard's death in 1153 and more than double that number by the end of the century. Yet in one important sense these austere new monastic orders were failures. Being exclusively agricultural and dwelling apart from society, these orders were unfitted to cope with religious discontent in the towns.

Heresy flourished particularly in the towns, where an increasing consciousness of sin and a demand for greater piety went largely unheeded by old-style churchmen. This fertile ground produced many heresies, among which the Albigensian and Waldensian were major ones.

Harking back to an early Christian heresy, the Cathari ("Pure") or Albigensians—so called because Albi in southern France was an important center—went to extremes in thinking of the world as the battleground of the opposing forces of good and evil. The Albigensians condemned many activities of the state and the individual, even condemning marriage for perpetuating the human species in this sinful world.

The Waldensians derived their name from Peter Waldo, a merchant of Lyons who gave his wealth to charity and founded a lay order, the Poor Men of Lyons, to serve the needs of the people. He had parts of the New Testament translated into French, held that laymen could preach the Gospel, and denied the efficacy of the sacraments unless administered by worthy priests. Because the Waldensian church still exists today in northern Italy, it has been called the oldest Protestant sect.

For ten years Innocent III tried to reconvert these heretical groups. Failing, in 1208 he instigated a crusade against the prosperous and cultured French region of Toulouse, where the Albigensian heresy was widespread. The crusade began with horrible slaughter to the cry of "Kill them all, God will know His own." Soon the original religious motive was lost in a selfish rush to seize the wealth of the accused. In time the Albigensian heresy was destroyed, along with the flourishing culture of southern France, and the Waldensians were scattered.

In 1233 a special papal court called the Inquisition was established to cope with the rising tide of heresy. The accused was tried in secret without the aid of legal counsel. If he confessed and renounced his heresy, he was "reconciled" with the Church on performance of penance. If he did not voluntarily confess, he could be tortured. If this failed, the prisoner could be declared a heretic and turned over to the secular authorities, usually to be burned at the stake. Until the Protestant Reformation of the sixteenth century, the Church was generally successful in its efforts to crush heresy.

The Franciscans and Dominicans. As a more positive response to the spread of heresy and the conditions which spawned it, Innocent III approved the founding of the Franciscan and Dominican orders of friars ("brothers"). Instead of living a sequestered existence in a remote monastery, the friars moved among their brother men, ministering to their needs and preaching the Gospel.

The Franciscans were founded by St. Francis of Assisi (1182?-1226), who rejected his father's riches and spread the gospel of poverty and Christian simplicity. Love of one's fellow men and all God's creatures, even "brother worm," were basic in the Rule of St. Francis, which was inspired by Jesus' instructions to his disciples

> to preach the Kingdom of God and to heal the sick. He said to them: "Take nothing with you for your trip: no walking stick, no beggar's bag, no food, no money, not even an extra shirt. . . . " The disciples left and traveled through all the villages, preaching the Good News and healing people everywhere.[5]

The second order of friars was founded by St. Dominic (1170-1221), a well-educated Spaniard whose early career had been spent fighting the Albigensian heresy in southern France. There he decided that to combat the strength and zeal of its opponents, the Church should have champions who could preach the Gospel with apostolic fervor. Dominic's order of friar-preachers dedicated themselves to preaching as a means of maintaining the doctrines of the Church and of converting heretics.

The enthusiasm and sincerity of the friars in their early years made a profound impact upon an age which had grown increasingly critical of ecclesiastical worldliness. But after they took charge of the Inquisition, became professors in

The simple piety preached by St. Francis is reflected in this altarpiece, painted only nine years after his death, which shows the characteristically austere saint surrounded by six scenes from his life. The marks on St. Francis' hands and feet are stigmata—symbolic wounds representing his identification with Christ—which he received after a period of prayer and meditation.

the universities, and served the papacy in other ways, the friars lost much of their original simplicity and freshness. Yet their message and zeal had done much to provide the Church with moral and intellectual leadership at a time when such leadership was badly needed.

THE INTELLECTUAL SYNTHESIS

The medieval renaissance. "The meeting of Roman decrepitude and German immaturity was not felicitous."[6] This concise characterization of early medieval civilization is especially relevant to the intellectual side of the period, and it remains a moot question among modern scholars whether the seventh century or the tenth was "the darkest of the Dark Ages." By the close of the sixth century even the most influential of early medieval popes, Gregory the Great, was contributing to the growing intellectual murkiness by voicing strong disapproval of secular literature, insisting that "the same mouth cannot sing the praises of Jupiter and praises of Christ." So feeble had the light of learning become by the end of the eighth century that Charlemagne found it necessary to order the monasteries to revive their schools and resume instruction in the rudiments of "singing, arithmetic, and grammar" (see p. 109).

In sharp contrast to the fate of his political achievements, Charlemagne's modest educational revival survived his death. At least partly as a result of this stimulus, western Europe by the late eleventh century was on the threshold of one of the most productive and energetic periods in the history of western thought—the medieval renaissance.

What was revived first of all during the medieval renaissance was intellectual curiosity, plainly evident from contemporary accounts, such as the following concerning an eleventh-century scholar from Liège:

> Olbert was not able to satiate his thirst for study. When he would hear of some one distinguished in the arts he flew there at once, and the more he thirsted the more he absorbed something delightful from each master. At Paris he worked at Saint-Germain and studied the Holy Faith which glowed there. In Troyes he studied for three years, learning gratefully many things. . . . He felt obliged to listen to Fulbert of Chartres who was proclaimed in the liberal arts throughout France. Afterwards just like the bees among flowers, gorged with the nectar of learning, he returned to the hive and lived there studiously in a religious way, and religiously in a studious manner.[7]

Scholasticism. Living "religiously in a studious manner" aptly characterizes the scholars of the medieval renaissance and points up an essential difference between medieval thought on the one hand and early Greek philosophy and modern scientific thought on the other. With but few exceptions, medieval man did not think of truth as something to be discovered by himself; rather, he saw it as already existing in the authoritative Christian and pagan writings handed down from antiquity. Spurred on by a new zest for employing reason (called logic or dialectic), medieval scholars of the twelfth and thirteenth centuries succeeded in understanding and reexpressing those elements in the Christian and pagan heritage that seemed significant to them. Since this task was carried out largely in the schools, these scholars are known as schoolmen—or scholastics—and the intellectual synthesis they produced is called scholasticism.

Each scholar formed his own judgments and earnestly sought to convince others. This led to much debate, often uncritical but always exuberant, on a wide range of subjects. Most famous was the argument over universals known as the nominalist-realist controversy. To the realists, who derived their views from Plato, only universal Ideas could be real and exist independently. To the nominalists, who were inspired by Aristotle, abstract concepts such as universal Ideas were only names (*nomina*) and had no real existence. Both realism and nominalism, when carried to their logical extremes, resulted in conclusions abhorrent to the Church. Realism became pantheism (the universe as a whole is God), and nominalism became materialism (the universe is composed solely of matter).

The contribution of Abélard. The extreme views of nominalists and realists, along with other examples of the sterile use of logic ("whether the pig is led to the market by the rope or by the driver"), outraged a brilliant young student named

Pierre Abélard (1079-1142), later a popular teacher at the cathedral school of Notre Dame in Paris. Like many bright students in all ages, Abélard succeeded in antagonizing his teachers, both realist and nominalist. "I brought him great grief," he wrote of one, "because I undertook to refute certain of his opinions."

Abélard's great contribution to medieval thought was freeing logic from barrenness and rerouting it to become a means to an end rather than an end in itself. Like others before him, Abélard emphasized the importance of understanding, but whereas the former had begun with faith, Abélard started with doubt. We must learn to doubt, he insisted, for doubting leads us to inquire, and inquiry leads us to the truth. Abélard's intellectual skepticism was not that of modern experimental science, however; he never transcended superimposed authority. He aimed to arouse intellectual curiosity in his students and turn it into useful channels, bringing reason to bear on inherited truths in order to achieve understanding.

In an epoch-making work, *Sic et Non (Yes and No)*, Abélard demonstrated his method. Listing 158 propositions on theology and ethics, he appended to each a number of statements pro and con taken from the authoritative writings of the Church. Abélard did not go on to reconcile these apparent contradictions, but he urged his students to do so by rational interpretation. Thus Abélard perfected the scholastic method of thinking which was used by his successors to assimilate and reexpress the pagan as well as the Christian heritage of the past. The resulting scholarly compilations constitute the crowning achievement of the medieval intellectual synthesis.

Abélard is remembered as a great lover as well as a great scholar—a rather uncommon combination. His ill-starred romance with his pupil, the learned and beautiful Héloïse, niece of the canon of Notre Dame, cut short his promising career as a teacher. The two lovers were married in secret, but Héloïse's uncle, falsely believing that Abélard planned to abandon Héloïse, hired thugs who attacked and emasculated the scholar. Both Abélard and Héloïse then sought refuge in the Church—Pierre as a monk and Héloïse as the abbess of a nunnery.

Reconciling classic and Christian thought. In the later twelfth and early thirteenth centuries the intellectual hunger of western scholars for more ancient Greek science and philosophy—but not Greek literature, which they were not yet ready to appreciate—led them to Muslim Spain. Thus western knowledge was expanded to include Muslim learning and such important classical works as Euclid's *Geometry*, Ptolemy's *Almagest*, Hippocrates' and Galen's treatises in medicine, and most of Aristotle's extant writings.

As his works became known, Aristotle became, in Dante's words, "the master of those who know," and his authority was generally accepted as second only to that of the Scriptures. But because the Church's teachings were considered infallible, Aristotle's ideas, as well as those of other great thinkers of antiquity, had to be reconciled with religious dogma. Using Abélard's methodology, the scholastic thinkers of the thirteenth century succeeded in this task of reconciliation.

Scholasticism reached its zenith with St. Thomas Aquinas (1225?-1274). In his *Summa Theologica* this brilliant Italian Dominican dealt exhaustively with the great problems of theology, philosophy, politics, and economics. After collecting the arguments pro and con on a given problem—for example, "Whether it is lawful to sell a thing for more than its worth?"—he went on to draw conclusions. (His answer to the problem cited reflects the great influence of Christian ethics upon medieval economic thought: "I answer that, it is altogether sinful to have recourse to deceit in order to sell a thing for more than its just price, because this is to deceive one's neighbour so as to injure him."[8])

St. Thomas' major concern was to reconcile Aristotle and Church dogma—in other words, the truths of human reason and the truths of faith. There can be no real contradiction, he argued, since all truth comes from God. In case of an unresolved contradiction, however, faith won out, because of the possibility of human error in reasoning. St. Thomas was so convincing in settling this conflict—the first clash between science and religion in the history of our western civilization—that his philosophy still has its followers today.

The decline of scholasticism. Having reached its zenith, scholasticism declined rapidly. The assumption that faith and reason were compatible was vigorously denied by two Franciscan thinkers, Duns Scotus (d. 1308) and William of Occam (d. c. 1349), who elaborated on Aquinas' belief that certain religious doctrines are beyond discovery by the use of reason. They argued that if the human intellect could not understand divinely revealed truth, it could hope to comprehend only the natural world and should not intrude upon the sphere of divine truth. Such a position tended to undermine the Thomistic synthesis of faith and reason. Realism and nominalism revived, the one promoting an increase in mystical, nonrational religion, the other contributing to the growing scientific spirit and to individualism and wordly concerns in general. For better or for worse, this trend toward the emancipation of human knowledge and action from the unifying authority of religion and the Church became a characteristic feature of western civilization.

After the thirteenth century scholasticism increasingly became a term of reproach, for its adherents were obsessed with theological subtleties, discouraged independent thought, and in general lost touch with reality. But it should be remembered that the scholastics sought to appropriate and make subjectively their own the store of Christian and pagan knowledge left to them by a more advanced civilization. In terms of their needs and objectives—an intelligible and all-embracing synthesis of faith, logic, and science—the scholastics were eminently successful, and people of our own age should not look askance at their accomplishments. Ironically, we today increasingly recognize the importance of reconciling science and faith in an age which has so much of the former and so little of the latter.

Medieval science. Because of the emphasis upon authority and the all-pervasive influence of the Church, the medieval atmosphere was not conducive to free scientific investigation. Those who studied science were churchmen, and their findings were supposed to illuminate rather than contradict the dogmas of the theologians. During the Early Middle Ages scientific knowledge was limited to such compilations as the *Etymologies* of Isidore, bishop of Seville. Written in the seventh century, this naive and uncritical scrapbook of information remained a standard reference work in the West for three centuries. Isidore believed that the real nature of a thing was to be found in its name, and so he usually introduced each item with an often fanciful etymological explanation:

> The liver [*iecur* in Latin] has its name because there is resident the fire [*ignis*] which flies up into the brain. . . . and by its heat it changes into blood the liquid that it has drawn from food, and this blood it supplies to the several members to feed and nourish them.[9]

The *Etymologies* has been called "the fruit of the much decayed tree of ancient learning."

When Greek and Arabic works were translated in the twelfth century, the West inherited a magnificent legacy of mathematical and scientific knowledge. Algebra, trigonometry, and Euclid's *Geometry* became available, and Arabic numerals and the symbol *zero* made possible the decimal system of computation. Leonard of Pisa (d. 1245), the greatest mathematician of the Middle Ages, made a great original contribution to mathematics when he worked out a method to extract square roots and to solve quadratic and cubic equations. On the other hand, Ptolemy's belief that the earth was the center of the universe—a fallacious theory destined to handicap astronomy for centuries—was commonly accepted.

Physics was based on Aristotle's theory of four elements (water, earth, air, and fire) and on his theories of dynamics—doctrines which took centuries to disprove, although some fourteenth-century nominalists did challenge Aristotle's theory that a heavy object falls faster than a light one. Chemistry was based on Aristotelian concepts, mixed with magic and alchemy. Like the Muslim alchemist, his European counterpart tried in vain to transmute base metals into gold and silver and to obtain a magic elixir that would prolong life; in both cases the attempts did much to advance chemistry.

Two notable exceptions to the medieval rule of subservience to authority were the emperor Frederick II and the English Franciscan Roger Bacon. Frederick had a genuine scientific interest in animals and was famed for his large traveling menagerie, which included elephants, camels, panthers, lions, leopards, and a giraffe. He wrote a remarkable treatise, *The Art of Falconry*, which is still considered largely accurate in its observations of the life and habits of various kinds of hunting birds. "We discovered by hard-won experience," he wrote, "that the deductions of Aristotle, whom we followed when they appealed to our reason, were not entirely to be relied upon."[10] At his Sicilian court Frederick gathered about him many distinguished Greek, Muslim, and Latin scholars (including Leonard of Pisa), and he wrote to others in distant lands seeking their views on such problems as why objects appear bent when partly covered by water. He indulged in many experiments; one was a test to determine what language children would speak if raised in absolute silence. The experiment was a failure because all the children died.

Roger Bacon (1214-1292) also employed the inductive scientific method—he coined the term "experimental science"—and boldly criticized the deductive syllogistic reasoning used by scholastic thinkers. His *Opus Maius* contains this attack on scholasticism:

> There are four principal stumbling blocks to comprehending truth, which hinder well-nigh every scholar: the example of frail and unworthy authority, long-established custom, the sense of the ignorant crowd, and the hiding of one's ignorance under the show of wisdom.[11]

Bacon never doubted the authority of the Bible or the Church—his interest lay only in natural science—yet his superiors considered him a dangerous thinker because of his criticism of scholastic thought.

Medieval universities. Roman schools had a curriculum of seven liberal arts, separated into two divisions: a *trivium* consisting of grammar, rhetoric, and dialectic; and a *quadrivium* of arithmetic, music, geometry, and astronomy. When the Roman empire in the West collapsed, the task of education fell to the monasteries, as we have seen. By 1150, however, monastic schools were overshadowed by the more dynamic cathedral schools established by bishops in such important cities as Paris, Chartres, Canterbury, and Toledo.

The renaissance of the twelfth century, with its revival of classical learning, its unprecedented number of students flocking to the schools, and its development of professional studies in law, medicine, and theology, led to the rise of new centers of learning—the universities, which soon eclipsed the monastic and cathedral schools. The word *university* meant a guild of learners, both teachers and students, analogous to the craft guilds with their masters and apprentices.

Two of the most famous medieval universities were at Bologna in northern Italy and at Paris. The former acquired a reputation as the leading center for the study of law. The students soon organized a guild for protection against the rapacious townspeople, who were demanding exorbitant sums for food and lodging. Because the guild went on to control the professors, Bologna became a student paradise. In the earliest statutes we read that a professor requiring leave of absence even for one day first had to obtain permission from his own students. He had to begin his lecture with the bell and end within one minute of the next bell. The material in the text had to be covered systematically, with all difficult passages fully explained.

At the university in Paris conditions developed differently. This university, which had grown out of the cathedral school of Notre Dame, specialized in liberal arts and theology and became the most influential intellectual center in medieval Europe. Its administration was far different from Bologna's. The chancellor of Notre Dame, the bishop's officer who exercised authority over the cathedral school, refused to allow the students or the masters to obtain control of the burgeoning university. Charters issued by the French king in 1200 and by the pope in 1231 freed the university from the bishop's authority by making it an autonomous body controlled by the masters.

The early universities had no campuses, and the masters taught in hired rooms. There were no dormitories, and students lived in rented rooms or pooled their resources to obtain housing on a cooperative basis. With masters' fees and living expenses to pay, the impoverished student labored under decided handicaps. Responding to such needs, philanthropic patrons such as Robert de Sorbon at Paris and John Balliol at Oxford founded student residences, called colleges, and provided endowments for masters who would live with the students.

The degrees available at medieval universities were similar to those offered today. The bachelor's degree became increasingly easy to obtain; by the late thirteenth century the major requirements were the payment of fees and a few years residency. At the same time, instruction in most universities became centered in the endowed residential colleges.

Latin literature. During the entire Middle Ages, virtually all the crucial communications of the Church, governments, and schools were in Latin. Undoubtedly the most splendid medieval Latin is found in the Church liturgy and in such great hymns as the *Dies Irae* ("The Day of Wrath") and the *Stabat Mater Dolorosa* ("There Stands the Sorrowing Mother"), which reflect the high level of religious feeling produced by the medieval reformation.

But any misconception that the Middle Ages were simply "other-worldly" and long-faced will be rudely shattered by glancing at the Latin poetry written during

the twelfth and thirteenth centuries by students. Known as Goliardic verse
because its authors claimed to be disciples of Goliath, their synonym for the devil,
it unhesitatingly proclaimed the pleasures of wine, women, and song:

163

The Intellectual
Synthesis

> 'Tis most arduous to make
>   Nature's self-surrender;
> Seeing girls, to blush and be
>   Purity's defender!
> We young men our longings ne'er
>   Shall to stern law render,
> Or preserve our fancies from
>   Bodies smooth and tender. . . .
>
> In the public house to die
>   Is my resolution;
> Let wine to my lips be nigh
>   At life's dissolution:
> That will make the angels cry,
>   With glad elocution,
> "Grant this toper, God on high,
>   Grace and absolution!"[12]

The Goliardic poets were brilliant at parodying and satirizing the ideals of their
elders. They substituted Venus for the Virgin, wrote masses for drunkards, and
were guilty of other blasphemies. Yet many of these poets later became respected
officials in the Church.

Vernacular literature. A rising tide of literature in the vernacular tongues
began to appear by the twelfth century, with the epic as the earliest form. The
greatest of the French epics, or *chansons de geste* ("songs of great deeds"), is the
late eleventh-century *Song of Roland*, which recounts the heroic deeds and death
of Count Roland in the Pyrenees while defending the rear of Charlemagne's army
(see p. 108). The great Spanish epic, the *Poema del Mio Cid,* is a product of the
twelfth century. These stirring epic poems, with their accounts of prowess in
battle, mirror the masculine warrior virtues of early chivalry (see p. 114).

By the twelfth century in the courts of a more sophisticated nobility that had
emerged in southern France, poets called troubadours were composing short,
personal lyrics dealing mainly with romantic love. These lines, written in
adoration of the lovely Eleanor of Aquitaine, are typical of the new preference for
songs of love over songs of war:

> When the sweet breeze
> Blows hither from your dwelling
> Methinks I feel
> A breath of paradise.[13]

Nothing comparable to these lines exists in the *chansons de geste*, but during the
last half of the twelfth century this new interest in romantic love fused with the
purely heroic material of the early epics. The result was the medieval romance, an
account of love and adventure, to which was often added a strong coloring of
religious feeling. Examples are Chrétien de Troyes' *Perceval* (see p. 115) and the

tales concerning King Arthur and his Round Table of chivalrous knights who variously pursue adventure, charming ladies, and the Holy Grail. In Germany about the beginning of the thirteenth century, the old saga material dealing with Siegfried, Brunhild, and the wars against the Huns was recast into the *Nibelungenlied* (*Song of the Nibelungs*).

All the foregoing literature was written for the aristocracy. The self-made burgher preferred more practical and shrewd tales. His taste was gratified by the bawdy *fabliaux*, brief, humorous tales written in rhymed verse; and the animal stories about Reynard the Fox, the symbol of the sly bourgeois lawyer who easily outwits King Lion and his noble vassals. In England during the fourteenth century the Robin Hood ballads celebrated robbing the rich to give to the poor and *Piers the Plowman* condemned the injustices of a social system that had brought on the peasant revolt in England (see p. 122 and quoted selection, p. 116).

Dante and Chaucer. The vernacular was also used by two of the greatest writers of the Middle Ages—Dante and Chaucer. Combining a profound religious sense with a knowledge of scholastic thought and the Latin classics, the Italian Dante (1265-1321) produced one of the world's great narrative poems. The *Divine Comedy*, which Dante said described his "full experience," is an allegory of medieval man (Dante) moving from bestial earthiness (hell) through conversion (purgatory) to the sublime spirituality of union with God (paradise). Dante describes how

> Midway this way of life we're bound upon,
>   I woke to find myself in a dark wood,
>   Where the right road was wholly lost and gone.[14]

Dante then accepts the offer of Virgil, symbol of pagan learning, to be his "master, leader, and lord" to guide him through hell and purgatory. But it is Beatrice, the lady whom he had once loved from afar and who is now the symbol of divine love, who guides him through paradise. At last Dante stands before God, and words fail him as he finds peace in the presence of the highest form of love:

> Oh, how fall short the words! . . .
> The Love that moves the sun and every star.[15]

In the *Canterbury Tales*, Geoffrey Chaucer (1340?-1400), one of the greatest figures in medieval literature, reveals a cross section of contemporary English life, customs, and thought. The twenty-nine pilgrims who assembled in April 1387 at an inn before journeying to the shrine of St. Thomas à Becket at Canterbury were a motley group. The "truly perfect, gentle knight," just returned from warring against the "heathen in Turkey," was accompanied by his son, a young squire who loved so much by night that "he slept no more than does a nightingale." The clergy was represented by the coy prioress who "would weep if she but saw a mouse caught in a trap,"[16] the rotund monk who loved to eat fat swan and ride good horses, the friar who knew the best taverns and all the barmaids in town, and the poor parish priest who was a credit to his faith. Also included in the group were the merchant who could talk only of business, the threadbare Oxford student, the miller with a wart on his nose, and the worthy wife of Bath, who had married five times and was now visiting Christian shrines in search of a sixth husband.

Chaucer's fame rests securely upon his keen interest in human nature and his skill as a storyteller. The Midland dialect he used was the linguistic base for the language of future English literature, just as Dante's use of the Tuscan dialect fixed the Italian tongue.

Rebirth of drama. Like Greek drama, medieval drama developed out of religious ceremonies; it was used by churchmen to instruct the faithful. The earliest forms were the mystery plays, which naively but forcefully dramatized Biblical stories, and the miracle plays, which described the miraculous intervention of saints in human affairs. At first the plays supplemented the regular service and were performed inside the church proper. As their popularity grew, they were presented either on the church steps or on a separate stage. By the fourteenth century another type, the morality play, had become popular. The actors personified virtues and vices, and the plot of the drama usually centered on a conflict between them. *Everyman*, an excellent example of a morality play, is still occasionally produced.

THE ESTHETIC SYNTHESIS

Early Christian basilicas. The earliest Christian churches imitated the plan of the Roman basilicas. In this design a rectangle is divided into three aisles: a central aisle, or nave, ending in a semicircular apse, and a lower-ceilinged aisle on each side. Parallel rows of columns separated the nave from the side aisles. The roof over the nave was raised to provide a clerestory—a section pierced by windows to illuminate the interior (see illustration, p. 166). In the fourth century the basilica plan was modified by the addition of a transept across the aisles between the apse and the nave. Graceful belltowers were erected separate from the church building; the "leaning tower" of Pisa is a famous later example.

Romanesque architecture. In the eleventh century occurred a tremendous architectural revival, marked by the recovery of the art of building in stone rather than in wood, as was common during the Early Middle Ages. At a much later date the name *Romanesque* came to be applied to this new style, because, like early Christian architecture, it was based largely on Roman models. Although details of structure and ornamentation differed with locality, the round arch was a standard

The rounded arches of this parish church in Rosheim in Alsace indicate that the main structure, built in the late twelfth century, was clearly Romanesque in style. The pointed arches in the belfry, however, accurately identify that part of the church as a later addition during the era of Gothic architecture.

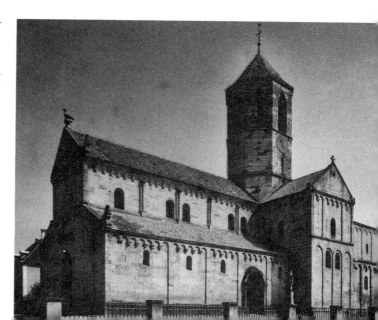

Romanesque feature. Both barrel and cross vaults (see p. 71) were used, particularly in northern Europe, where the need to build fireproof churches made it impractical to follow the common Italian practice of using flat wooden roofs. While there was often one long barrel vault over the nave, the aisles were divided into square areas or bays with a cross vault over each bay. Thick outside walls and huge interior piers were necessary to support the heavy stone barrel and cross vaults. (In time diagonal ribs were built along the groins of the cross vault, transforming it into the ribbed-groin vault.) Because the walls would be weakened by large window apertures, the clerestory windows were small or nonexistent. Thus the northern Romanesque interior was dark and gloomy, the exterior massive and monumental.

Gothic architecture. Just as the *Summa Theologica* of St. Thomas Aquinas and the *Divine Comedy* of Dante represent the best intellectual expressions of the medieval spirit, so the Gothic cathedral is the ultimate artistic expression of the age. Each of these masterpieces represents a different aspect of the attempt to organize everything into an overall pattern that would glorify God.

The transition from Romanesque to Gothic was a gradual process, which reached its culmination in the thirteenth century. The initial step was the use of pointed rather than round arches in the ribbed-groin vaults. This solved the technical problem of cross-vaulting the nave, which, being wider than the aisles, could not be divided into the square bays required by Romanesque cross vaults. Thus light ribbed-groin vaults, whose sides were of different length to fit the rectangular bays of the nave, replaced the heavy barrel vault, and the roof of the nave could be raised to permit the use of large clerestory windows. The thrust of the vaults over both the nave and the aisles was concentrated on a few strong structural supports. Part of the weight was carried down to the ground by columns

The Gothic age was the culmination of the Middle Ages, and the cathedral was the concrete synthesis of Gothic ideals. With his knowledge of weights and thrusts, the Gothic architect was able to raise his building to unprecedented heights and open it dramatically to light. The result, as evident in the cathedral at Cologne, is one of the most compelling unities of form and feeling in all of architecture.

The unified effect of the fully developed Gothic style is one of awesome, but ordered, intricacy, as the photograph of the entire front of Amiens Cathedral demonstrates. Vaults, arches, buttresses, and weighted pinnacles were important structural elements in the Gothic style of architecture.

within the building, and part by flying buttresses at points along the walls. With such vaulting and buttresses, the weight of the roof was largely shifted off the walls. Large stained-glass windows were set into the walls between the buttresses. The dark, somber interior of the Romanesque churches gave way to the jeweled light of the Gothic interiors.

Sculpture and stained glass. Most Romanesque and Gothic sculpture served an architectural function by being carved to fit into the total composition of a church. Many Gothic statues are masterpieces both in their fully developed craftmanship and the grace and nobility of their content. The relationship of the earlier Romanesque sculpture to the later Gothic reduplicates in large part that of archaic and classical sculpture in ancient Greece (see p. 54).

Like sculpture, medieval painting in the form of stained-glass windows was an integral part of architecture. Composed of small pieces of colored glass held together in a pattern by metal strips which both braced the glass and emphasized the design, stained glass was an art whose excellence has not been duplicated in modern times. By adding various minerals to molten glass, thirteenth-century craftsmen achieved brilliant hues. Details such as hair were painted on the glass. The object, however, was not realism but the evoking of a mood—to shine with the radiance of heaven itself.

PART THREE

THE TRANSITION TO
MODERN TIMES

So far in our study of history, we have encountered a number of societies which emphasized the group at the expense of the individual—societies such as that of ancient Egypt, for example, or of medieval Europe. (A similar collectivism characterizes many parts of our contemporary world.) In other societies, such as that of classical Greece, individualism counted for more than collectivism. During the period of transition from medieval to early modern times, the interests and rights of the individual were again in the ascendant. In the political sphere, this emphasis upon individualism was manifested by the creation of centralized, authoritarian states; in the realm of thought and art, it produced the Renaissance; in the area of religion, it split Christendom during the Reformation; and in the field of exploration, it resulted in the discovery and colonization of the Americas and the opening of the East to western trade.

In the realm of thought, Italian scholars known as humanists discovered in the literature of ancient Greece and Rome the same emphasis on individual freedon which was rapidly gaining momentum in their own day, and with this spirit of individualism sprang up an unashamed delight in the beauties and joys of life. Heeding Protagoras' ancient maxim that "Man is the measure of all things" and revolting against medieval authority and asceticism, Renaissance man was impelled by a new spirit of independence, a new hunger for experience. The creative vigor of the Italian Renaissance in literature, thought, and the fine arts surged throughout Europe, resulting in one of the most fruitful epochs in the cultural history of mankind.

Carried into the religious sphere, the resurgence of individualism shattered the universal supremacy of the Church and gave rise to the religious diversity of the modern western world. The followers of Luther, Calvin, and Zwingli substituted the authority of the Scriptures for that of the Roman Catholic Church and interposed no priestly mediator between the individual and his God.

Protestant-Catholic strife was the common denominator of the anarchic era of the Religious Wars, whose turbulence caused all classes to support strong rulers who could restore order. By the middle of the seventeenth century the national monarchs of France, Spain, and England, as well as the rulers of the smaller territorial states in Germany and Italy, were largely absolute in authority within their own frontiers and free agents in the domain of international affairs. Following the principles of political behavior systematized by Machiavelli, these sovereign states pursued power, prestige, wealth, and security. No moral or religious scruples were allowed to interfere with these objectives. It was considered axiomatic that a state had no permanent enemies or friends—only permanent interests. This maxim was illustrated by the manner in which alliances based on the new diplomatic technique of balance of power were formed on the European chessboard. We shall see that right up to the present day the great powers have continued to alter their alliances in deference to the exigencies of the balance of power. It is also noteworthy that since balance-of-power diplomacy was the product of a felt need to preserve the security and independence of the new sovereign states, it reflected an early recognition of the interdependence of the European state system. The present-day movement toward European economic and political unity can be viewed as the latest expression of this recognition.

The first large-scale example before 1650 of a successful countertrend to the increasing centralization of the monarch's power was the revolt of the Dutch from Spain. The establishment of the Dutch Republic in the name of people's rights foreshadowed the later and more famous revolts against absolutism which would establish constitutional government in England during the last half of the seventeenth century and in North America and France by the end of the eighteenth.

The right of a sovereign state to conduct its foreign affairs—especially the waging of war—without hindrance was challenged during this period by the opposing principle that states should accept some limitation of their freedom of action in international affairs. Ever since the early seventeenth century, when peace-loving men began to think of limiting wars and the need for international law, national sovereignty and internationalism have been in competition. Sovereignty has gotten the best of it by far, but this has not discouraged efforts to avert wars and subordinate disputes to the rule of law.

Finally, the economic structure of western Europe was transformed radically during this period, and Europe became the economic center of the world. The quickening of economic life abetted the rise of an enterprising middle class, whose members were the chief supporters and benefactors of the system of economic individualism known as capitalism. Furthermore, overseas expansion stimulated trade, increased wealth, and introduced to European markets an abundance of products previously scarce or unknown. So important was the new trade and its many influences on European life that it is referred to as the Commercial Revolution.

From the mid-point of the seventeenth century, European civilization—the most creative, expansive, and aggressive on earth—was to be the dominant and pervasive influence in world history. Thus one of the main themes of modern history is the rise of the West to dominance over the globe, just as the loss of that dominance since the Second World War is a major theme of contemporary history.

CHAPTER 8
MAN IS THE MEASURE

The Renaissance: 1300-1600

In Italy during the fourteenth and fifteenth centuries men began to view the thousand years that had elapsed since the fall of Rome as the "dark ages"—a time of stagnation and ignorance—in contrast to their own age which appeared to them resplendent in wisdom and beauty. They exuberantly proclaimed that they were participating in an intellectual and esthetic revolution sparked by the "rebirth" (*renaissance*) of the values and forms of classical antiquity. Modern historians have accepted the term *Renaissance* as a convenient label for this exciting age of intellectual and artistic renewal.

The spirit of the Renaissance was more than a mere cult of antiquity, a looking backward into the past. The men of the Renaissance were the harbingers of the modern world, energetically and enthusiastically engaged in reshaping their political, economic, and religious environment, in pushing back geographical boundaries and extending the limits of human knowledge. Renaissance culture strikingly exhibits belief in the worth of man and his desire to think and act as a free agent and a well-rounded individual.

The Renaissance did not burst forth simultaneously in all parts of Europe. It originated in the fourteenth century with a relatively small, educated group dwelling in the cities of central and nothern Italy, and not until the sixteenth century did it cross the Alps and bring an end to the Late Middle Ages in France, Germany, and England. It was in sixteenth-century England that the underlying optimism and dynamism of the entire Renaissance period was epitomized by Shakespeare:

> O, wonder!
> How many goodly creatures are there here!
> How beauteous mankind is! O brave new world,
> That has such people in't![1]

The waning of the Middle Ages.   By the fourteenth century there was a marked decline in medieval institutions and ideas. The feudal social structure was weakening before the growing power of the middle class, which sided with the new monarchs and thrived on the revival of trade and the growth of towns. The threat of armies using gunpowder was revolutionizing warfare at the expense of armor-clad knights. Heresy and schism racked the Church, and its temporal power was increasingly being challenged by aggressive national monarchs.

An empty formalism replaced the creativeness that had given the twelfth and thirteenth centuries their unique forms of expression. Scholars still held learned disputations at the universities, but scholasticism was unable to satisfy the growing interest in man and society. In art the Gothic style of the twelfth and thirteenth centuries, superb in its balance and restraint, had given place to exaggeration and flamboyance. Decoration and ornamentation became ends in themselves.

Meanwhile, sophisticated Italian urban society no longer found medieval ideals of other-worldliness and asceticism satisfactory. Pious religious themes were not so engaging as satires directed against a sometimes corrupt clergy and the outworn conventions of chivalry. Concerned with a new set of values and searching for new modes of expression, thinkers and artists found what they wanted in the literature and art of Greece and Rome.

Renaissance individualism.   In a sense, the Renaissance is the history of individual men expressing themselves brilliantly, and often tempestuously, in art, poetry, science, religion, and exploration. While the medieval way taught the unimportance of this life, stressed its snares and evils, and smothered the individual with a host of confining rules and prohibitions, the Renaissance beckoned man to enjoy beauty, to savor the opportunities of this world, and to be himself, regardless of restraints. Above all, the new spirit called upon its followers to adopt the concept of *l'uomo universale* ("the universal man" or "the complete man"). Life was best lived when the human personality showed its versatility by expression in many forms: advancement of the mind, perfection of the body, cultivation of the social graces, and glorification of the human form in the arts.

Humanism and the classical revival.   In medieval times the writers of antiquity had been interpreted within the framework of the Christian religion and usually cited as authorities to bolster Church dogma. Although many aspects of antiquity were avoided because of their disturbingly pagan quality, churchmen did make use of pagan literature for allegorical narratives which were Christian in char-acter. Consequently, the true nature of the classical legacy was generally distorted or obscured.

In fourteenth-century Italy a new perspective was attained and a fresh appreciation of classical culture emerged. Successors to a small group of medieval teachers of grammar and rhetoric, the representatives of this new movement called themselves humanists, a name derived from the *studia humanitatis*, or "humanities," which Roman authors had used in the sense of a liberal or literary education.

Medieval scholastic education had emphasized the sciences and professional training in law, medicine, and theology at the expense of the "arts," or literary side of the curriculum. Hence the scholastics had centered their attention on

Aristotle's scientific writings and other ancient works on astronomy, medicine, and mathematics. Stimulated by a rebirth of men's interest in the problems and values of human living, the humanists reversed this medieval emphasis and called attention to the importance of an education in the humanities—history, grammar, rhetoric, poetry, and moral philosophy. The humanists disdained the sciences because, as Petrarch—the first of the Italian humanists—wrote:

> . . . they help in no way toward a happy life, for what does it advantage us to be familiar with the nature of animals, birds, fishes, and reptiles, while we are ignorant of the nature of the race of man to which we belong, and do not know or care whence we come or whither we go?[2]

Thus, despite the fact that both the humanist and the scholastic looked to the past and venerated its heritage, they differed widely in their choice of the ancient material to be revered.

Humanists and scholastics also differed in the manner in which they saw themselves in relation to the writers of ancient times. While the scholastic always felt himself inferior to the ancients and looked up to them as son to father or pupil to teacher, the typical humanist in his exultant individualism saw himself equal to the ancients and boldly hailed them as man to man and friend to friend. At the beginning of his *Divine Comedy* Dante described medieval man's reliance upon the authority of the ancients in allegorical terms. Dante (medieval man) is lost in the "dark wood" which is this life until he is rescued by Virgil (a favorite medieval symbol of ancient wisdom), who thereafter guides him along the right path. "Losing me," Virgil is made to say to Dante, "ye would remain astray."

The noticeably different attitude of the humanists was well expressed by one of their few medieval forerunners, John of Salisbury (d. 1180): "Most delightful in many ways is the fruit of letters that, banishing the irksomeness of intervals of place and time, bring friends into each other's presence. . . . "[3] It was in this spirit that Petrarch wrote his *Letters to Ancient Authors*, addressing Homer, Plato, Cicero, and others in familiar terms and sharing with them his own thoughts and experiences. This feeling of equality with ancient authors was also behind the humanists' practice of stuffing their own writings with apt quotations from the classics. The humanists' purpose, however, differed from that of the scholastics, who also quoted extensively from the ancients; as the humanist Montaigne explained in his essays (see p. 183), he quoted the ancients not because he agreed with them but because they agreed with him!

Petrarch and Boccaccio. The "father of humanism" is a title that has been given to Francesco Petrarca, better known to us as Petrarch (1304-1374). Resentful as a youth of his father's desire to have him study law at Bologna, he turned to reading Virgil and Cicero for consolation. The ancients wrote of the joys of this world, and their attitude toward life struck a sympathetic chord in Petrarch. A product of medieval beliefs and attitudes, he nevertheless could not accept a depreciation of man's importance in the scheme of things or a constriction of his mental horizons. And thus he condemned the arid logic of scholasticism and the extent to which medieval education was governed by dead tradition. He himself was not a careful scholar and never learned Greek, yet this versatile rebel had a profound influence upon his contemporaries and gave humanism its first great impetus.

Another early humanist was Giovanni Boccaccio (1313-1375), who began his career as a writer of poetry and romances. In 1348 the calamitous Black Death struck—a disaster which wiped out nearly two thirds of Florence's population. Boccaccio used this event to establish the setting of his masterpiece, the *Decameron*. To escape the pestilence, his characters—three young men and seven young women—sought seclusion in a country villa, where they whiled away the time by telling each other stories. Boccaccio suffused the hundred tales of the *Decameron*, based on the old *fabliaux* (see p. 164) and on chivalric accounts, with a new and different spirit. Recounted by sophisticated city dwellers, the tales satirize the follies of knights and other medieval types and express clearly the contempt which had developed for the old, and by then threadbare, ideals of feudalism. Many tales are bawdy and even scandalous—a charge which Boccaccio undertook to refute:

> Some of you may say that in writing these tales I have taken too much license, by making ladies sometimes say and often listen to matters which are not proper to be said or heard by virtuous ladies. This I deny, for there is nothing so unchaste but may be said chastely if modest words are used; and this I think I have done.[4]

The *Decameron* offers a wealth of anecdotes, portraits of flesh-and-blood characters, and a vivid (although one-sided) picture of Renaissance life.

The *Decameron* closed Boccaccio's career as a creative artist. Largely through the influence of Petrarch, Boccaccio gave up writing in the Italian vernacular and turned to the study of antiquity. He attempted to learn Greek, wrote an encyclopedia of classical mythology, and went off to monasteries in search of classical manuscripts. By the time Petrarch and Boccaccio died, the study of the literature of antiquity was growing throughout Italy.

The search for manuscripts. The search for classical manuscripts became a mania, and before the middle of the fifteenth century works by most of the important Latin authors had been found. The degree of difference between humanist and scholastic attitudes is indicated by the ease with which the early humanists recovered the "lost" Latin literary masterpieces: they were found close at hand in monastic libraries, covered by the undisturbed dust of centuries. The books had always been there; what had been largely lacking was a mature and appreciative audience of readers. In addition to these Latin works, precious Greek manuscripts were brought to Italy from Constantinople during the fifteenth century.

Individual scholars had their favorite ancient authors, both Greek and Roman, but the highest universal praise was reserved for Cicero. Compounded of moral philosophy and rhetoric, his work displayed a wide-ranging intellect which appealed to many humanists. The revival of the art of writing classical Latin prose was due largely to the study and imitation of Cicero's graceful, eloquent, and polished literary style.

Late Italian humanism. As a result both of their rebellion against the Aristotelian emphasis upon natural science and of their search for a classical philosophy that stressed moral purpose and even mystical religious values, many humanists gravitated to Platonism during the fifteenth century. A factor in this revival was the study of Plato in the original Greek, particularly at Florence where Cosimo de' Medici, one of the great patrons of the Renaissance, founded the informal club that came to be known as the Platonic Academy. Its leader, Marsilio Ficino

(1433-1499), who always kept a candle burning before a bust of Plato, made the first complete Latin translation of Plato's works.

Ficino also sought to synthesize Christianity and Plato, much as St. Thomas Aquinas had done with Aristotle. In his principal work, *Theologia Platonica*, Ficino viewed Plato as essentially Christian and Plato's "religious philosophy" as a God-sent means of converting intellectuals. He coined the expression "Platonic love" to describe an ideal, pure love, and this concept found its way into much of Renaissance literature.

Despite its great attraction for many humanists, Platonism still had a formidable rival in Aristotelianism, which was concerned chiefly with natural philosophy, logic, and metaphysics. The most influential Aristotelians were the Latin Averroists, followers of the Muslim philosopher Averroes (see p. 103). The Averroists followed Aristotle in teaching that matter is eternal and in denying the immortality of the soul. Since such views were contrary to the Biblical story of creation and the belief in personal immortality, the Averroists advocated the doctrine of "double truth"—a truth in philosophy need not be valid in religion.

By the fifteenth century, the University of Padua had become the center of Aristotelianism, which reached its peak in the next century. By championing a secular rationalism that kept philosophy separate from theology, its adherents helped create an environment necessary for the triumph of scientific thought in the seventeenth century. As we shall see in Chapter 12, the new developments that Aristotelianism encouraged were to overthrow Aristotle's own brilliant but outmoded theories in physics and other fields of science.

Although the Italian humanists condemned medieval restrictions, they themselves became subservient to the authorities of antiquity. By the late fifteenth century theirs was a closed culture whose boundaries had been set by ancient Greece and Rome, so that the only course open to them was to retravel the ground, not to explore uncharted territory. Late Italian humanists were so dominated by Roman and Greek forms that they tended to imitate rather than to create for themselves. Their passion for Ciceronian Latin became pernicious; too often their writings were rich in form but barren in content. Worse still, their preoccupation with classical Latin retarded the growth of a much more vital vernacular literature.

ITALIAN RENAISSANCE ART

Transitional period in painting and sculpture. The spread of humanistic influence resulted in a renewed and valuable emphasis upon the freedom and dignity of man as an individual and the importance of his place in the cosmos. This interest was manifested not only in literature but also in painting and sculpture, and it marks the beginning of Renaissance art.

The greatest figure in the transitional art of fourteenth-century Italy was the Florentine painter Giotto (1266-1336), who, it was said, "achieved little less than the resurrection of painting from the dead." While earlier Italian painters had copied the unreal, flat, and rigidly formalized images of Byzantine paintings and mosaics, Giotto observed from life and painted a three-dimensional world peopled with believable human beings dramatically moved by deep emotion. He human-

Renaissance artists presented traditional subject matter in
novel ways. Giotto's "Lamentation over the Dead Christ," one of
thirty-eight frescoes painted for the Arena Chapel in Padua,
lends a new drama and a new credibility to a familiar Biblical
story.

ized painting much as Petrarch humanized thought and St. Francis humanized religion.

Quattrocento art.   The lull in painting that followed Giotto, during which his technical innovations were retained but the spirit and compassion that make him one of the world's great painters were lost, lasted until the beginning of the *quattrocento* (Italian for "four hundred," an abbreviation for the 1400's). In his brief lifetime the Florentine Masaccio (1401-1428) completed the revolution in technique begun by Giotto. He largely mastered the problems of perspective, anatomical naturalism of flesh and bone, and the modeling of figures in light and shade rather than by sharp line. Masaccio was also the first to paint nude figures whose counterparts can be found in classical, but not in medieval, art.

Inspired by Masaccio's achievement, most *quattrocento* painters constantly sought to improve technique. This search for greater realism was abandoned by Sandro Botticelli (1447-1510), who used a highly sensitive, even quivering, line to stir the viewer's imagination and emotion and to create a mood in keeping with his subject matter, frankly pagan at first but later deeply religious. His "Primavera," which centers on the figure of Venus, is an allegorical painting depicting the return of spring. It has been called a *quattrocento* love-in.

In the meantime progress was being made in sculpture, and it, like painting, reached stylistic maturity at the beginning of the *quattrocento*. In his bronze doors

As a master of line, Botticelli is probably unsurpassed in the western world. His "Primavera," which centers on the figure of Venus, is an allegorical painting depicting the return of spring. It has been called a *quattrocento* love-in.

for the baptistery in Florence, Lorenzo Ghiberti (1378-1455) achieved the goal he had set for himself: "I strove to imitate nature as closely as I could, and with all the perspective I could produce." These marvels of relief sculpture, which drew from Michelangelo the declaration that they were worthy to be the gates of paradise, depict skillfully modeled human figures—including some classically inspired nudes—which stand out spatially against architectural and landscape backgrounds.

Ghiberti's younger contemporary in Florence, Donatello (1386-1466), visited Rome to study the remains of antique statuary. Divorcing sculpture from its architectural background, Donatello produced truly freestanding statues based on the realization of the human body as a functional, coordinated mechanism of bones, muscles, and sinews, maintaining itself against the pull of gravity. His "David" is the first bronze nude made since antiquity, and his equestrian statue of Gattamelata the *condottiere* (professional soldier) is the first of its type done in the Renaissance. The latter clearly reveals the influence of classical models and was probably inspired by the equestrian statue of Marcus Aurelius in Rome.

More dramatic than either of these equestrian statues is that of the Venetian *condottiere* Bartolomeo Colleoni, the creation of Andrea del Verrocchio (1453-1488). A versatile Florentine artist noteworthy as a sculptor, painter, and the teacher of Leonardo da Vinci, Verrocchio designed the statue of Colleoni to permit one of the horse's forelegs to be unsupported—a considerable achievement. The posture and features of the *condottiere* convey dramatically a sense of the supreme self-confidence and arrogance usually associated with Renaissance public figures.

Renaissance architecture, which far more than sculpture reflects the influence of ancient Roman models, began with the work of Filippo Brunelleschi (1377-1446). As a youth Brunelleschi accompanied Donatello to Rome where he employed measuring stick and sketchbook to master the principles of classical architecture. Returning to Florence, Brunelleschi constructed the lofty dome of the cathedral, the first to be built since Roman times. Although strongly influenced by classical architecture, Brunelleschi's buildings in Florence, which include churches and palaces, were not just copies of Roman models. Employing arcades of Roman arches, Roman pediments above the windows, and engaged Roman columns and other decorative motifs, Brunelleschi re-created the Roman style in a fresh and original manner.

The High Renaissance, 1500-1530. During the High Renaissance the center of artistic activity shifted from Florence to Rome and Venice, where wealthier patrons lived and where consequently greater opportunities were available to artists. The popes were lavish patrons, and the greatest artists of the period worked in the Vatican at one time or another. It did not seem inconsistent to popes and artists to include representations of pagan mythological figures in the decorations of the papal palace, and thus the Vatican was filled with secular as well as religious art.

The great architect of the High Renaissance was Donato Bramante (1444-1514) from Milan. Bramante's most important commission came in 1506 when Pope Julius II requested him to replace the old basilica of St. Peter, built by the emperor Constantine, with a monumental Renaissance structure. Bramante's plan called for a centralized church in the form of a Greek cross surmounted by an immense dome. The exterior of St. Peter's exemplifies the spirit of High Renaissance architecture—to approach nearer to the monumentality and grandeur of Roman architecture. In Bramante's own words, he would place "the Pantheon on top of the Basilica of Maxentius." Bramante died when the cathedral was barely begun, and it was left to Michelangelo and others to complete the work.

High Renaissance architects also produced magnificent palaces and other secular buildings. Their decorative features show how classical details blended in a new fashion resulted in an impressive and refined structure. From the sixteenth century on, all Europe began to take to the new architecture.

The painters of the High Renaissance inherited the solutions to such technical problems as perspective space from the *quattrocento* artists. But whereas the artists of the earlier period had been concerned with movement, color, and narrative detail, painters in the High Renaissance strove to eliminate nonessentials and concentrated on the central theme of a picture and its basic human implications. By this process of elimination, many High Renaissance painters achieved a "classic" effect of seriousness and serenity.

Leonardo, Raphael, and Michelangelo. The great triad of High Renaissance

Bramente designed St. Peter's in the shape of a Greek cross with a dome similar to that of the Pantheon. After his death, however, his plan was modified. Michelangelo redesigned the dome—which has been called the greatest achievement of Renaissance architecture—and later a long nave was added to the front of the church, giving it the form of a Latin cross rather than of a Greek cross.

painters consists of Leonardo da Vinci, Raphael, and Michelangelo. An extraordinary man, Leonardo da Vinci (1452-1519) was proficient in a variety of fields: engineering, mathematics, architecture, geology, botany, physiology, anatomy, sculpture, painting, music, and poetry. He was always experimenting, with the result that few of the projects he started were ever finished.

A superb draftsman, Leonardo was also a master of soft modeling in full light and shade and of creating groups of figures perfectly balanced in a given space. One of his most famous paintings is the "Mona Lisa," a portrait of a woman whose enigmatic smile has intrigued observers for centuries. Another is "The Last Supper," a study of the moment when Christ tells his twelve disciples that one will betray him. Last of the great Florentine painters, Leonardo combined an advanced knowledge of technique with deep psychological insight into many facets of human nature.

The second of the great triad of High Renaissance painters was Raphael (1483-1520). By the time he was summoned to Rome to aid in the decoration of the Vatican, Raphael had absorbed something of Leonardo's intellectuality and Michelangelo's "body dynamics" and grandeur. His Stanze frescoes in the Vatican display a magnificent blending of classical and Christian subject matter and are imbued with a clarity and breadth of vision expressive of the High Renaissance at its best. Considered by some critics as unrivaled in the mastery of space composition, Raphael was equally at home in handling a single figure or in grouping masses.

The individualism and idealism of the High Renaissance have no greater representative than Michelangelo Buonarroti (1475-1564). Stories of this stormy and temperamental personality have helped shape our ideas of what a genius is like. Indeed, there is something almost superhuman about both Michelangelo and his art. His great energy enabled him to complete in four years the entire work of painting the ceiling of the Vatican's Sistine Chapel, an area of several thousand square yards, and his art embodies a superhuman ideal of man. With his unrivaled genius for rendering the human form, he devised a wealth of expressive positions and attitudes for his figures in scenes from Genesis.

Michelangelo considered himself first and foremost a sculptor, and this *uomo universale*, who also excelled as poet, engineer, and architect, was undoubtedly the greatest sculptor of the Renaissance. The glorification of the human body, particularly the male nude, was Michelangelo's great achievement. Fired by the grandeur of such newly discovered pieces of Hellenistic sculpture as the Laocoön group (see p. 58) and strongly influenced by Platonism, he expressed in art his idealized view of man's dignity and majesty. Succeeding Bramante as chief architect of St. Peter's, Michelangelo designed the great dome, and was in the midst of creative activities when he died, almost in his ninetieth year, in 1564. He had long outlived the High Renaissance.

The Venetian school. Venice offered a congenial environment to artists. A prosperous merchant-prince could well afford to play the role of patron of the arts; trade with the East provided Venetians with luxuries and comforts which added splendor and color to daily life; and the beauty of the city itself would attract the eye of any artist. There is a sensuousness in the Venetian painting of this period which is evident in the artists' love of decoration, rich costumes, radiant light and color, and striking nude figures.

Giorgione (1478-1511), like Botticelli, used classical themes and idyllic landscapes in his paintings. But unlike the Florentine master, who made his mythological figures imaginative and idealized, Giorgione's muses and Venuses were lovely Venetian models.

The pictures of Titian (1485?-1576) contain sensuous beauties of color and atmosphere. During his long working life he proved himself a master of a wide variety of subjects ranging from religion to pagan mythology. His portraits, which earned him the greatest fame among his contemporaries, show the Venetian love of color and texture of rich fabrics.

High Renaissance music. In contrast to the single-voiced or homophonic music—called plainsong or Gregorian chant—of the early Middle Ages, the later medieval composers wrote many-voiced, many-melodied, or polyphonic music. Polyphony often involved a shuttling back and forth from one melody to another—musical counterpoint. By the fifteenth century as many as twenty-four voice parts were combined into one intricately woven musical pattern. The composers of the High Renaissance continued to produce complicated polyphonic

Michelangelo's pursuit of a perfect Idea, as Plato described it, is evident in the compelling beauty of this marble figure depicting "Dawn" on the Medici tombs. The sculptor's passionate belief in man's godlike form and heroic qualities are plainly evident in this face. The group of figures on the Medici tombs achieve the integrated unity that marked all of Michelangelo's accomplishments in such varied fields as painting, sculpture, architecture, and poetry.

music, but in a calmer and grander manner. Compared with the style of his predecessors, that of Josquin des Près (d. 1521), the founder of High Renaissance music, "is both grander and more simple . . . ; few dissonances are used, and the rhythms and forms used are based on strict symmetry and mathematically regular proportions. Josquin handled all technical problems of complicated constructions with the same ease and sureness one finds in the drawings of Leonardo and Raphael."[5] During the sixteenth century, also, instruments such as the violin, spinet, and harpsichord developed from more rudimentary types.

The Renaissance in Italy stimulated many new forms of secular music, especially the madrigal, a love lyric set to music. The madrigal found favor in England, while French *chansons* and German *lieder* added to the growing volume of secular music.

THE NORTHERN RENAISSANCE

The northward spread of the Renaissance. By the beginning of the sixteenth century the stimulating ideas current in Italy were spreading north of the Alps and combining with indigenous developments to produce a French Renaissance, an English Renaissance, and so on. Here also wealthy burghers patronized the work of artists and scholars, but the prime sponsors of the northern Renaissance were often the kings of the new national states. By importing artists and learned men from Italy or supporting native geniuses, the rulers added brilliance to their courts.

Perhaps even more important in the diffusion of the Renaissance and later in the success of the Reformation was the invention of printing in Europe. The essential elements—paper and block printing—had been known in China since the eighth century. During the twelfth century the Spanish Muslims introduced papermaking to Europe, and in the next century block printing became known in the West. The crucial step was taken in the 1440's at Mainz, in Germany, where Johann Gutenberg and other printers invented movable type by cutting up old printing blocks to form individual letters. Gutenberg used movable type to print papal documents and the first published version of the Bible (1454).

Within fifty years after Gutenberg's Bible had been published, all the major countries of Europe possessed the means for printing books. It is said that the prices of books soon sank to one eighth of their former cost, thus placing books within the reach of a multitude of people who formerly had been unable to buy them. In addition, pamphlets and controversial tracts soon were widely circulated, and new ideas reached a thousand times more people in a relatively short span of time. In the quickening of Europe's intellectual life, it is difficult to overestimate the effects of the printing press.

Erasmus and northern humanism. The intellectual life of the first half of the sixteenth century was dominated by Desiderius Erasmus (1466?-1536). Born in Rotterdam, but always a wanderer unattached to any country, Erasmus was *the* scholar of Europe, and his writings were read eagerly everywhere. Perhaps his most famous and influential work is the satirical *In Praise of Folly*. Folly, the term used in the Middle Ages as a synonym for human nature, is seen as the source both of much that is good in life and of much that is amiss. The failings of every class in society are exposed: merchants ("they lie, swear, cheat, and practice all the intrigues of dishonesty"), lawyers ("they of all men have the greatest conceit of their own abilities"), scholastic philosophers ("that talk as much by rote as a parrot"), and scientists ("who esteem themselves the only favourites of wisdom, and look upon the rest of mankind as the dirt and rubbish of the creation"). Most roughly handled are churchmen, in particular monks, who are "impudent pretenders to the profession of piety," and popes, cardinals, and bishops, "who in pomp and splendour have almost equalled if not outdone secular princes." While his satire is sometimes harsh, Erasmus was himself balanced, moderate, and intolerant only of bigotry, ignorance, greed, and violence.

In Praise of Folly points up a significant difference between the northern humanists and their Italian predecessors. While both were repelled by much that seemed to them wrong in the life of their day, their reactions took different forms. The typical Italian humanists followed the course set by Petrarch: "In order to forget my own time I have constantly striven to place myself in spirit in other ages. . . . "[6] Disdaining such escapism, the great majority of nothern humanists faced up to reality and became reformers of their society's ills. They also went further in broadening their interest in ancient literature to include early Christian writings—the Scriptures and the works of the Church Fathers. This led them to prepare new and more accurate editions of the Scriptures (Erasmus' Greek edition of the New Testament became famous and was used by Luther) and to compare unfavorably the complexities of the Church in their own day with the simplicity of primitive Christianity. Since the northern humanists held that the essence of religion was morality and rational piety—what Erasmus called the "philosophy of Christ"—rather than ceremony and dogma, it is not surprising that the Church became a major target of their reforming zeal.

Sir Thomas More's Utopia. The most significant figure in English humanism was Sir Thomas More (1478-1535), who is best known for his *Utopia*, the first important description of an ideal state since Plato's *Republic*. In this work, still popular with critics of society's evils, More castigated his age by using as his spokesman a fictitious sailor who contrasts the ideal life he has seen in Utopia (The Land of Nowhere) with the harsh conditions of life in England. More's denunciations centered on the new acquisitive capitalism, which he blamed for the widespread insecurity and misery of the lower classes. More felt that governments

> are a conspiracy of the rich, who, in pretence of managing the public, only pursue their private ends, . . . first, that they may, without danger, preserve all that they have so ill acquired, and then, that they may engage the poor to toil and labor for them at as low rates as possible, and oppress them as much as they please.[7]

In Utopia, by contrast, no man is in want because the economy is planned and cooperative and because property is held in common. Utopia is the only true commonwealth, concludes More's imaginary sailor: "In all other places, it is visible that while people talk of a commonwealth, every man only seeks his own wealth: but there, where no man has any property, all men zealously pursue the good of the public."

More was the first of the modern English socialists, but his philosophy should not be considered a forerunner of the socialism of our day. His economic outlook was a legacy from the Middle Ages, and his preference for medieval collectivism over modern individualism was of a piece with his preference for a Church headed—medieval style—by popes rather than kings, a view that prompted Henry VIII to execute him for treason (see p. 198).

Rabelais. One of the best known of the French humanists was Francois Rabelais (1494-1553). A brilliant, if coarse, lover of all life from the sewers to the heavens, Rabelais is famed for his *Gargantua and Pantagruel.* Centering on figures from French folklore, this work relates the adventures of two genial giants of tremendous stature and appetite, to whom were ascribed many marvelous feats.

In the course of his pungent narrative, Rabelais inserted his views on educational reform and his humanistic belief in man's inherent goodness and ability to solve his problems by reason. He made vitriolic attacks on the abuses of the Church and the shortcomings of scholastics and monks, but he had little patience with overzealous Protestants either. What Rabelais could not stomach was hypocrisy and repression; and for those guilty of these tendencies, he reserved his choicest invective. He bid his readers to flee from that

> rabble of squint-minded fellows, dissembling and counterfeit saints, demure lookers, hypocrites, pretended zealots, tough friars, buskin-monks, and other such sects of men, who disguise themselves like masquers to deceive the world. . . . Fly from these men, abhor and hate them as much as I do, and upon my faith you will find yourself the better for it. And if you desire . . . *to live in peace, joy, health, making yourselves always merry,* never trust those men that always peep out through a little hole.[8]

Montaigne. The last notable northern humanist was the French skeptic Michel de Montaigne (1533-1592). At the age of thirty-eight he gave up the practice of law and retired to his country estate and well-stocked library, where he studied and wrote. Montaigne developed a new literary form and gave it its name—the essay. In ninety-four essays he set forth his personal views on many subjects: leisure, friendship, education, philosophy, religion, old age, death, and so forth. He did not pretend to have the final answer to the subjects he discussed. Instead, he advocated open-mindedness and toleration—rare qualities in the sixteenth century, when France was racked by religious and civil strife.

Montaigne condemned the pedantry into which humanism and humanistic education had largely degenerated by the end of the sixteenth century, arguing that "To know by heart is not to know; it is to retain what we have given our memory to keep."[9] Even today's student may have cause to listen sympathetically to the following words:

> Our tutors never stop bawling into our ears, as though they were pouring water into a funnel; and our task is only to repeat what has been told us. I should like the tutor to correct this practice . . . I want him to listen to his pupil speaking in his turn.[10]

Montaigne's final essay, entitled "Of Experience," which developed the thought that "when reason fails us we resort to experience," is an acknowledgment of the bankruptcy of humanism and a foreshadowing of the coming triumph of scientific thought.

Cervantes, creator of Don Quixote. The transition from feudal knight to

Renaissance gentleman finds its greatest literary expression in a masterpiece of Spanish satire, *Don Quixote de la Mancha*, the work of Miguel de Cervantes (1547-1616). By Cervantes' day knighthood had become an anachronism, though its accompanying code of chivalry still retained its appeal. It remained for a rationalist like Cervantes to show up the inadequacies of chivalric idealism in a world that had acquired new, and intensely practical, aims. He did so by creating a pathetic but infinitely appealing character to serve as the personification of an outmoded way of life.

Don Quixote, the "knight of the woeful countenance," mounted on his "lean, lank, meagre, drooping, sharp-backed, and raw-boned" steed Rozinante, sets out in the Spanish countryside to right wrongs and uphold his lady's and his own honor. In his misadventures he is accompanied by his squire, the much less gallant but infinitely more realistic Sancho Panza, whose peasant adages and hard-grained common sense serve as a contrast to the impractical nature of his master's chivalric code. Tilting at windmills, mistaking serving wenches for highborn ladies and inns for castles, and lamenting the invention of gunpowder as depriving ardent knights of a chance to win immortality, Don Quixote is, on the surface at least, a ridiculous old man whose nostalgia for the "good old days" is a constant source of grief to him. Thus the story represents a superb satire directed against the outworn ideology of the Middle Ages.

And yet *Don Quixote* is still more. Cervantes instilled in his main character a pathos born in large measure of the author's own career of frustrated hopes and ambitions. As a result, Don Quixote becomes more than a romantic lunatic; he serves to embody that set of ideals which each of us would like to see realized but which we must compromise in a world that has other interests to serve.

William Shakespeare. Like Greek drama, medieval drama developed out of religious ceremonies (see p. 51). A complete divorce of the Church and stage did not occur until the middle of the fifteenth century when the Renaissance era of drama began in Italian cities with the performance of ancient Roman comedies. Imitating the ancient models they admired, French and Italian writers followed what they believed were the rigid conventions of the classical drama and, to a large extent, catered to the aristocracy. By contrast, Spanish and English playwrights created a theatrical environment that was at once more socially democratic, more hospitable to national themes, and less concerned with classical models.

The spring of lyric song that bubbled up in the England of Henry VIII formed a veritable stream of verse that sparkled through his daughter Elizabeth's countryside. Her reign (1558-1603) climaxed the English Renaissance and produced such a galaxy of talented writers that some scholars have felt it necessary to go back as far as Athens in the fifth century B.C. to find an age as prodigal of literary genius. Strongly influenced by the royal court, which served as the busy center of intellectual and artistic life, their writings were highly colored, richly romantic, and often wildly extravagant in spite of all their poetic allusions to classical times.

The supreme figure in Elizabethan literature and perhaps in all literature is William Shakespeare (1564-1616), who wrote thirty-eight plays—histories, comedies, and tragedies. His historical plays reflected the patriotic upsurge experienced by Englishmen as their country grew stronger and more prosperous. For his comedies and tragedies, Shakespeare was content in a great majority of cases to borrow plots from earlier works. His forte lay in his creation of characters—perhaps the richest and most diversified collection conceived by the mind of one man—and in his ability to translate his knowledge of human nature into dramatic speech and action. Today his comedies are played to enthusiastic audiences, but it is in his tragedies that the poet-dramatist runs the gamut of human emotions and experience. Shakespeare possessed in abundance the Renaissance concern for man and the world about him. Hence his plays deal first and foremost with man's personality, passions, and problems. In such works as *Romeo and Juliet, Measure for Measure*, and *Troilus and Cressida*, the problems of love and sex are studied from many angles. Jealousy is analyzed in *Othello*, ambition in *Macbeth* and *Julius Caesar*, family relationships in *King Lear*, and man's struggle with his own soul in *Hamlet*. Shakespeare's extraordinary ability to build every concrete fact and action upon a universal truth makes his observations as applicable today as they were when first presented in the Globe Theater. Small wonder that next to the Bible, Shakespeare is the most quoted of all literary sources in the language.

Developments in painting. Before the Italian Renaissance permeated the artistic circles of northern Europe, the painters of Flanders had been making significant advances on their own. Outstanding was Jan van Eyck (1385?-1440), whose work has been called "the full flowering of the spirit of the late Middle Ages,"[11] for he continued to paint in the realistic manner developed by the illuminators of medieval manuscripts. Van Eyck also perfected the technique of

Northern Renaissance painting began to be affected by the Italian tendency toward naturalism and secularism at the end of the fifteenth century. In this detail from "Landscape with the Fall of Icarus" Pieter Brueghel the Elder has depicted an ancient myth as though it occurred in contemporary Flanders. Icarus (lower right) plunges into the water unnoticed by the herdsman and farmer, who continue their work.

oil painting, which enabled him to paint with greater realism and attention to detail.

The first talented German painter to be influenced deeply by Italian art was Albrecht Dürer (1471-1528) of Nuremberg. Dürer made more than one journey to Italy, where he was impressed both with the painting of the Renaissance Italians and with the artists' high social status—a contrast with northern Europe, where artists were still treated as craftsmen. Because he did not entirely lose many of the medieval qualities of the milieu in which he worked, his own work is a blend of the old and the new; but among German artists he went farthest in adopting the rational standards of Italian art. His "Knight, Death, and Devil" fuses the realism and symbolism of the Gothic with the nobility of Verrochio's statue of Colleoni. In the long run Dürer became better known for his numerous engravings and woodcuts than for his paintings.

Another German painter, Hans Holbein the Younger (1497-1543), was less imaginative than Dürer; but whereas the latter lived principally in Germany and interpreted its spirit, the younger artist worked abroad, especially in England, and as a result his painting acquired a more cosmopolitan character. In his numerous portraits, northern realism and concern for detail continues evident.

While many Flemish painters lost their northern individuality in the rush to adopt Italian techniques, Pieter Brueghel the Elder (1525?-1569) retained a strong Flemish flavor in his portrayal of the faces and scenes of his native land. He painted village squares, landscapes, skating scenes, peasant weddings and dances just as he saw them, with a reporter's eye for detail. He also took Biblical or mythological themes and depicted them as if the events were taking place in the Flanders of his own day. The depiction of everyday scenes in realistic fashion is known as *genre* painting; and in this medium, Pieter Brueghel and the Flemish school as a whole remained unexcelled.

CHAPTER 9

HERE I TAKE MY STAND

The Protestant and Catholic Reformations

On October 31, 1517, a professor of theology named Martin Luther nailed some papers on the door of a church in Wittenberg, Germany. It was the custom of the day for a man who wanted to engage in a scholastic debate with another to post his propositions publicly. In this respect Luther's action was not unusual, yet the forces he set in operation altered the entire religious pattern of the western world.

At first Luther believed that it might be possible to reform the Church to the conditions existing in early Christian times. From this standpoint the religious upheaval which he did so much to set in motion can be logically designated as the Reformation. On the other hand, because the struggle shattered western Christendom permanently, it can be described from a broader historical viewpoint as a revolution—the Protestant Revolt. The sixteenth century also witnessed a significant revival of Roman Catholicism itself. This renewal of the traditional faith was not solely a Counter Reformation in the sense that it represented a belated response to the challenge of Protestantism. As modern scholars have demonstrated, a strong Catholic Reformation had been gathering momentum even before Luther posted his theses.

The Reformation had both its negative and its positive aspects. In the name of God, men persecuted and killed their fellow men. Rulers anxious for absolute power used the conflicts engendered by the religious upheaval to serve their own political ends. Yet, much as in the early centuries of Christianity, when the blood of the martyrs became the seed of the Church, so the struggles of the sixteenth century, led by men afire with conviction and ready to sacrifice their lives for what they believed, renewed and stimulated the religious consciousness of western Europe. Luther declared: "Here I take my stand"; and in a broad sense this affirmation was echoed by Zwingli in the Swiss cantons, by Calvin at Geneva, and by the Catholic Church at the Council of Trent. Such staunch and uncompromising assertions of honest differences of doctrine gave institutionalized Christianity the new religious vitality and intellectual diversity that were to leave their mark on almost every phase of life in the West and bequeath us a rich legacy of values.

The end of the medieval papacy.   We have seen in Chapter 7 how the universal Church, headed by the pope, reached its zenith with the pontificate of Innocent III in the thirteenth century. During the next two centuries, the Late Middle Ages, the Church was to experience a disintegration similar to that which had already fatally weakened its great medieval rival, the Holy Roman Empire. Initially instrumental in undermining the international character of the papacy were national monarchs who, supported by parliaments or by local bishops organized as national Church councils, were strong enough to challenge papal power. The first such successful challenge occurred a century after Innocent III during the pontificate of Boniface VIII (1294-1303), who is with good reason called the last of the medieval popes.

When the strong English and French kings, Edward I and Philip II, took the unprecedented step of taxing the great wealth of the Church in their lands, Boniface emulated Innocent III in threatening to depose the "impious king," as he termed Philip. But Boniface gave way when Philip, with the support of the Estates-General, prohibited the export of money to Rome.

A final and more humiliating clash with the French king had long-range implications for the papacy. When Boniface boldly declared, in the most famous of all papal bulls, *Unam Sanctam* (1302), that "subjection to the Roman pontiff is absolutely necessary to salvation for every human creature," Philip demanded that the pope be tried for his "sins" by a Church council. In 1303 Philip's henchmen broke into Boniface's summer home at Anagni to arrest him and take him to France to stand trial. Their kidnaping plot was foiled when the pope was rescued by his friends, but, shocked and humiliated, Boniface died a month later. In the words of one of Philip's advisers, the thunder of papal bulls had become mere verbiage as compared with the sword of the king of France.

The Avignon papacy.   The success of the French monarchy was as complete as if Boniface had been dragged before Philip. Two years after Boniface's death, a French archbishop was chosen pope. Taking the title of Clement V, he not only exonerated Philip but praised his Christian zeal in bringing charges against Boniface. Clement never went to Rome, where feuding noble families made life turbulent, but moved the papal headquarters to Avignon in France, where the papacy remained under French influence from 1305 to 1377. During this period, the so-called "Babylonian Captivity" of the papacy, papal prestige suffered enormously. The English, Germans, and Italians accused the popes and the cardinals, who were also French, of being instruments of the French king, and the English Parliament forbade papal appointment to Church offices in England and restricted the carrying of appeals to the papal *curia*.

The Avignon papacy added fuel to the fires of those anticlerical critics who were attacking Church corruption, papal temporal claims, and the apparent lack of spiritual enthusiasm. Deprived of much of their former income from England, Germany, and Italy, and living in splendor in a newly built fortress-palace, the Avignon popes expanded the papal bureaucracy, added new Church taxes, and collected the old taxes more efficiently. This produced renewed denouncements of the wealth of the Church and demands for its reformation.

The Great Schism.   The return of the papacy to Rome in 1377 led to an even greater disaster for the Church. A papal election was held the following year, and the College of Cardinals, perhaps influenced by a shouting mob milling around the

Vatican, elected an Italian pope. A few months later the French cardinals declared the election invalid and elected a French pope, who returned to Avignon.

During the Great Schism, as this split of the Church into two allegiances was called, there were two popes, each with his college of cardinals and capital city, each claiming universal sovereignty, each sending forth papal administrators and taxing Christendom, and each excommunicating the other. The nations of Europe gave allegiance as their individual political interests prompted them. In order to keep that allegiance, the rival popes had to make concessions to their political supporters and largely abandoned the practice of interfering in national politics.

The Conciliar Movement.   Positive action to end the Great Schism came in the form of the Conciliar Movement, a return to the early Christian practice of solving Church problems by means of a general council of prelates (see p. 78). In 1395 the professors at the University of Paris proposed that a general council, representing the Universal Church, should meet to heal the Schism. A majority of the cardinals of both camps accepted this solution, and in 1409 they met at the Council of Pisa, deposed both pontiffs, and elected a third man. But neither of the two deposed popes would give up his office, and the papal throne now had three claimants.

Such an intolerable situation necessitated another Church council. In 1414 the Holy Roman emperor assembled at Constance the most impressive Church gathering of the period. For the first time voting took place on a purely national basis. Instead of the traditional assembly of bishops, the Council included lay representatives and was organized as a convention of "nations," with each nation having one vote. Through the deposition of the various papal claimants, the Great Schism was ended in 1417, and a single papacy was restored at Rome.

The Conciliar Movement represented a reforming and democratizing influence in the Church, aimed at transforming the papacy into something like a limited monarchy. But the movement was not to endure, even though the Council of Constance had solemnly decreed that general councils were superior to popes and that they should meet at regular intervals in the future.

The restoration of a single head of the Church, together with the inability of later councils to bring about much-needed reform, enabled the popes to discredit the Conciliar Movement by 1450. Unfortunately, while the popes hesitated to call councils to effect reform, they failed to bring about reform themselves. The Renaissance popes were more concerned with Italian politics and patronage of the arts.

Wycliffe, Huss, and Savonarola.   Throughout the fourteenth and fifteenth centuries the cries against the worldliness and corruption of the clergy increased and heresy intensified. In England a professor at Oxford named John Wycliffe (1320?-1384) assailed not only Church abuses but certain Church doctrines. Because Wycliffe believed that the Church should be subordinate to the state, that salvation was primarily an individual matter between man and God, that transubstantiation as formally taught by the Church was false, and that outward rituals and veneration of relics were idolatrous, he has been called the dawn-star of the Protestant Revolt. Wycliffe formed bands of "poor priests," called Lollards, who taught his views; and he provided the people with an English translation of the Bible, which he considered the final authority in matters of religion. Although Wycliffe's demands for reform did not succeed, the Lollards, including the famous John Ball (see p. 122), spread a more radical version of his ideas until the movement was driven underground early in the next century.

In Bohemia—where a strong reform movement, linked with the resentment of the Czechs towards their German overlords, was under way—Wycliffe's doctrines were propagated by Czech students who had heard him at Oxford. In particular, his beliefs influenced John Huss (1369?-1415), an impassioned preacher in Prague and later rector of the university there. Huss' attacks on the abuses of clerical power led him, like Wycliffe, to conclude that the true Church was composed of a universal priesthood of believers and that Christ alone was its head.

Huss' influence became so great that he was excommunicated. Later the emperor gave him a safe-conduct to stand trial for heresy at the Council of Constance. Huss refused to recant his views, and the Council ordered him burned at the stake in spite of his safe-conduct. This action made Huss a martyr to the Czechs, who rebelled against both the German emperor, who happened also to be king of Bohemia, and the Church. The Czechs maintained their political and religious independence for more than a generation before they were crushed. In the sixteenth century the remaining Hussites merged with the Lutherans.

A man whose career reflected all the major religious currents of the age—anticlericalism, mysticism, puritanism, reform, and heresy—was the Dominican friar Savonarola (1452-1498). A famed preacher who could fan the emotions of his audiences into a frenzied religious enthusiasm, Savonarola in 1494 helped oust the Medici bosses from Florence and became master of the city. For four years he worked to turn Florence into a republic of Christ, invoking the wrath of God upon worldly living and sinful luxuries. Bands of teenagers were organized to go about the city collecting and burning "vanities"—fashionable clothes, wigs, ornaments, and secular books and paintings. Savonarola also bitterly denounced the iniquities of Pope Alexander VI, who was deeply engaged in extending the Papal States and enlarging the fortunes of his family. "He preaches poverty," Savonarola said of the pope, "but his pockets are lined with coin." Claiming to be commissioned directly by God, Savonarola appealed to the rulers of Europe to summon a general council to oust the pope, whom he called Antichrist, and to reform the Church. "Come," he implored, "Christ wishes to revive His Church." But Savonarola lacked the power even to maintain his hold on the fickle Florentines. Tired of puritanism, they celebrated when the friar's enemies had him burned as a heretic in the great square of Florence. Savonarola, Wycliffe, and Huss were soon to be hailed by Luther and the Protestants as forerunners of their movement.

THE PROTESTANT REFORMATION

Martin Luther.   The first Church reformer to succeed where so many others had failed arose in Germany. But here a movement that began as a typical call for the reform of abuses soon became a revolt against the traditional doctrines and institutions of the Roman Catholic Church. The ultimate goal of Martin Luther and other Protestant leaders was a return to the original biblical Christianity, rejecting what they considered to be later human inventions such as the ecclesiastical hierarchy, monasticism, and most of the sacraments. Not ecclesiastical abuses but perversions of faith and doctrine became the main concern of Protestant reformers.

The son of a German peasant who by virtue of thrift and hard work had become a petty capitalist, Martin Luther was born on November 10, 1483. Young Martin received a sound education which included university studies, but he accepted as a matter of course the prevalent beliefs in witchcraft and other superstitions. The story goes that he once threw an inkpot at a devil whom he thought he saw leering at him. In 1505 he became a member of the mendicant order of Augustinian monks, a move which met with scant favor from his practical father, who wanted his son to study law. In 1508 Luther received an appointment as a lecturer at the new University of Wittenberg, and a few years later he became professor of theology.

In the meantime Luther had struggled with and solved for himself the spiritual problem that confronted many people in his time: In view of God's absolute power and man's powerlessness, how can man be certain of salvation for his soul? For many years Luther probed deeply this problem of eternal salvation. Finally, in 1515, while contemplating St. Paul's Epistle to the Romans (1:17), he came upon these words: "For therein is the righteousness of God revealed from faith to faith: as it is written, The just shall live by faith." Luther believed that his quest for spiritual certainty had been solved:

On his way home from the Diet of Worms, which had decreed him a heretic and outlaw, Martin Luther was "captured" and sent to a remote castle, Wartburg, on the orders of his protector, Frederick the Wise of Saxony. Safe from the Church's vengeance, Luther in this study at Wartburg translated the New Testament into German.

Night and day I pondered until I saw the connection between the justice of God and the statement that "the just shall live by his faith." Then I grasped that the justice of God is that righteousness by which through grace and sheer mercy God justifies us through faith. Thereupon I felt myself to be reborn and to have gone through open doors into paradise.[1]

By concluding that man was saved only by his trust and faith in the "sheer mercy" of God, Luther had come to his famous doctrine of justification by faith, as opposed to the Roman Church's doctrine of justification by faith *and* good works—the demonstration of faith through virtuous acts, acceptance of Church dogma, and participation in Church ritual.

The implications of Luther's doctrine were enormous. If salvation could come only through a personal faith in God's mercy, then an interceding priesthood became superfluous, for each man would then be his own priest. But Luther himself had no idea as yet where his views would eventually lead him and half of Christendom. It required a financial abuse by the Church to bring on the religious revolt.

Tetzel and indulgences. Leo x, a cultured scion of the Medici family, "who would have made an excellent Pope if he had only been a little religious,"[2] wanted to complete the magnificent new St. Peter's in Rome, but he lacked money for the costly enterprise. Papal agents were sent to Germany to sell indulgences as a means of raising money. One of these agents, a Dominican named Tetzel, discharged his mission "in the German archbishopric of Mainz in a manner which would be recognized in America to-day as high-pressure salesmanship."[3]

Church doctrine held that although the sacrament of Penance absolved the sinner from guilt and eternal punishment, some temporal punishment remained. An indulgence was a type of good work, to be compared with praying, visiting shrines, and contributing to worthy causes, and like all good works it was a means of remitting or pardoning the temporal penalty for sins. Theologically, the concept of indulgences rested on the theory of a "treasury of merits," which held that Christ, the Virgin, and the saints had won merit far in excess of their own needs and had thereby created a vast storehouse of good works. By means of indulgences the Church was able to draw upon and distribute this surplus to help those who felt they had not rendered sufficient penance to extinguish the punishment which they deserved.

It was the abuse attending the sale of indulgences to raise money that provoked Luther's initial protest. The common folk thought that a payment of money would buy God's grace and insure their salvation, and Tetzel exhorted them to give liberally for themselves and for their dead relatives in purgatory who were "crying to them for help."

Development of Luther's ideas. On October 31, 1517, Luther, following a university custom, posted ninety-five propositions (theses) on the subject of indulgences on the church door at Wittenberg, at the same time challenging anyone to debate them with him. The following are typical:

  6. The pope has no power to remit guilt, save by declaring and confirming that it has been remitted by God; . . .

21. Therefore those preachers of indulgences are in error who allege that through the indulgences of the pope a man is freed from every penalty.

36. Every Christian who is truly contrite has plenary remission both of penance and of guilt as his due, even without a letter of pardon.[4]

Luther wrote the ninety-five theses in Latin for the edification of his fellow theologians, but they were soon translated into the common tongue and six months later were well known throughout Germany. At first the Church at Rome did not seriously trouble itself, and Leo x dismissed the matter as a mere "squabble among monks."

In 1519 Luther debated with the eminent Catholic theologian John Eck at Leipzig. Luther maintained that the pope ruled by virtue of human rather than divine authority and was not infallible, that Church councils did not exist by divine right either and could also err, and that Scripture constituted the sole authority in matters of faith and doctrine. When Eck pointed out that such views were similar to those of Wycliffe and Huss, Luther boldly declared that "among the opinions of John Huss and the Bohemians many are certainly most Christian and evangelic, and cannot be condemned by the universal church."[5]

Yet in spite of these wide theological divergences, Luther continued to speak with affection of his "mother Church," which he hoped could be reformed and remain unified. By basing his position squarely on the doctrine of justification by faith alone, however, Luther found himself propelled by its implications to a position far removed from that of the Church.

Following the Leipzig debate, Eck initiated proceedings at Rome to have Luther declared a heretic. Luther in turn decided to put his case before the German people by publishing a series of pamphlets. In his *Address to the Nobility of the German Nation*, Luther called on the princes to reform ecclesiastical abuses, to strip the Church of its wealth and worldly power, and to create, in effect, a national German Church. Among numerous other proposals contained in this influential treatise, Luther urged a union with the Hussites, claiming that Huss had been unjustly burned at the stake.

The Babylonian Captivity of the Church summarized Luther's theological views. He attacked the papacy for having deprived the individual Christian of his freedom to approach God directly by faith and without the intermediation of the priesthood, and he set forth his views on the sacramental system. To be valid, a sacrament must have been instituted by Christ and be exclusively Christian. On this basis Luther could find justification only for Baptism and the Lord's Supper (his term for the sacrament known to Roman Catholics as the Holy Eucharist). Luther rejected the doctrine of transubstantiation on the grounds that a priest could not perform the miracle of transforming bread and wine into the Body and Blood of the Lord. Nevertheless, he believed in the real presence of Christ in the bread and wine of the sacrament. In Luther's view, the bread and wine coexist with the Body and Blood without a change of substance.

Luther's third pamphlet, *The Freedom of a Christian Man*, which was dedicated to the pope in the slight hope that reconciliation was still possible, set forth in conciliatory but firm tones Luther's views on Christian behavior and salvation. He did not discourage good works but argued that the inner spiritual freedom which comes from the certainty found in faith leads to the performance of good works. "Good works do not make a man good, but a good man does good works."[6]

The breach made complete. In June 1520 Pope Leo x issued the bull *Exsurge Domine* ("Arise, O Lord, . . . Arise all ye saints, and the whole universal Church, whose interpretation of Scripture has been assailed'"[7]), which gave Luther sixty days to turn from his heretical course. When Luther publicly burned the bull amid the applause of students and townsmen, he propelled himself into a showdown with Rome. In January 1521 Leo x excommunicated Luther.

Meanwhile, Charles v, who had recently been crowned emperor, found himself in a difficult situation. He was aware of popular German feelings and was not anxious to see papal power reconsolidated in his domains, yet he was bound by his oath to defend the Church and extirpate heresy. Moreover, Charles was orthodox in his own religious beliefs. It was decided that Luther should be heard at the emperor's first Diet, which was held at Worms. Summoned under an imperial safe-conduct, Luther was asked whether he intended to stand by everything he had written. He stood before the assembly and replied firmly:

> Your Imperial Majesty and Your Lordships demand a simple answer. Here it is, plain and unvarnished. Unless I am convicted of error by the testimony of Scripture or (since I put no trust in the unsupported authority of Pope or of councils, since it is plain that they have often erred and often contradicted themselves) by manifest reasoning I stand convicted by the Scriptures to which I have appealed, . . . I cannot and will not recant anything, for to act against our conscience is neither safe for us, nor open to us.
>
> On this I take my stand [*Hier stehe Ich*]. I can do no other. God help me. Amen."[8]

In May 1521 the Diet declared Luther a heretic and outlaw. He was, however, given protection by the elector of Saxony, in whose strongest castle he lived for almost a year.

During this period Luther began the construction of an evangelical church distinct from Rome. He wrote incessantly, setting forth his theological views in a collection of forceful sermons for use by preachers, in correspondence with friends and public figures, and in a treatise condemning monasticism. (In 1525 Luther married an ex-nun who had left the cloister after reading this treatise.) Luther also translated the New Testament into German, a monumental job accomplished in only eleven weeks. Later he translated the Old Testament. Luther's Bible was largely responsible for creating a standard literary language for all Germany.

Luther and the Peasants' War. Luther's teachings spread quickly through central and northern Germany. Pious persons who wanted the Church reformed embraced the new cause. Worldly individuals who believed that it would afford an opportunity to appropriate Church property also aided the movement, as did ardent nationalists who saw in it a means of uniting Germany. The emperor, meanwhile, was too deeply involved in a struggle with the French and the Turks to stamp out the new heresy (see p. 210).

Encouraged by Luther's concept of the freedom of a Christian man, which they applied to economic and social matters, the German peasants revolted in 1524. Long ground down by the nobles, the peasants included in their twelve demands the abolition of serfdom "unless it should be shown us from the Gospel that we are serfs"; a reduction of "the excessive services demanded of us, which are increased from day to day"; the fixing of rents "in accordance with justice"; and an end to "the appropriation by individuals of meadows and fields which at one time belonged to a community."[9] Luther recognized the justice of these demands, but when the peasants began to employ violence against established authority he turned against them. In a virulent pamphlet, *Against the Thievish and Murderous Hordes of Peasants*, Luther called on the princes to "knock down, strangle, and stab . . . and think nothing so venomous, pernicious, or Satanic as an insurgent."[10]

The revolt was stamped out in 1525 at a cost of an estimated 100,000 peasant dead, and the lot of the German peasant for the next two centuries was probably the worst in Europe. Politically and economically conservative, Luther believed that the equality of all men before God applied in spiritual but not in secular matters. This philosophy alienated the peasants but made allies of the princes, many of whom became Lutheran in part because it placed them in control of the church in their territories, thereby enhancing their power and wealth.

The religious settlement in Germany. At a meeting of the Diet of the Empire in 1529, the Catholic princes, with the emperor's support, pushed through a decree that the Mass must not be interfered with anywhere. This meant that while Lutheran activities were restricted in Catholic regions, those of the Catholics could be carried on even in Lutheran areas. In answer, the Lutheran leaders drew up a protest, and from this incident the word *Protestant* derives. The next Diet, meeting at Augsburg in 1530, was presented with a statement of Christian doctrine from the Lutheran viewpoint designed to conciliate the two parties. The Catholics refused to accept this statement, known as the Augsburg Confession, which became the official creed of Lutheranism.

The emperor now made public his intention to crush the growing heresy. In defense, the Lutheran princes banded together in 1531 in the Schmalkaldic League, and between 1546 and 1555 a sporadic civil war was fought. A compromise was finally reached in the Peace of Augsburg (1555), which allowed each prince to decide the religion of his subjects, gave Protestants the right to keep all Church property confiscated prior to 1552, forbade all sects of Protestantism other than Lutheranism, and ordered all Catholic bishops to give up their property if they turned Lutheran.

The effects of these provisions on Germany were profound. The Peace of Augsburg confirmed Lutheranism as a state religion in large portions of the Empire. Religious opinions became the private property of the princes, and the individual had to believe what his prince wanted him to believe, be it Lutheranism or Catholicism. Furthermore, by formally sanctioning state religion and thus enhancing a prince's power, the Peace of Augsburg added to Germany's political disintegration.

In 1546, during the Schmalkaldic War, the founder of the new faith died. Luther's career had been molded by an absolute conviction of the rightness of his beliefs, which goes far to explain both his driving power and his limitations. As Luther himself put it: "I myself will in no wise hearken to aught that is contrary to my doctrine; for I am certain and persuaded through the Spirit of Christ, that my teaching . . . is true and certain."

Lutheranism in Scandinavia. In 1525 the Grand Master of the Teutonic Knights who ruled Prussia (see p. 143) turned Lutheran, dissolved the order, secularized its lands, and declared himself duke of Prussia. With this exception, outside Germany Lutheranism permanently established itself as a state religion only in the Scandinavian countries. Here emerging modern monarchs welcomed the opportunity to obtain needed wealth by confiscating Church property and needed power by filling Church offices with Lutherans who preached obedience to constituted authority. This was particularly the case in Sweden where Gustavus Vasa led a successful struggle for Swedish independence from Denmark. In 1523 he was elected king, and soon thereafter he declared himself a Lutheran and filled his empty treasury from the sale of confiscated Church lands. In Denmark, which also ruled Norway, the spread of Lutheranism was encouraged by the king. In 1537 an ordinance, approved by Luther, established a national Lutheran church with its bishops as salaried officials of the Danish state.

Zwingli in Switzerland. Meanwhile, Protestantism had taken firm root in Switzerland. In the German-speaking area of that country—particularly in Zurich—the Reformation was led by Ulrich Zwingli (1484-1531). Like Luther, who was the same age, Zwingli repudiated papal in favor of scriptural authority, preached justification by faith, attacked monasticism and clerical celibacy, and drastically revised the sacramental system. But the differences between the two leaders proved irreconcilable when they met in 1529 at the University of Marburg, founded two years earlier as the first Protestant university in Europe. Whereas Luther looked on baptism as a means of helping to regenerate the individual, Zwingli considered it only a means of initiating a child into society. Nor did he believe with Luther that the real presence of Christ was found in the Lord's Supper. To Zwingli, who had been trained as a humanist and was therefore more of a rationalist than Luther, the bread and wine were only symbols of Christ's body and blood.

Zwingli was an ardent Swiss patriot who had once served as chaplain with Swiss mercenaries in Italy. The Swiss Confederation, comprising thirteen cantons, was a by-product of the weakness and disunity of the Holy Roman Empire. Originating in 1291 as a defensive union of three cantons, the Confederation expanded and repulsed all attempts of the emperors to exercise jurisdiction over it. Switzerland's independence was won by the valor of its hardy peasant pikemen, whose prowess became so famed that foreign rulers and popes eagerly sought their services. Garbed in colorful Renaissance costumes, Swiss mercenaries still guard the Vatican.

In 1531 war broke out between Protestant and Catholic cantons, and Zwingli was slain in battle. The war ended in the same year with an agreement that anticipated by a quarter of a century the Peace of Augsburg in Germany—each canton was allowed to choose its own religion. This settlement was largely responsible for keeping Switzerland from taking sides in the great religious wars that subsequently engulfed Europe. Furthermore, it helped set the policy of neutrality which the Swiss have followed to our own day.

John Calvin. The most famous sixteenth-century Protestant leader after Luther was John Calvin (1509-1564). A Frenchman of the middle class, Calvin studied theology and law at Paris, where he became interested in Luther's teachings. About 1533 he had what he called a "conversion," whereby he abandoned Catholicism and fled to the Protestant city of Basel in Switzerland. Here in 1536 he published the first edition of his great work, the *Institutes of the Christian Religion*, the most influential synthesis of Protestant theology ever written. Influenced by his legal training, Calvin's *Institutes* is a masterpiece of logical reasoning.

Whereas Luther's central doctrine was justification by faith, Calvin's was the sovereignty of God. "Both Calvin and Luther had an overwhelming sense of the majesty of God, but whereas for Luther this served to point up the miracle of forgiveness, for Calvin it gave rather the assurance of the impregnability of God's purpose."[11] God was omnipotent and for His own purposes had created the world and also man in His image. Since Adam and Eve had fallen from a state of sinlessness, man was utterly depraved and lost:

Carrying these doctrines to their logical conclusions, Calvin defined man's relation to God in his famous doctrine of predestination. Since God is omniscient, He knows the past, present, and future. Consequently, He must always know which men are to be saved and which men are to be damned eternally. Man's purpose in life, then, is not to try to work out his salvation—for this has already been determined—but to honor God. While Calvin did not profess to know absolutely who were God's chosen—the elect—he believed that exemplary living in accordance with a strict moral code was a "sign of election."

Calvin's emphasis upon the sovereignty of God led him to differ with Luther on the relationship of church and state. To Luther the state was supreme, but to Calvin the church and its ministers, as representatives of the sovereignty of God, must dominate. Calvinist church government in turn was democratically oriented in that it was based on the authority not of bishops but of synods or presbyteries, elected bodies composed of ministers and elders. Although Calvin upheld lawful political authority, he also approved of rebellion against a tyranny "which overrides private conscience." Thus, wherever Calvinism spread it carried with it the seeds of representative government and of defiance against despotism.

Calvinist Geneva. In 1536 the Protestants of Geneva invited Calvin to become their leader, and there he put his ideas on government into effect. Calvin believed it was the duty of the elect to glorify God by establishing a theocracy that would be governed according to scriptural precept. Although the Bible was the supreme authority, the chief instrument of government was the Consistory, or Presbytery, a council of ministers and elders which made and enforced the laws. Calvin in turn dominated the Consistory, which showed great zeal in disciplining the community and punishing or removing any person found guilty of unseemly behavior. Penalties were inflicted for being absent from sermons or laughing during the church service, for wearing bright colors, for swearing or dancing, for playing cards, or for having one's fortune told by gypsies.

In regard to more serious offenses, Calvin acted with a severity common to the Reformation age. When the Spanish physician Servetus sought refuge in Geneva, having fled from Catholic persecution because he was a Unitarian who denied the doctrine of the Trinity, Calvin had him burned for heresy. "Because the Papists persecute the truth," Calvin explained, "should we on that account refrain from repressing error?"

The spread of Calvinism. From Geneva, Calvinism spread far and wide, imbued with its founder's spirit of austerity and a self-righteousness born of confidence in being among the elect of God. Many of its leaders studied at the Academy (today the University of Geneva), which trained students from other countries in Calvin's theology. In France, Calvinism made influential converts among both the bourgeoisie and the nobility. Known as Huguenots, the French Calvinists remained a minority but, as we shall see in the next chapter, their importance far outweighed their numbers. In Scotland the fiery Calvinist John Knox successfully challenged the authority of the Roman Church (see p. 199), and in Germany and the Netherlands Calvin's teachings formed the basis for the German and Dutch Reformed churches.

Henry VIII's quarrel with Rome.   In Germany the revolt against the Church was primarily religious in nature, although it possessed political implications; in England the situation was reversed. There the leader was a monarch, Henry VIII (1509-1547), not a priest. Henry broke with Rome not for theological reasons but because the pope would not annul his marriage to Catherine of Aragon, daughter of Ferdinand and Isabella of Spain, whom he had married for dynastic reasons.

Catherine had given Henry a daughter, Mary, but no son, and Henry was convinced that a male heir was necessary if the newly established Tudors were to endure as a dynasty and England kept from reverting to anarchy. Catherine was the widow of his brother, and Church law forbade a man to marry his brother's widow. A special papal dispensation had been granted for the marriage, but Henry claimed the dispensation was not valid and in 1527 asked Pope Clement VII to revoke it.

Normally the pope might have acquiesced to Henry's wishes, for other popes had granted similar favors to monarchs and Henry had been loyal to the Church. In answer to Luther he had written a *Defense of the Seven Sacraments* (1521), in which he castigated Luther as a "poisonous serpent," the "wolf of hell," and the "limb of Satan." The pope gratefully bestowed on Henry the title "Defender of the Faith"—a title which English monarchs still possess. But much as he might have wished, the pope could not support Henry in his desires. The emperor Charles V, who was also king of Spain and the most powerful monarch in Europe, was a nephew of Catherine and threatened the pope if he declared the marriage null and void. Clement decided to wait before giving his answer, hoping that in the meantime events would resolve themselves.

But Henry would not wait. He obtained from Parliament the power to appoint bishops in England without papal permission, designating Thomas Cranmer as archbishop of Canterbury. In 1533 Cranmer pronounced the king's marriage to Catherine invalid and legalized Henry's marriage to coquettish Anne Boleyn, whom he had secretly married three months earlier. At last goaded into action, Clement VII excommunicated Henry and maintained that Catherine alone was the king's true wife.

Establishment of the Anglican Church.   In 1534 Henry severed all connections with Rome. A compliant Parliament passed the famous Act of Supremacy, which stated that the king "justly and rightfully is and ought to be supreme head of the Church of England." It also enacted the Treason Act, which declared liable to the death penalty anyone who called the king a "heretic, schismatic, tyrant, infidel, or usurper." Turning on his old friend, Henry had Sir Thomas More (see p. 182) beheaded because he would not acknowledge the sovereign as head of the English Church.

To replenish the royal coffers and to gain popular support, Henry, working through Parliament, dissolved the monasteries and sold their lands to the nobles and gentry. Thus Henry acquired accomplices, in a sense, in his conflict with Rome. But Henry and Parliament could not have effected such sweeping changes if many Englishmen had not been anticlerical.

In the same year (1539) in which Parliament acted to dissolve the monasteries, it also passed the Six Articles, which reaffirmed the main points of Catholic theology. By this act, both the Catholic who denied the supremacy of the king and the Protestant who denied the validity of transubstantiation were to be punished severely. Thus England threw off the supremacy of the pope without at that time adopting the Protestant faith; the elements of Protestantism in the English Church crept in after the break with Rome.

After Henry's death in 1547, his frail ten-year-old son mounted the throne as Edward VI. During his reign the growing Protestant party in England became ascendant. The Six Articles were repealed; priests were no longer held to their vows of celibacy; and the old Latin service was replaced by Cranmer's Book of Common Prayer, written in English, which brought the service much closer to the people and exerted a powerful influence on the development of the language. In 1553 the Forty-Two Articles defined the faith of the Church of England along Protestant lines.

Under the devoutly Catholic Mary (1553-1558), the unfortunate daughter of the still less fortunate Catherine of Aragon, Catholicism was reinstated, and three hundred Protestants, including Archbishop Cranmer, were burned at the stake. But with the accession to the throne of Anne Boleyn's red-headed and fiery-tempered daughter, Elizabeth I (1558-1603), the Anglican Church took on a strong Protestant character. Realizing the political necessity for religious peace, Elizabeth worked hard to achieve a compromise settlement. Although the Church of England remained a state church under the control of the monarch, Elizabeth astutely changed her title from "Supreme Head" to the more modest "Supreme Governor." In accepting the Bible as the final authority, and in recognizing only Baptism and Holy Eucharist as Christ-instituted sacraments, Elizabeth's Thirty-Nine Articles (1563) were essentially Protestant, although many articles were ambiguously phrased in an effort to satisfy both parties. Much Catholic ritual was preserved, along with the ecclesiastical government of bishops in apostolic succession.

Presbyterianism in Scotland. The religious revolt in Scotland was largely the work of the zealous reformer John Knox (1505?-1572), who had become a disciple of Calvin in Geneva. After returning to his native Scotland in about 1559, Knox became the leader of a group of Protestant nobles who wished to overthrow both the jurisdiction of the Roman Catholic Church and the monarch—Queen Mary Stuart, whose husband was king of France. In 1560 the Scottish Parliament severed all ties with Rome and accepted Knox's Articles of the Presbyterian Church, modeled after Calvin's views on theology and church government. When the beautiful but ill-fated queen returned from France one year later she found her bleak kingdom alienated from her own Catholic views. Her seemingly scandalous behavior (see p. 213) and her steadfast Catholicism led the Scots to depose her in 1567 in favor of her Protestant son James.

The Anabaptists. The most radical among those who rejected the religious establishment of the time were the Anabaptists ("rebaptizers"), so called because they denied the efficacy of infant baptism. They formed many sects led by self-styled "prophets" who carried to extreme Luther's doctrines of Christian liberty, priesthood of all believers, and return to primitive Christianity. Centered in Switzerland, Germany, and the Netherlands, the Anabaptists set themselves apart from the sinful world and followed the example of early Christians in sharing their worldly goods with one another. On occasion they employed force to purify society and establish a New Jerusalem. Mainly, however, they believed in the separation of church and state and advocated pacifism and the love-ethic. Today some portion of their spirit lives on among such groups as the Mennonites, the Amish, and the Quakers.

THE CATHOLIC REFORMATION

Origins. By the 1530's the Church had rallied its forces and had begun to take the offensive against the inroads of Protestantism. This renewal of strength, known as the Catholic Reformation—or Counter Reformation—penetrated all areas of the Church. New monastic orders adapted monastic life to the needs of the time, the papacy headed a program of vigorous reform, and the Church regained much ground lost to the Protestants. Climaxing the whole movement was the Council of Trent, where the Church boldly reaffirmed its traditional doctrines and flatly refused to compromise in any way with the Protestants.

The Catholic Reformation should not be viewed solely as a retaliatory movement to stem the rising tide of Protestantism. Before Luther had posted his ninety-five theses, evidence of renewed vitality and internal reform was visible in the Roman Church.

One of the prime examples of this resurgence occurred in Spain under Ferdinand and Isabella, ardent Catholics as well as autocrats. To deal with Moors, Jews, and heretics, the "Catholic Sovereigns" requested and got papal permission for a separate Spanish Inquisition under their control (see p. 136). The Inquisition soon came to dominate the Spanish Church, making it virtually a state church, and moved on to the problem of religious reform. Under the able Grand Inquisitor, Cardinal Ximenes (d. 1517), both the secular clergy and the monastic orders were invigorated by a renewal of spirit, discipline, and education—the latter including the scholarly study of the Bible at the University of Alcala, founded by Ximenes as a means of training able bishops. Thus Spain became a model Catholic state, where Protestantism would make few converts.

Reformist monasticism. In response to the same forces that had produced monastic reform during the earlier medieval reformation (see Chapter 7), a number of new monastic orders sprang up in the first half of the sixteenth century. Prominent among them were the Theatines, a body of devoted priests who undertook to check the spread of heresy by concentrating upon the regeneration of the clergy; the Capuchins, an offshoot of the Franciscan order inspired by the original spirit of St. Francis, who became notable for their preaching and for the care of the poor and the sick; and the Ursulines, whose special task was the education of girls. Reflecting both the reforming zeal of the new orders and the mystical reaffirmation of faith that characterized most reformers, Protestant as well as Catholic, was the order of barefoot Carmelites and their founder, the Spanish nun St. Theresa. These devout sisters slept on straw, ate no meat, and lived on alms.

Loyola and the Jesuits. The Society of Jesus, better known as the Jesuits, founded by the Spanish nobleman and ex-soldier Ignatius Loyola (1491-1556), played a vital role in the Catholic Reformation. While recovering from a severe battle wound, Loyola experienced a mystical religious conversion and vowed to become a soldier of Christ and "serve only God and the Roman pontiff, His vicar on earth." His "Company [*Societas*] of Jesus," founded in 1534 and given papal authorization in 1540, was organized along military lines with Loyola as "general." Members were carefully selected, rigorously trained, and subjected to an iron discipline. One of the classics in the field of religious literature, Loyola's *Spiritual Exercises*, a work of great psychological penetration based on his own mystical religious experience, was used to inculcate disciplined asceticism and absolute obedience to superior authority. In addition to the usual monastic vows of chastity, obedience, and poverty, the Jesuits took a special vow of allegiance to the pope. As preachers, educators, and confessors to monarchs and princes, the Jesuits had remarkable success in stemming and even reversing the tide of Protestantism, particularly in Poland, Bohemia, Hungary, Germany, France, and the Spanish Netherlands (modern Belgium). In addition, the Jesuits performed excellent missionary work in America and Asia.

Papal reform and the Council of Trent. A new era was at hand for the Church when Paul III, who reigned from 1534 to 1549, ascended the papal throne. He chose outstanding men as cardinals and appointed a commission to look into the need for reform. Their report listed the evils requiring correction, and Paul made plans to call a general council to carry out needed reforms.

The Catholic Reformation came to a climax in the Council of Trent, which met in three sessions between 1545 and 1563. Rejecting all compromise with Protestantism, the Council restated the basic tenets of Catholic doctrine. It declared salvation to be a matter of both faith and good works, and it affirmed the source of doctrine to be not only the Bible, as interpreted by the Church, but also the "unwritten traditions, which were received by the Apostles from the lips of Christ himself, or, by the same Apostles, at the dictation of the Holy Spirit, and were handed on and have come down to us. . . . "[12] The Council also reaffirmed the seven sacraments, with special emphasis on transubstantiation, decreed that only Latin be used in the Mass, and approved the spiritual usefulness of indulgences, pilgrimages, veneration of saints and relics, and the cult of the Virgin.

At the same time, the Council sought to eliminate abuses by ordering reforms in Church discipline and administration. Such evils as simony, absenteeism, the abuse of indulgences, and secular pursuits on the part of the clergy were strictly forbidden. Bishops were ordered to supervise closely both the regular and the secular clergy, appoint reputable and competent men to ecclesiastical positions, and establish seminaries to provide a well-educated clergy. The clergy, in turn, were requested to preach frequently to the people.

In addition to freeing the Church of its worst abuses and formulating its doctrines clearly and rigidly, the Council of Trent strengthened the authority of the papacy. The pope's party in the Council, ably led by Jesuit theologians, defeated all attempts to revive the theory that a general council was supreme in the Church. And when the final session of the Council voted that none of its decrees were valid without the consent of the Holy See, the Church became more than ever an absolute monarchy ruled by the pope.

EFFECTS OF THE RELIGIOUS UPHEAVAL

Religious division, education, and intolerance. By 1550, with Protestantism predominant in northern Europe, the unity of western Christendom was split irreparably. The Catholics accepted the authority of the pope and stressed the need for a mediatory priesthood. The Protestants placed their faith in the authority of the Bible and held that every Christian could win salvation without priestly mediation. But since the latter differed among themselves in their interpretation of the Bible and the methods of church organization, in time numerous separate Protestant sects arose.

Another by-product of the religious upheaval was a new interest in education, already broadened by the intellectual and moral concerns of the humanists. Each faith wanted its youth to be properly trained in its teachings. The Jesuits in particular developed a school system so superior that even many Protestant youths attended. Protestant emphasis upon the importance of Bible reading encouraged the promotion of universal education; Luther, for example, insisted not only that the state should establish schools but that "the civil authorities are under obligation to compel the people to send their children to school."[13]

On the debit side the Reformation era witnessed an intensification of religious intolerance. There seems little choice between Catholics and Protestants in the degree of their detestation for one another and for religious liberty in general.

Religion was not a subject which was taken lightly by Luther's contemporaries. Feelings of morbid unworthiness and guilt were not uncommon; Luther himself was prey to these emotions. In "The Seven Deadly Sins" Hieronymous Bosch shows each of the traditional sins being macabrely punished in hell.

Each religious sect assumed that salvation came through it alone, and all were equally intolerant when they had the power to be so. In the words of Sebastian Castellio (d. 1563), a one-time follower of Calvin who wrote a protest against the execution of Servetus:

> Although opinions are almost as numerous as men, nevertheless there is hardly any sect which does not condemn all others and desire to reign alone. Hence arise banishments, chains, imprisonments, stakes, and gallows and this miserable rage to visit daily penalties upon those who differ from the mighty about matters hitherto unknown, for so many centuries disputed, and not yet cleared up.[14]

How can we call ourselves Christians, Castellio asked in effect, if we do not imitate Christ's clemency and mercy?

> O Creator and King of the world, dost Thou see these things? Art Thou become so changed, so cruel, so contrary to Thyself? When Thou wast on earth none was more mild, more clement, more patient of injury. . . . O blasphemies and shameful audacity of men, who dare to attribute to Christ that which they do by the command and at the instigation of Satan![15]

Unfortunate, too, was the break between the humanists and the Protestants, which began when Luther broke with the Church. Although both groups wanted to reform the Church by removing its abuses and returning to the practices and faith of early Christianity, Erasmus could say of Luther's revolt: "I laid a hen's egg: Luther hatched a bird of quite different breed."[16] The humanists, in other words, desired reform, not revolution. Furthermore, because they exalted the rationality and innate goodness of man, the humanists disagreed with the strong Protestant emphasis on man's depravity and the necessity of salvation by superhuman means. As Luther saw it, "The human avails more with Erasmus than the divine."[17]

Protestantism and capitalism.   The Renaissance encouraged a new individualism in economic matters, which contributed to a breakdown of the guild system and to the rise of the individual capitalist entrepreneur (see Chapter 11). While Luther continued to accept the medieval concept of the "just price" and the ban against usury (receiving interest on money loaned), with the Calvinists investment of capital and loaning of money became respectable. Calvin encouraged enterprise by teaching that a man's career was a "calling" assigned to him by God and success in his calling was a sign of election to salvation. Indeed, it has been asserted that:

> Calvin did for the bourgeoisie of the sixteenth century what Marx did for the proletariat of the nineteenth, . . . the doctrine of predestination satisfied the same hunger for an assurance that the forces of the universe are on the side of the elect as was to be assuaged in a different age by the theory of historical materialism. He . . . taught them to feel that they were a chosen people, made them conscious of their great destiny in the Providential plan and resolute to realize it.[18]

Union of religion and politics. In most cases the religious division of Europe followed political lines. In Germany the Peace of Augsburg gave the ruler of each state the right to decide the faith of his subjects, thus controlling the church in his realm. Similarly, rulers of other countries, both Catholic and Protestant, developed national churches, so that much of Europe was divided religiously into an Anglican Church, a French Church, a Swedish Church, and so on. Religious uniformity was the ideal of the rulers of all states. Political and religious developments continued to be closely related for a century after 1550.

CHAPTER 10
THE STRIFE OF STATES AND KINGS

Power Politics and the New Diplomacy: 1500-1650

By acquiring a historical perspective we can do much to illuminate today's events and problems and bring them into focus. The period from 1500 to 1650 is particularly significant; it can serve as a laboratory in which we can watch the genesis and development of the statecraft of modern times.

The central factor in this troubled period was the rise of the competitive state system, involving the actions of independent and sovereign nations. These budding nations exhibited three fundamental features that contrasted sharply with the characteristics the same territories had possessed in earlier, feudal times: they had strong and effective central governments, their citizens displayed increased national consciousness, and their rulers claimed sovereignty—that is, supreme power within the boundaries of their own states. As we shall see in this chapter, these states were expansionist and aggressive, taking every opportunity to grow more powerful at the expense of weaker nations.

The decline of the medieval Church and the religious revolt in the sixteenth century ended the Church's role as the arbiter of right and justice in disputes between secular rulers. The rulers of the sovereign states were thus completely free and untrammeled in the arena of international politics. Would one state be able to dominate all the rest? Would there be varying degrees of power among states without any one becoming supreme? Would these independent and sovereign nations be able to establish a pattern of cooperation, ensuring thereby a measure of peace and political amity in the western world? These fundamental questions were answered in Europe between 1500 and 1650. And the way in which they were answered set the pattern of international relations from that day to this.

The one hundred fifty years following 1500 are among the bloodiest and most complex in European history. The story of these years is chiefly one of battles, alliances, and treaties—in a word, drum-and-trumpet history. Yet running through the wars and complexities of this period two major threads can be discerned: the emergence of the modern diplomatic technique of the "balance of power" as a means of providing some degree of equilibrium to the new European state system, and the rise and fall of Spain as the dominant power in Europe.

Sovereignty replaces suzerainty.   Both the medieval ideal of universal empire and Church and the medieval actuality of decentralized feudalism were undermined by the rise of strong monarchs who defied popes and put down rebellious nobles. The century before 1500 had witnessed much disorder, civil conflict, and war; more and more, people looked to their kings to provide the state with a measure of stability and security. Rulers also took an active part in stimulating the economy of their nations, and in return they obtained from the bourgeoisie larger revenues which they used to expand administrative bureaus and government services. Of great importance was the fact that kings could now afford to hire soldiers for standing armies—monarchs were no longer dependent upon the irregularly available feudal forces. Moreover, the king's army could easily squelch the retainers of a rebellious noble. Thus the power once distributed throughout the feudal pyramid was concentrated in the hands of the ruler.

The theory of centralized unchallenged authority—that is, sovereignty—was given its first comprehensive expression by a French lawyer and university professor, Jean Bodin (1530-1596). Dismayed by the disorders of the religious wars in France (see p. 213), Bodin attacked both the feudal idea of contract and the universalism of empire and Church in his work *Concerning Public Affairs.* He supported the power of the monarch and his right of sovereignty, which he defined as "unlimited power over citizens and subjects, unrestrained by law."[1] According to Bodin, the king was free of all restraint save some rather shadowy limitation exercised by God and divine law.

The advent of power politics.   Equipped with a standing army, royal courts, and new sources of revenue and backed by the growing support of the bourgeoisie, a European monarch was master in his own nation by the beginning of the sixteenth century. And, equally significant, he was his own master in foreign affairs. The Church was no longer an international arbiter, and the factionalism of the Protestant Reformation was soon to reduce appreciably the Church's claim to universal influence. It is interesting, however, to note that the Christian church, both Protestant and Catholic, after World War ii, has shown the will to exert its influence as an arbiter between nations. Especially noteworthy was the famous encyclical of Pope John in 1963, *Pacem in Terris (Peace on Earth),* calling for world peace and understanding. The international arena now consisted of a number of free agents who could keep what they could defend and take what they wanted if they had sufficient force. A nation-state depended for survival on the exercise of its power, and war was the chief instrument at hand. Thus statecraft became the politics of power, and the competitive state system emerged.

The rise of modern diplomacy.   The development of the competitive state system gave rise to the practice of modern diplomacy. Rulers needed to be informed about the plans and policies of their rivals; states fearful of attack from stronger foes had to seek out allies; and, after wars had been fought, agreements between victor and vanquished required negotiations.

Medieval popes customarily sent envoys to reside at royal courts, but modern diplomatic practice had its real birth among the fiercely independent city-states of northern Italy. The republic of Venice—"the school and touchstone of ambassadors"—was particularly active; its authorities maintained diplomatic archives and sent their representatives throughout Europe with elaborate instructions. To act as a safeguard against poisoning, trusted cooks were part of a diplomat's retinue, but ambassadors' wives were forbidden to accompany their husbands on diplomatic missions for fear they might divulge state secrets. About 1455 the first permanent embassy in history was sent to Genoa by the duke of Milan. Within a short time most of the important nations of the day followed suit and posted representatives in European capitals.

Balance-of-power politics. One of the most important achievements of the new diplomacy was the technique known as the "balance of power," whereby a coalition of states could checkmate the swollen power of one or more rival states and thereby restore equilibrium. Balance-of-power politics then and later aimed not so much at preventing war as at preserving the sovereignty and independence of individual states from threatened or actual aggression. Yet as international relations more and more took the form of alignments aimed at preserving the balance of power, a sense of the interdependence of the European state system developed. The strong movement toward European unity in our day is the latest manifestation of this sense of interdependence.

The sixteenth century was the formative period for the behavior pattern of modern nations in international affairs. Unrestrained by religious or ethical scruples, the sovereign governments were about to begin an era of international strife with the quest for power as their only guide to success. With disunited Italy as a pawn in the game, the counters on the chessboard began to move.

ITALY: CASE STUDY IN POWER POLITICS

Charles VIII and the Italian Wars. Because of Louis XI's success as a statemaker (see p. 134), his son Charles VIII (1483-1498) entertained grandiose notions of imitating the exploits of Hannibal and Charlemagne by invading Italy, conquering Naples, and eventually wresting Constantinople from the Turks. In 1494 Charles crossed the Alps at the head of thirty thousand well-trained troops and initiated the Italian Wars that were to last intermittently until 1559. At first the expedition was little more than a holiday for the French. Charles' cavalry, pikemen, and light, quick-firing cannon won easy victories, and he soon took possession of Naples.

This quick conquest alarmed the rulers who had previously acquiesced to Charles' plan. Ferdinand of Spain suspected that Charles might next try to conquer the Spanish possession of Sicily, and the Holy Roman emperor became uneasy at the prospect of French dominance in Italy. In addition, Venice feared for its independence and took the lead in forming a league which also included the Papal States, the Holy Roman Empire, and Spain. Called the Holy League, it was the first important example of a coalition of states formed to preserve the balance of power in Europe. Its armies drove Charles out of Italy in 1495, thus halting French designs on the peninsula for the moment.

End of the first phase of the Italian Wars. Following the death of Charles VIII in 1498, his successor, Louis XII, invaded Italy. The counters again moved on the chessboard: alliances were made and then broken, pledges went unhonored, and allies were deserted. Ferdinand of Spain offers a particularly good example of duplicity and treachery. Louis XII accused Ferdinand of cheating him on at least two occasions. Hearing this, Ferdinand scoffed: "He lies, the drunkard; I have deceived him more than ten times."[2]

In the first phase of the Italian Wars—which ended in 1513 with the French again ejected from Italy—one can see the new power politics at work, without benefit of rules and indeed without benefit of any moral or religious scruples. The only important objectives were glory, power, and wealth. In attaining these objectives "necessity knows no law," as Renaissance lawyers liked to observe. The conflict over Italy clearly prophesied the mode of future relations among modern sovereign states.

Machiavelli and Machiavellian politics.   The primer for diplomacy and power politics was written by Niccolò Machiavelli (1469-1527), historian, playwright, and official in the Florentine republic. Outraged at the cavalier manner in which invaders had smashed their way into his beloved Italy, Machiavelli mourned his native land as being

> more a slave than the Hebrews, more a servant than the Persians, more scattered than the Athenians; without head, without government; defeated, plundered, torn asunder, overrun; subject to every sort of disaster.[3]

Machiavelli's wide acquaintance with the unprincipled politics of the early Italian Wars produced his cynical and ruthless attitude toward men and politics. *The Prince*—one of a half-dozen volumes that have helped form western political thought—was written as a guide for an audacious leader who would use any means to win and hold power, free Italy from invaders, and end Italian disunity. A realist who wanted his leader-statesman to understand the political facts of life as they had been operating in Europe, Machiavelli wrote:

> A prudent ruler . . . cannot and should not observe faith when such observance is to his disadvantage and the causes that made him give his promise have vanished. If men were all good, this advice would not be good, but since men are wicked and do not keep their promises to you, you likewise do not have to keep yours to them. Lawful reasons to excuse his failure to keep them will never be lacking to a prince.[4]

Machiavelli did not, of course, invent the precepts of ruthlessness in politics. Rulers had dishonored treaties and used force to attain their ends before *The Prince* was written. What Machiavelli did was to accept the politics of his day without any false illusions. He gave his prince many suggestions for survival and conquest in the brutal world of unrestrained power.

> In the actions of all men, and especially those of princes, where there is no court to which to appeal, people think of the outcome. A prince needs only to conquer and to maintain his position. The means he has used will always be judged honorable and will be praised by everybody, because the crowd is always caught by appearance and by the outcome of events, and the crowd is all there is in the world. . . . [5]

Although "Machiavellian politics" is generally a term of condemnation, it should be noted that Machiavelli had an idealistic end in view: to "bring good to the mass of the people of the land" of Italy.[6]

EUROPEAN EMPIRE OR SOVEREIGN STATES?

Charles V.   The manner in which the rulers of Europe practiced power politics is shown clearly by the events in Europe during the first half of the sixteenth century, a period often referred to as the Age of Charles v.

Charles' grandfather, Maximilian i, Archduke of Austria and Holy Roman emperor, had added the Netherlands and Franche-Comté to his realm by marrying Mary of Burgundy. (Franche-Comté was that part of Burgundy not seized by Louis xi; see p. 135). Maximilian's son (Charles' father) had married a daughter of Ferdinand and Isabella of Spain. Thus, by a calculated policy of dynastic marriages, the Austrian Hapsburgs enjoyed a position no ruler since Charlemagne had held. Following his father's death in 1506, Charles became ruler of the Netherlands; in 1516 his maternal grandfather, Ferdinand, bequeathed him Spain and its overseas empire and Naples and Sicily. The death of his other grandfather, Maximilian, gave him Austria and left vacant the throne of the Holy Roman Empire, to which Charles was elected in 1519 as Emperor Charles v.

Charles' efforts in protecting his dispersed territories, together with his dream of restoring royal authority and religious unity in Germany, led many of his contemporaries to believe that he sought to dominate all of Europe. Although he was essentially conservative and moderate, Charles found himself with too many irons in the fire; he was constantly frustrating plots, crushing rebellions, and repelling invasions in his many dominions.

Charles' problems were inextricably connected with the activities of Francis i of France, Henry viii of England, and Suleiman, ruler of the Ottoman empire. Out of the interplay of their rivalries unfolded the bloody drama of the first half of the sixteenth century.

New moves on the chessboard.   The basic cause of Franco-Hapsburg rivalry was the fact that Charles' possessions encircled the realm of Francis i (1515-1547). In 1515, just before Charles v came into his inheritance, Francis invaded Italy, occupied Milan, and so set the stage for the renewal of the Italian Wars. Across the English Channel, Henry viii followed the events closely, aiming to use his state, with its small population of 2,500,000, as a counterweight in the Franco-Hapsburg rivalry. Believing Francis to be militarily stronger than Charles, Henry allied himself with the Hapsburg emperor in order to check French power.

The test of strength began as Charles' forces drove the French from Milan. Francis soon recaptured it, but at the battle of Pavia (1525) the French were defeated and Francis was taken prisoner. Realizing that he had miscalculated, Henry viii executed a sudden about-face, deserting Charles and supporting France and a coalition of lesser powers against the Hapsburgs. This use of England's power to equalize the strength of Continental rivals is a spectacular example of what now became the cornerstone of English foreign policy. Time and again in modern history, England has employed balance-of-power diplomacy to maintain European equilibrium.

Suleiman, ruler of the Turks.   The Ottoman empire, which reached the height of its power under Suleiman the Magnificent (1520-1566), was far stronger than any European state. The outstanding feature of its efficient administrative and military system was the dominant role played by slaves. Although Christians were granted a separate religious and civil status under the leadership of their bishops, every five years between 2,000 and 12,000 Christian boys from the ages of ten to fifteen were enslaved and brought to Constantinople. There they were converted to Islam and trained to enter the administration, where even the post of grand vizier was open to them, or the army. In the latter instance they served as Janissaries, the elite 12,000-man core of the Turkish standing army, who were fanatical in their devotion to Islam.

The powerful Ottoman empire was still expanding. Suleiman's predecessor had given Europe a respite by turning eastward to conquer Syria and Egypt, but Suleiman resumed the advance westward. With the European states politically and religiously at odds, Suleiman faced no concerted resistance. In 1521 he captured Belgrade, the key fortress of the Hungarian frontier, and in 1526 on the plain of Mohacs the Janissary infantry crushed the cavalry of the Hungarian magnates. The Hungarian king and many of his magnates were killed, and Suleiman moved on to plunder Buda without organized resistance.

The king who perished at Mohacs had ruled both Hungary and Bohemia. Terrified by the prospect of new Turkish attacks, the Bohemians and the Hungarians offered their vacant thrones to Ferdinand, brother-in-law of the dead king and brother of Charles v. Since most of Hungary had been occupied by the Turks, Furdinand's rule extended only over the northwest portion of that country. Thus a Turkish victory placed the destiny of Hungary and Bohemia in the hands of the Hapsburgs and established the Turks as a threat on Charles' Austrian borders.

Religion and politics on the chessboard.   Following his release from captivity in 1526, after making promises he had no intention of keeping, Francis i decided upon an alliance with Suleiman. The enemies of the French king protested loudly against this "unholy alliance," but power politics took precedence over religion in both Paris and Constantinople.

Indirectly, the Turks aided the Protestant cause in Germany. In 1529 Suleiman's armies besieged Vienna, but supply difficulties and Hapsburg resistance forced the attackers to retire. To deal with the Turkish threat, Charles, who had been planning measures against the Lutherans, was forced to arrange a truce with the Protestant princes to gain their support against the Turks.

Suleiman now turned to the Mediterranean where Tunisia and Algeria became Ottoman vassal states and bases for Turkish pirates, known as corsairs, who preyed on Christian shipping and raided the coasts of Spain and Italy. The strength that Charles might have amassed to crush the French monarchy was diverted to his besieged lands bordering on the Mediterranean. A truce in 1544 halted the French-Hapsburg struggle, and Charles could at last concentrate his efforts on the German states, where in 1546 the Lutheran struggle flared into civil war. With France aiding the Lutherans and the Catholic princes giving only half-hearted support to Charles lest he become powerful enough to dominate them, the Schmalkaldic War ended in 1555 with the compromise Peace of Augsburg (see p. 195). The Lutheran faith received official sanction, and Charles was thwarted in his cherished aim of restoring religious unity to Germany.

In 1556, five months after the Peace of Augsburg, the weary and discouraged emperor retired to a monastery. He turned over the Hapsburg possessions in central Europe to his brother Ferdinand, who was elected emperor, and gave

POLITICAL DIVISIONS
OF EUROPE ABOUT 1500

▬▬▬ Boundary of The Holy Roman Empire

Spain, the Netherlands, and his Italian possessions to his son Philip. Thereafter two Hapsburg dynasties, one Spanish and the other Austrian, ruled in Europe. A legend has it that Charles spent the two remaining years of his life trying to make several clocks keep exactly the same time—apparently an allegory suggesting that he was faced with so many problems that he could never settle all of them.

Significance for modern times. The eventful Age of Charles V had laid down much of the political and religious foundation for modern Europe:

1) It had been decided by force of arms that no single state was to dominate all of Europe. The balance of power was maintained.

2) German and Italian national growth was further stunted. Italy had been a battleground since 1494, and when the Italian Wars finally ended in 1559, Milan and Naples were Spanish possessions and Spain was to dominate Italy for nearly two hundred years.

3) Charles' wars with France and the Turks prevented him from applying pressure on the Lutherans and so saved the Reformation in Germany.

4) The Peace of Augsburg confirmed France's hold on the bishoprics of Metz, Toul, and Verdun in Lorraine, which the French had occupied during the Schmalkaldic War. French expansion toward the Rhine had begun, with momentous consequences for the future.

5) The advance of Ottoman power in Europe meant that Turkish control over the Balkans was handed down to later European statesmen as an explosive legacy. The alliance of France with Turkey, which also gave the French trading rights and a protectorate over the Holy Places in the Near East, became an enduring though irregular factor in European diplomacy.

6) The history of the first half of the sixteenth century made it quite clear that diplomacy a la Machiavelli was to be the order of the day. Deceit, treachery, surprise attacks, and broken promises were written into the record.

FAITH AND NATIONALITY IN WESTERN EUROPE

Era of the Religious Wars. While the threat of Hapsburg domination of Europe had been lessened after Charles v divided his lands, the Continent was still to witness convulsive rivalries and a century more of warfare. The period from roughly the middle of the sixteenth century to the middle of the seventeenth century is often referred to as the Era of the Religious Wars, for the religious issues which flamed forth from the Protestant upheaval—particularly that most international form of Protestantism, Calvinism—colored every political conflict.

Zenith of the Spanish state. The Era of the Religious Wars began in 1556 when Philip II, the son of Charles v, became king of Spain. It seemed that this devout monarch, with his vast possessions both in Europe and overseas, would realize his objectives of dominating the former and of advancing the cause of the Catholic Reformation. The auguries at the outset seemed promising. After Suleiman's death in 1566 the Turkish advance in the Mediterranean continued, and in 1570 the Turks captured the Venetian island of Cyprus, the last Christian outpost in the area. At the pope's urging, Christian Europe turned to Philip, the champion of the Catholic faith, to block Turkish expansion. A Holy League was formed to raise a great fleet and destroy Ottoman naval power in the Mediterranean. Spanish and Venetian warships, together with the smaller squadrons of Genoa and the Papal States, made up a fleet of over two hundred vessels which was joined by volunteers from all over Europe. In 1571 the League's fleet and the Turkish navy clashed at Lepanto, on the western side of Greece. The outcome was a decisive victory for Christian Europe; Ottoman sea power was crushed, never to be restored as a major threat to Christendom.

Seeking to make his rule absolute in the Netherlands, Philip excluded the local nobility from the administration, maintained an army of occupation, and introduced the Inquisition to stop the advance of Calvinism. It continued to spread, however, and in 1566 a series of violent anti-Catholic and anti-Spanish riots broke out. At the same time Philip proposed new and oppressive taxes, including a 10 percent sales tax, which antagonized most Netherlanders, Catholic as well as Protestant. Under the Dutch leader, William the Silent of the House of Orange, discontent flared into open revolt in 1568. When William the Silent was assassinated by a young Catholic fanatic and the Spanish stepped up their efforts to destroy the new republic. At this critical moment Elizabeth I of England, fearing that Philip planned to use the Netherlands as a base for an invasion of England, rushed troops to the aid of the United Netherlands. The destruction of Philip's Armada by England in 1588 (see below) further weakened Spanish ability to crush the Dutch.

In 1609 a twelve years' truce was signed, which recognized the partition of the Netherlands along the line where the fighting had stopped. Not until the end of the Thirty Years' War in 1648 did the Dutch gain from the Spanish formal recognition of their independence. For more than two hundred years the southern provinces remained in the hands of the Hapsburgs, first as the Spanish Netherlands and then as the Austrian Netherlands. In 1830 they achieved independence as the state of Belgium.

The English throne: Protestant or Catholic. Philip also had designs on England. In 1554 he married Mary Tudor, Catholic daughter of Henry VIII and queen of England. Her premature death removed for the time being any danger of Spanish domination; and Mary's successor, her half-sister Elizabeth, was regarded as both heretical and illegitimate by Catholic Europe. Elizabeth resorted to every subterfuge and trick available to her in the duel with Philip of Spain. Using her sex as a diplomatic weapon, she carried on long flirtations with the brothers of the French king, thereby helping to prevent an alliance between France and Spain. In addition she sent covert assistance to the Dutch, aware that their rebellion was sapping Spanish strength.

Elizabeth also secretly encouraged her sea captains to prey upon Spanish shipping and to attack the rich Spanish settlements in the New World. The most famous of Elizabethan Sea Dogs, Sir Francis Drake, sailed into the Pacific, plundered the western coast of Spanish America, and, after circumnavigating the globe, arrived in England with a hold full of gold and silver.

Aware of Elizabeth's duplicity, Philip planned to gain control over England by placing Mary Stuart on the English throne. But a plot against Elizabeth's life, in which Mary was obliquely implicated, was discovered. Parliament was convinced that as long as Mary lived, Elizabeth's life would be endangered, and therefore, in 1587, Elizabeth signed Mary's death warrant. At the same time the resourceful queen not only aided the embattled Dutch, but also the Protestant cause during the French Religious Wars; and Spanish shipping was constantly harassed by Elizabeth's raiders. Rebuffed in his efforts by the indomitable Elizabeth, Philip turned to force. A huge invasion fleet, the Spanish Armada, was launched in 1588 against England. The redoubtable Elizabethan Sea Dogs outmaneuvered and outfought the clumsy Spanish galleons. A severe storm, the famous "Protestant wind," completed the debacle; and the Armada limped home. This defeat meant that England would remain Protestant, that it would soon emerge as a dominant sea power, and that the Dutch rebellion against Spain would succeed.

The Wars of Religion in France. Soon after France and Spain ended their long conflict over Italy in 1559, France underwent one of the most terrible civil conflicts in its history. By 1560 its Calvinist Huguenots numbered about one million out of a population of sixteen million. Because the royal Valois line was nearing an end with no heirs to inherit the throne, ruthless rivalry existed between the noble house of the Bourbons, which was Protestant, and that of Guise which championed Catholicism. This was the setting for the series of civil wars, partly religious and partly political, that broke out in 1562. During this period the most powerful individual in France was Catherine de Medici, the Queen Mother, who

With the threat of Spanish invasion, Elizabeth gave the English people an example of courage and resolution. This portrait was painted during her reign.

was completely cynical in statecraft. Seeking to maintain the power of her weakling sons, she attempted to steer a middle course between the rival factions. But as the Huguenots grew stronger she resolved to crush them. Thus Catherine is blamed for the terrible Massacre of St. Bartholomew's Day on August 24, 1572 when some ten thousand Huguenots were slain. Civil war continued, however, and Philip II entered the conflict on the side of the Catholics. He hoped first to extirpate Protestantism in France and then to control French policy, thereby gaining valuable support in crushing the Dutch revolt and in conquering England. Finally, in 1589 after assassins had eliminated all rivals, the Protestant Bourbon prince Henry of Navarre became King Henry IV of France. Philip's intervention was checked by the dispatch of English troops by Queen Elizabeth, and by 1595 the civil war was over and Philip was forced to withdraw. Realizing that most of his countrymen were Catholic and that all were weary of strife, Henry accepted the faith of Rome supposedly saying, "Paris is well worth a mass." While accepting Catholicism as a means of achieving national unity, Henry sought to protect the liberties of the Huguenots in his Edict of Nantes (1598). Their religious liberties were given certain guarantees with the right to fortify some of their towns.

The failure of Philip II. Philip's failure in France was the last of his many setbacks. His final opponent, Henry IV, provided some fitting last words on Philip's hopes for Spanish dominance in Europe: while witnessing the departure of Spanish troops from Paris, Henry called out, "Gentlemen, commend me to your master, but do not come back."

While in the eyes of his Spanish subjects Philip was a wise, moderate, pious, and hardworking monarch, his enemies singled him out as a detestable example of trickery, cruelty, and religious intolerance. Yet Philip was not equal to Elizabeth in duplicity and diplomatic cunning, and it must be remembered that nearly all sixteenth-century European monarchs believed that the relentless persecution of nonconformists was essential to the welfare of the state. Philip's failures cannot be attributed to defects ingrained in his nature but to the fact that, in general, he was less skillful than his opponents in the game of power politics.

Most important, perhaps, is that Philip unwittingly pitted himself against the growing feelings of nationalism. Patriotism thwarted Philip's ambitions in the Netherlands and in England, and it also contributed to the failure of his intervention in the French religious wars.

Despite Philip's failures, Spain still enjoyed the reputation of being the first power in Europe. Spanish soldiers were the best on the Continent, and Spain's wealth from its vast overseas possessions seemed inexhaustible. Moreover, Spanish writers, scholars, and painters were outstanding; in fact, the last half of the sixteenth century and the first half of the seventeenth are usually regarded as the zenith of Spanish culture.

In the seventeenth century, however, Spanish power rapidly declined. Bad economic policies (see Chapter 11) coupled with continued overexertion in the game of power politics proved too great a burden for a nation of only eight or nine million people. The last of the so-called religious conflicts, the Thirty Years' War (1618-1648), accelerated the decline of Spain and left France the dominant state in Europe.

The Thirty Years' War. The final and climactic phase of these political rivalries tinctured with religion was the Thirty Years' War. At the outset in 1618 rebellious Protestant Bohemia was defeated by the Catholic emperor, Ferdinand

II. This victory was followed by the entry of Protestant Denmark and Sweden into the fray, both interested in reducing the power of the Catholic emperor. An uneasy truce was achieved in 1635.

The peace never went into effect, however, for Cardinal Richelieu, the chief adviser of the French king and the actual head of the government, decided that France would be secure only when the Hapsburgs of Austria and Spain, whose lands ringed France on three sides, had been defeated. Richelieu earlier had given secret aid to the German Protestants, the Danes, and the Swedes; now, in 1635, he came out in the open and the struggle became primarily a dynastic contest between Bourbons and Hapsburgs. The Swedes and the German Protestants kept the Austrian Hapsburg armies busy in Germany while French arms were concentrated against the Spanish Hapsburgs. In 1643 at the battle of Rocroi in the

Nördlingen, a town in Germany, was besieged during the Thirty Years' War, which was similar to modern fighting in that both countryside and towns suffered widespread destruction and civilians were killed in great numbers. This picture would indicate that the artillery bombarding Nördlingen must have created havoc among the crowded buildings and their occupants.

Spanish Netherlands the legend of the invincibility of the Spanish infantry came to an end.

The Peace of Westphalia. Peace negotiations began in 1644 without a cease-fire agreement, but they proceeded slowly. The delegates wrangled endlessly over such questions of protocol as who was to enter the conference room first and where they were to sit, and the fortunes of war frequently altered the bargaining power of the rival diplomats. Finally, in 1648, the longest peace negotiation on record ended in a series of treaties collectively known as the Peace of Westphalia. (Spain, however, stubbornly refused to make peace with France until 1659.)

A recapitulation of the various provisions of the peace would be very complex; suffice it to say that France moved closer to the Rhine with the acquisition of much of Alsace; Sweden and the Protestant state of Brandenburg made important territorial gains along Germany's Baltic coast; and Holland and Switzerland—the latter having successfully resisted its Hapsburg overlords since 1291—were granted independence. The Calvinists were given recognition in Germany, and Protestants were allowed to retain the Church lands they had taken before 1624.

The Peace of Westphalia permanently ended Hapsburg dreams of reviving the authority of the emperor in Germany. The sovereignty of the more than three hundred German states was recognized, with each state having the right to coin money, make war, maintain armies, and send diplomatic representatives to foreign courts. Henceforth the Hapsburg emperors worked to form a strong Danubian monarchy out of their varied Austrian, Bohemian, and Hungarian possessions.

The great significance of the Peace of Westphalia was that it symbolized the emergence and victory of the sovereign state which acknowledged no authority higher than its own interests and was prone to assume what Thomas Hobbes three years later called "the position of gladiators." More specifically, the conference established the basic principle underlying the modern state system—the essential equality of all independent sovereign states. It also instituted the diplomatic procedure of convening international congresses in order to settle the problems of war and peace by negotiation.

Thus the struggle against the Hapsburg encirclement of France begun by Francis I against Charles V early in the sixteenth century ended more than a century later. Changes had been wrought in the relative powers of nations. Both England and Holland had become great sea powers, and their commercial prosperity was increasing rapidly. The golden age of Spain was over, and France emerged as the greatest power in Europe. Although reports of devastation, population decline, and cultural retrogression in the Germanies have perhaps been exaggerated, the Thirty Years' War left a grievous legacy and thwarted German progress for a century. But by demonstrating that Protestants and Catholics were unable to exterminate each other, the Thirty Years' War—indeed, the entire Era of the Religious Wars—greatly promoted the cause of religious toleration in Europe.

THE CONTINUING SENSE OF EUROPEAN INTERDEPENDENCE

Proposals for keeping the peace. The irresponsible use of power was the outstanding feature of international politics in the late sixteenth and early seventeenth centuries. But gradually powerful rulers and diplomats realized that frequent wars threatened the growth of European trade and commerce and menaced even the existence of civilized society in the West. We have seen some of the early steps taken to improve international relations—the establishment of consular and diplomatic services, the formation of alignments to preserve the balance of power, and the first use of a general European peace congress to adjust conflicting interests after a great war. In addition, trade agreements and treaties formed the crude beginnings of a system of international law. Although these varied measures all too often had a negligible effect on the continued use of war as the means of settling disputes among nations, they reflect a continuing sense of the interdependence of the European state system—the Concert of Europe, as it would later be called.

The increased destructiveness of warfare aroused the dismayed protests of many sixteenth-century humanists—Erasmus, for example, asserted that "war is sweet only to the inexperienced." In the early seventeenth century students of international affairs made some specific recommendations that are of particular interest today.

In 1623, Emeric Crucé, an obscure French monk, published a plan to eliminate war by means of an international organization which, he claimed, would be "useful to all nations, and agreeable to those who have some light of reason and the sentiment of humanity." The central idea in his work was that all wars were harmful and their abolition would allow governments to devote themselves to the arts of peace. To this end he proposed that a permanent corps of ambassadors from all over the world be maintained at Venice as an international assembly for the settlement of all disputes through negotiation and arbitration. Crucé acknowledged that his plan for a seventeenth-century "United Nations" was in advance of his time, but added:

> I have wished, nevertheless, to leave this testimony to posterity. If it serves nothing, patience. It is a small matter to lose paper and words. I have said and done what was possible for the public good, and some few who read this little book will be grateful to me for it, and will honor me, as I hope, with their remembrance.[7]

Either the first Bourbon monarch, Henry IV, or his chief minister, the Duke of Sully, devised the plan known as the Grand Design, which called for the establishment of a European federal union headed by a council of representatives from all states. The council was to secure disarmament and to control an international police force which would back its decisions by force. Each state was to contribute troops and money according to its strength. Despite its theoretical and utopian character, the Grand Design "shows that at the very moment when the modern national state, centralized within and dividing Europe into mutually hostile camps, emerged from the ruins of medieval unity, the ablest minds realized that eventually a new unity would have to be built out of these distinct entities, a United States of Europe. . . ."[8]

Grotius and international law. A number of European scholars were also at work laying the foundation for a science of international law by developing the principle that the nations formed a community based upon natural law. The first to obtain a hearing outside scholarly circles was Hugo Grotius (1583-1645), a gifted Dutch historian, theologian, practicing lawyer, and diplomat. In 1625 appeared *On* *the Law of War and Peace*, the work which gained Grotius instant fame and lasting recognition as the founder of international law. "Such a work," he declared, "is all the more necessary because in our day, as in former times, there is no lack of men who view this branch of law with contempt as having no reality outside of an empty name." And he continued:

> I have had many and weighty reasons for undertaking to write upon this subject. Throughout the Christian world I observed a lack of restraint in relation to war, such as even barbarous races should be ashamed of; I observed that men rush to arms for slight causes, or no cause at all, and that when arms have once been taken up there is no longer any respect for law, divine or human; it is as if, in accordance with a general decree, frenzy had openly been let loose for the committing of all crimes.[9]

Grotius endeavored to set forth a new code of international conduct based not upon the authority of the Church but on what he termed the fundamental idea of the law of nature. The law of nature was in turn founded on the dictates of reason, morality, and justice. If civilization was to endure, Grotius argued, humane considerations should prevail in the councils of the mighty, and rules of conduct binding all men should be established.

More realistic than his contemporaries Crucé and Sully, Grotius did not propose to eliminate war entirely. He sought instead to outlaw "unjust" wars and limit the effects of "just" wars. Wars were justified only to repel invasion or to punish an insult to God. Grotius' appeal fell largely upon deaf ears. Machiavelli's *The Prince* enjoyed more popularity in European palaces than *On the Law of War and Peace.*

CHAPTER 11
SEEK OUT, DISCOVER, AND FIND

The Expansion of Europe and the Commercial
Revolution (1450-1750)

> "Be it known that we have given and granted . . . to our well-beloved John
> Cabot . . . full and free authority, leave, and power to sail to all parts,
> countries, and seas of the East, of the West, and of the North, under our
> banners and ensigns . . . to seek out, discover, and find whatsoever islands,
> countries, regions or provinces of the heathen and infidels whatsoever they
> be, and in what part of the world soever they be, which before this time have
> been unknown to all Christians . . . ."[1]

So began the letter patent from Henry VII of England authorizing John Cabot in
1497 to make a voyage which was one day to constitute England's claim to vast
stretches of the New World. Columbus and other mariners received similar
instructions from the sovereigns who authorized their voyages to "seek out,
discover, and find" what lay beyond the horizon. Braving vast, uncharted oceans,
these mariners persisted in their quest until the earth had been girdled and the
"banners and ensigns" of Europe had been planted on every continent.

Who wrought this miracle? First, there were the sea captains—da Gama, who
made the first ocean voyage from Europe to India; Columbus, who introduced
Europe to a New World; and Magellan, whose expedition ventured ever westward
until its weary survivors had sailed completely around the world and dropped
anchor once more in their home port. Close on the heels of such captains came the
conquistadores—the "conquerors"—resourceful and ruthless soldiers like Cortés
and Pizarro, who laid the foundations for a vast European empire by overwhelming flourishing native cultures in the New World.

Then came the task of exploiting what had been found and won. The European
powers took advantage of the claims of their discoverers and explorers in one of
two basic ways—through trade or by colonization. In Africa and Asia the
emphasis was on trade; Europeans carried on their business from forts, acting as
foreign merchants rather than as settlers. The story of European expansion in the
New World, on the other hand, is largely that of colonization, of the transplanting

of European civilization to a new and exotic environment. The territories in the Americas were treated as extensions of the mother countries.

Thus a handful of adventurers, ranging beyond the horizon in quest of El Dorado, the lengendary city of gold which symbolized their hopes and dreams, set in motion a train of events which resulted in the European domination of the world—a domination that did not end until our own day.

CAPTAINS AND CONQUISTADORES

Medieval maps and adventurers. Early medieval maps were curiosities rather than documents of fact. They included lands which no man had ever seen; the oceans were shown abounding in sea dragons, while drawings of elephants and more fanciful animals were used to fill up empty land spaces, thereby adding to the picturesqueness of the map as well as conveniently concealing the ignorance of the map maker. Arabic works on astronomy and geography, acquired in the thirteenth century, proved that the earth was a sphere and greatly expanded geographical knowledge. Of greatest significance for the development of scientific geography, however, was the recovery in 1409 of Claudius Ptolemy's *Geography* (see p. 73) with its elaborate map of the world. Although this second-century work added greatly to current knowledge, it contained a number of errors, two of which encouraged Columbus and other fifteenth-century explorers to sail boldly across the uncharted oceans. Ptolemy exaggerated the size of the known continents so that the distance between western Europe and eastern Asia appeared much smaller than it really is, and he underestimated the circumference of the world by five thousand miles.

Medieval adventurers also contributed to geographical knowledge, some of which influenced Columbus and his fellow explorers. The earliest prime examples were the Norsemen, who reached Iceland in the last half of the ninth century (see p. 111). In about 982 Eric the Red, son of a Norwegian noble, was banished from the Norse settlements in Iceland and sailed west to Greenland, which may have been discovered earlier in the century by Celtic refugees from Ireland, fleeing Viking raids on their homeland. Eric founded two settlements on the western coast of Greenland, which existed until about 1500 when they mysteriously vanished. It now appears that the first European to set foot on the North American coast was Bjarni Herjolfson. In 985 Bjarni was blown off course while sailing from Iceland to Greenland and made a landfall in Newfoundland. About fifteen years later Leif, son of Eric the Red, retraced Bjarni's route and named the country *Vinland* (Wineland) because of its wooded, vine-covered shore. A number of other voyages were made to Vinland, whose lumber was highly prized in treeless Greenland. Apparently no permanent settlement was made in Vinland, although archaeologists have recently discovered what appears to be the remains of a Viking camp in Newfoundland at L'Anse au Meadow.[2] But monumental as these voyages were, their implications were lost on contemporary Europeans, and they added little or nothing to European knowledge of geography.

In the thirteenth and fourteenth centuries a number of Europeans, many of them Christian missionaries, journeyed overland to the Far East. The most famous of these travelers was the thirteenth-century Venetian merchant, Marco

Polo, who spent seventeen years in China and wrote one of the world's outstanding travelogues. But these exploits had little permanent effect because of political changes in Asia in the last decades of the fourteenth century. The Mongol dynasty in China, which had been friendly to European missionaries and merchants, was overthrown, and the succeeding rulers proved anti-Christian. Meanwhile, the belligerent heathen Turks stood astride the eastern Mediterranean. These two developments put an end to further European penetration into the Orient, although trade continued at certain terminals controlled by the Muslims.

Trade routes to the East.   The three major routes by which trade flowed from the Far East to Europe had existed since Roman times. The northern one cut across Central Asia and the Caspian and Black seas to Constantinople (Byzantium); the middle route went by sea along the coasts of India and Persia through the Persian Gulf and the Euphrates valley to Antioch; and the southern route utilized the monsoon winds to strike across the Indian Ocean and up the Red Sea to Alexandria in Egypt. During the fifteenth century the commerce that flowed westward to Europe was rich indeed, even though the expansion of the Turks greatly reduced the importance of the northern route across Asia. The most important imports into Europe were spices—pepper, cinnamon, nutmeg, ginger, and cloves—highly valued as condiments and preservatives for food. Also in great demand were Chinese silk, Indian cotton cloth, and various precious stones.

The Mediterranean carrying trade in oriental goods was in the hands of Venice and other Italian city-states, which wielded an extensive and lucrative monopoly. Since the Arabs held a similar monopoly east of the Mediterranean, oriental goods were sold in the West at many times their price in India. As the demand for the products of the East increased during the latter half of the fifteenth century, the rulers of the new nations of western Europe became aware that an adverse balance of trade was draining their coined money away to Italy and the East. They determined to find new trade routes of their own, and, as rulers of powerful nation-states, they had the resources to support the stupendous feats of discovery and conquest that were needed.

The Portuguese voyages.   It was the Portuguese who spearheaded the drive to find oceanic routes that would provide cheaper and easier access to oriental products. The man who set in motion the brilliant Portuguese achievements in exploration and discovery was Prince Henry the Navigator (1394-1460), whose original goal was to tap at its source the gold of Guinea (the Gold Coast) on the underside of the great bend of Africa. This major source of Europe's gold was in the hands of Muslim middlemen of North Africa and the Sahara. By the time of Henry's death the Portuguese had reached Guinea and had raised their sights to the spices of India. In 1488 Bartholomew Diaz rounded the southern tip of Africa, from which point he noticed that the coast swung northeast. But his disgruntled crew forced him to turn back. Pleased with the prospect of soon finding a direct sea route to India, King John II of Portugal named the great cape rounded by Diaz "Cape of Good Hope."

Vasco da Gama commanded the first Portuguese fleet to reach India. Three ships left Lisbon in 1497 and, after rounding the Cape, crossed the Indian Ocean to Calicut in twenty-three days. The Arab merchants in Calicut sought to preserve their trading monopoly by delaying the return voyage, and it was not until 1499 that da Gama dropped anchor in Lisbon. He had lost two of his ships and one third of his men through scurvy and other misfortunes, but his one cargo of pepper and cinnamon was worth sixty times the cost of the expedition.

Lured by such fantastic profits another expedition set sail the following year and established a permanent base south of Calicut at Cochin. The Portuguese soon acquired a monopoly over trade in the Indian Ocean, and by 1516 their ships had reached Canton in China. The king of Portugal assumed the impressive title "Lord of the Conquest, Navigation, and Commerce of Ethiopia, Arabia, Persia, and China."

The New World. Meanwhile, Spanish ambitions for riches and prestige were realized through the exploits of a Genoese sailor named Christopher Columbus (1451?-1506). Influenced by Marco Polo's overestimate of the length of Asia and Ptolemy's underestimate of the size of the world, Columbus believed that Japan was less than 3000 miles from Europe (the actual distance is 10,600 nautical miles) and that it could be reached in one or two months by sailing westward. He tried unsuccessfully to interest the rulers of Portugal, England, and France in his enterprise before Queen Isabella of Castile agreed to sponsor his voyage. On August 3, 1492, Columbus set sail from Spain with three small ships and ninety men. On October 12 he landed on a small island in the West Indies. After he returned to Spain, Columbus announced that he had found the route to Asia, and the Spanish monarchs proclaimed him "Admiral of the Ocean Sea, Viceroy and Governor of the Islands that he has discovered in the Indies."

Even after da Gama's voyage had opened up the eastward route to India, Columbus steadfastly refused to acknowledge that what he himself had dis-

This map, published in the fifteenth century but based on one designed by Ptolemy in the second century, represents the first attempt to project the curved surface of the earth on a flat surface. The outline of the European continent (upper left) is fairly accurate.

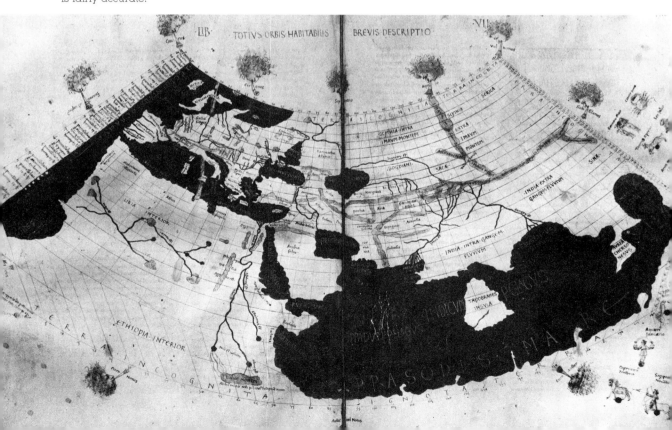

covered was in fact a massive obstacle on the route to the Far East. Although he made three more voyages to the New World in a vain attempt to find a direct opening to the Asian mainland, Columbus had already changed the course of history, though he did not know it. A New World had been revealed, and the entire history of Europe was soon to be affected by the discovery of the new lands.

Columbus' first voyage had destroyed Portugal's monopoly over discovery. Some sort of compromise had to be worked out between the two countries, and the Spanish monarchs invited the pope to define the pagan areas which Spain and Portugal might claim. In 1493 the pope issued the Bull of Demarcation, which drew a line from north to south running one hundred leagues west of the Azores and proclaimed that all heathen lands west of this line as far as the Indies were reserved for Spain. The Portuguese protested, claiming that this arrangement would confine their operations too closely to the African coast. By the Treaty of Tordesillas (1494) Spain agreed to have the line moved farther west. This new demarcation later enabled Portugal to claim Brazil after Pedro Cabral's sighting of South America in 1500 while sailing to the Indies. In 1529 another treaty fixed a similar demarcation line in the Eastern Hemisphere.

The search for riches drove the Spaniards to organize many expeditions to chart the coastlines and to penetrate the interior of the New World. Having heard from Indians of a vast ocean only a short distance to the west, Vasco de Balboa led a band of 190 Spaniards across the Isthmus of Panama. On September 25, 1513, Balboa climbed to the summit of a hill from which he beheld the Pacific Ocean—and in that act paved the way for European exploration of the largest single portion of the world's surface.

Ferdinand Magellan, a Portuguese navigator in the service of Spain, found a sea route into the Pacific. Encouraged by Balboa's discovery of the short distance between the two oceans, Magellan believed it was possible to sail around South America just as Diaz had rounded Africa. In August 1520 Magellan made his memorable discovery of the strait which bears his name. His five small ships made their way between huge ice-clad mountains and through tortuous passages. After a terrifying thirty-eight days they sailed out upon the western ocean, which looked so calm after the stormy straits that Magellan termed it "Pacific." Then followed a harrowing ninety-nine day voyage across the Pacific to Guam, during which rats had to be eaten for food. Magellan was slain by natives in the Philippine Islands (which he claimed for Spain), and only one of his ships returned to Spain in 1522 by way of India and the Cape of Good Hope. Its cargo of spices paid for the cost of the entire expedition. Magellan's tiny vessel had taken three years to circumnavigate the world, but henceforth no one could doubt that the earth was round and that the Americas constituted a New World.

The Conquistadores.   While the Portuguese soon profited from their hold on the rich oriental trade, the Spaniards found that the islands and coasts of the New World did not immediately produce the harvest of riches which they had eagerly sought. Such wealth was not to be found along the seashore but in the unknown hinterland, where rich indigenous cultures flourished. Penetration of inland areas was the work of the *conquistadores,* the courageous but independent-minded and often brutal conquerors who looted whole native empires and planted the Spanish flag from California to the tip of South America.

In the same year that Magellan set forth (1519), the Spanish governor of Cuba dispatched Hernando Cortés on an expedition to Mexico, from which had come rumors of a great Aztec empire, flowing with gold. Montezuma, ruler of the

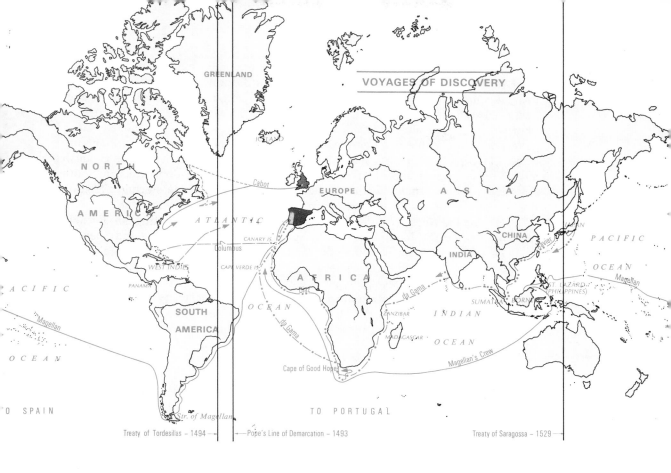

Aztecs, had thousands of warriors, while Cortés had about six hundred men. But the Spaniards were equipped with horses, armor, and gunpowder, all unknown to the Aztecs. Crossing the coast lands and the mountains, the Spaniards entered the valley of Mexico. Cortés treacherously made a virtual prisoner of Montezuma and through his cooperation ruled peacefully until a popular uprising gave the Spaniards an excuse to plunder and destroy the capital. Yet Cortés was more than a plunderer; he built a new City of Mexico on the site of Montezuma's capital and demonstrated administrative skills in adapting the former Aztec confederacy to Spanish rule.

Using Mexico and the West Indies as bases, the Spanish explorers searched what is now the southern part of the United States for the treasures which rumors planted there. That the expeditions failed to find gold or other riches does not detract from the tremendous progress they made in opening up new and potentially wealthy areas.

The conquest of the Incas in Peru was carried out with less skill and more enduring ill effects than Cortés' exploit in Mexico. Obsessed by tales of a rich and mighty empire in South America, a tough, illiterate peasant's son named Francisco Pizarro determined to explore and conquer it. In 1531 Pizarro sailed from Panama with 180 men and 27 horses. Landing on the Peruvian coast, the small band made its way across the barren mountains into the interior, where they seized the Incan monarch Atahualpa.

Attempting to buy his freedom by paying a huge ransom, Atahualpa offered to have a room measuring seventeen by twelve feet filled to a height of some seven feet with plates and vessels of gold and to have it filled twice over with silver. Despite this magnificent ransom, the Spaniards did not release the emperor but instead sentenced him on trumped-up charges to be burned to death. In the end, because Atahualpa accepted Christian baptism, he was merely strangled. The imprisonment and death of its ruler rendered the highly centralized Incan government incapable of effective, organized resistance; and Pizarro soon captured the capital. Not until near the end of the sixteenth century was Spanish authority securely established over Peru. In time Spanish dominions in South America formed a huge, uninterrupted semicircle, while the Portuguese took possession of the vast hinterland of Brazil.

Search for the Northwest Passage.   It was not long before the English, French, and Dutch were seeking to emulate the successes of the Portuguese and Spanish. In 1497—the same year in which da Gama embarked for India—John Cabot, an Italian mariner financed by the merchants of Bristol in England, sailed across the North Atlantic in a small ship manned by only eighteen men. After a turbulent six weeks' voyage, the expedition dropped anchor off the northern coast of the New World. When Cabot returned to England, Henry VII rewarded him with £10, the title of Grand Admiral, and the right to make another voyage. Cabot made his second voyage in 1498, coasting along the eastern shore of America in a vain attempt to find a passage to the Orient.

Cabot was the first European after the hardy Norse sailors to land on the mainland of North America; and, what was most important, his discovery laid the foundation for England's claim to the whole rich continent. Thus for £10 and a title England eventually acquired all of Canada and the territory along the Atlantic coast which constituted the thirteen American colonies.

For the next hundred years English seamen, including Henry Hudson, tried in vain to reach China through the illusive Northwest Passage, a sea route believed to exist north of Canada. Although similar expeditions trying to reach China by way of the Northeast Passage above Russia also failed, one of them reached Archangel and was granted trading privileges by Tsar Ivan the Terrible (see p. 146).

France also joined in the search for the Northwest Passage. In 1523 Francis I commissioned the Florentine mariner Giovanni da Verazzano to investigate the coast from North Carolina to Newfoundland. Eleven years later Jacques Cartier was sent on the first of two voyages that explored the St. Lawrence River as far as the present city of Montreal. These expeditions gave France its claim to sovereignty over eastern North America, a claim which duplicated England's.

Not until after its Wars of Religion did France resume its activities in the St. Lawrence region. Sponsored by the energetic first Bourbon ruler, Henry IV, Samuel de Champlain not only founded the first successful French overseas colony at Quebec (1608) but also journeyed over the lake which bears his name and westward to the Great Lakes. In 1673 Louis Joliet, a fur trader, and Father Marquette, a Jesuit missionary, reached the Mississippi River and followed it as far south as Arkansas in the hope of finding a short route to the Pacific. Nine years later René de La Salle explored the Mississippi to its mouth, taking possession of the entire territory and naming it *Louisiana* in honor of Louis XIV.

Dutch interest in the New World coincided with the rise of Holland to a position of political independence and great economic strength during the first half of the seventeenth century. Dutch ambitions to find a shorter route to the Far East caused them to hire the English explorer Henry Hudson, who in 1609 sailed up the river that now bears his name. In 1621 the Dutch West India Company was founded for the purpose of trading in western Africa and the Americas. As part of its work, the company founded New Amsterdam on Manhattan Island in 1624 and permanently colonized Guiana, Curaçao, and Aruba in the Caribbean area.

EUROPE INVADES THE EAST

The Portuguese empire. Until the fifteenth century civilizations in the Near East, India, and China had been fully as advanced as those in Europe; and in some areas and in some aspects of culture they had surpassed the West. After 1450, however, western Europe began to experience an astonishing resurgence—a "rebirth" which was reflected in the rise of powerful and well-administered nation-states, the increase of wealth and trade, the growing importance of the bourgeoisie, and the intellectual and artistic achievements of humanist scholars and artists. In contrast to the energetic West, the East was less dynamic both culturally and politically. Therefore, the contact between East and West in the fifteenth century was not a meeting of equals. With its effective political organizations, disciplined armies, and energy and ambition, Europe took advantage of the other continents; the wider world became the servant of the West. The expansion of Europe and its mastery of much of the world is generally referred to as imperialism. Many of the conflicts and tensions in contemporary world politics find their source to a large degree in the imperial systems created by the West during this first great age of imperialist expansion.

To ensure their toehold in Africa, the Portuguese built fortified posts along the coast, began to develop a colony in Angola, and settled traders on the island of Zanzibar. Early in the sixteenth century Afonso de Albuquerque, the greatest of all Portuguese viceroys, saw that Portugal could wrest commercial supremacy from the Arabs only by force, and he therefore devised a plan to establish forts at strategic sites which would dominate the trade routes and also protect Portuguese interests on land. The western end of the Arab trade routes was partially sealed off: Ormuz at the mouth of the Persian Gulf was captured, but the attempt to close the entrance to the Red Sea at Aden was only temporarily successful. To obtain a major base for a permanent fleet in the Indian Ocean, Albuquerque in 1510 seized Goa on the coast of India, which the Portuguese held until 1961. From Goa the Portuguese dominated the Indian ports that had supplied the Arab traders.

Albuquerque next set about securing control of the trade with the East Indies and China. His first objective was Malacca, which controlled the narrow strait north of Sumatra through which most Far Eastern trade moved. Captured in 1511, Malacca became the springboard for further eastward penetration. The first Portuguese ship reached Canton on the south coast of China in 1516, but it was not until 1557 that the Portuguese gained a permanent base in China at Macao, which they still hold. About 1516, also, the first trading post was established in the rich Moluccas, or Spice Islands, source of the finest spices.

Thus Portugal, through its control of most of the traffic between India and Europe as well as the trade between India and the Far East, developed the first European commercial empire. Portugal's greatest poet, Luis de Camoëns, in 1572 celebrated his compatriots' overseas achievements in a memorable epic poem, *The Lusiads* ("The Portuguese"):

In golden treasures rich, distant Cathay,
And all the farthest Islands of the East,
And all the seas, to them shall homage pay.[3]

Dutch and English in the East. Portugal's star was destined to set for many reasons, not the least of which was attacks on their commercial empire launched by the Dutch and the English. Two events facilitated Dutch encroachment on the Portuguese monopoly of oriental trade. One was the Netherlands revolt against Spanish rule, and the other was the Spanish acquisition of Portugal. The Dutch looked on Spain's trade and colonies as fair game, and when the two crowns of the Iberian peninsula were joined in 1580, they felt free to attack Portuguese territory in eastern waters. Furthermore, the Dutch had previously enjoyed a rich trade carrying oriental goods from Lisbon to the ports of northern Europe; this traffic

Portuguese ships are shown anchored at the port of Macao on
the Chinese coast in this sixteenth-century engraving.

AMACAO.

ceased when Spain took control of Portuguese ports. If Dutch trade was to survive, the Hollanders had to capture its source in the East.

In the 1590's a number of Dutch companies were formed to finance trading expeditions to the Far East. Because competition lowered their profits, in 1602 the companies amalgamated into the Dutch East India Company which received from the government the right to trade and rule in the area stretching from the Cape of Good Hope eastward to the Strait of Magellan. It was the Dutch East India Company that broke the power of the Portuguese in the Spice Islands.

The governor-general of the East Indies who was appointed in 1618, Jan Pieterszoon Coen, laid the foundations for the Dutch empire in the East Indies. Whereas Albuquerque had felt that it was sufficient to occupy strategic points along the sea routes, Coen believed that the Dutch had to control the actual areas of production as well. He built a fortified trading station at Batavia on Java, a site which eventually became the capital of the Dutch East Indies, including Sumatra and the Moluccas. Dutch monopoly of the spice trade became complete after they drove the Portuguese from Malacca (1641) and Ceylon (1658), the latter the main source of cinnamon. In 1652 the Dutch established a colony at Cape Town on the southern tip of Africa as a port of call on the long journey to the Far East.

The English meanwhile were staking out claims in India at the expense of the Portuguese. In 1600 Queen Elizabeth incorporated the English East India Company, granting it a monopoly of trade from the Cape of Good Hope eastward to the Strait of Magellan. By 1622 the company had put the Portuguese posts on the Persian Gulf out of business, and in 1639 it acquired Madras on the east coast of India. Through political stratagems, bribes, diplomacy, and exploitation of weak native rulers, the company prospered in India, where it became the most powerful political force in the subcontinent.

Europeans unwelcome in China and Japan. When the Portuguese first arrived in Canton in 1516, they were given the same privileges that Arab merchants had enjoyed for centuries. But the Portuguese behaved very badly, scorning the customs of the sophisticated inhabitants, and treating the "heathen" with arrogance and cruelty.

However, because trade was mutually profitable to both Chinese and foreign merchants, in 1557 the Portuguese were granted the right to trade at Macao. There, under close surveillance and subject to many strict regulations, the "ocean devils" conducted business. Stemming from this period is the mutual suspicion and hostility which characterized Sino-European relations in the nineteenth and early twentieth centuries.

A somewhat friendlier contact occurred when Jesuit missionaries arrived in China during the second half of the sixteenth century. They converted many important persons at the imperial court and in the provinces, thereby gaining protection for Christians generally.

About 1542 three Portuguese ships from Macao were driven far off their course and landed at one of the southern Japanese islands. Before long, others were welcomed as traders. Hearing about Japan after he had sailed from Lisbon for the Far East, St. Francis Xavier went there and started to convert the inhabitants. After Xavier's death, his work was carried on by Jesuit and other missionaries. By 1600 Japanese converts to Christianity numbered around 300,000.

Suspicion on the part of the Japanese rulers that Christianity was endangering the status quo was reinforced by the bigotry of many Christians and by economic exploitation on the part of unscrupulous Portuguese merchants. The Japanese began persecuting the missionaries and their converts, and in 1638 Japan cut itself off from the outside world: "For the future, let none, so long as the Sun illuminates the world, presume to sail to Japan, not even in the quality of ambassadors, and this declaration is never to be revoked on pain of death."[4] Except for a small, closely watched Dutch post at Nagasaki, the islands were closed to western contact until 1853.

THE COMMERCIAL REVOLUTION

The nature of capitalism. In the period between 1450 and 1750 Europe underwent a great economic transformation which is associated with the shift from a town-centered to a nation-centered economy, the extension of European influence throughout the world, and the rise of capitalism. The period is usually termed the Commercial Revolution because commerce and the activities of merchants were central to the great economic progress of the age.

Capitalism is commonly defined by economists as an economic system in which capital, or wealth, is invested in order to produce more capital. Thus capitalism is an expanding economic system, ever producing more wealth. Other important characteristics of capitalism are the private ownership of the means of producing wealth (land, raw materials, ships, factories, and so on), and a sharp cleavage between capitalists and wage workers, which was not present in medieval guilds and manors or in modern socialism. The driving force behind capitalism is the securing of profits.

Much of the history of the five hundred years between the midpoint of the fifteenth century and the present day is concerned with the virtues and sins of capitalism, its defense and condemnation, and its development (as in the United States) or rejection (as in the Soviet Union). Its history can be traced in four distinct stages.

The first stage—commercial capitalism—was underway at least by 1450 and continued on into the eighteenth century. Most of these early capitalists, protected and encouraged by governmental controls, subsidies, and monopolies, made their profits from commerce.

Beginning about 1750, the second phase—industrial capitalism—was made possible by the accumulation of vast amounts of capital and its investment in machinery and the factory system of manufacturing. During the resulting Industrial Revolution the industrialist replaced the merchant as the key figure in the capitalistic system.

In the last decades of the nineteenth century, when the ultimate control and direction of large areas of industry came into the hands of financiers, industrial capitalism gave way to finance capitalism. The establishment of mammoth industrial conglomerations and their management by men largely divorced from ownership were the dominant features of this third phase.

Since the great world depression of the 1930's, the state has played an increasingly dominant role in the capitalistic system, one well-known manifestation in the United States being the New Deal and its successor programs. This fourth phase is commonly known to economists as state capitalism.

Mercantilism. The body of economic theory and practice that accompanied commercial capitalism is called mercantilism—a system of governmental regulation of economic matters in order to increase the wealth of the state. In the words of Francis Bacon, its purpose was "the opening and well-balancing of trade; the cherishing of manufactures; the banishing of idleness; the repressing of waste and excess by sumptuary laws; the improvement and husbanding of the soil, the regulation of prices . . . ."[5] A similar program of stimulation and regimentation had characterized the economic life of medieval towns; now, under mercantilism, the new territorial state superseded the town and its guilds as the regulator of the economy. (In France the guild system was retained as the state's agent in regulating industry.) Mercantilism declined after 1750, when a new group of economic theorists challenged such basic mercantilist doctrines as the belief that the amount of the world's wealth is relatively fixed and that one nation can increase its wealth only at the expense of another.

Among the major tenets of mercantilism was bullionism, a doctrine which stressed the importance of accumulating precious metals. Mercantilists emphasized state power as the chief objective of economic policy, and "money," they liked to say, "is the sinews of war." The New World was a source of fantastic amounts of bullion for sixteenth–century Spain, the first great mercantilist state. Each spring two well-guarded fleets left Seville or Cádiz, one heading for Mexico and the other for Panama. Laden with silver from the Andes and Mexico, the convoys returned to Spain in the autumn at great risk. After a rendezvous at Havana the combined fleets ran the gauntlet back to Spain. Pirates and buccaneers were ever ready to swoop down on stragglers, as were warships of rival powers. Yet most of the treasure reached Spain, where the crown received its royal fifth.

A second and corollary tenet of mercantilism was that a nation should maintain the most favorable balance of trade possible: it should export more than it imported so that foreign nations would have to pay the difference in precious metals. Only raw materials that could not be obtained at home were to be imported; after these materials had been manufactured into finished articles, they were then to be exported. Government subsidies, such as the granting of monopolies and the use of protective tariffs, encouraged the home production of manufactured goods.

Mercantilists believed that when raw materials were native, the profit to the home country was 100 percent. Therefore, if a country could not supply its own materials, it should acquire colonies from which they could be procured. Furthermore, colonies constituted not only sources of supply for raw materials but also markets for finished products. Because the mother country did not want competition for its infant industries, colonies were prevented from engaging in manufacturing. In addition, the colonies were prohibited from trading with foreign powers.

Decline of the early commercial centers. During the Middle Ages the central agency of European trade was the town. In northern Europe trade had been dominated by the confederacy of towns in the Baltic area known as the Hanseatic League (see p. 120). After the fifteenth century, however, the League rapidly declined, a victim of mercantile rivalry from the rising nation-states of Denmark, Sweden, and Russia. The absence of a strong central government in Germany left the League without adequate protection.

In southern Europe the merchants of the Italian city-states, with Venice in the lead, had for centuries acted as the great middlemen of Europe because they controlled the lucrative Asiatic trade. But the Portuguese smashed the Italian monopoly by discovering a new sea route to India and by obstructing the Red Sea and Persian Gulf routes that led to the Mediterranean ports. In addition, the Italian Wars of the sixteenth century (see Chapter 10) had a disastrous effect upon the prosperity of the Italian cities.

Portugal, temporarily paramount. With its limited population, Portugal could not permanently administer and protect an empire scattered over three continents. During the sixteenth century emigration, plague, and famine reduced the country's population from one and a half million to less than one, and the Portuguese were unable to man their ships and fortresses adequately. In 1580 Portugal came under the Spanish crown, and when it regained its independence in the following century, it retained only a few small possessions in the Far East, some islands in the mid-Atlantic, Brazil, and Mozambique and Angola in Africa. The economic power of Portugal ebbed away, not from lack of initiative so much as from lack of resources to support so great a task.

The economic decay of Spain. The decline of Spain's economic might cannot be explained so simply. This nation apparently had everything—and failed. During the sixteenth century Spain had far more gold and silver than any of its rivals; and to this wealth was added that of Portugal and its possessions. Yet the wealth and power lavishly displayed during the reign of Philip II (1556-1598) were only surface deep. Agricultural production declined, and the countryside was depopulated because wool was Spain's chief export and the government favored the sheep ranchers by granting them the right to graze their flocks everywhere, even on the cultivated land. Religious persecution and the expulsion of the Jews and Moors had deprived Spain of many of its skilled financiers and craftsmen. Since the Church and the upper classes were exempt from taxation, the tax burden fell disproportionately on the peasants and the middle class.

An outward symbol of wealth, the rich flood of bullion from the Americas wreaked havoc in the Spanish economy by causing inflation. From 1500 to 1600 Spain experienced a fivefold rise of prices, a condition which attracted a stream of lower-priced products from France, Flanders, and England, to the detriment of Spanish manufacturers. Spain's riches were drained off to purchase foreign manufactured goods—and even grain—and to pay the costs of Philip II's wars.

Antwerp's period of glory. As Spain and Portugal declined, the commercial center of Europe moved northward to Antwerp. To this great Flemish port came Europe's merchants and bankers. Antwerp was made a toll-free port, and in 1531 the city fathers set up a merchants' exchange—the bourse—which, unlike the medieval fairs, operated continuously as an international commercial and financial center. It was said that Antwerp did as much business in one month as Venice in two years. Various institutions of modern capitalism evolved at Antwerp. Its bourse developed into the first stock exchange, trading in the shares of joint-stock companies. Life and property insurance came into use. But the spectacular prosperity of Antwerp was short-lived; in 1576, during the wars of the Netherlands against Spain, the city was sacked, and in 1585 the Dutch occupied the mouth of the Scheldt River and cut off the city's access to the sea. Henceforth Antwerp's trade and finances were largely appropriated by the Dutch city of Amsterdam.

Holland's golden age. During most of the seventeenth century Holland, with a population of two million, was the principal commercial, financial, and manufacturing country in Europe. Markedly successful were both the Dutch East India Company and the West India Company, private joint-stock companies which were authorized to acquire and govern overseas territory, negotiate treaties, and wage war. The Dutch built better ships than their rivals and operated them more efficiently; their lower freight rates gained for them a monopoly on the carrying trade of Europe. The Dutch policy of religious toleration attracted artisans from abroad, and Holland became the leading industrial nation of Europe. Dutch exports included textiles, salted herring, glazed pottery, fine jewelry, and printed books. Trade, in turn, made Amsterdam the center of banking and credit.

Nevertheless, like Portugal, Holland was a small nation, and larger neighbors were presently to overtake it. Rivalry with England and France led to a series of wars during the latter half of the seventeenth century, and the Dutch lost much of their carrying trade to the English. Yet Dutch skill, together with the retention of the East Indies, enabled Holland to remain a significant factor in world commerce and finance.

France's rise and decline. With a population of about fifteen million in the seventeenth century, France replaced Spain as the premier nation of Europe. Its abundant economic resources were assiduously cultivated by Colbert (1619-1683), Louis XIV's astute minister of finance, who sponsored the colonization of Canada and chartered a number of trading companies, which established slaving stations in Africa and also trading posts in both India and the Caribbean sugar islands. Colbert also subsidized French industry by protecting it with high tariffs and granting monopolies, tax reductions, and loans without interest. Although his aggressive mercantilist policies worked well at first, the merits of his program were gradually offset by evils inherent in the system. In retaliation for Colbert's restrictions against foreign imports, other nations refused to purchase French farm products and wines. Furthermore, monopolies were increasingly unpopular with businessmen, who also became irked by governmental regulations and controls by the old medieval guilds.

In addition, it has been estimated that between 1685 and 1715 France lost a million subjects through warfare, the surrender of colonies, and the drain of emigration. The revocation of the Edict of Nantes in 1685 resulted in the flight from France of a large group of industrious Huguenots, who took their capital and skills as artisans to neighboring countries. And the worldwide duel for empire between France and England during the first half of the eighteenth century (see Chapter 13) was a disaster for France. England emerged as Europe's dominant commercial and colonial power.

Rise of England's sun. Although England was inferior to France in area, fertility of soil, and population (between four and five million), this island kingdom had many factors in its favor which more than compensated for its disadvantages. Geographical isolation discouraged military conquest from the Continent—the last successful invasion by a foreign power had taken place in 1066—and the English economy had not been burdened by the cost of maintaining large standing armies. After the union of England and Scotland in 1707, internal trade flourished in the largest customs-free area in western Europe. The aristocracy and upper middle class which controlled Parliament also controlled the principal trading and banking companies so that the growth of new enterprises was more rapid than anywhere else in Europe. The gradual control of the seas, the establishment of trading posts in exotic lands, and the shrewd policy of taking overseas territory as its booty from successful European wars enabled England to gain commercial benefits and to build the world's largest empire.

The first important step in the rise of England's sun came in 1651 with the passage of the first Navigation Act forbidding the importation of goods into England or its dependencies except in English ships or in ships of the country producing the goods. The act was aimed at the Dutch carrying trade, and it provoked the first of three maritime wars with Holland. England soon outstripped both Holland and France and by 1750 had laid the foundation for its economic domination of the world in the nineteenth century.

We shall see that England's textile industry, having freed itself from the restrictions of the guild system, was no small factor in accounting for its economic growth. Daniel Defoe, the author of *Robinson Crusoe,* maintained that the woolen industry was of greater value to England than the rich mines of Peru and Mexico were to Spain.

More imports in Europe's markets.   The discovery of sea routes to both Asia and the Americas provided an unparalleled impetus to the expansion of European commerce. The spice trade was especially profitable because there was no refrigeration, and slightly spoiled food could be made palatable by seasoning it with cloves, cinnamon, or pepper. Cloths from the East—calicoes, chintzes, and ginghams—became popular. The textile workers of England became so incensed at the foreign competition that they demanded a prohibition on the import of these inexpensive cotton fabrics, which they maintained were "made by a parcel of heathens and pagans that worship the Devil and work for 1/2*d.* a day."[6] Among other imports from Asia were silks, carpets and rugs, precious stones, porcelain, brassware, and the all-important beverages, tea and coffee.

From the New World came a variety of products which revolutionized the eating and drinking habits of the Europeans. The food supply of Europe was greatly improved by the addition of potatoes, corn, and tomatoes. From the Caribbean islands came one of the most valuable imports, sugar, which supplanted honey as a sweetener. An abundant supply of fish, primarily cod, came from Newfoundland's Grand Banks; and warm furs were obtained by trappers penetrating the interior of North America. The sacred beverage of the Aztecs, cocoa, found its way to Spain and thence throughout Europe. The use of tobacco, like sugar, spread rapidly among rich and poor alike. It was used mainly in the form of snuff or for smoking in pipes. Both Church and state sought unsuccessfully to stamp out tobacco.

While gold and ivory from Africa enriched Europe directly, the most important African export enriched the European powers indirectly. This export was that most misery-ridden produce—slaves. Prince Henry the Navigator sent home the first African slaves, and the Portuguese dominated the slave trade throughout the sixteenth century. In the seventeenth century the Dutch drove the Portuguese out of the Guinea coast, and other Europeans, particularly the Dutch and the English, became active in the slave trade.

The chief market for African slaves was Spanish America, where the colonists soon discovered that the native Indians were poor workers. The Spanish government contracted with the traders of other nations who exchanged their cargoes with local African chiefs for slaves, most of whom were prisoners captured in Africa's continual tribal wars. "A woman slave might change hands for a gallon of brandy, six bars of iron, two small guns, one keg of powder, and two strings of beads; a man slave might cost eight guns, one wicker-covered bottle, two cases of spirits, and twenty-eight sheets."[7] The voyage across the Atlantic to America cost the lives of from 10 to 25 percent of the Africans—inhumanly packed as they were in evil-smelling, suffocating quarters below deck—but the remainder were profitably disposed of at their destination. Estimates are that in three centuries between twenty and fifty million Africans were brought to the Americas. During the sixteenth and seventeenth centuries more Africans than Europeans arrived in the New World.

The price revolution.   The gold and silver brought into the European market from the New World in enormous quantities had a more direct effect on Europe's economy than any other product of Africa, Asia, or the Americas. By the middle of the fifteenth century Europe had been confronted with a severe shortage of gold and silver, caused both by the depletion of European mines and by increasing demands for currency to finance the new standing armies and navies and to pay for spices and other luxury commodities. But the critical situation was partially relieved by the development of new European mines, by imports of gold from West Africa, and, above all, by the unprecedented quantities of precious metals from the mines of Spanish America. Since very little of this precious metal remained permanently in Spain, price levels throughout western Europe were upset; between 1500 and 1650 commodity prices more than tripled.

This price revolution affected all classes. Merchants and manufacturers were benefited, but laborers were harmed because wages lagged behind prices. Except in parts of England, the landowners of western Europe, most of whom had rented their land to peasants on long-term leases, suffered because their incomes were fixed. The peasants, on the other hand, benefited from rising prices for their farm products. In Europe east of the Elbe, however, the situation was reversed. Here the landowners benefited from the rising price and growing market for grain in the west by the twofold process of increasing production and enserfing their peasants, who during the Middle Ages had been freer than those in western Europe. The subjection of the east European peasantry—as a means of obtaining a cheap labor force—contrasts sharply with the freedom of western Europe's peasant renters and farmers. Through the centuries the Elbe would continue to divide Europe economically and socially, and today it divides communist and capitalist Europe.

Banking becomes big business.   One indicator of the resurgence of commerce was the growth of banking and related business practices. The word *bank* derives from the Italian *banca,* meaning "bench," on which medieval Italian moneylenders sat in the marketplace to carry on their business. When a man failed, the people broke his bench, and from this custom came the word *bankrupt,* or "broken bench." During the Late Middle Ages moneylending became indispensable to the administration of both national monarchies and the Church so that the traditional prohibition on usury was often ignored.

Large-scale banking was first developed in Italian cities, where merchant bankers arranged bills of exchange and negotiated loans. By 1350 some eighty banking houses were in business in Florence alone. In the fifteenth century the most illustrious of these families was the Medici, who established branch offices all over western Europe and acted as financial agents for the popes. Loans also were made to rulers who were continually in need of funds to carry on their wars.

The greatest of the sixteenth-century bankers were the Fuggers of Augsburg in Germany. They repeated the pattern set by the Medici, loaning money to the Church (half of the money collected by Tetzel from the sale of indulgences went to repay a Fugger loan), to Charles v to finance his election as emperor, and to the Spanish and Austrian Hapsburgs. The Hapsburg loans were secured by mining concessions, and the Fuggers gained a virtual monopoly on silver and copper mining in central Europe and silver and mercury mining in Spain. For decades the

Fuggers realized an average yearly profit of over 30 percent, but they went bankrupt in 1607 when Spain for the third time defaulted on its loans.

By the seventeenth century the resources of banking families like the Fuggers were inadequate to meet the needs of the time, and private banks were superseded by public banks chartered by the government. The first of these public institutions was the Bank of Amsterdam, chartered in 1609. Its main purpose was to facilitate trade by the conversion of various currencies into credits called bank money, which because of its standard value came to be preferred to coins. In 1694 the Bank of England was chartered as a means of financing England's wars. In return for a large loan to the government at 8 percent, the bank was granted a monopoly on such banking operations as issuing paper bank notes and marketing the government's securities.

With banking there naturally evolved new financial techniques. Despite the increase in precious metals after 1500, the supply could not keep pace with the increase in trade, and the Bank of Amsterdam began the practice of issuing loans against its deposits. Because it found that it could safely loan larger sums than had been deposited, the Bank of Amsterdam thus initiated a new and effective means of expanding credit. Likewise, bank notes came to replace gold and silver currency, and merchants developed the method of raising ready money known as discounting. Instead of waiting months to cash a bill of exchange owed to them, they sold it before its due date for something less than its face value. Banks in particular offered this service, holding the discounted bills until they matured at full value.

Progress was also made in commercial arithmetic and in bookkeeping. Double-entry bookkeeping was well known in Italy by 1500 and in western Europe a century later. By listing a transaction either as a *debit* (meaning, "he owes") or a *credit* ("he believes" a promiser will carry out his promise), a businessman could readily determine his status in terms of profit and loss.

Financing commercial companies. Unprecedented difficulties resulted from trading at long distances overseas in strange lands, and it was natural that those involved should form companies to seek state aid and to share losses as well as profits. The companies were of two types—regulated and joint-stock—and both were chartered, regulated, and granted monopolies by the state. In the regulated company individuals financed their own businesses and abided by the rules the group had accepted to protect the trade in which the members had a mutual interest. The earlier companies were of this nature.

The joint-stock companies involved an association of capital as well as of men. The members put their money into a common fund and gave over the management to a board of directors. Because of its advantages, the joint-stock company became almost universal. As many people as wanted could contribute capital, and stock might be transferred as the owner saw fit. The joint-stock company had a permanent legal personality that did not expire, whereas the regulated company was not a legal entity, and in case of damages each member had to sue or be sued individually. The vast corporations of today grew out of this early type of business organization.

The creation of joint-stock companies gave impetus to the growth of stock exchanges, because the shares could be easily transferred from one person to another like any other commodity. A stock exchange made it easier to accumulate capital from many different sources, thereby enabling very large commercial companies to be formed.

Another method of sharing losses besides the joint-stock company was insurance. Since the loss of his vessel might well ruin an individual merchant, it came to be the practice to distribute losses among a group of traders by means of insurance. Interested merchants drew up an agreement by which each was responsible for a percentage of any possible loss. Because the merchants signed their names at the bottom of this document, the practice came to be known as underwriting. The most famous of all marine insurance groups, Lloyd's of London, came into being about 1688. Lloyd's was not a stock company but an association of shipowners, merchants, and underwriters who first met together in a London coffee house owned by Edward Lloyd. Since its modest beginnings, Lloyd's has grown steadily and branched out into other forms of insurance.

Speculation and business bubbles. Toward the end of the seventeenth century, the accumulation of capital brought about a mania for speculation in the shares of joint-stock companies in England, France, and Holland. The two most notorious speculative companies were the South Sea Company in England and the Mississippi Company in France.

The financiers of the South Sea Company assumed the British national debt of about £9,000,000 in return for a 6 percent annual interest payment and a monopoly of British trade with South America and the islands in the South Seas. The price of company stock rose rapidly until it was far above the value of the company's earnings. In 1720, with a £100 share selling for £1,060, the huge speculative bubble burst when shareholders lost confidence and began to sell. Many lost not only their savings but also property they had mortgaged in the hope of getting rich quickly.

The Mississippi Company had a similar history. Formed to promote trade with France's Louisiana territory, where it founded New Orleans in 1718, the company soon acquired a monopoly on all French colonial trade. In addition, the company assumed the national debt and was granted the right to collect all indirect taxes in France and to operate a central bank with the privilege of issuing paper money. Speculative fever combined with currency inflation to bid up the company's stock to fantastic heights. Thousands suffered losses when shareholders began to unload and the company went bankrupt in 1720.

The demoralizing failure of these schemes left a legacy in both countries. In England Parliament passed the "Bubble Act," which drastically restricted the right of incorporation. In France distrust of paper money and the government's credit and solvency continued for generations.

The domestic system. The impetus of commercial expansion caused an important change in the organization of industry, particularly that of textiles. Beginning in Italy in the fifteenth century and in England in the sixteenth, the guild system was gradually superseded by the domestic, or putting-out, system. It operated in this fashion: a merchant capitalist would buy raw materials, assign them to artisans to be worked on at piece rates in their own homes, take the finished product, and sell it to his customers. Thus, between producer and customer, a middleman intervened—the capitalist entrepreneur. Because work was no longer planned and conducted by master and apprentice under one roof, this system widened the gulf between employer and employee, capitalist and worker.

The domestic system had many advantages. The accumulation of capital in the hands of the entrepreneur made possible the purchase of raw materials in greater bulk and allowed for marketing of finished products on a larger scale than had been possible under the guild system. The domestic system also contributed to an increased specialization of skills within an efficient system of overall production; an employer could have his raw wool sent to spinners, then to weavers, and finally to dyers. Many of the poorer agricultural laborers, and their women and children, could increase their income by doing piece-work in their cottages. The capitalist employer, on the other hand, could operate without the restrictions imposed by the urban guilds.

The domestic system persisted for two hundred years in England, although sometimes workers were brought together in central shops long before the beginning of the machine age and the factory system proper. In France, however, where the guilds were retained as agents of the mercantilist state in controlling industry, the guild system remained strong. Hence industrial production in France lagged behind that in England, where industry was less restricted by guild practices.

Innovation in agriculture. Although agriculture still provided the majority of Europeans with their livelihood, in parts of England, especially, the advent of commercial capitalism wrought significant changes. The profit-making potentialities in farming attracted enterprising entrepreneurs, who bought up large tracts of land. Because the possession of land had always been the mark of nobility, the *nouveaux riches* consolidated their position in polite society by acquiring estates and marrying into the landed gentry. The alliance between land and trade created a powerful new group in Parliament—a class which promoted legislation favorable to its own needs and desires. But the satisfaction of the profit motive had a beneficial effect upon English agriculture; by the eighteenth century capitalist landowners were applying efficient business methods to the management of their estates. They encouraged the use of new tools and crops and were sympathetic to new ideas in stock breeding and soil development.

Jethro Tull, for example, advocated careful plowing of the land, planting seeds in neat rows by the use of a drill he invented, and keeping the plants well cultivated as they grew to maturity. By mixing clay and lime into the soil, Viscount Charles Townshend restored the fertility of land that had once been worthless swamp and sand. He also suggested crop rotation as a method of soil restoration superior to the wasteful custom of allowing good farm land to lie fallow. He was so enthusiastic over turnips, his pet crop for livestock feed, that he was nicknamed "Turnip Townshend." Through the select breeding of choice animals, Robert Bakewell raised larger livestock, improved the quality of the meat, and increased the quantity of milk available from his dairy cattle.

The enclosure movement. The practice of enclosing open lands, a development which had begun in England even before Tudor times, was accelerated by the changes in farming methods. Aided by special acts of Parliament, members of the capitalist landowning class enclosed the common lands, where for hundreds of years English villagers had grazed their cattle. Many also evicted their tenants or purchased the small farms owned and operated by the sturdy, independent yeomen. The demand for wool in the textile industry resulted also in the enclosure of large tracts of arable land for sheep raising.

The enclosure movement led to controversy which reached a climax in the last half of the eighteenth century. The advocates of enclosure justified amalgamation of small agricultural holdings and common lands by claiming that new methods of stock breeding and crop rotation could not otherwise be practiced. From an economic standpoint, enclosure was inevitable, and the enclosure movement resulted in a more careful use of a greater amount of land than had been available before. Better and more food was thus made available for a population on the verge of rapid increase. Like most drastic economic changes, however, the enclosure movement spelled misery and dislocation to a large number of countryfolk. The destruction of the yeoman class and the depopulation of many villages was ruefully pondered by Oliver Goldsmith in his poem, "The Deserted Village":

> Ill fares the land, to hastening ills a prey,
> Where wealth accumulates, and men decay.
> Princes and lords may flourish, or may fade;
> A breath can make them, as a breath has made;
> But a bold peasantry, their country's pride,
> When once destroyed can never be supplied. . . .
> Ye friends to truth, ye statesmen, who survey
> The rich man's joy increase, the poor's decay,
> 'Tis yours to judge how wide the limits stand
> Between a splendid and a happy land.

The saga of the yeoman's misfortunes did not end with their departure from the villages; its finale took place in the cities. When the story of industrial capitalism is taken up in Chapter 16, we shall view the bleak and harsh environment of displaced rural people as they labored long and hard in grimy factories and lived as best they could in ugly, disease-ridden slums.

PART FOUR
CHARTING THE PRESENT

The story of Europe and the New World in the period from 1650 to 1815 forms one of the most complex chapters in world history. Following the challenge to the ideas and institutions of the Middle Ages posed by the Renaissance, the Reformation, and the great religious wars, the search for principles of order became a constant theme among scientists and in literature and the fine arts.

A succession of fresh concepts about the universe (in the seventeenth century), about society (in the eighteenth century), and about man (in the nineteenth century) brought profound changes in knowledge and attitudes which we in our century have built upon in turn. Today's science and technology affect every aspect of our lives—the electricity that powers our machines and lights our houses; our global transportation and communication networks; the medical discoveries that prolong man's life span; and even the quantity and quality of the food we eat. All these advances were made initially possible by a vast increase in men's understanding of the physical world in the seventeenth century, and in particular by the development of the scientific method. We regard the landing of astronauts on the moon and the photographing of Mars from close range as modern triumphs. And so they are, but they have taken place because certain scientists in the seventeenth century discovered the laws of motion and gravitation, while later others unraveled the complexities of electromagnetism. Similarly, our present understanding of the structure of the physical universe was brilliantly illuminated by Einstein, yet he was the first to acknowledge his own debt to the work of one of history's towering geniuses, Isaac Newton.

Science's discoveries and methods in early modern times had a pervasive effect upon thought and art. Reason was exalted, and an intellectual revolution occurred known as the Enlightenment. For many thinkers, religion lost its emotional fervor and became a philosophical creed. In this Age of Reason, literature was guided by the mind rather than by the heart, painting was restrained, while architecture adopted neoclassical canons and sought balance in both form and spirit. In Paris, where the cult of reason reached its zenith, the salon was the temple of cultivated society in which cosmopolitan Europeans exchanged their views on life during witty and often brilliant conversations. Intellectual and aesthetic pursuits emulated a mathematical precision akin to the geometrical elegance with which the formal gardens of Versailles were laid out. But logic cannot dictate to the emotions, and the Age of Reason gave way in time to Romanticism with its outpourings from the well-springs of human passion. In our own turbulent century, those passions have taken forms both wonderful and terrible, so that the upsurgings of a world in transition seem far removed from the ideal of ordered calm of the Enlightenment. Yet science today continues to search for regularities present throughout the natural phenomena of the world, while our transforming society seeks in turn for common denominators in standards and behavior which can be both constant and universally applicable.

Nowhere has this search for order during the past four centuries been more assiduously sought than in the political arena. Two opposing ideologies emerged in early modern times to dominate Western societies. The first was absolutism, which held that all power must be concentrated in a royal autocrat answerable only to God. The highwater mark of absolutism occurred under Louis xiv of France. But a rival belief contended that power and order must be vested in the people as a whole—and the revolutions of the eighteenth century voiced this ideology which was to inspire the whole liberal-democratic movement of modern times. The struggle between absolutism and democracy has continued unabated into our century with the kings replaced by dictators, who have claimed to act from a mandate inspired, not by God, but by "blood and soil" or the "inevitability of historical forces." For its part, liberal democracy has encouraged religious tolerance and freedom of inquiry and made man the focus of attention—his freedom, his happiness, and his potentialities as an individual capable of bringing order and purpose into his own life and society.

Yet this liberalism and rationalism have operated *within* but not *between* states. Humanitarian values did not touch international affairs which were dominated by the competitive state system. Here each nation was a law unto itself, any weak neighbor was a potential victim, and force remained the final argument. In this state of international anarchy, the European nations evolved the balance of power to check the grandiose ambitions of national rulers, whether Louis xiv or Napoleon. In our own century the League of Nations and the United Nations were created to try to bring order and security into an anarchic international environment. Given science's discovery of atomic energy and its application to thermonuclear weapons, the struggle is now between global order and global suicide.

CHAPTER 12

NEW DIMENSIONS
OF THE MIND

Science, Thought, and the Arts in the
Age of Reason: 1600-1800

The first phase of the transition from medieval to modern times in the western world ended about 1600, to be followed by an even more epochal period of intellectual change. So important were the changes in this latter period that the intellectual movement they comprised is identified as the Enlightenment and the time span in which they occurred is known as the Age of Reason. In the broadest sense, the Age of Reason can be thought of as comprising the seventeenth and eighteenth centuries. The spirit and purpose of the Enlightenment were eloquently expressed by one of its spokesmen, the *philosophe* Baron d'Holbach, who wrote: "Let us then endeavor to disperse those clouds of ignorance, those mists of darkness, which impede Man on his journey, which block his progress, which prevent his marching through life with a firm and steady step. Let us try to inspire him . . . with respect for his own reason—with an inextinguishable love of truth . . . so that he may learn to know himself . . . and no longer be duped by an imagination that has been led astray by authority . . . so that he may learn to base his morals on his own nature, on his own wants, on the real advantage of society . . . so that he may learn to pursue his true happiness, by promoting that of others . . . in short, so that he may become a virtuous and rational being, who cannot fail to become happy."[1]

This message indicates how rapidly the heritage of the Middle Ages was being left behind, together with its strong emphasis upon faith, authority, and man's preparation for the next world. The thinkers of the Age of Reason believed in happiness and fulfillment in this world; they regarded mind rather than faith as the best source of guidance and were suspicious of emotion, myth, and supernaturalism. The chief support of the cult of reason was science, with its new laws and methods. The supreme achievement of the Enlightenment, however, was not in discovering additional scientific laws but rather in translating the advances of science into a new philosophy and world view.

Exaltation of science, faith in reason, and belief in humanitarianism led writers and thinkers of the Enlightenment to carry on a strenuous campaign of reevaluation of all aspects of society. They were positive that reason could solve all human problems. All thought was colored by a belief in progress and by a vigorous optimism regarding mankind's improvability. In religion a movement known as Deism, reflecting these views, sought to establish a "rational" faith; and in the study of mankind, the foundations were laid for the systematic disciplines of the social sciences.

Literature, music, and the fine arts were affected profoundly by the cult of reason. Everywhere there was supreme confidence in logic, a tendency to minimize spirit and emotion, and a close attention to the forms and rules which had characterized the classical era in Greece and Rome, when the splendor of human reason had first been extolled.

THE SCIENTIFIC REVOLUTION

From "authority" to "facts."   The transition from the Middle Ages to early modern times represents a shift in emphasis from "authoritative" truth to "factual" truth. Medieval thought had enthroned theology as the "queen of the sciences" because the scholastics sought to relate human knowledge to ultimate divine purposes. Hence they made little distinction between a "fact" and a theological "truth." In their world view man was seen to be dependent upon a divine order in which God was responsible for mankind's origin and destiny alike. The medieval mind had also associated this earthly life with the loss of Eden and the physical world with the works of Satan. In order to justify modern man's extension of his environmental powers, it was first necessary to adopt a new attitude, namely, that God had revealed His divine purpose both in scripture and in nature. As a consequence, interest shifted progressively to discovering the processes and laws governing the natural world. Instead of concentrating their attention on *why,* or final cause, men concerned themselves with *how,* or the manner of causation.

Important consequences derived from this conceptual shift. Men continued to regard scriptural revelation as providing certainty in the subjective world of faith and ethics. But increasingly they employed their reasoning powers to discover in the objective world of nature the principles of causation—and to do so in terms that were both mathematical and mechanical. Eventually this rationalistic emphasis upon the scientific method was to affect virtually every area of human activity, including the evolution of religious thought into Deism.

Progress of the scientific method.   The birth of modern science is often regarded as marked by the publication in 1543 of Copernicus' heliocentric theory which denied that the earth was the center of the cosmos. This revolutionary theory challenged the teachings of religion and the traditional ideas concerning the nature of the universe and man's place in it. By the last half of the seventeenth century the Copernican system and the progress made in other branches of science besides astronomy had produced a change in man's outlook upon the world that is considered one of the greatest revolutions in the history of human thought. When Charles Darwin in the nineteenth century wrote that "science and her methods gave me a resting place independent of authority and tradition," he was describing what has been frequently called the fundamental faith of modern western man.

Basic to the growth of science was the development of the scientific method, a systematic and logical way of seeking truth. In the search for facts, this new servant relied on curiosity, healthy skepticism, and reason rather than faith. The foundations of the new method were laid in the first half of the seventeenth century by Francis Bacon in England and René Descartes in France.

Bacon's attack on unscientific thinking. In his *Novum Organum (The New Instrument),* published in 1620, Sir Francis Bacon (1561-1626) described the course which science and a scientifically oriented philosophy should take. First, man must cope with four major prejudices (in Bacon's famous term, *Idols*) which had so far obstructed human progress. The Idols of the Tribe are the prejudices inherent in human nature itself; in particular, they represent the tendency to see only those facts which support an opinion one wishes to entertain. The Idols of the Cave are prejudices fostered in the individual by his particular environment—the circumstances of his birth, childhood, education, and so forth. The Idols of the Market Place are false opinions which spread when men consort together. Lastly, there are the Idols of the Theater, resulting from men's tendency to become attached to particular theories, schools of thought, and philosophies and to hold on to them long after the logical basis for their continuance has disappeared.

If better results were to be obtained, new ways of thinking and of approaching the world of nature had to be devised. Here we come to Bacon's famous method of induction, by which he advocated a systematic recording of facts derived from experiments. These facts would lead to tentative hypotheses which could then be tested by fresh experiments under different conditions. Eventually it should prove possible for men to arrive at universal principles and scientific laws.

Bacon himself was an indifferent scientist. The significance of his work lies in the fact that he set forth a program to direct the course of scientific and philosophical inquiry at the time when the traditional modes of thought were crumbling. Bacon also forecast the vast importance of the new science in enabling man to conquer his environment. In his *New Atlantis* (1627)—his description of a utopian society—emphasis is centered on a research institute called "Solomon's house," where experimentation and invention were subsidized and directed toward the goal of "the enlarging of the bounds of Human Empire, to the effecting of all things possible."[2]

Descartes, champion of the deductive method. Experimentation is not the only approach to scientific knowledge, as the mathematical approach attests. The mathematical approach is to begin with a self-evident axiom and then, by logical reasoning, to deduce various inferences. Applied to scientific investigations as a whole, this type of approach—known as the deductive method—advances by logical steps from simple self-evident truths to more complex truths. It was the achievement of René Descartes (1596-1650) to make brilliant use of this method of reasoning in his attempt to extend the mathematical method to all fields of human knowledge. Bacon had called for "minds washed clean of opinions," and Descartes began by being prepared to doubt everything except the fact of his own doubting. And if he doubted, he must in fact exist—hence his famous expression *Cogito, ergo sum* ("I think, therefore I am").

For Bacon, experiment was the next step in the quest for truth. Although Descartes by no means rejected the value of experimentation, he placed reliance above all on the attainment of knowledge through reason. By logical deduction,

Descartes built up a concept of a unified, mathematically ordered universe which operated like a perfect mechanism; in this universe, supernatural phenomena were impossible and everything could be explained rationally, preferably in mathematical terms.

Some scientists criticized Descartes for not having made sufficient use of experiment, even as he had criticized Bacon for weakness in mathematics. As we well know, the experimental and mathematical methods are complementary. Before the mid-point of the seventeenth century, the two methods had been combined by Kepler and Galileo. Thus a revolution in scientific thinking had been effected, and the foundation of modern science and modern philosophy had been firmly laid.

Science takes to the heavens. It was in astronomy that science made its first spectacular advance. For over a thousand years western Europe had accepted the view of Ptolemy, a Greek scholar of the second century A.D., that the earth was stationary. Rotating around it were concentric, impenetrable, crystalline spheres to which were attached the sun, planets, and fixed stars. The Ptolemaic system as expressed in the geocentric (earth-centered) theory was incorporated into the scholastic system of the Church. By the middle of the seventeenth century, however, a revolution in man's conceptions of the heavens had been attained.

Copernicus (1473-1543) was a Polish contemporary of Martin Luther and Michelangelo. During visits to Italy for study, he read widely in the classical authors and was much impressed by the Platonist philosophy that beauty was supreme and that mathematics was the ideal science. As a mathematician, Copernicus found parts of the Ptolemaic theory "not sufficiently pleasing to the mind" and began to seek a more pleasing combination of circles to express the motions of the planets. He obtained such a model by assuming that the earth moves "like any other planet," while the sun stands still in the middle of the planetary orbits. Near the end of his life, he was persuaded to publish his views under the title *Concerning the Revolution of Heavenly Spheres* (1543). In this work he refuted the theory that the earth remained stationary in the middle of the universe, contending instead that it rotated every twenty-four hours upon its axis from west to east and that it made an annual movement around the sun. As early as 1539 Luther attacked Copernicus' views as contrary to the truth of the Bible. Not until 1616, however, did the Catholic Church place Copernicus' book on the *Index of Prohibited Books* "until corrected," from which it was removed in 1620 after only minor revisions.

Johann Kepler (1571-1630), a brilliant German mathematician with a strong leaning toward Platonic idealism, quickly adopted the Copernican theory. While working with data on the movements of Mars, Kepler had to account for the apparent irregularities in that planet's perplexing orbit. After patiently applying one mathematical hypothesis after another, he was able to verify that the planet did not move in a circular orbit but described an ellipse. He then proceeded to assume that the other planets also traveled in elliptical orbits. Another planetary law discovered by Kepler was that the pace of a planet accelerated as it approached the sun. After reading Gilbert's book on magnetism (see p. 248), Kepler concluded that the sun emitted a magnetic force that moved the planets in their courses—an idea that formed a valuable basis for Newton's theory of gravitation.

An Italian contemporary of Kepler, Galileo Galilei (1564-1642), discovered new facts to verify the Copernican theory but, as he wrote to Kepler:

. . . I have not dared to make [it] known, as I have been deterred by the fate of our teacher Copernicus. He, it is true, won undying fame amongst some few, but amongst the multitude (there are so many fools in the world) he was only an object of scorn and laughter.[3]

In 1609 Galileo made a telescope, and with it he discovered mountains on the moon, sunspots, the satellites of Jupiter, and the rings of Saturn. Thrilled with these discoveries, Galileo publicized his findings and beliefs. In 1616 he was constrained by the Church to promise that he would not "hold, teach, or defend" the heretical Copernican doctrines; and in 1633 he was forced to make a public recantation of his heretical doctrine. A legend has it that Galileo, upon rising from his knees after renouncing the idea that the earth moved, stamped on the ground and exclaimed, "Eppur si muove!" ("But it does move!")

Galileo was also the first to establish the law of falling bodies, proving that, irrespective of the weight or the size of the bodies, their acceleration is constant (the increase of velocity being thirty-two feet per second). Thus another entrenched belief inherited from the ancients was refuted: Aristotle's contention that bodies fall to earth at speeds proportional to their weight.

Newton and the law of gravitation. Great as the contributions of Kepler and Galileo had been to astronomy, their individual discoveries had yet to be united into one all-embracing principle or law which would explain the motion of all bodies in the planetary system and present the universe as one great unity operating according to unalterable principles. This goal was realized by Isaac Newton (1642-1727), the most illustrious scientist in the Age of Reason.

At the age of only twenty-four, Newton had made all his important discoveries; the law of gravitation, the principles of calculus, and the compound nature of light. Although he had already discovered the principle of gravitation, he was not able to prove it mathematically until 1685. Two years later his momentous work was published in Latin under the title *Philosophiae Naturalis Principia Mathematica (Mathematical Principles of Natural Philosophy).* By this work all laws of motion, both celestial and terrestrial, were synthesized in a master principle for the universe, the law of gravitation, which was expressed in a concise, simple, mathematical formula: Every particle in the universe attracts every other particle with a force varying inversely as the square of the distance between them and directly proportional to the product of their masses.[4] The publication of the *Principia* climaxed nearly a century and a half in which scientists had struggled against static tradition and intolerant authority.

Advances in mathematics. Meanwhile, mathematicians had been keeping abreast of the work of the astronomers and physicists and providing them with new tools. Indeed, as Galileo pointed out, mathematics was the language of science; of necessity these two fields had to progress hand in hand. Mathematical calculation was greatly simplified by the invention of time-saving devices and by the development of new forms of mathematical analysis. Decimals were introduced in 1585 and logarithms in 1614. Eight years later the slide rule was invented, followed in 1645 by the first adding machine. The degree to which these devices speeded up computation is indicated by the saying that John Napier, the Scotsman who invented logarithms, doubled the lives of his fellow mathematicians by halving the time involved in solving intricate problems.

Two new branches of mathematical analysis helped make the seventeenth century the great age of science. Descartes "discovered the foundations of a wonderful science" (the words of his enthusiastic announcement) by uniting algebra and geometry into a unified discipline. The result, analytic geometry, permitted relationships in space to be translated into algebraic equations—a development of obvious value to astronomers, for example, since it helped them to represent astronomical phenomena in mathematical symbols and formulas.

Algebra was next applied to motion. The result was calculus, the greatest mathematical achievement of the seventeenth century, worked out independently by Newton and a German philosopher of remarkable versatility, Gottfried Leibnitz. This new calculus enabled scientists to consider quantitatively such problems as the movement of heat and the motion of stars, to compute quickly the content of circles, and to calculate stresses. Newton himself used it to arrive at and to prove his law of gravitation.

The dawn of modern medicine. We have seen the spectacular discoveries made in astronomy and mathematics. Meanwhile, scientific progress was being made in other branches of knowledge, with medicine being one of the first to be placed upon a scientific foundation.

Paracelsus (1493-1541), a contemporary of Copernicus, was an egotistical, opinionated German-Swiss physician who was so annoyed with the tyranny of tradition in his field that he advocated instead the value of experimental science. The gist of his teachings was that since the human body was basically chemical in its construction, the prescription of chemicals was in turn required to cure disease. He appears to have been the first to use such drugs as silver nitrate, copper vitriol, and arsenic and antimony compounds and to introduce the zinc oxide ointment commonly used today for treatment of skin diseases. One of his most original books dealt with the peculiar ailments of miners—the poisonous effects of metallic dusts that penetrated their skin, lungs, and mucous membranes.

Another scientist to find himself at odds with the followers of Galen and Hippocrates was Andreas Vesalius (1514-1564), a native of Brussels. Although he did not deny the merits of the Greek authorities, Vesalius contended that in medical schools, attention should first be given to the actual dissection of human bodies. At the age of twenty-three, Vesalius became a professor at the famous University of Padua. He was perhaps the first professor to perform dissection in the classroom. In 1543, within a few weeks of the appearance of Copernicus' masterpiece, Vesalius published his treatise *The Fabric of the Human Body.* This work exposed the errors made by classical scholars, showed the true structure of the human body, and by its revolutionary approach achieved for anatomy what Copernicus' book did for astronomy.

Foundations of modern chemistry. During the seventeenth and eighteenth centuries chemistry came a long way from medieval alchemy, but it would not become an exact science until the phlogiston theory of combustion could be disproved. This theory contended that in all inflammable things there existed a combustible substance called phlogiston (from the Greek "to set on fire"), which was "a principle of fire, but not fire itself." Destruction of the phlogiston theory was the remarkable achievement of the eighteenth-century French scientist Antoine Lavoisier.

Supporters of the old theory maintained that phlogiston was removed during combustion. By using chemists' scales in his experiment, Lavoisier proved that nothing was given off, that, on the contrary, something was added. From this evidence Lavoisier reasoned that burning is a process in which "dephlogisticated air" is taken from ordinary air and unites with the substance consumed. By decomposing the red powder he had obtained by burning mercury, Lavoisier conclusively proved his thesis; the loss of weight of the powder was exactly equivalent to the weight of the dephlogisticated air given off. To the element so essential in combustion Lavoisier gave a new name—*oxygen.*

In his experiments on combustion Lavoisier also discovered the law of the conservation of matter—that matter cannot be created or destroyed. With the knowledge that weight is a constant and that the scientist, aided by his balance, can accurately determine by weight the substances in any compound, measurements in chemistry could be made with the precision required of an exact science.

Beginnings of electricity. Only three hundred years ago practically nothing was known of electricity and its seemingly magical potentialities. The scientist William Gilbert was the first to use the term *electricity,* which he derived from the Greek word for amber *(elektron).* In his work *De Magnete* (1600) Gilbert described the attraction between magnets as well as the forces which are created when bodies such as amber are rubbed.

Another great name in electricity is that of Alessandro Volta. In 1800 Volta, an Italian physicist, found a new way of generating electricity; he was able to make it flow continuously instead of discharging itself in one spark. Volta's apparatus consisted of a set of glass tumblers containing water and a little sulfuric acid. In each solution two plates, one copper and one zinc, were immersed. The copper plate of one glass was wired to the zinc of the next. Electricity flowed through the connecting wires; the free copper plate carried a positive charge and the free zinc plate, a negative charge. Thus Volta's machine—the direct ancestor of modern electric cells and batteries—produced electricity simply but effectively. Volta's name has been immortalized in the term used for a unit of electrical measurement, the volt.

Another science which made remarkable advances during the eighteenth century was geology. Here the most important figure was a Scottish gentleman farmer, James Hutton. His two-volume work, *Theory of the Earth* (1795), completely overthrew the catastrophic theory then current, which taught that the earth's surface was the result of sudden catastrophic action. In brief, Hutton maintained that behind all the various formations of the earth's surface two fundamental processes are at work in a constant and relatively imperceptible manner. The two processes are disintegration, or decay, and reconstruction, or repair. Through the action of water and wind and chemical decomposition, the former continually wears away the earth's surface. The process of reconstruction takes place as the material carried off and deposited on ocean, lake, and valley floors constantly forms new strata. By changing the concept of the earth as a static thing and stressing the immensity of geological time, Hutton gave the world an entirely new time perspective.

THE CRISIS IN THE EUROPEAN CONSCIENCE

The spiritual crisis. In the latter half of the seventeenth century much of western Europe was undergoing a revolution—not in the realm of politics but in the minds of men. As a result of the impact of the scientific revolution, with

Newton's discoveries as its crowning achievements, a new concept of a universe without supernatural or miraculous forces came into being. This universe could be understood; it was a smooth-running machine with all parts fitting into a harmonious whole. Scientists now were inclined to regard God not as a personal deity but as the embodiment of scientific natural law which operates the universe and holds the stars in their courses. "The ideal of a clockwork universe was the great contribution of seventeenth-century science to the eighteenth-century age of reason."[5]

By contrast to the harmony and reasonableness of the natural world revealed by the scientists, society and its institutions seemed more and more archaic and the world of man seemed one governed by intolerance, prejudice, strife, and unreasoning authority. But in the face of the teachings of science, many men were convinced that their world of religion, law, and government could also be brought under the control of reason.

The problem of how to reconcile old faiths with new truths had become, in the words of a noted French scholar, the "crisis in the European conscience."[6] Scholars and thinkers, therefore, set about seeing what could be reconciled between the old and new, what faiths if any might be left intact, and what should be completely discarded.

The dualism of Descartes. According to Descartes, reason was the chief source of knowledge. By logical methods of thought, the nature of reality, the existence of God, and the existence of the human self could be demonstrated. Descartes divided ultimate reality into two substances: mind and matter. He argued that there was no connection between the two realms except by God's intervention. The first was the realm of faith and theology, impenetrable and unknowable to science; the second was that of reason and the laws of nature, subject to the understandable processes of science. Thus Descartes, a loyal Catholic, sought to reconcile the old and the new by his system of philosophical dualism.

Spinoza and pantheism. Born in Holland to well-to-do Jewish refugees who had fled from the Inquisition in Portugal, Baruch Spinoza (1632-1677) was another thinker who sought to reconcile spirit and matter. Following the methods of Descartes, Spinoza strove to build a mathematical philosophy: his *Ethics* (1633) is filled with geometric axioms, postulates, and theories. But Descartes' dualistic system was rejected by Spinoza, to whom mind and matter were manifestations of one substance—nature, or God. In other words, the universe and God are one. While Spinoza was alive, both Jews and Christians persecuted him, but his true spirituality later was better understood. He has been called "the God-intoxicated man."

Locke and empiricism. In the main, the Continental philosophers were rationalists who believed that knowledge is gained through reasoning. By contrast, English thinkers tended to believe that knowledge came only from sensory experience, a school of thought known as empiricism. Its founder was John Locke (1632-1704), who felt that there was too much abstruse and flighty thought in Europe.

In 1690 Locke published *An Essay Concerning Human Understanding,* which sought to analyze the human mind. According to him, the mind at birth is like a blank tablet *(tabula rasa),* and the experience gained through the senses is recorded on this tablet. Unlike the rationalists on the Continent, Locke maintained that, of itself, the mind has no innate power to grasp reality. In acquiring knowledge, however, the mind is not completely passive. Locke believed that reflection also played a role: by the process of association, the mind combines new and old impressions to form a new idea.

Locke's empiricism was of fundamental importance in the cultural development of modern Europe. A true son of the Age of Reason, Locke believed that investigation of such basic philosophical questions as the existence of God and the fundamentals of morality would lead men to a state of universal reasonableness and thereby free them from the necessity of relying blindly on authority.

Deism: a solution to the spiritual crisis. By the end of the first quarter of the eighteenth century the crisis in the European conscience had eased. After this time most intellectuals pegged their faith to the new science and the new philosophy.

Upon this rationalistic, scientific basis they built their religion. Known as Deism, it stripped Christianity of most of its traditional dogmas. God—thought of as an impersonal force—became in their eyes the First Cause, the custodian of the world machine, the master "clockwinder" of the universe. God had been necessary to create the universe, but once the universe had been set in motion, its immutable laws could not be altered. It was regarded as useless to invoke the intercession of God to bring about a deviation from the laws of nature. Men must rely upon reason, not miracles, to solve the problems of society.

The Deistic concept of a "natural" religion included only a few basic beliefs: the existence of God as master of the universe, the necessity of worshiping God, the atonement by man for his sins, the doctrine of immortality, and the view that the aim of religion is virtue, or sensible living. All religions were to be based on these simple and rational essentials; anything additional was extraneous and not worth squabbling about. Deists maintained that if all creeds would give up or at least minimize their "extraneous" dogmas, religious intolerance and bigotry would cease. The God of Deism was universal and acceptable to all. It mattered little what He was called. In the words of Alexander Pope:

> Father of all! in every age,
> In every clime adored,
> By saint, by savage, and by sage,
> Jehovah, Jove, or Lord![7]

The *philosophes*, critics of society. By 1750 France was so decidedly the intellectual center of Europe that it has been said "an opinion launched in Paris was like a battering ram launched by thirty millions of men."[8] Here a group of thinkers and writers known as the *philosophes* brought the Age of Reason to its climax. The term *philosophes* cannot be translated as "philosophers," because they were not philosophers in any strict sense but rather students of society who analyzed its evils and advocated reforms.

Voltaire, prince of the *philosophes*. More than any other thinker, Voltaire (1694-1778) personified the skepticism of the eighteenth century toward traditional religion and the evils of the time. He enjoyed exercising a caustic pen, soon ran afoul of the law, twice was imprisoned in the Bastille, and finally was banished to England for three years. Upon his return to France, Voltaire again championed tolerance, popularized the science of Newton, fought for personal liberty and freedom of the press, and acted as an influential propagandist for Deism. He turned out a prodigious number of works: histories, plays, pamphlets, essays, and novels. In his correspondence—estimated at ten thousand letters—he wittily spread the gospel of rationalism and scathingly attacked the abuses of his day. Voltaire's short fictional satire *Candide* (1759) was a biting attack on the easy optimism of some *philosophes* and the view that this world is "the best of all possible worlds."

Voltaire achieved his greatest fame as the most relentless critic of the established churches, Protestant and Catholic alike. He was sickened by the intolerance of organized Christianity and disgusted by the petty squabbles which seemed to monopolize the time of many priests and clergymen.

Diderot and the *Encyclopédie*. Voltaire had many disciples and imitators, but his only rival in spreading the gospel of rationalism and Deism was a set of books—the famous French *Encyclopédie,* edited by Denis Diderot (1713-1784). The *Encyclopédie* constituted the chief monument of the *philosophes,* declaring the supremacy of the new science, championing tolerance, denouncing superstition, and expounding the merits of Deism. Its seventeen volumes contained articles whose authors—tradesmen as well as scientists and philosophers— criticized in a moderate tone unfair taxation, the slave trade, and the cruelty of the existing criminal code.

Kant and the *Critique of Pure Reason*. The German philosopher Immanuel Kant (1724-1804) symbolized the revival of the heart and of faith. Thoroughly aroused by the exaggerated skepticism and materialism of the age, he determined to shift philosophy back to a more sensible position without giving up too much of its "rational" basis. Kant's answer, contained in the *Critique of Pure Reason* (1781), marked the end of eighteenth-century natural philosophy and ushered in philosophical idealism, so important in the first part of the nineteenth century.

To resolve the conflict between mind and matter, Kant resorted to dualism. Beyond the physical world, which is the legitimate realm of science or "pure reason," lies the world of "things-in-themselves," he believed, where science can never penetrate and which is the legitimate realm of faith or "practical reason." Kant put as the basis of religious faith not reason, which is subject to experience, but an absolute innate moral sense, a conscience which is independent of experience yet able to distinguish between right and wrong. On this basis, Kant believed that free will and the existence of God could be proven. Reason cannot prove that there is a just God behind the world as it is, but our moral sense demands such a belief. Thus there are truths of the heart above and beyond those of the head.

The new humanitarianism. Pervading the thought of the Enlightenment was a deep concern for the welfare of mankind. Belief in the helplessness of man and the depravity of human nature was superseded by recognition of man's mental and moral dignity.

"It was the special function of the Eighteenth Century," wrote the English historian Trevelyan, "to diffuse common sense and reasonableness in life and thought, to civilize manners and to humanize conduct."[9] Notable among its humanizing functions was the emergence of the antislavery movement in England, spearheaded by the Quakers and the Methodists. The agitation against slavery found its foremost champion in William Wilberforce (1759-1833), who, beginning in 1789, introduced motions in the House of Commons to end trafficking in human misery, until in 1807 the slave trade in British territories was legally abolished. Not content with this victory, Wilberforce carried on his crusade to free all slaves in the British empire, a goal that was reached in 1833, the year in which he died.

One of the outstanding characteristics of the eighteenth century was its cosmopolitanism. During the long period in which France was at war with most of Europe, English thinkers and their *philosophe* friends in Paris could fraternize with no difficulty. Proud of belonging to the European "republic of letter," the intellectuals of the time were gravely concerned with the problem of war. Voltaire made a scathing attack on war in *Candide,* and several works were written urging the creation of machinery to enforce peace.

TOWARD A NEW SCIENCE OF MAN

Birth of the social sciences.   One of the great achievements of the eighteenth century was the application of the methods of science to the better understanding of man. The *philosophes* believed that by such application the laws governing society could be discovered. As one of them observed: "I believed that morals should be treated like all other sciences, and that one should arrive at a moral principle as one proceeds with an experiment in physics."[10] This spirit of inquiry led to important innovations in the writing of history and the creation of those studies known today as the social sciences—political science, economics, anthropology, and psychology. In addition, important advances were made in criminology and education.

The ideas of progress and human perfectibility—concepts basic to the temper of the eighteenth century—were expressed most clearly by the Marquis de Condorcet, a member of the circle of *philosophes* around Voltaire. In his famous *Progress of the Human Mind* (1794) Condorcet asserts that there are no limits to human perfectibility and declares that progress will come by abolishing inequalities between nations, by securing equality for all men within nations, and by improving the human race in mind and body.

The writing of history.   The greatest historian of this period was an Englishman, Edward Gibbon (1737-1794). Gibbon shared the rational spirit of his day, and his *Decline and Fall of the Roman Empire* (1776-1787) was a vehicle for his ideas. He exposed the evils of tyrannical rulers and attacked the "barbarism and religion" that in his view had weakened the greatness of classical Roman culture.

Voltaire was also a historian of no mean merit, creating a new form, or school, of history, one that forsook the old reliance on wars and the foibles of rulers. He was interested in capturing "the spirit of the times" and in describing the progress and influence of ideas; in short, Voltaire approached history as an account of the evolution of civilization.

Men like the Italian Giovanni Battista Vico studied the "philosophy" of history—not the "what happened" so much as the "why." In his important *Principles of a New Science* (1725) Vico discussed the operation of laws in history, stressing the idea that every age is imbued with a certain "psychology," mood, or point of view and that each age is not only the product of the one preceding but also the creator of the next.

Other social sciences.   The eighteenth century witnessed notable advances in political science, the study of government. In Chapter 13 we shall read of the writings of Hobbes, Bossuet, and Locke, and note the work of the *philosophes*

Rousseau and Montesquieu as they analyzed the machinery and purposes of government.

Economics as a distinct subject for study emerged in the last half of the seventeenth century, much of it justifying the policy of mercantilism. Later, the Scotsman Adam Smith (see p. 282) and a number of the French *philosophes* known as the physiocrats made important contributions to economic principles that were dominant down to the twentieth century.

As efforts were made to classify human races and to make comparative studies of various groups of people, the first halting steps were taken toward a science of anthropology. Much of the information used for these studies was provided by the writings of explorers, traders, and missionaries.

The science of criminology was established by the Italian Cesare Beccaria, whose *Essay on Crimes and Punishments* (1764) contained the plea that prison terms should be deterrents to crime rather than punishments for crime. Shortly thereafter, John Howard in England stressed the need for efficient prison administration and maintained that the chief aim of imprisonment should be reformation of the criminal.

THE ARTS IN EARLY MODERN TIMES

The "anti-Renaissance" style: Mannerism. In Italy, where the Renaissance had initially burst forth, a countermovement in art appeared in the sixteenth century. There artists—who so often act as barometers to register sensitive changes in the cultural atmosphere—responded to the stresses of the Protestant and Catholic Reformations. The result was the development in Italian painting of a new, "anti-Renaissance" style called Mannerism. No longer was the artist working in that spirit of calm and balance, of harmony and proportion, which had prevailed in Renaissance art at its finest. The Mannerist artist lived instead in a state of doubt and indecision, and his work reflected those tensions. Technically speaking, Renaissance painters had mastered the problems of space and perspective, so that the artist placed his figures in balanced relationships enriched by vigorous and harmonious colors. By contrast, Mannerist painters such as Tintoretto (1518-1594) often defied the rules of perspective in order to obtain an oblique and even twisted point of view; their lines might be agitated, their designs asymmetric. They did not hesitate to distort the human figure in order to achieve emotional intensity.

Outside Italy the Mannerist style found its greatest achievements in the works of El Greco ("the Greek"). Born in Crete as Domenico Theotocopuli, El Greco (1547-1614) studied in Italy and later settled in Toledo in Spain. He was not concerned with depicting nature realistically but distorted space and perspective to create an often eerie world of the imagination. To achieve dramatic effects, he used *chiaroscuro* (strong contrasts of light and shade) and abrupt transitions in color. El Greco's paintings are easily recognizable for their elongated figures (see illustration, p. 254). To us he appears amazingly "modern," and his works have had a decided influence upon twentieth-century painting.

Triumph of the Baroque style. Meanwhile, other developments had been pushing aside the doubts characteristic of Mannerism and were helping create a style expressing the varied facets of the seventeenth century: its intellectual zest, religious exaltation, sensuality, and violence. By announcing its regeneration with majestic voice, the Church of the Catholic Reformation indirectly exerted a powerful influence on the development of a new style of artistic expression—one that would proclaim the message of the revived Church with pomp and circumstance. This new style was the Baroque.

The Baroque style sought to synthesize two major traditions, one derived from the Middle Ages, the other from the Renaissance. The medieval esthetic tradition was transcendental in its purpose and marked by religious intensity, while the Renaissance was more natural in its conception and technically brilliant. In his synthesis the Baroque artist sought by the skill and grandeur of his treatment to arouse the strongest possible emotions in the beholder. As a result, by an

El Greco, the master of the Mannerist style, was deeply influenced by Tintoretto. Carrying the revolt against Renaissance style even further, El Greco distorted his figures to obtain the desired emotional intensity. In "St. Martin and the Beggar" the elongation gives the beggar's body a suggestion of weightlessness.

emphatic use of color, gesture, ornamentation, and movement, he developed a style that tended to be grandiose and exaggerated. In keeping with the spirit of the times, moreover, the Baroque gave expression to two new forces in Europe: the Catholic Reformation and royal absolutism (see Chapter 13). "In its sacred branch it discharged the mighty task of realizing and consolidating a Catholic reform of art, of emphasizing the aesthetic and emotional side of religion. In the secular field it ministered to the pomp and pride of princes. To both church and throne it lent effulgence."[11]

The Baroque style merged painting, sculpture, and architecture in new, large-scale combinations marked by heroic proportions and dramatic arrangements of light and space. One of the creators of the Baroque in painting whose influence permeated western Europe was the Flemish artist Peter Paul Rubens (1577-1640). An artist of prodigious gifts, Rubens chose dramatic themes from both pagan and Christian literature. Truly Baroque is his sensuous use of rich textures, as shown in his painting of flesh, satin, armor, and the hides of horses.

The Dutch masters: Hals, Vermeer, Rembrandt. The first half of the seventeenth century was a golden age for Holland. Prosperous and comfortable, the burghers often acted as patrons of the arts. Their tastes in paintings differed greatly from those of kings, prelates, and aristocrats. These Dutch merchants and bankers favored familiar scenes of the flat lush countryside, seascapes in all seasons, and comfortable household interiors.

The robust Frans Hals (1580-1666) possessed a vigorous style that enabled him to catch with particular success the spontaneous, fleeting expressions of his portrait subjects. His canvases provide us with an interesting gallery of types— from cavaliers to fishwives and tavern denizens. As for Jan Vermeer (1632-1675), the subtle delicacy with which he handled the fall of subdued sunlight upon interior scenes has never been equaled. His few canvases raised *genre* painting to perfection, and today each commands a king's ransom.

The finest of Dutch painters—and one who ranks with the outstanding artists of all time—was Rembrandt van Rijn (1606-1669). His straightforward and realistic works gained him fame at an early age, but his later work declined in popularity as his style became more subtle. He concentrated progressively in his portraits on psychological and emotional qualities, and his work exhibits a strong element of the dramatic, which links Rembrandt to the mainstream of Baroque style (see illustration, p. 256).

Baroque architecture. The Baroque style endowed architecture with a new emotional significance, dynamism, and fluidity. Where the architecture of the Renaissance is severe and self-contained and emphasizes symmetry and "squareness," the Baroque sweeps us off our feet by subjecting us to an almost physical pull. It is a magnificent stage set, full of visual illusions intended to arouse an emotional response.

The capital of the new Baroque architecture was Rome, and the most renowned seventeenth-century architect of the Baroque school was Giovanni Lorenzo Bernini (1598-1680). He designed the colonnades outside the Basilica of St. Peter's, and his plan is typical of the Baroque use of vast spaces and curving lines. Besides being an accomplished architect and painter, Bernini was also a magnificent sculptor (see his "St. Theresa," p. 257), as were many other artists of the Baroque. In fact, the architect acted also as a sculptor, painter, and interior decorator, for the integration of Baroque art reached the point where it was difficult to see where one art left off and another began.

After 1600 the Baroque style spread over much of Europe, being favored both by the Catholic Church and by rulers whose palaces were designed to serve as symbols of power and magnificence. The Baroque features of the luxurious palace of Louis XIV at Versailles (see p. 264), an ideal which nearly every European prince hoped to attain, include the sweeping composition of its vast facade as well as its formal gardens with their imposing fountains, formal statuary, and elegant rows of hedges. In the interior, the silk and velvet draperies, rich marbles, and gilded carving created a background for profuse painted decoration.

Classicism and the arts. Even during the heyday of the Baroque in the seventeenth century, many of the arts continued to follow the tenets of classicism often reinforced by the cultivation of reason. This was generally true of all the arts in England and of some of the arts, particularly literature, in France.

By the eighteenth century a great classical revival, usually called Neoclassicism, was under way in all the fine arts as well as literature. Inspired in part by the order and symmetry of the world as revealed by science, and in part by a reaction against the Baroque, the creative artists of the Age of Reason were noteworthy for their rationalism, sophistication, balance, and selfcontrol. Furthermore, the Enlightenment was a continuation of Renaissance humanism and its revival of antiquity, coupled with the new scientific outlook. In literature and the arts there was a respect for definite rules and conventions. The men of the time felt

In "The Syndics" Rembrandt painted a group of bourgeois Dutch capitalists. Self-confident and self-righteous Calvinists, these successful men wielded power not only in the great trading companies but in the government as well.

spiritually akin to Rome's Augustan Age and strove to exhibit the same stability, refined polish, and control over emotion. In consequence, every work of art tended to have a cold, rational aspect, whether it was a philosophical poem by Pope or a dainty symphony by Haydn. Inspiration sprang from the intellect, not the heart; from reason, not emotion. Generally speaking, classical forms were slavishly imitated; to writers the style of expression was considered so all-important that many of them were content to express old ideas so long as they were elegantly phrased.

The wittiest comedies of the period were those of Molière. As a true voice of the Age of Reason, he believed that moderation and good sense were the keynotes of life and that any deviation from reasonable behavior was fair game for comedy. With rapier-like wit, he spoofed the pretensions of learned females and the aspirations of the social climbing bourgeoisie. But like all great writers, Molière created characters that were universal figures as well as individuals of his own time.

Alexander Pope. The foremost exponent of Neoclassicism in English literature was the poet Alexander Pope (1688-1744). In his most famous poem, *An Essay on Man* (1733), Pope reduced to a series of epigrams the philosophy of his day.

Bernini's Baroque sculpture for a side altar in a small Roman church depicts a vision of St. Theresa. Describing her mystical experiences, St. Theresa once told of a moment of ecstasy and pain in which an angel pierced her heart with a flaming arrow. As the saint ascends to heaven on a cloud, the angel approaches her and she swoons.

Reflecting the strong note of optimism so characteristic of the Enlightenment, Pope accepted the cosmos thus:

> All are but parts of one stupendous whole,
> Whose body nature is, and God the soul . . . .
> All nature is but art, unknown to thee;
> All chance, direction, which thou canst not see.
> All discord, harmony not understood;
> All partial evil, universal good;
> And, spite of pride, in erring reason's spite,
> One truth is clear: *Whatever is, is right.*[12]

The English novel. In conformity with the emphasis on clarity and simplicity in an age of science and reason, the eighteenth century was in general an age of prose. This contributed to the growth of a new literary form—the novel. Daniel Defoe's *Robinson Crusoe* (1719) is sometimes called the forerunner of the modern novel, but the title is probably better deserved by Samuel Richardson's *Pamela* (1740-1741), written in the form of letters. In line with the rationalistic temper of the age, Richardson's servant-girl heroine succeeds in holding her lecherous employer at bay with lectures on moral philosophy until virtue at length has its reward and the reformed rake proposes marriage.

With Henry Fielding the novel achieved full stature. Disgusted with Richardson's "goody-goodness," Fielding achieved fame by parodying the latter's smug sentimentality and, as the author of *Tom Jones* (1749), by composing one of the great novels in English literature. The hero Tom is a high-spirited, good-hearted young man who is continually being exploited by self-seeking worldlings and led astray by designing females. Finally, after many comic adventures, he learns eventually that he must check his natural impulsiveness with good sense and reasonable behavior.

In keeping with the Age of Reason's attack on irrational customs and outworn institutions, this period produced masterpieces of satire, such as Voltaire's *Candide.* One of England's outstanding satirists was Jonathan Swift, whose *Gulliver's Travels* (1726) ridicules the pettiness of man's quarrels, wars, and vices.

The Neoclassical style in architecture. About midway in the eighteenth century, a reaction set in against Baroque, manifesting itself in a return to the intrinsic dignity and restraint of what a contemporary called "the noble simplicity and tranquil loftiness of the ancients." In England, where the classical style had resisted Baroque influences, the great country houses of the nobility now exhibited a purity of design which often included a portico with Corinthian columns. Outstanding as examples of Neoclassicism in colonial America are Mount Vernon and the stately mansion of Thomas Jefferson at Monticello. Interest in the classical style carried over through the nineteenth century, and today in the United States many libraries and government buildings are classical in derivation.

Painting and sculpture. The arts of painting and sculpture in the Age of Reason were dominated by the tastes of the aristocracy. In France Boucher and Fragonard mirrored the artificiality and idleness in which the aristocrats at Versailles, sometimes thinly disguised as Greek gods and goddesses, spent their lives. In England the most famous beauties of the day and many prominent men sat for portraits painted in the "grand manner" by Sir Joshua Reynolds or Thomas Gainsborough.

Two great nonconformists painters, William Hogarth in England and Francisco de Goya in Spain, strove to reproduce realistically the life around them in the gutter, the tavern, and the royal court, sometimes using their art to draw attention to the evils of the day. Typical of Goya's abhorrence of brutality is his stark series of etchings depicting "The Disasters of War" (see illustration below).

In sculpture the works produced in the eighteenth century were mostly imitations of classical forms and personages, such as Venus. Houdon's "Portrait of Voltaire" is a well-known example of Neoclassical sculpture at its best.

Developments in music. In the seventeenth century the Baroque spirit was manifested in music by the development of new forms of expression. For the first time instrumental music—in particular that of the organ and the violin family—

Goya's work often pointed up a moral. The harsh realism of this scene was a warning against brutality. This etching is one of the series entitled *The Disasters of War*, which were the outcome of a journey through Aragon at the time when it was devastated by the French invasion of 1808.

became of equal importance with vocal music. Outstanding among Baroque innovations was opera, which originated in Italy at the beginning of the seventeenth century and quickly conquered Europe. With its opulence, highly charged emotional content, and sweep of expression, opera was almost the perfect musical expression of the Baroque style. Here again we find an integration of the arts: dramatic literature, music, and acting, with the skills of the painter employed for elaborate stage settings.

The elaboration of polyphonic music during the Baroque era culminated in the sumptuous effects of the deeply religious music of Johann Sebastian Bach (d. 1750), the prolific German organ master and choir director. Bach's equally great contemporary, the German-born, naturalized Englishman George Frederick Handel (1685-1759), is known for his large, dramatic, and mostly homophonic operas, oratorios, and cantatas; he is best known today for his religious oratorio, the *Messiah* (1742).

To composers living in the latter half of the eighteenth century, the style of the Baroque masters Bach and Handel seemed too heavy and complex. Like the other arts of the Age of Reason, music now exhibited greater clarity and simplicity of structure and a strict adherence to formal rules and models.

New musical forms reflected new trends in instrumental music. As symphonies, sonatas, concertos, and chamber music appeared, music became more than the mere accompaniment to religious services and operatic performances. The chamber music played in courts and salons was written for woodwinds and brasses as well as strings. Thus the modern orchestra developed along with the symphonic form.

The music of the latter half of the eighteenth century, with its emphasis on technical perfection of form, melody, and orchestration, was summed up in the work of the Viennese composers Franz Joseph Haydn and Wolfgang Mozart. The prolific Haydn wrote over one hundred symphonies in addition to numerous other works. For his part, Mozart, a child prodigy who at the age of six was composing minuets, wrote forty-one symphonies, climaxing his career with a trio of famous operas, *The Marriage of Figaro, Don Giovanni,* and *The Magic Flute.*

CHAPTER 13
L'ETAT, C'EST MOI

Absolutism and the Politics of Power: 1650-1775

The century following the Peace of Westphalia (1648) was a vitally important period in European politics. In the weighing scales of power and military might, the modern hierarchy of nations was being established. Some of the old political structures were decaying: the Holy Roman Empire, Poland, and the empire of the Ottoman Turks. Such powerful nations as Spain and Sweden were passing their golden ages and slipping into a tranquil state of ineffectuality in the realm of international affairs. In contrast, France and England were dynamic and aggressive; Prussia, Russia, and Austria had achieved stability and were advancing rapidly into the category of first-class powers.

By 1700 commercial and colonial rivalry added to the intense competitive spirit existing in Europe and culminated in the worldwide duel for empire between France and Great Britain. Great Britain, as the leader of various coalitions and the self-appointed caretaker of the Continental balance of power, emerged victorious over France and the monarchical despotism it symbolized. In England the successful Revolution of 1688 heralded the triumph of aristocratic liberalism—the rule of Parliament and of law. The most wealthy and influential elements in society controlled the government, and their support made for a stronger and more united government than that operating from Versailles. The English government thus proved fit to achieve victory in foreign diplomacy and warfare.

The interplay of international rivalries during the last half of the seventeenth century and the first three quarters of the eighteenth century had many significant implications for modern times. In this period it was determined that North America would be mainly Anglo-Saxon in culture; British rule was firmly established in India; and Britain's sea power gained the world-wide supremacy it was to hold well into the twentieth century. This period also saw the rise of the Prussian type of absolutism—the militaristic state—and the birth of the Russian policy of pursuing access to the Baltic and Mediterranean seas.

THE SYSTEM OF ROYAL ABSOLUTISM

Architecture of absolutism. In the period from 1650 to 1775 the royal architects of the national state system reached the height of their power. During this age of absolutism the king was in theory and in fact an autocrat responsible to God alone. The outstanding example of the absolute monarch was Louis XIV of France, who is said to have once exclaimed to his fawning courtiers, "L'état, c'est moi" ("I am the state").

Under the system of absolutism the king's power touched every aspect of his subjects' existence. He was the supreme and only lawgiver—the fountain of justice. As head of the church he decided what religion his subjects were to follow and persecuted those who dissented. The worship of God was a matter of state, not the preserve of the individual conscience. The king regulated every phase of economic life, from the establishment of new industries to working conditions and standards of quality. In addition, he was the arbiter of manners and fashion, the patron of arts and letters, and the personification of national glory. An obedient bureaucracy and a powerful royal army enforced his will.

Although such a system of all-pervasive absolutism is abhorrent to us today, in the seventeenth century it was generally unquestioned and often very popular. A powerful king stood for order, efficiency, security, and prosperity—values willingly exchanged for the uncertainties of upheaval and bloodshed such as had been experienced during the turmoil of the preceding Era of Religious Wars.

Bossuet and Hobbes: defenders of absolutism. The new absolute state was explained and rationalized by a number of political theorists. Jacques Bossuet (1627-1704) was a prominent French churchman who had been entrusted with the education of Louis XIV's son and was finally elevated to the position of bishop. Utilizing the doctrine of the divine right of kings, Bossuet composed a brilliant justification of absolute monarchy. He argued that a king is a holy thing and that his throne is the throne of God himself. Thus a king need render account of his acts to no one.

In the long run, it was Thomas Hobbes (1588-1679) who composed the most penetrating and influential justification of absolutism. To this English student of the new scientific thought, absolutism was not to be defended by resort to religion. In the *Leviathan* (1651) Hobbes drew upon science and its servant, psychology. From the excesses of the religious wars in France, the Thirty Years' War in Germany, and the Civil War in England (discussed later in this chapter), Hobbes discovered what he believed to be the essential nature of man when not restrained by law. A pessimistic, cynical observer of human conduct, Hobbes saw man "as a wolf to his fellow man" and mankind as essentially selfish and cruel. Before law and authority came into existence men lived under the adverse conditions of the state of nature, in which

> there is no place for industry . . . no culture of the earth . . . no arts; no letters; no society; and which is worst of all, continual fear, and danger of violent death; and the life of man, solitary, poor, nasty, brutish, and short.[1]

To create a workable society and escape from the intolerable evils of the state of nature, men had gladly surrendered all their rights and powers to a sovereign government, an action which bound them to an irrevocable contract. Hobbes' Leviathan, the sovereign state, could be any one of a number of forms of government. But, to Hobbes, monarchy was the most effective and desirable, for only thus could peace and security be maintained. There was no right of revolution, even against tyranny.

LOUIS XIV: THE EPITOME OF ABSOLUTISM

Inheritance of Louis XIV. The best example of political absolutism is offered by France in the days of Louis XIV, who reigned from 1643 to 1715. This proud Bourbon monarch inherited a realm which had been made powerful during the preceding fifty years. The previous century, the sixteenth, had been a sorry period in France's history. Wars with the Hapsburgs had been followed by religious civil wars that almost destroyed the nation. The reign of Henry IV (1589-1610), however, brought peace and laid the foundations of the great nation which was to enjoy economic, military, and intellectual leadership in the seventeenth century.

The death of Henry left Louis XIII, a boy of nine, on the throne, with the queen mother as regent. During the next fourteen years Henry IV's achievements were slowly undermined, until in 1624 Cardinal Richelieu, the clever protégé of the queen mother, became the real power behind the throne. For eighteen years the biography of Richelieu was truly the history of France. As chief advisor to Louis XIII, the "grim cardinal" set about restoring and furthering the accomplishments of Henry IV. He strove to exalt the power of France in Europe and of royal authority within the state. Richelieu himself loved power; while he made his royal master the first man in Europe, he made the king the second man in France.

Under Richelieu's direction the structure of absolutism quickly took shape. Castles of the nobility were torn down, officials of the central government called *intendants* replaced the nobility as the chief administrators in the provinces, and the Estates-General—a body that might have challenged the power of the king—was not summoned. In foreign affairs Richelieu was equally decisive and crafty. As we have already noted (p. 216), his intervention in the Thirty Years' War struck a staggering blow against the Hapsburgs and helped make France the greatest power in Europe.

After the deaths of Richelieu in 1642 and Louis XIII in 1643, the throne of France was again occupied by a child, Louis XIV, who was less than five years old. Richelieu had anticipated this emergency, however, by grooming a promising young Italian, Cardinal Mazarin, to be adviser to the regent. Mazarin governed France with a firm and efficient hand during the minority of the king, although the royal authority was seriously challenged by civil outbreak. For six years (1648-1653) France was convulsed by disorder. This civil war—a reaction against the excesses of the now powerful royal administration, known as the Fronde—had no effect in tempering absolutism. In fact, the violence of the struggle served to convince many Frenchmen that the only alternative to royal absolutism was anarchy.

Following the death of Mazarin in 1661, Louis XIV, then twenty-three years old, took over the personal management of state affairs. He found his people obedient and docile; Henry IV, Richelieu, and Mazarin had done their work efficiently.

Louis XIV the Sun King. Believing implicitly in the divine right of kings, Louis chose the sun as the symbol of his power. His courtiers dubbed him *Le Roi Soleil* (the Sun King), and he was also known throughout Europe as the Grand Monarch. Louis labored to enhance the power and prestige of the crown, which he frequently defended in haughty style.

The palace of the Louvre in Paris had been good enough for his predecessors, but Louis wanted a more magnificent symbol for his greatness. On barren marshland a few miles from Paris, Louis ordered the construction of the palace of Versailles. The total cost of construction probably exceeded one hundred million dollars. The marshland was transformed into a beautiful park surrounding the palace, whose facade was more than a quarter mile in length. The symmetry in the design of formal gardens and surroundings for the palace reflected the orderliness that Louis XIV, throughout his long reign, tried to impose on the society of his age.

Today the palace of Versailles is merely a historical monument, a symbol of royal elegance and glittering court life that has no place in our modern world. But two hundred years ago it was the most fashionable spot in Europe. During the day the French nobles promenaded with their king among the groves, terraces, and fountains of the park or hunted and hawked in the nearby woods and meadows. At

The palace of Louis XIV at Versailles was painted by Pierre Putée shortly after the central chateau was finished. Its exuberant decoration and splendor is typical of the Baroque style.

night lords and ladies in powdered wigs, silks, and laces attended balls, masquerades, and concerts.

Just as science followed the rule of law, so life and manners conformed to the rules of etiquette. Studied elegance, formal manners, extravagant expressions of courtesy, and witty but superficial conversation all too often constituted the base of polite society, and manners were more important than morals. Palace etiquette was carried to ridiculous extremes; the "cult of majesty" resulted in the king's being treated practically like a god. Louis was surrounded by fawning sycophants and servile courtiers, and his every action was made a regal ceremony based on the strictest precedent. For example, a nobleman of designated rank was required to dry the king after his bath, and only a very illustrious noble could hand the king the royal shirt or breeches during the public ceremony of dressing.

Louis' absolutism: the balance sheet. During the late seventeenth century France was the premier nation of Europe. In nearly every aspect—the splendor and formality of Versailles, the functioning of the central government, the organization of the military services—the absolute state of Louis XIV was the model.

Louis worked hard at what he called "the business of being king." He increased the powers of the *intendants* instituted by Richelieu; reorganized the army, making it the largest (nearly 400,000 men by 1703) and most modern in Europe; and instituted a wide variety of economic reforms to strengthen the French economy and increase revenue. Louis was fortunate in having as his finance minister the able Colbert, whose aggressive mercantilist practices (see p. 230) enabled a surplus to be accumulated in the royal treasury.

The positive side of Louis' reign—his own administrative zeal and the financial genius of Colbert—was counterbalanced by some unfortunate manifestations of Louis' lofty concept of the dignity of his office. The pomp and ceremony of Versailles is an example; Louis moved in a world of glitter and luxury, isolated from his people.

One extemely unwise act was the revocation of Henry IV's Edict of Nantes, which had guaranteed religious freedom for the Protestant Huguenots. To an absolute monarch like Louis, complete uniformity within his state was a cherished ideal, and legal toleration of religious nonconformity was a serious flaw in the system of absolutism. Therefore, in 1685, Louis revoked the Edict and caused thousands of industrious Huguenots to flee to other lands, taking with them skills and knowledge which were to enrich the enemies of France.

Finally, and most important of all, Louis squandered the resources of his realm in his passion for military conquest. War had become an all-important function of the state which required efficiency, organization, and discipline. Important changes were made in tactics and weapons: the improvement of firearms and the introduction of the bayonet eliminated the pike as the main infantry weapon; artillery and fortification methods were improved and so, in turn, were siege methods for the reduction of fortresses. Indeed, the tactics for siege warfare devised by Vauban, Louis' military engineer, established the principles which governed that science until the twentieth century.

Possessing the strongest army and the most capable generals of the age, Louis embarked on a series of wars to attain for France her "natural boundaries" by extending French territory eastward to the Rhine at the expense of the Spanish and Holy Roman empires. Louis' chief motive was not security for France but prestige for the monarchy.

France threatens the balance of power. Louis engaged in four wars between 1667 and 1713. During the first two wars the French king tried unsuccessfully to take over first the Spanish Netherlands (modern Belgium) and later Holland. Louis' third effort against various districts mainly in Alsace and Lorraine were again thwarted by an anti-French coalition under the leadership of William of Orange.

The last of the four conflicts, the War of the Spanish Succession (1702-1713), was fought over control of the Spanish throne. The death of the childless king of Spain left the Spanish throne open to the conflicting claims of distantly related princes of both Hapsburg Austria and Bourbon France. In his will the dying king left this great prize to Louis xiv's grandson, Philip. All Europe realized that, with his grandson as king of Spain, Louis would have an empire rivaling in its extent and power the possessions of Charles v in the sixteenth century. Louis defied the Austrian claim and European sentiment by accepting the Spanish throne for Philip. In answer to Louis' menacing move to dominate Europe, England organized another coalition against him. From 1702 to 1713 French armies fought the combined forces of this Grand Alliance in Spain, Italy, France, Germany, and the Low Countries. The allies were blessed with a remarkable English commander, John Churchill, the duke of Marlborough, an ancestor of Winston Churchill. Marlborough's most famous victory was the battle of Blenheim (1704); not until the French Revolution would French armies again terrorize Europe.

Treaty of Utrecht. In 1713 the War of the Spanish Succession ended with the forces of France considerably weakened and the Grand Alliance split by petty rivalries. Comparable in importance to the Peace of Westphalia, which had ended the Thirty Years' War, was the series of treaties signed at Utrecht between France and the members of the alliance. As a result of this peace settlement, a fairly satisfactory balance of power was maintained on the Continent for nearly thirty years without any major wars.

The most important terms of the Utrecht settlement were as follows: (1) Louis' grandson, Philip v, was permitted to remain king of Spain so long as the thrones of France and Spain were not united. (2) France was allowed to retain all of Alsace. (3) The Spanish empire was divided: Philip v retained Spain and Spanish America, while Austria obtained Naples, Milan, Sardinia, and the Spanish Netherlands (Belgium)—thereafter called the Austrian Netherlands. (4) England gained important colonies from France and Spain: Nova Scotia, Newfoundland, and the Hudson Bay territory, and valuable Mediterranean naval bases in the Balearic Islands and at Gibraltar. (5) As a reward for joining the Grand Alliance, the duke of Savoy was given Sicily and the title of king, and the Hohenzollern elector of Brandenburg was recognized as "king of Prussia." (In 1720 Savoy ceded Sicily to Austria in exchange for Sardinia.)

The significance of several provisions in this peace should be noted. The accession of the Bourbons to the throne of Spain after almost two centuries of Hapsburg rule marked the end of an era. The long-standing French-Spanish rivalry was now replaced by a strong French-Spanish family alliance since Bourbons occupied the two thrones. The English acquisition of important colonies and naval bases marked an important stage in the rise of Great Britain to world power. The treaty also gave recognition to two aggressive ruling families, the House of Savoy and the House of Hohenzollern. In the nineteenth century the House of Savoy would succeed in unifying Italy, and the Hohenzollerns Germany.

Consequences of Louis' wars. In 1715 Louis XIV died, leaving behind him a kingdom demoralized and debiliated by costly wars. France continued to be a first-class power and French culture was universally admired and imitated, but in retrospect we can see that Louis' reign did much to discredit the system of absolutism. He left behind a record of misery and discontent that paved the way for the French Revolution and the bloody downfall of his dynasty.

Louis' four wars strengthened the guiding principle of international diplomacy in modern times—the concept of the balance of power (see Chapter 10). To prevent France from dominating Europe, coalition after coalition had been formed. England was the balance wheel in the maintenance of this delicate equipoise, throwing support from one side to the other in order to maintain the balance of power on the Continent.

EVOLUTION OF CONSTITUTIONAL MONARCHY IN ENGLAND

James I and Parliament. The victory of England over France involved more than just the matter of English superiority in arms or diplomacy. It was the triumph of a system of government set in a mold different from that of Louis XIV's absolutism. This new political form has been termed *aristocratic liberalism* and defined as "government in accordance with the agreed decisions of bodies which were drawn from a limited class but acted after free discussion and with some degree of tolerance and of consideration for the governed."[2] For hundreds of years English institutions had been developing slowly in the direction of constitutional, representative government.

Tudor monarchs had restored order and successfully defied Spain. Following the defeat of the Armada, Parliament began to assert itself, especially after the death of Elizabeth, last of the Tudor line. Her successor was the king of Scotland, who ruled England as James I from 1603 to 1625. He was an enthusiastic advocate of the divine right of kings. Disregarding the temper of his new English subjects and their institutions, James made it plain that he meant to be an absolute monarch. In 1611 he dissolved Parliament and ruled without it until 1621. Complicating this political issue was religion. Some Englishmen were content with their Anglican Church as it then was. Others wanted to reinstate some aspects of the Catholic ritual. Another group, the Puritans, sought to "purify" every vestige of Catholicism from their Church. Many of this latter group belonged to the urban middle class, which also resented James' arbitrary rule and heavy taxation.

Charles I and Parliament. James' mistakes were repeated by his son Charles I (1625-1649)—and to an even greater degree. Like father, the son espoused the divine right of kings, was contemptuous of the rights of Parliament, and supported the pro-Catholic or High Church faction in the Anglican Church.

Insisting on absolute royal power, Charles opened his reign with stormy debates with Parliament; but in return for revenue grants he agreed in 1628 to the famous Petition of Right—a reenactment of the "ancient rights of Englishmen." The most important provisions denied the monarch the right to tax without parliamentary consent or to imprison a freeman without just cause. Charles' capitulation was only temporary, and from 1629 to 1640 he ruled England without calling Parliament. During this period he resorted to methods of taxation which alarmed all property owners and which the supporters of Parliament considered illegal. In addition, Charles punished those who opposed his efforts to promote High Church Anglicanism.

Civil War.   Charles' misrule eventually forced him to convene Parliament; and tension quickly developed between two antagonistic groups. The Royalists, supported mainly by the great landowners, opposed the extreme reforms urged by the Puritans. The Parliamentarians were strongly anti-Catholic and demanded a further reduction of the king's prerogatives. Civil War erupted in 1642, and within four years the king's armies had been defeated. A major factor in this triumph was the leadership of Oliver Cromwell, a military genius of the first order. His God-fearing, irresistible force became known as Cromwell's Ironsides.

Meanwhile Cromwell's army had become disenchanted with faction-rid Parliament. Controlled by the so-called Independents, it proceeded to purge all of its rivals from this body. Following a brief trial, the army controlled Parliament, then brought Charles to trial for treason, and executed him in January 1649.

The Protectorate and Cromwell.   Abolishing the House of Lords, the House of Commons proclaimed England a republic—the Commonwealth. But in 1653 the army, still distrusting Parliament, overthrew the Commonwealth and set up a new form of government, the Protectorate, in which Oliver Cromwell held the office of Lord Protector, assisted by a new Parliament. The structure and operation of the government was based on a constitution called the Instrument of Government, the first written constitution of modern times.

Now virtual dictator of England, Cromwell endeavored to achieve a religious settlement for the nation. Amid the rivalries between Independents, Presbyterians, Royalists, Scots, and others, he had been forced to assume the role of dictator, but at heart Cromwell was a moderate, believing in religious toleration for all Protestants and constitutional government. It was impossible, however, to reconcile the religious factions. The last three years of Cromwell's life were filled with disappointment and trouble. Although he did not favor it, his more extreme Puritan colleagues muzzled the press and foisted on a pleasure-loving folk hateful prohibitions which closed the theaters and stamped out wholesome as well as unwholesome popular amusements.

Cromwell died in 1658 amid rising discontent with his rule. One contemporary observer claimed: "it was the joyfulest funeral I ever saw for there were none that cried but dogs . . . ."[3] Seemingly, Cromwell's work had been a failure; yet his firm opposition to royal despotism and his advocacy of religious toleration were priceless legacies from the kingless decade. The Civil War and the Commonwealth had also generated a substantial body of liberal and democratic thought.

The magniloquent John Milton (1608-1674), author of the great Puritan epic, *Paradise Lost* (1667) and a member of Cromwell's administration, espoused political freedom in opposition to tyranny. Arguing that men are born free, that kings are elected deputies without power except that given by their subjects, Milton maintained that a republic is "held by wisest men of all ages the noblest, the manliest, the equallest, the justest government . . . ."[4] One of his best known tracts is *Areopagitica* (1644), an impassioned plea for freedom of the press:

Who kills a man kills a reasonable creature, God's image; but he who destroys a good book, kills reason itself, kills the image of God, as it were in the eye. Many a man lives a burden to the earth; but a good book is the precious life-blood of a master-spirit, embalmed and treasured up on purpose to a life beyond life . . . .We should be wary therefore . . . how we spill that seasoned life of man, preserved and stored up in books; since we see a kind of homicide may thus be committed . . . whereof the execution ends not in the slaying of an elemental life, but strikes at that ethereal and fifth essence, the breath of reason itself, [and] slays an immortality rather than a life . . . .[5]

A group known as the Levellers—made up of small merchants, farmers, and artisans, many of whom were in Cromwell's army—advocated democracy and a written constitution guaranteeing equal rights to all. Another group, known as the Diggers, deplored the existence of private property and unequal wealth. Such groups as the Levellers and Diggers eventually died out, but the slow ferment of their ideas influenced English political life.

Ironically enough, the Puritans—champions of liberty against the Stuarts—ruled England in more autocratic fashion than had Charles I. Oliver Cromwell was succeeded as Lord Protector by his son, who lost control of the army and resigned in less than a year. To most Englishmen the restoration of the monarchy seemed the only solution.

Restoration of Charles II. When the exiled Charles Stuart, son of the late king, returned to England as Charles II in 1660, it was with the implicit understanding that he should rule through Parliament. Thus the English monarchy was made responsible to a representative body, in sharp contrast to the pattern of absolutism on the Continent. However, the king still wielded considerable power. He could veto laws; he commanded the militia; and unless he committed a breach of law serious enough to warrant his deposition, Parliament had no weapon other than its control of the national pocketbook to compel him to do its will. It was to circumvent this Parliamentary control over the pursestrings that Charles II made a secret treaty with Louis XIV behind the backs of his anti-French subjects. In return for an annual subsidy from the French government, Charles agreed to make England Catholic and to become an ally of France.

In 1672 Charles suspended the operation of laws directed against English Catholics and Protestant Dissenters. Since the English had come to associate Catholicism with the menace of strong foreign foes and with despotic government, a political crisis resulted. One year later Parliament passed the Test Act, which excluded all Catholics and Dissenters from public office. Among its victims was the king's brother James, a staunch Catholic.

One notable consequence of the controversy between Charles and Parliament was the gradual rise of amorphous, but recognizable, political groupings that were forerunners of political parties as we define such groups today. To thwart Charles' pro-Catholic tendencies, some members of the House of Commons formed the Whig party, which stood for the supremacy of Parliament, Protestantism, and the interests of the business classes. The Whig motto was "life, liberty, and property." Similarly, a group drawing heavily upon the landed gentry for support began to form, championing "the king, the church, and the land"—the Tory party. Such vague associations to support particular Parliamentary interests did not function as a two-party system, however, before the end of the Stuart dynasty (1714).

A second important consequence of the conflict between king and Parliament was the passage of the Habeas Corpus Act in 1679. Anyone believing himself unjustly imprisoned could obtain a writ of *habeas corpus,* which compelled the government to explain why he had lost his liberty. Later this safeguard against arbitrary imprisonment became part of the Constitution of the United States.

James II and the Revolution of 1688. When Charles II died in 1685 and his brother James ascended the throne, the Whig opposition, and many Tories, soon came to believe that the cause of popular liberty and the Anglican Church were in serious danger. James adjourned Parliament after it refused to repeal the Test and Habeas Corpus acts and by royal order suspended all laws against Catholics and Dissenters. He also appointed many Catholics to important positions.

When James' second wife, a Catholic, unexpectedly gave birth to a son in 1688, the threat of a Catholic succession cost James his remaining Tory support. An invitation from both Whigs and Tories was extended to William of Orange, ruler of the Dutch, to assume the English crown. This choice was dictated by two factors: William was the husband of Mary, the older daughter of James II and the Protestant next in line to the throne; he was also considered the champion of Protestantism in Europe. In November 1688 William set sail for England and landed without opposition. The discouraged James, forsaken by his army, fled to France.

The Bill of Rights. Parliament offered the crown to William and Mary as joint sovereigns—an offer contingent on their acceptance of a declaration of rights, later enacted as the Bill of Rights. This declaration provided (1) the king could not suspend the operation of laws; (2) no taxes were to be levied or standing army maintained in peacetime without the consent of Parliament; (3) sessions of Parliament were to be held frequently; (4) freedom of speech in Parliament was to be assured; (5) subjects were to have the right of petition and were also to be free of excessive fines, bail, and cruel punishment; and (6) the king must be a Protestant. The Bill of Rights has exercised a tremendous influence on the development of constitutional government. The first ten amendments to the Constitution of the United States show their debt to the English declaration of 1688.

Results of the Glorious Revolution. The events which placed William and Mary on the English throne are referred to by Englishmen as the Glorious, or Bloodless, Revolution. Without bloodshed Parliament had deposed the old line of kings and laid down the conditions under which future English sovereigns were to rule. The theory of divine right was discredited, and Parliament was on the road to becoming the dominant element in government. In foreign affairs the events of 1688 resulted in a switch from the pro-French policy of Charles II and James II. Acting as the champion of Protestantism on the Continent, William used England's resources to check the designs of Louis XIV.

Significant as they were, the achievements of the Revolution were limited. The Bill of Rights and subsequent legislation guaranteed certain fundamental rights to the common people, but the nation was now governed by a small, wealthy minority of merchants, gentry, and landed nobility. However, the development of such concepts as popular sovereignty and the right of revolution which were established in England by the Revolution of 1688 were later to have a profound influence on the world's governments and peoples.

Lock's justification of the Revolution of 1688. John Locke, as we have seen (p. 249), was one of the most eminent thinkers of his period. In his "Of Civil Government," the second essay in *Two Treatises of Government,* published in 1690, Locke justified the overthrow of James II by expounding the following ideas:

Before government was established, all men, living in a state of nature, possessed certain natural rights. These rights consisted principally of the rights to life, liberty, and property. While life in a state of nature was not frighteningly ruthless, as Hobbes supposed, it was unsatisfactory because society was handicapped in many ways by the absence of government. There was no superior agency to enforce the law of nature, which is a body of rules ensuring the equality of all men and every man's enjoyment of his natural rights. Since men in a state of nature arrived at different interpretations of natural law, uncertainty and conflict often resulted.

Therefore, by common consent, an agreement, or contract, was entered into by which a sovereign was set up with power to govern and enforce the laws of nature. Through this contract the people give up some of their rights to the government, but their basic natural rights are in no way surrendered. Finally, the social contract is bilateral, or binding upon parties. The government, for its part, can demand the obedience of the people, but the people may also expect that the government will keep its part of the contract by not in any way abridging the natural rights of the people. If these rights are violated, if the government rules unwisely and tyrannically, the people have a perfect right to overthrow their rulers. In short, the people are the real rulers, the custodians of popular sovereignty, which gives them the right of revolution. Thus, unlike Hobbes, Locke used the social contract theory to challenge rather than to support absolutism. His ideas were to find new expression in the American and French revolutions a century later.

Genesis of cabinet government. During the century following the Revolution of 1688 there slowly evolved what is known today as cabinet government—government by an executive committee, headed by a prime minister, which rules in the king's name but in reality is the instrument of the majority party in the House of Commons. A unique British contribution to the art of government, the cabinet system has spread to many parts of the world.

The evolution of cabinet government began during the reign of William III and Mary (1689-1702). William soon discovered that only when all his ministers were of the same party as the majority in Commons did the government function smoothly. Decisions were still frequently made by the monarch, sitting in conference with his ministers, but by 1714, at the end of the reign of Williams' successor, Queen Anne, the cabinet—as it was now known—was a distinct factor in policymaking.

Since neither William nor his successor Anne had any surviving children, the Hanoverian dynasty ascended the throne in 1714. Cabinet government began to assume its unique character during the reign of the first two Hanoverian monarchs, George I and II. During the reign of the latter, Robert Walpole, as leader of the Whig party, was the real head of the government and the first prime minister from 1721 to 1742.

Walpole established the principle that the entire cabinet had to act as the single administrative instrument of the House majority and that cabinet unanimity was a necessity. If any member refused to support the official policy, he had to resign. When Walpole eventually lost his majority in the Commons, he resigned. This act confirmed the principle that the executive branch of government—in theory the king but in practice the prime minister and cabinet—must resign when its policies are no longer supported in the Commons.

Pretensions of George III. With the reign of George III the cabinet system, in

As can be seen from the first map, Russia expanded outward from a nucleus around Moscow. Vigorously pursuing his country's goal of a "window" on the Baltic Sea, Peter the Great succeeded during the Great Northern War in wrestling valuable coastline from Sweden (see second map). By 1796 Catherine the Great had augmented Russia's holdings by the Partition of Poland.

effect, went into temporary eclipse. Coming to the throne in 1760 he was determined to "be a king," as his mother had long urged. In short, his object was to destroy the cabinet system by becoming his own chief minister. George III did not aspire to be a tyrant or to rule as a divine-right monarch; rather, he wished to rule as a "Patriot King," above political parties and in accordance with his own ideas.

It took George III only a few years to destroy the power of the Whigs and to secure control of Parliament. By 1770 all effective opposition to the king had been swept away, for George had filled the Commons with supporters known as the "King's Friends," bought by royal favors and pensions. For twelve fateful years George III was the effective head of the government. In this period Great Britain's thirteen North American colonies waged their successful war for independence.

The disaster to British arms in America dealt the king's policies and methods a crushing blow. In a sense, by gaining their liberty, the Americans helped the Britons gain theirs. In 1780 the House of Commons resolved "that the influence of the crown has increased, is increasing, and ought to be diminished."[6] By 1782 George III had to dismiss Lord North, his subservient prime minister, and employ ministers who were willing to make concessions to public opinion.

In 1783 George III called the twenty-four year-old son of the great war leader William Pitt (see p. 278) to be prime minister. Undoubtedly the king expected to control the youthful statesman, but he more than met his match. A new Tory party, reinvigorated by Pitt's leadership, took firm control of the affairs of state. The king was no longer consulted on the day-to-day details of government and only occasionally tried to intervene. When the king's mental instability and final insanity removed royal influence from governmental affairs, the prime minister and his cabinet colleagues assumed full control.

From the Glorious Revolution of 1688 until another great peaceful revolution in 1832, England was the perfect example of aristocratic liberalism. Ingrained in this English system was a habit of political thought that gave room for reform to take place very gradually, until ultimately the narrow oligarchical liberalism of the late seventeenth century broadened into the full democracy of the late nineteenth century.

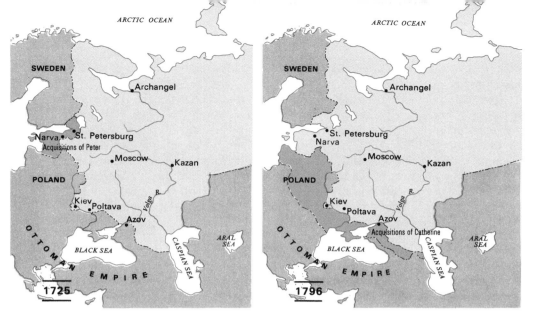

THE RISE OF RUSSIA

Peter the Great's "window on the sea." In 1682 a new era in Russian history began with the accession of Peter I, who soon showed himself to be master of his unruly state, which was still a world apart from western Europe. The fourth member of the Romanov dynasty that had secured the throne in 1613 at the end of Russia's "Time of Trouble" (see p. 146), Peter grew up without benefit of discipline or formal education. But this six-foot-nine-inch giant possessed an excellent mind and such great stores of energy that his contemporaries contended that "he works harder than any *muzhik* [peasant]." Having a sound appreciation of what was essential for Russian progress, Peter pursued three basic policies during his long reign: (1) to obtain an outlet, "a window on the sea," (2) to Europeanize his people, and (3) to make his power absolute.

Peter first turned his attention to the Turks, who blocked Russia's way to the Black Sea. It took two expeditions to conquer Azov from the Turks, and Peter realized that he must learn from the West how to modernize his army and build a navy. He organized a Grand Embassy whose dual object was to secure allies against the Turks and to observe the most advanced European methods of warfare, government, industry, and education. Traveling as plain Peter Mikhailov, Peter visited Holland, England, and Germany. In Holland Peter worked as a common ship carpenter in order to learn Dutch methods of shipbuilding at first hand.

Peter obtained some seven hundred technicians from the West but no allies against the Turks. He therefore decided to direct his energies away from the Black Sea to the Baltic. His ambition for "a window on the sea" next led him to make war against Sweden which controlled most of the Baltic's shores. After initial reverses, Sweden was decisively defeated at Poltava (1709). This victory amazed westerners and made them conscious for the first time of Russia's power. Peter's coveted access to the sea came in the form of four provinces situated south and east of the Gulf of Finland. This thrust to the sea continued into the nineteenth century toward the Mediterranean and became an accomplished fact of Russian naval power in the 1970's.

Attempts to westernize Russia. Peter resolved to change the age-old customs of his people in spite of their own opinions and desires. He instructed his male subjects to cut off their long beards, encouraged the adoption of European breeches instead of the flowing oriental robes which many men wore, and attempted to end the seclusion of women. Crude as he was, Peter endeavored to introduce the manners of polite European society into his country. At tremendous cost in treasure and human life, western architects built the new capital of St. Petersburg as "a window opened upon Europe." replacing Moscow, the center of Russia's old way of life.

Responsible for the revision and simplification of the old Russian alphabet, Peter also established printing presses, promoted the study of foreign languages, sent many young men to western Europe to study, and started new schools for advanced training in engineering, navigation, and accounting. In the economic field he was a staunch mercantilist who sought to make his country as nearly self-sufficient as possible. Some of Peter's reforms, such as the establishment of new industries, failed shortly after his death. In addition, his aggressive program of westernization provoked much hostility, including that of the Church. Furthermore, Peter did nothing to alleviate the arduous lot of the Russian peasants, more than half of whom had been reduced to serfdom by their landlords with the consent of earlier Romanov tsars.

Absolutism of Peter the Great. Peter the Great accelerated the molding of Russia into an absolutist state. All vestiges of local self-government were removed, and Peter continued and intensified his predecessors' requirement of state service for all nobles. They were compelled to serve in the army, in the government, or in industry, and to send their sons abroad for study. In return, this "service nobility" was granted a free hand in dealing with their serfs.

The Church also became a tool of the state when Peter abolished the office of patriarch and appointed a Holy Synod of bishops to govern the Church. The new body was dominated by a layman called the procurator, who represented the tsar. For the next two hundred years the Church served as one of the most powerful agents and supporters of Russian absolutism.

Worn out from his exertions in politics and his excesses in drinking and brawling, Peter died in 1725 at the age of fifty-three. He had firmly established absolutism in Russia and ended its isolation from the West. Russia was now ready to play an important part in European history, but nearly forty years were to pass before an equally ambitious and ruthless monarch appeared on the Russian throne.

Catherine the Great. Catherine II was a German princess who married the Russian heir to the crown. Finding him half insane—"a moronic booby"—Catherine tacitly consented to his murder. It was announced that he died of "apoplexy," and in 1762 she became the ruler.

Catherine contributed to the resurgence of the Russian nobility that began after the death of Peter the Great. State service had been abolished, and Catherine delighted the nobles further by turning over most governmental functions in the provinces to them. The condition of the serfs, on the other hand, became so bad—for example, Catherine legalized the selling of serfs separate from the land—that in 1773 a terrifying peasant uprising occurred. Inspired by a Cossack named Pugachev ("Hang all the landlords!"), the rebels threatened to take

Moscow before they were dispersed. Catherine had Pugachev drawn and quartered in Red Square, but his specter continued to haunt her and her successors.

This brilliant and unscrupulous monarch waged war successfully against the decaying Ottoman empire and advanced Russia's southern boundary to the Black Sea (see p. 273). Then, as we shall see later in this chapter, by plotting with the rulers of Prussia and Austria she annexed half of Poland and pushed the Russian frontier westward into central Europe. By the time of her death in 1796, Catherine's expansionist policy had made Russia a major European power.

THE EMERGENCE OF PRUSSIA

The Great Elector.   If the rise of Russia was remarkable, the development of Prussia was even more amazing. History has scarcely a parallel example of the manner in which one royal house, the Hohenzollern, expanded its territory and exalted its power by fair means or foul.

The earliest Hohenzollerns were unimportant nobles occupying a castle on the heights of Zollern in south Germany. In 1417 a member of the family, who was one of the seven German electors (see p. 141), was made ruler of the unpromising Mark of Brandenburg, one of the border provinces carved out of Slavic lands east of the Elbe during the Middle Ages. By turning Lutheran during the Reformation, the Hohenzollerns gained wealth from seized Church properties, and the elector increased his authority as head of the new church in Brandenburg. During the seventeenth century successive rulers expanded Hohenzollern lands on the lower Rhine and in East Prussia.

The Hohenzollerns were threatened with ruin during the Thirty Years' War, when Brandenburg was occupied by the Swedes from 1630 to 1643. Frederick William (1640-1688), known as the Great Elector, was determined to build a strong monarchy that would prevent such humiliations in the future. This meant the creation of a modern standing army and centralized bureaucracy, and the elimination of opposition from the nobility. Frederick William's small but effective army cleared his lands of foreign troops and made good his claim to eastern Pomerania (along the Baltic coast) at the Peace of Westphalia. After the war he increased the army to 30,000 men and laid the foundations for a civil service which governed the scattered Hohenzollern possessions directly from Berlin. The bureaucracy and the army remained the two main pillars of the Prussian state down to modern times.

The Great Elector also promoted economic progress in his domains. Immigrants were brought in—diligent Dutch farmers, harassed Jews, and (after Louis xiv revoked the Edict of Nantes) thousands of skilled Huguenots.

The Prussian nobility (Junkers) were encouraged to accept the new powerful state in return for important concessions—a monopoly of the key positions in the army and the bureaucracy, freedom from taxation, and a free hand in dealing with their peasants. As a result the rural masses of Prussia—as well as Russia and Austria, where a similar policy was followed—were forced deeper into serfdom at a time when the peasantry of western Europe had long been emancipated.

"An army which possesses a State."   By the opening of the eighteenth century Prussia, as the combined lands of the Hohenzollerns now came to be called, had almost reached a position where it could embark on more ambitious and agressive programs of expansion. The contribution of Frederick William I (1713-1740) was necessary, however, before this new phase in Prussian history could begin. He firmly believed that the destiny of Prussia, an artificial combination of lands without defensible frontiers, lay with its army. During his reign the army increased to 83,000 men—in size the fourth army in Europe and without a doubt the most efficient. As his contemporaries put it: "Prussia is not a State which possesses an army, but an army which possesses a State."[7]

King Frederick William also completed the task of creating a modern central-ized government, run by a trained and efficient civil service and obeyed by a docile citizenry, who were told by their crusty king: "No reasoning, obey orders." He has well been dubbed "the Potsdam Führer," for it was through this ruler, with his maxims of "order, discipline, and work" and "Salvation belongs to the Lord, everything else is my business," that Germany developed its tradition of subordination to the state and blind confidence in the military point of view.

Frederick William I had high hopes for his son Frederick, who was subjected to a Spartan training. But Frederick loved music, art, and philosophy, and at eighteen he attempted to flee to France. Caught, he was forced to witness the beheading of his accomplice and best friend and was then subjected to more years of severe training and discipline. As the old king neared his last days he is supposed to have said: "O my God, I die content, since I have so worthy a son and successor." Frederick William was correct; his son was eventually to become the greatest soldier of his day and a master of Machiavellian diplomacy. Frederick II (1740-1786), known as Frederick the Great, brought Prussia fully into the arena of European politics (see below). He also continued his predecessors' work of building a powerful Prussian state at home.

POWER POLITICS AND THE DUEL FOR WORLD EMPIRE

Seeds of conflict. In 1740 Europe had not seen a major war for a generation—not since the Peace of Utrecht in 1713 had brought the War of the Spanish Succession to a close. Political and economic forces were at work, however, which would in 1740 plunge the Continent into war, and the third quarter of the eighteenth century was to witness a series of destructive conflicts. France and Britain were becoming bitter rivals over commerce and colonies; Prussia under Frederick the Great was well armed and eager to secure additional territory; Russia under Catherine the Great was in a position to renew the expansionist policy of Peter the Great; and a fifth great power, Austria, had emerged along the middle Danube as the Hapsburgs, having failed as Holy Roman emperors, concentrated upon organizing their family lands into a monarchy capable of holding its own in the competitive state system.

As the vigor and acquisitive appetites of the five major powers mounted, three once great states were lapsing into impotence. Spain was no longer a power to be reckoned with, and the Ottoman Turks no longer inspired fear. Following the death of Suleiman the Magnificent in 1566, the Ottoman empire had begun a gradual decline marked by the defeat at Lepanto in 1571 and the loss of Hungary

THE GROWTH OF PRUSSIA,
1648-1795

- Prussia in 1648
- Acquired 1648-1688
- Acquired 1688-1740
- Acquired 1740-1786
- Acquired 1786-1795

to Austria in 1699. It was now caught in a net of intrigue woven by Russia and Austria. Poland still loomed large on the map of Europe, but it lacked strong government and natural boundaries and was to become the most notable victim of aggression by powerful neighbors.

From 1688 to 1713, during the last three of Louis XIV's wars, England had not only been pitted against France on the Continent but the two states had also begun a long duel on a worldwide stage for colonial possessions in North America, the West Indies, and India. As the eighteenth century progressed, this colonial rivalry became increasingly intense. In line with the philosophy of mercantilism, one London merchant expressed the clash of economic interests in this fashion: "Our trade will improve by the total extinction of theirs."[8]

England came to realize that it could best checkmate French ambitions in Europe by destroying French commerce and sea power in North America and India. When war resumed on the Continent in 1740, the English had perfected the practice of obtaining and subsidizing allies to keep the French occupied in Europe while the bulk of British troops, especially naval forces, concentrated on the task of conquering the colonies and destroying the commerce of the French overseas, where distance served to neutralize France's advantages as a land power. The French, on the other hand, divided their energies by trying to play the game of power politics in Europe and at the same time endeavoring to compete with England over colonies. The result was to spell failure for France in both areas.

War of the Austrian Succession.   Sparked by Frederick the Great's seizure of Austrian Silesia, war raged in Europe from 1740 to 1748 with Prussia, France, and

Spain seeking to wrest territory from Austria. England, interested in the balance of power, entered the conflict on the side of Austria together with Holland and Hanover. A feature of the war was that it broadened into a worldwide conflict involving European colonies in India and North America. Peace was signed at Aix-la-Chapelle with no conclusive result, except Frederick's retention of Silesia. Rivalries continued to smoulder and in less than a decade blazed forth in another major war.

The Diplomatic Revolution. The duel for world empire between England and France reached a decisive stage in the Seven Years' War (1756-1763), known in American history as the French and Indian War. The war was preceded in North America and India by preliminary skirmishes between English and French forces, and in Europe by a very significant regrouping of alliances in which two sets of traditional enemies became allies.

Thirsting for revenge against Frederick the Great, Maria Theresa turned to her country's hereditary enemy, France, and suggested to Louis xv that an alliance be formed against Frederick. The determining factor in Louis' decision to accept the Austrian offer was his realization that the English had replaced the Hapsburgs as France's most dangerous enemy. In the spring of 1756 Louis signed a pact whereby France joined Russia, Sweden, and various states in the Germanies as allies of Austria. (Five years later Spain was to join this coalition by declaring war on Great Britain.)

To check French ambitions on the Continent, England in the meantime had made an alliance with its recent foe, Prussia. So thoroughly had the traditional alignment of powers been reversed that this new grouping of nations—Austria and France vs. England and Prussia—is referred to as the Diplomatic Revolution of the eighteenth century. Such Diplomatic Revolutions were to become commonplace in more modern times: the *Entente Cordiale* in 1904 when old foes, England and France, became allies; and after World War II when the victorious United States became an ally of both Germany and Japan, her recent enemies.

The Seven Years' War. Frederick the Great applied the match to the international powder keg in 1756, making the droll observation: "If Austria is pregnant with war, I shall offer the service of the midwife."[9] Quickly attacking the coalition, he aimed heavy blows at Austria before France and Russia could threaten him. But he soon was attacked on all sides. With brilliant strategy Frederick marched and wheeled his forces, winning battles but despairing of ever winning the war.

In the colonial phase of the Seven Years' War, Great Britain at first suffered severe defeats. But the crisis ended when a remarkable statesman, William Pitt the Elder, became prime minister in 1757 and, like Winston Churchill in 1940, gave England new heart and a new war strategy. He developed a successful global strategy of war, known as his "system," which consisted of (1) providing large subsidies of money to Prussia, (2) destroying French sea power and thus preventing men and supplies from reaching the French possessions overseas, and (3) dispatching well-equipped English forces to the colonies to conquer the isolated French armies.

In 1759 one French fort after another fell in North America: Duquesne, Louisburg, Niagara, and Ticonderoga; and the defeat of France in North America was sealed when General Wolfe vanquished Montcalm's forces and captured Quebec. In India there was a similar chronicle of victories, climaxed by the defeat of the ruler of Bengal by Robert Clive at the decisive battle of Plassey (1757). The

**THE PARTITION OF POLAND
1772-1795**

- ☐ To Prussia
- ▨ To Russia
- ▨ To Austria
- Boundary of Poland after the
  first partition, 1772
- Boundary of Poland after the
  second partition, 1793

English commander's victory laid the foundation for nearly two hundred years of British rule in India.

The victories won by Great Britain contrasted markedly with the ordeals suffered by Prussia in holding off the combined armies of Austria, France, and Russia. Frederick was saved by the narrowest of margins when a new tsar recalled his armies from the gates of Berlin and withdrew from the war in 1762. Unable to continue without Russian support, Austria sued for peace in 1763. Prussia's hold on Silesia was confirmed, and the Continental phase of the war ended.

Treaty of Paris. In 1763 peace was also concluded between Great Britain and France and Spain. The Treaty of Paris provided for French cession to England of Canada and all the territory east of the Mississippi River. Spain ceded Florida to England and, as compensation, received from France the Louisiana territory including New Orleans. This marked the end of French rule in North America. France regained its trading posts in India as well as Martinique and other rich islands in the West Indies. The British also returned Havana and Manila to Spain.

By the Treaty of Paris, Great Britain became the greatest colonial, commercial, and naval power in the world. That a country of 6.5 million should triumph over a nation such as France, with a population of 23 million, was remarkable.

Partition of Poland. The eighteenth century offers many illustrations of the callous and cold-blooded manner in which wars were precipitated, promises broken, and allies deserted. Yet today, in an age accustomed to accepting the right of national self-determination, the most shocking example of completely un-principled statecraft was the ruthless partition of Poland by Prussia, Russia, and

Austria. Without natural barriers to aid in its defense, Poland was a handicapped nation. In addition, it was dominated by a reactionary nobility whose insistence on retaining its feudal "liberties" rendered the central government virtually powerless.

The first partition of Poland, in 1772, came about as a result of international tensions produced by the decline of the Ottoman empire. Austrian opposition to Russian designs on the Crimea and Moldavia brought the two states close to war. Frederick the Great, fearing that Prussia would be drawn into the conflict, then persuaded Catherine the Great to satisfy her territorial ambitions at the expense of helpless Poland. Frederick also aimed at annexing West Prussia (the Polish Corridor) in order to link East Prussia with the main body of Hohenzollern possessions. Maria Theresa of Austria reluctantly agreed to participate in the partitioning. In a wry comment on Maria Theresa's action, Frederick epitomized the ruthlessly competitive nature of international relations: "She wept, but she kept on taking."

In 1793, and again in 1795, while the rest of Europe was distracted by the French Revolution, Poland was again partitioned, Austria abstaining from the second operation. By the third partition Poland ceased to exist as an independent state. Under the alien rule of three different governments, the Poles continued to hope for the resurrection of their nation. Their faith was not rewarded until after the First World War, when an independent Polish nation was established.

CHAPTER 14
THE RIGHTS OF MAN

Revolution in the Western World: 1776-1815

The political changes that occurred during the last quarter of the eighteenth century and the first quarter of the nineteenth were world-shaking. John Locke's justification of the Glorious Revolution as a revolt against tyranny was a forerunner of the eighteenth-century attacks on the existing order. Physiocrats condemned the oppressive restraints of mercantilism, and *philosophes* attacked the irresponsible despotism of absolutism. Some monarchs heard the voice of reform and tried to uproot the evils of the Old Regime, but the momentous reforms that made the period from 1776 to 1815 a watershed in western political history were not imposed by authoritative decree from above but by revolutionary action from below.

In this chapter we shall follow the actions of the thirteen colonies as they successfully defy Britain and achieve their independence, we shall witness the overthrow of an ineffectual French king and watch a new republic rising from the bloodshed of revolution, and we shall observe the struggle of colonials in Latin America to throw off the shackles of repressive Old World regimes.

The rise of republican France was a challenge to despotic regimes throughout Europe, and the result was intermittent warfare on the Continent from 1792 to 1815. In the midst of this troubled era Napoleon came to power. Turning the new-born republic into a tool for conquest, this self-styled "man of destiny" threatened all Europe until defeat at Waterloo finally crushed his dreams of empire.

Before this period from 1776 to 1815, little is heard of the rights of the people; after it, representative government is in the ascendancy. Ever stronger voices speak forth for the rights of citizens, for bills of rights and constitutions—political concepts which have had an immeasurable influence on the course of western civilization.

Criticism of existing governments.   Not only the *philosophes* of the Enlightenment, but the middle class, too, found much that was irrational and indefensible in the institutions of the day. Perhaps the most important factor in middle-class discontent was the government-controlled economy of mercantilism (see p. 230). Convinced that capitalism had outgrown the need for state assistance with its accompanying controls, the bourgeoisie were ready for a system of free enterprise. As early as the seventeenth century English merchants had denounced the hoarding of bullion, advocating instead that "the exportation of our moneys in trade of merchandise is a means to increase our treasure."[1] This growing concern for freedom of trade led the middle class to support the physiocrats, eighteenth-century economic thinkers who, as their name indicates, shared with *philosophes* the viewpoint that all human activity—economic, social, and political—was subject to natural laws similar to those governing the physical universe.

The physiocrats, laissez faire, and Adam Smith.   The physiocrats believed that money should circulate naturally, much as the blood does in the human body, and that all economic activity should be freed from artificial restrictions. They believed in a "free market," the concept which implies that natural forces of supply and demand should be allowed to regulate the conduct of business without interference from the government. In short, governments should adopt the policy of laissez faire (letting business alone).

The most influential advocate of laissez-faire economics was a Scottish professor of moral philosophy, Adam Smith (1723-1790). In 1776 his systematic formulation of the new science of economics, *An Inquiry into the Nature and Causes of the Wealth of Nations*, was published. Smith was indebted to the physiocrats for his views of personal liberty, natural law, and the position of the state as a mere "passive policeman." He argued that increased production depends largely on division of labor, with each individual—and each nation—performing the work for which he is best fitted. Following this thesis, Smith maintained that every individual is and ought to be motivated by self-interest:

> It is not from the benevolence of the butcher, the brewer, or the baker, that we expect our dinner, but from their regard to their own interest. We address ourselves, not to their humanity but to their self-love, and never talk to them of our own necessities but of their advantages. . . . Every individual is continually exerting himself to find out the most advantageous employment for whatever capital he can command. It is his own advantage, indeed, and not that of society, which he has in view.[2]

Smith looked on all fixing of wages, guilds and trade unions that limit apprenticeship, and tariffs and other governmental interference as injurious to trade, and he scoffed at the mercantilists' view that the wealth of a nation depends on achieving a surplus of exports, amassing bullion, and crippling neighboring countries. He insisted that trade works for the benefit of all nations the world over and that a country cannot thrive and its trade flourish if its neighbors are not prosperous.

Philosophes urge political reforms. Working with the physiocrats as they sought to remove outworn economic abuses, the *philosophes* carried on an offensive against tyranny, misgovernment, and unjust laws. The reform movements of the physiocrats and the *philosophes* were inseparably connected, for only by obtaining efficient and rational government could essential economic reforms be carried through.

The *philosophes* militantly advocated the end of arbitrary government and the adoption of such rights as civil liberty, trial by jury, and freedom of expression— freedoms which they construed as implicit in natural law. By expressing the belief that laws and institutions could be based on a natural law as immutable as Newton's laws of physics, they helped undermine the edifice of absolutism.

Montesquieu and *The Spirit of Laws*. Montesquieu (1689-1755), a French nobleman, was the most systematic and comprehensive student of government during the first half of the eighteenth century. His most important work was *The Spirit of Laws* (1748), a massive study of the salient features of numerous governments. Unlike the English philosopher Locke and many of the *philosophes*, Montesquieu did not use the deductive method of analysis. He began not with the universal principles or natural laws but with facts. His method was to describe and analyze actual governments, both past and present, and then to show how they reflected the environment in which they functioned. In *The Spirit of Laws* Montesquieu concluded that all governments conformed to certain specific factors of geography, economics, and race, which varied from country to country. Since the value of any governmental system depended on its relation to these specific factors, there could be no single "best" form of government.

Montesquieu was a relentless critic of tyranny and a champion of liberty. Although he did not endorse any one form of government, he admired the limited parliamentary monarchy of England. In the separation of executive, legislative, and judicial powers, he found the bulwark of liberty. Actually, Montesquieu misinterpreted the operation of the unwritten English constitution, for with its cabinet system of government England was moving toward unity of powers. However, this concept of separation of powers greatly influenced the planners of the American Constitution.

Rousseau and the *Social Contract*. Jean Jacques Rousseau (1712-1778) was one of the most enigmatic and significant persons of his time. Although believing in the general objectives of the *philosophes,* Rousseau distrusted reason and science. He gloried in impulses and intuitions, trusting emotions rather than thoughts, the heart rather than the mind. His early hand-to-mouth existence and the rebuffs and ridicule he suffered from polite society contributed to his hatred of the Old Regime and the status quo. He was also influenced by the ideal of the "noble savage" who lived "without faith . . . law . . . [with] neither king, nor judge, nor priest . . . nor taxes, nor prisons."[3]

Rousseau's most important work and indeed one of the most influential books on political theory in modern times was his *Social Contract* (1762), which opens with the stirring statement: "Man is born free, but is everywhere in chains." In this work Rousseau endeavored to construct a theory of government based on the consent of the governed while reconciling the conflicting demands of individual liberty and social organization. In Rousseau's ideal society an individual surrenders all his natural rights—as envisaged by Locke—to the group and yet retains his freedom if the government follows what is called the "General Will," which is defined as any action that is right and good for all; hence by obeying the General Will the individual is really obeying what is in his own best interest.

Rousseau defined the social contract in a way that emphasized the sovereignty of the people. By means of the social contract each individual surrenders his natural rights to the state, meaning the people as a whole. The people and the state are therefore identical, but the government is something quite different—it is merely the executive agent of the people's will.

Rousseau was hailed as the champion of democracy. But it is also true that his doctrine of the General Will later came to be used by ambitious despots. Claiming that he alone knew what constituted the General Will, a shrewd leader could justify his seizure of power. It is one of history's ironies that the *Social Contract*, written to justify democracy, was used later on to justify dictatorship.

Faith in enlightened despotism.   The majority of the *philosophes* believed that the most logical way to attain desirable reforms was through the rule of an "enlightened despot": secure a well-meaning, intelligent monarch imbued with the philosophy of the Enlightenment and all would be well. In a sense, this theory of government was akin to the Platonic ideal of a society where philosophers would be kings. A few eighteenth-century monarchs were progressive, sincerely believing in the ideas of the *philosophes*. Major figures who were touched by the Enlightenment and became (or seemed to become) enlightened despots were Frederick the Great of Prussia, Catherine the Great of Russia, and the Austrian emperor Joseph II. The most sincere of the enlightened despots was Joseph II, the son of Maria Theresa. Joseph's reforms included the abolition of serfdom, toleration for Protestants and Jews, advancement of public education, equality of taxation, and centralization of the administrative and court systems.

Failure of enlightened despotism.   But enlightened despotism was incapable of rooting out the deep-seated evils of the Old Regime. No matter how sincere and devoted to reform, an enlightened ruler such as Joseph of Austria could not achieve success against the entrenched power of the nobility and Church and the ignorance of the peasantry.

In most cases enlightened absolutism was nothing but a facade, a mere playing at reform because it was fashionable. "The Enlightenment was a fashion in Russia," it has been observed, "never a fact." Before her death in 1796, Catherine no longer quoted her "dear *philosophes*" or proclaimed their ideas. She had repressed a widespread peasant's rebellion with savage cruelty, and she had been frightened by the French Revolution, "the enemy of God and of the Thrones," as she called it.

As the last phase of authoritarian absolutism, enlightened despotism more often aimed at strengthening the power of the state than at increasing the public welfare. Reforms were imposed from above on people who had not been educated to political realities. In the words of the British ambassador in Berlin: "The Prussian Monarchy reminds me of a vast prison in the centre of which appears the great keeper, occupied in the care of his captives."[4] The successful reform movements were to come from below, from the revolutionary action of the people. It is noteworthy that in 1789, one year before Joseph II died a broken-hearted failure, a bourgeois revolution with a program in large part similar to Joseph's exploded in France. This French Revolution, inspired in part by the American Revolution, would end absolutism in France and sound its death knell throughout Europe.

Opposition to mercantilism. In 1776, with George III in full command of the British government, there began the stirring revolt that created in the western world a new nation, based on the political ideas espoused by Locke and Montesquieu. Many historians believe that the American Revolution was not so much a revolt against the tyranny of George III as a revolt of the American middle class against Britain's mercantilistic economic policy. In accord with the prevailing view that colonies existed for the benefit of the mother country, British navigation laws and other restrictive acts required the colonists to trade only with Britain and prohibited them from competing with British manufactured goods. For about a century these acts were not rigidly enforced, but finally the day of reckoning came.

After the Seven Years' War, Britain was saddled with a debt of nearly $700 million. The added expense of maintaining a strong force of British regulars in America, made necessary by a serious uprising of Indians in the Northwest in 1763, was therefore especially troublesome. The prime minister, George Grenville, having decided that the colonists should bear some of the expense of their own defense, induced Parliament to enact a series of acts designed for this purpose. A storm of protest arose in America, especially to the Stamp Act (1765), which levied duties on dice, playing cards, and—to the chagrin of newspaper publishers. lawyers, and merchants—on newspapers and legal and commercial documents. The Americans raised the constitutional principle of "no taxation without representation"; the British countered with the argument that Americans were indeed represented in Parliament because the members of that body represented not only the kingdom but the entire empire.

A revolution in minds and hearts. Although Britain's taxation measures precipitated the rebellion, it would be a mistake to interpret the American Revolution as resulting solely or even primarily from economic causes. Like all great historical movements, the American Revolution was a complex phenomenon. While admitting that the new taxes were ill timed, that they came too rapidly, and that the British government followed a confused policy of advance and then retreat under pressure, many historians deny that British mercantilism discriminated heavily against the colonists. The American colonies enjoyed a high degree of prosperity.

Agreement is growing among historians that the American Revolution was not so much brought about by a "cause" as by "conditions." As John Adams wrote in 1818:

> But what do we mean by the American Revolution? Do we mean the American War? The Revolution was effected before the war commenced. The Revolution was in the minds and hearts of the people. . . . This radical change in the principles, opinions, sentiments, and affections of the people, was the real American Revolution.[5]

It has been said that the separation movement really began when the first Englishman set foot on the soil of America. Many colonists had suffered religious persecution in the mother country and felt little love for their homeland. Many other colonists never had any connection with Britain. In 1775, out of a population of nearly three million, almost 40 percent were of non-British stock, mainly from Ireland and southern Germany. Of course, many other colonists considered themselves loyal Britons and opposed the break with the mother country.

The British colonial majority, however, prided themselves on their rights as Britons, rights stemming back to the Magna Carta. They had read the political writings of Montesquieu and Voltaire, and they accepted Locke's contract theory and the concept of the sovereignty of the people.

In summary, these were the conditions which predisposed the colonies to revolution: a fierce spirit of freedom, experience in self-rule in the colonial assemblies, the impact of liberal political ideas from the writings of the French *philosophes*, and the lessons of the Puritan Revolution and the Revolution of 1688 in Britain.

The war against Britain.   Following the imposition of the stamp tax, events moved rapidly toward open hostilities. Colonial boycotts of British goods and British retaliatory measures, skirmishes at Lexington and Concord between British troops and colonial militia, and the well-organized movement for independence, led by such radicals as Samuel Adams and Patrick Henry, heightened sentiment against the mother country. On July 4, 1776, the revolt of the American colonies was formally proclaimed in the Declaration of Independence.

With the outbreak of war, Britain's state of unpreparedness was quickly exposed. After its victory in the Seven Years' War, Britain had failed to build up any alliance system to offset the enmity of its vanquished enemies, Spain and France. The British armies and fleets were woefully neglected; commanders found it impossible to put fifteen thousand regulars in the field in America.

The struggle dragged on for seven years. Colonial forces were puny and colonial supplies inadequate, but the revolutionary cause was immensely strengthened by the courage, determination, and skill of its leaders—Washington, patient patriot and dedicated commander; Franklin, sage diplomat and famous scholar; Madison, skilled student of government; Jefferson, ardent and courageous champion of freedom: and Hamilton, adept politican and Washington's wartime aide. The defeat of the British general Burgoyne in October 1777 and the alliance with France in the following year turned the scales in favor of the colonies.

The participation of France, seconded by Spain and Holland, widened the conflict into another European colonial war. In essence, this conflict was a great world struggle, with Britain, devoid of allies, fighting in the West Indies, the North Atlantic, West Africa, and India as well as in North America. Faced with the active coalition of France, Spain, and Holland—plus a league of neutrality composed of Russia, Sweden, and Denmark—Britain granted independence to the thirteen colonies in 1783. They were now free to make their own destinies, unhampered by constraints from Europe.

Constitutional government.   Before the conflict with Great Britain ended, the American colonies ratified the Articles of Confederation (1781), setting up a loose league of independent states under a weak central government. This system produced civil strife and confusion, and tariff and boundary disputes raged between the states.

At this juncture a group of public-spirited men, including Hamilton, Madison, and Washington, urged the establishment of a strong central government. Their efforts led to the Constitutional Convention, which met at Independence Hall in Philadelphia from May to September 1787. After much debate between the advocates of a strong central government and those favoring sovereign states, a brilliant compromise was reached—the Constitution of the United States—which assured the supremacy of the federal government without making puppet governments of the states. In April 1789 George Washington took the oath of office as first president under the Constitution.

The American Constitution embodied certain fundamental principles. The first was the doctrine of popular sovereignty—all power ultimately resides in the people. Constitutional provisions required the participation of the people in amending the Constitution and denied this right to the national government acting alone. Another principle, revolutionary in its day, was that of limited government, which safeguards the rights of the people by setting up definite bounds and restraints on the actions of their public officials. A third important feature was the principle of federalism. In most countries all power resided in the central government, but in the United States power was divided between the state governments and the national government.

Separation of powers was a fourth fundamental aspect of the new Constitution. The powers and duties of legislature, judiciary, and executive were carefully defined. Thus Congress makes the laws, the president applies and enforces them, and the courts interpret them. However, by a fifth feature—checks and balances—careful provision was made so that no one of the three governmental departments could become too independent or too powerful. The president, for example, can veto laws passed by Congress. But the legislature can by a two-thirds vote pass bills over the president's veto. In like manner, the Supreme Court stands as an ultimate safeguard because it can declare any law unconstitutional.

Finally, the Constitution contains a sixth basic principle, the protection of the rights of the individual, although in reality this principle appears in the first ten amendments to the Constitution—the Bill of Rights—instead of in the Constitution proper. No laws can be made encroaching upon freedom of religion, press, and speech, and all persons are safeguarded from arbitrary arrest and imprisonment.

THE FRENCH REVOLUTION

The Old Regime in France. In the eighteenth century France suffered greatly from the indifference and incompetence of its rulers. Lack of uniformity in legal codes, tariff boundaries, weights and measures, and taxation added to the confusion and inefficiency of government.

Discrimination and injustice prevailed in the social structure; birth, not intelligence or achievement, assured success and social position. Of France's total population of 25,000,000 people, only 200,000 belonged to the privileged classes—the clergy and the nobility. These two groups controlled nearly half of the nation's land, monopolized the best positions in the Church, army, and government, and evaded much of the taxation. The peasants—80 percent of the population—were saddled with intolerable burdens. The *taille*, a land tax; the tithe, levied by the Church; the *gabelle*, a tax on salt; and various other taxes took nearly half of a peasant's income. In addition, while the practice of serfdom had practically disappeared, peasants suffered from many vestiges of medieval social discrimination. Many nobles were absentee landlords who squandered their income from peasant tenant farmers and sharecroppers in ostentatious expenditures at Versailles.

The French middle class had wealth without responsibility, intelligence without authority, and ability without recognition. Practical and businesslike, they resented playing second fiddle to a parasitic nobility and were disgusted at the inefficiency of government. The extravagance of the royal court, the unfair methods of tax collection, the absence of a sound system of national bookkeeping, and the continuance of mercantilistic controls especially called forth censure. The middle class sought economic freedom and above all a constitutional monarchy in which they would be dominant.

Conditions in France were not the worst in Europe. France had the most prosperous middle class outside of England, and the peasants were better off than in any other Continental country. The revolution came to France because the middle class was keenly aware of the evils of the Old Regime.

In the background were the ideas of the *philosophes* and physiocrats. By criticizing the evils of the times, stimulating discontent—especially among the bourgeoisie—and offering a logical picture of what a well-ordered society might be, they created a widespread atmosphere of grievance and supplied political and economic philosophies for the future.

The financial crisis.   In France the impact of the American Revolution was deep and widespread; the Americans showed the French how an antiquated government could be removed. But the most immediate influence of the American Revolution upon France was acceleration toward bankruptcy. Participation in the American Revolution had cost France nearly $400 million. When Louis xvi and his advisers proposed a program of tax equalization that would have put French finances in order, the nobility flatly turned it down. They insisted that the king convene the Estates-General, which they expected to dominate and thereby regain the power they had lost to the monarchy during past centuries.

The Estates-General, inactive since 1614 (see p. 263), was composed of representatives of the First Estate (the clergy), the Second Estate (the nobility), and the Third Estate (the middle class and the peasants). As a gesture to the bourgeoisie, the Third Estate was granted twice the number of representatives allowed each of the other two estates. According to custom the three estates were expected to vote by orders—that is, by estates rather than as individuals. This would mean that any scheme of reform formulated by the Third Estate could always be defeated by a two-to-one vote at the hands of the two privileged estates.

The National Assembly.   The calling of the Estates-General in 1789 precipitated a demand for reform all over France. For the guidance of the delegates to the assembly, the people prepared *cahiers* (lists) of grievances. The *cahiers* included demands for personal liberty, a national legislature to make the laws, a jury system, freedom of the press, and abolition of unfair taxation. Thus the *cahiers* presented a program of wide but moderate social and economic reform.

After six weeks of wrangling on the question of whether voting should be by order or by head, the members of the Third Estate assembled at an indoor tennis court and solemnly took the Tennis Court Oath, declaring that they would not disband until a constitution had been drawn up. A royal official sent to order the Assembly to disband was told by the defiant leader Mirabeau, "Sir, go tell your master that nothing but bayonets will drive us out of here." Louis weakly yielded, and the Third Estate, augmented by a few members of the other orders, declared itself the National Constituent Assembly of France.

Collapse of absolutism. All over France millions followed the events at Versailles. Peasants and city workers grew bold at the capitulation of the king, and in July 1789, disorders and riots broke out throughout the land. In the cities, houses of the nobility were sacked; in the country, peasants demolished the castles of their lords. Everywhere it was manifest that royal government in France was collapsing. Following a rumor that the king was concentrating troops at Versailles as a means of browbeating the Assembly, a Parisian mob on July 14 attacked the Bastille, a grim fortress and the hated symbol of the Old Regime, and slew its defenders.

The National Constituent Assembly was in session from June 1789 until October 1791. During this period the Assembly passed more than two thousand laws and effected a peaceful and moderate revolution. In the words of one historian, "No other body of legislators has ever demolished so much in the same brief period."[6] By the August Decrees, serfdom was abolished (there were still some serfs in Alsace and Lorraine), old game laws were repealed, manorial courts were swept away, and tithes and all other fees of the Church were ended. It was declared that henceforth on, taxes were to be collected from all citizens irrespective of rank, the sale of judicial and municipal offices was to cease, justice was to be freely dispensed, and all citizens, regardless of birth, were eligible for any office. In addition the Constituent Assembly ended restrictions on the conduct of business and encouraged individual enterprise by abolishing guilds and prohibiting trade unions.

The Assembly also substantially changed the status of the Church. Monasteries were dissolved and all Church property confiscated. The former Church lands were used as collateral for paper money called *assignats*. By the Civil Constitution of the Clergy, the Church was secularized. Bishops and priests were now elected by the people, paid by the state, and required to swear allegiance to the new constitution of France.

The Declaration of the Rights of Man. Before drawing up the new constitution, the Assembly produced a document which summarized the principles upon which the new regime should be based—the Declaration of the Rights of Man. Its most important provisions were:

The excesses of the French Revolution are typified by the guillotine, the instrument used during the Reign of Terror to behead thousands of Frenchmen, including Louis XVI, whose head is being displayed to the crowd. Ironically, the guillotine was first recommended by a Paris physician, Joseph Ignace Guillotin, who wanted a more humane method of punishment instead of the feudal tortures used to execute criminals. Before the Revolution only the nobility were allowed the relatively painless death of decapitation.

1. Men are born and will remain free and endowed with equal rights. . . .

2. The end and purpose of all political groups is the preservation of the natural and inalienable rights of Man. These rights are Liberty, the Possession of Property, Safety, and Resistance to Oppression. . . .

4. Liberty consists in being able to do anything which is not harmful to another. . . .

6. The Law is the expression of the will of the people. . . . the Law must be the same for all. . . .

9. Every individual . . . [is] presumed innocent until he has been proved guilty. . . .

10. None is to be persecuted for his opinions, even his religious beliefs, provided that his expression of them does not interfere with the order established by the Law.

11. Free communication of thought and opinion is one of the most precious rights of Man. . . .

17. The possession of property being an inviolable and sacred right, none can be deprived of it, unless public necessity, legally proved, clearly requires the deprivation, and then only on the necessary condition of a previously established just reparation.[7]

The Declaration of the Rights of Man embodied the spirit of constitutional government and political liberalism underlying the Glorious Revolution in England and the revolt of the thirteen colonies in America. This French pronouncement appealed immediately to reform groups in all European nations, and during the nineteenth century it inspired many peoples to throw off the yoke of their own old regimes.

The Legislative Assembly. By September 1791 the National Constituent Assembly had formulated a new constitution which made France a limited monarchy. The chief organ of government was an elected single-chamber legislature called the Legislative Assembly. Louis XVI was given only a suspensive veto over legislation, a device which could retard action by the Assembly but could not block its will indefinitely. No longer could the king use the formula of Louis XIV, *L'état, c'est moi;* the monarch was now "Louis by the grace of God and the Constitution, King of the State."

Despite the rights guaranteed in the Declaration of the Rights of Man, the suffrage was given to only a minority of "active" citizens—those who paid a specified minimum amount of direct taxes. Thus one of the striking features of the French constitution of 1791 was its reflection of the interests of the influential bourgeoisie.

This first phase of the French Revolution has been called the Bourgeois Revolution. After relatively little violence France had become a constitutional monarchy with the upper middle class in control. Their concern now was to "stabilize" the Revolution by blocking further change.

The peasants were among the many elements in France that were discontented with the new government. Although the Constituent Assembly in the August Decrees had ruled that many privileges, such as possession of serfs, labor service, and hunting and fishing rights, were to be abolished without compensation, other old manorial dues and obligations were to be commuted into money payments. Most peasants, however, defied the government and refused to make the payments. Hatred against men of property and their agents in the Legislative Assembly grew.

The common people of the cities were especially disgruntled. The cost of living and unemployment were increasing, and they saw no hope of relief in a government from which they were excluded. Largely illiterate and motivated by emotion, these urban workers could be aroused to wild passions of frenzy by eloquent leaders, and as time passed they became increasingly dangerous.

Factions in the Legislative Assembly. The division of opinion in the country at large was mirrored by factionalism in the Assembly itself. About one third of the deputies were conservatives; they made up the party of the Right, which supported the king and was satisfied with the achievements of the moderate revolution. Seated in the middle of the Assembly was the party of the Center, made up of representatives who had no particular program or principles. Next to the apathetic Center were the deputies of the Left, dynamic and aggressive young radicals who distrusted the king, were dissatisfied with the constitution of 1791, and wished the Revolution to continue. From the very start the enemies of the constitution assumed the leadership of the Legislative Assembly and worked for its down fall.

Leaders of the Jacobin movement. The enthusiastic radicals who were determined to advance the Revolution formed various clubs in Paris that were centers of agitation and revolutionary propaganda. The most important of these organizations met in an abandoned Jacobin (Dominican) monastery and took the name "Society of the Friends of the Constitution Meeting at the Jacobins in Paris." Their program was the overthrow of the monarchy and greater justice and opportunity for the masses. Soon, Jacobin Clubs sprang up all over France.

Most prominent in Jacobin circles were Jean Paul Marat, Georges Jacques Danton, and Maximilien Robespierre. As champion of the masses, Marat founded the newspaper *L'Ami du Peuple (Friend of the People)* and carried on a campaign for direct action by the people until 1793 when he was struck down by an assassin's dagger. Robespierre was deeply influenced by the works of Rousseau and became a fanatical reformer who quietly bided his time until he possessed the necessary power to establish an ideal republic based on virtue and justice. Danton, unlike the theorist Robespierre, was a practical republican who had little use for utopias.

Opposition to the Legislative Assembly outside France. Also plotting against the Assembly were many reactionary émigré nobles who had fled France when the Revolution wiped out their ancient privileges. Most of them had taken refuge in various states along the Rhine, where they found receptive ears for their conspiracies against the French government. Leopold II of Austria, brother of the French queen, became concerned over her safety and, with the king of Prussia, issued the Declaration of Pillnitz (August 1791), which declared that the restoration of absolutism in France was of "common interest to all sovereigns of Europe."

Egged on by the radicals, France declared war on Austria in April 1792. Prussia shortly afterward entered the conflict as an ally of Austria. Yet, while eager for war, the French were utterly unprepared for it. During the summer of 1792, fortress after fortress fell to the invaders. On July 27 the Duke of Brunswick, commander of the allied forces invading France, issued a manifesto declaring that his object was "to restore to the king . . . the legitimate authority which belongs to him." He added that he would destroy Paris if the royal family was harmed.

Inauguration of the Republic.   The reply to the manifesto was the insurrection of the ninth and tenth of August instigated by radical Jacobin leaders. They set up a revolutionary "Commune" which controlled Paris and intimidated the Legislative Assembly into deposing Louis XVI and calling for the election, by universal male suffrage, of a National Convention to draw up a new constitution. As head of the Paris Commune, Danton became dictator of France.

The Legislative Assembly came to an end on September 20, 1792, when the National Convention held its first meeting. The following day the Convention abolished monarchy in France and proclaimed September 22, 1792, as beginning Year 1 of the Republic. France was now a republic, the former king Louis XVI a prisoner in fear for his life, and the first phase of the French Revolution—that of moderate reform—a failure.

The National Convention remained in session three years. At the outset it was faced with serious problems: (1) foreign armies had to be driven out of France; (2) a vital decision had to be made as to what should be done with the king: (3) revolts throughout the country had to be suppressed; (4) a republican constitution had to be framed; and (5) the social and economic reforms initiated between 1789 and 1791 had to be completed and put into action.

Danton proceeded with alacrity to increase the armed forces and give them new spirit. During the autumn of 1792 the tide of foreign invasion receded as French armies took the offensive. They occupied the Austrian Netherlands (Belgium), the Rhineland, and Nice and Savoy.

In November 1792, after its armies had reached the Rhine, the National Convention declared that "France will grant fraternity and assistance to all peoples who shall desire to recover their liberty." This announcement in essence proclaimed an international revolution. In December the Convention stated that "it considered itself called to give liberty to the human race and to overthrow all thrones" and declared war on tyrants. It was also announced that in all countries conquered by the French, the inhabitants had to accept the principles of the Revolution; property belonging to counterrevolutionaries and to the Church was to be seized.

Trial and execution of Louis XVI.   The fate of Louis XVI was soon settled. The Girondists, the moderate element among the Jacobins, wished to postpone the king's trial for treason until after the war, but radical Jacobins demanded his death. A follower of Robespierre echoed Jacobin sentiment when he declared:

> The death of the tyrant is necessary to reassure those who fear that one day they will be punished for their daring, and also to terrify those who have not yet renounced the monarchy. A people cannot found liberty when it respects the memory of its chains.[8]

The execution of Louis XVI was carried out on January 21, 1793. On the scaffold the king acted with quiet dignity and splendid fortitude. A French historian has declared: "he was greater on [the scaffold] . . . than ever he had been on his throne."[9]

Pressures inside and outside France.   In the face of French aggression—which, at the least, threatened the balance of power in Europe—Britain, Spain, Holland, and Sardinia joined Prussia and Austria in the First Coalition to wage war on the French Republic. Of all France's foes, Britain became the most implacable. From 1793 to 1815 Britain and France were at war almost continuously. In the spring of

1793 the armies of the First Coalition converged on France. The Revolution was again in peril.

In addition to this foreign menace France was rent by internal strife as moderate and radical factions fought for control of the National Convention. More representative of the bourgeois moderate revolution and of provincial support for federalism, the Girondists feared mob violence and radical reforms; to them the Revolution had gone far enough. By contrast, the Jacobins were tough realists who sided with the urban masses, welcomed more bloodletting, and were determined to advance the Revolution. The Jacobins finally ousted their rivals from the Convention and placed them under arrest. Some of the Girondists, however, escaped to the country, where they organized a rebellion against the tyranny of the radicals in Paris. Meanwhile, royalist Catholics rose again in rebellion. These disorders weakened the economy of the country, and bread riots broke out in Paris.

The Reign of Terror. To deal with the internal and external dangers, the National Convention entrusted its power to twelve men known as the Committee of Public Safety. It also passed a decree making liable to arrest every person of noble birth, anyone who had any contact with an émigré, and anyone who could not produce a certificate of citizenship. The Committee of Public Safety inaugurated the Reign of Terror. Thousands of suspected royalists were arrested and thrown into prison. After a summary trial, many of them were thrown into carts—the tumbrels—and taken to the public square to be guillotined. Perhaps as many as five thousand persons were executed in Paris; in the provinces the number was probably twenty thousand.

The "nation in arms." With subversive activity crushed on the home front, the leaders of the Republic turned their attention to the foreign danger. To meet its enemies, France forged a new weapon, the "nation in arms." Compulsory military service was introduced and the country was mobilized for war. During 1794 and 1795 the new French armies carried out a series of great campaigns. The citizen armies of the Republic were motivated by a spirit not found in the professional and mercenary armies of their opponents. The French citizen-soldier believed he was fighting for his own liberty and for the right to enjoy the fruits of the Revolution.

By 1795, with Spain and Prussia no longer offering effective resistance to the French, the First Coalition had almost been dissolved. Holland was allied with France, Belgium was annexed outright, and French troops controlled all the territory up to the Rhine. In three years the Republic had gained the "natural frontiers" that Louis XIV had dreamed about. By 1795 only Britain, Austria, and Sardinia remained at war with France.

Social and economic changes. Among the significant reforms achieved during the period of the National Convention (also known as the Jacobin Republic) were the plan for a national system of education, abolition of slavery in French colonies, final eradication of manorial dues and obligations without compensation, and the establishment of a metric system of weights and measures. The welfare of the lower classes was promoted by placing ceilings on prices and by selling the confiscated estates of the émigrés. As a result of the latter measure, France became a land of small proprietors, and the once radical French peasant became a conservative.

Reaction against the Terror. In the autumn of 1793 the Reign of Terror reached its height. The Girondists who had been expelled from the National Convention were executed, and the guillotine also claimed the queen, Marie Antoinette. By controlling the all-powerful Committee of Public Safety, Robespierre was now the dominant force in the government.

By the spring of 1794 there was no longer any justification for continuance of the Terror. But to the fanatical Robespierre, a "republic of virtue" had to be achieved, in which there would be no excesses of wealth, where every citizen would serve the public good, and where justice and love would prevail. To attain this utopian Jacobin commonwealth, Robespierre believed that "the people's prejudices must be destroyed . . . its habits altered, its vices eradicated, and its desires purified."[10] While a bewildered Paris looked on, many courageous leaders of the Revolution who dared to disagree with his fanatical views were executed. Among them was Danton, who wished to end the policy of terror. Disgusted at the bloodshed, the members of the Convention finally arrested Robespierre and sent him to the guillotine.

Thousands of suspects were now freed, the Paris Commune was dissolved, and the extraordinary powers of the Committee of Public Safety were swept away. In Paris gangs of young men attacked Jacobins, and in the provinces there was a veritable "White Terror" against the radicals. The Jacobin Clubs were closed and the Catholic churches were reopened. Conservatism was now the order of the day. It was not that the people wanted to go back to the old days. They wanted to see the gains of the Revolution safeguarded and perpetuated, but they were tired of extremists and fanatics.

THE NAPOLEONIC PERIOD

The Directory. The National Convention now drafted a new republican system of government, the Directory, which was composed of two legislative chambers and a weak executive body of five members called directors. The right to vote was restricted to some twenty thousand property owners.

Assuming power in 1795, the Directory faced opposition from extremists on the right and on the left. The royalists were so bold as to foment an insurrection in Paris, which an obscure young general named Napoleon Bonaparte dispersed with a "whiff of grapeshot." In the spring of 1796 a radical working-class leader named "Gracchus" Babeuf plotted to seize the government and introduce a socialist economy. He ended as a guest of "Madame Guillotine"—and a martyr for modern Communists to honor—while the workers continued to suffer from inflation and unemployment.

Napoleon rises to power. Determined to smash the remnants of the First Coalition, the Directory commissioned three armies to invade Austrian territory. Two of these forces failed, but the one led by Napoleon Bonaparte crossed the Alps in 1796 and crushed the Sardinians and the Austrians. Following a less successful campaign in Egypt directed against the British, Napoleon returned in 1799 to a France again in a state of crisis. A newly formed Second Coalition threatened to invade the country, and inflation threatened the economy. Faced with financial ruin and invasion, the French turned to the one man they believed could save the day—Napoleon. Sensing the mood of the nation, Napoleon in 1799 swept the Directory from power and established a new government called the

NAPOLEONIC EUROPE

- France in 1789
- Acquisitions of Napoleon to 1810
- Dependent States of Napoleon
- Allies of Napoleon
- → Napoleon's Campaigns

Consulate—ostensibly a republic but with nearly all power centralized in the thirty-year-old First Consul, Napoleon. The new constitution was approved by the people in a plebiscite; the vote was 3,011,007 to 1,526.

After becoming First Consul, Napoleon quickly scattered the forces of the Second Coalition. The Austrians were compelled to sign the Treaty of Lunéville (1801), and although Great Britain was not defeated, France and England arranged a truce in 1802.

Napoleon's domestic reforms. The First Consul then turned his attention to domestic reforms. The system of local government was reorganized to provide a completely centralized governmental structure, making for efficiency at the expense of liberty. Graft and inequality in tax collection were ended, economies in public expenditures were effected, and most important, the Bank of France was established. The Catholic Church was now restored in France, but without its former power and wealth. Also, a well-organized system of public education was introduced.

Napoleon's most famous accomplishment was his codification of the numerous laws and decrees of the Revolution and some 360 local law codes. Completed in 1804, the great Civil Code was written with precision and clarity; it guaranteed many achievements of the French Revolution, such as religious toleration and the abolition of privilege. The Code Napoléon, as it was renamed in 1807, has exerted a marked influence upon the law of other countries, and Napoleon later claimed that he was prouder of it than of his forty battles.

Napoleon at the height of his power. When Napoleon declared himself emperor in 1804, a grateful and contented people overwhelmingly approved his action in another plebiscite. The First French Republic was now no more.

Just before Napoleon assumed the crown of emperor, war between Great Britain and France broke out once more. Napoleon welcomed war. During 1803 and 1804 he directed extensive preparations for an invasion of England, but the inability of Napoleon's naval forces to gain control of the approaches to England and the formation of the Third Coalition (composed of Great Britain, Russia, Austria, and Sweden) compelled him to march eastward against his Continental enemies in 1805. Meanwhile Napoleon's hopes of securing control of the seas and invading or at least starving out Britain were ended rudely in the smoke of Trafalgar (October 1805). In this decisive naval battle Lord Nelson defeated the combined French and Spanish fleets. Undaunted, Napoleon crushed the armies of Austria and Russia at Austerlitz, the most brilliant of his victories. In 1806 he occupied Berlin after the Prussians, still basking in the reflected glory of Frederick the Great, declared war.

By 1808 Napoleon ruled over a France which extended from the North Sea to the Pyrenees and included much of Italy. He had placed several of his relatives on the thrones of nearby countries. Prussia and Austria were impotent before French power, and Russia appeared to be only a Napoleonic satellite.

By 1808 it was apparent that British sea power was the all-important obstacle standing in the way of Napoleon's mastery of Europe. Safe behind warships, British factories turned out more and more war goods. British commerce and wealth increased, while French trade declined. Great Britain imposed a naval blockade against Napoleonic Europe. Seeking to crush Britain's economy by imposing a counterblockade, Napoleon prohibited the entry of British vessels into countries under his control, a policy known as the Continental System. Fundamentally, the war was now a struggle between the sea power and industrial superiority of Britain and French military power on the Continent.

Reaction against French imperialism. Ostensibly "liberators" of subject people in Europe, Napoleon's armies disseminated the French revolutionary ideals of "liberty, equality, fraternity." But as Napoleon became more and more imperialistic, the people he had "emancipated" realized that they had merely exchanged one despotism for another. In posing as the champion of the Revolution, Napoleon had sown the seeds of nationalism and liberty which were to prove his undoing.

The occupation of Portugal (1807) and Spain (1808), in order to shore up the Continental System, proved to be the first crack in the facade of Napoleon's Grand Empire. In both nations guerrilla warfare soon broke out, and a British expeditionary force joined the fighting against the French invaders.

Invasion and retreat in Russia. Napoleon made a major misstep when, after a quarrel with Alexander I of Russia, he launched an invasion of the tsar's realm in 1812. The campaign was a catastrophe. Although Napoleon's Grand Army fought its way to Moscow, the enemy forces remained intact, and the Russians' scorched-earth strategy prevented the invaders from living off the country. While the French occupied Moscow, fires broke out, destroying three fourths of the city. After spending thirty-three days in the empty shell of Moscow vainly waiting for the tsar to agree to a peace, Napoleon gave the order to retreat.

As the Grand Army marched west along the frozen Russian roads, it rapidly disintegrated. Guerrilla forces hovered about the retreating columns, continually pouncing on stragglers. In the bitterly cold weather, campfires were inadequate, shoes soon wore out, and thousands died in the snow. Out of the 611,000 men who had crossed the Russian frontiers in June, a tattered fragment of about 100,000 was able to make a wintry escape from Russia to Germany.

Downfall of Napoleon. Prussia and Austria now joined Russia in the "War of Liberation." English troops commanded by the Duke of Wellington, "The Iron Duke," cleared French armies out of Spain, and in 1813 at Leipzig the allies inflicted a disastrous defeat upon Napoleon in the Battle of the Nations. Napoleon, however, spurned a peace offer:

> What is it you wish of me? That I should dishonour myself? Never. I shall know how to die, but never to yield an inch of territory. Your sovereigns, who were born on the throne, may get beaten twenty times, and yet return to their capitals. I cannot. For I rose to power through the camp.[11]

After Leipzig the empire of Napoleon tumbled like a house of cards. In March 1814, allied forces entered Paris. Two weeks later the French emperor abdicated his throne, receiving in return sovereignty over Elba, a little island between Corsica and Italy. Nearly one year later, in February 1815, Napoleon eluded the British fleet, landed in France, and after a tumultuous welcome entered Paris and

A romanticized painting by the Scottish artist Orchardson shows the defeated emperor Napoleon brooding on the deck of the British ship, the H.M.S. Bellerophon, which carried him to his final exile.

raised another army. In haste, the allies dispatched the British and Prussian armies toward France.

At the Battle of Waterloo in Belgium (June 18, 1815), Napoleon was outgeneraled and defeated by Wellington and soon thereafter sought asylum with the British. He hoped to live in exile either in England or the United States, but the British, taking no more chances, shipped him off to the bleak mid-Atlantic island of St. Helena, five thousand miles from Paris. Here, in 1821, he died of cancer at the age of fifty-one.

Accomplishments of Napoleon. Napoleon's rise to power is one of the most remarkable stories in all history, and his significance in history cannot be dismissed with only a negative verdict. It is true that his wars killed perhaps as many as six million people, but his interference throughout Europe spread French revolutionary ideals and kindled nationalism. In Germany, in addition, he contributed toward ultimate unification by allowing the larger principalities to annex their smaller neighbors, thus reducing the number of German states from more than three hundred to thirty-nine. He also did away with the hoary old Holy Roman Empire.

Napoleon is especially important because he preserved and disseminated many of the results of the French Revolution. In France he firmly established and safeguarded the social and economic gains of the Revolution, most of which benefited the middle class. The same can be said of French-occupied Europe: "the sale of sequestrated properties, the sweeping away of old feudal enclaves and immunities, the opening of careers to men of talent, . . . the liberation of the internal market from restrictive tolls and guilds . . . all helped to promote the growth and raise the social status of the bourgeoisie."[12] Outside of France after 1815 the Old Regime was restored, but the seeds planted by Napoleon in his self-styled role as "the son of the Revolution" could not be uprooted. During the nineteenth century they would come to flower as the middle-class movement called liberalism.

DISCONTENT AND REVOLUTION IN LATIN AMERICA

Climate for revolution. The wars for independence in Spanish America during the first quarter of the nineteenth century were another manifestation of the cycle of revolutions initiated by the Glorious Revolution in Britain in 1688 and followed by the American Revolution in 1775 and the French Revolution in 1789. All these movements sprang from the same body of political ideals.

A good deal of discontent existed in eighteenth-century Spanish America. The Creoles (Spaniards born in the colonies) resented the haughty *peninsulares* (the Spaniards sent from the homeland) who monopolized all the highest governmental positions. The rising young Creole generation feasted on the ideas of Montesquieu, Voltaire, and Rousseau. Although such works were banned after 1790, they were smuggled into Spanish America in great numbers.

While government policy was reformist, it could not keep pace with the growth of liberal ideas, especially after the American and the French revolutions. The high degree of censorship and control infuriated the young intellectuals. There was, of course, no hint of the government giving people a greater voice in politics.

While not so rigid, mercantilism was still in force, the courts were often corrupt, and the *peninsulares* dominated the Creoles and *mestizos* (those of mixed Spanish and Indian blood).

Toward independence. Only a spark set off by the Napoleonic wars was needed to ignite the revolutionary flame in Spanish America. When the news reached the colonies that Napoleon had unceremoniously removed the Bourbons and placed his brother Joseph on the throne, deep resentment stirred in Spanish America. The colonial authorities proclaimed their loyalty to Ferdinand VII, the former king, who was now interned in France. In a number of colonies liberal Creoles in 1810 ousted local officials and took charge, all the while proclaiming their loyalty to the absent Ferdinand. This "legal" phase of the revolution took place in Venezuela, the Argentine, New Granada (modern Colombia), and Chile.

The legal phase of the revolutionary movement was of short duration. Radical leaders demanded independence and an end to the fiction of loyalty to Ferdinand. In 1811 the independence of Venezuela was proclaimed, but successful royalist counterattacks ended the republican regime, and by 1815 Simón Bolívar (1783-1830), leader of the rebels in Caracas, was in exile.

Other uprisings in Lima, La Paz, and Quito had been equally unsuccessful, while a premature bid for self-government in Mexico also met with disaster.

The Liberators in action: Bolivar and San Martin. In 1814, following the defeat of Napoleon, Ferdinand VII was released by the French and was welcomed deliriously in Spain. Although the king might have rallied his subjects in the colonies by generous concessions, he ignored this opportunity and reimposed the Old Regime with all its hateful aspects. Soon embittered, the colonial independence forces rose from defeat to gain a complete triumph. This was the achievement of the Liberators, Simón Bolívar and José de San Martín (1778-1850), aided by a group of devoted and efficient lieutenants.

Bolívar began his comeback early in 1817. With a small force he defeated the Spanish armies in northern South America. The most dramatic incident of his victorious campaign was the successful crossing of the formidable Andes. The Republic of Gran Colombia (made up of modern Colombia, Venezuela, and Ecuador) was established, and Bolívar was named the first president of this huge new state.

Further south, in the Argentine, San Martín prepared for a spectacular offensive against the royalist forces. In 1817 he led his army over the Andes in a desperate three weeks' march, surprising and defeating the Spanish forces in Chile. Aided by a former British officer, Lord Cochrane, who won naval supremacy in the waters off Peru, San Martín transported his troops to this viceroyalty in 1820. In 1821 he entered Lima, where he formally announced the independence of Peru. The two liberators met in 1822. At this meeting basic differences in policy and strategy developed. Thereupon, without any recriminations, San Martín withdrew from the scene and spent the remainder of his life abroad. After San Martín's withdrawal, Bolívar was left to dominate the scene. In 1824 his army delivered the knockout blow to Spanish power by winning a decisive victory at Ayacucho, situated on a high Peruvian plateau nearly twelve thousand feet above the sea. Here the last Spanish viceroy in the New World surrendered. By 1825 the revolution had run its successful course.

Independence won in Mexico and Brazil. Royalist elements in Mexico were deeply offended by the revolution of 1820 in Spain and the brief triumph of the liberal party (see p. 345). Therefore, in 1821, the conservatives supported Agustín

LATIN AMERICA 1826

European Colony

By 1826 European holdings in South America had all but disappeared as a wave of revolutions, following the precedent set in England, France, and the United States, broke the old colonial pattern.

de Iturbide (1783-1824), a military man of dubious reputation. Joining the rebel forces holding out in the mountains, he proclaimed the independence of Mexico. After plans to establish a monarchy in Mexico under a Spanish prince fell through, Iturbide proclaimed himself emperor. Guatemala also announced its independence, though for a time it seemed likely to fall under Iturbide's rule.

Independence also came to Brazil, where the members of the royal house of Braganza had arrived in 1808, in flight from Napoleon's armies. Fond of their new abode, the Braganzas remained in Rio de Janeiro after Portugal was freed of the French armies of occupation. Under the paternalistic hand of King John, industries grew, commerce flourished, and European traders and bankers helped the cause of colonial development.

In 1820 a revolution in Portugal put the liberal party in power. Unfortunately, the colonial policy of the new government was reactionary, and King John decided that his presence was needed in Lisbon. Before he left, he told his young son Pedro, who was acting as regent: "If Brazil demands independence, grant it, but put the crown upon your own head." Shortly after his father's departure, Pedro ripped the Portuguese colors off his uniform and shouted, "Independence or death!" The Brazilians defeated the Portuguese garrison troops with the help of a British naval force. In December 1822 Pedro was crowned emperor of Brazil, under a parliamentary system of government.

Both the North American and the Latin American revolutions enjoyed the leadership of remarkable men, and both were civil wars in which a part of the colonial population remained loyal to the mother country. But there were important differences. In Spain and Portugal only a small percentage of the people favored the colonies; in England a substantial portion of the population did. And in Spanish America fighting ranged over larger areas and was more bloodthirsty and cruel. While freedom brought political unity to the United States, in Spanish America it was the harbinger of internal turbulence and political fragmentation.

Much of the history of the nineteenth century is concerned with the struggle to extend the French Revolution's heritage of patriotic nationalism, representative government, and intellectual, religious, and economic freedom. The use of violence to achieve these goals was an ominous part of the Revolution's legacy for the future.

PART FIVE

EUROPE'S CENTURY

Great international conflicts often leave a legacy of tensions and problems. In 1815, following the defeat of Napoleon, the peacemakers at the Congress of Vienna sought to return to the traditional status quo. But the dislocations of many years of war had unleashed new historic forces, mainly nationalism and democracy, that demanded recognition. It took some fifty years of revolutions and wars before Europe settled down to some semblance of tranquility. Likewise since World War II, our contemporary world has been undergoing the throes of change often accompanied by violence. No one can foretell the outcome of this postwar period; whether 1945 ushered in an indefinite succession of tensions and upheavals, or whether we are approaching compromises and solutions that will insure a reasonable measure of stability and cooperation between nations and their peoples.

During the past two decades many observers have been bewildered by the shifts in great-power relations. Former antagonists of the United States, such as Japan and Germany, have become close allies and Russia, a war time colleague, developed into a disturbing rival. A study of nineteenth-century international relations is especially illuminating in this regard. During this period nearly every great European power was, on occasion, both an ally and also a foe of its neighbors. History demonstrates that no nation has permanent friends, only enduring interests. Witness the recent rapprochement between the United States and mainland China.

A study of the nineteenth century's internal affairs shows that the middle class enjoyed a monopoly of power and wealth. The appearance of Marxian socialism did little to improve the lot of the masses. This gospel of the proletariat was not to come into its own until the Russian revolution of 1917. In the latter decades of the nineteenth century, however, the workers' status improved by the efforts of unions, the growth of universal suffrage, and the spread of free education. At the same time Europe advanced economically by giant strides. In power, wealth, and intellectual activity it became the center of the world. This ascendancy was attributed to the remarkable advances of science and technology. It was widely believed there was no limit to the blessing which they would bring to mankind. In contrast the twentieth century has awakened to the perils of uncontrolled science, both as a weapon of war and industrially as a pollutant of cities, air, and streams.

Notwithstanding its numerous accomplishments, Europe in 1914 was plunged into catastrophic war. How did this disaster come about? The explanation lies both in the forces which made the century one of such bitter struggle and in those which made it a period of great promise. Nationalism eventually became narrower and more bellicose, and laissez-faire economics led to imperialistic rivalries. The rise to preeminence of science encouraged the translation of scientific Darwinism into social Darwinism, and this fallacious emphasis on the "survival of the fittest" led to racism, unbridled competition, and militant nationalism. Thus, despite a century of unprecedented scientific, technological, and social advances, the promise which they had offered was placed in mortal jeopardy by a military conflagration which spread beyond the confines of Europe itself to embroil peoples all over the world. And when the holocaust died down four years later, Europe had ceased to be the arbiter of mankind's destiny.

CHAPTER 15
ROMANTICS
AND REALISTS

Thought, Art, and Science: 1800-1914

Between 1750 and 1850 society was reshaped by several major historical forces. Among them was the romantic movement, which reached its height in the nineteenth century. An intellectual and esthetic reaction against eighteenth-century rationalism and classicism, romanticism permeated other fields in addition to literature and the arts. In particular, as we shall see, it interacted closely with the political movement of nationalism. These two forces shared a strong faith in the idea of progress, the perfectibility of man and his society. Even as the martial strains of the "Marseillaise" had carried the revolutionaries of France to triumph, so new "marching songs" in the form of poems, symphonies, and paintings accompanied the new era. European poets, composers, and painters of the romantic school sought new techniques of expression along with new subject matter, new harmonies, and new color patterns. Spurred on by their enthusiastic faith in man, the romanticists rebelled against both the intellectual standards of the previous century and all forms of political oppression and social injustice.

Buoyed by their firm conviction that "God's in his heaven—All's right with the world,"[1] the Victorians faced the second half of their century with optimism. After 1850, however, marked changes took place in the intellectual and social environment. The members of the prospering middle class still had little reason to doubt that theirs was the best of all possible worlds—but was God in His heaven? Between the latest findings of science and the traditional religious faith on which their beliefs and moral values rested, a great conflict had arisen. The mid-Victorians had been brought up to believe that the creation of the world and the forms of life thereon had been an act of God and that nature revealed the workings of His moral law. But when Darwin in 1859 put forward his famous thesis that species were continually evolving through a ceaseless struggle for existence among living things and that the survival or extinction of all species depended on their adaptability, nature was seen as simply a blind life-and-death struggle, stripped of all morality. This harsh and uncompromising doctrine set off a bitter debate between many advocates of science and those of religion.

This period was distinguished by unprecedented scientific advancement. In addition to the work of Darwin and his associates in biology, fundamental discoveries were made in physics, such as in thermodynamics and electrodynamics, in chemistry with the arrangement of the periodic table, and in medicine with the development of the germ theory of disease. A new model of celestial mechanics was provided by Einstein, while Freud delved into hitherto little-understood levels of human consciousness. On the other hand, there also developed a cult of science whose practitioners were too often guilty of intellectual arrogance and of a dangerous oversimplification of human affairs. With such people it became all too easy to think of social needs and human values solely in materialistic terms.

In literature, painting, and sculpture, the impact of scientific and technological achievements took the form of realism, later extended into a facts-of-life school known as naturalism. At the same time, an increasing number of writers protested against injustices perpetrated in a society where cutthroat competition was defended and human exploitation excused as immutable elements in the struggle to survive. Still other artists, reacting against the badly mechanistic view of man, devised new movements in the arts—expressionism and symbolism—each with special techniques for representing the subjective feelings of the individual.

THE TRIUMPH OF ROMANTICISM

Romanticism and classicism compared. The Age of Reason was supplanted in the nineteenth century by an intellectual and cultural environment dominated by certain new trends. Among them was a widespread faith in the idea of progress— the perfectibility of man and his society—and the artistic and intellectual movement known as romanticism.

In contrast to the rationalism of the eighteenth century, with its exaltation of self-restraint and artistic self-discipline, the romanticism of the early nineteenth century was characterized by strong elements of individualism, idealism, and revolt against all rules and accepted authority.

To the classicist, man is a rational, finite being—an integral member of a society which is governed in accordance with law and well-defined rules of conduct. Within this well-ordered social structure, man finds fulfillment, even as, in his intellectual and artistic expression, he emphasizes form and order and harmony. To the romanticist, on the other hand, man is a creature of feeling no less than of thought. He seeks ever after the infinite because he is not simply a cog in a finite human society but instead an irreplaceable part of nature and the whole creative process. The romanticist argues that society's laws and rules of conduct serve only to confine the natural soaring instincts of man. While the classicist insists upon the overruling claims of society, the romanticist supports the right of self-determination, whether of the individual or of any group of like-minded individuals—for example, a nation. Where the classicist's esthetic ideal is manifested in elegance, symmetry, and order, the romanticist is charmed by the "natural," the wild, and the unruly. The classicist finds beauty in logic and in acceptance of what exists; the romanticist makes it synonymous with feeling and with longing after the ultimate.

The preromantics: Rousseau and Goethe. Jean Jacques Rousseau, whose *Social Contract* (1762) has been termed the Bible of the French Revolution, was a romanticist who believed that the human heart is the infallible source of wisdom, that we should trust in our instincts, that man is capable of constant improvement, and that men find their truest happiness in nature. Rousseau helped popularize the cult of the "noble savage" and urged mankind to return to a more "natural" form of society by abandoning artificial conventions and institutions. He proved a most potent influence both on the political rebels of his own century and on the romanticists of the next.

The works of Johann Wolfgang von Goethe (1749-1832) constitute the finest example of the transition from eighteenth-century classicism to nineteenth-century romanticism. At Weimar, which he made the intellectual center of Germany, Goethe turned out lyric poems, novels, and plays. By far the greatest of his works is *Faust* (Part I published in 1808, Part II in 1832). Based on an old German legend, this verse drama relates the story of an aging scholar, Faust, who makes a pact with the devil, Mephistopheles. In return for twenty-four years of youth and pleasure, Faust gives his soul to the archfiend. In Goethe's adaption the legend becomes the vehicle for a magnificent philosophical discussion of the trials and triumphs of the human soul. Faust is saved—but only because he ultimately rejects self-gratification and accepts service to his fellow man. This theme is in harmony with the tenets of romanticism. Goethe demands, on the one hand, a full realization of the individual personality through a multitude of experiences—intellectual, sensual, and spiritual alike—even at the risk of losing salvation. On the other hand, he seeks an integration of the now-developed personality with the collective good of the nation or society to which the individual must dedicate his gifts.

Romanticism in literature. In the early nineteenth century romanticism assumed many different aspects—all of them products of a state of mind in rebellion against accepted values. One was a strong interest in the folkways, ballads, and romances of the Middle Ages. Several of Goethe's contemporaries in Germany reflected this concern, while in France, Victor Hugo (1802-1885) recreated the medieval past in romances such as *Notre Dame de Paris*. In Britain, meanwhile, Sir Walter Scott (1771-1832) had stirred the imagination of contemporaries by his collection of Scottish border ballads, his antiquarian studies and narrative poems about the formative years of the Scottish national state, and his famous adventure story of medieval chivalry, *Ivanhoe* (1819).

In 1798 two young English poets, William Wordsworth (1770-1850) and Samuel Taylor Coleridge (1772-1834), published a volume of verse called *Lyrical Ballads*. In its preface Wordsworth defined poetry as "the spontaneous overflow of powerful feelings recollected in tranquillity"—a concept at once romantic and very much at odds with the views of the previous century. Wordsworth believed that by contemplating nature in all its aspects, reality could be grasped intuitively—a view associated with the philosophy of transcendentalism, which was in turn taken up by Emerson and other New England intellectuals.

For his part, Coleridge stressed another facet of romanticism—delight in the supernatural and exotic. Especially vivid are the descriptions found in his *Rime of the Ancient Mariner* and *Kubla Khan*. Coleridge's interest in the nonrational and irrational elements in human experience would be shared later by Freud and other psychologists; these elements are often described in literature in terms of fantasy, symbolism, dream states, and the supernatural.

The romantic poet rebelled against the constraints of his society. Thus the handsome, impulsive George Gordon, Lord Byron (1788-1824), gloried in the cult of freedom, and when the Greeks rose against the Turks in 1821 (see p. 345), he joined the cause of independence and died of fever in Greece. His friend Percy Bysshe Shelley (1792-1822) believed passionately that human perfectibility was possible only through complete freedom of thought and action.

Unlike Shelley and Byron, John Keats (1795-1821) was not a social critic or rebel. Of prime importance to him was the worship of beauty—it was the motive and message of his poetry. Thus, in the concluding lines of *Ode on a Grecian Urn* (1820), he tells us that: "Beauty is truth, truth beauty—that is all/Ye know on earth, and all ye need to know." Thus Keats exemplifies an important aspect of the romantic movement—estheticism, or the acceptance of artistic beauty and taste as a fundamental standard, superior to ethical and other standards.

Romantic nationalism in literature. In glorifying the uniqueness of the individual and his rights, romanticism exhibited a close affinity with another powerful emotional force of this period—nationalism. With its emphasis upon the uniqueness of particular groups, nationalism was a potent historical catalyst among the peoples of nineteenth-century Europe. During this period feelings of nationalism came more and more to imply the willingness of an individual to live and die for his country. His loyalty to the state transcended all other loyalties. Unhappily, too, extreme nationalism implied that a state could do no wrong and that self-interest was the only test for its behavior. Here again we see the close affinity between romanticism and nationalism—the former advocating unrestricted self-expression for an individual, and the latter demanding unrestricted self-determination for a group.

The excesses of the French Revolution and Napoleon's perversion of its principles alienated many of the romanticists. But the pendulum swung back again as a result of the system of political reaction set up in 1815 by the Congress of Vienna (see Chapter 17). Some of the notable romanticists again became the champions of nationalism and revolution. In France, the leading figure was Victor Hugo, who expressed hostility toward tyranny at home and abroad, espoused the aspirations of the common man, and was a staunch supporter of the struggle for Greek independence. In Russia, where nationalism had been greatly stimulated by the people's heroic resistance to the Napoleonic invasion in 1812, still other romantic rebels were attracting the sympathetic response of the reading public (and also the hostile attention of the tsar's secret police). The greatest of the Russian romanticist poets was Alexander Pushkin, whose unrestrained personal life and literary lyricism justify his being called the "Byron of Russia." His subject matter was largely derived from Russian tales and folklore, and his dramas and his verse novel *Eugene Onegin* (1831) had a strong nationalistic appeal. Like Byron, Pushkin denounced tyranny and the reactionary movement which had set in after the Napoleonic Wars.

Revolt against classical painting. The romanticist painters rebelled against classical models and the emphasis upon precise draftsmanship because they felt that color was more important than drawing and that subject matter should give unhampered scope to the imagination and emotions. Old legends and exotic and picturesque scenes, such as were to be found in North Africa and the Near East, became popular. One of the first major rebels was Eugene Delacroix, a French artist whose flamboyant canvases convey the heightened emotional approach of the romanticists.

The effects of the cult of nature were no less marked on romantic painting than on poetry. Artists were inspired to look at nature with a fresh appreciation. The English painter John Constable (1776-1837) was in some respects the creator of the modern school of landscape painting. Another English painter whose originality created a profound stir was J. M. W. Turner (1775-1851). Gifted with a vivid sense of color and a powerful imagination, Turner was particularly adept in creating atmospheric effects (see "Dutch Fishing Boats" below).

The Gothic revival in architecture.   Until about 1830 architecture in Europe and America was based largely on classical models (see p. 256). But after 1830 occurred the great period of the Gothic revival, in which towers and pointed arches became the chief characteristics of architectural design. The revival was stimulated in England by the romances of Sir Walter Scott, whose own residence at Abbotsford was designed along Scottish baronial lines; while in France the

Landscape painting acted as a pivotal point of inspiration in nineteenth-century art. Romantic painters, such as J. M. W. Turner, used the form not only as a point of departure from the somber classicism of the eighteenth century but as a means of expressing the vitality of nature. In "Dutch Fishing Boats," by means of bold brushwork and a brilliant treatment of light (later adopted by the Impressionists), Turner couples man and nature in a swirling canvas, a reflection of the heightened emotionalism and idealism of his day.

movement gained impetus from the publication of Victor Hugo's melodramatic novel of fifteenth-century life, *Notre Dame de Paris*.

Romanticism in music. The nineteenth century brought radical changes in music; the regularity of the minuet, the precision of the sonata, and the limitations of the small chamber orchestra were not adequate to express the powerful forces of romanticism.

The genius who broke the classical mold and revitalized music was the German composer Ludwig van Beethoven (1770-1827), a titan who acted as a bridge between classicism and romanticism. A lover of nature and a passionate champion of freedom and the rights of man, Beethoven unleashed emotional forces never before heard in music. While retaining the classicist's sense of proportion in the structure of his works, he added flexibility to music forms by developing new harmonies and enlarged the scope of the orchestra to handle them. In short, Beethoven succeeded in freeing music from arid formalism.

The momentum of the forces which Beethoven set in motion carried through the entire century. Johannes Brahms (1833-1897) is generally regarded as the greatest symphonic composer of the second half of the century, but the age is studded with names of great composers—Chopin, Schubert, Liszt, Franck, and Tschaikovsky, to name only a few. This was an age marked by an outpouring of romantic symphonies, symphonic overtures, and concertos, all of which exploited the new and varied effects made possible by an orchestra which had been greatly expanded.

As a result of significant changes in political and economic conditions, music was now supported chiefly by the middle classes and maintained by their thriving commercial prosperity.

THE RISING TIDE OF SCIENCE

The theory of evolution. The nineteenth century witnessed the spread of a doctrine which was to have powerful repercussions on science, philosophy, and religion. This was the theory of evolution—namely, that all complex organisms have developed from simple forms through the operation of natural causes and that no species is fixed and changeless. The scientist chiefly responsible for furthering the evolutionary hypothesis was Charles Darwin (1809-1882). After studying medicine and preparing at Cambridge University for the ministry, Darwin became a naturalist. From 1831 to 1836 he studied the specimens he had collected while on a surveying expedition with the ship *Beagle*, which had sailed along the coast of South America and among the Galápagos Islands. In 1859 Darwin's views appeared under the title *The Origin of Species by Means of Natural Selection, or the Preservation of Favored Races in the Struggle for Life*. In this work he contended:

> . . . that species have been modified, during a long course of descent . . . chiefly through the natural selection of numerous successive, slight, favourable variations; aided in an important manner . . . by the direct action of external conditions, and by variations which seem to us in our ignorance to arise spontaneously.[2]

The Origin of Species was to prove one of the most significant books in scientific literature, revolutionizing concepts about the origin and evolution of life on the planet. Furthermore, this pioneer work brought into the open the mounting differences between science and theology over the Biblical account of creation.

Darwin's next bombshell was *Descent of Man and Selection in Relation to Sex*, published in 1871. In this work Darwin applied the principle of natural selection to human beings and reached the explosively controversial conclusion that man's ancestors were probably monkey-like animals related to the progenitors of the orangutan, chimpanzee, and gorilla.

There are five main points in the Darwinian hypothesis. First, all existing vegetable and animal species are descended from earlier and, generally speaking, more rudimentary forms. Second, species evolve through the inheritance of minute differences in individual structures due to the direct effect of the environment. Third, in the struggle for survival, the fittest win out at the expense of their rivals. Fourth, a species may also be altered by the cumulative workings of sexual selection, which Darwin declared is "the most powerful means of changing the races of man." Finally, some variations seem to arise spontaneously, a view of Darwin's which pointed toward the doctrine of mutation.

Biology after Darwin. By the close of the nineteenth century scientists were in virtual agreement regarding the general validity of Darwin's hypothesis, though, as we shall see, it was later modified in certain important respects. Meanwhile, largely as a result of Darwin's unifying principle of evolution, biology was progressively transformed from a descriptive science into a search for genetic relationships between living organisms.

One of the most significant developments in biology concerned the question of heredity. In the 1870's the German biologist August Weismann, basing his investigation on an earlier theory that all living things originate and develop in very small structural units, or cells, distinguished two types of cells. One type—the somatic cell—dies with the individual, while the other—the germ cell—transmits through reproduction a continuous stream of protoplasm from one generation to the next. Later, Weismann produced experimental evidence that germ cells, which transmit hereditary characteristics, are not affected by changes in the somatic cells—in other words, that acquired characteristics cannot be inherited.

An Austrian monk, Gregor Mendel (1822-1884), formulated definite laws of heredity on the basis of experiments with the crossing of garden peas. Because he published his important findings in an obscure scientific journal, his work was overlooked until about 1900. Mendel's laws not only proved a valuable help in the scientific breeding of plants and animals but also demonstrated that the evolution of different species was more complex than had been deduced by Darwin.

From the work of Mendel and Weismann, biologists began to conclude that the nuclei of the germ cells possess chromosomes which carry the characteristics of an organism. Further research substantiated the mutation theory, which states that sudden and unpredictable changes within the chromosomes can be transmitted by heredity to produce new species.

Modern medicine emerges. Probably the most important single advance in medicine during the latter part of the nineteenth century was the substantiation of the germ theory of disease. The validation of this theory by Louis Pasteur and his younger disciple, the German bacteriologist Robert Koch, came as a result of a search for a cure for anthrax, a fatal disease which in the late 1870's was destroying over 20 percent of the sheep in France. Pasteur and Koch discovered that anthrax bacteria could be grown in a culture of meat-broth jelly and that the injection of the bacteria into a healthy animal produced anthrax. In 1881 Pasteur inoculated twenty-five sheep with weakened anthrax bacteria and left the same number unvaccinated. Later, all fifty were given a virulent form of the disease; the unvaccinated animals died while the treated sheep remained sound. With the establishment of the principle that the injection of a mild form of disease bacteria will cause the formation of antibodies which will prevent the inoculated person from getting the virulent form of the disease, the end of such scourges as typhoid and smallpox was in sight.

In 1885 Pasteur showed that by the injection of a vaccine an animal could be made resistant to rabies *after* having been bitten by a mad dog. For his part, the brilliant Koch discovered the organisms that caused eleven diseases, including tuberculosis and cholera. As a result of the work of Pasteur and Koch, the twin sciences of bacteriology and immunology were established on a firm footing.

Chemistry and related fields. Meanwhile modern chemistry had been securely founded on the atomic theory advanced by an English Quaker schoolmaster, John Dalton (1766-1844). This pioneer believed that all matter is made up of invisible particles, or atoms, which remain unchanged upon entering or leaving any chemical combination. Moreover, the basic substances or elements which are to be found in the world of matter differed by virtue of the size and weight of the atoms composing them.

It now became possible to arrange chemical elements according to their atomic weights, beginning with the lightest, hydrogen. It was seen that the elements fell into groups of eight which possess similar properties. In 1869 the Russian chemist Dmitri Mendeléeff (1834-1907) drew up his periodic table, in which all the known elements were classified according to their weights and properties. From gaps in this table, chemists were able to deduce the existence of still other undiscovered elements.

Revolution in physics. Until the nineteenth century scientists had believed previously that heat was a mysterious fluid called "calorie," but research showed that friction generated heat in proportion to the amount of energy expended. After physicists had found out how much mechanical energy was required to raise the heat of any given body, it became possible, in 1847, to formulate the first law of thermodynamics. This law states that the sum total of energy in the universe is constant—it cannot be either created or destroyed but can only be transformed from one form to another. Meanwhile scientists engaging in the converse problem of transforming heat into energy found that heat can in fact never be completely converted into energy. From their experiments emerged the second law of thermodynamics: although the total amount of energy in the universe remains constant, the amount actually available is always diminishing through its transformation into nonavailable, or dissipated, heat.

Nineteenth-century scientists prepared the way for the use of electricity as a source of power. The most prominent figure in the field of electrodynamics during the earlier part of the century was Michael Faraday (1791-1867). In 1831 Faraday produced an electric current by rotating a copper disk between the two poles of a horseshoe magnet, thereby inventing the first electric dynamo. This simple dynamo made possible the development of the electric motor, the transmission of large currents over long distances, and (later in the century) the invention of the electric telegraph, the telephone, and electric lights.

Electromagnetism and radiation. In his famous work *A Treatise on Electricity and Magnetism* (1873), the Scottish scientist James Clerk-Maxwell advanced the theory that "electricity is matter moving in waves like those of light and radiant heat," thereby linking optics and electricity; and he maintained that light, radiant heat, and invisible ultraviolet radiation are all electromagnetic phenomena.

Working with the electromagnetic theory of light, a German physicist named Heinrich Hertz was able to demonstrate in 1886 the existence of electromagnetic waves—as predicted by Clerk-Maxwell—and to measure their velocity. It was these "hertzian waves" (later known as radio waves) which provided the theoretical basis for Marconi's subsequent invention of wireless telegraphy. In addition, Hertz' studies of the optical properties of these waves led to his discovery of photoelectricity, which was fundamental for the development of television.

Toward the end of the century two new events occurred in the field of electrical research that were to have equally far-reaching repercussions. In 1895 a ray which could penetrate a nontranslucent mass was discovered, and, because the nature of this strange phenomenon was not at first understood, the term *x-ray* came into use. Shortly thereafter, it was learned that uranium gives off similar rays. Then in 1898 the French scientist Pierre Curie and his Polish wife Marie extracted radium from pitchblende, an ore of uranium, and the world began to be conscious of the potency of radioactivity. Radiation was soon utilized in medicine.

Studies of the scattering of x-rays led to the conclusion that electricity is composed of particles which are constituent parts of atoms. This deduction led to the electron theory—namely, that the atom contains negatively charged particles known as electrons. The next major step in understanding the structure of the atom was made in 1911 by the British physicist Ernest Rutherford, who advanced the theory that each atom has a central particle, or nucleus, which is positively charged. Later, scientists determined that the atom is like a miniature solar system; most of the weight is concentrated in the central, positively charged nucleus, around which the negatively charged electrons revolve. These discoveries smashed one of the foundation stones of traditional physics—the belief that the atom was indivisible and solid. The way was now clear to demonstrate conclusively that the universe is composed not of matter in the traditional sense but of atomic energy.

Quantum and relativity theories. Traditional physics received another jolt from the research of the German physicist Max Planck (1858-1947). Planck had been studying radiant heat, which comes from the sun and is identical in its nature with light. He found that the energy emitted from a vibrating electron proceeds not in a steady wave—as traditionally believed—but discontinuously in the form of calculable "energy packages." To such a package Planck gave the name *quantum*—hence the term *quantum theory*.

Planck's quantum theory, which was to prove invaluable in the rapidly growing study of atomic physics, found support in the studies of Albert Einstein (1879-1955). In 1905 Einstein contended that light is propagated through space in the form of particles which he termed *photons*. Moreover, the energy contained in any particle of matter, such as the photon, is equal to the mass of that body multiplied by the square of the velocity of light, which is a constant figure. The resulting equation—$E = mc^2$—provided the answer to many long-standing mysteries of physics—for example, how radioactive substances like radium and uranium are able to eject particles at enormous velocities and to go on doing so for millions of years. The magnitude of the energy that slumbers in the nuclei of atoms could be revealed. Above all, $E=mc^2$ shows that mass and energy are convertible.

In 1905 Einstein also revealed his epoch-making Special Theory of Relativity, which called for a radically new approach to explain the concepts of time, space, and velocity. For example, he maintained that time and distance are interrelated, that the mass of a body increases with its velocity, and that, as mentioned previously, mass and energy are convertible, i.e., $E=mc^2$.

In 1915 Einstein produced his second installment, or the General Theory, in which he incorporated gravitation into relativity. He showed that gravitation was identical to acceleration and that light rays would be deflected in passing through a gravitational field—a prediction confirmed by observation of an eclipse in 1919. The theory of relativity has been subsequently confirmed in other ways as well; thus the interconversion of mass and energy was dramatically demonstrated in the atomic bomb, which obtains its energy by the annihilation of part of the matter of which it is composed.

The universe as conceived by Einstein is not Newton's three-dimensional figure of length, breadth, and thickness but a four-dimensional space-time continuum in which time itself varies with velocity. Such a cosmic model calls for the use of non-Euclidean geometry. Einstein's theory has reoriented our attitude toward the structure and mechanics of the universe, and its relativistic implications have permeated not only this century's scientific theories but our philosophical, moral, and even esthetic concepts as well. Moreover, Einstein's contribution aptly illustrates one of the yardsticks sometimes employed to measure "progress." According to this yardstick, progress occurs when our knowledge and understanding of the phenomenal world are enlarged. Thus Einstein's theory of gravitation covers all the explanations provided by Newton's theory of gravitation and also "fits the facts" in a still wider field where the other fails.

Freud and psychoanalysis. Probably the most famous name associated with psychology is that of the Austrian Sigmund Freud (1856-1939). Placing far greater stress than any predecessor on the element of the unconscious, Freud pioneered in psychoanalysis. This form of psychotherapy is based on the theory that mental symptoms express forbidden desires which are not consciously acknowledged. Freud treated emotional disturbances by bringing deeply repressed, "pathogenic" motives and memories to the surface with the help of dream interpretation and free association. He believed that the source of all adult adjustments and maladjustments is the Oedipus complex, whereby a child is sexually drawn to the parent of the opposite sex and jealous of the other parent. In revealing the hertofore unappreciated intricacies of the human mind, Freud had a far-reaching influence upon the understanding of human behavior. He made current a whole new vocabulary, employing such terms as *libido, id, ego, inhibition, fixation, defense mechanism,* and *repressed desire.* The twentieth-century outlook on man, expressed in such fields as literature and art, owes much to the influence of Freud.

THE CULT OF SCIENCE

Science versus faith. With its spectacular successes in both pure research and technological application, science gripped the popular imagination of the pre-1914 generation to an extent never before equaled. Science was elevated to a cult by means of which all human problems were to be solved. Many men and women became skeptical and uneasy about whatever could not be proved in the laboratory.

It can be readily seen that a conflict was certain to ensue between the traditional doctrines of religion and the new scientific tenets, especially those of Darwinism. Thomas Huxley, a strong popularizer of Darwin's theories, contended that for the advocate of science "skepticism is the highest of duties; blind faith the unpardonable sin."[3] Certainly, established religion was thrown on the defensive, and many of the most sensitive minds of the period suffered anguish and even despair in their attempts to reconcile their religious beliefs with the new scientific tenets.

As time went on, however, more than one thinker came to believe that the evolutionary theory supplemented rather than contradicted the basic tenets of faith. As they saw the bounds of the universe pushed back by science, they perceived growth and development in the constant changes and felt that God was revealing Himself to man through the evolutionary process. Interestingly enough, Darwin himself had expressed a similar view in the conclusion of his *The Origin of Species:*

> When I view all beings not as special creations, but as the lineal descendants of some few beings which lived long before the first bed of the Cambrian system was deposited, they seem to me to become ennobled. . . . There is grandeur in this view of life, with its several powers, having been originally breathed by the Creator into a few forms or into one; and that, whilst this planet has gone cycling on according to the fixed law of gravity, from so simple a beginning endless forms most beautiful and most wonderful have been, and are being evolved.[4]

The science of man.   The apostles of science were also anxious to place human institutions on a scientific foundation. Such was the intention of the noted French student of society, Auguste Comte (1798-1857). Comte held that the history of mankind had passed through three stages of evolution. The first two of these, the theological and the metaphysical, had outlived their usefulness. Now the time had arrived to embark upon what he called the positive stage, in which scientific standards of observation and judgment would dominate. At the apex of all the social sciences, Comte placed the study of man in society, a new science to which he gave the term *sociology.*

Social Darwinism.   One American thinker at the close of the nineteenth century wrote:

> The life of man in society, just like the life of other species, is a struggle for existence. . . . The progress which has been and is being made in human institutions and in human character may be set down, broadly, to a natural selection of the fittest habits of thought and to a process of enforced adaptation of individuals to an environment which has progressively changed with the growth of the community and with the changing institutions under which men have lived.[5]

Here we see clearly how the concept of the survival of the fittest was used to explain not only the development but the progress of both human institutions and human character. Although Darwin himself had confined the principle of natural selection to the sphere of biology, others eagerly applied it to the field of human affairs. This application of Darwin's principles to man and his efforts was called "social Darwinism"; it became a vogue that swept western thought in the late nineteenth century. It also became a convenient doctrine for justifying various economic and political theories.

Herbert Spencer (1820-1903), an English philosopher from whom Darwin borrowed the phrase "survival of the fittest," was one of those who regarded society as a living organism. Spencer opposed any interference by the state with the natural development of society. The sole function of the state, in his view, was negative—namely, to ensure freedom of the individual, who if left alone through enough generations would become perfect. Spencer used this doctrine to advocate unfettered business competition and to oppose all state aid to the poor, whom he regarded as unable to compete successfully in the struggle for survival and consequently better eliminated. At the same time, he favored private charity to develop altruistic traits in the donors.

The "justification" of racism and war. The pseudoscientific application of a biological theory to politics, whereby a nation is regarded as an organism, constituted possibly the most perverted form of social Darwinism in the period under review. It led to racism and anti-Semitism (see p. 374) and was used to show that only "superior" nationalities and races were fit to survive. One was Comte Joseph Arthur de Gobineau (1816-1882), who argued that the different races are innately unequal in ability and worth and that the genius of a race depends upon hereditary and not environmental factors. The white peoples were alone capable of cultural creativity, which in turn could be destroyed by racial intermixture.

Social Darwinism was also employed to justify the use of military power to ensure that the "fittest" state would survive. Most influential as an advocate of war was the German philosopher Friedrich Nietzsche (1844-1900). His ideal, the superman, was characterized by bravery, strength, egoism, arrogance, and ruthlessness. Nietzsche challenged the world with: "You say, 'A good cause sanctifies even war,' but I say, 'A good war sanctifies every cause'!" Nietzsche viewed Christianity with contempt because he regarded gentleness as weakness and humanitarianism as protection of the unfit and spineless. Likewise, he ridiculed democracy and socialism for protecting the worthless and weak and hindering the strong.

Developments in philosophy: pragmatism and vitalism. Philosophy had been profoundly influenced by the implications of Darwin's work. Stressing the roles of change and chance in nature, the Darwinian theory strengthened the trend away from absolute standards.

Among American philosophers arose a school known as pragmatism. Led by the noted psychologist William James (1842-1910), the pragmatists argued that men think for the practical purpose of getting on with the job of living; and since the validity of any idea lies not in its approximation to some ultimate truth but in its ability to effect desired action, it must be tested by its logical or empirical results. As James put it, "An idea is 'true' so long as to believe it is profitable to our lives." Pragmatism, in effect, rejected any concept of truth or reality as absolute. Although it has been credited with bringing formal philosophy out of the clouds and relating it more concretely to the major scientific and intellectual trends of the day, the pragmatic approach resulted in a strongly utilitarian bent on the part of some of its adherents, with whom truth became indistinguishable from success.

Influenced by contemporary scientific currents in both biology and physics but differing widely from pragmatism was the philosophy of Henri Bergson (1859-1941). Bergson attributed evolution to a spontaneous creative force which he called the vital impulse (*élan vital*). Nothing is fixed; everything in life changes ceaselessly. The intellect is incapable of grasping the true nature of reality, which flows like an uninterrupted stream, and instead cuts reality up into discontinuous parts in much the same way that a movie film divides a single action into separate pictures. Bergson believed, however, that man has another faculty, intuition, which is capable of grasping life in terms of wholes. This, he maintained, is the ability employed by artists.

Bergson's philosophy of vitalism, which made its greatest impact in the years preceding World War I, represented a revolt against scientific determinism. While making use of the Darwinian thesis of change, it conceived evolution to be creative and not a blind struggle for survival. With its insistence that mental processes could not be reduced to simple mechanistic terms, this vitalistic philosophy was to influence many intellectuals of the time.

FROM REALISM TO EXPRESSIONISM

The realistic novelists. By 1870 writers were not only responding in various ways to the growing cult of science and to the impact of philosophical rationalism; they were also in revolt against the now-spent romanticism that survived in the form of sentimentalism. A down-to-earth attitude had become the order of the day. The nineteenth-century realists did not hesitate to describe in graphic detail social and personal problems which had hitherto gone unmentioned because they were not "nice." Their creed was to chronicle without comment, to photograph without touching up.

This new trend in literature had already been foreshadowed in the works of Charles Dickens (1812-1870). He painted in vivid colors the everyday life of the middle classes and the poor—and especially the struggle of the individual against the worst excesses of industrial expansion and social injustice. In *Oliver Twist, Dombey and Son, Hard Times, Bleak House,* and *David Copperfield,* to name but a few of his major works, Dickens blended romantic and realistic elements by combining a fundamental optimism and belief in progress with trenchant attacks upon existing slum conditions, the miseries of the poor, and the inhuman debtors' prisons.

Another pioneer in realistic writing was the French novelist Honoré de Balzac (1799-1850), the author of *La Comédie Humaine* or "The Human Comedy," a panorama of ninety volumes concerning French city and country life in the first half of the nineteenth century. In his novels the crudities and avarice of the French petty bourgeoisie were depicted in detail. The first thoroughgoing French realist was Gustave Flaubert (1821-1880). His masterpiece, *Madame Bovary* (1856), describes how the boredom of a romantic-minded young provincial wife led her into adultery, extravagance, and ultimately suicide. By implication Flaubert was pointing to the pitfalls of romanticism as a way of life.

Realism served as the keynote for the most important novelists of the late nineteenth century. Count Leo Tolstoy's epic novel *War and Peace* (1869), a magnificent tapestry of life in Russia during the Napoleonic invasion of 1812, stripped every shred of glory or glamour from that conflict. His *Anna Karenina* (1877) relentlessly detailed the story of two lovers who openly defy social conventions. Another great Russian novelist, Feodor Dostoevski, traced the causes and effects of murder in two masterpieces of suspense and psychological analysis, *Crime and Punishment* (1866) and *The Brothers Karamazov* (1880).

In the hands of some writers realism developed into an extreme form of presentation known as naturalism. The naturalists wished to apply scientific objectivity to their subject matter and to deal with their characters as with animals in a laboratory, whose every move was determined by environment or heredity. The most outstanding practitioner of this literary doctrine was Émile Zola, who made a case study twenty volumes long of a middle-class family. In this series of

Rodin's statue of Balzac gives a powerful impression of the French author. Using techniques that he gleaned from Michelangelo's vibrant figures emerging from rough blocks of stone, Rodin has been described as the most influential sculptor of the late nineteenth century.

works, which included *Nana* (1880) and *Germinal* (1885), Zola employed a clinical approach, amassing huge notebooks of information on such subjects as the stock market and the mining districts before describing these settings.

The problem play: Ibsen and Shaw. The exposure of social problems was an important aspect of the new literary realism. The problems facing *fin de siècle* (end of the century) society were more subtle in character than the obvious injustices of child labor and cholera-infested slums, which had monopolized the attention of social critics earlier in the century. Thus, perhaps, was provided the impetus for the development of a new, sophisticated form of drama called the "problem play."

The dramas of the Norwegian Henrik Ibsen were the first of the problem plays. One of his best known works is *A Doll's House* (1879), in which he assailed marriage without love as being immoral. In other plays he attacked social greed masked by conventional respectability and delineated with great sensitivity the human dramas latent in the strains and stresses of ordinary life. A disciple of Ibsen and, like the Norwegian, an ardent assailant of bourgeois complacency, was the brilliant Irish playwright George Bernard Shaw. In a series of shrewdly satirical and highly diverting stage successes, he cajoled, bullied, and shocked the English-speaking public into reassessing their conventional attitudes on a variety of social subjects, ranging from private and public morality to militarism and religious beliefs.

All the writers of this period were not proponents of the realistic school. Some, like Oscar Wilde in England, made a cult of their revulsion against the crudities and vulgarity of a realism-ridden age. To them, the only valid standard was "art for art's sake." Still other writers sought new standards and modes of expression. A group of poets known as the symbolists, found for the most part in France during the last two decades of the nineteenth century, made use of images, archaic and mystical terms, and other devices in order to convey the inner feelings of an individual or group.

Realism in painting. The major trends in literature between 1870 and 1914 were paralleled by developments in painting in the same era. Already, by the 1850's various artists in France had been rebelling against traditional subject matter and techniques. Feeling that the canvases exhibited on academy walls were for the most part too "respectable" and hence artificial, they chose instead to paint life as they saw it.

Gustave Courbet, probably the outstanding French realist, expressed his contempt for religious and Neoclassical themes when he mocked: "Show me an angel and I will paint one." When he looked at nature, he consciously dropped the affectations of both the romanticists and Neoclassicists and painted uncompromising, often brutal canvases. Courbet's view that "realism is an essentially democratic art" was shared by his compatriot Honoré Daumier, who knew Parisian life intimately. His lithographs were biting satires of life among the bourgeoisie, in the courts of law, and in political circles.

Impressionism in France. Preoccupied with problems of color, light, and atmosphere, the Impressionists sought to catch the first impression made by a scene or object upon the eye, undistorted by the intellect or any subjective attitude.

An outstanding Impressionist was Pierre Auguste Renoir, who skillfully employed color to capture flesh tones and texture. Renoir painted all sorts of subjects, among them the opera, landscapes, and houseboats on the Seine. His canvases all reveal his rich sense of color; the sunlight plays across his paintings, giving the sense of a passing moment held in paint (see the "Canoeists' Luncheon" below).

To France must go credit for the development not only of this new style of painting but of related techniques in other arts as well. The outstanding sculptor of the late nineteenth century, Auguste Rodin, has been described as the father of modern sculpture. He infused his work with a realistic honesty and vitality that made him the object of stormy controversy during much of his lifetime. Sharing with the Impressionist painters a dislike for studied finality in art, Rodin preferred to let the imagination of the beholder play on his sculpture. Rodin's technique of rough finish shows to advantage in his bronze works. By this technique the sculptor achieved two effects: a glittering surface of light and shadow and a feeling of immediacy and incompleteness that emphasized the spontaneous character of the work.

Post-Impressionism. Paul Cézanne (1839-1906) sought in his painting to simplify all natural objects by emphasizing their essential geometric structure. As Cézanne said, everything in nature corresponds to the shape of the cone, the cylinder, or the sphere. Proceeding on the basis of this theory, he was able to get

Auguste Renoir, the French Impressionist, used vibrant color and scintillating light to achieve delightful visual effects. Many of his paintings, such as "Canoeists' Luncheon," portray the pastimes of the lower and middle classes in informal outdoor scenes.

below the surface and give his objects the solidity which had eluded the Impressionists. Yet, like the latter, he made striking use of color—in his case, to establish the relationships of his objects in space. The successful pioneering work of Cézanne was to have important consequences.

One or two other late nineteenth-century painters were also successful, by reason of their individualism, in contributing to the rise of Post-Impressionism. One was Vincent van Gogh (1853-1890), a Dutch painter whose short life of poverty and loneliness was climaxed by insanity and suicide. In many of his paintings he employed short strokes of heavy pigment which accentuated forms and rhythms. Van Gogh was concerned not with presenting simply a photographic representation of what lay before him but wanted to convey also the intense feelings evoked in himself by his subject. As a consequence, he was ready to distort what he saw in order to depict these sensations, even as Cézanne had abandoned perspective where necessary so as to concentrate on form and spatial relationships.

Expressionism and Cubism.   Continuing to experiment, artists became increasingly concerned with painting what they felt about an object rather than the object itself. The Expressionist school was intent on conveying subjective feelings. Among the early Expressionist—or *les fauves* (the wild beasts), as they were derided by their critics—was Henri Matisse, who had learned to simplify form partly from African primitive art and had studied the color schemes of oriental carpets. His decorative style was to influence design strongly in our own day.

Experimentation took still other subjective forms. We have already noted that in order to achieve a sense of depth and solidity, Cézanne used geometric shapes and depth relationships on the two-dimensional painting surface. Further developments along these lines resulted in the emergence of a new school—Cubism. Cubists would choose an object, then construct an abstract pattern from it. In doing so, they went far beyond the traditional manner of reproducing the object from one vantage point; instead, they viewed it from several points of view simultaneously. In a Cubist canvas one might see a given object—say a violin— from above, below, outside, and inside, with all the dissected elements interpenetrating. Such a pattern is also evident in "Three Musicians" by the Spanish artist Pablo Picasso, probably the most influential single figure in twentieth-century painting.

Architecture reflects the machine age.   Aided by advances in industry and technology, architects were now able to design structures that could span greater distances and enclose greater areas than had hitherto been possible. Whereas high buildings had formerly required immensely thick masonry walls, a metal frame now allowed the weight of the structure to be distributed on an entirely different principle and permitted a far more extensive use of glass than ever before. Outstanding among the pioneers in this new architecture was Chicago's Louis Sullivan (1856-1924). Like others, Sullivan perceived the value of the skyscraper in providing a large amount of useful space on a small plot of expensive land, such as that in Chicago's Loop or in Manhattan. Unlike others, he rejected all attempts to disguise the skeleton of the skyscraper behind some false facade and boldly proclaimed it by a clean sweep of line. Sullivan's emphasis upon the functional was to have far-reaching influence.

One of Sullivan's pupils, the brilliant Frank Lloyd Wright (1869-1959), was meanwhile originating revolutionary designs for houses. Wright interwove the interiors and exteriors of his houses by the use of terraces and cantilevered roofs (see the Robie House below). He felt that a building should look appropriate on its site; it should "grow out of the land." His "prairie houses," with their long, low lines, were designed to blend in with the flat land of the Midwest. Much that is taken for granted in today's houses derives directly from Wright's experiments at the turn of the century.

Impressionism and experimentation in music.   In the early years of the period 1870 to 1914, romanticism was still the main style in the musical world. Brahms and Tschaikovsky were offering the public new orchestral works, and Verdi and Wagner were writing operas.

A striking departure from musical tradition occurred with the rise of the French school of impressionism, whose foremost exponent was Claude Debussy (1862-1918). Just as the painters of the period had achieved new atmospheric effects by their technical innovations, so composers now engaged in "tone painting" to achieve a special mood or atmosphere. Such an effect is immediately recognizable in Debussy's prelude "L'Après-midi d'un faune" ("The Afternoon of a Faun"), which astounded the musical world when it was first performed in 1892.

A number of other composers rebelled strongly against romanticism and engaged in striking experimentation. Breaking with the major-minor system of

An excellent example of Frank Lloyd Wright's "prairie houses," the Robie House, built in 1909 in Chicago, shows the hallmarks of that style—long, low lines, a close interrelationship with the site, and groups of horizontal windows.

tonality, which had been the foundation of western musical tradition since the Renaissance, some of them began to make use of several different keys simultaneously, a device known as polytonality. Outstanding among such composers, Igor Stravinsky (1882-1971) has done for modern music what innovators like Picasso have done for modern painting. Unlike the romanticists, Stravinsky was less concerned with melody than with achieving his effects by means of polytonality, dissonant harmonies, and percussive rhythms.

CHAPTER 16

THE INDUSTRIAL REVOLUTION AND ITS INFLUENCE

The Industrial Revolution: 1750-1900

During the nineteenth century the landscape of many countries was being transformed by the forces of industrialism. Factory towns with their smoke-belching chimneys were springing up in western Europe, linked in turn by new railway networks and steam-driven engines. The owners of these factories and railroads—the bourgeoisie, or middle class—were rapidly propelled to the top of the social heap. In the political sphere, the bourgeoisie attained a dominant voice in government; in the economic sphere, they often profited from the doctrine of laissez faire, or economic liberalism, and piled up increasing wealth. But in time angry voices cried out against the poverty and social injustice resulting from bourgeois acquisitiveness and laissez-faire liberalism. Most trenchant and influential was that of the German socialist Karl Marx. As a result, much of the history of the western world after 1848, the year in which the *Communist Manifesto* was proclaimed, concerns the duel between the forces of capitalism and communism.

In the latter part of the century, electricity and other new forms of energy accelerated man's technological capabilities to produce more goods and raise living standards; transportation and communication networks expanded across continents and oceans and telescoped time-distance relationships; and Europe became the workshop of much of the world. At the same time the earlier fear of class warfare waned as governments showed increasing solicitude for their peoples' economic and social needs. Illiteracy was being reduced by the spread of public school systems. The franchise was being broadened; parliamentary government and mass suffrage were crowding out aristocratic plutocracy; political liberty was on the march.

The growth of big business spurred workers to unite in order to protect their own interests. The socialist movement was growing, but many of its members now embraced a policy of gradual reform instead of violent revolution. In Russia, however, reform was nowhere in sight; and the pressures of the new industrialism were mounting towards explosion.

THE TRIUMPH OF THE MACHINE

Interpretations of the Industrial Revolution. With the advent of industrialism, the economic life of Europe was modified drastically—a transformation called the Industrial Revolution. The first historian to give wide currency to the term was Arnold Toynbee of Oxford, the uncle of the famous British historian Arnold J. Toynbee. In *Lectures on the Industrial Revolution of the 18th Century in England* (1844) Toynbee pointed out that: (1) the beginning of the Industrial Revolution was sudden, starting in the year 1760; (2) the effects of the revolution were both sudden and cataclysmic, rudely overturning the whole edifice of society; (3) the Industrial Revolution quickly pervaded all quarters of British manufacturing and for a substantial period was wholly an British phenomenon; and (4) for many decades the effects of the revolution upon the common people were completely evil.

This traditional interpretation has been criticized in recent years by various economic historians who assert that the change was less a revolution than a speeding up of technological evolution. Nevertheless, this accelerative process, and the economic and social changes which resulted, can still justify the use of the term *Industrial Revolution* as long as we set it within a larger chronological framework. During the Middle Ages there emerged a new machine technology which involved the exploitation of water and wind as important sources of energy (see Chapter 5). In the eighteenth century men came to rely on steam derived from coal and increasingly replaced wood with iron. This new technical phase—which was unique in its exploitation of new forms of energy and new raw materials and which called for new forms of economic and social organization—is part of the Industrial Revolution.

Changes in the textile and smelting industries. During the eighteenth century in Britain the growing demand for cotton cloth, recently introduced from India, led to a series of inventions designed to increase and cheapen the methods of production. In 1733 John Kay, a spinner and mechanic, patented the first of the great textile inventions, the flying shuttle—a spring device that propelled the shuttle across the loom and permitted one person instead of two to weave wide bolts of cloth. By 1785 all the devices necessary for the full mechanization of the spinning and weaving processes had been introduced.

Until 1784 iron was available only in an impure state—cast iron which would break rather than bend and which was too brittle to withstand hard strains and heavy blows. In that year a method was invented for making iron malleable by burning the impurities out and leaving the iron clean and tough. The molten iron was then stirred with a long rod, a technique known as "puddling." Widespread adoption of this process enabled Great Britain to produce cheap wrought iron.

In the 1850's the smelting and refining of iron ore were substantially improved by Sir Henry Bessemer. With his new process, steel could be manufactured quickly and cheaply; in fact, between 1856 and 1870 the price of British steel fell to one half the sum formerly charged for the best grades of iron. At the same time production increased sixfold.

Steam power for trains and ships. With improvements in machinery came corresponding improvements in power. About 1705 an English mechanic, Thomas Newcomen, had devised an "atmospheric engine" in which a piston was raised by injected steam, the steam condensed, and the piston returned to its original position as it cooled off. Used to pump water from coal mines, Newcomen's invention doubled the depth in the ground at which coal could be worked but consumed large quantities of coal, which the mines could supply cheaply but which factories could not.

The transformation of the atmospheric engine into the true steam engine was the achievement of James Watt (1736-1819). Using steam to force the piston back and forth inside a closed cylinder, Watt devised a separate condenser to control the supply of steam. The first steam engines were used for pumping; after 1785 they were employed in cotton manufacturing; and still later they were adapted to the needs of the steam locomotive and the steamship.

In Britain the era of canal building was cut short by the advent of railroads. Before the locomotive was perfected, iron rails had been installed on public streetcar lines and in mines to reduce the friction on the wheels of horse-drawn vehicles. The forty miles of track between Stockton and Darlington in England served as a testing ground for the improved locomotive built in 1825 by George Stephenson, the brilliant son of a poor miner. Five years later, when his *Rocket* attained the terrifying speed of thirty-six miles an hour, the railroad era was on its way. Soon other countries began to lay the shining rails for locomotive transportation. In the United States the federal government subsidized the construction of the Union Pacific and Central Pacific railroads to connect Omaha and San Francisco. With their completion in 1869, it became possible to cross the entire North American continent by rail.

With the advent of the Industrial Revolution mechanization took over many tasks once performed by hand. An illustration from Diderot's famous *Encyclopedia* shows textile workers operating the spinning mule, which was powered by water.

Although others had used steam to propel boats earlier, the man who reaped the lion's share of glory for this feat was Robert Fulton, who used a Watt engine to drive his *Clermont* 150 miles up the Hudson River in 1807. About thirty years later Samuel Cunard initiated regular transatlantic passenger steamship service.

Britain, "workshop of the world." It was Britain's undisputed leadership in the Industrial Revolution that explained the tremendous volume of the nation's exports, its accumulation of vast amounts of capital, and its long-held position as the world's commercial center. Britain enjoyed a virtual monopoly in some manufacturing techniques until after 1870.

There were reasons for Britain's technological leadership. On this small island were rich deposits of coal and iron to supply the needs of industry. The wool of British sheep, unsurpassed in quality, provided essential raw material for some of the nation's textile mills. In the nineteenth century Britain's stable government catered increasingly to the interests of the trading and industrial classes, and its unrivaled navy not only protected the country from invasion but also kept open the routes for the merchant fleet. There was also surplus capital, accumulated from trade with America and the Orient. Finally, Britain concentrated on staple goods, adaptable to mass production and mass consumption, whereas France, for example, specialized in luxury commodities demanding individual craftsmanship.

Industrialization outside Britain. During the nineteenth century industrial progress was much slower in France than in Britain. The development of heavy industry lagged. There was a shortage of coal, and although the output of iron ore increased about 65 percent between 1830 and 1865, the deposits of ore were not conveniently located.

Early in the nineteenth century the progress of industrialism in Germany was retarded by political disunity, the conflict of interests between nobles and merchants, and, as in France, the existence of the guild system, which discouraged competition and innovation. But after the formation of a tariff union, the Zollverein, which by 1842 included most of the German states, industry was stimulated by the wider trade advantages now available. After 1850 improved methods in metallurgy were introduced, and in the next twenty years the output from German furnaces increased fourfold. Coal production likewise mounted rapidly.

Belgium also achieved rapid industrial growth, helped initially by the adoption of British manufacturing techniques. During the nineteenth century, in fact, Belgium produced more coal and iron than its much larger neighbor, France, and Belgian railroad construction boomed until this small nation boasted a greater railroad mileage per capita than any other country. Meanwhile the Belgian factories and mills turned out quantities of lace, carpets, cutlery, and iron products.

By the 1840's factories and railroads had become important in the United States; by 1860 American textile, iron, steel, and shoe industries were developing rapidly. At mid-century, large-scale corporate enterprises had begun to replace small-scale businesses, and after 1861 the government was usually in the hands of legislators friendly to corporate enterprise, instead of under agrarian control as it had been in earlier decades. Protective tariffs were passed with the hope of assuring American manufacturers a ready home market, and the power of the states to regulate business was restricted; thus the basis was laid for large-scale industrial development, already stimulated by military needs during the Civil War.

By 1870 the nation was crisscrossed with railroads, the northeastern part of the country was heavily industrialized, and new factories and mills were springing up everywhere.

Outside the industrial pale were Italy, Spain, Portugal, the nations of eastern Europe and the Balkans, and Russia, where industry either barely existed or grew very slowly. And before 1870 industrialism made little progress in South America, Africa, the Middle East, and Asia.

New markets for new goods. An important result of industrialism was the increase in productivity. In some industries productivity increased a hundredfold; in others, as much as a thousandfold. It soon became apparent that home markets alone were not able to absorb all the goods the factories could produce, and western European powers therefore began searching for trade outlets all over the world. International trade required a network of world transportation, a need which was met by the development of the railroad and steamship. The world was becoming an integrated economic unit.

Accompanying the mounting demand for overseas markets was the need for raw materials. These aims led to the European penetration of African and Asian lands. Isolated and primitive peoples were brought into touch with western culture by traders seeking markets and raw materials. And with these traders usually came officials and troops to take over territories as protectorates or colonies. Thus in the nineteenth century, and increasingly after 1871, the great industrial powers of Europe pursued a program of imperialism by which vast chunks of Asia and practically all of Africa came under European political and economic control.

Changing population trends. The best markets for the new products were still in Europe, where the industrial era was accompanied by a substantial and continuous increase in population. It has been estimated that Europe in 1800 had about 175 million people, whereas by 1900 it had 400 million.

Up to early modern times populations were checked by food scarcity, pestilence, and high infant mortality. Now the growing agricultural productiveness of European countries, achieved through intensive farming and the adoption of the techniques of scientific agriculture, supported larger populations. Because of the spread of transportation facilities, Europe was also able to import more food from other continents. In addition, achievements in medicine resulted in a lowered death rate. Infant mortality was reduced; in the eighteenth century it had been not uncommon for a mother who bore ten children to lose seven of them. By the latter part of the nineteenth century medicine and public health were slowly but surely conquering the dreaded plagues—cholera, typhus, and smallpox.

An increasing majority of the population were city dwellers. First in Britain, then in Belgium, France, and Germany, and later in other parts of the world, old cities outgrew their boundaries, and many new ones were founded. In general, from 1750 down to the present people have more and more tended to concentrate in cities, while population in the country has declined.

The factory, symbol of the new order. The most important symbol of the new industrial order was the factory, for here was the site of the machinery and power that made industrialism possible. The factory system did not replace the cottage or domestic system of home manufactures overnight; the two existed side by side for decades. Until 1815 the hand-loom weaver in Britain did not suffer substantially, but after that he was forced to compete with machines that could produce more goods at lower cost. As a result, weavers had to accept lower and lower wages to compete with the cheaper goods made by the power looms. Ultimately, they lost their hopeless battle and were forced to move to the communities where the new factories offered employment.

This displacement of human skills by machinery, known as technological unemployment, remained a constant source of fear as the Industrial Revolution spread. Even today the twentieth-century advance in labor-saving machinery—automation—is causing serious concern to factory workers and their union leaders.

Wretched working conditions. The first factories thrown together during the extraordinary rise of such industrial centers as Manchester and Birmingham were lacking in the most elementary sanitary and safety facilities; horrible cases of mangling were a common occurrence among the factory workers. Furthermore, under British common law, any accident a worker might suffer was considered a result of his own negligence, for which the employer could not be held responsible. There was no system of workmen's compensation or health insurance; an injured worker was likely to be thrown out in the street destitute and his job given to one of the thousands who had flocked to the new cities in search of employment.

Despite the innovation of "labor-saving" machinery, the worker was certainly not saved any labor. Each day the factory bell summoned him to long hours of monotonous drudgery. Women were forced by poverty to work until a day or two before delivery of their children and then to report back to work shortly after the child was born.

Children were the most unfortunate victims of the factory system. The mills employed some youngsters only four or five years of age, and in the coal mines children were used to carry baskets of coal up ladders. Children working in the mills received almost no education, for schooling was neither compulsory nor free. The facilities for obtaining even the most rudimentary training were insufficient, and evening schools were of little benefit to children who had to toil twelve hours during the day.

Ugly, disease-ridden slums. If we had visited a working-class district in Manchester early in the nineteenth century, we should have seen whole blocks of jerry-built homes, thrown together back to back by speculators so that the rear rooms had no windows. The houses faced on narrow, unpaved alleys or courts in which garbage and sewage were dumped. The living quarters for factory workers were chronically overcrowded and lacked adequate sanitary facilities. No wonder epidemics such as cholera were frequent. In 1842 a commission reported that the deaths caused by filth and lack of public sanitation outnumbered the loss in any wars that Britain had fought in modern times.

THE MIDDLE CLASS TRIUMPHANT

Liberalism: its meaning and impact. Unlike romanticism and nationalism, liberalism was associated almost exclusively with the middle class. Let us see why.

Like romanticism, liberalism vigorously affirmed the dignity of man and the "pursuit of happiness" as his inherent right. Like the philosophy behind the American and French revolutions, the liberal philosophy was an outgrowth of the philosophy of the Enlightenment. But where romanticism accepted revolution as a justifiable means to give expression to the "rights of man," liberalism stood for gradual reform through parliamentary institutions. And where both the rationalists and the romanticists tended to speak of man in the abstract—that is, "Man"—and to conceive of him as a philosophical ideal in opposition to, say, the "state" or the "king," nineteenth-century liberals thought in terms of individual men who shared certain basic rights in common, who worked together to obtain parliamentary majorities and political power, and who made use of that power to ensure that each of them would be given a maximum of freedom from state or external authority.

In the economic sphere liberalism was expressed in the doctrine of laissez faire—competition among individuals with a minimum of governmental interference or regulation. The textbook of this school of thought, Adam Smith's *Wealth of Nations*, postulated that society benefited most from competition, which brought the more intelligent and more efficient individuals the greater rewards. Although governments were responsible for the protection of life and property, the hands of government should be kept off business; the best interests of society would be served by permitting the natural "laws" of supply and demand to operate unimpeded (see also p. 282).

In the new industrial societies the bourgeois entrepreneurs had everything to lose from revolution and everything to gain from governmental protection of property rights. To win such protection, however, they had to obtain a dominant voice in government. As government immediately after the Napoleonic Wars was largely controlled by the nobility and landed classes, this meant in turn that the middle class had to secure a limited extension of the suffrage—an extension that would give them the vote without granting voting privileges to the working classes. Thus the members of the middle class demanded political power commensurate with their steadily increasing economic strength. In Britain this goal was attained in 1832 with the passage of the Reform Bill (see p. 346).

We might pause here to note the change that has taken place regarding the meaning of *liberalism*. The term still stands for reform, in contrast to conservatism with its defense of the status quo or to radicalism with its demands for immediate, drastic change. But in the economic sphere especially, liberalism has undergone a profound modification. Unlike his nineteenth-century predecessor, the twentieth-century liberal believes that the state should take an active role in minimizing the extremes of wealth, in balancing the great power enjoyed by big business and big organized labor, in conserving natural resources, in providing social security, and in actively opposing racial discrimination.

The triumph of laissez faire.   The bourgeoisie achieved their success in the era of industrial capitalism, which superseded the predominantly commercial, or trading, phase of business (see Chapter 11). In industrial capitalism profits were made primarily from investment in machinery and raw materials and from utilization of other people's labor. At first controlled and administered by factory owners, the new industrial capitalism soon resulted in important changes in business organization. The corporation, which could raise and utilize large sums of capital, became the characteristic form of business organization, largely replacing individual proprietorship and partnership, both of which proved inadequate to meet the needs of the factory system.

With the triumph of the middle class in the nineteenth century, we find also the triumph of their economic philosophy—laissez faire. This theory, known as "economic liberalism," held that it was impossible to correct the social evils of industrialism. Each man, enjoying free choice, could only improve his own circumstances by hard work, economy, and limiting the size of his family. Economists offered so little hope for improvement of the economic status of the common people that economics came to be known as the "dismal science."

Malthus' theory of population. Among the gloomier prophets was Thomas Robert Malthus (1766-1834), an English clergyman whose fame rests on his *Essay on Population* (1798). This study asserts that "the power of population is indefinitely greater than the power in the earth to produce subsistence for man."[1] In his own day Malthus could accurately point to a comparatively limited food supply and a population that was increasing by leaps and bounds. From this evidence, he deduced that the inevitable lot of the mass of mankind was misery, as the birth rate would always outrun the food supply. Malthus' only solution to what he believed to be a permanent problem was self-restraint in reproduction.

Laissez-faire theory popularized and modified. Jeremy Bentham (1748-1832), a wealthy British jurist, devised the doctrine of utilitarianism, or philosophical radicalism, based on the two concepts of utility and happiness. He correlated these two terms by saying that each individual knows what is best for himself and that all human institutions should be measured according to the amount of happiness they give—Bentham's celebrated "pain and pleasure" principle. Bentham believed strongly that the function of government should be the securing of as great a degree of individual freedom as possible, for freedom made for happiness. Utilitarianism has been defined as "the greatest happiness for the greatest number."

John Stuart Mill (1806-1873) did not believe that the interests of the manufacturers would necessarily coincide with the interests of the workers; he advanced the theory that government should, if necessary, pass legislation to remedy injustices. Mill felt that when the actions of businessmen harmed people, the state should intervene for their protection. While admitting that the maximum freedom should be permitted in the processes of production according to natural law, he insisted that the distribution of wealth depends on the laws and customs of society, and these can be changed by the will of men. He upheld the rights of property and of free competition but only within reasonable limits. The liberty of the individual should be subordinated to the wider interest of the group. In this thought there are the germs of what came later to be known as the welfare state. John Stuart Mill's ideas gained influence slowly; and, until well past the middle of the nineteenth century, laissez-faire liberalism held its ground with little change.

Theory and practice diverge. The philosophy of laissez faire seemed logical and was, in fact, a positive aid to social and economic progress. However, a wide gulf soon appeared between theory and practice. Because of monopolistic practices and secret collusion between competitors, the operation of competition did not always ensure fair prices. Nor did competition ensure the survival of honest and efficient businesses. Underhanded and unfair competition often wrecked the more ethical and scrupulous firms.

It also became increasingly difficult to reconcile the great wealth enjoyed by a few with the poverty borne by the many. Furthermore, legislation prevented them from achieving anything like an equal bargaining position with their economic masters. Drastic laws, such as the Combination Acts of 1799-1800 in England, forbade unions on the grounds that they would restrain trade. Strikes were classed as conspiracies, and strikers were harshly punished. While emphasizing the necessity for "freedom," the proponents of laissez faire completely disregarded the individual worker's lack of bargaining power.

The middle class in Victorian Britain. By the 1840's Britain had entered a new era which coincided with the long reign (1837-1901) of the staunchly respectable Queen Victoria. This age was best symbolized by the opening of the Great Exhibition in London in 1851—a monument to the cult of material progress where one might see the latest wonders of an ever accelerating industrialism. "Material progress seemed, as by some new law of nature, to have been showered without stint on a people who rated industriousness, business efficiency, and private enterprise among the major virtues. This situation induced in large sections of the upper and middle classes a mood of comfortable complacency which later generations have found the most unattractive of Victorian characteristics. . . . "[2] But reaction against mid-Victorian self-satisfaction was soon to swell into a chorus of attacks, both moderate and radical, upon the existing social order.

CHALLENGES TO THE EXISTING ORDER

Social criticism: Arnold and Ruskin. The state of culture in his day profoundly disturbed the English poet and essayist Matthew Arnold (1822-1888). Arnold believed that the materialistic standards of an industrialized society were completely incompatible with the great humanistic values inherited from Greece and the Renaissance. In his view, mid-Victorian culture was beset by personal self-seeking and lack of social purpose and moral strength. At one end of the social structure were the aristocrats, whom Arnold dubbed "Barbarians" because they were ignorant of the great western cultural inheritance and spent their lives in idleness and worldly pleasures. At the other end was the "Populace," the working class, which was now emerging from its traditional state of poverty and ignorance but which could, unless properly educated and directed, smash much that was irreplaceable in our civilization.

Then there was the middle class, about which Arnold was perhaps most concerned, since its members were now dominant in society. Arnold called them "Philistines" because they neither understood nor cared about culture in its humanistic terms. This new industrial bourgeoisie, he argued, thought only of power and riches and saw in the external signs of change proof of spiritual advancement. Philistinism led a man "to value himself not on what he is . . . but on the number of the railroads he has constructed."[3] In Arnold's judgment, state education was necessary in order to restore humanistic values and to make available to all classes in society the best of man's cultural heritage.

Another influential critic was John Ruskin (1819-1900). A leader of the protest movement often called the Esthetic Revolt, Ruskin believed wholeheartedly in the basic integrity and common sense of the people, for whom he advocated socialistic reforms and widespread education. Ruskin wrote eloquently to free his age from the ugly consequences of a soulless industrialism and to reform the arts and handicrafts, many of which were being destroyed by cheap mass production. Although Ruskin and his associates were not able to stem the tide of tasteless goods pouring from the machines, they helped stimulate a new appreciation of craftsmanship.

Stirrings of reform: Factory Acts. As critics of the existing order continued their protests, a movement to reform the worst evils of the Industrial Revolution gathered momentum. In Britain the landowning aristocracy constituted a powerful force in this camp. Resenting the rise of the *nouveaux riches* mill owners in the cities, the nobles were willing to curb middle-class power by passing Factory Acts setting various restrictions on woman and child labor and excessively long working hours. Although the Tory squires had little use for democracy, they possessed a humanitarian spirit and resented the callous indifference of the urban bourgeoisie toward human rights. Even among the factory owners themselves, a few men such as Robert Owen (see p. 334) realized that altruism and profits made a good team. If the conditions of the workers were improved, their efficiency and productivity would likewise rise.

The first effective Factory Act in Great Britain was passed in the year 1833. This law forbade the employment in textile factories of children under nine, restricted the hours of labor for children between nine and thirteen to forty-eight a week and the hours of children between thirteen and eighteen to sixty-eight, and made it illegal for anyone under eighteen to work at night. Government inspectors were to help administer the act. This piece of legislation prompted such manufacturers as John Bright to exclaim that it was "most injurious and destructive to the best interests of the country" and violated "the liberty of the subject" and "freedom of contract"—as though children of nine had freedom of contract in bargaining with mill owners.

Other reforms in Britain gradually whittled away at the old doctrine of laissez faire by broadening state regulation of economic enterprise. As industrialization spread, other countries tended to pass regulatory legislation similar to that in Britain. In 1836 Massachusetts passed the first act regulating child labor in the United States.

For their part, women had acquired a somewhat improved status. Women's colleges began to appear, and nursing by women was raised to professional status as a result of the initiative displayed by Florence Nightingale during the Crimean War. Sent to the military hospitals in the Crimea, the "Lady with the Lamp" brought about a complete change in the treatment of the wounded. Under her efficient charge, medical facilities were improved so that the terrible mortality due to cholera, dysentery, and gangrene was materially reduced.

By the 1840's there had been substantial modification of the middle-class theory of laissez faire. The state was increasingly expanding its jurisdiction over industry, protecting workers in mines, factories, and on the railways. In addition, philanthropy by private individuals was doing much to make life easier and fuller for the masses. Yet despite these reformist efforts, there was evidence of a growing rift between the bourgeoisie and the workers. In Disraeli's novel *Sybil* (1845), the author points out that Queen Victoria really rules over two nations

> between whom there is no intercourse and no sympathy; who are as ignorant of each other's habits, thoughts, and feelings, as if they were dwellers in different zones, or inhabitants of different planets; who are formed by a different breeding, are fed by a different food, are ordered by different manners, and are not governed by the same laws . . . THE RICH AND THE POOR.[4]

This rift intensified the rising class consciousness among the mass of the working people. In doing so, it contributed to the emergence of yet another major theory in the intellectual history of the nineteenth century, namely, socialism, which proposed complete social reconstruction.

The emergence of socialism. Attacking the nineteenth-century capitalistic system with its laissez-faire philosophy as both unplanned and unjust, socialists or communists (the two terms were once used synonymously) condemned the concentration of wealth and called for public or worker ownership of business. Above all, they insisted that harmony and cooperation—not ruthless competition—should control economic affairs. Generally convinced of the goodness of human nature, they dreamed of a happy future when

> there will be no war, no crimes, no administration of justice, as it is called, no government. Besides there will be neither disease, anguish, melancholy, nor resentment. Every man will seek, with ineffable ardor, the good of all.[5]

A sketch from an early edition of *Bleak House* illustrates the way in which Charles Dickens satirized the aggressive, middle-class "do-gooders" whose willful and stern philanthropy was often worse than no philanthropy at all. When the particularly aggressive Mrs. Pardiggle visited, the poor bricklayer, lying on the floor, answered the prying questions he knew were forthcoming: "An't my place dirty? Yes, it is dirty—it's nat'rally dirty, and it's nat'rally onwholesome; and we've five dirty and onwholesome children, as is all dead infants, and so much the better for them, and for us besides. . . . How have I been conducting myself: Why, I've been drunk for three days; and I'd been drunk four, if I'd a had the money."

This humanitarian idealism, a legacy of the Enlightenment, was typical of the theorists who created the early socialist movement.

Utopian socialism. The early socialists of the nineteenth century are known as the Utopians. (They were so called by Karl Marx later in the century, and the name has persisted.)

A reformer and Utopian socialist was Robert Owen (1771-1858), a successful mill owner in Scotland, who made New Lanark, the site of his textile mills, into a model community. Here, between 1815 and 1825, thousands of visitors saw neat rows of workers' homes, a garbage collection system, schools for workers' children, and clean factories where the laborers were treated kindly and where no children under eleven were employed. In 1825 Owen migrated to the vicinity of Evansville, Indiana, where he founded a short-lived Utopian colony called New Harmony.

Partly because of the impracticality of such colonies as New Harmony, which were usually based upon the somewhat naive notion that men naturally loved one another (or could be educated to love one another) and that men could live happily together in a communal society were it not that capitalist competition set man against man; partly because the Utopians made no practical, large-scale attempts to meet the problems of the depressed nineteenth-century industrial classes as a whole; and partly because ultimately Marxist socialism supplanted it—Utopian socialism failed.

Anarchism. Another socialist school of thought that became known as anarchism grew partly out of the ideas of the French theorist Pierre Proudhon (1809-1865), who wrote pamphlets urging the organization of society on a purely voluntary basis. The anarchists insisted that human nature is inherently good but is warped and depraved by authority. They repudiated all governmental compulsion, proposing instead free cooperation among the members of society. Proudhon's dictum, "Property is theft," was widely repeated by radicals everywhere.

In discussions on how to achieve their ends, the anarchists heard advocates of divergent tendencies—on the one hand, pacifists and humanitarian philosophers who were content to dream about a perfect society; on the other, devotees of violence. A member of the latter group was Michael Bakunin, an expatriate Russian revolutionary who insisted that God, the family, and the state must all be repudiated and that only when the world was without law would it be free (see p. 363).

Karl Marx and "scientific" socialism. Born in the Rhineland, at Trier (Treves), of German-Jewish parents who had been converted to Christianity, Karl Marx (1818-1883) obtained his doctor's degree after studying the philosophical ideas of George Wilhelm Friedrich Hegel (1770-1831). Failing to find a career in university teaching, he was forced to make a precarious living as a journalist. He went to Paris, where he became interested in socialistic ideas and, while there, he began his lifelong friendship with Friedrich Engels (1820-1895), the son of a wealthy German factory owner. In 1845 Marx was expelled from France by the authorities, and with Engels he went to live in Brussels.

In January 1848 Marx and Engels published the famous *Communist Manifesto*. This stirring document contained practically all the elements of what they came to call "scientific" socialism. It opened with an ominous declaration: "A spectre is haunting Europe—the spectre of Communism." The *Manifesto* called for an implacable struggle against the bourgeoisie, proclaimed the inevitable revolution and the triumph of the masses, and closed with a stern warning:

The Communists disdain to conceal their views and aims. They openly declare that their ends can be attained only by the forcible overthrow of all existing social conditions. Let the ruling classes tremble at a Communistic revolution. The proletarians have nothing to lose but their chains. They have a world to win. Working men of all countries, unite![6]

The revolutions of 1848 (not in the least influenced by Marx, an obscure figure at the time) were welcomed by Marx as the dawn of a new era, the birth of a new society. Going to Germany to assist in its arrival, he was forced to flee when the revolutionary movement collapsed. From that time until his death in 1883, he lived a life of penury in London, supported largely by contributions from friends, especially Engels. Nearly every day Marx would make his way to the British Museum, where he collected material for his various books, especially *Das Kapital (Capital)*.

Basic theories of Marx. No matter what one may think of Marxian socialism, no one can doubt that *Das Kapital* (1867-1894) constitutes one of the most influential books of modern times. In the mid-twentieth century nearly half of the world has been organized on the basis of its teachings.

The following are the basic theories of Marx's socialist system:

(1) The materialistic conception of history: "economic determinism." Marx believed that economic forces basically determine the course of history; all other supposed factors—patriotism, religion, art—are only "ideological veils." For Marx, all history could be explained in terms primarily of the social organization best adapted to the current means of economic production. When the economic organization of any era changed, it took the whole social and ideological structure with it to a new phase of history.

(2) "Dialectical materialism." Hegel, whose philosophy Marx had studied, felt that history is not just a matter of chance. It is dynamic and unfolds as the result of a definite plan or process of change. History is made up of a number of cultural periods, each the expression of a dominant spirit or idea. After fulfilling its purpose, the period is confronted by another contradictory idea or set of values. In Hegelian phraseology the traditional "thesis" is challenged by the new "antithesis." Out of this struggle there emerges a "synthesis" of old and new. Then the cycle starts all over again. Thus, to Hegel, history is a process of unfolding, determined by an absolute purpose or idea, which orthodox Hegelians called God; the machinery of change was called "historical dialectic."

Marx adopted this concept of change—the dialectic—but modified Hegel's approach in an important respect. To Marx the combatants were material forces, not ideas. History became a series of clashes between the exploited and the exploiting group: slave against master in ancient Greece, plebeian against patrician in Rome, serf against lord in the Middle Ages. The bourgeoisie, who by means of the organization of trade and the Industrial Revolution had created a new urban and industrial society, were now opposed by the modern industrial proletariat. The bourgeoisie themselves had helped create the factory system of production—and with it their own nemesis, the proletariat. It was inevitable that when the proletariat realized its true power, it would overthrow its natural enemy, the bourgeoisie. Out of this conflict would appear the new synthesis, the classless society, the ultimate social organization of the modern industrialized era.

(3) The concept of "surplus value." Here Marx borrowed from the laissez-faire economists who held that economic value represented "congealed labor." Only

human labor, Marx argued, can create new economic values. But under the capitalist system, the worker is not fully paid for all the values he creates. Suppose, for example, that a worker could produce in six hours the necessary economic values to supply his needs. However, the employer, as employers often did in the nineteenth century, keeps the worker producing goods for, say, twelve hours. The employer is in possession of a "surplus value" of six working hours, which he has "expropriated" from the worker. From this "stolen" surplus value the employer draws profits and capital. The workers are thus robbed of the fruits of their toil and become progressively poorer. Meanwhile, there is a concentration of capital in fewer hands as the most ruthless of the bourgeoisie destroy more and more of their competitors, forcing them into the ranks of the proletariat.

(4) The inevitability of socialism. Because the masses cannot buy all the goods they produce, economic crises, with overproduction and unemployment, will become the rule. Finally comes the day when the proletariat rises up and takes over the means of production. Then, says the *Manifesto:* "The knell of capitalism is sounded. The expropriators are expropriated."[7] In the apocalyptic new society private property will be abolished, exploitation of one class by another will cease, class warfare will end, and the millennium, a virtual heaven on earth, will arrive.

Devoting most of his ammunition to attacking the obvious injustices of unreformed nineteenth-century industrial society, Marx paid comparatively little attention to the kind of society that would supersede the bourgeois state. He once remarked that he had no interest in "writing the kitchen recipes of the future."

Weaknesses in Marxist doctrine. Certain weaknesses and inconsistencies in Marx's arguments were soon perceived. In interpreting history, Marx sees at work in all ages his "dialectical materialism," the class struggle. Yet in some miraculous fashion this "dominant" feature of history is to disappear when the communist society is established.

Furthermore, there is something ironic in Marx's term *scientific socialism* (i.e., based upon supposed inevitable laws of social development "scientifically" observed and explained by Marx) "in contrast to the Utopian variety." With his talk of a final social stage in which there would be no coercion and no exploitation and with his vague notions about the organization of his ideal society, he really was akin to utopian dreamers of all ages.

By explaining all social and intellectual phenomena in terms of economics and class struggle, Marx's theory denied the importance of intellectual and idealistic influences. And yet Marxism itself as a body of ideas about history and social change became in time a great intellectual influence and historical force. A major difficulty which Marxists encountered was the patriotism of most European workers. Faced by a choice between supporting national interests, as in World War I, and supporting Marxist tenets about the class nature of war under capitalism, most European workers chose to support their nations. Nationalism was a stronger influence than socialism.

THE NEW INDUSTRIALISM

Chief characteristics. The second half of the nineteenth century saw a new surge of technological and industrial development of such magnitude that it has sometimes been called the Second Industrial Revolution.

Between 1870 and 1914 the new industrialism displayed the following characteristics: (1) New sources of energy, particularly electricity and the power produced by the internal combustion engine, were introduced. (2) New materials including steel and a variety of lighter metals and alloys were employed, along with a host of synthetic products and new types of explosives. (3) Mass production methods involved the use of interchangeable parts and the assembly line, which came into its own in the automobile age when Henry Ford began turning out Model T's. (4) Industry increasingly allied itself with the laboratory; invention became systematic rather than accidental, involving research teams. (5) New and faster means of mass transportation provided a new capacity to disperse industry and decongest factory towns and to plan for the social improvement of the human landscape (though large-scale social planning had to await later decades in the present century).

New inventions.   This new stage of industrialism was marked by a veritable avalanche of inventions. In 1876 a working dynamo was invented that could produce electricity in any required amount. With the harnessing of this new form of power, the western world entered the age of electricity, which now ran its factories, lighted its homes and city streets, and moved its tramcars. The self-taught American genius, Thomas Edison, supervised the construction in New York City of the world's first central electric power plant, and many of his more than 1200 patents involved machines powered by electricity.

The field of communications was revolutionized by the introduction of electrical devices. The first telephone was invented by Alexander Graham Bell in 1876, and in 1895 Guglielmo Marconi revealed his brainchild—wireless telegraphy. Three years later wireless messages were being transmitted across the English Channel, and within six years, across the Atlantic.

No less a revolution was taking place in transportation. In the 1880's a successful internal-combustion engine using gasoline as fuel was constructed and then applied to a bicycle and a carriage. From these crude beginnings came the motorcycle and the automobile. During this period man acquired wings. In the 1890's attempts were made to construct a heavier-than-air craft with propellers run by internal-combustion engines. The climax came at Kitty Hawk, North Carolina, on December 17, 1903, when Orville and Wilbur Wright succeeded in keeping their fragile biplane aloft for twelve seconds.

The spread of industrialism.   Between 1870 and 1914 the world could be divided into three economic areas. The highly industrialized area was concentrated in western Europe, in the northern United States and in Japan. In the area just beginning to be touched by industry were such countries as Italy, Spain, the Balkan states, Russia, and Canada. The third area, consisting of all of Africa, the Middle East, and all of Asia except Japan, was outside the industrial realm. This third zone can be called "the world of empire," for most of its vast territories were colonies of the industrial powers or objects of foreign exploitation.

Great Britain was the pioneer in industrialization. But after 1870 new and vigorous competitors, primarily the United States, Germany, and Japan, became important industrial nations. In 1870 Britain had more textile spindles and looms and produced more coal and iron than all the rest of the world. By 1910 it had only 40 percent of the spindles and 30 percent of the looms of the world and produced only 26 percent of the world's coal and 14 percent of the world's iron. In banking and shipping, however, Britain still led the pack. Its ships carried 40 percent of all the world's commerce, and London was the world's main source of capital.

Although Britain had an "unfavorable" balance of trade (imported more goods than it exported), it received nearly a billion dollars annually from overseas investments, shipping fees, insurance, and banking services. These "invisible exports" kept Great Britain out of the red.

After the conclusion of the Civil War, industrialization in the United States proceeded at an amazing rate (see p. 388). In 1860 the total value of American manufactures was less than $2 billion; by 1900 the figure was nearly seven times as large.

The unification of the German empire was in part responsible for the astounding growth of German industrialization. The Germans concentrated primarily on the development of such new enterprises as the chemical and electrical industries. The government played a decisive role in this expansion by designing tariffs to aid the new industries and by setting up technical schools to train personnel. In the chemical industry the Germans seized undisputed first place—by 1900 they produced four fifths of the world's dyestuffs—and in the electrical industry Germany's skilled technicians were soon producing intricate equipment destined for all countries of the world.

After isolated Japan had been opened to the West in the mid-nineteenth century, industrialization was introduced. Economic changes came with pell-mell rapidity: the labor market was large, and workmen could always be found to work at a low wage, enabling the Japanese manufacturer to undersell his rivals in other nations. The government aided industrialization by subsidizing railroads and steamship lines, and large supplies of coal were available. Specializing in textiles, Japan created serious competition for the mills of Manchester. The pace of industrialization in Japan is best indicated by the following facts: in 1870 no manufactured goods were exported; in 1906 the value of manufactures exported had reached $100 million.

The growth of world trade.   The new industrialism set in motion strong forces binding the world into one interdependent economic unit. The tremendous increase in manufacturing productivity caused the most highly industrialized regions of the world to see new markets in the backward zones. There was also a demand for huge quantities of raw materials—cotton, tin, oil, tea, coffee, wheat, sugar, and timber. In 1860 world trade amounted to slightly more than $7 billion; in 1913 the figure was nearly $42 billion.

Materially aiding this world economic interdependence was what might be termed the export of people. The higher standard of living and lower death rate in western Europe led to an unparalleled increase in population. From 1870 to 1914 the European continent registered an increase of 100 million people. At the same time a quarter of that number migrated to the great unsettled regions of North and South America, to Australia, and, to a lesser extent, to South Africa. This vast movement of people helped to develop backward and underpopulated lands and also created expanding markets for European goods.

Business consolidates.   In the rush of new products and factories, businessmen became aware of the advantages of consolidation. By being big, a business could enjoy the economies of mass production, could buy raw materials in huge amounts and at low prices, and could use its power to crush competition and, if necessary, to lobby for favorable government legislation. In addition, big business could effectively discourage unionism, could place labor agitators on a black list, and, in the event of a strike, could employ strikebreakers.

Business consolidation took the form not only of larger corporations but also of mergers and alliances of separate units. One form was the trust, in which a body of trustees held a majority of the stock and thus controlled the wage, price, and merchandising policies of the several companies involved. Another form was the holding company, in which a corporation was organized to perform the same functions as the more informal trust. In Europe business integration took the form of huge industrial combines known as cartels. These great industrial units were hooked together from country to country in international affiliates controlling such products as steel or rubber.

To create and operate such huge industrial organizations required larger sums than the manufacturer could ordinarily provide; as a result, capitalism passed into a new stage of development. Just as commercial capitalism had been replaced by industrial capitalism in the eighteenth century, industrial capitalism in the last two decades of the nineteenth century was superseded by finance capitalism. As the financial houses arranged for the vast amounts of capital investment demanded by industry, more and more control of business fell into their hands. In this era the financier rather than the manufacturer became the dominant figure in the business arena.

With the growth of the size of the business unit, gains in economy and efficiency were registered. But there were also danger signals. In too many instances key industries providing services or commodities vital to the health and well-being of society were dominated by a few huge enterprises controlled by a relative handful of men.

Workers unite. In response to the seemingly all-powerful position of big business in wage bargaining and in reaction against management's tendency to regard workers merely as commodities, the workers began to organize into trade unions. In 1824 the harsh Combination Acts were repealed in Britain, and from this time on workingmen had the legal right to organize and to bargain peacefully with employers, though legal restrictions continued to limit trade union activity. For a long time the authorities vigorously opposed strikes, thereby restricting the strength and effectiveness of the unions.

In the meantime workers on the Continent turned more and more to unions as a means of obtaining their demands for higher wages, shorter hours, and more healthful working conditions. In France in 1864, workers were allowed by law to combine for strikes. During the 1860's trade unionism made progress in Germany, as it did in the United States, where the number of local unions multiplied almost fourfold between 1861 and 1865.

The first unions were craft unions made up of skilled workers. Then unskilled wage earners were organized. Some of the unions formed were industrial unions, taking in all the workers employed in one industry. In this case, when any given group of workers felt compelled to strike, all union men in the industry would join them. As another means of gaining strength, associations of unions, such as the British Trade Union Congress, were formed on a national basis. In 1881 a federation of autonomous craft and industrial unions was founded in the United States with a membership that soon numbered in the millions. This was the American Federation of Labor, headed by Samuel Gompers; it became the most powerful voice of American workers.

The immediate result of the growth of unionism was better protection for the working masses, a stronger voice when it came to collective bargaining with the bosses, and consequently higher wages. While in some instances labor organizations sought to overthrow the capitalist system, the vast majority of unions both in

Europe and in the United States were moderate and gradualistic in both their aims and methods.

NEW ECONOMIC AND SOCIAL FORCES

The new trends.   From the standpoint of conditions in 1848, it looked as though Marx's predictions in the *Communist Manifesto*—the inevitability of revolution and the destruction of capitalism and the bourgeoisie—would come true. But the latter part of the nineteenth century and the decade preceding the First World War saw improvement in three basic areas: (1) the granting of such basic political rights as universal suffrage, civil liberties, and free expression of opinion; (2) an increase in the democratic distribution of wealth, also known as economic democracy; and (3) the spread of education.

Democratic distribution means, simply speaking, more equal sharing in the wealth of a nation. The growth of labor unions gave workers more bargaining power with their employers, and they used this power to gain better wages. It has been estimated that the "real" wages of workers (the amount of goods that their wages could actually buy) increased 50 percent in industrial nations between 1870 and 1900.

Not only did real wages improve, but the state increasingly guaranteed the popular standard of living. More and more governments made it their business to provide such benefits as unemployment insurance, old-age pensions, and accident compensation. Because this social legislation was paid for out of tax revenues, Britain introduced a graduated income tax, by which every individual paid a sum relative to his earnings.

Business management became less exclusively a monopoly of the capitalists. Labor unions began to assert their right to have some say in the operation of industry, and government itself assumed the right to regulate and control great industries when the public interest was involved. Governments, moreover, sought to prevent the unrestrained exercise of economic power by the enactment of legislation such as the Sherman Anti-Trust Act and the Clayton Act in the United States. However, the effective direction of big business in the highly industrialized western nations was not fully taken in hand until the advent of world depression in the 1930's.

The final aspect of the democratic movement in the second half of the nineteenth century was education. As the result of an education bill passed in 1870 under Gladstone, school attendance in Britain jumped from one to four million in ten years. Similar acts were passed in France, Germany, the Low Countries, and Scandinavia. Although educational progress lagged in southern and eastern Europe, with 80 percent of the people of Russia and the Balkans remaining illiterate, by 1900 free and compulsory elementary education became almost universal in western Europe.

Liberalism fades; the welfare state appears.   Only through the drastic modification and weakening of the middle-class doctrine of laissez-faire liberalism could the government's increased solicitude for the masses have come about. The expansion of a government's responsibilities for the economic security of all its people pointed toward the welfare state. That government moved away from laissez-faire liberalism and in the direction of the welfare state must be regarded as one of the fundamental trends of the late nineteenth century.

Socialism compromises. In the early 1870's the growth of socialism was slow; but as the decade progressed, the movement gained momentum. The Social Democratic party, organized in Germany in 1875, became the strongest of its kind in Europe and a model for similar parties in other nations. In the 1880's Marxist parties also arose in Italy, Austria, Scandinavia, and the Low Countries. In France the socialist movement—discredited by the Paris Commune of 1871—broke into a number of acrimonious factions. British socialists placed their faith in parliamentary reform rather than in any uprising of the proletariat. The most important socialist group was the Fabian Society, organized in 1883 and including such brilliant intellectuals as George Bernard Shaw, Sidney and Beatrice Webb, and H. G. Wells. (The Fabian group derived its name from the cautious Roman general Quintus Fabius Maximus, who wore down his enemy Hannibal by being content with small gains.) Chiefly through the efforts of the Fabian Society, the Labour party was formed in 1900 with the support of trade unions and various socialist groups. Much of the credit for British social legislation goes to the Labour party, which supported the Liberal party's program before World War I.

Moderate socialists were not limited solely to Britain, for the Fabian gospel of moderation—or revisionism, as it came to be called—spread to the Continent. Encouraged by a general improvement in the lot of the common man, the socialists became less revolutionary and more willing to cooperate with governments which were genuinely interested in raising the standards of living of the working people. In the 1890's the movement grew rapidly.

Orthodox Marxism in Russia. By 1900 the picture of workers "having nothing to lose but their chains" had been substantially altered in western Europe by the advance of social legislation and the rise of "real" wages. But if Marx could have risen from his grave in that year, he would have found in Russia the "1848" he once described in the *Communist Manifesto*. Here industrialization was just gaining momentum, and bewildered peasants seeking work in city factories were shamefully exploited. There were no traditions of peaceful reform, gradualism, or compromise in Russia—only the memory of ruthless government suppression and of equally violent attempts at retaliation. It was natural, therefore, that when socialism appeared in Russia, its adherents passionately embraced Marx's original doctrines of class war and revolution. While the tsars still reigned, the socialist leaders were preparing for the day when the people would overthrow the regime and win control of the government. One such leader was Lenin.

Born Vladimir Ilich Ulyanov in a small city in the Volga River valley, Lenin (1870-1924) grew up in moderate and respectable circumstances provided by his father, a teacher of physics. In 1887 his elder brother was arrested for plotting against the life of the tsar and was executed. Shortly thereafter, Lenin began to read his dead brother's copy of *Das Kapital* and joined a secret Marxian discussion club. He was arrested in 1895 and sentenced to exile in Siberia. After he was released in 1900, he and his wife made their way to Switzerland. There, Lenin helped to found the socialist papaer *Iskra* (*Spark*), whose motto was "From the spark—the conflagration."

Lenin stood for a socialism whose weapon was violence and whose creed allowed no compromise with the bourgeoisie. While Marx believed that capitalism would break down of its own accord, Lenin wanted to smash it.

Lenin also disagreed with Marx on the dictatorship of the proletariat. Engels and Marx did not envisage a police state but rather a republic of workers. Engels in 1891 wrote: "If anything stands, it is that our party and the working-class can only come to power under the form of a democratic republic. This is the specific form of the dictatorship of the proletariat."[8] Lenin had other notions. His dictatorship of the proletariat would be highly centralized. The shattering impact of World War I would give Lenin and his followers the opportunity to seize power.

CHAPTER 17

NATIONALISM AND AUTHORITARIAN REGIMES

Reaction and Revolution: 1815-1850;
The Politics of Power: 1850-1914

After the final defeat of Napoleon, the statesmen of the great powers assembled at the Congress of Vienna to resume the interrupted task of building a new Europe. Their solutions were conservative. Old dynasties were restored, national aspirations of peoples such as the Germans, Belgians, and Poles were ignored. Liberalism was placed in cold storage. International machinery known as the Congress System—or the Concert of Europe—was created to defend the conservative settlement.

But revolts began as early as 1820, broke out again in 1830, and reached a climax in 1848. These uprisings were partially successful. Greece and Belgium attained independence; France repudiated repressive government. But national aspirations, expressed in a rash of revolutions in 1848, were tragically frustrated in Italy, Germany, and Austria.

The history of Europe from 1850 to 1871 chiefly concerns the attainment of national unity in Germany and Italy. While liberal aspirations before 1850 had been sparked by much idealism and romanticism, the era of nation-making after 1850 was attended by cold diplomatic calculations and military force. The march of events now came under the direction of two consummate practitioners of *Realpolitik*—Bismarck of Prussia and Cavour of Savoy. In a series of wars and maneuvers, carefully calculated, Italy and Germany were united by 1871, and two new states joined the family of European nations.

During the remainder of the nineteenth century, Germany and Austria-Hungary remained essentially authoritarian. As for Russia it continued to be both repressive and backward, a complete anachronism to modern forces of change.

REACTION AT VIENNA AND THE CONGRESS SYSTEM

The Congress of Vienna. In September 1814, during Napoleon's exile at Elba, a brilliant gathering of diplomats and rulers assembled at Vienna to remake the map of Europe. The leading delegates were Tsar Alexander of Russia, Lord Castlereagh of Great Britain, Talleyrand of France, and Prince Metternich. The leadership of this last-named statesman initiated a reactionary era, now termed the Age of Metternich, which lasted until 1848. Many Europeans, especially those of the middle class, hoped that the peacemakers would be guided by the principles of nationalism and democracy—the twin ideologies of the French Revolution. Unfortunately, the Congress was in no mood to respect these aspirations.

In the reestablishment of the European political order, four principles were followed: (1) legitimacy, (2) encirclement of France, (3) compensations, and (4) balance of power. It was agreed that, wherever possible, the legitimate rulers who were in power before their deposition by Napoleon should have their thrones restored to them. Following this principle, all the rulers who had been established by Napoleon were removed except Bernadotte of Sweden. In their place the traditional dynasties were restored. In the person of Louis XVIII, the Bourbon House was restored in France, and other Bourbon rulers were returned to their thrones in Spain and in the kingdom of Naples. The House of Savoy reigned again in Sardinia and the House of Orange in Holland.

In the reconstruction of the political boundaries of Europe, the keynote again was the restoration of the past. France was reduced to substantially its former size; Spain, Holland, and other former Napoleonic possessions regained their independence. The Holy Roman Empire with its multitude of miniscule states was dissolved; and in its place the German Confederation of states was created under the domination of Austria. Various territorial changes were arranged. The Austrian Netherlands (Belgium) was given to Holland, Prussia gained extensive territory along the Rhine, and Austria gained Lombardy and Venetia in northern Italy. Sweden acquired Norway, and Russia retained Finland. England obtained colonies and naval bases, notably the Dutch holdings of Ceylon and South Africa. In general the map of Europe looked much as it had before the French Revolution.

Certain features of the map of Europe were modified in accordance with the principle of encirclement. The allied statesmen were resolved that a protective belt should be fashioned to surround France, hem it in, and prevent any future French aggression. When the Austrian Netherlands (Belgium) was turned over to Holland, it was to make this country a stronger barrier on France's north; Savoy, belonging to the kingdom of Sardinia, was enlarged in order to block any French invasion of Italy; and Prussia was given extensive territory along the Rhine.

The principles of compensation and balance of power prompted much jockeying among the great nations. For example, in granting compensation for the loss of the Austrian Netherlands, Austria was given Lombardy and Venetia in northern Italy and part of the Adriatic coast as well. When Sweden agreed to allow Russia to retain Finland, Sweden's compensation was Norway. The diplomats also had to create a new balance of power among the nations. Among the Big Four there existed deep jealousies. Prussia coveted all of Saxony, while Austria feared growing Prussia. Russia wanted to expand by securing all of Poland. And Britain believed that an enlarged Russian state would menace the balance of power and—indirectly—British security. Talleyrand arranged a secret treaty, pledging to use force if necessary to restrain Prussia and Russia. Confronted by this threat, Russia and Prussia reduced their claims for more Polish and Saxon territory.

The Congress System. The most serious mistake made at Vienna was disregarding nationalism. The Italian desire for unity was ignored, Germany was kept weak and divided, mainly by Austrian influence. Nationalism was also violated in the case of Norway and Belgium, and the Poles remained under foreign rulers.

The great powers were determined to maintain the status quo, and their Quintuple Alliance was designed to crush the growth of liberalism and nationalism. In effect after 1820 the Congress System became a trade union of kings for suppressing the liberties of people.

Rebellions against the Congress System began almost immediately. A general uprising in Spain in 1820 and in the kingdom of Naples and Sicily led to intervention by Austrian and French troops. In both countries brutal repression obliterated the liberal movements. But after this initial success the conservative alliance rapidly waned. Britain refused to support intervention in Latin America against the newly independent republics, and the American president spelled out the Monroe Doctrine (1823) which warned the world that the United States would not countenance any interference in the western hemisphere.

Meanwhile, in the Balkans the subject peoples of the Turks were restless and often rebellious. Montenegro gained independence in 1799 and Serbia some autonomy in 1826. Liberals were especially interested in the struggle of Greece for freedom. Following a revolt against Turkish rule in 1821, the great powers intervened and forced the sultan to recognize Greek independence and to grant some measure of self-rule to the Rumanians. This event was a serious blow to Metternich's Congress System. Yet the victory of nationalism in the Balkans was incomplete, and revolts against remaining Turkish rule were to continue during much of the nineteenth century.

FRANCE, ENGLAND, AND THE REVOLUTIONS OF 1830

The July Revolution in France. The defection of Great Britain from the conservative alliance had heralded its demise, and by 1829 it was no longer an effective instrument of international repression. In 1830 additional sledgehammer blows fell upon Metternich and his backward-looking colleagues.

While the monarchy had been restored in France under Louis XVIII, considerable rights had been granted to all citizens. Everyone was now equal before the law. Freedom of speech and of religion were guaranteed, and arbitrary arrest was forbidden. Moderate as these reforms seemed, they had the backing of only a minority. The lower bourgeoisie, the students and intellectuals, and the urban laborers wanted a more democratic constitution and the vote; at the other extreme the nobles and clerics of the Ultra faction thought the privileges were far too radical. Throughout this period, the real political power was retained by the nobility and the upper bourgeoisie.

During the reign of Louis XVIII a characteristic feature of modern French politics emerged—the multi-party system. Numerous loosely organized factions appeared, and it became necessary for ministries to be formed of men from a coalition of parties in the legislature instead of from one majority party, as in England. Thus the basis was laid for a pattern of government by frequently unstable parliamentary coalitions.

For nine years Louis XVIII's government was not challenged but in 1824, with the accession of Charles X, unrest rapidly mounted. When in 1830 the king gagged the press and limited the franchise, Parisians rose in rebellion. The then narrow streets were blocked by barricades behind which armed revolutionaries defied the king's forces. After three days of violence the king fled ignominiously to England. This July Revolution gave France a new king, Louis Philippe, with a definitely bourgeois outlook. The vote was extended to the moderately wealthy but still did not include the lower middle class and the common people. Having ostensibly accepted his crown from the people, Louis Philippe was the "citizen king", in contrast to Louis XVIII and Charles X, who had claimed to rule by divine sanction. Thus the principle of the sovereignty of the people supplanted the principle of divine right.

Nationalism in Poland and Belgium. Word of the July Revolution spread rapidly throughout Europe. The semi-independent kingdom of Poland revolted against Russian overlordship only to be defeated by the tsar's armies in the summer of 1831. The national Diet was abolished, and Poland sank to the status of an ordinary Russian province, governed directly by Russian officials in St. Petersburg.

The Belgians were more fortunate. Announcing their independence and adopting a liberal constitution, they successfully defended their freedom against a Dutch army. After centuries of foreign rule—under Burgundy, Spain, Austria, and Holland—the Belgians had finally secured their independence. A treaty declaring Belgium to be a "perpetually neutral state" was drawn up in 1839 and signed by the great powers. This was the treaty which Germany dismissed as a "scrap of paper" when its troops invaded Belgium in World War I.

The reform movement in England. The first decade after 1815 was a period of reaction in England as well as on the Continent. Instead of sympathizing with the plight of the poor and unemployed, the aristocrats saw in their discontent only the evil of Jacobin influence from the French Revolution. In the late 1820's, however, a series of reforms were enacted. These bills abolished capital punishment for over one hundred offenses, created a modern police force for London, began the recognition of labor unions, repealed old laws which forbade non-Anglican Protestants to sit in Parliament, and by the Catholic Emancipation Bill gave equal rights to members of the Catholic faith. The basic problem of gross inequalities in the suffrage remained.

There had long been a need for reform in Parliament. Representation in the House of Commons had virtually no relation to the population; it has been estimated that 3 percent of the population dictated the election of the members. Many "pocket" boroughs were under the control of political bosses who dictated the choice of the voters. In various depopulated "rotten" boroughs, members of Parliament were elected to represent areas which boasted only a handful of people or no longer contained any inhabitants. On the other hand, new and rapidly growing industrial towns, such as Manchester with 140,000 inhabitants and Birmingham with 100,00, had no representatives.

Supported by the rising middle class and the workers, the government introduced a bill to abolish the rotten boroughs, widen the franchise, and give representation to the new industrial towns. Defeated in the Commons at the outset, the bill was again introduced and passed, only to be defeated in the House of Lords. After the bill had been introduced a third time, the king, William IV, finally threatened to create enough new peers who would vote for the bill in order to pass the measure in the House of Lords. This threat forced the Lords to pass the bill.

The Reform Bill of 1832 transferred the balance of power from the landed gentry to the middle class and emphasized the growing supremacy of the

Commons over the Lords. The important fact is that, while the great Reform Bill did not represent an immediate substantial widening of the franchise (the working class was still disenfranchised), the bill indicated a new sensitivity to popular forces and thus constituted an initial step in breaching the wall of political privilege.

Immediately following the first Reform Bill, several other notable reforms were enacted, such as the abolition of slavery in the British Empire and the first important Factory Act.

The Chartist movement.   In the early 1830's a strong popular movement known as Chartism had developed in England. Its leaders published the People's Charter, containing six demands: universal suffrage, secret voting, no property qualifications for members of Parliament, payment of members so that poor men could seek election if they wished, annual elections to Parliament, and equal electoral districts. Twice, in 1839 and in 1842, the Chartists presented their petition, with over a million signatures, to the House of Commons. In each case the government ignored the petition.

In 1848, following the news of the February Revolution in France (see p. 349), a third petition was presented to Parliament, which again rejected the demands. A militant minority among the Chartists planned an armed insurrection in protest, but their plans were divulged by an informer and the ringleaders seized. The bulk of the English people, Chartists or otherwise, apparently preferred to avoid violence as an instrument of political and social reform. Although the Chartist movement subsquently declined, within the next century all but one of its demands—annual elections to Parliament—were enacted into law, forming the very foundations of modern British democracy.

Another reform came with the repeal of the Corn Laws, which were protective duties on grain. By the middle of the nineteenth century the population had increased to such an extent that English agriculture could no longer feed the country, and the price of bread rose alarmingly. Repeal of the Corn Laws in 1846 made possible the import of low-priced wheat from abroad, and cheaper food for the masses.

By mid-century Britain was a wealthy nation taking pride in the stability of its political institutions. The pattern of restraint and of gradual social and political reforms, so characteristic of England's history for the next hundred years, had been firmly established. Britain would move forward by evolutionary rather than revolutionary reform.

REVOLUTION RENEWED IN WESTERN EUROPE

France under Louis Philippe.   Throughout western Europe by the year 1848 discontent was rife. Idealistic romantics dreamed of liberty, practical businessmen sought the control of government, and city workers desired democracy and a more equal distribution of the profits of industry. The new forces of discontent were particularly strong in France. Since 1830 France had been ruled by the bourgeois monarch, Louis Philippe, who prided himself on being the representative of the business interests of his country. France was fairly prosperous, and the government, while not democratic, was moderate and sensible. On the debit side, it soon became apparent that the July Monarchy had little concern with the lower classes. What Louis Philippe failed to perceive was that new economic and social forces were at work which were bound to affect the political structure as well. The Industrial Revolution, entering France from England at an increasing tempo during his reign, was fattening the bourgeoisie whom he so sedulously represented, but it was also swelling the ranks of the politically conscious proletariat and creating those wretched conditions which gave rise to socialism, with its aim of redesigning the whole economic and political system.

Louis Blanc (1811-1882), a socialist theorist and journalist who had a large following among French workers, demanded that the state guarantee the "right to work" by establishing "national workshops" owned and operated by the workers. The discontented industrial workers concentrated in Paris and other growing factory towns, added their demands for reform to the moderate requests of the lower bourgeoisie, who simply wanted the vote for themselves, and those of the intellectuals who were devoted to republican principles.

Another cause of the government's general unpopularity was the corruption that pervaded the administration. Officials speculated with public funds, army commissions were sold, and a series of scandals in high society rocked the country. In addition, the reign of Louis Philippe was colorless and dull. "Business before national honor" seemed to be the king's policy in foreign affairs.

In his early years on the throne the "king of the bourgeoisie," Louis Philippe, made a point of walking about the streets of Paris in a frock coat and top hat and carrying a walking stick like any solid middle-class citizen. For a time he allowed ordinary citizens to flock through his palace, much as their American contemporaries poured through the White House during the presidency of Andrew Jackson.

349

Central Europe:
The Rise
of the
Nationalistic
Spirit

Frenchmen began to think back fondly to the immortal deeds of the great Napoleon and yearn for national glory once again.

The Revolution of 1848. In February 1848 a Parisian insurrection once more turned into a political revolution. Again, as in 1830, mobs of excited citizens began to congregate and the barricade—the inevitable symbol of revolution—appeared. More than 1500 barricades were thrown up in Paris. Republican leaders proclaimed a provisional revolutionary government, and Louis Philippe fled to England. Universal suffrage was immediately established, giving France a full political democracy.

The new regime, known as the Second Republic, had a brief and inglorious existence. Created without real preparation, it was hamstrung by the complete inexperience in democracy of both its officials and the newly enfranchised common people. In addition, the reformers who had been united in their opposition to Louis Philippe broke into diverse factions after his removal. Sparked by rivalry between bourgeois groups and radical revolutionaries, a violent insurrection known as the "June Days" broke out. The unemployed workers hoisted a red flag as the sign of revolution—the first time that the red flag appeared as the symbol of the proletariat. With the cry of "Bread or Lead," these Paris workers erected barricades and sought to overthrow the government. Not since the Reign of Terror had the capital witnessed such savage street fighting. The insurrection was crushed after much loss of life. It left the working class with a bitter hatred of the bourgeoisie and the bourgeois element with a deep and lasting fear of left-wing violence.

Louis Napoleon and the Second Empire. The bloody upheavals in Paris produced a wave of reaction throughout the country. When the election for the presidency of the new republic was held, the victor was not one of the revolutionaries who had founded the new government but a hitherto obscure bearer of the magic name *Napoleon*—Louis Napoleon, nephew of Napoleon I. He considered himself, not the legislature, as representing the national will. In December 1851, while serving as president under a constitution that did not permit him to succeed himself, Louis Napoleon forcibly dissolved the government, which had played into his hands by attempting to abolish universal male suffrage. Imitating the methods of his illustrious uncle and anticipating the techniques of modern dictators, he then carried out a plebiscite which gave almost unanimous support to his action. In 1852 Napoleon proclaimed himself emperor. The Second Republic was no more. France still did not seem to be ready for republican institutions.

CENTRAL EUROPE: THE RISE OF THE NATIONALISTIC SPIRIT

The Old Regime maintained in Austria. During the revolutions of 1820 and again in 1830, there had been sympathetic vibrations of unrest and minor insurrections in the German states and the Austrian empire. In the main, however, the political arrangements made at Vienna in 1815 were not seriously challenged. Under the strong hand of its chief minister, Metternich, Austria continued to be a bulwark of reaction throughout its sphere of influence among the multitude of states in Germany and Italy.

Nationalism menaced not only the Hapsburg domination of Germany and Italy but also the Austrian state itself, for the Austrian empire did not constitute a nation but rather a bewildering jumble of diverse nationalities. Austria proper, the seat of the governing house of the Hapsburgs, was German. To the east of Austria was the great plain of Hungary, the home of the Magyars, who were originally of Asiatic origin and spoke a language not related to most European tongues. All around the fringes of the Austrian and Hungarian center were primarily Slavic peoples: Czechs, Slovaks, and Poles to the north, Rumanians to the east, and Serbs, Croats, and Slovenes to the south. In addition, south of Austria were the large provinces of Lombardy and Venetia, purely Italian in population. In this polyglot Austrian empire the Germans were the ruling nationality. Although they comprised only about 20 percent of the total population, they constituted the bulk of the upper and middle classes, controlling the government, the Church, the bureaucracy, and the army. In appearance, then, Austria was German, but it was actually "a Slav edifice with a German facade." Only by excluding the ideas of nationalism and popular government could this ramshackle empire be kept intact.

The middle class in the empire was very small; the great bulk of the inhabitants were peasants, either serfs, as in Hungary, or virtual serfs who owed half their time and two thirds of the crops to their lords. Government was autocratic, and the regional assemblies or Diets possessed little power and represented only the nobility.

The Frankfurt Assembly. Notwithstanding the stern opposition of Metternich, supported by most of the German rulers, nationalism and political liberalism advanced in the German states after 1815. Much of the inspiration for this movement was derived from the romantic nationalism so strongly expressed by German professors, poets, and philosophers (see Chapter 15). The echo of the 1848 Revolution in France did not take long to reach discontented liberals and workingmen throughout Europe, leaving only Russia and Turkey untouched.

In March, 1848, serious rioting broke out in Berlin with the Prussian monarch forced to promise a constitution and support for a united Germany. Two months later the Frankfurt Assembly, representing the various German states and Austria met to create a constitution for a united Germany. Such a document was approved but the Assembly wasted valuable time debating academic issues. This lull gave the conservatives time to rally their forces. The Prussian king regained control of Berlin, and the liberal cause collapsed in Germany. The loose German Confederation, dominated by Austria still existed.

Revolts in Austria, Hungary, and Bohemia. In the meantime the nationalist spirit was increasing among the Magyars of Hungary. Czechs, Poles, Croats, Serbs, and Bulgars also began to take pride in their distinctive national cultures, to agitate for national independence where it was lacking, and to feel a sense of kinship and common destiny with all Slavic groups.

In March 1848 Vienna was rocked by revolt, as was Berlin. Metternich was forced to flee to England. Led by a magnetic nationalist, Louis Kossuth (1802-1894), the Hungarian Diet proclaimed its independence, tied only to Austria by a common sovereign. The emperor accepted this change and granted the same concession to the Czechs in Bohemia. A liberal constitution was also promised for Austria together with the end of serfdom. But the wave of reform subsided quickly. Various nationalities in the empire began to quarrel. With the end of serfdom the peasants became conservative supporters of the old regime. Royal authority from Vienna was effectively restored. In the summer of 1848 Hungarian

resistance collapsed with the intervention of Russian troops. Kossuth escaped and found refuge in the United States. The incompetent emperor was then induced to abdicate in favor of his young nephew, Francis Joseph.

NATIONAL RESURGENCE IN ITALY

Mazzini and the Risorgimento. After 1815 the Hapsburgs ruled over some unhappy provinces in the north and northeast sections of Italy and dominated the little independent states throughout the peninsula. It was perhaps natural that this frustrated land should produce the most famous exemplar of romantic nationalism, Guiseppe Mazzini (1805-1872), the son of a professor at the University of Genoa. Fired by the revolutionary zeal of romantic poets such as Byron, Mazzini in the 1820's joined the *Carbonari*, a secret revolutionary society. In 1830 Mazzini was implicated in an unsuccessful revolution against the royal government of Sardinia and was imprisoned for six months. Following his release, he established a new patriotic society known as Young Italy. Appealing mainly to students and intellectuals, he initiated a new phase of the Italian nationalist movement known as the *Risorgimento* (Resurgence).

Mazzini was intensely religious, and to him loyalty to the nation came midway between a man's loyalty to his family and that to his God. But unlike leaders of nationalism later in the century, who arrogantly preached the superiority of their own people, Mazzini believed that the people of every nation should work for the benefit of their brothers throughout the world.

The year 1848 saw a rash of revolutions on the Italian peninsula in which the king of Sardinia took a leading role. He also voluntarily promulgated a liberal constitution. But these advances soon faltered. Austrian forces defeated the Sardinian king and then helped restore old systems of government throughout Italy.

The final episode was the fall of the Republic of Rome. Early in 1849 Pope Pius IX was compelled to flee from Rome which was then declared a republic with Mazzini at its head. This action brought a wave of indignation in many quarters of Europe. Louis Napoleon, seeking to gain the approval of French Catholics and conservatives sent an expeditionary army which crushed the Roman republic in 1849. The restored pope was now bitterly hostile to all liberal and national ideas.

THE REVOLUTIONARY ERA IN RETROSPECT

Why democratic movements failed. The account of the rise and fall of the short-lived Roman republic ends the story of the widespread struggles for reform from 1848 to 1852. Looking back from the perspective of more than a hundred years, we can now see that the failure of the democratic movement in Europe in 1848 was one of the most decisive happenings in modern history; it helped shape the course not only of the nineteenth century but also that of the twentieth. What accounted for the failure?

One factor was excessive nationalism. It had been Mazzini's hope that men could be good Europeans as well as solid nationalists; but the events of 1848 showed that Europeans, whether democrats or reactionaries, were first and last Italians or Czechs or Germans, as the case might be. Kossuth, for example, refused to recognize the same national rights for the Croats and Serbs that he demanded for his own Magyar people. The problem posed to the men of 1848 was how to devise arrangements that would allow the various national groups to exercise political rights and enjoy cultural autonomy within some larger unit of cooperation. No progress was made in this direction.

Another element was the fact that romantic idealism was shown to be ineffectual in the realm of practical affairs. The idealist, the pacifist, and the internationalist were completely discredited. After 1848 romanticism in politics was superseded by the doctrine of realism, which placed its faith in power and resorted to any means to gain its ends.

Perhaps the most significant factor explaining the failure of the revolutions of 1848 was the emergence of class struggle as a factor in European politics. Since the peasants had little interest in revolution once the old feudal obligations had been removed, the movement became primarily the product of the middle class and the large-city workers. The leaders of the former wanted to transfer power from the aristocrats and upper bourgeoisie into their own hands; spokesmen for the latter wanted a social and economic change that would guarantee them a fair share in profits and in political control. In numerous instances a revolution was effected by a coalition between workers and bourgeoisie, but this cooperation soon broke down. The importance of the bloody June Days in Paris cannot be overestimated. The excesses of the Paris mob horrified both the intellectual and the bourgeois. By the end of 1848 it seemed that the observations of Marx and Engels in the Communist Manifesto issued on the eve of the revolutions of 1848 (see p. 334) might be justified—that perhaps there was an irreconcilable gulf between proletariat and bourgeoisie that could be resolved only by force.

The unfinished business of 1848. In spite of the overall failure of the revolutions of 1848, there were important immediate gains. Serfdom was not restored in the Austrian empire; Sardinia maintained its liberal constitution; and all the German states—even Prussia—had parliaments, even if most of them were not of the democratic variety. But the frustrations of 1848 left much unfinished business; for the next two decades the armies and diplomats of Europe were caught up in two great movements: the unification of Italy and of Germany. This era of nation-making is important not only for what happened but also for the attitudes of those involved. Political objectives were neither confused with the romantic dreams of poets nor modeled on the utopias imagined by idealistic intellectuals. Instead they were practical goals, ruthlessly pursued by such pragmatic statesmen as Cavour and Bismarck.

Metternich's place in history. As one looks back on this turbulent revolutionary era with its clash of opposing ideas, two symbols stand out in bold relief—the barricades and Metternich. In recent years some historians have been more kind in evaluating the Austrian statesman than were his contemporaries. Appalled by the chaos and conflict of the twentieth century, which they attribute to breakneck change, the fanaticism of nationalism, and the frequently emotional basis of politics in twentieth-century mass democracy, these scholars see a praiseworthy stability in the conservative system championed by Metternich from 1815 to 1848. Yet a complete absence of change is not better than too much change. Metternich failed to understand that the art of real statesmanship must provide for the attempt to bring together, in reasonable equilibrium, the best of the old forces and the most promising of the new. As a British historian has observed: "He saw no mean between revolution and autocracy, and since revolution was odious, he set himself to repress that which is the soul of human life in society, the very spirit of liberty."[1]

NATION-MAKING IN ITALY

Common denominators in Italian and German unification. The two most important achievements of nineteenth-century European nationalism were the unifications of Italy and Germany. This addition of two new, powerful nation-states radically altered the European state system.

Italy and Germany were built around a dynamic nucleus—the kingdom of Sardinia, whose center was the mainland territory of Piedmont, and the kingdom of Prussia. Both Italy and Germany had a common obstacle to national unity—Austria, since 1815 master of central Europe. In the case of Italian unification, however, a special complication was the existence of the Papal States, ruled from Rome by the pope. The Italian nationalists were faced with the problem of stripping this important religious leader of his secular powers and absorbing his territories into a united Italy without incurring the wrath of the Catholic powers in Europe.

Both the German and the Italian unifications were ultimately achieved not by romantic poets or intellectuals but by the dispassionate calculations of practical statesmen who exercised the art of diplomacy divorced from ethical considerations. This kind of statecraft is known as *Realpolitik*; in Germany it became identified with the policy that Bismarck called "blood and iron."

In the early 1850's Italy still remained what Metternich had derisively called it—"a geographical expression." The first phase of Mazzini's *Risorgimento* had failed. A new era now began with the career of Count Camillo Benso di Cavour (1810-1861), one of the most important statesmen of the nineteenth century. In 1852 he became prime minister of Sardinia. Well aware that Sardinia alone could not oust the Austrians from the Italian peninsula, Cavour determined to find an ally for his cause. The first move was to join France and Britain against Russia in the Crimean War (see p. 377). This step appeared ridiculous but it enabled Cavour to speak at the peace conference where he called attention to Italy's grievances.

The Austro-Italian War.   Cavour's speech impressed Napoleon III who agreed to assist Sardinia in case of war with Austria. France promised to help eject Austria from the Italian provinces of Lombardy and Venetia. Sardinia was then to rule over all of northern Italy. In return France would receive from Sardinia two provinces—Nice and Savoy.

Within a year Cavour tricked Austria into war. A French army intervened and the Austrian forces were driven out of Lombardy. Before the allied armies could

THE UNIFICATION OF ITALY 1859–1870

■ Kingdom of Sardinia to 1859
■ To Kingdom of Sardinia 1860
□ Annexed to Kingdom of Sardinia 1861; establishes Kingdom of Italy
□ To Kingdom of Italy 1866
■ To Kingdom of Italy 1870

The kingdom of Sardinia was the nucleus of a unified Italy. Through the wily diplomacy of Count Cavour, Lombardy was added to Sardinia in 1859. A year later Tuscany, Modena, and Parma voted to join the growing cluster; and Garibaldi led Naples and Sicily in revolution. Venetia and the Papal States were the last to come in.

invade Venetia the French emperor—realizing that he had started a movement destined to unite all of Italy—made a separate peace without consulting his ally. Cavour was furious, but in 1859 he agreed to a peace settlement that added Lombardy to Sardinia. A year later under British auspices a number of small Italian states voted to join Sardinia.

Garibaldi and his Red Shirts. The center of interest now shifted to southern Italy and to a new leader, Giuseppe Garibaldi (1807-1882), who had been a follower of Mazzini. Secretly subsidized by Cavour, Garibaldi recruited one thousand tough adventurers, his immortal Red Shirts. In 1860 this audacious force invaded and conquered the reactionary pro-Austrian kingdom of Naples and Sicily. When Garibaldi planned to set up a separate government, Cavour rushed troops to Naples; and Garibaldi surrendered his power to the king of Sardinia. By November 1860 Sardinia had annexed the former kingdom of Naples and Sicily and all the papal lands except Rome and its surrounding territory, known as the Patrimony of St. Peter.

Unity achieved. Italy's first parliament met at Turin in February 1861. A new nation of 22 million citizens had been created, but the task had not yet been completed. Austria still controlled Venetia, while Rome and the Patrimony of St. Peter were still under papal control. Cavour, who died in 1861, did not live to see the full fruits of his works, but he realized that a united Italy was not far off. Although many have criticized his duplicity, he himself made no attempt to hide the true nature of his methods. He once said: "If we did for ourselves what we do for our country, what rascals we should be."[2]

In the decade following Cavour's death, Italian policy followed his principles. By acting as an ally of Prussia during the war between Prussia and Austria in 1866, Italy obtained Venetia. And when the Franco-Prussian War broke out in 1870 and French troops were withdrawn from Rome, Italian troops took possession of the Eternal City. In 1871 Rome became the capital of a unified Italy.

Italy still faced serious problems. The country had few natural resources, and the interests of the industrial north often clashed with those of the agricultural south. Furthermore, a religious issue seriously weakened the state, the seizure of Rome, the last remnant of the Papal States, had alienated the pope. Terming himself "the prisoner of the Vatican," the pope called on Italian Catholics to refrain from voting. In an attempt at conciliation, the Italian government passed the Law of the Papal Guarantees, by which the pope was to have the Vatican as a sovereign state and was to be given an annual sum of $600,000. Although this offer was rejected, the law was not repealed.

In the field of politics, the people lacked experience in or aptitude for constitutional government. Seventy-five percent of the population was illiterate in 1861, and the franchise was very restricted. As late as 1904 only 29 percent of the adult male population could vote, and of this group only 38 percent actually went to the polls. Political life also suffered from unstable coalitions.

Another grievous burden for the country was its leaders' ambition to have Italy play a grand role in the world and thus fulfill the dreams of greatness built up during the *Risorgimento*. Too much money was spent on the army, and national resources were squandered in the unrewarding pursuit of empire in Africa.

Early in the twentieth century liberals joined socialists in demanding such reforms as compulsory education, freedom of the press, and better working conditions for the masses. As a result, in 1912 laws were passed providing for universal suffrage and for payment of deputies in parliament.

THE TRIUMPH OF BLOOD AND IRON IN GERMANY

Prussia and the German nationalistic movement.   Although the German revolution of 1848 and the Frankfurt Assembly failed to achieve their liberal-national purposes, the nationalist movement in Germany was far from dead. It was accelerated by a group of remarkable German historians who saw in the Italian struggle a clear example to follow. Economic factors also proved to be significant in the German unification movement. Of special importance was the Zollverein, or customs union, initiated by Prussia in 1834, which instituted free trade throughout Prussia and the territories of other member states (but excluded Austria). By 1842 most of the German states belonged to the Zollverein. This tariff union not only demonstrated that closer economic cooperation was good business for the various states but also strengthened the interest of the German middle class in the nationalist movement.

Prussian government and public administration were modern and efficient. Civil servants were well trained, honest, and highly devoted to the service of the state. The hierarchy of government bureaus and departments was logical and functional. By the middle of the century the general citizenry of Prussia attended public schools far in advance of those found in any of the other great powers, or in the United States; and Prussian higher education enjoyed an enviable reputation throughout Europe. By 1850 Prussia was rapidly building up the strength to compel central Europe to do its bidding, but it was twelve years before there appeared the man who was to formulate the necessary orders.

**THE UNIFICATION OF GERMANY
1815–1871**

- Prussia 1815-1866
- Annexed by Prussia 1866
- Joined Prussia in forming the North German Confederation 1867
- Joined with Prussia to form the German Empire 1871
- Alsace-Lorraine ceded to German Empire by France 1871
- German Confederation 1815-1866

Bismarck and his policy of blood and iron. The unification of Germany was achieved through the genius of a consummate statesman, Otto von Bismarck (1815-1898). The future German chancellor grew up a typical Prussian aristocrat, or Junker, an enemy to all liberal ideas and an uncompromising supporter of the Prussian state and its king.

In 1862 Bismarck was called to be Prussian prime minister. His appointment coincided with a serious constitutional crisis: the king wished to strengthen the army, but the Chamber of Deputies would not approve the necessary appropriations. Following Bismarck's advice, the king successfully defied the legislature and levied the necessary taxes without its consent.

With meticulous care Bismarck prepared for the task of building a powerful new German empire. He was a superb master of diplomatic intrigue and a practitioner of *Realpolitik*—the "politics of reality." Boldly, he declared:

> Germany does not look to Prussia's liberalism, but to her power. . . . The great questions of the day are not to be decided by speeches and majority resolutions—therein lay the weakness of 1848 and 1849—but by blood and iron![3]

Wars against Denmark and Austria. In 1864 Bismarck invited Austria to join Prussia in waging war on Denmark, the issue being the status of two duchies bordering on Prussia and Denmark—Schleswig and Holstein—which were claimed by both Denmark and the German Confederation. The Prussian army, aided by Austrian forces, easily smashed the Danish defenses; the administration of Holstein was awarded to Austria, while Schleswig came under Prussian rule.

Bismarck next proceeded to pick a quarrel with his recent ally. Hostilities broke out with Austria in 1866 with the armies of Prussia completely victorious. To avoid humiliating Austria, Prussia offered moderate terms. The old German Confederation was dissolved, supplanted by the North German Confederation under Prussian domination. Austria and the south German states were excluded. Prussia annexed Holstein along with Hanover and a number of small states to the south, thus at last bridging the gap between its various territories.

The Franco-Prussian War. Two barriers remained to Bismarck's plans for a united Germany under Prussian leadership—France with its centuries-old policy of keeping Germany disunited and weak, and the south German states with their distrust of Prussia. Both obstacles were removed when Bismarck succeeded in maneuvering Napoleon III into declaring war on Prussia.

As early as 1865 Napoleon III in a fateful conference with Bismarck had allowed himself to be completely hoodwinked. In return for vague promises—the German statesman mentioned securing for France "perhaps the Palatinate and the Rhine frontier, perhaps Luxemburg, perhaps part of Belgium or Switzerland"[4]— the French emperor pledged himself not to interfere in any Austro-Prussian war. After the conflict had been decided by a Prussian victory, Bismarck announced that he had no recollection of promises made to France. Napoleon III thereupon specifically raised the possibility of French compensation at the expense of Belgium, and an agreement was drawn up in which Bismarck backed this claim in return for French recognition of the federal union of all German states. Bismarck next saw to it that the document was made public in England, the nation where it would do the most harm to France. The British became openly hostile to Napoleon III, and Bismarck thus made certain that there would be no British support of France in case of war. At the same time, by supporting Russia during the Polish revolt in 1863 and by offering Austria a moderate peace in 1866, Bismarck successfully isolated France from these two states.

Too late, Napoleon III realized that a great rival power was in the making and that France could no longer claim to be the "mistress of Europe." France declared war in July 1870, and amid wild enthusiasm and shouts of "On to Berlin" the French regiments marched to the front. But there was no comparison between the superbly trained Prussian hosts and the badly disorganized French army. The French suffered reverse after reverse. In September came the crowning disaster—the surrender at Sedan, where an entire French army and the emperor himself were forced to capitulate. New leaders emerged to carry on resistance against the German forces, and Paris withstood a siege of four months before surrendering. By the Treaty of Frankfurt, France lost Alsace and part of Lorraine to Prussia and was required to pay a huge indemnity. Many Frenchmen never forgot this humiliation. History was to give France a chance to retaliate after World War I.

The Second (Hohenzollern) Reich.   During the Franco-Prussian War the south German states, moved by patriotic enthusiasm, had joined the North German Confederation. Thus the common struggle against France removed the last obstacle to national unification. In January 1871, in the Hall of Mirrors at the palace of Versailles, King William of Prussia was proclaimed German emperor.

This well-known cartoon, "Dropping the Pilot," appeared in the English magazine *Punch* in 1890, following the dismissal of Bismarck as chancellor of Germany. Kaiser William II, determined to dominate German government personally, watches from the ship of state as the former helmsman leaves the vessel. Despite the change in leadership, however, the tradition that Bismarck represented continued into the twentieth century, as Germany followed a course of ardent nationalism and military aggressiveness.

The new German empire (Reich)—a federal union of twenty-six states with a population of about 41 million—included the kingdoms of Prussia, Bavaria, Saxony, and Württemberg, various grand duchies and duchies, three city republics, and the imperial territory of Alsace-Lorraine.

Headed by the German emperor, the imperial government consisted of a legislative upper house, the Bundesrat, representing the ruling houses of the various states; and a lower house, the Reichstag, representing the people. The 61 members of the Bundesrat voted as instructed by their royal masters. The 397 members of the Reichstag were elected by manhood suffrage, but they had little power. Thus the Hohenzollern empire had a few parliamentary trappings, but behind this facade of democracy was the dominant power of reactionary Prussia.

The office of German emperor was vested in the Hohenzollern dynasty so that the king of Prussia was at the same time kaiser of the empire. The kaiser wielded considerable power in military and foreign affairs. As king of Prussia, he also controlled seventeen votes in the Bundesrat. No amendment to the constitution could pass this body if opposed by fourteen votes. Prussia also controlled the chairmanships of practically all the standing committees in the Bundesrat.

Appointed by the emperor and responsible to him alone, the chancellor was the actual head of the government. Unlike the situation in the English House of Commons or the French Chamber of Deputies, the German chancellor could defy or ignore any action taken by the legislature, especially the Reichstag. In 1871 Bismarck was appointed the first imperial chancellor.

As the architect of German nationalism, Bismarck completed his most important work by 1871, although he remained chancellor of the German empire until 1890. To achieve his ends, he had used ruthless means. But perhaps, as in the case of Cavour, he felt that circumstances left him no alternative. It was a tragedy for the world that to Bismarck blood and iron seemed essential in forging a united Germany, for his successes strengthened the notion that war is a national business that can be made to pay big dividends.

Bismarck's Red and Black menaces. The Chancellor's achievements in foreign affairs were impressive, but, in the domestic realm he experienced two notable setbacks. His attempt to curb the influence of the Catholic Church, his "Black Menace," was a definite failure. Again Bismarck's repressive measures against the socialist movement, his "Red Menace," only increased its adherents. In order to wean the working masses away from radicalism, important measures such as health, accident, and old age insurance were passed. But these did little to weaken German socialism.

Kaiser William II. In 1888 William II, the grandson of William I, became German emperor. Just as Bismarck had stamped his policies and personality on the German nation for the more than twenty years that he was chancellor, so this young man was the focus of German history from 1890 to 1918.

In addition to having a strong militaristic bent, William was an ardent champion of the divine right of kings. He constantly reminded those around him that "he and God" worked together for the good of the state. Berliners, astounded at his wide if superficial interests, humorously said: "God knows everything, but the kaiser knows better." The loud dress, flashy uniforms, and oratorical outbursts of the emperor sprang from an inferiority complex, which probably had its origin in the withered left arm that he had had from birth. Restless and emotionally unstable, he was continually making undiplomatic speeches and casting off insulting phrases that alarmed and sometimes infuriated governmental circles in Europe.

William II came to the throne determined to dominate the German government personally. To the kaiser's mind it was "a question whether the Bismarck dynasty or the Hohenzollern dynasty should rule."[5] For two years the tension between emperor and chancellor mounted. Finally, in 1890, William rudely dismissed Bismarck.

Reasons for despotism. Despite advances in industry and science, Germany remained a "political kindergarten." There were several reasons why despotism existed in such a prosperous and advanced country. First, the nation had militaristic leanings. It had achieved its unity by blood and iron. Any liberal movement would, if necessary, be crushed by the armed forces, which were passionately loyal to the Hohenzollern dynasty. At the heart of this militarism were the aristocratic Prussian Junkers, who disdained business, gloried in war, and had an austere sense of their duty to the state.

What we may term the German tradition also played its part. The people had long been taught to serve the Prussian state unquestioningly and to look to their leaders for guidance. As the Germans expressed it: "Alles kommt von oben" ("Everything comes down from above"). The people also gave the government unquestioning loyalty because it was efficient and solicitous of their material welfare. Bismarck's social insurance program succeeded in keeping the German masses contented.

Another factor which kept most of the Germans in line was the school system. The masses went to the *Volksschule,* where they were given excellent training in the three R's and were taught obedience to the state. The businessmen and landed aristocracy, on the other hand, sent their sons and daughters to an altogether different school system that led to the university and produced the elite that ruled the nation. German education trained many followers and a few leaders.

The democratic movement. Notwithstanding the strength of autocracy, a remarkable democratic movement, whose spearhead was the Social Democratic party, manifested itself in Germany as the twentieth century dawned. Despite the opposition of the emperor and his conservative supporters (William II called the socialists a "treasonable horde"), the vote cast by the Social Democrats continued to increase during William's reign as it had under Bismarck. In 1914 this party could claim the support of one third of the German voters.

The outbreak of war in 1914 was to nip in the bud the promising democratic movement. As a result, revolution was later substituted for evolution, and the German people achieved a republic before they had been sufficiently trained to govern themselves.

THE DUAL MONARCHY: AUSTRIA-HUNGARY

Establishment of the Dual Monarchy. As we have seen, the collapse of the liberal and nationalist movement in the Austrian empire in 1848 was followed by stern repression. An undisguised system of absolutism was imposed upon all peoples in the empire. Included in this system was the centralization of all governmental administration in Vienna and an active policy of Germanizing the non-Teutonic subject peoples.

These reactionary measures were doomed, however, by the defeat of Austria in

1859 by France and Sardinia. The old ways were thoroughly discredited, and Vienna realized that if the empire was to survive, the demands of the subject nationalities would have to be appeased. As a result, in 1861 a new imperial constitution was framed in which representatives were to be elected from the various provincial parliaments to a central, imperial Diet. The Hungarians, however, who were by far the strongest of the subject nationalities, demanded concessions which would virtually make Hungary an independent state. The resulting impasse ended following Austria's disastrous defeat by Prussia in 1866 when the emperor offered to establish the Magyars as equal partners in ruling the empire. The offer was accepted, and in 1867 the constitution known as the *Ausgleich* (Compromise) was promulgated.

Setting up a unique form of government, a Dual Monarchy known as Austria-Hungary, the *Ausgleich* made the Hapsburg ruler king in Hungary and emperor in Austria. Each country had its own constitution, offical language, flag, and parliament, but finance, defense, and foreign affairs were under ministers common to both countries. These common ministers were supervised by the "Delegations," which consisted of sixty members from the Austrian parliament and an equal number of representatives from the Hungarian legislature.

Problems in the Dual Monarchy. While the Germans of Austria recognized the equality of the Magyars of Hungary, these two dominant nationalities made few concessions to the aspirations of their subject nationalities (see map below). Increasingly restive under alien rule, these peoples wanted the right to govern themselves. In some cases, as in Bohemia, the people wanted to set up a new

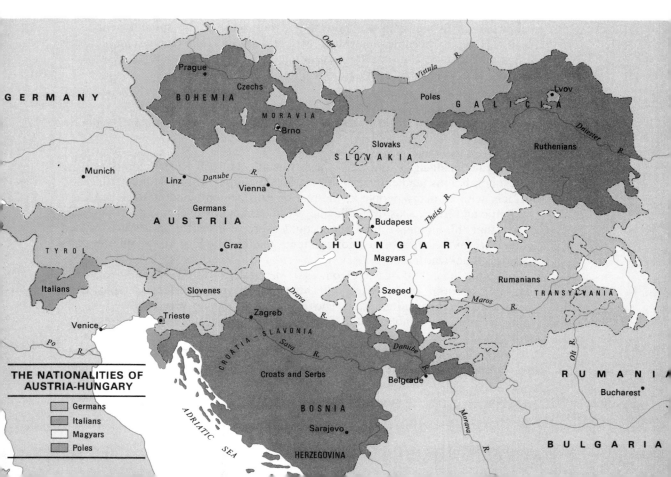

THE NATIONALITIES OF AUSTRIA-HUNGARY

- Germans
- Italians
- Magyars
- Poles

independent nation; or, in the case of the Italians and the Serbs, the goal was to join their countrymen living in adjacent national states.

Although the bicameral legislature in Austria was elected by general manhood suffrage after 1907, political life continued to be dominated by wealthy German businessmen and the landed aristocracy. The latter monopolized the leading positions in government, the army, and parliament. Strong racial and national antipathies also impeded the functioning of what, on paper, seemed a liberal constitution. Political parties were not based primarily on political principle but on nationality. Each major group—Czechs, Poles, Slovenes, and Italians—feared and detested the German ruling elite, and too often each disliked the other national groups. Although Austria gave its subject nationalities substantial local self-government, this concession had little mollifying effect.

If democracy was weak in Austria, it was practically nonexistent in Hungary. Here the aristocracy firmly held the reins of power, and the Magyars refused to share political control with the other nationalities—Croats, Serbs, Slovaks, and Rumanians—who were under their rule. Hungary was agricultural, with a small landowning class dominating a great mass of backward, landless peasants.

Despite the difficulties to which the existence of the Dual Monarchy gave rise, the defenders of the empire could point to the military strength and international influence it gave to a large part of eastern and southern Europe. Above all, the empire exhibited a certain economic unity, for its various parts complemented each other well. Hungary, for example, produced wheat; Croatia and Slavonia exported cattle and swine; Bohemia and Austria were important industrial centers; and the great capital city of Vienna was the heart of the empire's banking and commerce.

In Chapter 18 we shall see how the restlessness of the subject peoples in Austria-Hungary became enmeshed with a Pan-Slav movement exploited by Serbia and Russia. Nationalism was ultimately to prove the undoing of Austria-Hungary and to involve Europe in the First World War.

RUSSIA: AUTOCRACY, ORTHODOXY, AND NATIONALISM

Autocracy challenged: the Decembrist Revolt. In 1850 Russia comprised the largest continuous land empire in the world. Containing a sixth of the earth's land surface, with as many people as the rest of Europe combined, it stretched from the Baltic and Black seas to the Pacific. At this time, however, the great potential power that this immense land giant could exercise in world affairs was hidden under the inefficiency of its government, the isolation of its people, and its economic backwardness.

Following the defeat of Napoleon, Tsar Alexander I (1801-1825) had been ready to discuss constitutional reforms, but though a few were introduced, no thorough-going changes were attempted. The pseudo-liberal tsar was followed by his younger brother Nicholas I (1825-1855), who at the outset of his reign was confronted by an uprising. The so-called Decembrist Revolt (December 1825)—the work of a small circle of liberal nobles and army officers was easily quashed and those involved were cruelly punished. Five were executed and over five hundred exiled to Siberia. This harsh retaliation made "December Fourteenth" a day long remembered and the inspiration for later revolutionary movements. It also made Tsar Nicholas ultrasensitive to revolution and liberalism. He turned away from the Europeanization program begun by Peter the Great and Catherine the Great and championed the maxim "Autocracy, Orthodoxy, and Nationalism."

Repression and radicalism. Under the reactionary Nicholas System, Russia became "frozen." Foreign visitors were carefully screened, and those with "dangerous ideas" were halted at the border. Foreign books were not permitted if they contained any tincture of liberalism. Schools and universities were placed under constant surveillance, and the students were provided with official textbooks. Police spies were everywhere. Would-be revolutionaries and often quite harmless liberals were packed off to Siberia; from 1832 to 1852 an estimated 150,000 persons were exiled there. As we noted earlier in this chapter, it was during Nicholas' reign that the Polish nationalist revolution of 1830 occurred. The treatment of Poland after the unsuccessful revolution was quite in keeping with the Nicholas System in Russia proper. Poland was reduced to a Russian province, and every attempt was made to stamp out Polish nationalism.

Although Russian liberalism had received a setback from the collapse of the Decembrist conspiracy, the reform movement continued. In the 1830's and 1840's the younger generation of the nobility began to study the ideas of French and English reformers. They also found inspiration in the work of two Russian authors, Alexander Herzen (1812-1870) and Michael Bakunin (1814-1876).

While the former was a moderate socialist, the latter was much more radical and is regarded as the father of Russian anarchism. He advocated terrorism as an agent of social change, calling it "the propaganda of the deed." He preached that anarchy—complete freedom—can be the only cure for society's ills.

Heavy-handed repression by Nicholas did not stifle the desire of Russian intellectuals for knowledge. One of them called this period "an amazing time of outward slavery and inner liberation." Liberals and reformers met in secret and argued during the long winter nights about freedom, the merits of parliamentary government, and the part Russia should play in world history.

The question of Russia's destiny had been brewing ever since Peter the Great's program of westernization had been put into operation early in the eighteenth century (see Chapter 13). Which path should Russia follow? Should it imitate Europe or renounce the West and return to the traditions of its past? The first road was championed by the so-called Westerners; the second by the nationalistic Slavophiles, who heaped scorn on the "decadent" West. The Slavophiles preferred the collectivism of the medieval Russian *mir*, or village community, to what they regarded as the dog-eat-dog individualism of the West. Presentday communism in Soviet Russia owes a debt to the age-old social pattern of the *mir* as well as to the doctrines of Karl Marx.

Alexander II abolished serfdom. Tsar Nicholas died with his philosophy in disrepute. One year earlier, in 1854, Russia had become involved in the Crimean War, a conflict fought primarily in the Crimean peninsula (see pp. 377–378). Since playing a major role in the defeat of Napoleon, Russia had been regarded as militarily invincible, but the reverses it suffered on land and sea in the Crimean War, the blunders committed by its generals, and the huge loss of its manpower exposed the rottenness and weakness of the Nicholas regime. Russia, it was said, was like a giant with feet of clay.

When Alexander II came to the throne in 1855, desire for reform was widespread. Many of his subjects, even the conservatives, believed that social and political conditions needed changing if Russia was to keep up with other European states. Although no liberal, the new tsar realized the necessity for moderate reform; his first move was against serfdom, which meant virtual slavery for more than 23 million peasants. An Emancipation Proclamation was issued in March 1861. The freed peasants, however, had to pay for their land over a period of forty-nine years to the government. The emancipation of the serfs was the single most important event in nineteenth-century Russian history. It was the beginning of the end for the landed aristocracy's monopoly of power. Emancipation brought a supply of free labor to the cities; industry was stimulated, and the middle class grew in numbers and influence. Above all, emancipation gave strong impetus to the liberal movement.

Nihilism. In the 1860's a remarkable movement known as Nihilism developed in Russia. For some time many Russian liberals had been dissatisfied by the empty discussions of the intelligentsia; they now launched a movement which aimed to put all things in Russia to the test of reason. Ivan Turgenev, in his novel *Fathers and Sons* (1861), described a Nihilist as "a man who does not bow down before any authority, who does not take any principle on faith, whatever reverence that principle may be enshrined in."[6] As might have been expected, this attitude of "nothing sacred" resulted in a radical reconsideration of the very basis of society. The Nihilists questioned all old values, championed the independence of the individual, and delighted in shocking the older generation. The Nihilists first attempted to convert the aristocracy to the cause of reform. Failing there, they turned to the peasants, and a veritable missionary movement ensued. Young college students became laborers and worked in the fields with the peasants. Others went to the villages as doctors and teachers to preach reform to the people. This "go to the people" campaign was known as the Narodnik movement (*narod*, "people").

Alexander abandons reform. Alexander II proceeded to carry out other reforms. In 1864 the elective principle was introduced in local government and trial by jury in criminal cases. City administration was improved by the creation of municipal councils.

Alexander, however, became disillusioned when his reforms failed to arrest discontent. In 1863 the Poles revolted and were crushed with harsh repression. In the meantime the Narodnik movement had collapsed. The government had tried to extirpate it; and the peasants, who could not understand it, rejected it. In response to the growing reaction of the government, a radical branch of Nihilists advocated and systematically practiced terrorism. One after another, prominent officials were shot down or killed by bombs. Finally, after several attempts, Alexander II was assassinated in 1881, on the very day he had approved a proposal to call a representative assembly to consider new reforms.

Autocracy and reaction under Alexander III. Unlike his father, the new tsar, Alexander III (1881-1894), was throughout his reign a staunch reactionary who revived the repressive system of Nicholas I and rigidly adhered to its maxim of "Autocracy, Orthodoxy, and Nationalism." A confirmed Slavophile, Alexander III believed that Russia could be saved from chaos only by shutting itself off from the subversive influences of western Europe. Publications were censored, and schools and universities were regulated to prevent students from learning "dangerous" ideas. One nation, one language, one church, and one government—an autocratic government—was the formula of administration. The Jews were bullied and sometimes massacred in terrible drives called pogroms, and thousands sought asylum in the United States.

Nicholas II and a new revolutionary movement. Alexander was succeeded by his son, Nicholas II (1894-1917), a weak man with little intellect and hardly any force of character. The Industrial Revolution, which had begun to exert a significant influence in Russia in the late nineteenth century, was quietly helping create forces that would finally overthrow this last "Tsar of all the Russias." Several distinct reform parties, either liberal or radical, emerged. The progressive elements among the businessmen and nobility formed the Liberals (Constitutional Democrats, or Kadets). They wanted a consititutional monarchy and believed in peaceful reform. The Social Revolutionaries combined socialism with the Narodnik tradition and advocated "the whole land to the whole people." Their specific goal was the distribution of the land among those who actually worked it—the peasants.

Another radical group was the Social Democrats, exponents of Marxist principles. Gathering their strength chiefly from the radical intellectuals and the workingmen in the cities, they believed in a complete social and economic as well as political revolution. In 1903 the party split into two wings—the Mensheviks, or moderates, and the Bolsheviks, or extremists. The Mensheviks believed that Russian socialism should grow gradually and peacefully and that the tsar's government should be overthrown and succeeded by a democratic republic in which the socialists would cooperate with bourgeois political parties. Working under a democratic system, the socialists would gradually become the dominant political force and would secure their socialistic society by parliamentary means. On the other hand, the Bolsheviks, under Nikolai Lenin (see p. 341), advocated the formation of a small elite of professional revolutionists, subject to strong party discipline, to act as the self-appointed vanguard of the proletariat. Although the Bolsheviks posed as democrats, they advocated seizure of power by force.

The government struck back energetically. Nicholas' minister of the interior organized diversionary outbursts of anti-Semitism among the people. Bands of thugs, called Black Hundreds, were organized to carry out pogroms and to attack liberals; and the fierce Cossacks were frequently used to carry fire and sword into rebellious regions. In the ranks of the revolutionists the government planted *agents provocateurs*, who incited the insurgents to murder officials and then exposed them to the police.

The revolution of 1905: Bloody Sunday. In 1904 the clash of rival imperialism in Manchuria and Korea (see p. 407) led to war with Japan. The Russian fleet was destroyed, and on land the Japanese gained victory after victory. With the ignominious defeat of its armed forces, the tsar's corrupt regime became the target for almost universal criticism.

Disorders spread throughout the land in the last months of 1904. On January 22, 1905, occurred the tragic incident known as Bloody Sunday. On this day a priest led an enormous crowd to the Winter Palace in St. Petersburg to present a petition to the tsar. When the procession reached the Winter Palace, Cossacks opened fire on the defenseless crowd, killing hundreds and wounding many more. This massacre shocked the world. Subsequently it was discovered that the priest had once been an agent of the secret police.

The Russian masses were so aroused over the Bloody Sunday massacre that a general strike was declared. The strikers demanded a democratic republic, freedom for political prisoners, and the disarming of the police. Soviets (councils of workers) appeared in the cities to direct revolutionary activity. Most business and government offices closed, and there was no gas, electricity, or (in some areas) water. The whole machinery of Russian economic life creaked to a defiant halt. Russia was paralyzed, and the government was helpless.

Results of the revolutionary movement. In October 1905 Tsar Nicholas reluctantly issued the famous October Manifesto, which promised "freedom of person, conscience, speech, assembly, and union." A national Duma (legislature) was to be called without delay, the right to vote was to be extended, and no law was to go into force without confirmation by the Duma. When the first Duma was convened in the spring of 1906, it proceeded to censure the government, demanding an investigation into the conduct of the Russo-Japanese War, autonomy for Poland and Finland, and the freeing of political prisoners. The tsar dissolved the Duma in midsummer because, he said, its members "would not cooperate." An appeal by the liberal leaders of the Duma was met by apathy on the part of the people. Sensing the decline of the revolutionary fervor, the tsar appointed a conservative prime minister, Piotr Arkadevich Stolypin, who mercilessly repressed all radical elements.

Yet Stolypin was no blind reactionary. Even without the tsar's full support, he managed to push through some significant agricultural reforms. All payments still owed by peasants under the Emancipation Law were abolished, and, with financial aid from the state, two and a half million peasants were enabled to withdraw from the village community (*mir*) and become private owners of their lands.

Although Nicholas II had been forced to make some concessions, the loyalty of the army, the staunch support of the Orthodox Church, and division among the opponents of tsarism enabled him to continue his autocratic and inefficient regime for the time being.

CHAPTER 18

HOPE AND HOLOCAUST

Parliaments and Political Reforms: 1850-1914;
Forces for Peace and War: 1871-1918

Because of its steady and peaceful progress toward democracy, Britain was regarded by many nineteenth-century liberals as the model nation. Fearful of the rising influence of the business class, the English nobility allied itself with the growing labor class, which became politically ambitious and demanded an effective voice in government. In addition, many among the well-to-do had real fear of revolution; to them it seemed better to grant concessions to the masses than to risk bloodshed such as Paris witnessed in 1848 and 1871. Under Disraeli, city workers got the vote; under Gladstone, suffrage was extended to agricultural workers. Finally, the Parliament Bill of 1911 made Britian an almost completely democratic state.

The second great democratic power of the late nineteenth century was France, which, for the third time, attempted to adopt a republican form of government after its Second Empire went down in humiliating defeat at the hands of Prussia in 1870. The first important act of the Third French Republic was the defeat of the Commune, a revolutionary body which brought about a violent and bloody civil uprising in Paris. As the nineteenth century came to a close, France was further convulsed by a series of crises that threatened to discredit, and even to overthrow, the Republic. Although by 1914 democratic France seemed to have ridden out the storm, the feuds and scandals of the past had left scars.

Democracy was weak or non-existent in Central and Eastern Europe. Twentieth century Nazi dictatorship, and that of Soviet Russia and its satellites, all have their roots in this failure of parliamentary government before 1914.

Meanwhile, with progress in science and technology came progress in destructive armaments; and while the power of military weapons increased, little was done to remove the causes that led nations to rely upon these weapons. If men could be said to have ascended to a new level of civilization in their scientific and intellectual attainments, their tactics and outlook in international affairs were often reminiscent of the jungle. Europe, with its progressive and brilliant yet menacing and unstable civilization, was now the center of the world. It was the central position this little continent enjoyed that gave its promise and peril world-wide implications. Fanned by old rivalries and callous ambitions, a spark in that center was to grow and spread and finally engulf the world in flames, creating the holocaust known as World War I.

For more than four years during this titanic conflict, Europe's youth, wealth, and industry were dedicated to destruction. With the entrance of the United States into the war in 1917 the bloody stalemate ended, and in the autumn of 1918 Germany collapsed and sued for peace.

TOWARD DEMOCRATIZATION OF BRITISH LIFE

End of the Victorian Compromise. From 1850 to 1914 Great Britain manifested a slow but orderly progression to broadened horizons of political democracy and social justice. The period from 1832—the year in which the first Reform Bill was passed—to 1865 is often described as the era of the Victorian Compromise. During this period an alliance of the landed gentry and the middle class worked together to dominate the government and keep the lower classes "in their stations." The members of the middle class believed that the political reforms— which had been in large measure of benefit to them alone—had gone far enough. Although some social reforms were granted, they were exceptions in the general atmosphere of middle-class complacency.

The symbol of this conservatism was Lord Palmerston, who dominated the direction of foreign affairs from the 1830's until his death in 1865 and ended his career by acting as prime minister during much of the period from 1855 to 1865. A viscount himself, he was quite satisfied with the rule of the aristocracy and the middle class.

The death of Palmerston and the entry of two new political leaders into the limelight heralded the beginning of a new era in British affairs. For a generation English politics was little more than the biographies of William Ewart Gladstone (1809-1898), a Liberal, and Benjamin Disraeli (1804-1881), a Conservative, who alternated with one another as prime minister from 1867 to 1880. Following the death of Disraeli, Gladstone continued to dominate politics until his retirement in 1894.

The son of a rich Liverpool merchant, Gladstone had every advantage that wealth and good social position could bestow. Entering Parliament in 1833 at the age of twenty-four, the young politician quickly made a name for himself as one of the greatest orators of his day, on one occasion holding the attention of the House of Commons for five hours while he expounded the intricacies of the national budget. At first Gladstone was a Conservative in politics, a follower of the Tory leader Robert Peel. But gradually he shifted his allegiance to the Liberal (Whig) party, which he headed as prime minister for the first time in 1868. Gladstone was a staunch supporter of laissez faire, the belief that government should not interfere in business. His record as a social and economic reformer, therefore, was not imposing. But in political reforms his accomplishments were noteworthy.

The great rival of Gladstone, Benjamin Disraeli, had few advantages of birth and social position. The son of a cultured Jew who had become a naturalized British subject in 1801, Disraeli was baptized an Anglican. He first made a name for himself as a novelist with *Vivian Grey* (1826). Unlike Gladstone, Disraeli swung from liberalism to conservatism in his political philosophy; he stood for office as a Conservative throughout his career and eventually became the leader of the Conservative (Tory) party.

By the time of Palmerston's death it was obvious that the Victorian Compromise could not be maintained any longer. With only one adult male out of six having the right to vote, English workmen had formed large organizations to agitate for the franchise. Both the Conservatives and the Liberals realized that reform must come, and each hoped to gain new political strength from the passage of a reform bill. In 1867 the Conservatives came into power and successfully sponsored a reform bill that added more than a million workers to the voting rolls. Although women and farm laborers still could not vote, Britain was well on its way to democracy.

Gladstone's "Glorious Ministry." To the dismay of Disraeli, the newly enfranchised voters brought the Liberals back to power in 1868 with Gladstone as prime minister. Gladstone's so-called "Glorious Ministry," which was to last until 1874, was one of great achievements.

The Education Act of 1870 was the first attempt to create a national system of education. In ten years, attendance in elementary schools jumped from one to four million. In the same year a merit system transformed the civil service, and the war office introduced reforms in army enlistment and promotion.

Other long-needed reforms included a surer and speedier system of justice, introduction of secret balloting (1872), and removal of some of the restrictions on labor union activity. Gladstone's energetic efforts to solve the Irish problem, described later, extended through his second and third ministries. By the early 1870's, however, the reforming zeal of the Glorious Ministry had run down, and Disraeli wittily referred to Gladstone and his colleagues in the House of Commons as a "range of exhausted volcanoes."

Disraeli and Tory democracy. The story of the continued growth of democracy in Great Britain resumes with the election of Disraeli as prime minister in 1874. Attacking standpat conservatism, he advocated what became known as Tory democracy—a political alliance formed between the landed gentry and the workers against the businessmen. In the landed gentry Disraeli saw England's natural leaders—champions of the common people, who were being exploited by the middle class, the modern counterpart of the medieval nobility.

The social legislation enacted under Disraeli's ministry (1874-1880) substantially advanced Britain toward what we know now as the welfare state. Public health facilities were improved, peaceful picketing and the right to strike were fully legalized, a food and drug act was passed, and housing programs were inaugurated.

Reform measures of Gladstone. Returning to power in 1880, Gladstone in 1884 sponsored the third Reform Bill, a measure extending the vote to agricultural workers. This statute brought Britain to the verge of universal manhood suffrage. Gladstone also obtained passage of the important Employers' Liability Act, which gave the workers rights of compensation in five classes of accidents. Apart from these measures, Gladstone concerned himself primarily with attempts to solve the Irish problem, the principal question in British politics in the late nineteenth century.

The Irish problem. Unrest and violence have been a part of Irish history for three hundred years. In the seventeenth century Britain settled large numbers of Scottish Protestant emigrants in northern Ireland in Ulster. Oppressive laws were also passed by which Irish Catholics were dispossessed of their lands, and in 1801 the Irish legislature was abolished. In 1845 the potato crop, the main staple of diet, failed, and a terrible famine ensued. Perhaps as many as 500,000 people died, and a huge exodus to America began—the beginning of the principal Irish Catholic settlements in the United States. In 1841 the population of Ireland was 8,770,000; in 1891 it was less than 5,000,000.

During the course of the nineteenth century various measures were taken to reduce the inequities between Catholics and Protestants. In 1829 Catholics were permitted to sit in Parliament, and Gladstone sponsored two land acts encouraging Irish peasants to become landowners. Above all he sought to solve a burning grievance by giving Ireland its own legislature with retention of British control only over such matters as foreign affairs. Two home rule bills were introduced but both were defeated in Parliament.

Finally, a third home rule bill was introduced and passed in 1914. The Ulsterites, however, strongly opposed the measure and prepared to fight incorporation into a Catholic Ireland, divorced from the government of Great Britain. Only the outbreak of war with Germany in 1914 prevented civil strife in Ireland. The 1914 act was never put into effect, and the question was not settled until 1921, when southern Ireland attained the status of a British dominion.

Rule of the new Liberals, 1905-1914. Gladstone's fight for Irish home rule split his party and paved the way for a decade of Conservative rule in Britain (1895-1905). Partly because Britain was enmeshed in foreign and imperial affairs, the Conservative party no longer adhered to Disraeli's Tory democracy and its program of social legislation. But by 1905 the need for social and political reform again claimed major attention. Over 30 percent of the adult male workers received a starvation wage of less than seven dollars per week. The pitifully small wages made it impossible for the workers to lay aside savings for increasingly frequent periods of unemployment. Numerous strikes gave evidence of discontent among the workers, and the newly founded Labour party (see Chapter 16) gained adherents. The Liberals, traditional champions of laissez-faire economics, decided to jettison their old ideas and embark on a bold program of social legislation. David Lloyd George (1863-1945), a leading member of the Liberal government, declared: "Four spectres haunt the Poor; Old Age, Accident, Sickness and Unemployment. We are going to exorcise them."[1]

Led by Prime Minister Herbert Asquith, Lloyd George, and Winston Churchill—the last-named just beginning his fabulous career—the Liberal party, with the aid of the Labour party, carried through Parliament a revolutionary reform program that provided for old-age pensions, national employment bureaus, and sickness, accident, and unemployment insurance. In addition, labor unions were not to be held financially responsible for losses caused an employer by a strike, and members of the House of Commons, heretofore unpaid, were granted a moderate salary. This last measure enabled men without private means, chiefly in the new Labour party, to follow a political career. The House of Lords had tried to obstruct this reform program. The result was the Parliament Bill of 1911 which, after bitter acrimony, was passed, taking away from the Lords all power of absolute veto.

The *Pax Britannica*. In nineteenth-century world affairs England's industrial might, its financial strength, and its smoothly functioning and stable government made it possible for this nation to play a unique role in world affairs. The very size of the British empire meant that Englishmen were involved in developments all over the globe. Enlarged and consolidated in the nineteenth century (see Chapter

19), the British empire consisted of 13 million square miles of land—the largest empire known to history. Although the *Pax Britannica* was not free of flaws or evils, in the absence of any world government there was a great deal to be said for a global system of law and defense which maintained stability in one quarter of the world's area.

FRANCE: PAINFUL PATH TO DEMOCRACY

Prosperity without liberty under Napoleon III. Since its establishment in 1852 (see p. 349), the Second French Empire of Napoleon III had prospered in both domestic and foreign affairs. Over a period of eighteen years, Napoleon III, the "emperor boss," gave his realm glory, prosperity, and, above all, order and discipline—nearly everything a great nation could desire, in fact, except liberty. Although the government structure retained the outward forms of a parliamentary regime, the suffrage was juggled to give the supporters of the emperor a safe majority in the legislature—which had little power anyway. An efficient secret police was established to hunt down "dangerous elements," the press was censored, and parliamentary debates were given no publicity.

But if the France of Napoleon III lacked liberty, it did enjoy prosperity. Large-scale industries and corporations developed, and in two decades production doubled. France sponsored the building of the famous Suez Canal (1859-1869), railway mileage increased fivefold, and steamship lines prospered. The condition of the masses was bettered in a number of ways, including the partial legalization of labor unions and the right to strike. An ambitious program of public works transformed Paris into a city of broad boulevards and harmonious architecture.

Successes and failures in foreign affairs. Napoleon III thought of himself as the first servant of the empire, devoted to the task of making the state prosperous and progressive. But though he claimed to be a man of peace, he was heir to the Napoleonic legend. He had no choice but to pursue a spirited role in international affairs.

For ten years Napoleon III's foreign policy was remarkably successful. Allying France with England in the Crimean War, the emperor gained the desired victory against Russia and appeared at the peace conference as the arbiter of Europe. In 1859 his support of Cavour in Italy against Austria earned him military glory and gained Nice and Savoy for France. Furthermore, during this period France secured a foothold in Indochina (the assassination of a French missionary providing the pretext to occupy the region around Saigon) raised the tricolor over Tahiti and other Pacific islands, completed the conquest of Algeria, and began to penetrate the Senegal River in West Africa.

Until 1861 Napoleon III could boast that France was mistress of Europe, but after this date the emperor seemed to lose his touch in foreign affairs, and the morale and efficiency of the Second Empire declined rapidly. In 1863, while the United States was distracted by civil war, Napoleon III embroiled France in the madcap scheme of placing Maximilian, a Hapsburg prince, on the Mexican throne. Some forty thousand troops were involved in this expensive adventure, which ended in the withdrawal of the French forces and the capture and execution of Maximilian by Mexican patriots. France suffered further humiliation in 1863 when the emperor talked boldly of aiding a Polish revolt against Russian rule and then failed to act.

Napoleon III's prestige at home and abroad reached a new low in 1866 when, as we saw in Chapter 17, his blunders contributed to the quick Prussian victory over Austria and the apparent certainty of a powerful united Germany rising on France's borders. To regain public support at home, Napoleon had gambled on a successful war with Prussia in which he unrealistically counted on Austrian and Italian aid. The result, as will be recalled, was complete disaster. Thus the glory of the Second French Empire and the power of its creator, Napoleon III, perished on the battlefield just as the empire of his uncle, Napoleon, had disintegrated before the unbending squares of British infantry at Waterloo. News of this debacle swept the discredited Second Empire from power, and a republic was proclaimed in Paris.

The Third Republic. Born in 1871 amidst the humiliation of military defeat, France's Third Republic went through many years of precarious existence before it achieved a firm and popular foundation. A new republican constitution was enacted in 1875 providing for the election by direct manhood suffrage of representatives to the Chamber of Deputies, the influential lower house. There was also a Senate, elected indirectly by electoral colleges in the major administrative districts, the departments. The president was elected by the legislature, and his powers were so limited as to make him merely a figurehead. The real executive was the ministry, or cabinet, appointed from whatever coalition of parties or factions held a majority in the legislature. As in England, the ministry was responsible to the legislature.

Dreyfus and anticlericalism. In the mid-1880's there began a series of crises which, lasting more than a decade, threatened the very existence of the Republic. The most critical was the Dreyfus affair which embittered French opinion and challenged the basic ideals of French democracy. Captain Alfred Dreyfus, the first Jewish officer to secure high military rank, was accused in 1894 of selling military secrets. Found guilty, he was condemned to the notorious penal settlement on Devil's Island. Gradually it became apparent that he was innocent and that anti-Semitic elements in the army supported by the Church had made him a scapegoat.

In 1899 the Dreyfus case was authorized for review, but even though another officer had admitted his guilt, political passions were so strong that Dreyfus was again found guilty. The president of France, however, pardoned Dreyfus. In 1906 the highest civil court in France found Dreyfus completely innocent, thus asserting the power of the civil authority over the military that had condemned him. The victorious Republic then purged the army of its reactionary officers.

The Church also had to pay for its alliance with the army during the Dreyfus affair. Convinced that the clergy was the Republic's main enemy—"at the botton of every agitation and every intrigue from which Republican France has suffered"—leading republicans demanded an end to Church interference in the affairs of state. As one republican stated, "I want the priest outside of politics. In the Church, yes; on the public square, on the platform, never."[2]

In 1901 all Church schools were closed, and in 1905 Church and state were formally separated with the abrogation of Napoleon's century-old Concordat with the papacy. Henceforth, the state ceased to pay the salaries of the clergy— Protestant and Jewish as well as Catholic. Furthermore, all Church property was taken over by the state, annual arrangements being made for the use of Church buildings.

The Third Republic in 1914. By 1914 France was a prosperous land of more than 39 million people, although a falling birth rate put it far behind the prolific Germans, who numbered 70 million. And after a century of wars, revolutions, and crises, French republicanism had finally attained stability and wide public support.

Most Frenchmen enjoyed basic democratic rights, such as manhood suffrage, freedom of the press, and equality before the law. They tended, however, to regard government not as a servant but as a meddling, would-be tyrant. In consequence, officials found it difficult to impose direct taxation, and the machinery of the state was severely handicapped by a lack of funds.

Reflecting the extreme individualism of the French was the multi-party political system. There were so many different political groups represented in the Chamber of Deputies that prime ministers had to form cabinets made up of diverse elements. Like unstable chemical compounds, these cabinets blew up under the slightest pressure. French prime ministers came and went with bewildering rapidity, at the whim of the legislature. In spite of these weaknesses, however, France in 1914 was regarded as the most important democracy on the Continent and one of the great powers of the world.

FORCES FOR PEACE AND WAR

Growing spirit of internationalism. As the nineteenth century came to a close, there was evidence of a growing spirit of internationalism and a deep yearning for peace among the peoples of the world. The growth of world trade, augmented by new marvels in transportation and communication, served to knit men together into a world community; and further evidences of such internationalism were numerous. In 1865 a conference which met in Paris to discuss the coordination of telegraph lines and the problem of rates established the International Telegraph Union, made up of twenty nations. To facilitate the handling of mail the world over, the Universal Postal Union was set up in 1875. As a protection for authors' rights, an agreement was drawn up in 1886 by an international copyright union. In 1896, as part of the growing internationalism, the ancient Greek Olympic games were revived. Held every four years, the games attracted participants from nearly every nation.

A dynamic peace movement also began early in the nineteenth century. The Pan-American Conference for promoting peace in the western hemisphere was organized in 1889. A decade later a disarmament conference was assembled at the Hague. The Hague Tribunal was created to settle international issues by arbitration.

The contributions of famous individuals were also important to the movement for world peace. Alfred Nobel, the famous Swedish manufacturer of dynamite, established the Nobel Peace Prize; and Andrew Carnegie founded the Carnegie Endowment for International Peace and built a Peace Palace at The Hague to be used for international conferences. (Ironically, the building was finished just before the outbreak of the First World War.)

Forces of antagonism. While some forces were working to bring about closer cooperation between nations and peoples, others were promoting distrust and rivalries. These antagonistic forces finally triumphed, and, as a result, Europe and most of the world with it were plunged into war in 1914. The underlying causes of this great conflict were the actions of national states in power politics, militarism, rival alliances, secret diplomacy, economic imperialism, and nationalism.

Europe in 1914 consisted of some twenty independent political units. Recognizing no higher authority, each of these states went its own way; international law was obeyed only if its dicta did not clash with a nation's interests. The great powers were ready to take advantage of any neighbor's weakness and to resort to war if the prize to be seized or the danger to be averted was substantial enough. War was an instrument of national policy, to be used whenever peaceful methods failed.

Living in this international anarchy the great powers engaged in an armament race. They also sought to strengthen their security by joining military alliances. These developments only poisoned the atmosphere of international relations and increased the prospects of war. In the 1970's some observers of international affairs drew a parallel between these pre-1914 tensions and those of their own day.

After 1870 the world's markets were viewed as a battleground. Industrial powers sought to secure control of areas rich in natural resources or valuable as markets. In some cases this economic imperialism led to war. Japanese designs upon the Asian mainland brought about war with China in 1894, and Great Britain fought the Boer War in South Africa in 1899-1902. Japan and Russia fought over Manchuria in 1904-1905, and Italy wrested Tripoli from Turkey in 1912.

The emotion of nationalism. Nationalism—particularly the narrow, blatant, and bellicose variety of the late nineteenth century—has been rightly regarded as one of the most potent causes of modern war. Among both subordinated and ruling groups, national loyalty was an intense, explosive emotion. Inflated patriotism became a new religion, the emotional adjunct to power politics. In the opinion of many observers, the most important fundamental cause of the First World War was rampant nationalism. As it turned out, the greatest danger to peace was the flame of nationalism that burned fiercely in the new Balkan nations (see p. 377).

In Germany, for example, the Pan-Germanic League was organized to spread the doctrine of the superiority of the German race and culture. The League was a leader in anti-English agitation; it supported German colonial ambitions; it sought to retain the loyalty of all Germans to the fatherland no matter where they were living in the world; and it worked to promote a policy of German power both in Europe and overseas.

Anti-Semitism and Zionism. Speaking of Pan-Germanism and Pan-Slavism, a famous historian refers to their development as the "seed time of totalitarian nationalism." These pernicious ideas of racial superiority were later to develop into the hideous campaign of extermination which Adolf Hitler and his Nazi henchmen carried out against certain supposedly inferior peoples, concentrating primarily on the Jews.

A foretaste of what racial nationalism would bring in the twentieth century was provided by the treatment of the Jews in the later nineteenth century. After suffering from many injustices and restrictions during the Middle Ages, the Jews in western Europe and in the Americas secured practically all the rights of full citizens after 1800. With this advance came new opportunities; and Jews in many countries made significant contributions to art, music, literature, and science. About 1850, however, a strong anti-Semitic movement began to appear in Europe.

German nationalists like Heinrich von Treitschke coined the phrase "The Jews are our calamity." In France anti-Semitism reached a climax in the Dreyfus affair. In eastern Europe the Jewish minorities suffered many injustices, but their hardest lot was in Russia. In the tsar's realm the Jews had to live in specified western provinces, the so-called Jewish Pale. They were forbidden to buy certain kinds of property; their admittance to schools was restricted; and they had to pay twice the taxes of corresponding non-Jewish communities. Used at times as scapegoats, many Jews were murdered in pogroms carried out with the encouragement of the government.

From the injustices of anti-Semitism in the last century grew the desire for a Jewish homeland. Thus the exaggerated nationalism of other peoples bred a nationalistic spirit among the Jews themselves. In 1896 a Hungarian Jew, Theodor Herzl, came forward with the program of Zionism, which had as its purpose the creation of Palestine as an independent state. Herzl claimed that the Jews were a distinct nationality and thus were entitled to have a country of their own. The first general congress of Zionists was held in Switzerland in 1897, and small-scale immigration to Palestine began.

THE LAMPS ARE GOING OUT

Bismarck's diplomatic footwork. After the conclusion of the Franco-Prussian War in 1871, the German chancellor was well aware that France would try to inflict revenge on Germany and take back Alsace-Lorraine. Therefore, Bismarck deliberately set out to isolate France diplomatically by depriving it of potential allies. In 1873 he made an alliance with Russia and Austria-Hungary, known as the Three Emperors' League; but at the Congress of Berlin (1878) he was forced to choose between the claims of Austria and those of Russia in the Balkans. Bismarck chose to support Austria because he trusted that empire more than he did Russia. He was afraid also that supporting Russia would alienate Great Britain.

A year later Bismarck negotiated the Dual Alliance with the Austrian government, and in 1882 a new partner, Italy, was secured, thus bringing into operation the Triple Alliance. The choice of Austria as a close ally in preference to Russia did not mean that Bismarck was reconciled to the loss of the latter's friendship. In 1881 the Three Emperor's League was renewed, but when rivalries between Austria and Russia in the Balkans made it impossible for these two powers to be in the same group, the alliance collapsed in 1887. To fill the gap, Bismarck negotiated a separate alliance with Russia called the Reinsurance Treaty.

Under the masterful hand of Bismarck, Germany retained hegemony over the European continent from 1871 to 1890. The chancellor had succeeded admirably in his diplomacy. Every effort was made to avoid challenging the interests of Britain, which continued its policy of "splendid isolation" from rivalries on the Continent. France had been kept in diplomatic quarantine without allies. Through amazing diplomatic acrobatics, Bismarck had managed to avoid alienating Russia while retaining an alliance with Austria.

In a single move, however, the preponderance of power built up by Bismarck was heedlessly cast away. In 1890 the new German kaiser, young William II, dismissed the old chancellor and took German foreign policy into his own hands. Foolishly allowing the Reinsurance Treaty to lapse, he permitted Russia to seek new allies. France immediately began to woo Russia; millions of French francs went to buy Russian bonds, and in 1894 France received what it had wanted for twenty years—a strong military ally. The Triple Alliance was now confronted by the Dual Alliance.

England ends its isolation. At the end of the nineteenth century Britain was involved in bitter rivalries with Russia in the Balkans and Afghanistan and with France in Africa. During the Boer War (see p. 395) all the great powers in Europe were anti-British. Only the supremacy of England's fleet effectively discouraged the development of an interventionist movement. More and more, Great Britain became disquieted by its policy of diplomatic isolation. It was these circumstances which explained British overtures to Germany in 1898 and again in 1901.

Kaiser William II refused Britain's suggestions for an alliance, which he interpreted as a sign of British weakness, and embarked on an aggressive policy known as *Weltpolitik* (world politics). He was determined not only to make Germany the first military power in Europe but to expand its influence in the Middle East and the Balkans, secure more colonies overseas, and build a battle fleet second to none. A huge naval program was initiated in 1900, providing for the construction of a fleet strong enough to jeopardize Britain's naval supremacy within twenty years. For England the supremacy of the royal navy was a life-or-death matter. Since food and raw materials had to come by sea, it was crucial that the royal navy be able to protect British shipping. The British were disturbed also at the tremendous strides made by German industry, as well as the Kaiser's threatening and irresponsible speeches and unpredictable behavior. Rebuffed and challenged by Germany, Britain turned elsewhere to establish friendly relations.

In 1904 Britain and France settled their outstanding differences and proclaimed the *Entente Cordiale*, a French term meaning "friendly understanding." The Entente Cordiale, together with England's alliance with Japan in 1902, ended Britain's policy of isolation and brought it into the diplomatic combination pitted against Germany's Triple Alliance. In 1907 Britain settled its problems with Russia, thereby establishing the Triple Entente. Great Britain made no definite military commitments in the agreements with France and Russia. Theoretically it retained freedom of action but, for all this, it was now part of the alliance system.

The Moroccan crises: 1905 and 1911. For a decade before the First World War, Europe experienced a series of crises brought about as the two alliance systems flexed their muscles and probed each other's strength. As each new diplomatic crisis arose, Europe teetered on the abyss of war.

The first serious diplomatic crisis occurred in 1905 over Morocco. France sought control of this territory in order to establish a stretch of contiguous dependencies from the Atlantic across the North African coast to Tunisia. Carefully timing his moves, the German chancellor arranged for the kaiser to visit the Moroccan port of Tangier, where he declared that all powers must respect the independence of the country. The French were forced to give up their immediate plans for taking over Morocco and agree to Germany's suggestion that an international conference be called at Algeciras (1906) to discuss the matter.

At this meeting the German hope that a rift might appear between the British and French did not materialize. On the contrary, all but one of the nations in attendance—even Italy—supported France rather than Germany. Only Austria remained at the side of Germany. It was agreed that Morocco should still enjoy its sovereignty but that France and Spain should be given certain rights to police the area. The events at Algeciras and the British agreement with Russia the following year (1907) filled the Germans with dread.

In 1911 a second Moroccan crisis heightened the tension. When France sent an army into the disputed territory "to maintain order," Germany countered by dispatching the gunboat *Panther* to the Moroccan port of Agadir. Great Britain came out with a plain warning that all its power was at the disposal of France. A diplomatic bargain was struck whereby France got a free hand in Morocco, and Germany was granted French holdings in equatorial Africa.

The Balkan nemesis. Although the two rival alliance systems had managed to avert an armed showdown over Morocco, these happy auguries were of no avail against the forces of rival imperialism in the Balkans. This area had been in almost constant turmoil during the nineteenth century. Various subject peoples, in Serbia, Bulgaria, and Rumania, had gained independence, usually accompanied by war and revolution. These gains were made at the expense of a decaying Ottoman Empire whose weakness also encouraged the ambition of Russia to gain control of the strategic Dardenelles—the gateway to the Mediterranean. Fearing this Russian naval presence would jeopardize her communications to India, Britain repeatedly blocked Russian designs and supported the Ottoman Empire. This international rivalry is often referred to as the Near Eastern Question which today still lingers in a new form—Arab-Israeli tension, heightened by Russian-American rivalry—endangering world peace. In 1854 a Russian attack on Turkey led to the

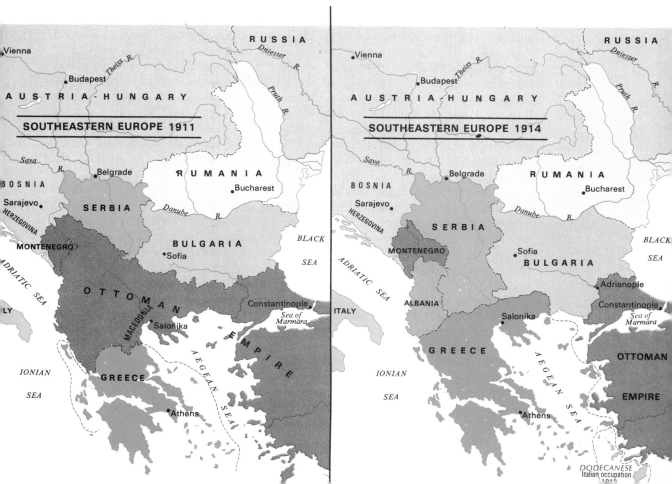

Crimean War. British, French, and Sardinian troops responded by invading the Crimea. Russia was forced to sue for peace and her advance was halted in the Balkans.

But Russian ambitions were only temporarily halted. In 1877 and 1878 it again waged war against Turkey only to have Britain and Austria at the Congress of Vienna force her to forego all gains. This conclave allowed Austria to "occupy and administer" the Turkish ruled provinces of Bosnia and Herzegovina, which were to be the scene of the incident setting off World War I. Russia now turned to a propaganda offensive—the movement known as Pan-Slavism. Assuming the role of protector of its "little brother Slavs" it encouraged revolts against Turkish rule and, more significantly, against Austrian control of its Slavic subjects. Both Germany and Austria were opposed to Russia's Pan-Slavic ambitions. German motives were largely economic; the Germans envisaged a great continuous economy stretching from the Baltic to the Persian Gulf. The Austrian concern in the Balkans was primarily defensive. A polyglot empire containing millions of Slavs, Austria-Hungary feared an expanding Serbia, egged on by Russia. To counter the advance of the Greater Serbia movement, Austria in 1908 annexed the provinces of Bosnia and Herzegovina, which it had administered since 1878. This high-handed move produced a dangerous crisis. Russia was furious and Serbia was equally exercised over the incorporation of more South Slavs into the Hapsburg domain. But because Russia had come out of its war with Japan (1904-1905) badly battered, it could not support Serbia against the combined might of Germany and Austria. In this crisis the Triple Alliance had humbled Russia and thwarted the plans of Russia's protégé Serbia.

In 1912 Serbia and its neighbors, especially Greece and Bulgaria, formed an alliance with the objective of expelling Turkey from Europe. The First Balkan War began later in that year and was quickly terminated as Turkish resistance crumpled. The victorious Balkan nations were not permitted to divide their spoils, however, and this led to the Second Balkan War. Denied Albania by Austria, the Serbs, supported by the Greeks, demanded territory originally promised to Bulgaria. Bulgaria attacked its former allies, and Turkey and Rumania in turn entered the war against Bulgaria, which was no match for its numerous opponents. A peace was signed by which Bulgaria gave its former allies most of the territory it had originally taken from Turkey. The Turks retained only a precarious toehold in Europe, the small pocket around Constantinople.

By the end of 1913 no permanent solution had been found to the Balkan problem. Austria was more fearful than ever of the Greater Serbia movement, and Serbian ambitions had grown larger, since its territory had doubled as a result of the recent wars. The Serbian prime minister is quoted as saying: "The first round is won; now we must prepare the second against Austria." As for Russia, its Pan-Slavic dreams had not been completely blocked but only interrupted. The dynamite in the Balkan bomb was the involvement of the major powers.

The archduke assassinated. The fateful spark came on June 28, 1914, when Archduke Francis Ferdinand, heir to the Austrian throne, and his wife were assassinated in the town of Sarajevo in Bosnia. This deed was the work of a young Bosnian student inspired by Greater Serbia propaganda. He and two associates received assistance from high Serbian officers, although the direct complicity of the Serbian government has not been proved. Even so, it seems unlikely that the government could have been ignorant of the plot.

Count Leopold von Berchtold, the Austrian foreign minister, believed that the assassination justified crushing, once and for all, the anti-Austrian propaganda and terrorism emanating from Serbia. Austria hesitated to act, however, without securing the support of its German ally. The kaiser felt that everything possible must be done to prevent Germany's only reliable ally from being weakened by such forces as Serbian terrorism, and so he assured the Austrian government of his full support. Thus Berchtold obtained a blank check from Germany. Vienna wanted only a local Austro-Serbian war, and Germany favored quick action to forestall Russian intervention.

The Austrian ultimatum and Russian mobilization. On July 23 a harsh Austro-Hungarian ultimatum was presented to the Serbs. Intending that the ultimatum be turned down, Berchtold demanded unconditional acceptance within forty-eight hours. On July 25 the Austrian government announced that Serbia's reply was unsatisfactory and mobilized its armed forces. Meanwhile the German chancellor urged Austria to negotiate with Russia, which was following developments closely. Russia realized that if the Austrians succeeded in humbling Serbia, Russian prestige in this area would suffer tremendously. The French in the meantime assured the Russians of their full cooperation and urged strong support for Serbia, while the British advised negotiations, but without success.

Fearful that Serbia would escape from his clutches, Berchtold succeeded on July 27, thanks in part to falsehood, in convincing the Hapsburg emperor that war was the only way out. On the following day, war was declared against Serbia. As the possibility of a general European war loomed, Berlin sent several frantic telegrams to Vienna. The German ambassador was instructed to tell Berchtold: "As an ally we must refuse to be drawn into a world conflagration because Austria does not respect our advice."[3] At this critical stage, when German pressure on Austria might have opened a path to peace, an event took place which wrecked any further attempts at negotiation. This was the Russian mobilization on July 30.

To Germany, the question of Russian mobilization was especially vital, because, in the event of war with Russia and its ally, France, Germany would be confronted with enemies on two fronts. The best plan seemed to be to launch a lightning attack against France, crush France, and then turn to meet Russia, which could ordinarily be expected to mobilize rather slowly. To allow Russian mobilization to proceed would jeopardize this strategy.

War declared. On July 31 the government in Berlin dispatched ultimatums to Russia and France demanding from the former cessation of mobilization and from the latter a pledge of neutrality. Failing to receive satisfactory replies, Germany declared war on Russia August 1 and on France August 3. On August 2 an ultimatum was delivered by the German ambassador in Brussels, announcing his country's intention of sending troops through Belgium. The Belgian cabinet refused to grant permission and appealed to Russia, France, and Great Britain for aid in protecting its neutrality. A majority in the British cabinet did not favor war, but with the news of the German ultimatum to Belgium, the tide turned. Sir Edward Grey, the British foreign secretary, sent an ultimatum to Germany demanding that Belgian neutrality be respected. This Germany refused to do, and on August 4 Great Britain declared war.

On the basis that Germany and Austria were not waging a defensive war, Italy refused to carry out its obligations under the Triple Alliance and for the time being remained neutral. In the latter part of August, Japan joined the Allies; and in October, Turkey, fearing the designs of Russia, threw in its lot with the Central Powers, Germany and Austria.

The question of war guilt. Germany made a serious blunder when its chancellor referred to the treaty of 1839 guaranteeing the neutrality of Belgium—signed by the European powers, including Prussia—as "a scrap of paper." Germany thus put itself morally in the wrong as a breaker of treaties, a position that lost it support and sympathy the world over. Equally important, Germany's declaration of war on Russia and France had brought on a general war.

The structure of the Treaty of Versailles, as we shall see later, rested in large part on the assumed "war guilt" of Germany. When the treaty was first written, scholars and laymen alike in the Allied nations sincerely believed that Germany was completely responsible for the war. In time it became increasingly clear that the problem was more complex than had been originally thought. Today most historians agree it is next to impossible to try to explain the war in terms of the actions of any one of the great powers. Rather, all the major participating nations must accept, in some measure, responsibility for the outbreak of the First World War. In the final analysis, it is needless to try to apportion the blame, for the tragedy was inherent in the prevailing order—or disorder—of international anarchy.

In the last few days of peace, diplomats strove desperately to avert general war. Through confusion, fear, and loss of sleep, the nervous strain among them was almost unbearable. Many broke down and wept when it was apparent they had failed. This atmosphere of anguish and gloom is reflected in a passage from Sir Edward Grey's autobiography:

> A friend came to see me on one of the evenings of the last week [before the war]—he thinks it was on Monday, August 3. We were standing at the window of my room in the Foreign Office. It was getting dusk, and the lamps were being lit in the space below on which we were looking. My friend recalls that I remarked on this with the words: "The lamps are going out all over Europe; we shall not see them lit again in our life-time."[4]

THE FIRST WORLD WAR

Scope of the conflict. Although the terrible struggle that racked mankind from 1914 to 1918 was fought chiefly on the European continent, it can justly be called the First World War. Altogether, twenty-seven powers became belligerents, ranging the globe from Tokyo to Ottawa and from Rio de Janeiro to Capetown. Tremendous fighting strength was mustered. The Central Powers—Germany, Austria, Bulgaria, and Turkey—mobilized 21 million men; their opponents, the Allies, mustered 40 million of whom 12 million were Russian. Since the Russian divisions were poorly equipped and often ineffectively used, these total figures are somewhat misleading in that they indicate a more decisive advantage than the Allies actually enjoyed. Furthermore, in the German army, the Central Powers boasted superb generalship and discipline, and they fought from an inner or central position and were therefore able to transfer troops quickly and efficiently to various fronts. In their favor, the Allies had greater resources of finance and raw materials; and Britain, helped by its empire, had the advantage of a splendid, powerful fleet with which to maintain control of the seas.

The grinding attrition of the war.   The belligerent nations went into battle in a champagne mood. Each side believed the conflict would soon be over, concluded by a few decisive battles, and each side believed its victory was inevitable. Allied naval supremacy cut off the Central Powers from vitally needed sources of raw material from overseas. Germany was therefore determined to strike a quick knockout blow to end the war. Pushing heroic Belgian resistance aside, German armies drove rapidly south into France. The invaders, however, were halted a few miles from Paris at the Battle of the Marne. At the same time a Russian thrust into East Prussia was hurled back with heavy loss. After much desperate fighting, battle positions were stabilized, and the "western front" was created in a solid line of opposing trenches stretching from the Channel to Switzerland. Toward the end of 1914 all combatants began to realize the terrible consequences of modern war. Single battles devoured hundreds of thousands of lives, and the toll during the first few months of conflict ran as high as a million and a half dead and wounded.

For the next two and a half years the war settled down to a weary and titanic conflict of attrition. While Italy joined the Allies in 1915, Russia ceased to be a major threat to the Central Powers. In the Balkans a British attempt to force the Dardanelles, thus opening a sea route to Russia, was a costly failure. The most savage fighting took place in France on the "western front." Here thousands of men lost their lives as they sought to cross No Man's Land in such blood baths as the Somme and Verdun. On the seas Britain turned back a German naval challenge at the crucial battle of Jutland in 1916.

Allies near the breaking point in 1917.   In 1917 British and French military strength reached its highest point, only to fall to unprecedented depths. Allied commanders were hopeful that the long-planned breakthrough might be accomplished, but a large-scale attack by the French was beaten back with horrible losses. French regiments mutinied rather than return to the inferno of no man's land. The British army meanwhile launched several massive offensives, only to lose hundreds of thousands of men without any decisive results. The Allies also launched unsuccessful offensives in Italy, where catastrophe threatened. Aided by the Germans, the Austrian army smashed the Italian front at the battle of Caporetto (1917), so vividly described by Ernest Hemingway in *A Farewell to Arms.* Italian resistance finally hardened, but collapse was barely averted.

This frustration of Allied hopes was deepened by the growing menace of the German submarine campaign. By 1917 shipping losses had assumed catastrophic proportions. In three months 470 British ships alone fell victims to torpedoes. Britain had no more than six weeks' supply of food, and the situation became critical for the Allies. But the very weapon that seemed to doom their cause was to prove their salvation, for the submarine brought the United States into the war on the Allies' side.

American sentiment lay with the Allies.   After Italy joined the Allies in 1915, the United States was the only great power remaining neutral. In 1914 President Wilson had announced the neutrality of the United States and declared that the people "must be impartial in thought as well as in action." The events of the following two years showed that this was no easy task.

From the beginning of the conflict, American sentiment was predominantly with the Allies. There was the strong tradition of friendship with France because of that country's help to the American colonies during the revolutionary war, and between Britain and America there were strong cultural ties of language, literature, and democratic institutions. British propaganda, moreover, had the

WORLD WAR I

- [ ] Triple Entente
- [ ] Central Powers
- [ ] Allies of Triple Entente
- [ ] Neutral nations
- → Allied thrust
- → Central Powers' thrust
  Battles:
- × Allied victory
- ⊗ Central Powers' victory

United States as its special target and was much more effective than that of the Central Powers.

Another factor favoring the Allied cause was the American belief that Germany had grossly violated international law by invading Belgium. Partly because of the kaiser's saber-rattling speeches, the German government was regarded as undemocratic, unpredictable, and unstable. In some circles it was believed that a German victory would upset the world balance of power and that a victorious and expansionist Germany might imperil American security.

As the war progressed, it became apparent that the British blockade would permit American trade to be carried on with only the Allies, and before long American factories and farmers were producing munitions and food exclusively for Great Britain and France. Industry expanded and began to enjoy a prosperity dependent upon the continuance of Allied purchases. Between 1914 and 1916

American exports to the Allies quadrupled. During 1915 and 1916 Allied bonds totaling about $1.5 billion were sold in the United States.

The United States' entrance into the war. The immediate cause of the United States entry into the war on the side of the Allies was undoubtedly the German submarine campaign. Blockaded by the British navy, Germany decided to retaliate by halting all shipping to the Allies. Its submarine campaign began in February 1915, and one of the first victims was the luxury liner *Lusitania*, torpedoed with the loss of more than a thousand lives, including more than one hundred Americans. This tragedy aroused public opinion in America.

In the fall of 1916 Wilson was reelected to the presidency. One of his election slogans was "He kept us out of war." But this boast was soon invalidated by the force of events. The discovery of German plots to embroil Mexico in the war against the United States and more submarine sinkings aroused violent American resentment. Finally the President asked Congress to declare war against Germany. This action was taken on April 6, 1917. The United States was now fighting, in the words of President Wilson, "to make the world safe for democracy." The spell of Wilson's lofty principles caused a great welling of idealism among Americans.

Germany's last effort. While the United States mobilized its tremendous resources of manpower and materials, the German government decided to win the war before American aid became effective. The British army had been bled white from the fruitless offensives of 1917, and the French divisions had barely recovered from the mutinies. Furthermore, the Russian war effort had collapsed. In the revolution of November 1917 the Bolsheviks seized power in Russia; and by the Treaty of Brest Litovsk early in 1918, they made peace with Germany. The terms were harsh. Russia lost 500,000 square miles of territory and 66 million people.

Freed from the necessity of fighting on the Russian front, Germany launched a series of great offensives against British and French positions in the spring of 1918. During one of these attacks a brigade of American marines covered itself with glory by halting a German onrush at Chateau-Thierry. A final effort was made against the French in July 1918. It was described as the *Friedensturm*, the peace offensive. Thus far German forces had made substantial gains but had not scored the essential breakthrough. By this time the momentum of attack was slowing down, and more than one million American "doughboys" had landed in France. The last German offensive was hurled back after a slight advance.

German collapse and armistice. The German drive had hardly been halted when the supreme Allied commander, Marshal Foch, counterattacked. Badly beaten and continually harassed, the German troops fell back in rapid retreat. By the end of October the German forces had been pushed out of most of France, and Allied armies were advancing through Belgium. The war of fixed positions separated by no man's land was over. With a preponderance of tanks, the Allies had smashed trench defenses and were now in open country.

On October 1 the German High Command urged the kaiser to sue for peace, and three days later the German chancellor sent a note to President Wilson requesting an end to hostilities. The president's reply notified the German government that peace was impossible so long as the autocratic regime in Germany existed. Although the German chancellor tried to retain the monarchy by introducing certain liberal reforms, it was too late. Revolution broke out in many parts of the country, the kaiser abdicated, and a republic was proclaimed.

While Germany was staggering under the relentless pounding of Foch's armies, the German allies were suffering even greater misfortunes. Bulgaria surrendered on September 30, and Turkey capitulated a month later. Austria gave up the struggle against Italy on November 3; nine days later the Hapsburg empire collapsed when Emperor Charles I fled Vienna for sanctuary in Switzerland.

At five o'clock on the morning of November 11, 1918, in a dining car in the Compiègne Forest, the German delegates signed the terms of the armistice presented to them by Marshal Foch. At eleven o'clock the same day hostilities were halted. Everywhere the news was received with an outburst of unrestrained joy. The world was once more at peace, confronted with the task of binding up its wounds and removing the scars of conflict. Delegates from the Allied nations were soon to converge on Paris, where the peace conference was to be held.

The participants of World War I experienced a tragic consequence of industrialization as the tools of peacetime prosperity became the weapons of wartime destruction. The "dogfight" between German and Allied planes was a typical scene during the Great War. Although the aircraft of those days are now obsolete, their maneuverability has never been matched.

CHAPTER 19
EXPANSION AND IMPERIALISM

New Europes Overseas and Imperialism: 1650-1914

In little more than two and one half centuries (1650-1914) the greatest human migration from the smallest of continents, Europe, had taken place. At the same time the slave trade brought vast numbers of Africans to the Americas. This enormous migration surpassed in scope such momentous human wanderings of the past as those of the Indo-Europeans into India and southern Europe and the historic incursions of the Germanic tribes into the Roman Empire. Transoceanic in character, this mass movement originated in Europe which, during this period, forged ahead of the rest of the world in industry, technology and science, wealth, and military power.

These advances were reflected in the tremendous increase in Europe's population that reached full tide in the nineteenth century. From 1815 to 1914 that continent's numbers increased from 200 million to 460 million; yet, during this time span, more than 40 million immigrants sought homes in the new Europes overseas. In 1815 there were less than 20 million abroad. By 1914 the figure had grown to 200 million. As many people of European stock lived outside Europe by this latter date as had been in it when Napoleon was defeated at Waterloo in 1815.

In the new areas of settlement—the Americas, South Africa, Australia, and New Zealand—new Europes were founded and developed. The immigrants took with them what has been aptly called their "cultural baggage"—their language, religion, folk habits, and religious institutions. Moreover, the most important developments in Europe after Waterloo—the ambitions of the middle class, the search of the masses for full political rights, the increased interest in a better standard of living, and the pervasive force of nationalism—all these became important factors in the overseas communities. Yet if the history of the new Europes is to be studied profitably in comparison with that of Europe itself, it should be remembered that certain common conditions and problems distinguished the history of these new nations: the challenge of geographical exploration, the problem of what to do with the indigenous peoples, and the search for a new national way of life. In the Americas there was also the problem of how best to treat the black, first as a slave and then as a free man. Furthermore, some historians have stressed the deep influence in all the new Europes of frontier life with its fostering of democracy, individualism, resourcefulness, and optimism. As a complete explanation of the course of history in the new Europes, this thesis has been overdone. But some of its relevance remains.

Before 1870 Europe had little interest in colonial expansion. But with the completion of the unification of Germany and Italy, the mounting of tariffs, and the need for markets, raw materials, and areas for investing surplus capital, the western nations avidly turned their attention to imperialism. The economic forces back of this expansion have usually been overemphasized, the psychological underestimated. By 1870 Europe had unbounded faith in its destiny and in its powers. What has been called "a certain indefinable national energy"[1] impelled nations such as France, Britain, and Germany to spread their rule, power, and culture. Love of adventure and scientific curiosity also impelled explorers and administrators to peg out colonial claims. In Europe's golden age of imperialism (1870-1914) its most eloquent spokesman, the English poet Rudyard Kipling, urged his countrymen:

"Take up the White Man's burden—
  Send forth the best ye breed—
Go bind your sons to exile
  To serve your captives' need . . . "[2]

In the Far East China was opened to the exploitation of the western nations in the 1840's and 1850's—somewhat before the real onset of imperialism. Japan avoided imperialism by a pell-mell adoption of western military and industrial techniques. In so doing, this feudal island kingdom was maintaining a long tradition of borrowing from the outside. Britain secured her hold on the entire Indian subcontinent as well as on Ceylon, Malaya, and Burma. The French acquired Indochina, and the Dutch exploited the riches of the East Indies. Russia expanded to the Pacific and marched southward to the passes of India and Afghanistan. Africa was the largest area to be partitioned. By the end of the colonial scramble only two independent states remained: Ethiopia and tiny Liberia. Even the United States, once a colony herself, joined the imperial act, acquiring such territories as the Philippines, Hawaii, and Puerto Rico.

At the outset this imperial mission had few critics, but after 1900 there rose a crescendo of denunciation against colonial rule. No matter what the ultimate verdict may be on the significance of Europe's intrusion into many parts of the world, this imperialistic thrust is an intriguing saga of intrepid explorers, dedicated missionaries, businessmen—avaricious or honest—and colonial officials, both good and bad. And most important, one can observe the impact of colonial rule upon the indigenous peoples as they seized upon such western dynamic traits as nationalism, democracy, science, and technology and began first to question and then to challenge the overlordship of their colonial masters.

NEW EUROPES IN THE AMERICAS

Brave new world. The revolutionary movements in Europe during the nineteenth century had a two-pronged problem: they faced the vestiges of a feudal order of lord and peasant in which political, economic, and social privilege was concentrated in an aristocratic class; or they faced restless nationality groups that sought to unite under their own government by throwing off alien rule—or both. The nineteenth-century movements in the United States were not quite the same, since there was no significant heritage of feudal lord and peasant relationship in *English* North America and no counterpart to the conflicts with outside powers over national unification that troubled the Germans, Italians, Serbs, and other peoples of central and southeastern Europe. In place of these problems the United States had two major and interrelated problems of its own—the annexation, settlement, and development of a sparsely populated continent, and slavery. Free land and unfree men: these were the sources of the many political confrontations that culminated in the Civil War, the greatest revolutionary struggle in nineteenth-century America.

In 1783, the year the United States became a sovereign country, the young nation could not be called a democracy. Six years later only one male in seven possessed the franchise. The influence of the western frontier helped move the fledgling nation closer to full democracy. As thousands of pioneers crossed the Appalachian Mountains into the frontier, land was to be had for the asking. Here social caste did not exist: one man was as good as another. From 1800 to 1860 the westward movement proceeded at a rapid pace.

Throughout most of the nineteenth century as the pioneers moved toward the Pacific, the West was to be a source for new and liberal movements. The election in 1828 of Andrew Jackson, spokesman of the common man, signalized the triumph of the democratic principle which set the direction for political development down to this day.

The Civil War.   The acquisition of new territory forced the issue whether slavery should be allowed in these areas. Slavery was a fundamental issue; from its existence stemmed many differences and tensions which separated the North from the South. In a sense the North and the South had become two different civilizations. The former was industrial, urban, and democratic; the latter was mainly agricultural, rural, and dominated by a planter aristocracy. The South strongly opposed the North's desire for higher tariffs, government aid for new railroads, and generous terms for land settlement in the West.

Soon after the inauguration of Lincoln as president, the southern states seceded from the Union and formed the Confederacy. The first shot of the Civil War was fired at Fort Sumter in 1861. Four agonizing years of conflict and the bloodiest war experienced by any western nation up to that time followed. The Civil War ended when General Lee surrendered to General Grant at Appomattox in April 1865; a few days later the joyful North was stunned by the assassination of President Lincoln. With the final collapse of the Confederacy before the overwhelming superiority of the Union in manpower, industrial resources, and wealth, the Civil War became the grand epic of American history in its heroism, romance, tragedy, and incalculable results.

In the largest sense the American Civil War can be explained in its relation to the great historical movements of the ninteeenth century—liberalism, democracy, and nationalism—which were transforming Europe. It was the desire for freedom that sparked the revolutions in Europe in 1830 and 1848; and likewise in the United States many people had come to believe that slavery was an inhuman and immoral institution. The sentiment of nationalism was equally strong in Europe and in the United States. Just as wars were fought to attain German and Italian unity, a great struggle took place in America to maintain national unity. If the causes of the American Civil War are complex, the all-important result was simple. It settled the issue of whether the United States was an indivisible sovereign nation or a collection of sovereign states. The Federal Union was preserved, and nationalism triumphed over the sectionalism of the South.

Industrial expansion. The victory of the North also foreshadowed an irresistible trend toward industrialism. In its lasting effects the economic revolution in the United States that followed the Civil War was more significant than the conflict itself. Railroads were built across broad prairies, and the first transcontinental railroad, the Union Pacific, was completed in 1869. Thousands of settlers swarmed westward.

Between 1850 and 1880 the number of cities with a population of 50,000 or more doubled. The number of men employed in industry increased 50 percent. In 1865 there were 35,000 miles of railroads in the country; eight years later this figure had been doubled. By 1900 the trackage was estimated to be about 200,000 miles, more than in all of Europe. In 1860 a little more than a billion dollars was invested in manufacturing; by 1900 this figure had risen to twelve billion. The value of manufactured products increased proportionately. In 1870 the total production of iron and steel in the United States was far below that of France and England. Twenty years later the United States had outstripped them and was producing about one third of the world's iron and steel.

In the age of rapid industrialism and materialistic expansion, many who pursued profits lost sight of ethical principles both in business and in government. In five years, between 1865 and 1870, the notorious Tweed Ring cost the city of New York at least $100 million. Ruthless financiers, such as Jay Gould and Jim Fisk, tampered with the financial stability of the nation. During General Grant's administration as president, the country was shocked by scandals and frauds. A new rich class, elevated to power and wealth overnight, failed to appreciate its responsibilities to society. Corruption in business was a blatant feature of the new economic order.

End of the era of expansion. For roughly a century the gospel of the new nation of America had been rugged individualism. As in Europe, government interference in business was unwelcome because it was felt that the individual should be free to follow his own inclinations, run his own business, and enjoy the profits of his labors. In an expanding nation where land, jobs, and opportunity beckoned, there was little to indicate that the system would not work indefinitely. By 1880, however, the end of the frontier was in sight. Free land of good quality was scarce, and the frontier could no longer act as a safety valve to release the economic and social pressures of an expanding population.

Between 1850 and 1900 the United States became the most powerful state in the western hemisphere, increased its national wealth from $7 billion to $88 billion, established an excellent system of public education, and fostered the enjoyment of civil liberties. But there were many disturbing factors in the picture. Unemployment, child labor, and industrial accidents became common in the rapidly growing industrial areas. In large cities, slums grew and served as breeding places for disease and crime. Strikes, often accompanied by violence, demonstrated the tension developing between labor and capital.

By 1890 a new challenge had arisen—the need for economic reform. At this point, as had happened in England and elsewhere at about the same time, a powerful movement whose object was the removal of economic inequalities began. The so-called progressive movement agitated for the elimination of sweatshops, of exploitation of foreign labor, and of waste of the nation's natural wealth. This era of the muckrakers lasted roughly from 1890 to 1914.

The success of the progressive movement was reflected in the constitutions of new states admitted to the Union and in their introduction of the direct primary, the initiative and referendum, and the direct election of senators. All these measures tended to give the common man more effective control of his government. After the enactment in 1887 of the Interstate Commerce Act, which had introduced federal regulation of the railroads, a steady expansion of governmental regulation of industry began.

The United States in 1914. In 1914 the United States was the most populous, rich, and influential of the new countries which had sprung from motherlands in Europe. In 1790 the population of the United States had been just under 4 million; the census of 1910 showed an increase to nearly 99 million. During the nineteenth century and the first decade of the twentieth century, more than 25 million immigrants had made America their new home. Since the days of George Washington, the national wealth had increased at least a hundredfold. Once the producer of raw materials only, the United States in 1914 was the greatest industrial power in the world. In 1900 it was producing more steel than Great Britain and Germany combined; and one of its concerns—United States Steel—was capitalized for $1,460 million, a sum greater than the total estimated wealth of the country in 1790. In 1914 many people in the United States and in the rest of the world failed to appreciate the significance of the amazing growth of the United States. Only World War I could give tangible proof that the New World nation had surpassed the power and economic importance of its mother country.

Early disappointments in freed Latin America. While the United States gained its independence, extended its authority from the Atlantic to the Pacific, and became a great industrial power, the people of Latin America had gained their independence from Spain and Portugal early in the nineteenth century. Nine new political units initially emerged. For most of these new nations the first half century was a period of disillusionment. Military leaders, or *caudillos*, seized power, revolts became endemic, and large states fragmented into puny republics.

The Spanish colonial system had offered American-born whites little responsibility or opportunity in government, and the tradition of autocracy and paternalism was a poor precedent for would-be democratic republics. The emphasis on executive power inspired later presidents, generals, landowners, tribal leaders, and even clerical officials to wield authority with extreme arrogance. Independent legislative organs never flourished. Spain's economic system encouraged concentration of land and other forms of wealth in a few hands and an extractive economy. Finally, the Church, with its great properties and its hold on education and welfare agencies, was to complicate the politics of every new nation.

The effects of the wars of independence were also ruinous. Some of the most productive areas were devastated. Hatreds and divisions long persisted. Also, many men who had fought the royalists remained armed, fond of a life of violence and pillage, and likely to group themselves about the *caudillos* who promised them adventure or gain in revolutions.

Racial disunity. When independence was achieved in the first quarter of the nineteenth century, there were from fifteen to eighteen million people in the former Spanish empire. About three million of these were whites, among whom were included almost all the property-owning and educated groups. (Immigration from Europe did little to increase their numbers until the last third of the century, when a deluge began.) About the same number of people were of mixed European and Indian blood. Called *mestizos*, they scorned the Indians but were usually not accepted by the whites, though they were steadily increasing in number and ambition during the period when new nations were being formed. During the nineteenth century at least half of the population in some states was Indian. Deprived of the small protection once offered by the Spanish crown, they either sank into peonage or lived in semi-independence under their tribal rulers. Finally in Brazil and most of the Caribbean islands, the blacks, most of them slaves, were in a large majority. Conflicts of interest quickly developed between these broad racial groups, particularly between the Creoles (white peoples born in the colonies) and the *mestizos*.

By the end of the nineteenth century, while some promising economic gains had been made in countries such as Mexico, Brazil, and Argentina, the continent was still plagued by political instability, and the masses continued to exist in dire poverty.

THE AMERICAS IN WORLD AFFAIRS

Retreat from isolation. During the first quarter century after gaining its independence, the United States fought a brief naval war with France, became embroiled with Britain in the War of 1812, and sent two expeditions to the Mediterranean to teach the Barbary pirates a lesson. These complications notwithstanding, isolationism became the cardinal principle of American foreign policy. In 1823 President Monroe warned the European powers not to intervene in the Western Hemisphere. This policy coincided with British interests and had the shield of the British fleet (see p. 370). Some modification of American isolationism became apparent in the two decades before 1860. The United States was instrumental in "opening up" Japan, became interested in the Hawaiian Islands, and purchased Alaska for the paltry price of $7,200,000. By the 1880's new forces began to emerge that were to carry the United States increasingly away from isolationism in the closing years of the nineteenth century. The United States began to seek an outlet for its vast national energy now that the frontier had disappeared and most of the fertile land was occupied. Foreign trade increased from a value of $393 million in 1870 to more than $1,333 million in 1900. Investments abroad in the same period increased from practically nothing to $500 million. At the same time, American missionary activity in Africa, in the Middle East, and in Asia greatly expanded. In common with the same intellectual trend in Europe, many American leaders were influenced by Darwinism, especially by its application to political affairs. The slogan "survival of the fittest" had its followers in Congress as well as in the British Parliament, the French Chamber of Deputies, and the German Reichstag. In order to be great, many argued, the United States must expand and must assume a vital role in world politics.

In consequence an American colonial empire appeared in the 1890's with the stars and stripes waving over Guam, Hawaii, the Philippines, and Puerto Rico. This urge to acquire dependencies did not long endure, however; by 1905 it was definitely waning. Nevertheless, the imperialistic urge was a manifestation, however fleeting, of deeper currents of history that were carrying the United States into the full stream of world affairs.

In Asia there was also evidence of the new dynamism in American foreign affairs. In 1899 the American secretary of state, John Hay, took the initiative in maintaining equal commercial rights in China for the traders of all nations, and the Open Door Policy in China became a reality. And in the melodrama of the Boxer Rebellion, the United States again was a leader rather than a follower.

In 1883 the building of a modern navy was begun, and by 1890 the buildup had accelerated greatly. Care was taken not to alarm isolationist circles, however, for the new ships were officially known as "seagoing coastline battleships," a nice nautical contradiction. When this naval program was initiated, the United States Navy ranked twelfth among the powers; by 1900 it had advanced to third place.

Theodore Roosevelt. The quickened activity of the United States in international affairs is best symbolized by the ideas and actions of Theodore Roosevelt (1858-1919). In his terms as president he was one of the leading figures on the world stage. At the request of the Japanese, he assumed the role of peacemaker in the Russo-Japanese War. The peace conference, which met at Portsmouth, New Hampshire, in 1905, successfully concluded a treaty. In 1910 Roosevelt received the Nobel Peace Prize.

Roosevelt was not always a man of peace, however. Whenever he believed the legitimate interests of the United States to be threatened, he had no compunctions about threatening to use force or actually using it. The most significant illustration of Roosevelt's determination to protect vital national interests took place in the Panama incident.

Frustrated by the dilatory maneuvers of Colombian authorities through whose territory the canal was to be built, Roosevelt engineered the creation of a new republic, Panama, which seceded from Colombia. In 1903 a satisfactory canal treaty was secured by the United States with the new nation, and the waterway was opened in 1914. By the twentieth century the United States had moved far from its traditional isolationism. This fact was attested by its increasing involvement in the affairs of Latin America.

The United States in Latin America. As the Industrial Revolution got into full stride, the great industries of Europe and the United States sought the rich raw materials of Latin America as well as opportunities to invest their surplus capital at high rates of interest. Too often corrupt officials bartered away the economic heritage of their lands. In many cases Latin American governments defaulted on their loans and as a result were threatened with armed intervention by European states, which were backing up the loans made by private creditors. To forestall any European intervention in Latin America, the American president in 1904 proclaimed the Roosevelt Corollary to the Monroe Doctrine. By it the United States reserved the power to intervene in Latin America to protect European creditors as well as its own. The United States proceeded to establish a customs receivership in the Dominican Republic and exercised similar control in Nicaragua and Haiti. Following the victorious conclusion of its war with Spain in 1898 it imposed a virtual protectorate over Cuba. The Monroe Doctrine was now being used not only for its original purpose of keeping out European political interference in Latin America but also as an agency for expanding the commercial interests of the United States.

The next manifestation of the imperialistic mood of the United States has been appropriately called dollar diplomacy, an American policy which prevailed from the Theodore Roosevelt through the Coolidge administrations. Dollar diplomacy referred to the coordinated activities of American foreign investors and the State Department, who worked in close cooperation to obtain and protect concessions for investors, especially in those sections of the Caribbean countries which produced sugar, bananas, and oil. From 1890 to 1914 this policy acutely affected nearly a dozen of the Latin American republics. The United States government could—and at times did—in the last analysis control the policies of these states.

Latin America in 1914. If Latin American nations had ever felt a grateful appreciation for the protective features of the original purpose of the Monroe Doctrine, this benign aspect was now forgotten in their concern over what they now chose to call the "Colossus of the North." Thus, by 1914 Latin American relations with the outside world, and especially with the United States, were neither healthy nor comforting. A century of independence had elapsed, but Latin America still lingered on the margin of international life.

BLACK AFRICANS IN THE NEW EUROPES

Forced migration for blacks. There was, however, another form of migration. Millions of Africans were seized and forcibly transplanted to the Americas. The slave trade in Latin America began shortly after 1502. As many native Indians died off and could not supply the mounting demand for the labor required by the plantations, the influx of black slaves increased rapidly. The first to be imported into Brazil came in 1538. By 1600 blacks formed the basis of the economy in Brazil, along the Peruvian coast, in the hot lands of Mexico, in Santo Domingo and Cuba, and in the mines of Colombia. By 1800 the population of Haiti was predominantly black or mulatto, and the African element was substantial in Brazil and Cuba and much less in the Dominican Republic, Panama, Venezuela, and Colombia.

A century after the African was brought to Latin America, he appeared in the English colonies to the north. The first Negroes were landed in Jamestown in 1619, but their status was uncertain for some fifty years. Between 1640 and 1660 there is evidence of enslavement, and after the latter date the slave system was defined by law in several of the colonies. The labor of white immigrant indentured servants —initially an important factor in these colonies—provided unfree, cheap labor for only brief terms and declined as the use of black, lifetime slaves proved to be a less costly labor supply for the plantations. In 1790 when the white population was just over three million, there were some 750,000 Negroes in the United States.

During the American Revolution there was a quickening of conscience about the rightness of slavery. For some people there was an embarrassing contradiction between the ideals of the Declaration of Independence and human bondage. The incipient antislavery sentiment waned, however, as concern mounted over a bloody slave insurrection in Santo Domingo, unrest among American slaves, and the unsettling economic and social consequences of liberal opinion. Slave rebellions in the early 1800's shocked many quarters. It was the Industrial Revolution in England, however, that did the most to fasten slavery on the economy of the southern states. An increased supply of cotton was needed for the new textile mills early in the nineteenth century. New technology and new lands made the plantation system more profitable, creating a rising demand for slaves even as the importation of slaves was ended in 1808. Eventually the belief in Negro inferiority was elevated into a pseudoscientific racist doctrine defending slavery.

Emancipation without equality. While human servitude was legally outlawed after the defeat of the Confederacy in the Civil War, the full "blessings of freedom" were denied to the "free" black during the remainder of the nineteenth century. In fact, while social Darwinists (see p. 314) upheld the rectitude of European imperialism's rule over the "lesser breeds" in Africa and Asia, an analogous American school of thought, based upon the spurious logic of biology, championed beliefs apportioning blacks a lowly and subordinate role in society. Following emancipation, blacks in the South were progressively disfranchised by state laws or by various devices such as poll tax requirements, literacy tests. property qualifications, and naked intimidation. A pattern of segregation in schools, restaurants, parks, and hotels was more thoroughly applied. Laws were passed prohibiting interracial marriage, and blacks were generally excluded from unions. Between 1885 and 1918 more than 2500 blacks were lynched in the United States. Blacks were generally poorly educated, socially denied, and economically depressed.

Notwithstanding numerous and often painful obstacles, however, black Americans in 1913, fifty years after the Emancipation Proclamation, could point to some solid advances: a professional class estimated at 47,000, at least 70 percent literacy, ownership of 550,000 homes, 40,000 businesses, and savings of some 700 million dollars. Their churches, banks, and insurance companies had become substantial institutions.

In addition to improving their own lot, blacks made rich and distinctive contributions to American culture. In music, folk spirituals are known all over the world, and modern rhythmic forms so dominant after World War I had their origin in black rhythm and blues. At the turn of the century Henry Ossawa Tanner was recognized as a distinguished painter specializing in biblical scenes. Receiving over fifty-seven patents for his various inventions, Elijah McCoy was a pioneer in perfecting automatic lubricating devices; appliances for lubricating railroad cars were not considered adequate without the "McCoy" trademark. The achievements of George Washington Carver in the field of agricultural chemistry illustrate the contributions of black Americans in science. W. E. B. Du Bois, a social scientist of national stature, began the first effective black protest early in the century. In the 1920's New York experienced its Harlem Renaissance, as such notable black writers as Alain Locke, Claude McKay, and Langston Hughes produced outstanding literature. The first phase of this Renaissance ended in 1930, but its dynamism and strength carried on and still continues.

Africans in Latin America. The history of African peoples in Latin America has generally been different from that north of the Rio Grande. Long contact of the Spanish and Portuguese with the dark-skinned Moorish people in the Iberian peninsula and their early African explorations had helped prevent the development of the form racism took in North America. There was also an important difference in the status of the slave in North and South America. In the former, the slave was regarded as a mere chattel with no legal or moral rights. In the latter, partly explained by the tradition of the Roman law and some influence of the monarchs and the Catholic Church, slaves had a legal personality and moral status. Thus while the slave status was generally considered to be perpetual, manumission was not difficult in Latin America. By 1860 free blacks outnumbered slaves 2 to 1 in Brazil, while slaves outnumbered freeblacks 8 to 1 in the United States. In 1888 slavery ended in Brazil without armed conflict.

There has been greater racial mixing in Latin America. The greatest meld of races—white, red, and black—in the history of the world has taken place. Perhaps more than half of the population has mixed blood. This intermingling may have eased racial tensions and made impossible North American practices such as segregation.

What did the African contribute to the new Europes of Latin America? Demographically, he helped fill the vast empty tropical spaces. Economically, he played a vital role in the production of colonial wealth as a herdsman, an artisan, and a farm worker. "During this era, the frontiers of European influence in the New World tropics were established on the base of African manpower."[3]

BRITAINS OVERSEAS

French and English rivalry in Canada. Europe not only sent immigrants to found new nations in the Americas, but Great Britain built a new family of nations in Canada, South Africa, Australia, and New Zealand. All of these societies retained special ties with Britain. While France first colonized Canada, a series of wars culminated in a British take-over of the colony in 1763 under the Treaty of Paris. The addition of an English population came as a result of the American Revolution when a large number of pro-British Tories migrated to Canada. During the next half century Canadian history was marked by quarrels between its French and English peoples. Fear of the United States, need of a common tariff policy, and a concerted effort to develop natural resources, finally led the Canadians to adopt a plan of national union. Under the British North American Act of 1867 Canada became a federal union of four provinces. In effect the new nation, while tied to Great Britain, was self-governing.

Canada has aptly been called "a classic instance of a two-fragment society,"[4] a pluralism that has seriously hindered its development. As we have seen, this dualism was not born with the British conquest in 1763. At this time the entire population was French, but an historic change began with the American Revolution, when English-speaking American Loyalists wishing to retain their British allegiance fled to Canada. In 1761 there were only 65,000 people in New France; by 1815 the population of all the British North American colonies had increased to 600,000, of whom only 250,000 were French. Between 1815 and 1850 a second wave of immigrants from Britain brought the entire population to 2,400,000, of whom less than one third were French. During the nineteenth century, and indeed down to the present, the population of French origin has remained between 28 and 31 percent of the total.

From the first arrival of significant numbers of British, the relations between the French and English have been strained. In his investigation of Canadian unrest in 1837, Lord Durham eloquently observed, "I found two nations warring in the bosom of a single state; I found a struggle not of principles but of races." In this reference to the ill will and on occasion downright hostility between English and

French Canadians, Durham singled out the most persistent and disturbing problem in Canadian national life.

The reasons are complex and numerous. The memory of the British conquest has often rankled the French; the English, on the other hand, have felt pride in this victory and in their tie to the mother country. There was also a clash in the religious field. New France was highly conservative, ruled by an authoritarian regime. When this political authority was removed, the Catholic Church in Quebec became the main defender and citadel of French Catholic culture. The English-speaking Canadians, however, tended to be antagonistic to this Catholic role.

Complicating the situation was the fact that the French minority was largely agricultural with a high rate of illiteracy. The French lived an unhurried existence, dominantly rural, suspicious of the outside world. Their education, often centered in convents and seminaries, was classical and theological in emphasis. The more secular-minded English, on the other hand, eagerly sought training in economics and science. It was natural, therefore, that the English dominated business. And while the federal constitution sought to create a bilingual society and a dual school system, the French were bitter over the progressive erosion of this guaranteed equality in the western provinces, where no appreciable French population developed. Tension was also generated by the inclination of some English Canadians to assume a pose of superiority; they denigrated French-Canadian culture and made little effort to learn French.

At the end of the nineteenth century, while Canada was a united federation in political structure, a common Canadianism had not been achieved. The French had no intention of being absorbed by the culture of the majority. How to create a single nationality comprised of two separate but officially equal cultures was to emerge in the mid-twentieth century as Canada's cardinal problem.

South Africa and Australia. In 1806 the Dutch Cape Colony came into British possession. From the beginning, the relations between the original Dutch settlers, called Boers, and British immigrants were strained. In 1836 in the Great Trek many Boers traveled inland where they established two small republics. Hoping to be left alone, they resented the influx of miners and businessmen following the discovery of gold in 1885. Resentment and ill will on both sides led to the Boer War (1899-1902), in which the British armies were victorious after hard fighting. In 1909 Boer and Britain joined hands creating the Union of South Africa in the tradition of a self-governing dominion. It was hoped that a new South African patriotism would result—a blend of English and Boer nationality.

The British connection with Australia began with the establishment of a convict settlement at Sydney in 1788. From this colony, later called New South Wales, five other settlements were founded. By 1850 they were enjoying a liberal form of self-government. Although gold was discovered in 1851, agriculture continued to be the mainstay of Australia's economy. Population grew slowly; in 1914 it was five million. In 1906 the six colonies formed a federal union known as the Commonwealth of Australia.

New Zealand's development. About a thousand miles from the Australian mainland is a group of islands, two of which are of particular importance. These lonely projections of British influence in the South Pacific constitute the self-governing Dominion of New Zealand. The total population of this country, which has an area five sixths the size of Great Britain, is just over 1,500,000. The earliest settlers were desperate convicts who had escaped from the penal settlements in Australia. The activity of other colonizers forced the British government to assume protection of the islands in 1840, and a treaty was signed by British agents guaranteeing certain rights, especially land rights, to the indigenous Maoris.

New Zealand gradually became a rich pastoral, farming, and fruit-raising country. The chief export, then as now, was wool. Later the development of refrigeration enabled large quantities of meat and dairy products to be shipped to foreign markets, especially to Great Britain.

COMMON DENOMINATORS OF THE NEW NATIONS

Immigration. The vast, fertile lands of the new Europes provided an almost magnetic attraction for the poor and landless peoples of Europe. A tremendous tide of immigration entered the new lands; it is estimated that 40 million emigrants sailed from their European homes from 1815 to 1914. By the latter date the number of people of European stock living in the new Europes totaled 200 million—a figure which is almost equivalent to the total population of Europe at the time of Napoleon's defeat.

For some 350 years this mass movement from Europe was accompanied by an equally significant forced migration from West Africa to the Americas. The number transported in the slave trade ran into the millions, and since many died from ill treatment at the time of capture and at sea during the nefarious Middle Passage—the forty-day voyage across the Atlantic—this trade perhaps cost Africa 50 million of its people; this estimate does not include the Arab slave trade from the East African coast.

In various and different ways the new Europes reflected the nineteenth-century movements that had originated in western Europe—nationalism, democracy, industrialism, and even imperialism. In addition, they had problems and opportunities which sprang specifically from factors and conditions shared in their new environments. These common denominators, with some variants, will be considered here.

Exploration. In all the new Europes vast spaces had to be explored, paths to the interior mapped, and natural resources evaluated. In what is now Canada, Alexander Mackenzie in 1789 traveled to the Great Slave Lake, then down the river that now bears his name to the shores of the Arctic. Four years later he crossed the Rocky Mountains to the Pacific and thus became the first European to traverse North America at its greatest width. In the United States the famous expedition of Meriwether Lewis and William Clark started from St. Louis in the winter of 1803-1804, blazed a trail through the unknown Northwest, and reached the Pacific two years later. For half a century the process of exploration and mapping continued, reaching its climax in John Frémont's expeditions to Oregon and California during the 1840's.

The most famous figure in the exploration of South America was the German naturalist Alexander von Humboldt, who from 1799 to 1804 carried on explorations in Mexico, Cuba, and South America; he investigated the valley of the Orinoco, crossed the Andes, and studied the sources of the Amazon. Although others have carried on the work he began, the huge Amazon basin—a tropical wilderness covering an area as large as the United States—has not been completely explored to this day.

Not until after the midpoint of the nineteenth century was the continent of Australia crossed from north to south. Between 1860 and 1862 John McDouall Stuart made three attempts before he successfully completed the journey from Adelaide to Van Diemen's Gulf. The penetration of the interior of South Africa differed from explorations in the other new Europes. It was achieved by the gradual expansion of white settlement in such valiant movements as the Great Trek rather than by expeditions of exploration, although discovery further north was accomplished by such men as Livingstone and Stanley (see p. 412).

Race problems in the new Europes. Race relations have been an important component in the history of most of the new Europes and have remained so in some. Estimates of the number of Indians in North America at the time of the coming of the white man are conjectural. In Canada the estimate is about 200,000; in the United States, about 850,000. Since the coming of the white man, the number of Indians in North America has been reduced by approximately half. In Canada, where the Indian population was not so great as in the United States, the Canadians encountered less difficulty with the natives as they moved westward to the Pacific. In the United States, however, there were frequent Indian wars and, generally speaking, a much more severe impact of an advanced civilization upon the culture patterns of the Indians. While in modern times some attempts have been made to help the Indian make a place for himself in contemporary urban society, these efforts have generally been inadequate. The Indian remains the most neglected and isolated minority in the United States.

The aborigines of Australia and Tasmania—numbering possibly 300,000 at the time of the arrival of the Europeans—could not withstand the ravages of new diseases and of the intoxicating liquors brought by the white men. Nor could they adapt themselves to new ways of life made necessary by the disappearance of their hunting lands. At times they were treated brutally: in some localities they were shot in batches; sometimes the whites got the natives drunk and then gave them clubs to fight each other for the amusement of the "civilized" spectators. The natives of Tasmania are now extinct, and the aborigines in Australia are a declining race.

In New Zealand the native Maoris had a more advanced culture than the Australian aborigines and were better able to stand up to the whites. After serious wars in the 1860's peace was finally secured, and slowly the Maoris accommodated themselves to the new world created by the whites. Since 1900 the Maoris have shared the same political rights and privileges as the European settlers and have obtained the benefits of advanced education. In the 1920's the pure Maori community was estimated to be fifty thousand. They now constitute 5 percent of the population, and their numbers are increasing.

In two of the areas colonized by European stocks, Latin America and South Africa, the indigenous peoples greatly outnumbered the white pioneers. Some authorities, for example, estimate that the population of Latin America in pre-Columbian days was at least 25 million. While a large percentage of these people died of disease, war, or famine following the initial European impact, in the long run native stocks did not dwindle away but substantially increased. There was much racial mixing between the Indians and Europeans, giving rise to the *mestizo*, and this mixed strain together with the Indian soon outnumbered the white population. Only in Argentina, Chile, and a few smaller states such as Costa Rica, Cuba, and Uruguay have European stocks overwhelmed the Indian.

Although the indigenous peoples in South Africa were not exterminated, neither were they given the opportunity to share in European civilization. The fierce fighting between the European frontiersmen (mainly the Dutch) and the Bantu caused constant misunderstanding and fear. Despite many political and economic disabilities, in the nineteenth century the South African natives showed a substantial increase in numbers. By 1904 the Europeans numbered about 1,150,000, as compared with about 7,000,000 others, mainly Bantu, "coloured,"* and a small community of Indians originally brought to the country as indentured workers from India. Unlike the situation in Latin America, the European minority—both English and Boer—have resolutely opposed any miscegenation with the indigenous Bantu peoples. Socially, politically, and economically there has been implacable segregation.

Isolation. Another common denominator in the new Europes was that generally the new nations remained outside the main current of world affairs in the nineteenth century. The British overseas nations accepted British leadership in international affairs. They were also effectively sheltered by the British fleet, a dependence that largely explains their reluctance to assert their complete independence.

During most of the nineteenth century the United States lavished its main efforts upon the exploitation of its vast natural resources and on the Americanization of the millions of immigrants who flocked to its shores. Evidence of its future role in world affairs became increasingly apparent, however, as the century drew to a close. In fact, the entrance of the United States onto the world stage was to be one of the cardinal factors in the drama of twentieth-century international affairs.

It would not be wholly correct to say that the nations of Latin America remained aloof from the flow of world politics. Politically unstable but rich in natural resources, these countries were tempting bait for great powers in Europe and also for the "Colossus of the North"—the United States. But the cruder imperialistic partitions and outright annexations so evident in Africa, China, and Southeast Asia were avoided. This lack of complete exploitation was due to luck rather than to the virtue of the outside powers. The national interests of the United States and to some extent of Britain coincided with the maintenance of the independence of various Latin American nations.

Progress of democracy. In general the liberal and equalitarian trends originating in western Europe found a fertile soil in the new Europes. Opposition to authority and to long-established traditions were at the heart of the revolutions that expelled the influence of Britain, Spain, and Portugal from the New World. Some historians have emphasized another factor in the progress of democracy—the influence of the frontier. Among the frontiersmen existed an absence of class distinctions, a refusal to truckle to authority, and a strong belief in the rights and capacities of the individual.

It is interesting that this frontier thesis worked in reverse in Australia. In this new Europe, land was not free or as productive as in the United States. As a result, in the remote "outback," vast sheep and cattle stations were established as rural capitalistic enterprises. On what has been called the "big man's frontier"[5]

Coloured is a special South African term used to refer to the Cape Coloured, a people of mixed racial ancestry.

there was little opportunity for the squatter and little man. This rural proletariat, therefore, escaped to the city. In this urban environment it supported radical and reformist causes that help explain the strong democratic trend in late nineteenth-century Australian politics. To a striking degree the same reverse frontier development occurred in Argentina.

In the United States the impediments to social democracy remaining after independence were largely removed by the 1820's; and during the remainder of the nineteenth century the country progressively perfected its democratic structure. In Canada the greatest stimulus to the growth of democracy was the achievement of responsible government. The trend toward social democracy evident in the United States was outstripped in Australia and New Zealand. In fact, New Zealand led the world in the direction of what is known as the welfare state.

With few exceptions, such as Mexico under the first Juárez administration, the Latin American republics in the nineteenth century paid mere lip service to the concept of social and political democracy. Society did not have the mobility existing in the United States and Canada. The new Latin American nations suffered from chronic political instability; changes in government came too frequently from bullets, not ballots.

Search for a nationality. Among all the new Europes, the United States has found the quest for nationality easiest. Its power, size, available resources, and heritage of freedom and the rule of law from its mother country have all contributed to a distinctive and recognizable national ideal. The greatest threat to national sovereignty—the Civil War—ended with the triumph of the forces of national union. In the nineteenth century the United States was the melting pot for thousands and thousands of immigrants; it stood for nonmilitarism and for the hope of the common man. And this democratic ideology consisted not only of faith but also of works.

The search for a national identity has not been easy in Canada. The establishment of the Confederation in 1867 increased nationalistic sentiment. But the Canadian, then as now, continued to be drawn like a magnet to the colossus of the south. He prefers baseball to cricket; he even joins affiliates of American labor organizations. Another problem complicating the search for a national identity is the existence of a closely knit French Canadian minority that tenaciously clings to its own language and culture. To some, Canada is a country with two nationalities: Toronto the symbol of one and old Quebec that of the other.

Nationalism has burned as brightly in each of the Latin American nations as in the other new Europes. In fact, the sentiment of nationalism has seemed the stronger as if in compensation for the obvious failures in political stability. The eight major administrative divisions in the late colonial era have fragmented into nineteen states—a process accompanied by costly and bloody wars. The whole of Latin America, however, exhibits a cultural homogeneity which has perhaps been some compensation for political turmoil.

Australia and New Zealand have found the search for nationality difficult. Remote from Europe, these islanders have clung to the traditions and ways of life of their forebears. New Zealanders brag about being more English than the English. This sentiment notwithstanding, a recognizable national character has developed in both countries—strongly equalitarian and fiercely nationalistic in its pride of the immensity and beauty of its lands.

Unlike Canada, where the original European community became a national minority in a new country created by the victorious British, the Union of South Africa has a majority of Boers instead of British in its European community. Of all the people of the new Europes, the South African Boers, who now call themselves Afrikaners, have developed the strongest sense of national identity. Continuously challenged by the alien culture of their English neighbors and potentially endangered by the Bantu majority, these beleaguered people have developed a distinctive, unbending culture. Two of its main pillars are a rigid Calvinism brought from Europe in the seventeenth century and a new language, Afrikaans, developed from the Dutch tongue. As in the case of Canada, a unicultural and national South Africa (at least as far as Europeans are concerned) has been weakened by the antipathy between its English and Afrikaner segments. In recent years, however, this division has been lessened by a common fear of Bantu domination and also by resentment directed against the outside world for its criticisms of South African racial policies.

THE DYNAMICS OF IMPERIALISM

Imperialism defined.   The word *imperialism* has come to mean many things to many people. Broadly speaking, the term refers to the extension of authority or control, whether direct or indirect, of one people over another. But we use the term *imperialism* in a more restricted sense to refer to the period from 1870 to 1914, when western Europe—which controlled much of the world's finance, commerce, military power, and intellectual life—extended its power over the peoples of the Orient and Africa.

The traditional periodization of nineteenth-century imperialism, which describes European expansion as lukewarm from 1815 to 1870 and thereafter as tumultuous and energetic, has recently been attacked by some British historians.[6] Dealing exclusively with British imperial history, they have sought to obliterate the differentiation between political and nonpolitical categories of British expansion, between "informal and formal" empires, putting both into "the vital framework" of nineteenth-century imperialism. It is pointed out that before 1870 Britain advanced its commercial interests by such informal means as political influence exerted upon weaker states, by the level of loans and trade treaties, and by the acquisition of strategic bases and trading sites that guarded British interests along the main routes of commerce. "Until the 1870's much of the empire was held, with the grand exception of India, by indirect interest rather than formal control." It was an empire of "trade not dominion."[7] Notwithstanding this form of British "indirect imperialism," the formal annexation of vast territories by Great Britain and other powers and the climax of imperial rivalries came after 1870. The term *imperialism*, therefore, is especially appropriate for this period in which the great colonial empires of modern times were acquired.

Waning European interest in colonization.   From the end of the Middle Ages to the close of the eighteenth century, a large part of Europe was expansive. Aggressive national states strove to stake out colonies and to monopolize overseas trade with their colonial possessions; the subsequent rivalries between nations helped bring on the great colonial wars of the eighteenth century. But by the end of that century interest in colonization declined. The loss of the thirteen colonies in 1783 dampened British ardor. By 1815 France had lost nearly all of its colonial possessions, and a few years later Spain and Portugal were forced to grant independence to most of their colonies. At the same time, the school of laissez faire argued that there were no advantages in possessing colonies and that the cost of defending them was an expensive burden. It was also believed that the whole world would soon be opened to free trade. Thus, between 1815 and 1870, as the gospel of free trade and laissez faire became dominant, colonial expansion was comparatively small.

Revival of imperialism.   When the tide turned, however, it came with a rush. In his six years as English prime minister, Disraeli annexed Fiji and Cyprus, fought a war against the Zulus in southeastern Africa, purchased a controlling interest in Suez Canal shares, and proclaimed Queen Victoria empress of India. Other European powers avidly followed Britain's lead, and early in the 1880's the colonial scramble began in earnest. The United States also felt the imperialistic urge.

This expansion of the western peoples had come about with amazing rapidity. It has been estimated that in 1800 fully one half of the world's surface was unknown to Europeans. A century later more land had been explored and acquired than in the entire period from the middle of the fifteenth century to the midpoint of the eighteenth. By 1914 the European nations could claim control of about 60 percent of the world's surface.

Economic motives for imperialism.   What were the motives behind this amazing expansion of western power? The most obvious and powerful were economic. Britain had been the home of the Industrial Revolution; by the middle of the nineteenth century other nations began to industrialize. To compete with British industry, these nations placed protective tariffs on imports. The free commerce of the early nineteenth century waned as tariff walls rose in the United States, Russia, France, and Germany. Great Britain and its new competitors—now producing a surplus of manufactured goods—began to search for trade outlets; building colonial empires appeared to be the solution to the problem.

Besides increased markets for European goods, colonies and trading posts could supply burgeoning industries with raw materials such as cotton, silks, rubber, exotic woods, tin, manganese, copper, and oil. And growing populations continued to increase the demands for foods raised in exotic lands.

Banks provided capital for trading enterprises and for the development of resources in distant lands. Money invested overseas could earn 10 to 20 percent. This impetus to wealth led one wag to remark that the French colonist was the franc. To safeguard these important investments and recover defaulted loans, European governments sometimes established spheres of influence or protectorates over the territories of weak native rulers and in certain cases subjected these lands to military occupation or to annexation.

Marxian socialists have stressed only the economic motives underlying imperialism. In his famous work *Imperialism, the Highest Stage of Capitalism* (1916), Lenin argued that the wages of the workers did not represent enough purchasing power to absorb the output of the capitalistic factories, and, moreover, that vast amounts of capital accumulated which could not be profitably invested in the home country. Therefore, to the Marxists, imperialism was an inevitable phase in the development of capitalism. That the profit motive in imperialism is strong is undeniable, but that it is the sole motive is false. It is also false that imperialism is a policy exclusive to capitalist powers, as can be proved by examples of Communist imperialism in the twentieth century.

Population pressures to expand. In the middle of the eighteenth century the population of Europe numbered about 140 million; by 1914 this figure had increased to 463 million. Hearing that land was more plentiful and jobs easier to secure overseas, no less than 9 million British subjects and 6 million Germans, to say nothing of the Italians, left their homelands. These migrations provided one of the greatest population movements in history.

But while some European statesmen, particularly in Germany and Italy, thought of the acquisition of new colonies as a means whereby their surplus population could be settled in vacant lands without escaping the political control of the motherland, this belief proved to be a delusion. Few Europeans migrated to the tropical colonies; the great majority made their new homes in the United States and the temperate regions of Latin America. In such areas the loyalty and support of these sons and daughters of Germany, Italy, and other nations were lost to the homeland.

Nationalism as a force for imperialism. While the economic forces behind nineteenth-century European expansion were strong, the psychological factors were equally important. A dominant factor was the new nationalism. Fresh from the achievement of national unification, Germany and Italy were eager to show off their new national strength; both demanded a place in the sun. In Great Britain also, a strong nationalist spirit existed. Britain was ready to take on any antagonist who stood in the way of its imperialistic ambitions.

Closely enmeshed with the nationalistic justification of imperialism was the philosophy of social Darwinism (see Chapter 15). Just as Darwin believed that progress in the biological sphere was measured by the survival of the fittest, so political and social theorists saw this concept of the "fittest" as an immutable factor in the onward march of civilization.

The military factor. If the use of force and the survival of the fittest were essential features of progress, then the military factor was important. A nation had to be strong enough to defend its interests. Colonies could be used as naval bases to protect a nation's commercial lifelines or to destroy those of a rival. Or a colony could be obtained as a buffer state to protect another colony against the designs of a rival.

Humanitarian and religious motives. The acquisition of colonies cannot be explained on economic, political, or strategic grounds alone, however. Many colonial administrators honestly felt that they were carrying the "white man's burden"—that it was a sacred task to bring the best aspects of western civilization to their undeveloped wards. The religious motive was likewise especially strong. In the nineteenth century British missionaries were particularly active, and there were large numbers of missionaries from France, Germany, and the Scandinavian countries.

Evaluating the motives of imperialism. In recent years there has been significant scholarly reexamination of the dynamics of nineteenth-century imperialism. In general the original overemphasis upon economic factors has been rectified. The scramble for territory in Africa, for example, has been shown to spring not so much from the economic competition between European states as from their international rivalries, stemming from problems of the balance of power in Europe that were extended to Africa.[8] Reflecting the mounting recognition of the role psychological factors play in human affairs, some scholars have turned to this area for an explanation of imperialism. One theory is that the nineteenth-century ruling classes purposely diverted the attention of the masses from their wretched living conditions by offering them the exciting diversion of adventure and glory in imperial enterprises.[9] Another ingenious explanation, influenced by the effect of "the dark powers of the subconscious," sees imperialism as the result of primitive aggressive instincts that still inhere in mankind. "Imperialism thus is atavistic in character. It falls into that large group of surviving features from earlier ages that play such an important part in every concrete social situation."[10] Thus nations sought colonies not so much as ends in themselves but rather for the satisfaction derived in fighting for them and in dominating them.

The final word on imperialistic motivation is a long way off, but it may be said at this time that no single simplistic cause is adequate. Stressing the importance of multiple causation and the fact that numerous motives recur but in different combinations, a student of African history has said that:

> The missionary movement will be important in one case, strategic considerations in another, economic motives in a third, and so on. We have now reached the paradoxical situation of knowing so much about European imperialism that generalization about its causes is almost impossible.[11]

IMPERIALISM IN ASIA

Manchu China and the West. In the middle of the eighteenth century China was ruled by the Ch'ing dynasty, which had been established by the Manchu. Descendants of Tatars who for centuries had lived in Manchuria, the Manchu appreciated Chinese civilization and adopted a conciliatory attitude toward their subjects. However, an uncritical acceptance and reverence for traditional thought (particularly Confucianism), augmented by the scholar rule of a civil service trained almost exclusively in the classics, had tended to make Chinese culture excessively backward-looking and conservative. Thus the amazing continuity which Chinese civilization had exhibited for thousands of years was gained at a heavy price. In addition, the prevailing attitude of superiority to the cultures of all other peoples was an unwholesome one for China, leading to what has been called "progressive sterility."[12]

Jesuit missionaries were active in China during the seventeenth century, occupying high positions at the Ming and Ch'ing courts. They made important contributions to Chinese scientific information and technology and helped the government survey its territories. While this diffusion of western knowledge was a factor in Ch'ing dynamism, the introduction of elements of Chinese culture into Europe by the Jesuits was more significant. The political and philosophical concepts they introduced played an important role in the intellectual climate of the European Enlightenment, and in the arts the stately homes of both England and France became graced by the decorative cult of *chinoiserie.*

Trade and the Opium Wars. Meanwhile a new factor, destined to have momentous consequences for China, had entered the scene: European trade. During the eighteenth century merchants from western Europe came to China in increasing numbers. Only with great difficulty was trade carried on, however. Foreign merchants were confined to Canton and the Portuguese colony of Macao.

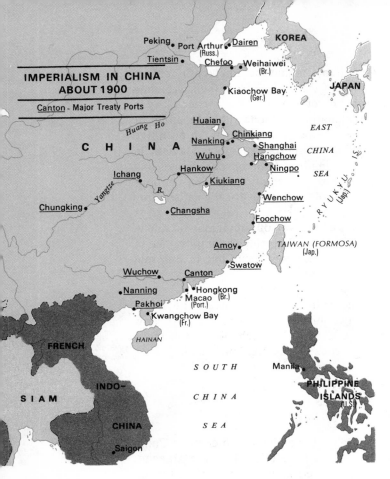

IMPERIALISM IN CHINA
ABOUT 1900

Canton - Major Treaty Ports

During the nineteenth century the western powers took advantage of the weakness of the Manchu dynasty to force greater trade concessions. As a result of the Opium Wars a number of ports were opened up to European ships and westerners were allowed new privileges, which, along with the importation of illegal opium by western traders, humiliated and angered the Chinese.

Nor would the Manchu government recognize or receive representatives of foreign powers.

European traders were irritated by the high customs duties the Chinese forced them to pay and by the attempts of Chinese authorities to curb the growing import trade in opium. In 1800 its importation was forbidden by the imperial government. Still, the opium trade continued to flourish. Privately owned vessels of many countries, including the United States, made huge profits from the growing number of Chinese addicts.

Early in the nineteenth century serious internal weaknesses developed in the Manchu empire. The standing army became corrupt, and rapacious governors fleeced the people. Weak emperors proved inadequate to meet the challenges of the time.

In 1839 war broke out with England—ostensibly over the opium traffic. But this was basically a secondary issue. As a Chinese historian has observed: "The war between China and England, caused superficially by the problem of opium prohibition, may actually be viewed as a conflict of Western and Eastern cultures."[13] Traditional China was no match for English military power, and in 1842 China agreed to the provisions of the Treaty of Nanking. Hong Kong was ceded to Great Britain, and certain ports, including Shanghai and Canton, were opened to British residence and trade.

In 1856 a second "Opium War" with England, aided by France, took place, and China was again defeated. By the terms of the Treaty of Tientsin (1858), new ports were opened to trading, and foreigners with passports were permitted to travel in the interior. Christians gained the right to propagate their faith and to hold property, thus attaining another means of western penetration. The United States and Russia obtained the same privileges in separate treaties, and China appeared well on the way to ultimate physical dismemberment and economic vassalage. Three provisions of these treaties, in particular, caused long-lasting bitterness among the Chinese: (1) extraterritoriality, (2) customs regulation, and (3) the right to station foreign warships in Chinese waters. Extraterritoriality meant that, in a dispute with a Chinese, a westerner had the right to be tried in his own country's consular court. Europeans argued that Chinese concepts of justice were more rigid and harsh than those in the West. But the Chinese felt that extraterritoriality was not only humiliating to China's sovereignty but also discriminative in favor of the western nations.

China beset from all sides.   The concessions to the "foreign devils" resulted in a great loss of prestige for the Manchu rulers. Serious internal difficulties further diminished their power, and the Taiping Rebellion of 1850 to 1864 almost overthrew the dynasty. That the Manchu dynasty managed to survive another half century was largely due to the statecraft of a remarkable woman, Tzu Hsi, the dowager empress, popularly known as "Old Buddha." From 1861 to her death in 1908, she was the real power behind the throne. Shrewdly and unscrupulously, Tzu Hsi crushed internal revolts and restored a measure of prestige to her homeland. Convinced that security for China lay in adhering to ancient traditions and customs, she encouraged antiforeign sentiment—an attitude her subjects shared. A relatively weak central government and general lack of national unity, however, made it impossible for China to resist foreign encroachments.

By 1860 Russia had annexed the entire area north of the Amur River; by 1885 France had taken Indochina and Britain had seized Burma; and in 1887 Macao was ceded to Portugal. China was too weak to resist these encroachments on its borders. But the crowning blow came not from the western nations but from Japan, a land which the Chinese had long regarded with amused contempt.

Trouble had brewed for some time between China and Japan, especially over the control of Formosa and Korea. In a dispute over China's claim to suzerainty in Korea, war broke out in 1894, and the brief Sino-Japanese struggle resulted in a humiliating defeat for China. By the Treaty of Shimonoseki (1895), China was forced to recognize the independence of Korea and hand over the rich Liaotung peninsula and Formosa.

The Chinese defeat was the signal for the renewal of aggressive actions by western powers, who forced Japan to return the strategic Liaotung peninsula to China. Shortly thereafter, the European powers made their demands of the Manchu. In 1897 Germany demanded a ninety-nine-year lease to Kiaochow Bay and was also given exclusive mining and railroad rights throughout Shantung province. Russia obtained a twenty-five-year lease to Dairen and Port Arthur and gained the right to build a railroad across Manchuria, thereby achieving complete domination of that vast territory. In 1898 Britain obtained the lease of Weihaiwei, a naval base, and France leased Kwangchowan in southern China (see map, p. 406).

A halt, or at least a hesitation, in the process of disintegration was brought about by the United States, not from high-minded desires but largely because Washington was alarmed at the prospect of American businessmen being excluded from China because the United States had no sphere of influence. In 1899

Secretary of State John Hay asked the major powers to agree to a policy of equal trading privileges. In 1900 several powers did so, and the famous Open Door Policy was born.

The Boxer Rebellion. The humiliation of the defeat by Japan had incensed the younger Chinese intellectuals, who agitated for reform. Sympathetic to their cause, the young emperor in 1898 instituted what came to be known as the "hundred days of reform." Unhappily for China, however, the reactionaries at court viewed all innovation with disfavor and formed a powerful faction about the dowager empress, Tzu Hsi. In September 1898 she imprisoned the emperor and took over the government.

After the suppression of the reform movement, a group of secret societies united in an organization known as the "Righteous Harmony Fists"; the members were called "Boxers" by westerners. At first the Boxers were strongly anti-Manchu because of the reactionary measures of "Old Buddha," but by 1899 the chief object of their hatred had become the foreign nations who were stripping China of land and power.

The Boxers started a campaign to rid China of all "foreign devils." Many Europeans were killed, and the legations at Peking were besieged. In August 1900 an international army forced its way to Peking and released the prisoners. China was then forced to apologize for the murder of foreign officials and to pay a large indemnity. The United States returned most of its share of the indemnity, which the Chinese government set aside to send students to American universities.

Only a decade after the conclusion of the rebellion, a revolution was to break out all over China, and in 1912 the Republic of China was proclaimed with Sun Yat-sen as president. This story of China's giant step into modern times will be discussed in Chapter 22.

Japan modernizes. At the beginning of the seventeenth century Japan was being ruled from Edo (now Tokyo) by the head of the Tokugawa clan, who in 1603 had made himself shogun. As a military dictator with a retinue of feudal lords and warriors, the shogun kept the country united and at peace. Meanwhile, the emperor—nominal head of the government—lived a meaningless existence at Kyoto.

As in the case of China, European merchants and missionaries posed a problem to the Japanese authorities. The shoguns insulated Japan effectively from the outside world by expelling the European traders and crushing Christianity. Nevertheless, despite the attempts of the shoguns, change could not be averted. There was remarkable economic growth, accompanied by rapid urbanization, the spread of education, and the rise of new social classes, especially young aggressive *samurai*, merchants, and intellectuals, many interested in western culture. Thus, in spite of Tokugawa isolationist policies, a new ferment was preparing the way internally for the "opening of Japan."

In 1854 an American naval flotilla forced the shogun to sign the Treaty of Kanagawa, the first formal treaty between Japan and a western nation. Ports were opened for the provisioning of ships and a limited amount of trade. With his prestige destroyed, the shogun in 1867 restored supreme authority to the emperor. The new leaders of this restoration clearly recognized that the West was the greatest threat to Japan and they proposed to modernize their country by making it a strong military and industrial power.

A new constitution was promulgated in 1889. Patterned after the German system, the cabinet was made responsible to the emperor alone, and final control of politics rested in the hands of the military clique. The constitution provided for a legislative Diet, but the property qualifications at first limited the electorate to a small number.

Many changes began to transform the land of the rising sun. Railways, telegraphs, and dockyards were constructed and warships were purchased from England. Foreign experts were employed to instruct in medicine, agriculture, engineering, and especially in military matters. In 1876 national conscription went into effect, and a modern military machine was created. Thus the new Japan avoided the dangers to sovereignty with which imperialism threatened such underdeveloped countries as China.

The world took note of this rapid transformation and was amazed when Japan in 1904 defeated Russia over rival claims in Manchuria and Korea. By the Treaty of Portsmouth, signed in September 1905, Japan acquired half of the island of Sakhalin, the leaseholds to the Liaotung peninsula and Port Arthur, and various Russian railway and mining rights in southern Manchuria. Japan's paramount position in Korea was also conceded, paving the way for Japanese annexation of that nation in 1910. Japan was now accepted as a first-class power.

The modernization of Japan was one of the amazing phenomena of modern world history. But there were some disturbing features in the way western technology and institutions were adapted by the Japanese for their own purposes. On the surface, Japanese government was liberal and parliamentary. In reality,

The influence of western technology and culture is evident in a Japanese woodcut of Yokohama harbor in the late nineteenth century. A steam locomotive carries passengers along the dock as Yokohama citizens dressed in western attire watch a ship set sail.

however, the constitution was ultra-conservative, giving the emperor and his cabinet dominant power. Though Japan was the first Asian nation to achieve a high degree of literacy, education was the tool of the government, and its primary function was to produce docile servants of the state. The press was subject to wide control and censorship. The army was used as a means of instilling conscripts with unquestioning loyalty and obedience to the emperor. In army barracks young soldiers learned that the noblest fate was death on the battlefield.

A prominent characteristic of Japanese culture was the meticulous attention paid to formal manners and "face." Like the Chinese, the Japanese took great pride in their dignity and status; to be shamed, degraded, or dishonored was a mortal offense. Awareness of these culture traits is basic to an understanding of Japanese reactions to the modern world and the policies that the rulers of Japan adopted to meet the challenges of the twentieth century. .

Imperialism in Southeast Asia and the Pacific.   At the southern tip of the Asian mainland, wedged between India and China and including a multitude of islands in the Indian and Pacific oceans, is the complex area of Southeast Asia. Its diverse peoples and countries began to come under European colonial rule with the arrival of the Portuguese and Spanish in the sixteenth century and the Dutch in the early years of the seventeenth. In the nineteenth century imperial control was completed when the British gained power over Ceylon, Burma, and Malaya and the French over Tahiti and Indochina. While European imperialism pushed eastward by way of the Indian Ocean into Southeast Asia, the United States, expanding westward, had reached the shores of the Pacific. By mid-nineteenth century it began to extend its influence and control into the Pacific area, ultimately securing control of Hawaii and the Philippines with naval bases at Pearl Harbor and Manila as well as Guam and Pago Pago in Samoa.

Throughout Southeast Asia, western rule made a substantial imprint. A plantation economy was established with foreign capital to develop the rich natural resources; vast quantities of petroleum, tin, coffee, tea, pepper, and other tropical products were produced for the world market. Chronic civil war and banditry were ended. Law and order, together with public health facilities, came in with colonial rule and brought about a rapid increase in population.

Throughout the colonial lands of Southeast Asia, the impact of European ways of life, and especially western education, created a new generation of nationalists. More and more irked with alien rule, this minority of young intellectuals finally aspired to complete independence. Little was done to satisfy these aspirations in the Dutch East Indies or in French Indochina. Britain provided some training in self-government in Burma and Ceylon, but it was in the Philippines that benevolent imperialism most consciously moved in the direction of ultimate freedom.

Notwithstanding substantial reservations in the minds of many Americans, there could be no doubt that by 1900 the United States sat astride the Pacific basin as did no other power. The consequences of this Pacific imperial posture were to become a major and costly constituent of American life in the twentieth century. A massive conflict with Japan, another in Korea, and a tragic war in Vietnam lay in the future. Whether such involvement was essential for American basic interests was to become a crucial and painful dialogue after the late 1960's.

British rule in India.   During the Mughul era in the seventeenth century, Europeans came to India to establish trading posts. As European infiltration continued, Mughul authority rapidly declined. The condition of India during this

After Robert Clive, as the servant of the British East India Company, had defeated the ruler of Bengal, thus becoming the real power in this province, he decided to continue the fiction of Indian authority. In this contemporary print Clive receives "Dewanee," the right to collect taxes, from the Mughul emperor.

time may be summed up in one word—misery. Marauding armies, nobles bent on gaining power, and officials who oppressed the people brought anarchy to India.

The collapse of the central government left the field open to a new authority. For more than one hundred years English and French trading companies had fought one another for supremacy. The French were finally defeated in 1760 and by 1818 the East India Company was master of the subcontinent.

The British Parliament, disturbed by the idea that a great business concern interested primarily in profits was controlling the destinies of millions of people, voted itself the power to control company policies and to appoint the highest company official in India, the governor-general. This system of dual control lasted until 1858. During this era important reforms were passed, such as the prohibition of *suttee* in which widows burned themselves on the funeral pyres of their deceased husbands. A comprehensive educational system, including universities was also introduced.

The rapid pace of modernization and the influx of disturbing alien ideas led to a serious rebellion in 1857, which was crushed only after fierce fighting. The mutiny ended the system of dual control, under which the British government and the

East India Company shared authority. The government terminated the company's political responsibilities in 1858; and a trained civil service was recruited from honor graduates of British universities. These men set out to rule India benevolently and efficiently.

By 1880 it was apparent that Indian nationalism was growing rapidly, the fruit of the influx of western ideas and technology. In 1885, with the aid of several Englishmen who had interested themselves in Indian political ambitions, the Indian National Congress was formed.

The British educational system served as one of the most potent forces back of the new movement. As Indians became acquainted with the story of the rise of self-government in England, the desire for the political freedom of their own land grew. Unable to obtain white-collar employment in governmental service and disdainful of manual labor, thousands of newly educated but unemployed Indian youths turned in wrath against the government. Confronted by the spread of violence, the British between the years 1907 and 1909 opened opportunities for Indian participation in the government. Moderate nationalists were satisfied for the time being, but their more radical comrades were not appeased. The twentieth century in India would see the spirit of nationalism become ever more insistent.

Britain and Russia in Central Asia. Ordinarily one does not think of tsarist Russia as a colonial power such as Britain or France. The reason is the manner of Russian expansion: unlike Britain, which had to expand overseas, the Russian empire grew from the center outward by a process of accretion. From the grand duchy of Moscow, the Russians pushed out into the great plain that surrounded them. Early in the nineteenth century, Russian armies and colonists pushed across the steppes north of the Aral Sea into Turkestan. By the 1870's the little states, or khanates, had been conquered. Russia had now pushed south to the frontiers of Afghanistan and India.

On the reverse side of the coin the defense of India's land frontiers and the control of all sea approaches to the subcontinent via the Suez Canal, the Red Sea, and the Persian Gulf became twin elements in British foreign policy during the nineteenth century. While the East India Company was consolidating its hold on India, Russian expansion had moved steadily eastward to the Pacific, then toward the Middle East, and finally to the frontiers of Persia and Afghanistan, both latter territories adjacent to India. Russia had annexed the kingdom of Georgia between the Black and Caspian seas in 1801 and had fought several wars with Turkey and Persia. As the Russians drove southward into the mountainous lands of the Caucasus, the indigenous people fought desperately but were finally overcome in the 1860's. Afghanistan and, to a lesser extent, Tibet continued to be serious areas of tension during much of the nineteenth century. Russian designs against the former were finally effectively blocked by Britain, and the intrusion of Muscovite influence into Tibet was countered by a British military expedition to Lhasa in 1904.

Anglo-Russian rivalry in the Middle East. The royal navy was in command of Britain's sea communications with India. A naval station at Aden guarded the entry into the Red Sea; and along the Arabian coast Britain, by treaty relations, controlled and protected a number of friendly minuscule sheikdoms, such as Muscat, Oman, Bahrein, and Kuwait. The maintenance of this sphere of influence blocked efforts of both Germany and France to secure footholds on the Persian Gulf. The former unsuccessfully sought to build a terminus on the gulf for its

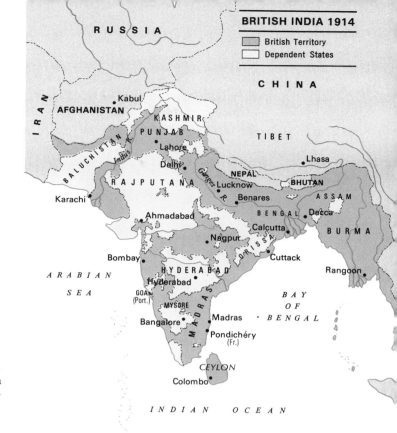

BRITISH INDIA 1914

British Territory
Dependent States

Dating back to the crucial Battle of Plassey in 1757, most of India was governed by the English. However, as can be seen from this map, some principalities remained independent.

projected Berlin to Baghdad railroad. In 1903 the British foreign secretary issued what has been termed a British Monroe Doctrine over this area:

> I say without hesitation, we should regard the establishment of a naval base or a fortified port in the Persian Gulf by any other power as a very grave menace to British interests, and we should certainly resist it by all the means at our disposal.[14]

While Britain had forestalled Russian influence in Afghanistan, the decline of Persian power and the mounting interference of Moscow into the shah's land caused grave concern in London. There was the possibility that the Russian Trans-Caucasian Railway might be extended south through Persia to the warm waters of the Persian Gulf; in this event, the government of the tsar might not only profit commercially but also construct a naval base that would be a potential threat to the British sea route to India. Persia was in no position to resist Russian pressure. Its government was corrupt, inefficient, the tool of a medieval parasitic aristocracy.

The Anglo-Russian entente. The upshot of this rivalry was that Britain and Russia ended their enmity in 1907 in Central Asia and the Middle East. Russia agreed not to interfere in Afghanistan and Persia was divided into three zones: the northern was a sphere of influence for Moscow, the middle was a neutral zone, and London had a free hand in the south. This understanding had been reached because of a mutual fear of German world ambitions on the part of Britain and Russia. We will see, however, that following the precipitous decline of British power at the end of World War II, Russia renewed her long range goal of achieving dominance in the Middle East. This possibility was viewed with considerable concern by the United States, a new entrant into the complicated rivalries of the Middle East.

THE GREAT AFRICAN COLONY HUNT

Exploration of Africa. The best area in which to follow the course of nineteenth-century imperialism is Africa, for nowhere else on the globe were colonial empires achieved so quickly. A great continent many times the size of Europe came almost completely under the control of European powers.

Late in the eighteenth century the opening of Africa began in earnest, and by 1835 most of northwestern Africa had been mapped by Europeans. The greatest of the European explorers was David Livingstone, a Scottish missionary who traversed vast barren wastes and jungles from the Cape of Good Hope as far north as Lake Tanganyika and from the Atlantic to the Indian Ocean. It was Livingstone who discovered Victoria Falls and the Zambezi River. "The very great doctor," as the natives called him, began his series of explorations in 1853. After his death in 1873, explorations of the interior were carried on by Henry Morton Stanley, a British explorer and journalist who had located Livingstone in 1871 and had casually greeted him, "Dr. Livingstone, I presume." By the end of the century Africa was no longer the "Dark Continent." The source of the Nile had been discovered, the courses of the Niger and Congo had been traced, and the world now realized the rich resources of Africa.

On the eve of the European scramble for Africa, only 10 percent of the continent was under the control of western nations. In 1875 the two most important European holdings were Algeria, administered by France, and Cape Colony, held by Great Britain. In South Africa there were Dutch farmers in two small republics, the Orange Free State and the Transvaal. Most of the other European holdings were mere coastal ports. The interior still remained a mysterious land.

Belgian interest in Africa. Stanley's explorations galvanized the European nations into action, although at first his ideas found little support except from the Belgian king. Leopold II, who in 1876 had organized the International African Association, enlisted Stanley in his service. The association, composed of scientists and explorers from all nations, was ostensibly to serve humanitarian purposes, but the crafty king had other motives. As an agent of the association, Stanley was sent to the Congo region, where he made treaties with several African chiefs and by 1882 obtained over 900,000 square miles of territory. Leopold organized his holdings into the Congo Free State, which he ruled personally, unchecked even by the Belgian parliament. Ruthless exploitation followed, including harsh forced labor on the rich rubber plantations. In the face of a rising tide of world indignation, Leopold was forced to turn over the Free State to the Belgian government which improved conditions in the colony, now named the Belgian Congo.

The British in Egypt. Meanwhile, in 1882 Britain occupied Egypt both to restore the country's financial stability and to secure control of the Suez Canal. Much was done to end corruption, to end the use of forced labor, and to build huge dams. Indeed, it has been said that the best record of imperialism is to be found in Egypt. Nevertheless, the twentieth century was barely under way before the Egyptians voiced a growing demand for self-government.

Organization of imperial policy. The occupation of Egypt and the acquisition of the Congo were the first moves in what came to be a precipitous scramble for African territory. In 1884 Bismarck convened a conference in Berlin to discuss the Africa problem. This assembly of diplomats paid lip service to humanitarianism by condemning the slave trade, prohibiting the sale of liquor and firearms in certain areas, and expressing concern for proper religious instruction for the natives. Then the diplomats turned to matters they considered much more important. They laid down the rules of competition by which the great powers were to be guided in seeking colonies. They agreed that the area along the Congo was to be administered by Leopold of Belgium, that it was to be neutral territory, and that in this area trade and navigation were to be free. No nation was to peg out claims in Africa without first notifying other powers of its intention. No territory could be claimed unless it was effectively occupied, and all disputes were to be settled by arbitration. In spite of these encouraging declarations, the competitors ignored the rules when it was convenient to do so, and on several occasions war was barely avoided.

The methods Europeans used to acquire land continued, in many cases, to involve the deception of the native peoples. Europeans obtained huge grants of lands by presenting ignorant chiefs with treaties which they could not read and whose contents they were not permitted to comprehend. In return, the natives were rewarded by bottles of gin, red handkerchiefs, and fancy-dress costumes. Since in many cases native custom reserved ownership of land to tribes, allowing individuals only the use of it, the chief granted land to European settlers with no idea that he was disposing of more than its temporary use. When later the settler claimed ownership, the natives were indignant, feeling that the tribe had been robbed of land contrary to tribal law.

The partition of Africa continues. The seizure and occupation of practically all of Africa took little more than two decades. In the 1880's Germany acquired three colonies on the west coast: Southwest Africa, Togoland, and Cameroons. In addition German East Africa was occupied. Britain obtained important territories such as Uganda, Kenya, Nyasaland, and Zanzibar. On the west coast the Union Jack had been hoisted over Nigeria, Gambia, Sierra Leone, and the Gold Coast. Added to these colonies was the Anglo-Egyptian Sudan, all important as the headwaters of the White Nile. During this same period Great Britain's influence in southern Africa expanded northward from Cape Colony to German East Africa. The main impetus in this drive north came from the British capitalist, Cecil Rhodes, who dreamed of an uninterrupted corridor of British territory from the Cape of Good Hope to Cairo.

France was also an energetic agent in this scramble for Africa. Along the Mediterranean she seized control of Algeria, Tunisia, and Morocco. The large island of Madagascar was also occupied. By 1900 the French controlled the largest empire in Africa, one which stretched westward from the Atlantic to the western Sudan and southward to the Congo basin.

While Portugal succeeded in retaining control of her huge possessions, Angola and Mozambique, first colonized in the sixteenth century, Italy's African ventures were mainly fruitless. An attempt to annex the ancient empire of Abyssinia in 1896 ended in the destruction of an Italian army. A piece of Red Sea coast and a slice of barren land on the Indian Ocean were obtained. Italy then shifted its attention to the Turkish territory of Tripoli forcing the Sultan's government to cede the area in 1912. This event temporarily marked the end not only of Italian expansion but also of the race for colonial empires by European powers.

The economic wealth of Africa surpassed the expectations of the most avid imperialist. By the first decade in the twentieth century it was the world's greatest producer of gold and diamonds. In addition, rich resources of tin, phosphates, and especially copper were uncovered. From the once "Dark Continent" poured rubber, coffee, sisal, palm oil, and cotton—products which became more and more essential for the great industrial nations of the world. The exploitation of these raw materials profited European enterprise rather than African.

Europe's impact on Africa. It was inevitable that the process of acculturation—that is, the social change caused by the interaction of significantly diverse cultures—should have been more profound and widespread in Africa than in India. In India some disintegration and modification of the culture occurred, but the main core of the ancient Hindu ways remained intact. This was not so in Africa, where for the first time the villagers were compelled to pay money taxes to a distant central authority. In most cases Africans had lived within a small tribal area of law and political affiliation. With the advent of imperial rule, dozens of formerly distinct—and often antagonistic—tribes were gathered together into one colony, as in the case of Nigeria. In some cases boundaries divided large tribes into two or three European colonial segments. Colonies, therefore, were usually not homogeneous nations in the modern sense, a fact later to prove a serious complication when these colonies became independent "nations" following World War II.

The process of colonization in Africa added up to the massive impact of a dynamic, self-confident, and technologically advanced civilization upon cultures that had been isolated from the mainstream of world affairs, politically and technologically arrested, and psychologically overawed. Kinship and family ties were weakened when villagers sought wage employment in distant towns or mines. In some areas, as many as 50 percent of the young males sought jobs in European mines hundreds of miles distant. Migrant workers sought money to pay the new hut taxes or to buy cheap, enticing European wares. Undoubtedly wage remittances from absent husbands raised standards of living, but the effect upon family ties and tribal loyalty was destructive. Old handicrafts declined as trade came to be dominated by Europeans and by Indian and Syrian merchants. The old ways of life were most disrupted in colonies that attracted European settlement, as in Kenya and Southern Rhodesia. In such areas Africans were limited to "native reserves" or to segregated areas in the towns. On occasion large tracts of land were allocated exclusively for European use. It was in these plural societies that racial tensions most rapidly developed.

For some fifty years after the African scramble began, the incidence of social change was uneven. In some remote areas Africans may never have seen a white man, let alone worked for him. But tribal life was gradually transformed by the introduction of new forms of land tenure, enforcement of alien systems of law, and the growth of a money economy. The obvious material superiority and military power of Europeans deeply impressed Africans. They sought consciously to imitate their rulers, to accept the white man's gods, and if possible to obtain a modicum of western education. The African in consequence became "detribal-ized" and often bewildered, alienated from much of his traditional culture but yet unable to understand and be part of the new.

Although the transformation of Africa was inevitable, it was unfortunate that this revolutionary change occurred so quickly and at the hands of intruders whose motives were so mixed and who too frequently denigrated all African culture, dismissing the African as barbarous and uncivilized. Perhaps colonialism was a necessary, if abrupt and rude, awakening. It *did* introduce peace between tribes, administrative techniques, communications, harbors, western education, and a money economy—all essential before any African area could develop into a modern state. Some scholars disagree; Basil Davidson contends:

> There is indeed nothing in that episode to show that these people could not or would not have worked this transformation for themselves, far less expensively in life and suffering and self-respect, without the coercion of outside interference.[15]

IMPERIALISM: THE BALANCE SHEET

Spread of imperialism. By 1914 some 283 million whites in Europe and the United States, together with about 54 million Japanese in Asia, directly controlled over 900 million non-Europeans, mainly in Africa and Asia, and dominated millions more in vast areas like China and Latin America. Britain, the greatest of the empire builders, boasted that "the sun never set" on its empire. Russia's colonial domain, mainly in central and eastern Asia, was at least half the size of Britain's empire. France was the third largest imperial power, with Germany a poor fourth. Belgium, Portugal, and Holland had substantial colonial holdings, though Italy made a poor showing. In 1914 the United States, as an imperial power, controlled over 700,000 square miles of territory outside the confines of continental United States. Its three most important possessions were Hawaii, Alaska, and the Philippines, but its shadow loomed gigantically over Latin America as well.

Imperialism: positive aspects. Today classical imperialism would find few, if any, enthusiastic supporters. However, the significance of western colonial rule in the scheme of world history is becoming clearer following the achievement of independence by a large number of colonies after World War II. It is now evident that many of the native peoples living under imperial rule took the ensuing law and order for granted. It should not be forgotten that the slave trade in tropical Africa was smashed in the mid-nineteenth century largely by British efforts, and that the French ended piracy in North Africa.

In many of the areas that came under imperial control, tribes or nations had been constantly at war with each other. This was especially true in Africa, Malaya, and the Dutch East Indies. One law was imposed over an entire area, providing advantages of political and economic unity heretofore unknown. As we shall see in a later chapter, the granting of independence revived the old tribal and sectional loyalties. Regions such as India broke apart; unity has been maintained with extreme difficulty in Indonesia. The recent breakaway effort of the Ibos in

Nigeria to create a new state of Biafra exemplifies the tendency toward a continued fracturing of the African political map.

On the economic front, western nations constructed roads, public buildings, postal, telegraph, and railway systems, and dams, while their businessmen dug mines, tapped oil fields, and established plantations. With the end of imperial control, many of these improvements remain, performing invaluable functions. Moreover, these underdeveloped areas still require the capital and technical skills of more developed nations.

Nor should the positive side of the ideological impact of imperialism be minimized. To civilizations, such as the Chinese, that were no longer dynamic, and to certain areas, such as tropical Africa, where modern technology had never existed, the West brought lively ideas of progress, nationalism, effective public administration, democracy, and faith in science. This ideological impact of nationalism and democracy, made possible by imperial rule, ultimately led to a demand for independence.

Among the most important agencies diffusing western ideas were the Christian missionaries. Their missions, hospitals, churches, schools, and colleges made a unique contribution. True, missionaries sometimes failed to respect or understand the intrinsic worth of indigenous culture. They believed such customs or beliefs undesirable because they were non-western or non-Christian. But much selfless labor also was devoted to humanitarian objectives in the world's colonial regions.

Imperialism: negative aspects. A strong anticolonial school in the West has produced a massive literature against imperialism. Thus its critics charge that it was imposed "by self-seeking interests which appeal to the lusts of quantitative acquisitiveness and of forceful domination surviving in a nation from early centuries of animal struggle for existence,"[16] Unquestionably imperialism had its ruthless and exploitative side. Large territories were taken by force or fraud, and on occasion lands were seized from native populations without compensation.

In the political and economic sectors, while imperial rule did create law and order, it was often achieved by perpetuating an indigenous hierarchical structure and endowing this elite with wealth and authority in return for maintaining a status quo that was advantageous for the imperial power. One result was to retard the development of national forms of representative government, of needed educational opportunities, or of the ability of the indigenous peoples to profit from the exploitation of their own natural resources. Often the construction of roads, transportation systems, hospitals, and schools was designed to serve the economic and societal interests of the colonial administrators and western business community so that the great masses remained both illiterate and at the bottom of the economic ladder, often at the bare subsistence level. Moreover, so well did western economic interests become entrenched that the eventual transfer of independence in the political sphere was seldom accompanied by a concomitant transfer of economic control and resources to the indigenous community, thereby creating a condition known as "neocolonialism."

On the sociological side, the large-scale destruction of culture patterns in Asia and Africa had massive repercussions. This is not to suggest that imperialism deliberately set out to practice either physical or cultural genocide. Rather, when drawing up an overall historical balance sheet, we must recognize that the penetration of western culture armed with a dynamic technology had a devastating impact which imperialism *per se* did little or nothing to alleviate. Whether the charge is valid or not, it is widely believed in the new Asian and African nations that imperialism accentuated the destructive forces inherent in western political, economic, and cultural penetration.

Finally, on the psychological side the Africans and Asians were subjected to the hauteur and superior-race attitudes of their rulers. They were treated and thought of too frequently as uncivilized heathen, barbarous in manner and backward in intelligence. It is only by understanding this racial denigration that one can appreciate the psyche of former colonial peoples—the assertiveness of their new national identity, their sensitivity to any hint of condescension, and their suspicion of the West in general and the former colonial imperialists in particular.

THE WORLD ADRIFT

World War I has been described as a major watershed in modern history. It closed a century of relative peace and ushered in what has been called the Age of Violence. It also marked the end of the era in which Europe was the center of the world in political influence, cultural creativity, and military and financial power. New continental centers were to arise to contend for supremacy on the world stage, especially in the decades after World War II.

First of the total technological conflicts, the 1914-1918 conflagration so shattered the international framework as to cause shock waves to jar the social environment for twenty anxious years until a second, and still more convulsive, holocaust engulfed mankind. The hopes of millions who had survived World War I that a better world would emerge were quickly shattered. Statesmen placed national ambitions and rivalries above the cause of international justice, and relied upon new sophisticated armaments while depriving the League of Nations of either the strength or support to keep the world secure during the troubled 1920's and 1930's.

In these years democracy began its struggle with new totalitarianisms. In war-exhausted Russia, Marxist tenets were embraced by revolutionaries, and a Communist society took shape under Lenin. On the extreme right, Mussolini subjected Italy to fascism. And the most frightening ideology of all, Nazism, grew to terrifying fruition in Germany, where the people staked their future on a madman named Hitler.

By the 1920's and 1930's the non-European world had discovered the concept of nationalism. In the Middle East, Arab national ambitions had flared in 1916 into a revolt against Turkish rule. The immigration of European Jews to Palestine led to conflict between Arabs and Jews—a portent of the warring struggle that was to become endemic following the creation of Israel after World War II. In North Africa, the Middle East, India, Southeast Asia, and Oceania the indigenous peoples were gathering strength to oust the Europeans and govern themselves, while in the huge colonial region south of the Sahara, Africans were beginning to stir restlessly, though here again nationalism would triumph only after another global war. China had already turned to revolution to become a republic, but throughout this period it remained poor and weak. In striking contrast Japan had continued its amazing technological, industrial, and military growth to become a world power with imperial ambitions in the Pacific.

The world depression in the 1930's encouraged the totalitarian movements to expand their despotism at home and to launch aggression abroad. From 1931 to 1939, starting with the Japanese invasion of Manchuria, their belligerence mounted. The older democratic nations tried appeasement, but the aggression continued. Finally, in 1939, the British and French took up arms in an attempt to stop Hitler's march of conquest. The Second World War began. Two years later the Soviet Union and the United States were forced into the struggle. By the time victory came to the Allies in 1945, millions of both soldiers and civilians were dead; and Hitler's Third Reich and the fascist states in Italy and Japan were totally defeated.

As in 1919 the victors were confronted with the immense task of rebuilding a great part of the world. This task was made more difficult by the knowledge of the failures of the peace of 1919 and the dismaying realization that as the Second World War was more encompassing and vastly more destructive than the First, so a Third World War would be much more shattering than the Second. Worse yet, the advent of nuclear weapons might bring about the annihilation of man.

The period spanning from 1914 through 1945 has been experienced by hundreds of millions of people still alive, so that its impact on the 1970's remains powerful. Prior to 1914 Western civilization implicitly believed in the fundamental validity of Christianity, parliamentary institutions, and capitalism, which seemed destined to spread all over the globe. This set of beliefs was reinforced by a comfortable assumption in human progress and perfectability, carried over from a prosperous nineteenth century. After World War I the democracies sought to build a "world fit for heroes to live in" and to "return to normalcy." But how does one return to a world whose assumptions had been blown to smithereens over the shell-pocked battlefields of Flanders? Instead of traditional certitude, there was now doubt and even despair. The old order was dying, but none knew the shape or values of the new order. And so these decades were shaken by inner turmoil, naked aggression, and social innovations as governments experimented with new ideologies and programs to improve the lot of the common man. The New Deal under Franklin Roosevelt was an example. Meanwhile technology was accelerating the tempo of change and at the same time annihilating the spaces which historically had separated people. Men were now flying the Atlantic and Pacific, and intricate communication networks were linking all the continents. In short, the way was being prepared for a new—a global—social order, whose shape would become progressively clear after 1945.

CHAPTER 20
THE WAGES OF WAR

The Course of Politics in the West: 1918-1930

When World War I ended, a weary world began the herculean task of transforming its efforts from those of war to peace. Underlying this transition was the prevalent belief that somehow the sacrifices made during the war would lead to a better life for all mankind. Accordingly, there were roseate predictions of the ultimate triumph of democratic institutions everywhere. A new international order was to be achieved by the creation of a world organization designed to outlaw war and encourage amity between nations.

Europeans generally viewed their continent's prospects optimistically. They were prone to believe that Europe could regain its preeminence in the world—in finance, industry, and military power. It soon became evident, however, that such hopes were not justified. The war's economic consequences were both underestimated and only dimly understood. Nations such as Great Britain had lost export markets; disagreements over war debts and reparation claims against former enemies, as well as runaway inflation, plagued various nations after 1918. Economic recovery was also hindered, and the general morale tarnished, by the destruction of millions of Europe's young men on the battlefields.

Against this background, and confronted by the defeated nations' belief that the peace treaties were unjust, the newly created League of Nations began its task of safeguarding world peace and encouraging international conciliation. In retrospect, it is hardly surprising that its record was not impressive. Its usefulness was also compromised by the refusal of the United States to become a member of the League.

The aftermath of war was characterized by an absence of dynamism in the parliamentary democracies. In Great Britain, France, and the United States, there seemed to be a lack of purpose, of vitality, and of confidence. While France and Britain failed to come to grips with their basic problems, the United States, mainly aloof from world affairs, concentrated on what appeared to be dazzling prosperity. During the postwar decade all three nations exhibited various symptoms of moral fatigue and disillusionment.

Russia, meanwhile, was being convulsed by an important political and social revolution. The overthrow of the tsarist regime ushered in a period of turmoil and innovation that was to have long-term consequences for the world at large.

But of more immediate international import were events in Italy and Germany. The ominous triumph of the Fascists in Italy was paralleled in republican Germany by the emergence of the racist and anti-democratic Nazi movement.

THE PEACE SETTLEMENT

Wilson's blueprint for peace.   Woodrow Wilson had declared that World War I was

> a war for freedom and justice and self-government amongst all the nations of the world, a war to make the world safe for the peoples who live upon it and have made it their own, the German people themselves included.[1]

In January 1918, in an address before both houses of Congress, the president had enunciated his famous Fourteen Points as the basis for a lasting peace. With this speech, Wilson made himself a new kind of world leader, representing not wealth and power but morality and justice. Millions of men and women, at home and abroad, in the Allied nations, in the enemy countries, and in neutral states, flocked to his standard. The Fourteen Points seemed to open the way not only for a speedy cessation of hostilities but for a peace that could endure.

The first five points were general in nature and may be summarized as follows: "Open covenants openly arrived at"; freedom of the seas in peace and in war alike; the removal of all economic barriers and the establishment of an equality of trade conditions among all nations; reduction of national armaments; a readjustment of all colonial claims, giving the interests of the population concerned equal weight with the claims of the government whose title was to be determined. The next eight points dealt with specific issues involving the evacuation and restoration of Allied territory, self-determination for submerged nationalities, and the redrawing of European boundaries along national lines. The fourteenth point in Wilson's speech contained the germ of the League of Nations: the formation of a general association of nations under specific covenants for the purpose of affording mutual guarantees of political independence and territorial integrity to great and small states alike.

Crosscurrents at the peace conference.   All the Allied powers sent delegations to the peace conference at Paris, but the vanquished nations were not accorded representation. This exclusion was not in the spirit of Wilson's idealistic pronouncements before the armistice.

Three personalities dominated the Paris Conference: Wilson, Lloyd George, and Clemenceau. In the eyes of the war-weary and disillusioned peoples of Europe, Wilson was a veritable Messiah. But it soon became apparent that he would be unable to prevent his ideals and promises from being sabotaged by the other Allied statesmen. Against the wily Lloyd George and the cynical Clemenceau, the idealistic American scholar had little chance of holding his own. In

Thirty-two Allied nations sent representatives to Paris to put the
stamp of finality and justice on the "war to end all wars." But
the settlements which came out of the Peace Conference
were marked by national rather than global interests, and by hostility
rather than assistance for the defeated nations. Four influential
men who clashed over their individual plans for a lasting peace
were David Lloyd George, prime minister of Great Britain; Vittorio
Orlando, prime minister of Italy; Georges Clemenceau, premier of
France; and Woodrow Wilson, president of the United States.

addition, certain factions in Congress were preparing to repudiate Wilson's
program. Handicapped by a cold and imperious personality, Wilson (1856-1924)
was so thoroughly convinced of the validity of his own ideas that he seldom
recognized a need to "sell" them to others and often refused to consider the
possibility of merit in the ideas of his opponents.

Lloyd George (1863-1945), the prime minister of Great Britain, came to the
conference just after a triumphant victory at the polls in which his party had
promised the electorate the "hanging of the kaiser" and the "squeezing of the
German lemon until the pips squeaked." He was determined to destroy the
commercial and naval power of Germany, to acquire the German colonies, and to
compel Germany to pay a large share of the cost of the war.

The strongest personality of the conference was the French premier—the
seventy-seven-year-old Clemenceau (1841-1929). His burning ambition was to

ensure the security of France in the future; his formula was restitution, reparations, and guarantees. Clemenceau had little confidence in what, to him, were the unrealistic and utopian principles of Wilson, observing, "Even God was satisfied with Ten Commandments, but Wilson insists on fourteen."

Prearmistice peace principles and secret treaties. The Germans had surrendered with the understanding that the peace would in general follow the Fourteen Points and coincide with Wilson's speeches. In February 1918 the president had announced, "There shall be no annexations, no contributions, no punitive damages"; on July 4 he had said that every question must be settled "upon the basis of the free acceptance of that settlement by the people immediately concerned."

Complicating the promises of Wilson, especially the Fourteen Points, were the secret treaties the Allies had made during the war, such as that by which Italy had been induced to enter the conflict.

President Wilson professed ignorance of the existence of the treaties, but their contents were common knowledge before the end of the war. Wilson may have believed that the secret agreements could be ignored, for he hoped to sway European statesmen to the necessity of founding the peace on his principles.

The League Covenant. When the statesmen assembled in their first plenary meeting on January 18, 1919, the first difficulty arose over the question of a league of nations. Wilson was insistent that the initial work of the conference must be to agree upon a covenant of a league of nations which was to be made part of the peace treaty. After much wrangling, the Covenant was approved by the full conference in April 1919. In order to gain support for the League, however, Wilson had to compromise on other matters. His Fourteen Points were thus partially repudiated, but he believed firmly that an imperfect treaty incorporating the League was better than a perfect one without it.

The Covenant of the League of Nations specified its aims: "to guarantee international cooperation and to achieve international peace and security." To implement this goal, Article x, the key article of the Covenant, stipulated that:

> The Members of the League undertake to respect and preserve as against external aggression the territorial integrity and existing political independence of all Members of the League. In case of any such aggression or in case of any threat or danger of such aggression the Council shall advise upon the means by which this obligation shall be fulfilled.[2]

Redrawing German boundaries. The conference also faced the task of redrawing German boundaries. Alsace-Lorraine was turned over to France without question, in accordance with one of the Fourteen Points. Three districts formerly belonging to Germany were given to Belgium, after a dubious plebiscite conducted by Belgian officals. Another plebiscite gave half of Schleswig back to Denmark.

Clemenceau was determined that a buffer state consisting of the German territory west of the Rhine should be established under the domination of France. In the eyes of the American and British representatives, such a crass violation of the principle of self-determination would only breed future wars; and a compromise was therefore offered Clemenceau, which he accepted. The territory in question was to be occupied by Allied troops for a period of from five to fifteen years; and a zone extending fifty kilometers east of the Rhine was to be demilitarized. In addition, Wilson and Lloyd George agreed that the United States and Great Britain, by treaty, would guarantee France against aggression. The importance of this pledge cannot be overemphasized.

Along Germany's eastern frontier the creation of the Polish Corridor, which separated East Prussia from the rest of Germany, raised grave problems. Large sections of German territory in which there were Polish majorities but also a goodly number of Germans were turned over to Poland. (The land in question had been taken from Poland by Prussia in the eighteenth century.) A section of Silesia was likewise given to Poland, but only after a plebiscite. Danzig, a German city, was handed over to the League for administration. All in all, Germany lost 25,000 square miles inhabited by some six million people.

The mandate system.   A curious mixture of idealism and revenge determined the allocation of the German colonies and certain territories belonging to Turkey. Because outright annexation would look too much like unvarnished imperialism, it was suggested that the colonies be turned over to the League, which in turn would give them to certain of its members to administer. The colonies were to be known as mandates, and praiseworthy precautions were taken to ensure that the mandates would be administered for the well-being and development of the inhabitants. Once a year the mandatory powers were to present a detailed account of their administration of the territories to the League. The mandate system as such was a step forward in colonial administration, but Germany nevertheless was deprived of all colonies, with the excuse that it could not rule them justly or efficiently.

Reparations.   Germany had accepted the armistice terms with the understanding that it was to pay for damage done to the Allied civilian population. At the conference the British and French delegates went much further by demanding that Germany pay the total cost of the war, including pensions. The American representatives maintained that such a claim was contrary to the prearmistice Allied terms and succeeded in achieving a compromise. It was agreed that, except in the case of Belgium, Germany was not to pay the entire cost of the war, but only war damages, which included those suffered by civilians and the cost of pensions. These payments, called reparations, were exacted on the ground that Germany was responsible for the war.

Other Allied demands.   Germany was required to hand over most of its merchant fleet, construct one million tons of new shipping for the Allies, and deliver them vast amounts of coal, equipment, tools, and machinery. In military matters the demands were even more drastic. Germany was permitted a standing army of only 100,000 men, the size of the fleet was drastically reduced, possession of military airplanes was forbidden, and munitions plants were to be placed under close supervision. The treaty also provided that the kaiser be tried by a tribunal "for a supreme offense against international morality and the sanctity of treaties" and cited some eight hundred German officials for trial on charges of war atrocities. But the kaiser had fled to Holland after the German revolution; and when that country refused to surrender him, no further steps were taken by the Allied governments, which had inserted the clause providing for the punishment of the kaiser largely for home consumption.

The Treaty of Versailles signed.   The Treaty of Versailles was built around the concept that Germany was responsible for the war. It stated explicitly that:

THE PEACE SETTLEMENT IN EUROPE

Newly Created States

Ceded Territories

The Allied and Associated Governments affirm and Germany accepts the
responsibility of Germany and her allies for causing all the loss and damage to
which the Allied and Associated Governments and their nationals have been
subjected as a consequence of the war imposed upon them by the aggression
of Germany and her allies.[3]

Before coming to Paris in April 1919 to receive the Treaty of Versailles, the
German delegation had been given no official information as to its terms. Upon
obtaining the treaty of May 7, the German foreign minister stated:

> It is demanded of us that we shall confess ourselves to be the only ones guilty
> of the war. . . . We are far from declining any responsibility . . . but we

energetically deny that Germany and its people . . . were alone guilty. . . . In the last fifty years the Imperialism of all the European States has chronically poisoned the international situation. . . . [4]

The menace of Allied invasion gave the Germans no alternative but to sign, and the government therefore instructed its delegates to accept the treaty for Germany "without abandoning her view in regard to the unheard-of injustice of the conditions of the peace." On June 28, on the anniversary of the assassination of Archduke Francis Ferdinand and in the Hall of Mirrors at Versailles where the German empire had been proclaimed in 1871, the treaty was signed.

After witnessing this ceremony, an American delegate wrote in his diary:

> I had a feeling of sympathy for the Germans who sat there quite stoically. It was not unlike what was done in ancient times, when the conqueror dragged the conquered at his chariot wheels. To my mind, it is out of keeping with the new era which we profess an ardent desire to promote. I wish it could have been more simple and that there might have been an element of chivalry, which was wholly lacking. The affair was elaborately staged and made as humiliating to the enemy as it well could be.[5]

Other World War treaties.　The Allies also concluded treaties with the rest of the Central Powers. The treaty with Austria, the Treaty of St. Germain (1919), legalized the nationalist movements of Czechs, Poles, and South Slavs and converted the rest of the empire into the separate states of Austria and Hungary. By the treaty terms, the Austrian empire was reduced in area from 116,000 to 32,000 square miles and in population from 28,500,000 to 6,000,000. *Anschluss*—union of the Germans in Austria with their kinsmen in the new German republic—was forbidden. The treaty also awarded Italy sections of Austria—the territory south of the Brenner Pass, South Tyrol, Trentino with its 250,000 Austrian Germans, and the northeastern coast of the Adriatic with its large number of Slavs.

By the Treaty of Sevres (1920) the Ottoman empire was placed on the operating table of power politics, dissected, and divided among Greece, Britain, and France. Two other treaties affected the Balkans. By the Treaty of Trianon (1920) Hungary lost territory to Czechoslovakia, Yugoslavia, and Rumania. The Treaty of Neuilly (1919) cut off Bulgaria from the Aegean Sea, imposed an indemnity, and provided for compulsory demilitarization. Bulgaria lost nearly one million subjects.

Evaluation of the peace settlement.　During the first postwar decade tons of paper and barrels of ink were used in hot justification or acrid denunciation of the peace settlement. On the whole, the peace settlement was inadequate and unrealistic. In his indictment of the economic provisions of the peace, the world-famous economist John Maynard Keynes wrote in 1919:

> The treaty includes no provisions for the economic rehabilitation of Europe, —nothing to make the defeated Central Empires into good neighbours, nothing to stabilise the new States of Europe, nothing to reclaim Russia; nor does it promote in any way a compact of economic solidarity amongst the Allies themselves; no arrangement was reached at Paris for restoring the disordered finances of France and Italy, or to adjust the systems of the Old World and the New.[6]

One of the weakest aspects of the peace settlement was the complete disregard of Russia. While the peace conference was in session, Russia was convulsed by civil war, complicated by the intervention of Japanese, American, French, and British troops. The Allied representatives at Paris disagreed on the policy to adopt toward the Communist government in Russia. The Soviets proposed to accept the huge prewar debts contracted by the tsar's government if the Allies would stop aiding the anti-Communist forces and restore normal commercial and diplomatic relations. The statesmen at Paris did not take this offer seriously, for they believed that the Communist government would soon collapse. Whether the new regime in Russia and the Allies could have reached some kind of an agreement leading to Russian participation in the peace settlement is uncertain, but the possibility was not seriously explored. George F. Kennan, an American authority on Soviet affairs, maintains that the sacrifice of this possibility had tremendous consequences for "the long-term future of both the Russian and American peoples and indeed of mankind generally."[7]

PROBLEMS OF STABILITY AND SECURITY

The "new world" and the powers. The prophecy that peace would usher in "a world fit for heroes" was quickly repudiated in the early troubled years of the postwar decade. The unity among the Allies wrought by the necessities of war did not long survive victory. During the Paris Conference and in the years following, serious differences emerged over such basic issues as reparations, war debts, disarmament, and the structure and functions of the League of Nations. Italy was angry with its former allies for being so niggardly with the spoils of war. Great Britain was ready to let bygones be bygones; the "nation of shopkeepers" was anxious to see prosperity return to central Europe. On the other hand, France feared a resurgent Germany and was determined to enforce all the peace treaties. And what of the vanquished? Germany was resentful of the peace settlement and determined to repudiate it. Hungary, Austria, and Bulgaria held similar views.

The shift to a peace economy. One of the chief obstacles to postwar peace was the confused and desperate situation into which the European economy had been plunged. It has been estimated that the cost of the war was about $350 billion. It was the financial consequences of war that did the most to continue the enmity between victors and vanquished and also to alienate the nations, formerly allies, which had defeated Germany.

The conflict had brought about many changes in world trade. Europe in particular had suffered a serious decline in its share of the world's commerce because of war blockades, the reduction of consumer purchasing power, the loss of shipping, and the capture of overseas markets by the United States, Latin America, and Japan. These economic setbacks were felt keenly by Germany and Great Britain. Furthermore, the peace treaties had multiplied national boundaries, which soon became obstacles to the flow of goods.

The inter-Allied debt problem. The most serious problem facing Europe as it strove to achieve a prosperous peace economy was the revolution in its financial position in relation to the rest of the world. In 1914 the United States had been a debtor nation, mostly to Europe, for the amount of $3.75 billion. The war reversed the situation, and in 1919 the United States was owed more than $10 billion by its fellow victors. This tremendous debt posed what economists call the transfer problem. Such international obligations could only be paid by the actual transfer of gold or by the sale of goods to the creditor country.

The various Allied powers in Europe had lent each other funds, with Britain acting as the chief banker. When their credits had been used up, they had turned to the United States for financial help. Britain owed huge sums to the United States but was still a net creditor of $4 billion because of its European debtors. France, on the other hand, was a net debtor of $3.5 billion.

France invades the Ruhr. It became apparent that the Allies had placed an impossibly heavy burden on Germany. In 1921 its total indemnities had been fixed at $32 billion. During the same year Germany made a payment of $250 million, which reacted disastrously upon its currency system. Upon the default of some of Germany's payments, French troops, supported by Belgian and Italian contingents, marched into the rich industrial German district of the Ruhr, undeterred by British and American opposition. Defying the French army, German workers went on strike. Many were imprisoned, and the French toyed with the idea of establishing a separate state in the Rhineland which would act as a buffer between Germany and France. While chaotic conditions in the Ruhr led to catastrophic inflation of German currency, the French gained little economic benefit from their occupation. Meanwhile, public opinion all over the world had been shocked by France's strong-arm tactics in the Ruhr.

Change for the better. Midway in 1923 the prospect of a tranquil and cooperative world seemed far off indeed. But while not apparent to the harassed statesmen of the period, the worst of the war's aftermath had run its course. The Franco-British quarrel, mainly over the Ruhr, was patched up, and French troops were evacuated from the Ruhr in 1924. In the same year a commission under the chairmanship of an American banker, Charles Dawes, formulated a more liberal reparations policy. Installments were reduced and extended over a longer period, and a large loan was floated to aid Germany's recovery. Reparations payments were now renewed, and the former Allies paid their debt installments to the United States on schedule.

Organization of the League of Nations. In 1919, the year of its establishment, the League of Nations constituted a promising agency for improving the status of mankind everywhere. At the outset, however, it suffered a great blow to its prestige: the United States refused to become a member of the League. President Wilson was both physically unable and politically maladroit in campaigning for Senate ratification of the League Covenant. In 1920 his program was repudiated at the polls, for the victory of Warren G. Harding, the Republican candidate for president, meant that the Covenant would never be ratified by the Senate.

The United States refusal to support the League was a fateful decision and, in retrospect, probably a serious blow to the cause of world peace. The League of Nations was the first ambitious attempt in world history to create an organization designed to prevent war and to promote international conciliation. Its main organs were a Council, an Assembly, and a Secretariat. The Council was the most important body, dominated by the great powers. It dealt with most of the emergencies arising in international affairs. The Assembly served as a platform from which all League members could express their views. It could make specific recommendations to the Council on specific issues; but all important decisions required the unanimous consent of its members, and every nation represented in the Assembly had one vote.

The Secretariat represented the civil service of the League. Numbering about seven hundred, the personnel of the Secretariat constituted the first example in history of an international civil service whose loyalty was pledged to no single nation but to the interests of all nations in common. All treaties made by members of the League had to be registered with the Secretariat; its fifteen departments had charge of the matters of administrative routine arising from the mandates and dealt with questions relating to disarmament, health problems, the protection of racial minorities, and any other problems which the League was considering.

In addition to the Council, the Assembly, and the Secretariat, two other important bodies were derived from the Covenant of the League. The first was the Permanent Court of International Justice, commonly referred to as the World Court. Its main purpose was to "interpret any disputed point in international law and determine when treaty obligations had been violated." It was also competent to give advisory opinions to the Council or Assembly when asked for them. (By 1937 forty-one nations had agreed to place before the World Court most of the basic international disputes to which they were a party.) The second international body affiliated with the League was the International Labor Organization. Pledged "to secure and maintain fair and humane conditions of labor for men, women, and children," this organization consisted of three divisions: a general conference, a governing body, and the International Labor Office.

The League as a peace agency.   The record of the League from 1919 to 1929 was one neither of dismal failure nor of complete triumph. Restrained optimism was the mood of its supporters. Its greatest handicap was the refusal of the United States to become a member. Such threats to peace as disputes between Sweden and Finland, Poland and Germany, and Britain and Turkey were resolved. When a great power defied the League, as in the case of Fascist Italy's quarrel with Greece, the organization proved impotent. Little progress was made in the field of world disarmament. On one occasion, perhaps because of its relative military weakness, Russia proposed complete disarmament to League members. This proposal did not get very far because the British delegates were suspicious of the Russian government's sincerity.

Other League activities.   While the effectiveness of the League as a peace agency is debatable, certain of its activities deserve high praise. The League supervised the exchange and repatriation of thousands of prisoners of war and saved thousands of refugees from starvation. With its assistance, Austria, Bulgaria, and Hungary obtained badly needed loans, and the League rendered valuable service in administering the region of the Saar Basin and the Free City of Danzig. The League's efforts in the fields of health, humanitarianism, and intellectual activity were especially noteworthy. The League investigated the existence of slavery in certain sections of the world, sought to control the traffic in dangerous drugs, and stood ready to offer assistance when great disasters brought suffering and destruction to any portion of the world's population. It published books and periodicals dealing with national and international problems of all kinds and broadcast important information, particularly in the field of health, from its own radio station.

Reaction sets in.   The postwar period witnessed an inevitable reaction against wartime controls. In the English-speaking democracies, which were the chief bastions of laissez-faire economics, governmental controls were thrown off with all possible speed. The slogan "back to normalcy" in the United States indicated a desire to return to prewar economic habits and creeds. And halted throughout most of the democratic-capitalist world were the strong prewar movements to advance social welfare legislation and to regulate traditional laissez-faire economics. An unhealthy inertia resulted in the suspension of badly needed socioeconomic reforms.

The national mood and psychology prevailing in the democracies, whether long-established or newly created, differed basically from the mood and psychology in the rising dictatorships. The democracies drifted into listlessness and futility, while the totalitarian states exhibited resolution, dynamism, and purpose, even though of a ruthless variety. Furthermore, during the postwar period the democracies had no burning sense of national injustice as did Germany and, to some extent, Italy. After their herculean efforts for victory, they suffered a kind of national weariness. Because victory had not solved deep-seated problems, there was a feeling of disillusionment in western Europe.

Unstable coalition governments in France. More than one million Frenchmen had been killed and some 13,000 square miles of French territory laid waste in the holocaust of World War I. Years later the nation would still feel the heavy loss of manpower and the economic devastation of a war that had been fought largely on French soil. While a commendable record was achieved in foreign affairs, especially the rapprochement with Germany, in internal affairs the country was plagued with inflation endangering the franc and a spurious prosperity. In addition, parliamentary government was hindered by a multiparty system and by the brief tenure of unstable ministries. In sum, the story of the Third French Republic in the 1920's is a mixed plot of progress and setbacks, of successes and failures. Fundamentally, a national spirit and a sense of purpose were lacking. The war had sapped the vigor of the French nation, and the unhealthiness and lack of dynamism characteristic of the postwar mood were evident.

Evolutionary socialism comes to Britain. The 1920's were not a tranquil period for Britain. During these dismal years unemployment and bitter labor disputes disrupted the nation. In 1924 Ramsay MacDonald became Britain's first Labourite prime minister. The goal of the Labour party was to introduce socialism slowly and within a democratic framework. During four years of power the Labour government registered some successes in foreign affairs but at home generated little dynamism in solving Britain's critical economic problems. Following MacDonald's defeat at the polls in October 1924, Britain was for the next five years led by a Conservative government under Stanley Baldwin, who was even less successful than his predecessor in providing vigorous leadership. Thus the decade following victory in 1918 saw an absence of forward-looking programs of economic development and reform and a seeming inability to measure up to the demands of a difficult new age. To many young British people, unemployed and maintained on a government pittance, the postwar period was aptly symbolized by a popular play of the time—*Love on the Dole.*

Change and ferment in the British empire. During this period serious tensions, mainly demands for home rule, were emerging in various parts of the British empire, mainly in India, Ceylon, Burma, and Egypt. An ominous trend was the growing antagonism between the Arab inhabitants of mandated Palestine and the Jewish Zionist immigrants (see Chapter 23). Happier developments were the attainment of home rule by the Irish Free State (the southern part of Ireland) in

1921 and Britain's recognition in 1931, in the Statute of Westminster, of a new national status for the dominions (Canada, Australia, New Zealand, and South Africa). Henceforth, the dominions and Great Britain were held together only by loyalty to the crown and by a common language, legal principles, tradition, and economic interests. Collectively these states were now known as the British Commonwealth of Nations.

Era of normalcy and big business in the United States. By 1919 wartime industrial expansion had won for the United States the supreme position in industrial equipment and wealth among the family of nations. Moreover, the nation had been transformed from a debtor nation to the world's greatest creditor. But while other nations increasingly looked to it for leadership, the United States turned away from the international scene. The wartime democratic idealism of President Wilson was shelved, the League of Nations was ignored, and isolationism triumphed over internationalism.

Internally, industrial strife and a wave of intolerance directed against immigrants, Catholics, Jews, and the League of Nations marked the postwar years. One important event was the ratification of the Eighteenth Amendment prohibiting the sale and possession of intoxicating liquors. However laudable its purpose, the law was broken by great numbers of citizens, and it strengthened the "bootleg" underworld and led to widespread violence and corruption.

In 1921 the inauguration of Warren G. Harding (1865-1923) as president on the platform of a "return to normalcy" ushered in a decade of Republican dominance. It soon became apparent that by "normalcy" the Harding administration meant resistance to pressure for such progressive measures as low tariffs and antitrust prosecutions. In foreign affairs the new president was bent upon isolationism and the repudiation of the League of Nations. In fact, the American ambassador in London was "instructed to inform the League's authorities that as the United States had not joined the League she was not in a position to answer letters from it."[8] Harding died suddenly in 1923, on the eve of the exposure of widespread corruption in his administration.

Harding's vice president and successor, Calvin Coolidge (1872-1933), advocated high tariffs and reduction of taxes. His credo was summed up in these words: "The business of the United States is business." The Democrats tried in vain to raise the issue of corruption so rampant during Harding's regime, but under the glow of rising prosperity the voters in the 1924 presidential elections decided to "keep cool with Cal" and the Republicans won easily.

Little outstanding legislation was enacted during the second Coolidge administration. A difficult problem was agriculture. Although farm income continued to decline while the fixed payments for debts contracted during agriculture's wartime expansion had to be kept up, bills to ease the farmers' plight were repeatedly vetoed by Coolidge. Other segments of the national economy enjoyed what appeared to be dazzling prosperity in 1927 and 1928. The stock market, mass production, high tariffs, large foreign loans, and installment buying—all seemed to be working together in harmony. These years marked the high tide of American big business and economic self-satisfaction.

When Herbert Hoover (1874-1964) took office in 1929, he was supported by a Republican Congress and a nation enjoying unbounded industrial prosperity. But this prosperity was one whose unhealthy foundations were destined to crumble in the early 1930's.

Prelude to revolution in Russia. Tsar Nicholas II and his subjects entered World War I in a buoyant mood of enthusiasm and patriotism. The weaknesses of the Russian economy, and the inefficiency and corruption in government, were hidden for a brief period under a cloak of fervent nationalism. By the middle of 1915, however, the impact of war was demoralizing the nation. Food and fuel were in short supply, war casualties were staggering, and inflation was mounting ominously. Strikes increased among the low-paid factory workers, and the peasants, who wanted land reforms, were restive. Confronted with these danger signals, the tsar showed little leadership.

The revolution begins. On March 3, 1917, a strike occurred in a factory in Petrograd. Within a week nearly all the workers in the city were idle, and street fighting broke out. On March 11 the tsar dismissed the Duma and ordered the strikers to return to work. These orders precipitated the revolution. The Duma refused to disband, the strikers held mass meetings in defiance of the government, and the army openly sided with the workers. A few days later a provisional government headed by the moderate liberal, Prince Lvov, was named by the Duma, and the following day the tsar abdicated. There is little evidence to indicate that there was a calculated conspiracy behind the overthrow, which has been termed "one of the most leaderless, spontaneous, anonymous revolutions of all times."[9] Thus far the revolution had been, on the whole, peaceful.

Many historians have analyzed the complex background and causes of the revolution. For a century or more the whole tsarist regime had become an anachronism, completely unable and unwilling to reform itself to meet the needs of its people. As an English historian has noted: "The complex revolutionary situation of 1917 was the accumulated deposit of Russian history, detonated by the explosion of war."[10]

Dominated by liberal middle-class representatives, the Duma hoped to achieve a political but not an economic revolution. Meanwhile the Marxian socialists in Petrograd had formed a soviet (council) of workers and soldiers' deputies to provide them the representation they lacked in the Duma. Determined that a thoroughgoing change should take place in accordance with Marxist teachings, the radical soviet cooperated with the provisional government for a few months.

In July, Lvov resigned and was succeeded by Aleksandr Kerenski, who was more progressive than his predecessor but not radical enough for the Bolsheviks. While Kerenski's government marked time, the Marxist soviet in Petrograd extended its organization all over the country by setting up local soviets. The new provisional government made a serious mistake when it decided to prosecute the war and honor its commitments to the Allies. Such a policy was increasingly unpopular with the masses, who were completely disillusioned by the heavy sacrifices demanded by the war effort.

Meanwhile Lenin, the exiled Marxist, who had been living in Switzerland, was anxious to return to Russia and transform the revolution according to his Bolshevik ideas. Hoping that widespread strife and chaos would cause Russia to withdraw from the war, Berlin helped Lenin return to Petrograd. A tumultuous reception by thousands of peasants, workers, and soldiers took place as Lenin's train rolled into the station. Lenin addressed the crowd with this message:

The people need peace; the people need bread; the people need land. And they give you—war, hunger, no bread; they leave the landlords on the land. . . . We must fight for social revolution, fight to the end, till the complete victory of the proletariat. Long live the worldwide Socialist revolution.[11]

Lenin's coup d'état. After many behind-the-scenes maneuvers, the soviets seized control of the government in November 1917, and drove Kerenski and his moderate provisional government into exile.

Lenin did not become a national hero overnight, however. In the free elections held to form a constituent assembly to frame a constitution, he and his followers were chagrined to receive just under 25 percent of the votes. When the assembly, which met in January 1918, refused to become a rubber stamp of the Bolsheviks, it was dissolved by the bayonets of Lenin's troops. With the dissolution of the constituent assembly, all vestiges of bourgeois democracy in Russia were removed. Moreover, this decisive step sealed the fate of the Mensheviks. Lenin next freed his regime from the war problem by the harsh Treaty of Brest Litovsk (1918) with Germany, although with great sacrifice of Russian territory.

The Bolshevik fight for survival. The worst was yet to come. A powerful group of counterrevolutionaries termed White Russians began to make war on the Bolsheviks. At the same time the Allied powers sent several expeditionary armies to Russia to support the anti-Leninist forces. The Allies were fearful that the Bolsheviks were in a conspiracy with the Germans because of the Treaty of Brest Litovsk; they also hoped the White Russians might renew hostilities against Germany. In the fall of 1918 the Bolshevik regime was in a perilous condition, opposed by Russia's former allies and challenged by internal foes.

To counteract this ominous emergency, a ghastly reign of terror was begun within Russia as the Red Army and the Cheka (the secret police) destroyed all enemies of the revolution as well as those who were only lukewarm in their support of the revolution. The royal family, under arrest since the outbreak of the revolution, was made to pay for all the years of cruel and inept Romanov rule. In July 1918 they were herded into a cellar and shot. By 1920 all White Russian resistance had been crushed, the foreign armies had been evacuated, and about one million White Russian anti-Communist refugees were scattered over the earth.

After the surrender of the Central Powers in November 1918, Allied intervention in Russia ceased, and the Bolsheviks were able to concentrate their energies against the White Russians. Other factors contributing to the Bolshevik victory were the do-or-die spirit of Lenin and his followers, the resentment against foreign intervention, and the lack of appeal of the White Russian movement, which sponsored no program of land and social reform.

Lenin's contribution to Marxist thought. As we have previously noted (see p. 341) Nikolai Lenin had made an important contribution to Marxist theory that set the pattern by which socialism in Russia would be guided. Opposing all democratic parliamentary procedures, such as an officially recognized opposition party, he believed that the new order should be established by a revolutionary "dictatorship of the proletariat" under Bolshevik leadership. The opposition group, the Mensheviks, charged that Lenin was confusing the dictatorship *of* the proletariat with the dictatorship *over* the proletariat, while they in turn were

A leader who stressed unity with the masses, Lenin addresses a group of Bolsheviks in this Russian painting by Serov.

accused of having capitulated to gradualism by adopting a revisionist program. Both groups agreed, though, that the socialist revolution could be consummated in Russia only as part of a general uprising of the proletariat throughout Europe. As we have seen, the Bolshevik-Menshevik feud continued until the Revolution of 1917.

As a Marxist, Lenin accepted the two-revolutions sequence—that is, that the proletarian-socialist revolution must be preceded by a bourgeois-democratic revolution. He interpreted the toppling of the tsarist regime in March 1917 and its replacement by a provisional government of moderates and liberals as the first (bourgeois) revolution. His coup d'état in November 1917 engineered the second or proletarian-socialist revolution. Lenin justified the dissolving of the constituent assembly on the grounds that a higher form of the democratic principle had now been achieved which rendered a constituent assembly superfluous: the proletarian-socialist revolution had vested all power in the Russian republic in the people themselves, as expressed in their revolutionary committees or soviets.

The state: theory and practice.   Many orthodox Marxists believed that once the dictatorship of the proletariat had liquidated the bourgeoisie, the way would be open for the progressive disappearance of the state and the abolition of the standing army and the bureaucracy, the two most characteristic institutions of the centralized bourgeois state. While Lenin thought that the state would eventually wither away, at the same time he believed that during the dictatorship of the proletariat the latter's power must be wielded by an "iron party" (the Bolsheviks).

Ironically enough, the events which transpired between his coup d'état in 1917 and his death seven years later served not to weaken but to strengthen the role of the state in Russia.

In this period occurred three major developments relating to the Communist party. (The Bolsheviks were renamed Communists in 1918.) First, all other parties were eliminated. Second, the function of the Communist party was modified. No longer charged with the overthrow of existing institutions, the party now became the controlling element within the new governmental machinery of the state; the concentration of authority and power in the party was justified as "democratic centralism." Third, within the party itself authority was consolidated in the hands of a small elite group, the Politburo, which was composed of five members with Lenin as the chairman. The second major organ of the party was the Secretariat for the Central Committee.

The state was known as the Russian Socialist Federated Soviet Republic (R.S.F.S.R.). As the power of this government grew and the anti-Bolshevik forces were repelled, the jurisdiction of the R.S.F.S.R. expanded. In 1922 the Union of Soviet Socialist Republics (U.S.S.R.) was established, consisting of four constituent socialist republics: the original R.S.F.S.R., the Ukraine, White Russia, and Transcaucasia.

The constitution, adopted in 1924, established a federal system of government based on a succession of soviets which were set up in the villages, factories, and cities and in larger regions. This pyramid of Soviets in each constituent republic culminated in the All-Union Congress of Soviets, which was at the apex of the federal government. But while it appeared that the congress exercised sovereign power, this body was actually governed by the Communist party, which in turn was controlled by the Politburo. So great did the authority of the Communist party become over the formation and administration of policy that before Lenin's death in 1924 it could be said without exaggeration that party and state were one.

The period of war communism. One of Lenin's central beliefs was egalitarianism. He championed the program of "from each according to his ability; to each according to his needs" and believed in the principle of "maximum income," by which no state employee would receive a salary higher than a qualified worker. Following both Marx and Engels, Lenin subscribed to the ultimate goal of large-scale collective farming and the elimination of private ownership of land.

The period from the consolidation of the Bolshevik Revolution in 1918 until 1921 is known as the period of war communism, when the Bolsheviks sought to apply undiluted Marxist principles to the Soviet economy. Banks, railroads, and shipping were nationalized; the money economy was restricted; and private property was abolished.

Strong opposition to this program soon developed. The peasants wanted cash payments for their products and resented having to surrender their surplus grain to the government. Many laborers grumbled at being conscripted to work in the factories, and former business managers showed little enthusiasm for administering enterprises for the benefit of the state. This period was also a time of civil war, when the White Russians, aided by the Allies, were attempting the overthrow of the Communist regime.

The early months of 1920 brought the most dangerous crisis yet faced by the government. The years of civil strife had left Russia in a state of confusion and disruption. Total industrial production had been reduced to 13 percent of what it had been in 1913. Added to the misery caused by wartime dislocations and the shortages caused by inept or wasteful management in the recently nationalized industries was the suffering that followed the crop failures of 1920. Famine marched over the land, bringing more than twenty million people face to face with starvation.

In the meantime serious controversy developed between Poland and Russia over their boundaries. War followed in 1920, and after defeating Russia, Poland annexed a large slice of its territory, thereby sowing the seeds of later conflict. During these turbulent years other areas of Russia were chopped off to form Finland, Estonia, Latvia, and Lithuania. While the collapse of the first Marxist state seemed imminent, Lenin remained indomitable.

The NEP. Confronted with the collapse of the nation, Lenin beat a strategic retreat in spite of strenuous opposition from his colleagues. He felt that the new regime had run into difficulties because it had been too eager to change everything at once. A return to certain practices of the capitalistic system was recommended, and the New Economic Policy, or NEP, was inaugurated.

The retreat from war communism operated from 1921 to 1928. The peasants were freed from the onerous wholesale levies of grain; after paying a fixed tax, they were allowed to sell their surplus produce in open market. Factories employing less than twenty men were returned to private management, and a graduated wage scale was granted to the workers in the state industries. Commerce was stimulated by permitting private retail trading. Although simon-pure Communists criticized the wealthy peasants or *kulaks* who benefited from the new order of things and dubbed the private businessmen "Nepmen," such compromise proved highly beneficial and the economy revived. The NEP was designed as only a temporary strategic retreat from the former outright socialist system; the state continued to be responsible for banking, transportation, heavy industry, and public utilities.

The NEP was Lenin's last outstanding achievement. In spite of broken health, Lenin worked unceasingly until his death in January 1924. His tomb in Moscow's Red Square is a Mecca for thousands of followers who come to pay homage to the creator of the first Marxist state in history.

Stalin vs. Trotsky: the politican and the intellectual. Upon the death of the one man in the party who had possessed unchallenged authority and whose decrees were binding, a struggle for power broke out, and conflicts of policy and personality appeared. Two rivals who took different sides on most issues were Trotsky and Stalin.

Leon Trotsky (1879-1940), whose real name was Bronstein, had turned to Marxism in his early youth and, like Lenin, had known exile. During the revolution Trotsky had come to the forefront. He was a magnificent orator; and by his personal magnetism and his demonic energy, he had led the Red Army to victory. During his hectic career Trotsky wrote an amazing number of brilliant and provocative articles and books. A theorist and scholar, this intellectual, professor-like leader had personal defects of arrogance and egotism which contrasted with the peasant shrewdness and cunning of his less colorful but more calculating rival.

Stalin, born Joseph Dzugashvili in 1879 in the Georgian region of Transcaucasia, was the son of a poor shoemaker. Admitted to a seminary to be trained for the priesthood, young Stalin was later expelled for radical opinions. Before the revolution he engaged in much activity in the underground and was sent into exile four times. In 1922 *Pravda* carried a brief announcement that the Central

Committee had confirmed Stalin as general secretary of the Secretariat—a decision that was to have momentous consequences after Lenin's death.

Trotsky, like Lenin, believed that the U.S.S.R. could not maintain itself indefinitely as a socialist island in a capitalist ocean and that it was therefore the duty of the Russian Communists to foster revolution elsewhere. Stalin, less the theorist than the political realist, viewed Trotsky's ideas of world revolution as premature. He noted that Marxism had made little headway outside of Russia, despite the existence of what from the Marxist standpoint were the most advantageous circumstances for revolution. The impoverished and war-disillusioned workers of Germany had not turned against the bourgeoisie, while in Italy socialist opposition had been crushed by Mussolini. Stalin advocated a new policy, which was to become known as "building up socialism in a single state."

In the struggle that ensued, Trotsky had the initial advantage of being one of the chief architects of the revolution and (second to Lenin) the best known Bolshevik in the Soviet Union. With his outstanding record and his mastery of ideological analysis, Trotsky not unnaturally expected to assume Lenin's mantle of leadership. But he reckoned without the political astuteness of Stalin, who had obtained a key administrative post in the party apparatus. Quietly and systematically, Stalin proceeded to shunt his rival aside. He placed his supporters in important posts in the government, asssumed the powerful chairmanship of the Politburo, and by 1927 had brought about the expulsion of Trotsky and his followers from the party. Trotsky was exiled and led a hare-and-hounds existence until 1940, when he was struck down by the ax of an assassin in Mexico, probably on Stalin's orders.

With a well-organized governmental structure and an obedient bureaucracy and with the Trotskyites either exiled or rendered powerless, Stalin was ready by 1928 to put a daring new program into operation. The NEP was to be scrapped and replaced by a Five-Year Plan, which called for a highly ambitious program of heavy industrialization and the collectivization of agriculture. In spite of breakdowns and failures, the first Five-Year Plan achieved amazing results (see Chapter 21), mainly because of the heroic sacrifices of the common people. Russia, an inert sleeping giant before 1914, now became industrialized at an unbelievable speed, far surpassing Germany's pace of industrialization in the nineteenth century and Japan's early in the twentieth.

Changes in Soviet society. While the Russian economy was being transformed, the social life of the people underwent equally drastic changes. From the beginning of the revolution, the government attempted to weaken the importance of the family. A divorce required no court procedure; and to make women completely free of the responsibilities of childbearing, abortion was made legal. The policy of "emancipating" women had the practical objective of increasing the labor market. Girls were encouraged to secure an education and pursue a career in the factory or the office. Communal nurseries were set up for the care of small children; and efforts were made to shift the center of the people's social life from the home to educational and recreational groups, the soviet clubs.

Most observers in the 1920's credited the regime with abandoning the tsarist policy of persecuting national minorities in favor of a policy of tolerance toward the more than two hundred minority groups in the Soviet Union. Medical services were extended. Campaigns were carried out against typhus, cholera, and malaria; the number of doctors was increased as rapidly as facilities and training would permit; and death and infant mortality rates steadily decreased. Education within a framework of Communist values was made available to millions of children.

In addition there was widespread religious persecution. Religious leaders were sentenced to concentration camps. Members of the party were forbidden to attend divine services. The Church was shorn of its powers over education, religious teaching was prohibited except in the home, and antireligious instruction was stressed in the school.

RISE OF FASCISM IN ITALY

Problems in postwar Italy.   During World War I the Italian armies had been badly mauled by their enemies, and Italy emerged from the peace conference a victor with only modest gains. The First World War aggravated the weaknesses of the Italian economy. The lira fell to a third of its prewar value, unemployment rose, and severe food shortages developed. People refused to pay their rent, strikes broke out in industrial centers, and workers seized factories. Italy's economic plight invited agitation by extremists from both Right and Left.

Mussolini and the birth of Fascism.   Within four years following the armistice in Italy, five incompetent premiers came and went. The situation seemed propitious for the appearance of a strong leader on the political stage. When he appeared, he was the jutting-jawed son of a blacksmith named Mussolini, and he bore the Christian name of Benito in honor of the Mexican revolutionary hero Benito Juárez.

Born in northern Italy, Benito Mussolini (1883-1945) had grown up in left-wing circles. Although he became editor of the influential Italian socialist newspaper *Avanti (Forward)* in 1912, he was far from consistent as regards his belief in socialism and its doctrinal opposition to "capitalist" wars. When a majority in the Italian Socialist party called for neutrality in World War I, Mussolini urged intervention. *Avanti* was taken from his control and Mussolini was expelled. Undaunted, he founded his own paper, *II Popolo d'Italia (The People of Italy)*, in which he continued to advocate Italian intervention in the war on the side of the Allies. As part of his campaign for Italian participation in the war, Mussolini organized formerly leftist youths into bands called *fasci*, a name derived from the Latin *fasces*, the bundle of rods bound about an ax which was the symbol of authority in ancient Rome. When Italy entered the war, Mussolini volunteered for the army, saw active service at the front, and was wounded. After his return to civilian life, he reorganized the *fasci* into the *fasci di combattimento* ("fighting groups") to attract war veterans. The ultimate purpose of these groups was to capture the control of the national government.

The march on Rome.   In the elections of 1919 the socialists capitalized on mass unemployment and hardship to emerge as the strongest party. Although the Fascists failed to elect a single candidate to the Chamber of Deputies, they succeeded in obtaining both approval and financial aid from industrial and landowning groups fearful of the triumph of Marxist socialism in Italy. Mussolini's black-shirted toughs broke up strikes and workers' demonstrations and, by beatings and overdoses of castor oil, "persuaded" political opponents of the error of their views. The central government remained virtually impotent during these outbreaks of violence.

Elections held in May 1921 resulted in a plurality for the liberal and democratic parties. A few Communists were elected to the Chamber of Deputies, and only thirty-five Fascists, among them Mussolini. In November Mussolini established the National Fascist party.

Events in 1922 conspired to favor Mussolini's bid for power. The liberal-democratic government of the day was ineffective, and the socialists were divided among themselves, while the ranks of the Fascists had been strengthened by the enrollment of thousands of disaffected bourgeoisie, cynical and opportunistic intellectuals, and depression-weary workers. The general strike called in August by the trade unions in order to arouse the country to the menace of Fascism was smashed. On October 24 a huge crowd attending a Fascist rally at Naples shouted "On to Rome!" When some fifty thousand Fascist militiamen swarmed into the capital, King Victor Emmanuel III invited Mussolini to form a new government.

Mussolini organizes the Fascist state.   Mussolini's first act as prime minister was the passage in 1923 of an enabling law which gave him dictatorial powers. By this means Mussolini acquired a temporary "legal" right to govern without democratic procedure. He quickly used his newly acquired power to dissolve all other political parties and thus completely eliminate opposton to his regime. The Fascist party was now in a position to recast the entire governmental apparatus.

The Fascist state was ruled by an elite in the party, which ruthlessly crushed all free expression and banished critics of the regime to penal settlements on islands off the southern Italian coast. Censorship of the press was established, and a tribunal for defense of the state was set up to punish any individuals not conforming to Fascist practices. Thus Fascist ideology was a continuation of the antirational, elitist cult of the leader or "great men" school prominent before 1914 and exemplified by such thinkers as Nietzsche. Fascism glorified force, accepting the tenets of social Darwinism. It was above all anti-democratic.

Parliamentary institutions of the pre-Fascist era were not destroyed overnight, but all real power in the new state was soon vested in the Fascist Grand Council, headed by Mussolini. During 1925 and 1926 the Italian cities were deprived of self-government. With all units of local and provincial government welded into a unified structure dominated from Rome, the Fascist administrative system constituted the ultracentralization of government.

In 1929 Mussolini negotiated the Lateran Treaty with representatives of the Roman Catholic Church. By the terms of this agreement, Roman Catholicism was recognized as the state religion in Italy; and Vatican City, a new state of 108 acres located in Rome itself, was declared fully sovereign and independent. In addition, the Vatican was promised sums amounting to $91 million. Thus the long-standing controversy concerning the relationship of Church and state in Italy was settled amicably.

The corporate Fascist state.   There is a marked difference in economic theory between Communist and Fascist states. The communists are determined to destroy private capital and to liquidate the managerial-capitalist class. The Fascist system, sometimes defined as state capitalism, aims to abolish the class war through cooperation between capital and labor, by the compulsion of the state if need be. In Communist theory, labor is the state itself; in Fascism, labor and capital are both instruments of the state.

Mussolini based his ideas of economics on the views of the syndicalists, who believed that industrial unions should be the cells of society and that a confedera-tion of these unions, or syndicates, should constitute the governing body of the state. Syndicalism was adapted to the objectives of Fascism, creating what is called the corporate state. Economically, Italy was divided into thirteen syndicates or corporations: six were formed from the ranks of labor, an equal number represented capital or management, and a thirteenth syndicate was established for the professions. Under the control of the government these bodies were to deal with labor disputes, guarantee adequate wage scales, control prices, and supervise working conditions. Strikes by workers and lockouts by employers were prohibited.

The corporate state also included the concept of economic functionalism—that is, the representation of all major national economic segments in the political process. In 1928, for example, a law set the membership of the Chamber of Deputies at four hundred. Eight hundred candidates were to be named by worker-employer groups and two hundred by various charitable and cultural organizations. From this master list the Grand Council then selected four hundred deputies. Mussolini liked to claim that the corporate state, embodying in theory a classless economic system together with economic functionalism, was one of Fascism's greatest contributions to political theory.

Fascism's glorification of the state and war. The concept of the "inevitability" of war, added to the exaltation of the state and of its "destiny," created a supernationalism whose adherents tended to interpret the right of self-determination in terms of the expansion of the Fascist state at the expense of other nations. A foretaste of Mussolini's contempt for peace and his defiance of the League of Nations soon became apparent when he humiliated Greece in 1923 by the bombardment of Corfu. Mussolini warned the world that Italy intended to expand or explode, and his encouragement of a high birth rate in conjunction with meager territorial and natural resources pointed in only one direction—imperialism.

Fascism has been defined as "the cult of state worship." In the Italian totalitarian state the individual had no significance except as a member of the state. The Fascists were taught "to believe, to obey, and to fight" *(credere, obbedire, combattere).* Fascist ideology governed the educational system. The first sentence pronounced by children at school was "Let us salute the flag in the Roman fashion; hail to Italy; hail to Mussolini." Textbooks emphasized the glorious past of the ancient Romans, the limitations imposed upon the present inhabitants by geography and western "plutocratic" nations, and the imperial destiny that awaited Italy's future development.

Mussolini provided the trappings of greatness while he talked of acquiring the substance. The ruins of imperial Rome were revered at the same time that new, ostentatious monuments, buildings, and official sculptures were erected. All public functions and displays of the state were clothed in propaganda, from the dedication of farm land salvaged from ancient swamps to the regime's vulgar displays of military might and its gigantic sports rallies.

As in the case of other dictatorial regimes, the Fascist social program had some commendable features, such as its slum clearance, its offensive against illiteracy, its campaign against malaria, and its system of child welfare clinics. To the casual observer the country seemed rejuvenated. For example, the notoriously erratic Italian trains now ran on time. But any positive achievements were more than outweighed by such nefarious results as the deification of war, excessive armaments budgets, and the fraudulent claim of the corporate state to protect the workers while it actually benefited the large landowners and industrialists. By

1930 Italy had the lowest standard of real wages in western Europe. The basic weakness and sham of Fascism, however, would not be exposed for another decade.

WEIMAR DEMOCRACY: THE REPUBLIC THAT FAILED

The Weimar Republic. The collapse of the imperial government in Germany at the end of the war provoked vigorous disagreement over the type of administration that was to replace it. The Communists wanted a complete social revolution as well as a political revolution, while the Social Democrats favored a democratic system in which the rights of private property would be safeguarded. In December 1918 and January 1919 the moderates and the radicals clashed violently; the Communists in Berlin were scattered and their leaders murdered. In a national election held to select a constitutional convention, the parties stressing moderation were triumphant, with the Social Democrats securing the most votes. The German revolution was democratic and bourgeois.

Problems of the Weimar Republic. The new constitution was adopted in midsummer of 1919 at Weimar, famous as the residence of Germany's greatest poet, Goethe. It provided for a president, a chancellor who was responsible to the Reichstag, and national referendums. The rights of labor were guaranteed, personal liberties were safeguarded, and compulsory education was planned for everyone up to the age of eighteen.

In spite of difficulties and the opposition of Communists and monarchists, the Weimar Republic restored political stability to Germany and surmounted serious financial problems. In 1923, when French and Belgian troops occupied the Ruhr, the wild inflation of the mark wiped out savings, especially of the middle class, and political moderates gradually lost their influence to ultranationalists and reactionaries. But after the French withdrew and the Dawes Plan enabled Germany to meet its schedule of reparation payments and to obtain large loans from abroad, the German economy took a turn for the better, and from 1925 to 1929 Germany enjoyed economic prosperity. Large public works projects were undertaken, industry was expanded, and Germany became the second largest industrial nation in the world. But disturbing forces were at work.

Factors favoring the growth of dictatorship. Germany in the late 1920's was a compound of numerous ingredients, many of which had been in existence for at least a century. With Prussia as their model, such men as Hegel and Treitschke had exalted the state at the expense of the individual; and the government of the kaisers had fostered despotism. Lack of experience in democratic government made the success of the Weimar Republic doubtful from the start. There were too many political parties; the army, which had never reconciled itself to the abolition of the empire, was not brought under effective civilian control; and the republic was too complacent and did not take the drastic measures essential to destroy the enemies of democracy. In short, "German democracy was utterly fair, legalistic, but not militant."[12]

Other difficulties threatening the new government stemmed from the resentments and frustrations engendered among the people by defeat in war. The powerful Prussian militaristic clique fanned the flames of discontent by fostering the legend that the Germany army had not been defeated on the field of battle but had been stabbed in the back by pacifist liberals and "decadent" democrats on the home front. The legend of the betrayal of the Fatherland was to be increasingly the refrain of those who came to favor Nazi militarism. The resurgence of strong feelings of nationalism was evidenced by the election to the presidency in 1925 of Field Marshal von Hindenburg, a stalwart Junker and hero of World War I.

The Treaty of Versailles embittered many Germans, and its use by the French to justify the invasion of the Ruhr sowed further seeds of hate. The so-called war guilt clause of the treaty, by which the Germans were forced to proclaim sole responsibility for starting the war—which most impartial historians have been unable to assign to any single nation—was particularly rankling.

The ultranationalists made effective appeals to the industrialists and landowners, who were convinced that the republic could not effectively discourage the internal threat of communism. As a result of the war and the postwar inflation, professional people, white-collar workers, and skilled tradesman feared the prospect of being dragged down to the level of the masses. Especially after the debacle of inflation, a deep sense of despair and futility fell upon the people. Blaming their elders for the catastrophe of 1918 and the humiliations that followed, German youth repudiated the past and sought a cause to redeem the Fatherland. They were vulnerable to the blandishments of any spellbinding would-be dictator.

Hitler's rise to prominence.   The creator and high priest of German fascism was Adolf Hitler (1899-1945), the son of a minor customs official in Austria. An orphan at the age of seventeen, Hitler went to Vienna in 1908 hoping to become an architect or artist. While in the Austrian capital, he read pamphlets written by racists and proto-Fascists who championed such ideas as the leader concept and social Darwinism and became interested in Marxist socialism and Pan-Germanism. He experienced dire poverty in Vienna and a few years later moved to Munich, where he earned a scanty living by selling drawings.

When war broke out, Hitler joined a German regiment and was sent to France. The armistice of 1918 found him in a hospital. He said later that news of Germany's defeat caused him to turn his face to the wall and weep bitterly. Following his return from the war front, Hitler was hired by the authorities in Munich as a special agent to investigate Communist and other extremist movements. In the line of duty he was asked to check on a small organization called the German Worker's party. Hitler joined this group, whose fervently nationalistic doctrine was at once antidemocratic, anticapitalist, anti-Communist and anti-Semitic.

Before long the movement took the name "National Socialist German Workers' party," and the words "National Socialist" (Nationalsozialistische) became abbreviated to "Nazi." In 1920 the party obtained a newspaper as a mouthpiece; soon thereafter the first of the paramilitary organizations, Storm Troops, or SA, was organized. Adopted as the emblem of the party was the swastika set against a red background signifying the community of German blood.

Hitler was now becoming better known. His remarkable oratorical gifts began to attract large crowds in Munich. With a kind of mystical exaltation, this charismatic leader had the uncanny ability to arouse and move mass audiences with his bombastic, passionate oratory. Likened to a "human phonograph," he has been termed the "greatest demagogue in history." Sometimes he would hire a dozen beer halls and dash from one to the other in an automobile, delivering fiery harangues at each. His initial political program called for land reform, the nationalization of trusts, abolition of all unearned incomes, and—in the field of foreign relations—a greater Germany to include all German-speaking peoples in Europe, the abrogation of the Versailles Treaty, and the restitution of Germany's prewar colonies. In 1923 Hitler staged his *Putsch*, or revolt, in Munich; coming prematurely, it failed, and he was sent to prison.

Mein Kampf. Before his release from prison in 1925, Hitler began to write *Mein Kampf (My Battle),* at once an autobiography and a long-winded exposition of Nazi philosophy and objectives. In this work Hitler contends that history is fashioned by great races, of which the Aryan is the finest; that the noblest Aryans are the German people, who are destined to rule the world; that the Jews are the archcriminals of all time; that democracy is decadent and communism criminal; that foreign expansion into the Russian Ukraine and the destruction of Germany's prime enemy France are rightful courses for the German people; and that war and force are the proper instruments of the "strong." Again and again his sentences drip with acid as he fulminates against the Jews, Russia, and France. With his irrational creed and his ritualistic gestures, badges, and uniforms, Hitler would one day surpass his predecessor Mussolini in Italy by becoming *Führer* (leader) of a new Germany based on despotism and terror.

CHAPTER 21

THE TRAGIC DECADE
AND GLOBAL CONFLICT

Depression and World War II: 1930-1945

On September 1, 1939, Hitler's legions marched into Poland, and the Second World War began. This outbreak of terrible violence marked the end of a tragic decade.

Ten years earlier the Wall Street stock market crash had ushered in a world-wide financial crisis—the Great Depression. Nation after nation fell victim to industrial decline, bank failures, deflated prices and profits, and commercial stagnation. People the world over suffered from lowered standards of living, unemployment, hunger, and fear of the future.

In desperation governments sought economic recovery by adopting restrictive autarkist policies—high tariffs, import quotas, and barter agreements—and by experimenting with new plans for their internal economies. The United States launched the New Deal, and Britain adopted far-reaching measures in the development of a planned national economy. In Nazi Germany economic recovery was pursued through rearmament, conscription, and public works programs. Observers in many lands saw in the gigantic economic planning and state ownership of the Soviet Union what appeared to be a depression-proof economic system and a solution to the crisis in capitalism.

The economic malaise of the 1930's gave dictators their chance: Hitler took over control in Germany, and a militaristic clique grasped the reins of power in Japan. In 1931 the Japanese pounced upon Manchuria, and when the League of Nations proved powerless to interfere, war between Japan and China raged intermittently throughout the decade. While China was fighting for its national existence, Italy conquered Abyssinia, fascism emerged triumphant from the Spanish civil war, and by a series of "incidents" Hitler swelled the territory of the Third Reich and increased its power. Faced with blatant aggression by the Axis powers (Germany, Italy, Japan), Britain and France abandoned their faith in collective security and the League of Nations and adopted a policy of appeasement. Meanwhile, the Soviet Union played for time to build up its own defenses, and the United States detached itself from the increasing world tensions by maintaining its traditional policy of isolationism. Finally driven to the limit by the

Axis, the European democracies and later the Soviet Union and United States took up arms to defend their independence and end the threat of world conquest.

Far more than World War I, World War II represented global conflict. Furthermore, the Second World War was a "total war" in that never before had civilian populations been so deeply involved. They were targets of the guns and falling bombs, and many were participants, often fighting beside the soldiers.

In many ways this was a new kind of war, not only in its enormous scope but also in its techniques and in its weapons. Technology made possible the mass bombing raids, the air-borne invasions, the amphibious assaults, the operations of carrier-based planes, the maneuvers of armored divisions, the coordinated efforts of the giant naval task force, and the mass murders of Nazi concentration camps; and science and technology combined to create the ultimate in efficiency and horror—the nuclear bomb.

DEPRESSION AND TOTALITARIANISM

Phony prosperity of the "roaring twenties." In 1929 the world's most prosperous nation was the United States. President Hoover declared in his inaugural address:

> Ours is a land rich in resources, stimulating in its glorious beauty, filled with millions of happy homes blessed with comfort and opportunity. . . . I have no fears for the future of our country. It is bright with hope.[1]

But despite the buoyant optimism in the United States and the apparent economic well-being in other countries, the world economy was in an unhealthy state. One by one, the cornerstones of the pre-1914 economic system—multilateral trade, the gold standard, and the interchangeability of currencies—were crumbling.

The desire for self-sufficiency, or autarky, led nations to manufacture goods or grow products at home, even though this policy was sometimes more expensive than importing what they needed. Then, to protect home products against competition from foreign imports, high tariff walls were raised. The United States led the movement toward higher tariffs. Other nations quickly retaliated with discriminatory tariffs against the United States and each other, American foreign trade seriously declined, and the volume of world trade steadily decreased.

The high tariffs had a crucial effect on the payment of war debts. As a result of America's high tariff, only a sort of economic ring-around-the-rosy kept the reparations and war-debt payments going. During the 1920's the former allies paid their war-debt installments to the United States chiefly with funds obtained from German reparations payments, and Germany was able to make these payments only because of large private loans from the United States and Britain. Similarly, American investments abroad provided the dollars which alone made it possible for foreign nations to buy American products. By 1931 the world was reeling from the worst depression of all time, and the entire structure of reparations and war debts collapsed.

Panic on Wall Street in 1929: the depression. On Wall Street the crash came in 1929, on October 24, "Black Thursday." "Prices fell farther and faster, and the ticker lagged more and more. By eleven o'clock the market had degenerated into a wild, mad scramble to sell. In the crowded boardrooms across the country the ticker told of a frightful collapse. . . . The uncertainty led more and more people to try to sell. . . . By eleven-thirty the market had surrendered to blind relentless fear. This, indeed, was panic."[2] Within a few weeks, stock prices had declined 40 percent. Fortunes were wiped out, business confidence was blasted, and the demand for goods plummeted. The growing paralysis in the American economy spread all over the world as the United States began to call in its foreign loans and decrease its imports.

The effects of the depression were catastrophic the world over. Governments could not balance their budgets, factories shut down, and harvests rotted in the fields. The price of wheat fell to the lowest figure in more than three hundred years.

During the years following the crash most nations strengthened their resolve to employ autarky as their guiding economic principle. To increase exports and decrease imports, quota systems were put into operation, and tariffs were boosted to new highs. The lives of the grower of cacao in the African Gold Coast, the coffee grower in Brazil, and the copra plantation worker in the Dutch East Indies were blighted, as were those of the factory worker in Pittsburgh, Sheffield, Lille, and Frankfurt. In the "land of plenty," one of the popular songs of the day was "Brother, Can You Spare a Dime?"

The depression had profound implications for politics. In the tragic thirties democracy in many nations went into eclipse as unemployed and starving masses turned to dictators who promised jobs and bread. The hardships of the depression formed a dismal backdrop on a political stage where dictators seized the leading roles.

Considering the shattering impact of this world economic malaise, there has been relatively little research and comprehensive literature about its background and causes. Was it the inevitable cornsequence of unwise peace treaties; was it the result of the economic losses and disruption of trade suffered by the belligerents during World War I; or was it mainly caused by the United States tariff and reparations policies compounded by a fanatical fever of stock speculation? A noted economist has called attention to a number of unhealthy conditions in the American economy: (1) the uneven distribution of income between the very rich and the extremely poor; (2) the lack of stability, honesty, and good management in the corporate structure; (3) an inherently unsound banking system; and (4) the lack of adequate economic intelligence available to business-men.[3] Although all these factors existed to some degree in other national economies, the United States occupied such a central position in world finance that any substantial reverse or breakdown in its economy inevitably had world repercussions. As the dean of a noted American school of business administration has stated: "I can only repeat that I think it was primarily of American domestic origin, though with many complicating circumstances."[4]

The Five-Year Plans in the Soviet Union. The years from 1929 to 1939 comprised a dark decade in Russia—a period of massive industrialization and of convulsive inner struggles as Stalin established a personal dictatorship both total and terrible. While in the capitalist countries factories and mines were idle or running on reduced schedules and millions were unemployed, the Soviet people worked many hours a day, six days a week, in an all-out attempt to revolutionize Russia's economic structure. For the first time in history, a government controlled all economic activity.

In 1928 Stalin proposed a Five-Year Plan, the first of a number of such schemes aimed at the relatively swift accumulation of capital resources through the buildup of heavy industry, the collectivization of agriculture, and the restricted manufacture of consumers' goods. Although capitalism in the form of the NEP was abolished, citizens were permitted to own certain types of private property—houses, furniture, clothes, and personal effects. They could not, however, own property which could be utilized to make profits by hiring workers. The only employer was the state.

A second Five-Year Plan, begun in 1933, sought to redress some of the mistakes of the first; greater emphasis was placed on improving the quality of industrial products and on manufacturing more consumers' goods. The year 1938 witnessed the initiation of the third Five-Year Plan, in which national defense became the major consideration. Industrial plants were shifted inland to the east, and efforts were made to develop new sources of oil and other important commodities.

The plans achieved remarkable results. Soviet authorities claimed in 1932 an increase of industrial output of 334 percent over 1914, and in 1937 a further increase of 180 percent over 1932. However, the high volume of production was often coupled with mediocre quality, and the achievements were secured only at an enormous cost in human life and suffering. At first a bare subsistence scale of living was imposed on the people by the burdensome expense of importing heavy machinery, tools, equipment, and finished steel from abroad. These purchases were paid for by the sale of food and raw materials in the world's markets at a time when the prices of such goods had drastically fallen. An even greater cost was the terrible loss of life brought about by the callous collectivization of agriculture. By a decree of February 1930, about one million *kulaks*—well-to-do farmers—were forced off their land and all their possessions confiscated. Many farmers consistently opposed regimentation by the state, often slaughtering their herds when faced with the loss of their land. In some sections they revolted, and thousands were executed. A serious famine broke out and several million peasants died of starvation.

Another casualty of the Five-Year Plans was Lenin's basic concept of economic equalitarianism. In 1931 Stalin declared that equality in wages was "alien and detrimental to Soviet production" and a "petit-bourgeois deviation." So much propaganda was used to implant this ideological twist that the masses came to accept the new doctrine of the inequality of wages as a fundamental Communist principle. Piecework in industry became more prevalent, and bonuses and incentives were used to speed up production.

The great purges. While the Five-Year Plans were forging ahead, Stalin was establishing an all-powerful personal autocracy. From 1928 to 1931 and again from 1935 to 1938, Stalin settled his accounts with all his rivals through barbaric purges. Old Bolsheviks who had been loyal comrades of Lenin, high officers in the Red Army, and directors of industry were liquidated. It has been estimated that between 5 and 6 percent of the total population passed through the pretrial prisons of the secret police. The climax to the purges came in 1940, when Stalin's archcritic Trotsky, living as an exile in Mexico, was murdered by a Soviet agent.

In 1936, notwithstanding the terror of his secret police, Stalin ostensibly turned to constitutionalism. A new constitution declared that: "All power in the U.S.S.R. belongs to the toilers of town and country as represented by the Soviets of Toilers' Deputies." On the surface many basic rights, such as free speech, secret ballot, and universal suffrage, were granted, together with a number of important economic and social rights. In practice, however, much of the new document was mere window dressing. The people, however, were given some feeling of participation in their government by means of parades, rallies, and carefully supervised elections. The liberal features of the new constitution also improved Soviet Russia's image abroad.

Crisis in Germany. World depression, accompanied by the cancellation of foreign loans to Germany and the withdrawal of foreign investments, was the culminating blow to the ill-fated Weimar Republic. In 1931 all banks were forced to close, and disorders broke out in many cities. A year later the number of unemployed had reached six million; and desperate, jobless workers roamed the streets shouting, "Give us bread." Night after night, police and military troops battled hungry mobs.

Up to this time the Nazi party had attracted only lukewarm support; there were but a handful of Nazi deputies in the Reichstag. By the summer of 1932, however, their number had swelled to 230, and the Nazis had become the largest political party. Hungry, frightened, and desperate, the impoverished masses turned to Hitler as a source of salvation. And, ironically enough, the rich also saw their salvation in Nazism. Alarmed at the growth of the German Communist movement, the great industrialists supported Hitler—a rabid anti-Communist—and his Nazi party as a shield against a proletarian revolution.

Once the Nazi movement began to gain popularity, Hitler and his master propagandist, Joseph Goebbels, utlized every type of persuasion to make the mass of the people permanent converts to Nazism. All over Germany huge meetings were organized. Then thousands of Storm Troopers marched into stadiums to

With crusading zeal, Hitler used every type of propaganda to make the German people permanent converts to Nazism: huge meetings, parades, sporting events. Here, Hitler makes his entrance at the annual Nazi rally in Nuremberg, where he made some of his most virulent speeches.

form a great swastika, while martial music, the roll of drums, and the trumpeting of bugles filled the air. At first, no speaker was seen on the platform, starkly illuminated by a huge spotlight. Then, as the suspense became almost unbearable, into the beam of light stepped Goebbels or, on major occasions, Hitler himself. For hours the speaker poured forth a torrent of words. "Germany is in ruins," "This is the result of reparations," "The Jews are behind all our woes," "It is only the Nazi party that can make Germany strong and prosperous, that will repudiate the reparations and make Germany's army and navy the fear of all Europe." Thrilled by these colossal displays and mesmerized by rituals and ranting speeches, the masses gave the Nazis increasing support.

Hitler becomes chancellor. For the Nazi party, 1932—when Hitler ran against the incumbent Paul von Hindenburg for the presidency of the German republic—was a crucial year. Although Hitler was defeated, Hindenburg asked the Nazi leader to join coalitions on two subsequent occasions. Hitler refused, demanding what was equivalent to dictatorial power.

It became increasingly difficult for the German ministries to carry on the government, and a second general election held in November was so costly to the Nazis that the party treasury almost went bankrupt. Some observers believed that the Nazis had passed the crest of their power. At this point, however, a clique of aristocratic nationalists and powerful industrialists, fearful of a Communist revolution and the growing strength of the trade union movement, offered Hitler the chancellorship. In January 1933 a mixed cabinet of nationalists was created with Hitler at the head. Because he did not have a clear majority in the Reichstag, Hitler called a general election for March 5. During the campaign, radio broadcasts were monopolized by Nazi propaganda, and Storm Troopers bullied and coerced the voters. But many Germans became disgusted with the strong-arm methods, and the Nazis needed a dramatic incident to clear a majority in the election.

Just before the election, fire gutted the Reichstag building. The blaze was blamed on the Communists, though there was strong suspicion that the Nazis themselves had started it. When the votes were counted, Hitler controlled 44 percent of the deputies. The added support of the Nationalists (another 8 percent) gave the Nazis a bare majority. Quickly the Reichstag passed the Enabling Act, which granted Hitler the right to legislate by decree for the next four years. The Weimer constitution was never formally—only effectively—abolished; the Reichstag continued as a phantom legislature, but nearly all political power was exercised by one organization, the National Socialist party.

A dread intimation of things to come was Germany's withdrawal from the League of Nations in 1933. Two years later, in defiance of the Treaty of Versailles, Hitler introduced conscription. When President von Hindenburg died in 1934, Hitler became both chancellor and president; he was known as Führer (leader), and the new regime was described as the Third Reich.*

Persecution of the Jews. Hitler ruthlessly uprooted and smashed the democratic institutions by which he was brought to power. All rival political parties were disbanded by force, and individuals who had spoken out against Nazism mysteriously disappeared after midnight visits from the dreaded Gestapo—the Nazi secret police. Concentration camps were built to house thousands of prisoners. It has been estimated that in 1933 nineteen thousand Germans

*The First Reich was created by Otto the Great in 962; the Second by Bismarck in 1871.

committed suicide and sixteen thousand more died from unexplained causes. Not until the end of World War II was the full horror of Nazi brutality revealed (see p. 463).

The doctrine of Aryan racial superiority was an integral part of Hitler's program, and the Jews bore the brunt of Nazi persecution. They were blamed for the Versailles Treaty, for all that was bad about capitalism, for revolutionary communism, for pacifism, and for internationalism—all represented as being facets of a Jewish plot to destroy Germany and seize control of the world. That such a fantastic tale was seriously believed by a considerable number of the citizens indicated the state of near psychosis into which Germany had fallen.

Once he was dictator, Hitler did everything to stifle and to destroy the Jews. They were prohibited from owning businesses, barred from public service, and deprived of citizenship. Marriage between "Aryans" and "non-Aryans" was forbidden. Six million Jews were killed in extermination camps, where the Nazis used the most refined techniques of science to carry out loathsome mass murders. The German commandant of one of these camps has described its methods:

> I used . . . a crystallized prussic acid dropped into the death chamber. It took from three to fifteen minutes to kill the people in the chamber, according to climatic conditions. We knew when the people were dead because their screaming stopped. We usually waited about half an hour before we opened the doors and removed the bodies. After the bodies were removed. our special commandos took off the rings and extracted the gold from the teeth of the corpses. . . . we built our gas chambers to accommodate two thousand people at one time. . . . [5]

Nazi propaganda and education. A Reich culture cabinet was set up to instill a single pattern of thought in literature, the press, broadcasting, drama, music, art, and movies. Forbidden books, including the works of some of Germany's most distinguished men of letters, were seized and destroyed in huge bonfires.

The school system was integrated with the German Youth Movement, which drilled and regimented boys and girls between the ages of ten and fourteen. The boys were taught above all else to be ready to fight and die for their Führer; the girls, to mother the many babies needed by the Third Reich. The German universities, once famous throughout the world for their academic freedom, became agencies for propagating such ideas as the racial myths of Nazism; and since Nazi doctrine elevated the state above all else, a movement was instigated to subordinate religion to the Hitler regime. Enrollment in the universities was limited to good Nazi material, and professors were dismissed by the score.

Public works and rearmament. In theory and in outward form, Nazism retained capitalism and private property. Business and labor, however, were rigidly controlled by the state. Labor unions were dissolved, and both workers and employers were enrolled in a new organization, the Labor Front. As in Mussolini's corporate state, the right of the workers to strike or of management to call a lockout was denied. Compulsory dues were taken from workers' wages to support Nazi organizations. As a sop, the government established the Strength Through Joy movement, which provided sports events, musical festivals, plays, movies, and vacations at low cost.

The government's attempts to solve Germany's economic problems included levying a huge tax load on the middle class and increasing the national debt by one third in order to provide work for the unemployed. To create jobs, the first Four-Year Plan, established in 1933, initiated an extensive program of public works and rearmament. The unemployed were put to work on public projects (especially noteworthy was a great network of highways, or *Autobahnen*), in munitions factories, and in the army. The program led to the production of vast armaments and to their eventual utilization in aggression against other states.

Nazism—Why? The rise and victory of the brutal, atavistic Nazi movement in such a culturally advanced nation as Germany must be regarded as one of the most momentous events of the twentieth century. How to account for this phenomenon and its leader, Hitler, constitutes one of the most complicated and fascinating problems in historical causation.

One school of thought has found the answer in the logical outcome of German history. Over the centuries national traditions had progressively united such elements as authoritarianism, submissiveness on the part of the individual, strains of unstable and explosive mysticism, anti-Semitism, and a belief in the superiority of the "Germanic-Nordic race." Other historians deny that a German national character had anything to do with Nazism; they assert that it was the understandable result of the catastrophic impact of the Treaty of Versailles and the depression. Marxist explanations see Fascism coming to power in Germany because of the Communist menace and its threat to a crumbling capitalistic system. Such arguments naturally emphasize the financial assistance Hitler received from German big business. The role of the army has also received attention. The army had always been an important, influential, and respected force in public life, and the military chiefs, unhappy with their lot under the Republic, gladly turned their support to Hitler in 1933.

Social psychologists maintain that the key is to be found in the psychological mood of the German people. Generally, the populace was in a condition of stress, insecurity, and frustration. The immediate post-1918 trends had had a painful effect upon all Germans, no matter what their social position. The depression, with its massive unemployment, political instability, and ineptitude of the leaders of the republic, left millions in a state of traumatic shock.

> Hitler succeeded not because of a conspiracy of the few but because his movement gave high hope to the many of solving the pressing psychological demands of a people living under conditions of acute stress. Defeated by war and broken by inflation, the uprooted, humiliated, and insecure Germans were attracted to Nazism because they felt that their personal problems would be solved by a movement that promised to supply everything they lacked as individuals: dramatic action, a sense of purpose, a feeling of power.[6]

Other nations, however, experienced shocks to their national lives, perhaps as traumatic as Germany's, and yet did not accept the extreme solution of Nazism. There were, then, certain elements in the German situation that were unique and conducive to a Nazi victory. Not least of these was the charismatic leadership of Hitler. Some observers maintain that there could have been no Third Reich without this perverted genius.

Parliamentary demoralization in France. The lack of vigorous leadership in the democratic nations and the mounting crisis in their capitalistic systems were best exemplified in France. Although the prosperity of the twenties carried over after other nations were engulfed in depression, in the early thirties France was faced with rising unemployment, budget deficits, the drying up of the lucrative tourist trade, and heavy military expenditures for security against a rearming Germany. Ministry after ministry was organized, only to collapse a few months later; citizens became more and more impatient with the government.

Disgust with the administration increased with the exposure of corruption in high places. A new government, the National Union, ignored pleas for constitutional reform and for a grant of increased power to the prime minister. The agent of the wealthy and privileged classes, the National Union grew ultraconservative but continued to rule under a variety of prime ministers.

In 1936 emerged the Popular Front, a coalition composed of liberal parties united in opposition to the conservative elements in the government. In June the Popular Front won a national election; and Léon Blum (1872-1950), a noted lawyer and writer, became premier. The Popular Front endeavored to stem the influence of fascist ideas, to improve the country's finances, and to bring about certain fundamental economic reforms. In particular, the Popular Front promised to "break the power of the two hundred families who control the economic life of the nation."[7] After only a year in office, however, Blum was forced to resign. Unfavorable trade balances, an enormous public debt, and an unbalanced budget proved too much for the Popular Front government. France swung back to conservatism. The forty-hour week was ended, and strikes were energetically suppressed.

The National Union and the Popular Front mirrored the widening chasm between the upper and lower classes. The working classes believed that the reforms of the Popular Front had been sabotaged and that a France ruled by a wealthy clique deserved little or no allegiance. On the other hand, some businessmen and financiers were horrified at the prospect of communism and flirted with fascism. While Frenchmen quarreled and France's economic strength was being sapped, Hitler's Germany, regimented and feverishly productive, was rapidly outstripping France in the manufacture of armaments. The ingredients for the tragic fall of France in the spring of 1940 had now been supplied.

"Muddling through" in Britain. It was inevitable that the depression would have catastrophic effects in the highly industrialized and heavily populated island of Britain. In two years exports and imports declined 35 percent, and three million unemployed roamed the streets.

A Labour administration, with James Ramsay MacDonald as prime minister, took office in 1929. Little was accomplished, and unemployment became more widespread as the depression deepened. When the Labour government fell, MacDonald retained his office by becoming the leader of a National Coalition government, which was primarily conservative. The bulk of the Labour party constituted the opposition.

Nothing spectacular was undertaken, but by 1937 a substantial measure of prosperity had been regained, and production registered a 20 percent increase over that of 1929. To achieve this comeback, much of what remained of laissez-faire policy was discarded. The government now regulated the currency, erected high tariffs, gave farmers subsidies, and imposed a heavy burden of taxation. The rich had a large proportion of their income taxed away, and what might be left at death was decimated by inheritance taxes.

The New Deal fights depression. In shocking contrast to the frenzied boom on the stock market, and the smug complacency of American businessmen in the

1920's was the economic paralysis which gripped the United States in 1930. By 1932, business failures numbered at least thirty thousand, and the number of unemployed was somewhere between twelve and fifteen million.

In the first few years after the crash President Hoover tried to prop up shaky businesses with government money in the hope that the benefits would filter down to the workers. Because the President believed that the government should not compete with private concerns, only a few public works projects were started. Hoover avoided federal relief, leaving to private charities and local governments the heavy responsibility for caring for the hungry. Toward the end of his term the depression steadily worsened, and thousands of people went hungry because they had no money for food.

The general dissatisfaction with the government was evidenced by the sweeping victory of Franklin D. Roosevelt (1882-1945), the Democratic standard-bearer, who was inaugurated in 1933. Under his leadership the New Deal, a sweeping program to cope with the national emergency, was put into operation. The three objectives of the New Deal were relief, recovery, and reform. Millions of dollars were appropriated for the relief of the unemployed, and vast sums were expended for the construction of public works in the belief that such activity would stimulate economic recovery. A combination work and relief program, the Civilian Conservation Corps, offered employment and education to thousands of young men. To encourage building activity, the Federal Housing Administration offered liberal terms to finance new homes, especially for low-income families. Most significant was the Social Security Act, passed in 1935. For the first time in the history of the United States, a comprehensive scheme for unemployment insurance and a plan for old-age benefits were introduced.

AGGRESSION AND APPEASEMENT

Japanese aggression in Manchuria.   The first challenge to world peace occurred in September 1931, when Japan moved into Manchuria. Unable to cope with the invader, the Chinese appealed to the League of Nations, which appointed a committee of inquiry. The committee report condemned the aggression while trying not to affront Japan, which nevertheless resigned its League membership two years later. The significance of the Manchurian campaign was dreadfully clear. A demonstration that a great power could embark on aggression without any effective opposition from League members marked the beginning of the collapse of the League.

When the Chinese resorted to a nationwide boycott of Japanese goods, the Japanese attacked Shanghai and early in 1933 began to push deeper into northern China. To slow down the invasion and give themselves a chance to prepare for the inevitable struggle, the Chinese agreed to the Tang-ku Truce, which recognized Japanese conquests in Manchuria and northern China. The truce remained in effect for about four years, while the Japanese consolidated their position and the Chinese wrestled with internal threats.

The united front in China.   In addition to the invaders, the Nationalist forces of Chiang Kai-shek had to contend with the Chinese Communists (see p. 477). The Chinese Communists demanded a united front against the Japanese, stating that the first objective of all China should be whole-hearted resistance against foreign imperialism and aggression. In order to achieve a united front, Mao Tse-tung agreed to end land confiscation and armed opposition to the Nanking government, to abandon the system of soviets, and to permit the incorporation of the Communist forces into the fight against Japan. Neither of the parties to the truce trusted each other, but they both feared the Japanese. China was unified just in time to meet the next Japanese thrust.

Japanese conquests continue. In 1937 fighting broke out again, this time around Peking. Farther south, Japanese troops captured Shanghai and advanced rapidly up the Yangtze valley to Nanking. The Chinese retreated westward, establishing a new capital at Chungking. In North China the Chinese armies were also forced to retreat, and the Japanese set up a government at Peking.

In 1938 Japan proclaimed the New Order in eastern Asia. Its objectives were the destruction of Chiang Kai-shek's regime, the expulsion of western interests in eastern Asia, and the establishment of a self-sufficient economic bloc to include Japan, Manchuria (which was renamed Manchukuo by the Japanese), and China.

Italy swallows up Abyssinia. Italian aggression in Abyssinia followed Japan's lead. As his first victim, Mussolini chose Abyssinia, the only important independent native state left in Africa and the nation which in 1896 had handed the Italians a humiliating defeat. Late in 1934 fighting broke out between the Abyssinians and the Italians, and in the following year the Italians made a wholesale invasion of Abyssinia. The limited sanctions imposed against Italy by the League proved ineffectual. Using bombs, mustard gas, and tanks, the Italians advanced swiftly into Abyssinia and crushed the resistance of Emperor Haile Selassie's valiant soldiers. The whole sorry story ended in July 1936, when the League's sanctions were removed.

Germany marches into the Rhineland. The conflict over Abyssinia gave Hitler his first big opportunity to use the military force he had been building up. In March 1936, while the wrangle over the sanctions against Italy was taking place, German troops marched boldly into the Rhineland in defiance of the Treaty of Versailles and the Locarno agreements. France immediately mobilized 150,000 troops, but Britain refused to support the use of force to compel Germany to withdraw. Many Britons thought it hardly worth while to risk war over Germany's demand to fortify its own territory.

Alliance of the Axis powers. Up until 1935 Germany had been diplomatically isolated in Europe, faced by the United Front of Great Britain, France, and Italy. But the Abyssinian incident and the imposition of sanctions broke up the United Front, and Italy became Germany's friend. In 1936 the friendship was formalized in the Rome-Berlin Axis, and one year later Mussolini followed Hitler's lead by withdrawing from the League. Japan, the third major member of the Axis powers, joined forces with Germany in 1936 with the Anti-Comintern Pact. A year later Italy subscribed to the agreement. On the surface the agreement was directed against the international activites of communism; in reality the pact was aimed at Russia. The members of the Rome-Berlin-Tokyo Axis were preparing for expansion.

Dress rehearsal in Spain. In 1936 civil war broke out in Spain, shattering that country and threatening to involve all of Europe. The Spanish republic had been established five years earlier. Long overdue reforms were enacted: new schools were constructed, great estates were broken up, and the army was purged of its parasitic officers. But the republic brought neither prosperity nor stability to

Spain. Reactionary groups tried to gain control of the government while left-wing groups resorted to terrorism. The middle-of-the-road reformist government became increasingly powerless to maintain order, and an uprising inspired by reactionary and military cliques began in July 1936.

The totalitarian powers—Italy and Germany—seized the opportunity to ensure a Fascist victory. Large numbers of Italian planes were made available to the Fascist insurgents, led by General Francisco Franco (1892-   ). Most of the regular army troops were faithful to Franco, and a quick victory was anticipated. But many groups stood by the Republic, and, as Communists gained increasing strength in the Republican government, the Soviet Union provided it with aid. Foreign Communists flocked to Spain, as did many idealistic anti-Fascists who were not Communists, including a number from Britain and the United States. The Republicans mustered stronger resistance than expected, and Franco's drive was checked at the outskirts of Madrid. Germany and Italy sent troops and equipment to the Fascists, while Russia sent matériel and personnel to the Loyalists at Madrid. Germany, Italy, and Russia tried out their new cannon and combat planes on Spanish battlefields. Internal dissensions weakened Russian assistance, which was not sufficient to offset German and Italian aid. In March 1939 Madrid fell, and the Spanish republic was no more. Franco, at the head of the new state, was endowed with absolute power. The Spanish civil war was not only a national catastrophe, which left permanent scars on a proud and gallant people, but also a dress rehearsal for the tragic global drama of World War II.

British appeasement and Allied weakness.   Neville Chamberlain (1869-1940), whose name was to symbolize the policy of appeasement, had become the British prime minister in 1937. Determined to explore every possibility for reaching an equitable understanding with the dictators, Chamberlain persisted in trying to ease international tension despite snubs from those he wished to placate and also warnings from some of his colleagues and from experts in the British foreign office. Chamberlain's policies were strongly supported in Britain. Many Britons had a feeling of "peace guilt"—namely, that Germany had been unfairly treated in the Treaty of Versailles. In other quarters, there was reluctant admiration for the Nazi regime and the belief that a strong Germany could serve as a buffer against Communist Russia. Most important, however, was the passionate and widespread desire for peace, arising from the war weariness and disillusionment suffered after World War I.

Hitler's Austrian coup.   In announcing the military reoccupation of the Rhineland in the spring of 1936, Hitler had stated, "We have no territorial demands to make in Europe." The course of events was to belie this statement. By 1938 the German army had amazing strength, the *Luftwaffe* was at its peak, and Hitler was ready to embark on a daring program of expansion. His "territorial demands" were to prove limitless.

Hitler's first victim was his neighbor Austria. Previously, in 1934, Hitler had attempted to annex Austria; and the Austrian chancellor, Engelbert Dollfuss, had been murdered by Nazi agents. Partly because of Mussolini's opposition, this *Putsch* (coup) failed. Four years later, after Mussolini had become his ally, Hitler tried again. The blow fell on Friday, March 11. American radio listeners were told at 2:15 P.M. that the Austrian chancellor had resigned, at 2:45 that German troops were crossing the frontier, and at 3:43 that the swastika had been hoisted over the Austrian chancellery. Meanwhile, Nazi agents in Austria took over the government; on Saturday German troops occupied most of the country.

Germany aspires to the Sudentenland.   After the Austrian coup, Hitler moved on to his next objective, the annexation of the Sudetenland, an area in Czechoslovakia bordering on Germany and peopled mainly by Germans. In September 1938 the Führer bluntly informed Chamberlain that he was determined to secure self-determination for the Sudeten Germans. Chamberlain then persuaded Edouard Daladier, the French premier, that a sacrifice on the part of Czechoslovakia would save the peace. When France, previously counted as an ally by the Czechs, joined Britain in pressing for acceptance of the Nazi demands, Czechoslovakia had little choice but to agree. Chamberlain gave this news to Hitler, only to discover that the German demands had increased considerably. Hitler demanded that within one week the Czechs evacuate certain areas and that all military matériel, goods, and livestock in these areas be turned over to the Germans immediately.

Munich seals the fate of Czechoslovakia.   On September 29, 1938, Hitler, Mussolini, Daladier, and Chamberlain met at the Nazi headquarters in Munich and for thirteen hours worked out the details of the surrender of the Sudetenland. No Czech representative was present. Though an outspoken ally of Czechoslovakia, Russia was completely disregarded. (French and British statesmen distrusted Russia and presumably thought that Hitler's hatred of communism would not permit the attendance of a representative from Moscow.) Not only were all of Hitler's demands accepted, but Poland and Hungary also received slices of Czechoslovakia. Munich brought relief to millions of Europeans half-crazed with fear of war, but it was still a question whether this settlement would be followed by another crisis. Many hoped for the best but feared the worst.

The mounting fears of French and British statesmen were confirmed in 1939. Early in March a bitter attack against the Czech government was inaugurated by the German press. Another coup was in the making. On March 14, Hitler summoned the Czech president, Hacha, to Berlin. Subjected to all kinds of threats during an all-night session, Hacha finally capitulated and signed a document placing his country under the "protection" of Germany. His signature was a mere formality, however, for German troops were already crossing the Czech frontier. Not to be outdone, Mussolini seized Albania the following month, and the two dictators celebrated by signing a military alliance, the so-called Pact of Steel.

The shock of the final conquest of Czechoslovakia and Hitler's callous violation of pledges made at Munich ended the appeasement policy of France and Great Britain. For the first time in Britain's long history, the government authorized a peacetime draft. A tremendous arms program was launched. In Paris, Daladier obtained special emergency powers to push forward national defense.

Isolationism in the United States.   The United States had been disillusioned by the results of the "war to make the world safe for democracy." Influential spokesmen asserted that World War I had been caused by the greed of munitions makers and stressed the centuries-old hatreds and rivalries in Europe; the United States, therefore, should insulate itself from these potent causes of international conflict. Reflecting this mood, Congress passed neutrality legislation between 1935 and 1937 which made it unlawful for any nation at war to obtain munitions from the United States.

The Polish question and the Nazi-Soviet pact.   It was Germany's aggression against Poland that precipitated the Second World War. The Treaty of Versailles had turned over West Prussia to Poland as a Polish Corridor to the sea (see map, p. 425). While 90 percent of the Corridor's population was Polish, the Baltic port city of Danzig was nearly all German. Late in March 1939 Hitler proposed to Poland that Danzig be ceded to Germany and that the Nazis be allowed to occupy a narrow strip of land connecting Germany with East Prussia. Chamberlain, with France concurring, warned the Nazi government that "in the event of any action which clearly threatened Polish independence," the British would "at once lend the Polish government all support in their power." In the months that followed the Allied warning, France and Britain competed with Germany for an alliance with Russia.

The Soviet Union had long been seriously concerned about the twin menaces of Nazi Germany and expansionist Japan. But while British and French negotiators attempted to convince the Kremlin that their nations really desired an effective alliance against Nazi Germany, the Nazi and Soviet foreign secretaries were secretly working out the details of an agreement. On August 23, 1939, Russia and Germany signed a nonaggression pact, an utterly cynical arrangement between two inexorably antagonistic foes.

Through this agreement Stalin gave Hitler a free hand in Poland, thus precipitating war between Germany and Britain and France. Russian political strategy was that such a conflict would give the Soviet Union time to build up its armaments and would weaken the antagonists. With the pact in his pocket, Hitler could attack Poland without fear of intervention by his great rival to the east. Furthermore, he believed that Britain and France would not dare oppose his ambitions. But France and Britain at last understood that if they wished to stop Germany from dominating all of Europe, they must fight.

Basic causes of Hitler's war. Undoubtedly Germany nursed a sense of grievance over what were regarded as the injustices of Versailles. The most important cause of the war, however, was the ruthless ambition of an irrational dictator to gain control of Europe and as much of the rest of the world as he could master. Aiding and abetting his sinister ambition was the strong, even obsessive desire of the democracies for peace. Because Britain and France had long turned the other cheek, Hitler believed that they would not fight under any provocation. Hitler scoffed at the democracies: "Our enemies are little worms. I saw them at Munich."[8]

THE WORLD DIVIDED

Blitzkrieg in Poland. Without a declaration of war, Nazi troops crossed the Polish frontier early in the morning of September 1, 1939, and the *Luftwaffe* began to bomb Polish cities. On the morning of September 3, Chamberlain sent an ultimatum to Germany, demanding that the invasion be halted. The time limit was given as 11 A.M. of the same day. At 11:15 he announced on a radio broadcast that Britain was now at war. France also declared war, and after an interval of only twenty-one years since World War I Europe was again plunged into conflict.

For the first time the world had the opportunity to witness the awesome power of Nazi arms. Polish resistance crumbled, and at the same time Russian forces attacked from the east. In less than a month Poland had been partitioned by the Russo-German treaty. Britain and France did not try to breach the Siegfried line along the Rhine. With their blockade and mastery of the seas, they hoped to defeat Hitler by attrition.

Dunkirk. All seemed to be going according to this plan during the winter of 1939-1940. There was little fighting along the Franco-German frontier during this period of the "phony war," or *Sitzkrieg*. Russia, however, took advantage of the opportunity to force Finland to cede substantial territory, but only after unexpected stubborn resistance. In the late spring there were signs that the Nazi High Command was not prepared to accept a long war of attrition. Neutral Norway and Denmark were invaded and occupied. A month later, in May 1940, German armies overran neutral Holland and Belgium. From the latter, armored columns knifed into France through an undefended gap north of the Maginot line. German forces swept to the English Channel trapping an Anglo-French army of nearly 400,000 on the beach at Dunkirk.

The reverses in Norway and a military crisis in France led to Chamberlain's resignation, and Winston Churchill (1874-1965) became prime minister of Great

Like this Frenchman, people from many nations were forced to watch the Axis powers take over their country while their own forces either laid down their arms or escaped into exile. For a while, Axis victory indicated to the world that an Allied defeat was very possible.

Britain. While he had intermittently occupied high office during his long career in Parliament, which dated back to 1900, Churchill had suffered numerous frustrations and in the 1930's enjoyed little popular support. At that time he was described as "a might-have-been; a potentially great man flawed by flashiness, irresponsibility, unreliability, and inconsistency."[9] Yet in 1940 Churchill's qualities of leadership rose to match his nation's peril. During the next five years he was the voice and symbol of a defiant and indomitable Britain.

Confronted with the prospect of destruction of the British army at Dunkirk, Churchill refused to be dismayed. Appearing before Parliament as the new prime minister he announced, "I have nothing to offer but blood, toil, tears, and sweat," preparing the people for a long and desperate conflict. By herculean efforts hundreds of small craft, protected by an umbrella of the Royal Air Force, successfully evacuated some 335,000 soldiers. An army had been brought home, but all its heavy equipment had been lost.

The fall of France. After Dunkirk, the fall of France was inevitable. Anxious to be in on the kill, Mussolini declared war against France and Britain. Designated an "open city" by the French, Paris fell on June 14. As the German advance continued, the members of the French government who wished to continue resistance were voted down; and Marshal Pétain, the eighty-four-year-old hero of Verdun in the First World War, became premier. Pétain immediately asked Hitler for an armistice, and in the same dining car in which the French had imposed armistice terms on the Germans in 1918, the Nazis and the French on June 22 signed the armistice agreement. France was split into two zones, occupied and unoccupied. In unoccupied France, Pétain's government at Vichy was supposedly free from interference, but in reality it was a puppet of the Nazis. And so the Third Republic, created in 1871 from the debris of defeat suffered at German hands, now came to an end because of a new blow from the same quarter. However, a remarkable patriot, General Charles de Gaulle (1890-1970), fled to London and organized a Free French government, which adopted as its symbol the red cross of Lorraine (flown by Joan of Arc in her fight to liberate France centuries earlier) and continued to aid the Allied cause throughout the war.

The crucial battle of Britain. With millions of Europeans already his captives and with millions more living in constant dread of his screaming dive bombers and clanking panzer divisions, Hitler demanded that the British lay down their arms. But in the face of almost hopeless odds, they rallied to the support of their homeland. Churchill's eloquent defiance of Hitler stirred not only his own countrymen but all of the free world:

> We shall go on to the end. . . . we shall defend our Island, whatever the cost may be, we shall fight on the beaches, we shall fight on the landing grounds, we shall fight in the fields and in the streets, we shall fight in the hills; we shall never surrender. . . . [10]

As a prelude to invasion, the Germans sought to gain control of the air over Britain. Their fighter and bomber squadrons crossed the Channel but were turned back with heavy losses by the R.A.F. All through the winter of 1940-1941, however, Britain continued to be racked by terrible raids. Night bombing destroyed block after block of Britain's cities; St. Paul's Cathedral in London stood as a solitary survivor in the midst of acres of desolation. Evacuating their children and old people and sleeping in air-raid shelters, Britain's people stood firm. Their air force retaliated in some measure by raiding the industrial cities of the Ruhr, and their naval forces remained on the offensive.

Italian failures and Nazi successes. Meanwhile, Mussolini was eager to share in the spoils. In October 1940 he invaded neutral Greece, but this thrust proved to be a costly failure. Other defeats were met in North Africa, and Abyssinia was recaptured by British forces. Hitler, on the other hand, continued to expand his domination over Europe. Rumania, Bulgaria, and Hungary became Nazi satellites. In the spring of 1941 Yugoslavia and Greece were overrun.

By the spring of 1941 nearly all of Europe had come under the iron heel of the Third Reich. Only Portugal, Switzerland, Sweden, and Turkey remained neutral. While ostensibly neutral, Spain under Franco was pro-Nazi. Britain, though still dangerous, was powerless to interfere on the Continent. The United States was profoundly disturbed over the Nazi successes but was still unprepared.

Hitler turns on the Soviet Union. Thwarted in his invasion plans of Britain, Hitler made the fatal decision to invade Russia. Stalin had no illusions about Nazi friendship. When he had signed the nonaggression pact with Hitler in 1939, Stalin had expected that in the event of war the antagonists would wear themselves out and suffer terrific losses. But now Hitler was master of western continental Europe. *Lebensraum* (living space) and badly needed raw materials could be had by expansion to the east.

In June 1941, without warning, a gigantic German attack was launched against Russia, even though many of Hitler's generals were apprehensive. Along a battlefront eighteen hundred miles long, nine million men became locked in struggle. At the outset, the Nazi armored panzer units were irresistible. Russian

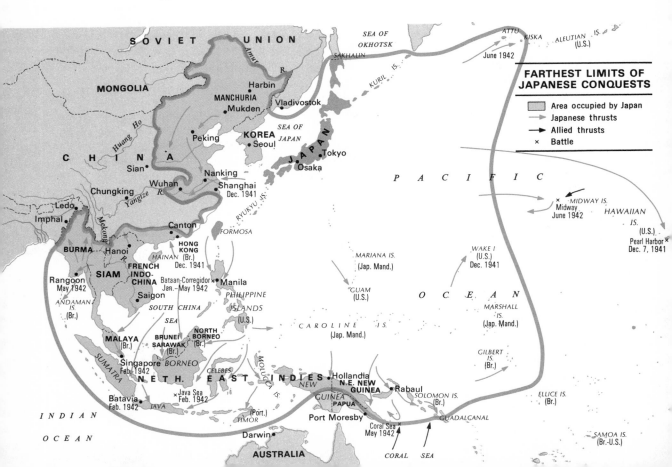

troops were killed or captured in enormous numbers. In October, Hitler's troops neared the suburbs of Moscow; Russia appeared to be on the verge of collapse. With the coming of winter, however, the Nazi offensive bogged down. Weapons froze, troops were inadequately clothed, and heavy snows blocked the roads. The German attack not only halted, but in the spring of 1942 the Russian army began to recover territory.

Pearl Harbor draws the United States into war. It was Japan's expansionist policy which brought the United States directly into the conflict. Confronted with Japanese ambitions for the New Order in Asia, the United States froze Japanese funds and refused to sell it war matériel. In spite of this pressure, Japan made the fateful decision to continue its expansion; in October 1941, General Tojo, an avid militarist, became premier.

On Sunday, December 7, while special "peace" envoys from Tokyo were negotiating in Washington, ostensibly to restore harmony to Japanese-American relations, Japanese planes attacked Pearl Harbor, the American bastion in the Pacific. Half the United States fleet was crippled, and planes were wiped out on the ground. On the following day Congress declared war on Japan. In a few days Italy and Germany declared war on the United States; and Britain, together with the dominions, the refugee governments of Europe, and the Central American republics, ranged themselves with the United States against Japan.

High tide of the Axis. After Pearl Harbor, Japanese power expanded over the Pacific and into Southeast Asia (see map, p. 460). Hong Kong, Singapore, the Dutch East Indies, Malaya, Burma, and Indochina were conquered. An American army was forced to cease its defense of the Philippines when it surrendered at Bataan. The Chinese, however, in their remote inland fortress-capital of Chung-king, managed to hold off the Japanese. The summer of 1942 was an agonizing period for the foes of the Axis. A new German offensive pushed deeper into Russia, threatening the important city of Stalingrad. Egypt was placed in peril when the gifted German general, Rommel, inflicted a decisive defeat on the British army in Libya. All over the globe the Axis powers were in the ascendancy.

The road to victory for the Allies. Imminent defeat was suddenly and miraculously transformed to hope of victory in 1942. Further Japanese expansion in the Pacific was halted by two American naval victories—Coral Sea and Midway—and at Guadalcanal American marines began the conquest of Japanese-held islands. In November 1942 British and American troops landed in North Africa, and Axis forces were defeated by the British at Alamein. By May 1943 all Axis troops in North Africa had been destroyed or captured. Hitler fared no better in Russia, where in February 1943 an entire German army was surrounded and captured at Stalingrad. The next Allied thrust was against Italy; in July 1943 Sicily was captured. The whole edifice of Fascism now collapsed. Mussolini was stripped of his office and was later kidnapped by Nazi agents. A new Italian government signed an armistice as Allied forces landed in Italy. Rome was not captured until June 1944, and German resistance continued in northern Italy until the end of the war.

By the end of 1943 the initiative had definitely passed to the Allies. Russian divisions pushed into Poland and wheeled south into the Balkans. On D-Day, June 6, 1944, a vast armada of ships landed half a million men on the beaches of Normandy. After violent fighting, British and American forces entered Germany in October. At the same time, Russian troops closed in from the east.

With victory in Europe in sight, Stalin, Roosevelt, and Churchill met at Yalta in

THE CREST OF AXIS POWER

- Allies and areas they controlled
- Axis nations
- Area occupied by the Axis
- Vichy France
- Neutral nations

Battles: Allied victory × Axis victory ⊗
Thrusts: → →

ARCTIC OCEAN

ATLANTIC OCEAN

FAEROE IS. (Den.)

SHETLAND IS. (Br.)

ORKNEY IS. Scapa Flow

NORTH SEA

IRELAND
Dublin

GREAT BRITAIN
Glasgow
Liverpool
Birmingham
Air battle for Britain July-Oct. 1940
London
Southampton

GERMANY
Hamburg
Hanover
Berlin
Cologne
Frankfurt
Dresden
Munich

NETHERLANDS May 1940
BELGIUM 1940
Dunkirk May-June 1940
Lux.

FRANCE
Nantes
Paris
Bordeaux
Lyons

VICHY FRANCE
Vichy
Marseilles

SWITZERLAND

NORWAY
Narvik
Trondheim
Apr. 1940
Bergen
Oslo
Goteborg

SWEDEN
Stockholm

DENMARK Apr. 1940
Copenhagen

BALTIC SEA

FINLAND
Helsinki

GULF OF BOTHNIA

WHITE SEA

Murmansk
Arkhangelsk
N. Dvina R.

Lake Onega
Lake Ladoga

Leningrad
Tallinn
ESTONIA
LATVIA
Riga
Pskov
LITHUANIA
Kaunas

SOVIET UNION
Kazan
Gorki
Moscow
Smolensk
Minsk
W. Dvina R.
Voronezh
Don R.
Volga R.
Sarat

POLAND
Danzig
Germany invaded Poland Sept. 1, 1939
Warsaw
Krakow
Lvov

Germany invaded Poland Sept. 1, 1939

CZECHOSLOVAKIA Mar. 1939
Prague
Vienna

AUSTRIA Mar. 1938

HUNGARY Oct. 1940
Budapest

Kiev
Kharkov
Dnieper R.
Dniester R.

RUMANIA Nov. 1940
Bucharest
Danube R.

Odessa
Sevastopol
Sea of Azov
Rostov

BLACK SEA

Trabzon

ITALY
Milan
Venice
Trieste
Genoa
Rome
Naples
Palermo
SICILY

YUGOSLAVIA Apr. 1941
Belgrade

BULGARIA Mar. 1941
Sofia

ALBANIA Apr. 1939

GREECE Apr. 1941
Salonika
Athens

TURKEY
Istanbul
Ankara
Smyrna
Adana
Aleppo
SYR

Kizil R.

CYPRUS (Br.)

Beirut
Damascus
PALESTINE
Jerusalem
TRANSJORDAN
SAUDI ARABIA

ADRIATIC SEA
TYRRHENIAN SEA
IONIAN SEA
AEGEAN SEA
CRETE

SPAIN
Madrid
Barcelona
Valencia

BALEARIC IS.
CORSICA
SARDINIA

MEDITERRANEAN SEA

MALTA (Br.)

Oran
Algiers
Bône
Tunis

ALGERIA
TUNISIA

LIBYA
Tripoli
Bengasi

EGYPT
Alexandria
Cairo
Suez Canal
Nile R.

RED SEA

La Havre
Loire R.
Rhine R.
Rhône R.
Elbe R.

the Crimea in February 1945 to discuss the peace arrangements. It was agreed that the Soviet Union could have a slice of Poland and territory and privileges in the Far East, a decision later severely criticized. It was also agreed that Russia would enter the war against Japan and that postwar Germany would be split into four zones. Yalta was the high point of the alliance. After this conference, relations between the Soviet Union and its allies quickly deteriorated.

As the Allied troops advanced through Germany, they uncovered the secret hell of Nazi inhumanity toward the people Hitler despised. In the concentration camps—Belsen, Buchenwald, Dachau, and others—they found the gas ovens which had destroyed millions of lives, the wasted bodies of slave laborers who had starved to death, and the living dead who had somehow survived torture and the cruel medical experiments to which they had been subjected. Between 1939 and 1945 the Jewish population in Nazi-occupied Europe had decreased from 9,739,200 to 3,505,800; and another 6,000,000 people—Poles, Czechs, Russians, and others—had also fallen victim to Nazi cruelty.

The Axis leaders did not live to see defeat. Mussolini, a cringing fugitive, was seized by anti-Fascist partisan fighters and shot to death; his mutilated body, with that of his mistress, was trussed up in the public square at Milan, an object of

The nightmare of Nazism is only suggested by these piles of bodies at the concentration camp at Belsen, Germany. These victims died of disease and starvation, but millions more—men, women, and children—were deliberately murdered.

derision and hatred. While street fighting raged in Berlin, Hitler committed suicide. His body and that of the mistress he had just made his wife were doused with gasoline and set afire. Nor did the great wartime leader of the United States live to see the end of the war, although he realized the imminence of victory. Franklin Roosevelt died suddenly in April 1945, less than a month before the German armies surrendered. The final surrender ceremony took place in Berlin on May 8, designated by President Truman as V-E Day, Victory Day in Europe.

End of the war.   While the Allied armies were finishing off the Germans, the Americans had been "island-hopping" their way to Japan, capturing in turn Tarawa, Kwajalein, and Saipan, after bloody struggles on the sandy beaches. In October 1944, with their victory in the battle for Leyte Gulf—the greatest naval engagement in all history—the Allies ended the threat of the Japanese fleet; and in January 1945 General MacArthur returned to the Philippines. The final phase of the war against Japan was unfolding. Only a few hundred miles from Japan, Iwo Jima and Okinawa were conquered; and from such advance bases, waves of American bombers rained destruction on Japanese cities. In the China-Burma-India theater, the Chinese, with American aid, were making inroads on areas previously captured by Japan. Plans were laid for an Allied invasion of Japan.

At this juncture Truman was informed that the atomic bomb had been successfully tested. Acting on the statements of his military advisors who asserted that only an invasion costing thousands of American lives would bring Japan to unconditional surrender, the president authorized the use of the awesome new weapon.

From the Potsdam meeting of the Allied leaders in July-August 1945 came a warning to the Japanese that the war against them would take a new and angry turn. When Japan refused to surrender, an American bomber dropped the most terrible weapon yet invented by mankind—the atomic bomb—on Hiroshima. As the mushroom-shaped cloud rose over the city, only charred ruins were left beneath; an expanse of approximately three miles square—and 60 percent of the city—was almost completely obliterated. The Japanese government estimated that 60,000 people died, 100,000 were wounded, and 200,000 were left homeless. Whether or not the use of the bomb was justified is still a question for debate, but the new weapon achieved its purpose. A few days after the dropping of a second atomic bomb on Nagasaki, the Japanese sued for peace. The surrender ceremony took place September 2 on board the battleship *Missouri,* almost six years to the day after Hitler had plunged the world into the Second World War.

In the final days of the war the explosion of two atomic bombs registered the awesome warning that world wars in the future would be suicidal for all concerned. Among the multitude of questions facing the postwar nations were the complexities of how to deal with the stockpiling of nuclear weapons by Russia and the United States, how to handle the proliferation of atomic bombs as more countries discovered the techniques of building them, and how to develop the peaceful uses of nuclear energy.

In the titanic struggle that was the Second World War there was no clearcut ideological alignment. The exigencies of battle helped conceal basic and even conflicting differences in ideology between Britain and the United States on one hand and Russia on the other. There is evidence to show that just before his death in April 1945, President Roosevelt had begun to realize that his attempt, through wartime military aid, to win the good will and friendship of the high officials in the U.S.S.R. had failed. Winston Churchill also sensed the chasm that was now opening when, just ten days before Germany's surrender, he wrote a personal letter to Stalin warning this third leader of the Big Three of the terrible consequences of an East-West feud. Yet the world, numbed by its suffering and exhausted by its efforts, did not understand the danger inherent in the opposing aims of the two ideologies and the vital need to prevent their clash. As the Second World War came to an end, the leadership of the European nations had diminished greatly, while the United States and Russia emerged as the two powerful—and opposing—nations.

PART SEVEN
TOWARD A NEW WORLD

"To survive, to avert what we have termed future shock, the individual must become infinitely more adaptable and capable than ever before. He must search out totally new ways to anchor himself, for all the old roots—religion, nation, community, family, or profession—are now shaking under the hurricane impact of the accelerative thrust."[1] Mankind has always been undergoing change, but never at our present rate. Consequently, we are challenged everywhere today to cope with the stress and disorientation—but also with the innovative opportunities—created by our technological and societal acceleration.

In the fast-changing decades since 1945, three major worlds have emerged, each with its recognizable way of life. The western world comprises almost all of the Americas, western and southern Europe, Australia and New Zealand, as well as South Africa and Japan. Stretching across the vast Eurasian heartland, from Berlin to Peking, is the Communist world. The underdeveloped nations of Africa and parts of Asia make up the Third, or nonaligned, World. The conflicting interests of these three worlds form much of the story of our times.

For most of the last 25 years, however, the fate of the world depended upon the rivalry and confrontation tactics of the western and communist power blocks, as summed up in the term *cold war.* Each armed itself with thermonuclear weapons and an intercontinental delivery system capable of annihilating the other. Although the United Nations was created in 1945 to keep the peace, it proved powerless to mediate between these blocs, so that the world had to depend upon a "balance of terror," with the two superpowers leading a number of regional security alliances. However, because of the dangers attending an increase in the number of countries possessing nuclear weapons and the massive financial burdens involved, Washington and Moscow have begun as of 1972 to limit strategic arms by treaty. Meanwhile, cold war bipolarity has given way to polycentrism. Not only have the former defeated Axis powers reemerged as dynamic and democratized societies, but both America's and the Soviet Union's allies have acquired greater freedom in world affairs.

The most dramatic changes have occurred in the Third World, where scores of former colonies in Asia and Africa are now independent. Their attainment of freedom was purchased at the price of new psychological, social, economic, and political problems; as a result numerous new countries have capsized into outright chaos. Yet the people of Africa and Asia are determined that their road from dependence to independence is irreversible.

In all three worlds entire societies are engaged in a new—and often seemingly frantic—search for identity. In western countries, such as the United States, minorities have been seeking to enter the mainstream of social development and be accepted as equal in all respects. In the Communist world the ideological postulates which helped channel the energies of an earlier generation along revolutionary avenues are increasingly resented by the youth as outmoded and constricting. In the Third World the search takes the form of rediscovering the values and forms of precolonial Asian and African cultures and of adapting them to meet the social and psychological needs of nation-building in this century.

Change is inherent in human affairs, and man has always been discovering new knowledge and solving new problems. This planetary process has now been accelerated beyond anything known in the past. A veritable knowledge and cultural explosion is revolutionizing the second half of the twentieth century. Some of the sciences are doubling their information almost every decade, while a communications revolution has broken down the traditional political and social barriers around the globe. The major problems confronting mankind cut across national boundaries: the population explosion, urbanization, the dwindling of nonrenewable natural resources, and pollution. Science and technology are at once contributing to the existence of these problems and proving essential to their solution. But will the traditional political and social institutions be able to transform themselves either swiftly or fundamentally enough to enable mankind to continue to survive—and prosper—on a plundered and polluted planet? These questions challenge today's youth, who are attempting to develop a new life style appropriate to their approaching role of responsible decision-making.

CHAPTER 22
THE QUEST
FOR WORLD ORDER

The West and Communism Since 1945

With the end of global conflict a great longing to return to the pursuits of peace motivated most of mankind. Statesmen of the victorious Allied powers met to draft peace treaties, while in San Francisco they organized a new international institution, the United Nations, in order "to save succeeding generations from the scourge of war, which twice in our lifetime has brought untold sorrow to mankind."

For a brief period these arrangements concealed the more profound consequences of the war, chief of which was the emergence of two superpowers, the United States and the Soviet Union, which now superseded western Europe as centers of power. They created rival political and military blocs, thereby restructuring the postwar world into a bipolar configuration. The resulting confrontation came to be known as the cold war, a struggle that was neither war nor peace in the conventional sense but a constant maneuvering for advantage combined with incessant glowerings and threats. For a quarter of a century the world had to live with this cold war, which spasmodically threatened to burst into uncontrollable nuclear holocaust.

An equilibrium of tension based on two military alliances in Europe—NATO and the Warsaw Pact—provided the basic structure of the world's power division, which was symbolized concretely by the Berlin Wall. Yet paradoxically, this uneasy equilibrium was to be disturbed less by the superpowers themselves than by changes within their respective blocs. Moscow and Washington experienced diminishing control over their client states, and both were challenged by the rising power of communist China. A bipolarized world was undergoing another transformation as new loci of power emerged.

In a thermonuclear age the three "worlds" have no alternative but to strive for a stable political order in which age-old competition and conflict must give way progessively to cooperation. In their respective styles, they all have to come to terms with the promise and problems of contemporary technology and its as yet incalculable impact on a global environment. And all peoples are engaged in a search for a new and relevant social and cultural identity in the last three decades of a century marked by seismic transformations. The century began with the Wright Brothers' inauguration of the space age and Einstein's Relativity Theory, has progressively altered the human landscape and all traditional modes of thought and behavior, and can be expected to continue to accelerate the tempo of change as Spaceship Earth hurtles towards the year 2000.

THE COLD WAR ABORTS THE GREAT HOPE

The United Nations—purposes and structure. The memory of the failure to build a lasting peace after World War I convinced Allied statesmen that the survival of civilization required an efficient international machinery to maintain peace and security. With this goal in mind, the representatives of fifty governments met at San Francisco from April to June 1945 and drafted the Charter of a new organization, the United Nations. To achieve its purposes, the United Nations was equipped with six major organs: the Security Council, to maintain peace and order; the General Assembly, to function as a form of town meeting of the world; the Economic and Social Council, to improve living standards and promote fundamental human rights; the Trusteeship Council, to advance the interests of dependent peoples; the International Court of Justice, to resolve disputes between nations; and the Secretariat, headed by a secretary-general, to serve the needs of the other major organs. Though lacking the sovereign powers of its member states, the United Nations was a more wide-reaching instrument than its defunct predecessor, the League of Nations.

The most controversial issue at San Francisco was over the right of veto in the Security Council. The smaller countries held that it was undemocratic for certain governments to be privileged to block the wishes of the majority, but the Big Five—the United States, the Soviet Union, China, France, and Great Britain—maintained that singly and collectively they had special interests and responsibilities in maintaining global peace and security. Realists recognized that given the actualities of power in 1945, peace could not be kept unless the five permanent members of the Council—in particular the Big Two—were willing to cooperate.

Advent of the Atomic Age. The United Nations Charter was signed on June 26, 1945; the first atomic bomb in history was dropped on Hiroshima some six weeks later, on August 6. This second event—and its timing—had two implications of far-reaching significance. First, the advent of nuclear weapons completely altered man's capacity to wage war and to destroy his physical and societal environment; second, because the Charter had been drafted in a prenuclear context, the newly established United Nations was not equipped with formal, far less specific, powers to internationalize the control of atomic energy for peaceful purposes only. Henceforth, those states with nuclear—and later thermonuclear—weapons would possess a life-and-death advantage over nonpossessors; at the same time, the very disparity in power relations would almost certainly propel the latter to bend every effort to acquire these weapons in the absence of any effective international control system. Consequently, the years following World War II were marked by the progressive acquisition of atomic weapons by the larger nations and by ineffectual attempts to limit the proliferation of nuclear weapons and to put brakes on what was to prove the most costly armaments race in history.

Problem of the ex-enemies. At the Potsdam Conference in 1945 the Council of Foreign Ministers of the Big Five was set up to draft the peace treaties. What proved to be roadblocks to international cooperation were treaties with the major ex-enemies, Japan and Germany. Postwar Japan was given a new and more democratic constitution, the national economy was liberalized, workers were encouraged to join trade unions, and the great trusts were broken up. A peace treaty between Japan and the West, signed in 1951 over Soviet objections, reestablished that country as a sovereign state, while a Japanese-American security pact made allies of ex-enemies less than ten years after Pearl Harbor.

It was in Germany that Allied and Soviet policies collided headlong. The defeated country had been divided into zones of temporary occupation; the eastern zone remained under Soviet control, while western Germany was partitioned into American, British, and French zones. Berlin, forming an enclave within the Soviet zone, was placed under four-power administration. This arrangement created serious tensions. Moscow closed its zone to western inspection, stripped the area of raw materials and industry, and in effect demonstrated its aim to keep Germany politically and economically impotent and to foster a Communist regime. With Germany physically and ideologically split, the two superpowers found themselves in serious confrontation in central Europe.

The Iron Curtain falls. Collaboration among the major Allies had won the war and was supposed to serve as the basis for postwar reconstruction and security, as the United Nations Charter attested. At the wartime Yalta Conference, pledges had been made to permit "free and unfettered elections" in Poland, but a Communist regime was imposed without reference to the will of the people. By 1947 similar governments had been forced on Rumania, Yugoslavia, Hungary, Bulgaria, and Albania, and the following year saw a Communist take-over in Czechoslovakia. Even before some of these events, Winston Churchill had warned at Fulton, Missouri, in 1946, "From Stettin in the Baltic to Trieste in the Adriatic, an Iron Curtain has descended across the Continent."

The bipolarization of Europe became progressively apparent. Soviet support of Communist guerrilla activities in Greece and territorial demands upon Turkey were countered by the dispatch of economic and military aid to Greece and Turkey by President Harry S. Truman (1884-   ) in 1947—a move usually regarded as recognizing the start of the cold war.

This American initiative was followed by an offer, announced by Secretary of State George C. Marshall, to help Europe solve its dire economic problems. Western European nations eagerly accepted this American proposal, which was, however, rejected by the Soviet Union for itself and the countries of eastern Europe. Congress subsequently appropriated billions of dollars to implement the European Recovery Program—better known as the Marshall Plan—which proved so effective that within four years the industrial production of the recipient nations had climbed to 64 percent over 1947 levels and 41 percent over prewar figures.

To enable western Germany to participate in the Marshall Plan, the western Allies helped create the new Federal Republic of Germany, which comprised West Germany and West Berlin. Almost immediately the Soviet Union established the German Democratic Republic in East Germany and began to apply pressure to gain control over West Berlin as well.

Collective security by regional alliances. Deadlocks in the United Nations and

**TERRITORIAL CHANGES
IN EUROPE AFTER
WORLD WAR II**

▢ Annexed by the Soviet Union
▢ Annexed by Poland
▢ Annexed by Bulgaria
▢ Annexed by Yugoslavia

The Allied agreements at Yalta encouraged the Communist nations to take over great stretches of territory after the Second World War.

its inability to guarantee international security, coupled with Soviet expansionism, led to the establishment of the North Atlantic Treaty Organization (NATO) in 1949. Composed of nations of western Europe (Great Britain, France, Belgium, Luxemburg, the Netherlands, Norway, Denmark, Portugal, and Italy) together with Iceland, the United States, and Canada, NATO was a regional alliance for mutual assistance in the North Atlantic area; in 1952 its territorial limits were extended to include Greece and Turkey. West Germany's entry into NATO in May 1955 was swiftly followed by the creation of the Warsaw Pact, which provided for a unified Communist military command in Soviet-dominated eastern Europe.

The Korean War. After Japan's surrender Korea had been divided into American and Soviet zones of occupation. The departure of occupation forces left behind two hostile regimes, each claiming jurisdiction over the entire country. On June 25, 1950, North Korean troops crossed the 38th parallel into South Korea. Washington immediately called for a special meeting of the United Nations Security Council, whose members demanded a cease-fire and withdrawal of the invaders. (The Soviet delegate was boycotting the Council at the time and was not present to veto its action.) When the demand was ignored, the Council undertook to furnish assistance to the South Korean government in order "to repel the armed attacks and to restore international peace and security in the area." After three years of costly fighting—during which the United States carried the brunt of the burden in defending South Korea while Communist China dispatched "volunteers" to assist the North Koreans—an armistice was secured in July 1953 and the status quo *ante bellum* was reestablished.

A new era in American-Soviet rivalry. With the death of Stalin in 1953, Soviet foreign policy shifted from crude brinkmanship to a more sophisticated approach. Nikita Khrushchev (1894-1971), the new leader, realized that nuclear war would be suicidal to all concerned. By enunciating the doctrine of "peaceful coexistence," he repudiated the Stalinist view that war between the socialist and capitalist worlds was inevitable. Rivalry between the two systems would continue, however, and Khrushchev boasted that in the near future the Soviet Union would overtake the United States economically, scientifically, and in the area of social justice. In his own words. "We shall bury you." Thus coexistence did not mean the end of tensions during Khrushchev's period of control in the Kremlin (1953-1964).

The early years of the 1960's were marked by dangerous tensions that threatened to engulf the superpowers in a nuclear conflict. A summit meeting convened in Paris in 1960 broke up angrily, the situation exacerbated by an American U-2 reconnaissance plane having been discovered and shot down over the Soviet Union. During the same year Khrushchev, speaking at the United Nations, demanded the resignation of the secretary-general, Dag Hammarskjöld, and denounced American foreign policy. The following year Moscow again demanded the withdrawal of Allied forces from West Berlin, and once more Washington refused to back down. Backed by Moscow, the East German government erected a wall between East and West Berlin, thereby blocking the escape route formerly used by thousands.

The most serious crisis occurred in 1962 within ninety miles of the United States mainland. Three years earlier Fidel Castro had wrested power from a right-wing dictatorship in Cuba and set about to transform the island into a Communist state and to create a springboard for the diffusion of Marxist revolution directed against United States hegemony in Latin America. A setback to the administration of President John F. Kennedy (1917-1963) occurred when some Cuban exiles, trained under American auspices, invaded their homeland in April 1961 and were decisively defeated at the Bay of Pigs. The following year the Soviet Union sought to install rocket sites in Cuba. To the United States, these missiles represented a dangerous threat to the cold war balance of power. Kennedy ordered a naval blockade set up around Cuba and demanded that Moscow withdraw the offensive weapons. Khrushchev in turn had the rockets removed after receiving assurances that the United States would respect Cuba's territorial integrity.

The Cuban imbroglio underscored the urgency of reducing the peril of atomic war. The result was a limited nuclear test ban treaty, signed in 1965 by Great Britain, the Soviet Union, and the United States, which outlawed the testing of nuclear devices in outer space, in the atmosphere, or under water. Although France (now a nuclear power) and Communist China (soon to become one) refused to sign, one hundred other states did. This test ban registered some lessening of tension, and relations between the superpowers improved in other ways. Scientific and agricultural exchanges were encouraged, and a "hot line" between the White House and the Kremlin was set up to prevent a communications breakdown and to facilitate understanding of their respective positions.

Developments in the western alliance. The United States had emerged from World War II with its landscape unscathed and its economy the most powerful in history. The burgeoning of this industrial power made possible the vast number of global activities undertaken by the American government after 1945: the expenditure of $128 billion (through 1967) for military and economic foreign aid; the maintenance of armed bases around the world; and the waging of two protracted wars in Asia.

Meanwhile, western Europe, assisted initially by the Marshall Plan, had made a remarkable recovery since the war-devastated days of 1945; and by 1964 its economic power stood next to the United States. Non-Communist Europe's economic advance was largely attributable to the creation in 1957 of the European Economic Community, better known as the Common Market. Its members— Belgium, France, Italy, Luxembourg, the Netherlands, and West Germany— aimed to abolish gradually all custom duties among them, to reach agreement on a common tariff, to facilitate a common trading market, and, eventually, to attain some form of political integration.

Britain's changing role. Perhaps Britain's most notable postwar achievement was the peaceful liquidation of its once vast empire (see Chapter 23). This imperial loss, coupled with domestic economic problems, caused British statesmen to develop a new posture in world affairs, such as seeking closer ties with countries across the English Channel. In 1971 Britain accepted an official invitation to join the Common Market (EEC), a decision taken despite a cleavage in British public opinion regarding its future impact on the country's role in world affairs. Henceforth, London had cast its lot with Europe's fortunes. In addition to the United Kingdom, the ECC's ranks were augmented at the beginning of 1973 by Ireland and Denmark.

Britain's most critical domestic problem has been the renewal—and intensification—of tensions between the Protestant majority and the Catholic minority in northern Ireland, or Ulster, which is an integral part of the United Kingdom. Mounting street fighting, sniping, and bombings led to London's abrogation of Stormont, Ulster's parliament, which to Catholics represented a legal-political weapon of the Protestant establishment. The year 1972 saw London having to bend every effort to prevent a further deterioration of antagonisms into outright civil war.

De Gaulle's France. Overwhelmed by defeat in 1940, France owed its resurgence primarily to General Charles de Gaulle (1890-1970), who dominated that country's political scene from 1958 to 1969. In giving France a status in world affairs which it had not enjoyed for decades, de Gaulle challenged two fundamental postwar theses: (1) NATO was indispensable for western security; and (2) the United States must maintain leadership in the western alliance. De Gaulle saw the situation differently. Post-Stalinist Russia was no longer expansionist in Europe, while a Germany split into two segments entrenched in rival power blocs offered little chance of upsetting the postwar equilibrium—nor were many people seriously interested in seeing Germany reunited. In short, the threat of war on the European landscape had receded over the horizon.

De Gaulle's distinctive French foreign policy rested on three pillars. He opposed Anglo-American hegemony in the West. He believed that a united Europe, hopefully under French leadership, would become a major force in world politics, along with the Soviet Union (if it did not join the new European structure), the United States, and China. He was also concerned with the Afro-Asian world, whose newly emergent nations in his opinion should not be committed to either the East or the West.

At home, de Gaulle was able to provide the strong leadership which France had formerly lacked; but in mid-1968 his regime was profoundly shaken by a student uprising and nation-wide strikes. In 1969 the president resigned and was replaced by his former prime minister, Georges Pompidou.

Resurgence in West Germany.   The dramatic story of West Germany's recovery from an occupied territory to membership in the western alliance began with the establishment of the Federal Republic in 1949 and the end of Allied occupation five years later. Under its aged but forceful chancellor, Konrad Adenauer (1876-1967), West Germany surged forward economically, while politically Adenauer welded his country's fortunes to those of the western nations.

In October 1969, for the first time in some forty years, the Social Democratic Party was able to form the government—under its leader and new chancellor, Willy Brandt—on election promises that included improved relations with Germany's Communist neighbors and the Soviet Union. In March 1970 the leaders of West and East Germany held direct meetings, followed a few months later by Brandt's trip to Moscow where he concluded an important treaty. By its provisions, the German Federal Republic and the Soviet Union renounced the use of force in the settlement of disputes; the parties accepted the concept of eventual reunification of the two Germanies; and for its part West Germany recognized the continued existence of the Oder-Neisse line as the western boundary of Poland. For his work in helping reconcile east and west Europe, Brandt was awarded the Nobel Peace Prize in 1971.

Meanwhile the remarkable strength of German industry and an economic prosperity unrivaled in Europe attested to West Germany's preeminence in the Common Market community, though 1972 saw slackening in its growth rate.

Latin America: reform or revolt.   The period following World War II witnessed much political instability and rising social unrest in the region. The only countries with continuous elected governments from 1950 to 1966 were Chile, Mexico, Costa Rica, and Uruguay. Between these dates fourteen governments were toppled by force, and dictatorial rule was imposed on more than half of the Latin American population. Political instability and the seeds of social upheaval spring from appalling socioeconomic disparities. Despite the region's great natural resources, the poverty of the average Latin American is cruel. Shanty towns on the edges of the large cities house thousands amid filth, disease, hunger, and vice. Life expectancy in Latin America is about forty; more than half of the adults are illiterate.

Four of the problems currently afflicting Latin American societies can be enumerated. First, agricultural productivity must be improved in order to lower food costs, increase supplies for both home consumption and export, and raise rural incomes. Second, the population explosion must be controlled; with a yearly increase around 3 percent, Latin America has the fastest-growing population in the world. In the mid-1960's the region's population was about 200 million; it is entirely possible that the figure will climb to 600 million by the year 2000. Third, national economies—especially those that are relatively developed—have suffered from inflation which has created far-reaching economic and social disturbances. Finally, Latin America must not only accelerate industrialization but also develop greater regional integration and better access to domestic and foreign markets.

These massive problems have made Latin America a battleground for opposing ideologies. Since 1948 the countries south of the Rio Grande have been aligned with the United States in the Organization of American States (OAS). Dominated by the "Colossus of the North," the OAS has sought to prevent socialist movements from acquiring control in Latin American countries. After 1959, when Castro was rapidly transforming Cuba into a Communist society, his attempts to export his brand of politics were countered by a boycott set up by the OAS. Under Castro, educational and health standards rose appreciably, as did living conditions among the peasantry, who comprised the great majority of the population. However, the professional and middle classes suffered losses in both living standards and personal liberties, and many thousands fled to the United States. The loss of these professional skills added to Castro's problems. which were already great because of Cuba's dependence upon a one-crop economy, sugar, and especially upon its export to other Communist countries.

In order to protect American interests and prevent the further spread of communism, President Kennedy initiated, with Latin American cooperation, the Alliance for Progress. For the first decade, the United States pledged $20 billion, to which the recipients were to add $80 billion. It was thus hoped that economic reforms could eradicate those conditions against which communism's attack was chiefly directed. But the Alliance has so far not made the progress originally expected.

Given the social traditions of paternalism and oligarchic rule, there has been little economic or political reform. Extreme inequalities exist in the distribution of income. According to a United Nation's estimate for 1965, half of Latin America's population received only 14 percent of the region's total income, while 31.5 percent went to top income brackets comprising only 5 percent of the population. Latin America is far from reaching the point of economic takeoff. It is still in a race between reform and revolt.

With the election of Marxist President Salvador Allende in 1970, Chile became the second Latin American country to attempt a Marxist solution to its problems of economic inequalities and dependence on foreign interests. Elsewhere on the continent other kinds of economic and political nationalism were plainly in evidence during the early 1970's.

Japan: economic and social transformation. In striking contrast to lethargically paced developments in Latin America stands the brilliant recovery and development of Japan since 1945. Allied-occupation reforms in the educational, social, and political spheres, together with close economic and political ties with the United States, made Japan a member of the western bloc—both the chief ally of the United States in Asia and its second largest trading partner.

The American alliance, however, caused considerable division in Japanese public opinion. Leftist groups tended to be anti-American, an attitude accentuated by the unpopularity in Japan of the war in Vietnam. The students were especially critical of the renewal in 1960 of their country's security pact with the United States, and its adoption set off a rash of riots. Despite the subsequent return of

Okinawa to Japan, continued American use of military installations on the island grated on national sensibilities.

Relations with neighboring mainland China were of growing concern to Japan. Since China offers an immense potential market, Tokyo made a limited trade pact with Peking in 1962. At the same time, as an ally of the United States, Japan followed a diplomatic policy of nonrecognition. When in 1972 President Nixon flew to Peking (see below), with Tokyo only being informed at the last minute, the Japanese government felt affronted and disturbed about its own international position. It perceived the need to reassess its postwar Asian policy and to find new accommodations with both China and the Soviet Union.

With the highest standard of living in Asia, a gross national product twice that of Latin America, and the status of the third largest industrial power, Japan enjoyed the longest sustained economic growth of any nation in the two decades following 1945. Throughout the world, in fact, Japan's phenomenal postwar economic growth was making its presence felt. The 1970's could be expected to see a growing involvement by Japanese businessmen and statesmen alike in the trade and politics of East and Southeast Asia, the latter region offering both raw materials and a potentially large market for Japanese exports. In addition, Tokyo was expanding trade with Canada, and in 1972 was planning joint economic ventures with Moscow in Siberia.

The fracturing of monolithic communism. Just as the structure and behavior pattern of the western alliance underwent profound changes in the quarter of a century following World War II, so a once monolithic Communist world was to find itself irretrievably shattered by inner tensions and conflicts. Briefly stated, the fracturing process was due to the inability of an ideology which professes to be international to contain, far less direct, the upsurge of historically nurtured nationalism within the geographical orbit which had been largely delimited by Soviet force.

Ravaged by war—with millions killed and many millions more left homeless, with cities blasted into rubble and vast areas of the countryside laid waste—the Soviet Union nevertheless faced the postwar years in a determined, aggressive mood. Early in 1946 the Soviet government inaugurated its fourth Five-Year Plan, designed to restore the war-damaged economy, accelerate heavy industry and the mechanization of agriculture, and expand the country's military capability.

Stalin died in 1953, his last years marked by brutality and a paranoid fear of even his close associates. On the eve of his demise there were ominous portents of yet another blood purge. The Stalinist regime has been described as combining "all the horrors of early industrialism, Victorian imperialism, political tyranny, and ideological infallibility into a single totalitarian whole."[1]

Following Stalin's death, the Soviet government announced that henceforth it would be guided by the "collective leadership" of the top Communists. It was not long, however, before the shrewd, stocky Ukrainian Nikita Khrushchev succeeded in making himself undisputed master of the Soviet world. The new premier gave top priority to heavy industry, so that steel production doubled between 1950 and 1957 and made possible a complex of plants throughout the country. The Seven-Year Plan, announced early in 1959, aimed at further strengthening the country's economic and military might and at surpassing the leading capitalist countries in per capita output. Many discounted these ambitious plans, but Khrushchev's ebullience sprang from his awareness of Soviet industrial and technological capabilities. His confidence was rewarded with the launching of the first space satellite, Sputnik, in 1957 and the moon rockets, Lunik I, II, and III, two years later.

Soviet imperialism and eastern Europe. After 1945, while western powers were relinquishing control over their extensive colonial holdings, the Soviet Union staked out a colonial area of its own in eastern Europe. Throughout eastern Europe, the Soviet Union effectively exercised political control, directed economic activities, and forbade any cultural or educational initiative that ran counter to Marxism-Leninism as interpreted by the Kremlin leadership.

Nevertheless, one Soviet satellite, Yugoslavia, broke Moscow's grip. Marshal Tito (1892-   ), a tough wartime resistance leader and top Communist in that country, at first went along with the Soviet "line." However, his national strength and geographical distance from Soviet forces enabled him to display a growing resentment of Russian interference. When Tito made a final political break with Soviet policy in 1948, he was encouraged by the western powers and held his ground despite Moscow's economic reprisals and threats of war.

Following the organization of the eastern zone of Germany into the German Democratic Republic, the East German regime proceeded to break up the large farms and expand heavy industry. As living standards stagnated, or in some instances declined, discontent mounted. Thousands of East Germans fled each week to West Germany; and in June 1953 severe food shortages, coupled with new decrees for longer working hours, touched off a workers' revolt, which was quickly put down.

Meanwhile national communism had been gaining ground in Hungary. The climax was reached in a widespread revolt in the fall of 1956, the creation of a popular government, and the withdrawal of Russian forces from Budapest. Reinforced Soviet troops, however, quickly returned to the capital where they stamped out the flames of national independence. Large numbers of freedom fighters died in the struggle, while more than 200,000 refugees fled to the West.

Communism triumphs in China. Another momentous transformation foreseen by few during the war was the swift victory of communism in China. During that conflict Chiang Kai-shek's Nationalist government and the Chinese Communist leaders had waged a common struggle against the Japanese invaders. The Communists emerged from the conflict with increased popular support and in control of an area containing some 90 million people as well as an army of 500,000 under the leadership of Mao Tse-tung.

Civil war broke out in October 1945. The Nationalists had failed to retain the loyalty of the masses and could be saved neither by American mediation nor by international relief supplies. Notwithstanding Chiang's attempts at limited reform, the long struggle with Japan had resulted in catastrophic inflation, a situation made more critical by widespread corruption among government officials. Above all, the Nationalist regime favored big business and had neglected the long-existing poverty and problems of the farmers. Chiang's strength collapsed in Manchuria in 1948, and the following year saw the complete rout of his armies. By the middle of 1950 Mao had become master of mainland China, and Chiang and a remnant of his forces fled to Formosa (Taiwan). The People's Republic of China, already established in Peking in 1949, was immediately recognized by the U.S.S.R., and subsequently the two countries formed a thirty-year alliance. However, largely because of United States opposition, attempts to gain for Peking the seat in the United Nations held by Nationalist China were not successful until 1971.

Reorganization in China. As in the Soviet system, all power in China was concentrated in the Communist party, governed by the People's Central Committee, whose members occupied the chief civilian and military posts. The day-to-day work of the committee was entrusted to a smaller Politburo headed by Mao, who was also chairman of the republic.

After checking two flagrant evils that had afflicted the Nationalist regime—namely, corruption and inflation—Mao's government began to grapple with China's basic problems: a desperately low standard of living, too many people on overworked land, and an urgent need for industrialization. Millions of acres, confiscated from their owners without compensation, were set up as state farms, and other land was organized into collectives. The first Five-Year Plan (1953-1957) showed significant economic growth, especially in heavy industry. Agriculture, on the other hand, tended to be neglected. A grandiose second Five-Year Plan was launched in 1958, and the "Great Leap Forward" began. The entire population was mobilized on the land and in the factories. In agriculture gigantic communes were set up, each served by public mess halls, dormitories, and nurseries. It soon became evident, however, that the Great Leap Forward had proved overly ambitious and ill planned. The communes failed to produce more food, industry bogged down in a mire of mismanagement, and severe floods compounded the economic fiasco.

The Sino-Soviet split. The 1950's had witnessed large-scale cooperation between Moscow and Peking and forms of Soviet assistance to China. These included cash loans, credits for industrialization, the training of thousands of Chinese students at Soviet universities and factories, and the dispatch of thousands of Soviet technicians to help build new factories, mines, and power plants in China. Throughout the 1950's the Soviet Union was China's principal source of machinery and other needed goods and its biggest customer.

On the other hand, during that same decade tensions were building up. Thus Mao made sure that the Russians abandoned their special position in Manchuria, including their half-ownership of the Chinese Eastern Railroad and the basing of Soviet troops in Port Arthur and Darien. For their part, the Kremlin leaders made clear that the supplies they provided the Chinese forces during the Korean war were not a gift but a loan which Peking was expected to repay, and in 1958 Khrushchev did not disguise his basic disagreement with China's Great Leap Forward. Moreover, both giants were competing in a prestige race to determine which one would be first to reach Marx's goal of pure communism and in the process could claim to be leader of the Communist world.

As far back as the seventeenth century, with the drive of tsarist governments across Eurasia to the Pacific, Sino-Russian relations had experienced serious tensions. In their advance, the Russians encountered Chinese subjects living in the Amur River valley and elsewhere. In time the newcomers acquired at Chinese expense some half a million square miles of what now comprises the Soviet Far East and much of Soviet Central Asia. In addition, the Soviets succeeded in transforming Outer Mongolia into a protectorate.

Like other European powers, Russia had gained territory when China was weak; now that the latter has acquired new strength—along with a thermonuclear capability—it seeks to regain as much of its former territory as possible. Territorial issues were raised publicly in 1963 when the Sino-Soviet split broke into the open, and since then tensions and armed conflict have intensified along the disputed borders as well as over the strategic province of Sinkiang, which contains important sources of oil as well as China's nuclear installation sites.

The Sino-Soviet power struggle can be described in terms of two epithets: the charge of "adventurism" which Moscow hurls at Peking, and of "revisionism" with which the latter assails the Kremlin leadership. Each claims to represent Marxism-Leninism in its pure form and charges the other with betraying world communism. The Soviet leaders argue that in a thermonuclear age, when hydrogen bombs could destroy the whole world, communism must coexist with capitalism. In their view, the Chinese leadership either does not sufficiently understand the ecological risks of a nuclear conflict or expects that sufficient numbers of the huge Chinese population would survive to ensure. Peking's primacy in any aftermath. In addition, Moscow charges Mao Tse-tung with substituting for Marx's teachings about labor-capital conflict his own revisionist doctrine that pits peoples of the "countryside" (the underdeveloped nonwhites of Asia, Africa, and Latin America) against those of the "city" (the developed white populations of Europe, the Soviet Union, and North America).

For their part, the Chinese Communists charge Moscow with maintaining the international status quo of which, as a superpower, it is a major beneficiary. Hence, the Kremlin's leaders have abandoned Marxist revolution in favor of reaching a détente with Washington in order to ensure continued American-Soviet hegemony over the world. Soviet warnings about the dangers of nuclear warfare need not discourage Communist revolutions which can be prosecuted without recourse to atomic weapons (as the Vietnam struggle attests). The present Kremlin leaders have revised Marxism to the point where they are reintroducing

No amount of American support could indefinitely prop up the corrupt Nationalist regime in China. This map shows the extent of the Communist territory in 1947; three years later they controlled the whole country.

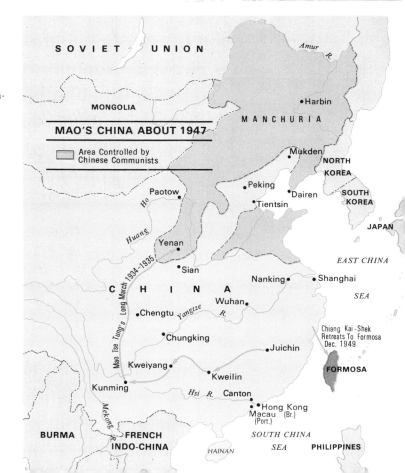

some elements of capitalism into the Soviet Union and its client states and are placing national interests before those of international communism. They must be replaced by leaders dedicated to a world Communist revolution.

Toward international détente. That the world has moved far from the rigid bipolarity of the Cold War period was dramatized by events in 1971-1972. The United Nations' decision to admit the representatives of communist China and to expel the Taiwan-based Nationalist regime was a belated recognition of the great-power status of Peking and the further impossibility of excluding it from the international mainstream. That the time was ripe to make major global accommodations had been realized by President Nixon even before China's admission to the United Nations. Perhaps the high-water mark of his 1968-1972 administration was this basic shift in foreign policy. Henry Kissinger, Nixon's chief security and foreign affairs assistant, defined this change as the "transformation from rather rigid hostility" to a new behavior of "restraint and creativity" that was designed not only to dampen dangerous crises but, hopefully, to avoid them altogether.

The two most spectacular examples of this new foreign policy orientation occurred when the President paid separate visits to Peking and Moscow. In July 1971 Kissinger was dispatched to Peking to arrange for the first trip of a United States president to a country with which Washington had no diplomatic relations. The presidential visit in February 1972 was largely ceremonial, though agreements were reached to increase scientific, cultural, and commercial exchanges. But of greater significance was the visible thaw in the two countries' decades-long cold war, the opening of new lines of communication at both the governmental and personal levels, and the initiation of a continuing dialogue on mutual interests and problems in Asia and the Pacific. The trip was expected to lead to the restoration of diplomatic relations between Washington and Peking.

The president's trip to Moscow in May 1972 took place soon after he had stepped up the aerial bombing of North Vietnam. That the Soviet government did not cancel the visit attested to the importance which it attached to this opportunity to improve Soviet-American relations. The most notable specific achievement was the signing of the first treaty coming out of the Strategic Arms Limitation Talks

Taken at a working session during Nixon's momentous visit to China in 1972, this photograph shows the key participants: (left to right) Chou En-lai, the interpreter, Mao Tse-tung, President Nixon, and Henry Kissinger.

(SALT). It limits the signatories to two antiballistic missile (ABM) sites each and freezes offensive missile weapons systems to their existing levels and to the completion of programs already under way. This treaty subsequently gained congressional approval and thereby paved the way to initiate a second SALT round starting in November 1972. Another outcome of Nixon's visit was an agreement on a joint manned-space mission in 1975—thus making outer space a region of cooperation rather than great-power rivalry. The two countries will also expand their scientific exchanges and commercial relations.

On his way home Mr. Nixon stopped off at Warsaw, where he signed an agreement with the Polish leader, Gierek, to establish a joint economic commission to increase trade between the two countries. Meanwhile, this growing détente between East and West in Europe was advanced by Willy Brandt's *Ostpolitik* policy, which stabilized West Germany's relations with its eastern neighbors. In addition a four-power agreement over Berlin, signed in June 1972, eased western travel to and from that isolated city and gave West Berliners thirty visiting days a year to East Berlin. This agreement, coupled with an exchange of Soviet-German documents confirming current boundaries in central Europe, paved the way for an all-European security conference, which the Russians wanted. A parallel discussion of mutual troop reductions, as advocated by the Americans, was also planned.

A number of factors were responsible for this burgeoning détente. Washington felt that the Soviet leaders sought a relaxation in international relations because of an urgent need to improve their economy—especially the consumer sector—by means of expanded foreign trade and importing sophisticated forms of technology from the West. An obsessive fear of Peking's future actions may have been another factor in Moscow's willingness to ease the tensions. From Moscow's standpoint, the recognition by Washington of nuclear equality and the West's acceptance of existing European frontiers were handsome diplomatic achievements. Russia felt that President Nixon had to make an accommodation because of the adverse American situation in Vietnam and to offset his economic and social problems on the domestic front. For their part the Chinese leaders had acquired new stature in the international environment and could exploit their

newfound relationship with Washington in their intracommunist rivalry with Moscow. In any case the three power centers had sensed that the old cold-war rigidities and postures were now counterproductive, and that 1972 presented them with a new point of international equilibrium. The future was fraught with possibilities for innovation, though no one could dare ignore the booby traps on the path ahead.

THE NEW SEARCH FOR IDENTITY

Domestic developments in the United States. The breakdowns within the western and the Sino-Soviet alliances were accompanied, throughout the 1960's, by important internal developments in the three great powers—the United States, the U.S.S.R., and the People's Republic of China—which inevitably affected their capacities on the international scene.

The 1960's found the United States involved in massive efforts to eliminate racial discrimination. Since the 1954 decision of the Supreme Court calling for desegregation of public schools, the nation had sought to make the Constitution's provisions real and substantial for every American. Integration in schools and public facilities and equal voting rights for black Americans, who comprise one tenth of the nation's population, have been the dramatic objectives of the overall civil rights issue. By the middle of the decade those rights had been largely enacted into law, mainly because of pressures brought to bear by the civil rights movement, which in the fifties and early sixties was characterized by nonviolence. From 1965 to 1968, however, the nation was rocked by violence in the ghetto slums of cities as far apart as Los Angeles, New York, Detroit, and Washington. It had become apparent that the legal extension of guaranteed civil rights to the black population was not a sufficient answer to the social and racial problems of the nation.

The urban violence that characterized the middle of the decade was closely linked to the continuing pockets of poverty in the world's wealthiest nation. The administration of President Lyndon B. Johnson (1963-1968) was marked by notable reforms on a broad domestic front, but by the mid-1960's many observers felt that too little was being done too late to help the cities solve their social and economic problems. Congress was slow in providing the massive funds required to improve the living conditions of the ghetto dwellers. One of the reasons was budgetary: the rapidly escalating costs of the Vietnam War made Congress reluctant to vote funds for internal development if that meant an increase in taxes.

Consequently, the internal struggle for economic rights, which had largely supplanted the struggle for civil rights, became more and more linked with the war in Vietnam, or, more precisely, the civil rights movement increasingly joined with the antiwar movement. Thus Dr. Martin Luther King, Jr., the Nobel laureate who had led the nonviolent civil rights movement, became a leader in the movement against the Vietnam War as well—until he fell victim to an assassin's bullet in 1968. Frustration with the slow pace of reform resulted in a more radical civil rights movement, and many younger Negro spokesmen began to demand political action and influence under the banner "Black Power." The more militant leaders, who also opposed the Vietnam war, emphasized that they were prepared, as they put it, to meet violence with violence in the attainment of their objectives of equal social, educational, and economic status for black Americans throughout the country.

The antiwar movement itself increased in importance as the war escalated. Beginning in the early 1960's with only a handful of urban and university intellectuals, by 1967 it included many of the most influential members of both houses of Congress from both political parties. On the nation's campuses and elsewhere, dissatisfaction with the draft laws and frustration at the slow progress being made in such fields as poverty legislation led to increasing disaffection with the government. Tens of thousands of young Americans sought refuge from military service in Canada.

Johnson did not seek reelection, and the 1968 presidential contest was won by the Republican, Richard M. Nixon (1913-   ).

Domestically, the Nixon administration showed a distinct shift toward a more conservative philosophy of government. Economically, it introduced restrictive fiscal and monetary measures to combat the country's inflation and its balance of payments problem. The weakness of the American dollar among the world currencies led to its devaluation, which made this country's goods more competitive abroad. Protectionism also took the form of new import restrictions against foreign products. However, as of June 1972, the American balance-of-trade deficit was running at a record height.

In 1968, Nixon had made law and order a major campaign issue, but during the next four years the national incidence of crime increased further. It loomed as an issue again in 1972, together with the sensitive busing question. The American public continued to be deeply concerned over the eroding purchasing power of the dollar and the high incidence of unemployment. The costs of running the country had meanwhile been soaring at all three levels of government, and their relationships in the raising and sharing of revenue were becoming critical. A high proportion of governmental expenditures was on education, and its increasing financial demands were being progressively resisted by local taxpayers and state legislators. It was ironic that at the same time thousands of college graduates in 1972 found job prospects reduced to the vanishing point.

The gross national product continued to rise, but more than half the national budget was still allocated to defence, despite the de-escalation of American involvement in Vietnam and the initial SALT agreements, which did not inhibit the Pentagon's request for large sums for new weapon systems. Again the question of national priorities would be a central issue in the 1972 presidential elections, given also such problems as urban renewal, outmoded transportation systems, and the continued deterioration of the natural environment. The American search for an identity—and a value system—appropriate to the 1970's was already in full swing.

The Soviet Union. On November 7, 1967, the Soviet Union celebrated the fiftieth anniversary of the Bolshevik Revolution. The half-century mark had been reached as the U.S.S.R. showed signs of political and social maturation and change. Symbolic of the maturity that the regime had achieved was the manner in which the leadership was changed in October 1964, when Nikita Khrushchev was ousted from power and replaced by a duumvirate composed of Aleksei Kosygin as premier and Leonid Brezhnev as chief of the Communist party. The change of power was carried out by a vote in the Central Committee of the Communist party; while it had many of the earmarks of a coup, Khrushchev was permitted to retire quietly and was occasionally seen in public in the following years. The new leadership consisted of men who were accomplished bureaucratic politicians and technocrats, and the caution with which they changed top governmental personnel and developed new policy moves indicated that they sought the support of public opinion rather than its repression through terror.

The 1960's witnessed the rise of new spokesmen in Soviet economic planning who were interested in the use of the profit motive and material incentives to increase consumer production. While the Twenty-Third Congress of the Communist party of the Soviet Union, which met in 1966, retained centralized planning as the keystone of the country's socialist system, it also introduced more liberal regulations based on the principles of a free market. A price system reflecting supply and demand as well as distribution and production costs was widely considered. By the end of 1966 some four hundred economic enterprises were operating under the new system.

The 1960's also witnessed growing pressure for the liberalization of intellectual life and greater freedom of artistic expression and experimentation. While some progress was made, it was far from steady, and the strong voices of the young poets like Yevgeny Yevtushenko, or again of novelists who revealed inhuman conditions in Soviet labor camps, were all too often drowned out by official censure at the trials of writers who had made the mistake of criticizing the regime too openly or of publishing in the west.

Developments in Communist Europe. The restiveness of Russian youth is directed against artificial restraints imposed by their own government; the restiveness, and occasional violent flare-ups, of their counterparts in eastern Europe is directed against the control and subordination of their national societies by alien, Soviet power in both the military and the bureaucratic sectors. Several factors appear responsible for the contemporary ferment in eastern Europe. One is the resurgence of nationalist feelings among peoples possessing long and proud societies. Another is recognition of the fact that since successful revolution against a neighboring superpower equipped with the most advanced military technology is seemingly impossible, changes in the theory and practice of government imposed by that neighbor should be attempted by evolutionary, peaceful means. Hence the growing insistence among the Communist satellites that the Kremlin accept the theory of many paths to socialism. As we have seen, Tito's Yugoslavia was the first to employ and successfully apply this theory, so that his "deviation" served as the initial augury of polycentrism.

In the 1960's Czechoslovakia provided the most dramatic example of the search of east Europeans to find a new, appropriate identity of their own by eroding the constraints of Russian-imposed ideology and behavior. During the previous decade, while discontent in neighboring countries had risen to the boiling point, as in East Germany, Poland, and Hungary, the Czechs had remained relatively passive towards their own Communist regime. But the forces of dissension were in the ascendancy, due to economic stagnation which antagonized the trade union membership, to a failure to initiate educational reforms which alienated the students, to the denial of civil liberties which frustrated the intellectuals, and to an inefficient bureaucratic regime which caused the more progressive Communist politicians to work for reforms within the existing system.

At last, reformist political forces, led by Alexander Dubcek, acquired power and instituted programs aimed at liberalizing and revitalizing the economic sector for the benefit of the consumer and labor force, at restoring freedom of the press and encouraging greater intellectual and commercial contacts with Czecho-slovakia's western neighbors, and at correcting Communist party errors of policy and behavior alike. Unhappily, this dramatic move to realize a new vision of democratic socialism was aborted on August 20, 1968, when Soviet tanks and armed forces invaded the country and completely suppressed the national movement. Following this intervention, the Kremlin leaders began systematically to force the Czech Communist reformers to abrogate their programs and finally ousted Dubcek and his associates from all decision-making offices.

The forces of reaction had apparently triumphed in Czechoslovakia. Yet despite this setback, it is doubtful whether Moscow can continue to suppress pressures in eastern Europe demanding liberalization of existing dogmas and governmental behavior. Late in 1970, economic discontent in Poland erupted into rioting, and forced the resignation of government leader Gomulka. The search for a viable, and acceptable, ideology goes on. The leader of Rumania, Nicolae Ceausescu, for example, insists on his country's sovereignty and freedom to develop an independent foreign policy that includes improving relations with the United States and other western nations, as well as with Moscow's most dangerous Communist competitor, China. Similarly, the Rumanian government is in turn experimenting with more liberal economic and social policies at home.

In short, in the Communist world as elsewhere, the appearance of the 1970's was witnessing continued polycentrism accompanied by the search for identity.

Communist China.   While the Soviet Union took fitful but evident steps in the direction of liberalization, the People's Republic of China rushed headlong into social and political radicalization. By the end of the 1950's it was evident that the solidarity which had characterized Chinese Communist leadership since the Long March in the mid-1930's was beginning to fracture. In the aftermath of the failure of the Great Leap Forward it became apparent that there were at least two groups divided over policy: the "liberals," who wanted to proceed slowly and carefully with economic development and social change, and the "radicals," who evidently were impatient to effect a drastic restructuring of Chinese society. It is probable that Mao Tse-tung was the leader of the radicals.

By the middle of the 1960's a perplexed world could perceive the development of a gigantic ideological and political conflict inside China. Mao Tse-tung and his supporters had organized a movement known as the "Red Guards," composed chiefly of bands of high school and college age youths whose primary responsibility was to attack the radicals' liberal opponents, to whip up ideological fervor, and to enforce a strict radical orthodoxy on the entire population. Temporarily placing political purification higher on the Chinese priority list than economic development, the Red Guards were, at first, permitted to interfere with production processes. Vast rallies and demonstrations were held in Peking; the Red Guards set out on cross-country marches in emulation of the Long March; the entire educational system from top to bottom was closed down for a year to permit the ideological correction of texts and teachers; and those considered the carriers of outmoded ways of life and thought were often physically attacked in their homes and on the streets.

Known as the "Great Proletarian Cultural Revolution," this radicalization movement was based ideologically on what came to be known as the "thought of Mao Tse-tung," conveniently summarized in "the little red book" entitled *Quotations from Chairman Mao Tse-tung.* This collection of excerpts from Mao's writings became the catechism of the Maoist movement, and memorization and repetition of quotations in speech and song were intended as an educational device to instill in everyone the essentials of Mao's thought. The study of Mao's thought was claimed to have efficacious results in all fields of human endeavor, from agricultural and industrial production to medicine and interpersonal relations.

Among the important issues the Cultural Revolution was meant to resolve was the question of "Red or expert?"; whether, in other words, basic technical and economic decisions should be made at all levels by the party, because of its adherence to the "general line" of Maoist thinking, or by technical personnel, thoroughly educated in their specialties but not always or necessarily ideologically pure. In other words, should politics or rational economic development occupy the prime position in the process of constructing a new China?

The Cultural Revolution appeared to be a device for deciding the issue on the basis of the doctrine that politics is always primary. Maoism considered the human element and "revolutionary correctness" more important than professional or technical training; dependence on the latter was considered "bourgeois thinking" and was the prime target of the Red Guards and their Cultural Revolution. As such, the Cultural Revolution must be seen as more than a power struggle between two factions within the Communist party. On another level, it was nothing less than an attempt to reorganize the pattern of thought of an entire nation, a gigantic campaign to remake the Chinese in the image of the "new socialist man." In contrast to traditional Marxists, who believed that a new, unalienated socialist man would emerge from the structures of socialist society, the Maoists apparently believed that a socialist society could only be built by the new socialist man.

Despite the intense radicalization of its internal politics, in foreign affairs China continued the essentially conservative policy it had followed since the end of the Korean War. Verbally bellicose, it exercised a self-restraint appropriate to the realities of international power, although numerous situations and incidents, such as the Vietnam War and American flights over Chinese territory, might have served as occasions for foreign adventures. In 1962, it is true, China came into direct armed conflict with India. China's primary aim in the Sino-Indian conflict, in addition to securing the frontiers of its Tibetan territory, was probably to demonstrate its strength in contrast to India's. Although undoubtedly tempted to enter actively the neighboring Vietnam situation, its contributions of military matériel and economic support appear to have been less than the Soviet Union's. Nevertheless, the Vietnam War remained, throughout the 1960's, the primary issue in Chinese foreign policy, as it was in the foreign policies of the Soviet Union and the United States as well.

Three views of man.   The great ideological divisions that characterized civilization after World War I not only survived World War II but have become more profound with the passing decades. As a result, today's citizen is assailed by grave doubts that go far deeper than the problem of choice among alternative policies to resolve specific political, social, or economic issues. The very nature of man and the structure of society are being called into question.

In the West, where philosophical liberalism has provided the basis for some of man's greatest achievements, the individual personality remains central to man's self-image. Each person is unique, and society should be structured to permit and encourage the individual to develop his personality to the fullest. Liberalism recognizes that society itself places limitations on individualism, that man can be truly free only in a society in which all men recognize and accept the limitations of law. Chaos is antithetical to the freedom that is necessary for individual growth and development. Man, the liberal holds, is capable of "making himself" and of fashioning his environment for the greatest good of the greatest number.

The liberal image of man is rejected, however, by the two other contending schools of ideology, the Soviet and the Chinese. Man, according to the Soviet Marxists, is the product of his material environment and of his relationship to "the means of production"—that is, to the social and economic relationships characteristic of his society. An individual is not the unique personality understood by the liberals but rather a member of a class, and it is his class status that determines his consciousness and his view of the world. Unlike the liberal, who believes that men should voluntarily join together to solve their problems, the Soviet Marxist sees men pitted against each other in an inevitable to-the-death struggle between social classes, a struggle which history dictates will be won by the "proletariat," the working class. To change man, society must be changed, and the most "enlightened" among men, those who are members of the Communist party, will lead mankind in the class struggle and the process of social change that will end in the emergence of the "new" man.

The Chinese Communists, though deriving a great deal of inspiration from the Soviet Marxists, offer a third view of man. According to them, man makes the world in which he lives: the world is essentially the product of man's conscious-

Mao Tse-tung's belief that the revolution must be based on peasant uprisings was rejected by the early Chinese Communist party and was counter to the Marxian doctrine held by Moscow. Here a young Mao gives a speech at a meeting of Chinese Communists.

ness. Therefore, the world can be changed, and man's new consciousness must be forged in the revolutionary struggle. Less materialistic than the Soviets, and laying greater emphasis on the necessity for change within each individual, the Chinese believe that man changes only within the collective community. At the same time, the Chinese are less deterministic and thus paradoxically less optimistic about man than either the liberals or the Soviet Marxists. They lay greater emphasis on struggle as an inherent part of man's nature.

CHAPTER 23

THE WEST AND THE THIRD WORLD

Africa, the Middle East, India, and Southeast Asia:
1914-1972

This chapter is divided into two main parts. The first describes the period from World War I to the onset of the 1930's, which was a prelude to the dramatic changes that were to transform Africa and Asia after 1945. Japan became a militarily powerful industrial state; and China deposed its Manchu dynasty, but the new republic was plagued by unrest and the rise of Communism. Above all, in the non-self-governing colonies it was a time of preparation for revolt against imperialism when nationalism developed its ideology and goals and obtained its leaders.

The latter part of this chapter describes the collapse of colonialism and the winning of independence by some five dozen former colonial dependencies. These new nations are now collectively known as the Third World in contrast to the western and Communist worlds.

This tripartite distinction is not completely clear-cut, however. There are marginal states, such as Afghanistan, Thailand, Iran, and Ethiopia, which are underdeveloped but not newly independent, and which have never been under colonial control—except for a very brief period in two instances. Latin America is usually included as part of the western world. Although most of its nations have been independent for much more than a century and have at least the forms of democracy if not the reality, they can be classified as underdeveloped.

The appearance of these Third World nations with their distinctive problems and aspirations constitutes one of the most significant features of our contemporary world, affecting all the major powers, not least those of the West. In the earlier periods of world history western and Afro-Asian affairs were mutually exclusive, but in the twentieth century the history of the West could hardly be understood without some consideration of the course of events in the non-West. Generally underdeveloped economically, urgently in need of foreign aid and technical assistance, often politically unstable—these conditions were reflected in the activities of the new states in the United Nations. At the same time these unstable situations invited big-power intrusions into such areas as the Middle East, Pakistan, and Vietnam.

Pan-Africanism and Negro nationalism.　In Africa opposition to imperialism grew during the World War I, as democracy and self-determination of nations were so widely publicized by President Wilson. American black leaders demanded greater recognition of black rights, particularly in Africa. Dr. W. E. B. Du Bois (1868-1963), editor of the influential newspaper *Crisis*, believed that the Paris Peace Conference should help form an internationalized, free Africa. He proposed the nucleus for a state of some twenty million people, guided by an international organization. At the war's end, Du Bois and other black American leaders journeyed to Paris in order to present their ideas in person to the delegates at the peace conference. While in Paris, Du Bois was instrumental in convening a Pan-African Congress with representatives from fifteen countries; the gathering urged that the former German colonies be placed under an international agency, not under the rule of one of the victorious colonial powers such as Britain.

Complementing the sentiments expressed at the Pan-African Congress were the ideals of black nationalism. In a convention held in New York in 1920, the members issued the Declaration of Rights of the Negro Peoples of the World, a document which went on record against racial discrimination in the United States and the "inhuman, unchristian, and uncivilized treatment" of the African in colonial empires.

The mandate system in Africa.　As a result of the Pan-African movement—coupled with a growing liberal sentiment in various nations, especially Britain—all territories conquered by the Allies in World War I were declared to be mandates. Article XXII of the League Covenant stated that the "well-being and development" of backward colonial lands was a "sacred trust of civilization." In essence, the mandate system was a compromise between annexation of the spoils of war by the victors and establishment of an international trusteeship. Parts of the Cameroons, Togoland, and German East Africa (Tanganyika) went to Great Britain. The remaining portions of the Cameroons and Togoland became French mandates. Belgium received the mandate of Ruanda-Urundi (also a part of German East Africa), while the former German colony of Southwest Africa was allotted to the Union of South Africa.

Annual reports from the governments administering the mandates were subject to the scrutiny and evaluation of the Permanent Mandates Commission. While the commission had no effective power to rectify unsatisfactory conditions in a mandate, it could place the matter before the eyes of the world. On numerous occasions the suggestions and criticisms of the commission were heeded by the mandatory powers.

Judgments of the mandate system, a radically new concept in colonial administration, have differed widely. To many critics, international supervision was a unique invasion of national sovereignty. To others, the Permanent Mandates Commission did not have enough power, especially the right to send its own observers into the mandated areas.

Impact of western colonial rule.　The two decades following World War I witnessed the first massive and pervasive impact of European culture upon the African, which, to some degree, penetrated to all parts of the continent. While in some isolated bush areas tribesmen lived in Neolithic isolation, in the new cities many Africans led lives almost wholly European, at least in externals. Under colonial rule Africans now had to obey the laws and regulations of white administrators as well as those of their tribal councils and chiefs. To pay for better roads, public buildings, health and agricultural departments, taxes now had to be paid in cash, forcing many Africans to seek employment outside of their tribal areas in the towns, in the mines, in menial domestic or government service or on plantations run by Europeans. Habits of living changed, new modes of dress were adopted, new farming methods designed to produce cash crops were introduced, and a desire to buy enticing imported goods developed.

Contact with European modes of life rapidly undermined old faiths, customs, tribal loyalties, and social institutions—a process known as detribalization. But the African as yet belonged exclusively neither to his old tribal world nor to that of the white man. No longer bound by his tribe's laws, he was uneasy about the courts and the law of the Europeans; while accepting Christian doctrines, he secretly believed in the powers of his tribal deities. No matter what the benefits of imperial rule might be, it was paternal at its best and exploitive at its worst. Perhaps it was necessary and indeed desirable that Africa be brought into the mainstream of world forces; but it was a profoundly disrupting experience.

While colonial systems of administration varied, few Africans, outside of their tribal affairs, were allowed to participate in the important organs of colonial government. In British and French colonies a modicum of training in self-government was available to a small minority.

New African leadership.   In spite of their limited opportunities, the creation of a small nucleus of African intellectuals was the most significant consequence of colonial acculturation. Educational opportunities were generally meager. The great mass of Africans never attended school, and only an infinitesimal fraction was able to secure the equivalent of a high school education. But a few ambitious and competent young men, such as Kenyatta, Senghor, and Nkrumah, did manage and then continued advanced studies abroad, mainly in Britain, the United States, and France. It was largely from their ranks that the future leaders of independent Africa were recruited. Both Nkrumah from Ghana and Dr. Benjamin Azikiwe from Nigeria, for example, studied at American universities and were later prominent in the new Africa. Their educational advantages gave them a renewed confidence in the destiny of Africa and a burning desire to have a part in ending colonial control. Thus, ironically, imperialism provided the essential dynamic for its eventual overthrow.

Segregation in the Union of South Africa.   The most explosive area in the period between the First and Second World Wars was the Union of South Africa. As we saw in Chapter 19 the British defeated the Boer settlers and in 1909 joined the Transvaal, the Orange Free State, the Cape Colony, and Natal to form the Union of South Africa, which became a self-governing dominion in the British Commonwealth. But union did not bring cooperation between the Boers and their former enemies, the British. The Boers obtained official recognition for their language, Afrikaans (developed mainly from seventeenth-century Dutch); they insisted on their own flag and national anthem; and they talked about secession from the Commonwealth.

While the rift between Briton and Boer was serious, more dangerous yet was the increasing gap between the whites and the blacks. In the Union the discontent of the African was the deepest, the confusing process of detribalization the most widespread. Numerically the Africans way outnumbered the whites, and after World War I the Europeans began to eye the statistics nervously. The figures disclosed that there were 5,500,000 pure Africans in the Union and 1,800,000 whites, just under 50 percent of them of British stock. In addition there were 200,000 Asiatics and 600,000 "coloured." Fearful of being overwhelmed by sheer numbers, many whites became convinced that the natives had to be kept separate from the European community socially and politically and that all political control must remain in the hands of the Europeans.

Segregation and the color bar spread rapidly in the 1930's; and a policy of racial discrimination, called *apartheid*, came into being. Africans were required to live on their tribal reserves. Only those who obtained special permission could work on farms owned by Europeans or in the cities; and in urban areas they were obliged to live in squalid, segregated "locations" and had to carry passes and identity cards under penalty of arrest and fine or imprisonment if found without them. Native labor unions were discouraged and strikes forbidden. In addition, governmental regulations or the white labor unions excluded Africans from certain skilled trades. Because of the enormous supply of unskilled native laborers, who would work for miserably low wages, uneducated Europeans—the "poor whites"—found it difficult to make a living. To favor this group, laws were passed earmarking certain jobs on the railroads and in city services for Europeans; wages for these jobs were raised, and the cost was paid by special subsidies. The practice was most discriminatory; the average wage for Europeans was just under four dollars a day, while that of the Africans was just over three dollars a week. In addition to the color bar in industry, the African was effectively barred from politics: he could not vote or hold office in any influential elective body or parliament outside his own tribal reserve. African unrest was manifested in the increasing crime rate in the cities, in the formation of underground organizations, and in the determined efforts to secure political rights.

Although the ferment of change and unrest began to be detected in other parts of Africa, only in the Union were nationalist aspirations widespread. The unappeasable upsurge of nationalism was to wait until after World War II.

TENSIONS IN THE ARAB WORLD

The Arab revolt. Just before the outbreak of the First World War, the Arabs within the Ottoman empire had reached the breaking point in their relations with the Turkish government. In 1913 an Arab Congress meeting in Paris demanded home rule and equality with the Turks in the empire. Because the Middle East was strategically important to Britain, the British government followed the rise of Arab discontent with great interest. During 1915 extensive correspondence was carried on between the British high commissioner in Cairo and Sherif Husein, guardian of the holy places in the Hejaz. In the event of an Arab revolt, Great Britain would recognize Arab independence except in those regions of coastal Syria which were not wholly Arab—presumably excluding Palestine—and in those which might be claimed by France. But British commitments were purposely vague, and the whole correspondence has been described as a "monument of ambiguity." In addition to the British alliance with the Arab nationalist movement, the indomitable desert warrior Abdul-Aziz ibn-Saud

(1880-1953), sultan of Nejd in south-central Arabia, was induced to adopt a policy of benevolent neutrality toward Britain. The wooing of the Arabs thwarted the Turkish attempt to rouse the whole Muslim Middle East by preaching a *jihad*, or holy war, against the British.

Late in 1916 the Arab revolt began. Husein raised the standard of rebellion in the Hejaz, proclaimed independence from the Turks, and captured Mecca for his cause. In the fighting that followed, the Arab forces were commanded by the third son of the Sherif Husein, Emir Faisal (1885-1933), who was assisted by a remarkable English officer, Colonel T. E. Lawrence, later known as Lawrence of Arabia. Under his command the Arabs took a decisive part in the last battle against the main Turkish forces in September 1918.

When the war ended, Syria was occupied by the victorious Allied forces; a small French force was located along the coast of Lebanon; Emir Faisal and his Arab forces were in the interior, grouped around Damascus; and the British controlled Palestine.

The Balfour Declaration. The most important pronouncement bearing upon the postwar history of the Middle East was Britain's declaration to the Jewish Zionist organization in 1917. Jewish aspirations to create a national home in Palestine had been rapidly growing after 1900. During the course of World War I, the British government—strongly influenced by Balfour, then foreign secretary—became convinced that its support of a Zionist program in Palestine would not only be a humanitarian gesture but would also serve British imperial interests in the Middle East. Thus in November 1917 Britain issued the Balfour Declaration which stated:

> His Majesty's Government view with favour the establishment in Palestine of a national home for the Jewish people, and will use their best endeavors to facilitate the achievement of this object, it being clearly understood that nothing shall be done which may prejudice the civil and religious rights of existing non-Jewish communities in Palestine. . . .

Zionists were disappointed that the Declaration did not unequivocally state that Palestine should be *the* national home for the Jewish people. In 1918 Great Britain made several declarations recognizing Arab national aspirations, and an Anglo-French pronouncement pledged the establishment of national governments "deriving their authority from the initiative and free choice of the indigenous populations."

The Middle East settlement after World War I. With Turkey defeated, the Arab leaders sought the independence they thought Britain had promised in the correspondence with Husein. At the Paris Peace Conference Emir Faisal, aided by Lawrence, pleaded the cause of Arab independence, but in vain. It became painfully clear that the problem of political settlement in the Middle East was a jumble of conflicting promises and rivalries. During the war years a number of important commitments had been made, starting with the British pledge in 1915 to Sherif Husein. In 1916, in the Sykes-Picot Agreement, Syria and Iraq had been divided into four zones, with Britain and France each controlling two. Palestine was to be placed under an international administration.

While the statesmen in Paris argued, a congress of Syrian leaders met in March 1920 and resolved that Faisal should be king of a united Syria, including Palestine and Lebanon. But in April the San Remo Conference of the Allied powers turned over all Arab territories formerly in the Ottoman empire to be administered as mandates. Syria and Lebanon were mandated to France; Iraq and Palestine, to Great Britain. To the Arabs the mandates were a poor substitute for independence and a flimsy disguise for imperialism.

From the Arabs' point of view, the peace settlement in the Middle East was a shabby piece of statesmanship compounded of ignorance, deception, and conflicting aims. Apologists for Britain and France point out that Britain made promises to France during the war because the British could hardly deny the requests of their most important ally, which had close missionary and educational ties in Syria. In 1916 Britain made its ambiguous pledge to Husein because of its desperate need for Arab friendship. Again, in the Balfour Declaration, Britain acted according to short-range interests; in order to swing the support of the world's Jews to the Allied cause and to maintain communications in the Middle East, Britain promised to open the Arab region of Palestine to Jewish settlement. It should be kept in mind that British statesmen sincerely believed that a Jewish national home could be reconciled with Arab interests; they had no idea of the massive influx of Jewish immigrants during the 1930's. The plain fact remains, however, that the Allied statesmen at Paris were profoundly ignorant of the intensity of Arab nationalism.

The French and British mandates. In 1920, following the San Remo Conference, a French army moved against Damascus and ejected Faisal from the throne. After this incident, France took over the mandate of Lebanon and Syria. Following a policy of divide and rule, the French attempted especially to woo the large Christian Arab groups in Lebanon. But they were not successful; the Arabs remained hostile. Strikes, demonstrations, and revolts were not uncommon.

Great Britain's vital interest in the mandate of Iraq was prompted largely by Iraq's rich oil resources, its growing importance in East-West air transportation, and its proximity to the Persian Gulf. But this interest did not prevent the British from taking steps to satisfy Iraqi nationalism after the outbreak of rebellion in June 1920. An Anglo-Iraqi treaty signed in June 1930 granted Iraq full independence, and in 1932 Iraq was admitted to the League of Nations. By these concessions Britain avoided the conflict that France experienced in Syria-Lebanon.

Arab-Jewish conflict in Palestine. Between the two world wars, Palestine was the most tempestuous area in all the Middle East, as Britain sought to protect its imperial interests and at the same time reconcile them with Zionism and Arab nationalism. Almost as soon as the mandate was set up, Arab riots broke out in Palestine. In 1919 the population was given at 700,000, with 568,000 Arabs, 58,000 Jews, and 74,000 others, mainly Christians. Realizing the apprehensions of the Arabs, the British sought to define the Balfour Declaration more precisely. While not repudiating Palestine as a national home for the Jews, the British government declared it "would never impose upon them [the Arabs] a policy which that people had reason to think was contrary to their religious, their political, and their economic interests."[1]

Such pronouncements and the fact that Jewish immigration was not large made possible a period of peace and progress from 1922 to 1929. As the Zionists reclaimed land, set up collective farms, harnessed the Jordan for power, and established many new factories, a veritable economic revolution took place.

Tel-Aviv grew into a thriving modern city, an excellent university was founded at Jerusalem, and Palestine became the center of a Hebrew renaissance.

The era of peace ended in 1929 when serious disorders broke out, mainly Arab attacks on Jews. Violence continued to erupt in the early 1930's as the Nazi persecution of the Jews brought about a steep rise in immigration to Palestine and threatened the Arabs' predominant position in the area.

Throughout the 1930's the "Palestine Question" was violently discussed in many parts of the world. Zionists argued that they had a historic right to the Holy Land, their original home, that Palestine had been promised to them in the Balfour Declaration and legalized by the League of Nations; that Jewish colonization constituted a democratic and progressive influence in the Middle East; and that Arab antipathy was mainly the work of a few wealthy effendis, since the mass of Arabs were profiting from the wealth being brought into Palestine. On the other hand, the Arabs argued that Palestine had been their country for more than a thousand years and declared that the Balfour Declaration did not bind them because they were not consulted in its formulation. They further insisted that much of Zionist economic development was not healthy because it depended upon subsidization of huge amounts by outside capital. Finally, they asked how could any people be expected to stand idly by and watch an alien immigrant group be transformed from a minority into a majority.

As war with the Axis powers loomed in 1939, Britain sought desperately to strengthen its position in the Middle East by attempts to regain Arab good will. A "white paper" was issued declaring that it was Britain's aim to have as an ally an independent Palestine established at the end of ten years, with guarantees for both the Arab and Jewish populations. During this ten-year period land sales were to be restricted. After the admission of 50,000 Jews, with the possibility of another 25,000 refugees from Nazi Germany, no more immigration would take place without the consent of the Arabs. The outbreak of World War II shelved the Zionist-Arab quarrel in Palestine; but after the war the controversy was to break out again with fatal virulence.

The problem of Egyptian sovereignty. While the Arabs in the mandates had been struggling for the right of self-determination, a parallel development was taking place in Egypt. When the British refused a delegation of Egyptian nationalists permission to attend the Paris Peace Conference and deported the spokesman of the group and his followers, the Nile valley rose in revolt.

After three years of disorder the government in London announced that Egypt was no longer a British protectorate. It was to be a sovereign state. Britain, however, was to remain responsible for the defense of the country, for the protection of foreign interests, and for communications vital to the British empire, above all the Suez Canal. Egypt grudgingly adapted itself to this declaration, made its sultan a king, and proclaimed a constitution in 1923. Anglo-Egyptian relations remained unsatisfactory, however, and frequent negotiations between the two governments were fruitless.

Respite in the long record of Anglo-Egyptian acrimony came about through the threat of Italian Fascist aggression in Africa following Mussolini's conquest of Abyssinia (see p. 454). In 1936 Britain and Egypt negotiated a treaty of alliance. In the case of war there was to be mutual assistance on a wide scale, and the status of the Sudan (theoretically under the dual sovereignty of Britain and Egypt but actually under British control) was to continue unaltered.

Aggressive nationalism in North Africa. Long before the outbreak of World War I, Algeria had become politically integrated with France; Tunisia had prospered under French rule and had maintained its native ruler, the bey; and the native sultan had also been retained in the protectorate France established in Morocco in 1911. Nevertheless, the storm signals of bitter nationalism had appeared, particularly in Morocco.

France deserves much credit for its colonial rule. Administration on the whole was just and efficient, the economy prospered, and living standards advanced. Nevertheless, a fundamental split existed, especially in Algeria, between the privileged Christian minority and the overwhelming Muslim majority.

Mustafa Kemal's rise to power in Turkey. At the turn of the century the decaying Ottoman Empire was a disreputable, vicious Oriental despotism. The sultan, Abdul-Hamid II, who could rule only with the aid of 40,000 spies, was overthrown in 1909 by a reform group called the Young Turks. But they in turn made themselves unpopular with their Arab subjects by their policies of Turkish supremacy and by their refusal to grant home rule. Defeat in World War I, the revolt of the Arabs, and the impotence of the sultan's government convinced some patriots that only the most drastic measures could save the Turkish nation. In addition, they were embittered by the harsh terms of the Treaty of Sevres (1920). It was bad enough to lose their empire, peopled by Arabs, but it was much worse to see their homeland, mainly Anatolia and the city of Smyrna, partitioned and invaded by the Greeks and Italians.

Imbued with a new spirit of nationalism, the patriots rallied around the military hero, Mustafa Kemal Pasha (1880-1938). An important figure in the Young Turks movement, Kemal was a born leader, thoroughly western in education and outlook. After the defeat of Turkey, he had been sent by the sultan to demobilize the Turkish troops in Asia Minor, but, disregarding his instructions, he had reorganized the troops and successfully defied the Allies.

A new government was set up in Ankara, and Kemal was selected as president and commander in chief. In 1921 Greek designs on Turkish territory were defeated by Kemal's armies. And in the following year the sultanate was abolished, followed by the establishment of a republic. The Allies agreed to a revision of Sèvres, and the Treaty of Lausanne, signed in 1923, returned to Turkey some Aegean islands and territory adjoining Constantinople. The heartland of Turkey—Anatolia—remained intact, and no reparations were demanded.

The new constitution was democratic in form, but in reality Kemal was a dictator who brooked no interference with his plans. His dictatorship does not belong in the same category as those fashioned in Nazi Germany, or Fascist Italy, or Communist Russia, however. In the new Turkey there was little of the cult of the superior race; the brutal efficiency of the purge and the concentration camp was practically unknown. Dictatorship was regarded as the rough but essential highway to parliamentary government. Kemal envisioned a dictatorship as a necessary stage in raising his people to that level of education and social well-being which democratic government requires.

Under his rule the old institutions and customs of a backward oriental state were transformed or replaced within a few short years. The caliphate, the sultan's spiritual leadership of the Muslim world, was abolished. The courts of the Greek Orthodox Church were discontinued, and new law codes were promulgated. Education was taken out of the hands of the Orthodox Church, and school attendance was made compulsory to the age of sixteen. Use of the fez by men and the veil by women was forbidden. Polygamy was prohibited. In addition, the western Gregorian calendar and European numerals were introduced, and the Latin alphabet replaced the Arabic. Thus, Turkey was rejuvenated by its indefatigable leader, who created a new capital at Ankara.

INDIA SEEKS TO RULE ITSELF

Gandhi's pressure for independence.　Many observers had predicted that in the event of war Great Britain would find India a serious liability. But when hostilities began, nearly all unfriendly acts against Britain ceased. By 1917, however, it became apparent that the Indian people expected compensation in the way of more self-government. Parliament's reply indicated that the goal to be attained in India was the gradual development of self-government within the British empire. In 1919 a measure of self-government was granted but Indian nationalism was not appeased.

The foremost nationalist leader in India was Mohandas K. Gandhi (1869-1948). Born of middle-class parents, Gandhi had been sent to London to study law; later he went to South Africa, where he built up a lucrative practice. During these years his standard of values changed completely. The new Gandhi repudiated wealth, practiced ascetic self-denial, condemned violence, and believed firmly that true happiness could be achieved only by service to one's fellow men.

Gandhi began his career as reformer and champion of his people in South Africa. The Indians there were subject to numerous restrictive laws which hampered their freedom of movement, prevented them from buying property, and imposed upon them special taxation. By the use of passive resistance, or noncooperation, Gandhi forced the government to remove some restrictions.

When he returned to his native land shortly after the outbreak of World War I, Gandhi was welcomed as a hero. During the war he cooperated with the British government, but disappointing concessions in the new constitution led him to announce his determination to force the British to give India self-rule.

In 1919 Gandhi introduced his campaign. A mass strike was declared in which all work was to cease and the population was to pray and fast. Contrary to Gandhi's plan, however, riots took place, Europeans were killed, and soldiers were sent to try to restore order. Although public gatherings were forbidden, a large body of unarmed Indians assembled at Amritsar. They were dispersed by gunfire, and several hundred were killed. All hope of cooperation between Indian and Briton was temporarily at an end. Arrested in 1922, Gandhi seemed to welcome being placed on trial; he assured the British magistrate that the only alternative to permitting him to continue his opposition was to imprison him. Sentenced to six years' imprisonment, Gandhi suffered a temporary eclipse.

There was little peace in India in the 1920's. During 1928 and 1929 a group of political experts from Great Britain, the Simon Commission, toured the country. The survey issued by the commission in 1930 suggested only a cautious advance in the direction of self-government. Meanwhile Gandhi initiated another campaign toward that goal.

British reform gestures.   A promising road to conciliation opened in 1930, when a series of round-table conferences was arranged in London. A new scheme of government was hammered out, providing for a federal union which would bring the British provinces and the states of the princes into a central government. In the provinces the existing system of semi–home rule was displaced by full autonomy, while in the federal government all powers were transferred to the Indians except defense and foreign affairs, which remained in the control of the British viceroy. From 1937, when this new Government of India Act came into operation, to 1939 the scheme of self-government worked smoothly. The possibility of federation, however, faded away as the native princes refused to enter the central government.

The Indian National Congress.   The new system of government failed to satisfy the demands of the Indian nationalists, who continued to espouse the cause of complete independence for India. The chief element in the nationalist movement was the powerful Indian National Congress, which had become the organ of the militant nationalists. Membership, estimated at several million, was predominantly Hindu but also included many Muslims and members of other religious groups. Soon after the First World War, the Congress had come under the leadership of

The great leader of the Indian independence movement was Gandhi. He is shown here just after he arrived in England in 1931 to attend a round-table conference on the future of India.

Gandhi, whose personal following among the people was the chief source of the party's tremendous influence.

In the 1930's Gandhi came to share his leadership with Jawaharlal Nehru (1889-1964), who came from a Brahmin family of ancient lineage. In his early youth Jawaharlal had all the advantages of wealth: English tutors, enrollment in the English public school of Harrow and later in Trinity College, Cambridge, where he obtained his B.A. in 1910 and was admitted to the bar in 1912. Upon his return to India, Nehru showed little interest in the law and gradually became completely absorbed in his country's fight for freedom.

A devoted friend and indeed a disciple of Gandhi, Nehru could not agree with the older leader's asceticism, mysticism, and his antagonism against western industrialism. At heart Nehru was a rationalist, an agnostic, an ardent believer in science, and a foe of all supernaturalism. Above all he was a blend of the cultures of both East and West, with perhaps the latter predominating. As he himself said: "I have become a queer mixture of the East and the West, out of place everywhere, at home nowhere. Perhaps my thoughts and approach to life are more akin to what is called Western than Eastern, but India calls to me."[2]

The Hindu-Muslim clash. India is a classic example of a plural society. The division in India was between the Hindus and Muslims and was known as the "communal problem." As Britain's imperial control over India began to show signs of ending, hostility between the two communities quickened. They were poles apart in culture and values. In a word, Islam and Hinduism represented a fundamental antithesis in nearly all facets of life. Many Muslims believed that in the event of independence they would be relegated to an ineffectual minority; in this sense the rivalry was a struggle for political power.

During the 1920's differences between Muslim and Hindu progressively developed. In the early 1930's the Muslim League, a political party, began to challenge the claim of the Indian National Congress to represent all of India. Its leader, Muhammad Ali Jinnah (1876-1948), originally a member of Congress and once dubbed by Indian nationalists as the "ambassador of Hindu-Muslim unity," had become alienated by what he considered the Hindu domination of Congress and its claim to be the sole agent of Indian nationalism. The Muslim League began to advance the "two-nation" theory, and in 1933 a group of Muslim students at Cambridge University circulated a pamphlet calling for the establishment of a new state to be known as Pakistan. This leaflet was a portent of momentous developments. In the fall of 1939 the Muslim League emphatically denounced any scheme of self-government that would mean majority Hindu rule.

NATIONALISM IN SOUTHEAST ASIA

Roots of decolonization. Southeast Asia underwent dramatic changes between World Wars I and II. Inspired by the Wilsonian ideal of "self-determination of peoples" or by the social revolutionary ideals of European socialism and the Russian Revolution, or by a combination of both, more and more Southeast Asian political, intellectual, and business leaders joined the anti-imperialist struggle, promoted national self-consciousness, and sought by one means or another the path to independence. The rise of Japan to the status of a world power indicated to

Southeast Asian elites that the West was not alone in its ability to master technology and politics for purposes of national renewal. Furthermore, the spectacle of westerners barbarously slaughtering westerners in World War I gave birth to grave doubts concerning the validity of the West's claim of being a civilizing agent. The imperialist powers continued to exploit their colonial possessions, apparently oblivious of the political ideals they had subscribed to during the First World War.

Throughout the area the elite became more assimilated into European culture as increasing numbers of young people went to the "mother countries" for education. The masses were hardly touched by this process, however, and the result was an increasing cultural and social dichotomy between the indigenous leadership and the people at large. With the exception of the United States in the Philippines and Great Britain in Burma and Ceylon, moreover, none of the imperialist powers undertook to prepare their colonies for self-government, as they had no intention of relinquishing them.

The Philippines. The United States established civil government in the newly won Far Eastern possession on July 4, 1901, under William H. Taft. President McKinley declared that the primary American aim was to prepare the Filipinos for self-government. The first elections were held in 1907, and by 1913 Filipinos dominated both houses of the island legislature, while an American remained as governor-general or chief executive. By 1935, when the Philippine Commonwealth was inaugurated with a new constitution and the promise of independence in ten years, the islands had developed a complex political structure and a sophisticated political life.

Economic developments, however, decreased Philippine independence at the same time that the islands were being prepared for political independence. Before the outbreak of World War II, four fifths of the Philippine exports went to the United States, and three fifths of its imports were American. Like most underdeveloped economies, the export trade was dominated by a very few products: hemp, sugar, coconuts, and tobacco. Independence, with its accompanying imposition of tariffs, would be economically difficult. Socially, the United States had prevented the development of a colonial-type plantation economy by forbidding non-Filipinos to own plantation lands. But native landlordism was rampant, and agrarian discontent manifested itself in brief uprising in the mid-thirties.

The Dutch East Indies. The growth of Indonesian self-consciousness and nationalism was paradoxically facilitated in the interwar period by the spread and increasing efficiency of Dutch rule. Stretched over 3100 miles of water, the numerous islands of Indonesia were integrated into political and communications systems by the Dutch. At the same time, the stringent limits put on the power and advancement of native elites led to bitterness and resentment. The colonial administration banned all discussions of any subject that might involve the concept of national independence. Even the name Indonesia was banned from official publications.

Burma and Malaya. India was the model for the development of Burmese nationalism and agitation for independence. British promises to promote Indian self-government created a similar demand in Burma; in 1937 Burma was administratively split off from India, and a parliamentary system was inaugurated with a Burmese prime minister under a British governor who was responsible for foreign relations, defence, and finance. Malaya, in contrast to Burma, did not develop a strong nationalist movement. Perhaps the major reason for this was the existence of large ethnic groups that distrusted each other more than they felt the need to make common cause against the British.

Indochina. The story of the Indochinese, and particularly the Vietnamese, struggle for independence is far too complex to be related here in anything but the most general terms. In fact, it has not yet ended. French rule in Indochina was in some ways the least enlightened of all the colonial regimes in Southeast Asia. Four fifths of the population was illiterate, and with over 21,000,000 people only about 500,000 children received any education at all, with only a few thousand receiving any higher education. French rule was characterized by political oppression, severe economic exploitation, and a rigid and stagnant traditional culture.

Revolution alone seemed the answer to Vietnam's problems. During World War I over 100,000 Vietnamese laborers and soldiers were sent to France, where many of them came into contact with liberal and radical thinking, which they then brought home. The Vietnam Nationalist party, patterned organizationally and intellectually on the Chinese Kuomintang, was denied any legal existence and, by the late 1920's, resorted to terrorism as the only form of political expression open to it. Communism rapidly became the major revolutionary ideology in the French colony. In 1920 a young Vietnamese calling himself Nguyen Ai Quoc ("Nguyen, the Patriot"), and later known to the world as Ho Chi Minh, participated actively in the formation of the Communist party in France. In 1930 he organized in Hong Kong what eventually became the Vietnamese (later Indochinese) Communist party. The 1930's in Vietnam were characterized by the spread of Communist ideas and organization, Vietnamese uprisings against French oppression, and strong repressive measures by the colonial government. As a result, the Communist party entered World War II as the major vehicle for the expression of Vietnamese nationalism.

THE ECLIPSE OF EMPIRE

War's impact on imperialism. In 1945, European colonies, controlling more than one billion people, dotted the globe. Within the colonial powers there was a grudging realization that the days of Kipling and the domination by white men in Africa and Asia were drawing to a close. It was believed, however, that this liquidation would be a slow process. Actually it took just about two decades.

The war accelerated forces already in existence; in competition with these influences, imperialism could not endure. In areas once remote and untouched by modern change, westernized elites grew rapidly. The process of urbanization created professional and merchant classes imbued with western political ideology. The presence of European troops had a disturbing effect. It sometimes exposed the vices of the white man, and not infrequently some anticolonial European liberals made secret contact with native leaders. Allied propaganda, with its emphasis upon a better postwar world and the crusade for democracy, tended to encourage Afro-Asian peoples to expect a "new deal" following the war.

One of the most important anticolonial forces emanated from the United States. Various private organizations published programs for the postwar period, most of them calling for some reform or even abolition of the colonial system. Journals, such as *Life* and *Time*, continually attacked the idea of empire in the modern world. Influential figures in American life added their support to anticolonialism. Sumner Welles, American Undersecretary of State declared:

> Our victory must bring in its train the liberation of all peoples. The age of imperialism is ended. The right of a people to their freedom must be recognized. The principles of the Atlantic Charter must be guaranteed to the world as a whole—in all oceans and in all continents.[3]

In the colonies the claim of European invincibility had been swept away by the shattering victories of Japanese arms at Pearl Harbor, Hong Kong, Singapore, and in Burma. These conquests led to the startling growth of nationalist movements in Asia—especially in Indonesia, French Indochina, Malaya, and Burma. Japanese occupation authorities carefully nourished anti-European sentiment. In India the western thrust of Japanese armies toward Bengal had caused the British government to make substantial concessions to Indian nationalist leaders. In 1942 the famous Cripps' Mission offered India independence within or without the British Commonwealth following the war.

During World War II Africa remained generally tranquil. But the lessons of Allied defeats and echoes of anti-imperialism reached educated African circles. In 1942 an African students' organization in London presented the government with a memorandum asking for "Internal Self-Government Now, with a definite guarantee of complete self-government within five years after the war."[4]

New colonial policies.   The various colonial powers were sensitive both to the demands of nationalism in the colonies and to the censure of world opinion against imperialism. In England, especially, a tired and perhaps more realistic younger generation no longer had any heart for empire. In fact, the British Labour party, which came into power in 1945, had always been anti-imperialistic. Toward the end of the war, however, the Labour party, supported by strong public opinion, realized the problems that would inevitably emerge with colonial independence and shifted its ground somewhat. It announced a policy of gradual advances toward self-government in many of the colonies, notably those in Africa, in the form of a partnership with Britain, which would provide substantial financial and technical aid.

During the war France also formulated a new program for its colonies. In 1944 a significant conference held in French Equatorial Africa stated:

> The chief aim of the colonial policy of the new France will be to ensure the material and moral development of the natives . . . while respecting their culture and civilization and having them participate, within the framework of a French Federation, in the evolution of Metropolitan France.[5]

France envisaged eventual self-government for its colonies but, unlike the British idea of Commonwealth, within a political structure dominated by Paris.

Other powers similarly denied that immediate independence was their policy toward their colonies. Belgium claimed that self-government in the Congo was chimerical within the foreseeable future. Portugal denied that Angola and Mozambique were colonies, maintaining, as it still does, that they were integral units of the homeland. (Very few colonists, however, had the opportunity to become educated and "civilized.") The Netherlands announced that its empire would form a commonwealth, each part having "complete self-reliance and freedom of conduct."

The chronicle of decolonization. These new colonial policies, based generally on programs of partnership between the imperial powers and their colonies, came too late. Nationalism would not be denied. Too much had happened during the war to undermine the traditional relationship of imperial overlordship and colonial subordination. The rapidity with which empires disappeared constitutes one of the great historic happenings of modern times. Their passing ended some four hundred years of what might be called the European phase of world history.

For a decade after 1945 it seemed possible that the new colonial policies might succeed, that independence might be gradually achieved. One of the first indications that the whole edifice of imperialism would quickly collapse came in the late 1940's when Indonesian nationalists demanded a complete break with the Netherlands. An ugly war ensued, and finally, in 1949, through UN mediation, the Dutch East Indies became Indonesia—a new nation. Largely with the help of the same international body, Libya, a former Italian colony, was tendered its freedom in 1951. Meanwhile, keeping its prewar promises, the United States had granted the Philippines independence in 1946. In the same part of the world France became embroiled in a tragically costly war while trying to restore some semblance of its authority in Indochina (see p. 510).

While not renouncing its program of enlightened guidance for the colonies, Britain realized that an exception would have to be made in the case of India which, during the war, had been given an unequivocal pledge of independence after the conflict. In 1947 this huge dependency gained its complete freedom as two nations: India and Pakistan. The following year the same status was granted to Burma and Ceylon. In the Middle East, Britain recognized the independence of Jordan in 1946 and two years later terminated its mandate of Palestine, an action that led to the creation of the state of Israel and a bitter war between this new nation and the Arab world.

Notwithstanding these cracks in the colonial structure, the new colonial programs appeared relatively successful, particularly in Africa. Appearances were deceptive, however, and mounting unrest in the West African colony of the Gold Coast forced Britain to give this colony independence as Ghana in 1957. In this same year Malaya became a sovereign state as Malaysia. Singapore, Malaya's major city and almost entirely Chinese in population, eventually broke away from the federation to become an independent member of the Commonwealth. It was now evident that nothing short of complete sovereignty could satisfy colonial nationalists. While on a tour of British Africa, Prime Minister Harold Macmillan acknowledged this fact when he declared: The wind of change is blowing through this continent, and whether we like it or not this growth of national consciousness is a political fact, and our national policies must take account of it.[6]

Africans rightly think of 1960 as their year. Eighteen new nations emerged, the most important being Nigeria and the Congo. France had enacted various reforms seeking to keep its African territories as autonomous republics under the jurisdiction of the French-directed Community. (Guinea, however, had elected to become completely independent in 1958.) This ingenious compromise, however, could not satisfy African aspirations. In 1960, therefore, all thirteen African republics within the French Community proclaimed their independence. While the old assimilationist dream of a great French imperial structure had ended, France did retain a unique status in its former colonies. Its culture persists in what can be called French-speaking Africa; and the new republics rely upon France for financial and technical aid.

By 1970 forty-three sovereign states could be identified, where in 1945 there had been only four. And in other parts of the world, colonies had practically disappeared from the map, with the exception of a few small oddments such as Gibraltar, Hong Kong, and various French islands in the South Pacific.

While not so spectacular as the triumphs of freedom in Africa or in South Asia, independence was achieved by various islands in the British West Indies, notably Jamaica, Trinidad and Tobago, and Barbados. The South American mainland colony of British Guiana also gained the same status as Guyana.

In retrospect, the eclipse of empires was an amazingly peaceful phenomenon. The British left India with warm words from Prime Minister Nehru: "It is rare in history that such a parting takes place not only peacefully but also with goodwill."[7] There had been bloodshed in the Dutch East Indies, post-independence riots between Hindus and Muslims in India and Pakistan, a tribal uprising of the Mau Mau in Kenya, and tragic hostilities in the Congo. But considering the many territories and the millions of people involved, the transition from colonialism to statehood had been remarkably tranquil.

The aftermath of independence. Many colonial peoples believed that the attainment of independence would usher in a golden age characterized by economic plenty, smooth-functioning governments, and proud national unity and purpose. There was euphoric optimism about what the future was to be following the exit of alien imperialists. Unfortunately, these hopes proved to be illusory.

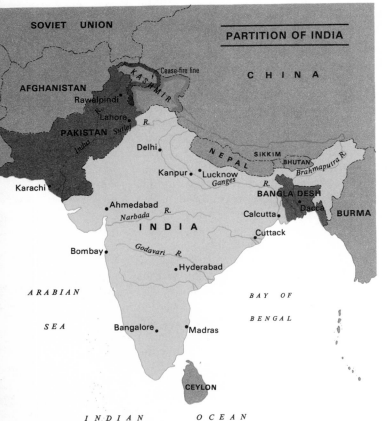

When Britain relinquished India in 1947, religious antagonism dictated the formation of two countries—Hindu India and Muslim Pakistan. In 1971 East Pakistan broke away to become a new nation, Bangla Desh.

Nearly all the new nations were confronted by serious problems, some challenging their very existence.

At the outset the new nations were confronted with the heavy costs of creating a diplomatic service as well as a military establishment. Economic and social development were urgently needed. In addition, there existed a psychological drive for national prestige symbols, leading, in some instances, to showy nonproductive facilities such as uneconomic air lines and costly government buildings and hotels. The initial imperative task was how to build and maintain national unity, how to weld disparate and sometimes antagonistic religious, cultural, and ethnic groups into one.

In many instances the new political entities in Africa and Asia are not the end result of a long historical process such as took place in medieval Europe, when small feudal principalities were hammered into homogeneous nation-states. Numerous Third World states never existed in their present dimensions and boundaries until they were created by the action of the imperial power that ruled them until independence. Nigeria, for example, encompasssing so many diverse and often hostile ethnic and tribal segments, was created by the force of British arms. It has been pointed out that the notoriously polyglot Hapsburg empire was more homogeneous than the present Congo or the Sudan.

The result has been serious regional problems often leading to conflict. When independence was achieved in India in 1947, the country split into two nations, Pakistan and India. In 1971 East Bengal seceded from Pakistan, creating a new nation Bangla Desh. Both Malaya and Indonesia have experienced traumatic racial problems and tribal rivalries have threatened the unity of a number of African nations. In addition the Third World countries initially formed democratic governments patterned after western models, but these—with the notable exception of India—have generally given way to military dictatorships or authoritarian one-party systems. Above all, the Third World nations have been endeavoring to raise the miserable living standards of their masses. In this struggle for economic development, foreign aid is a critical factor. During 1967 the underdeveloped nations received grants and loans totaling $12 billion. Ideally this aid should be even more massive, but it can only be a palliative unless political stability and governmental efficiency can be maintained together with a reduction in population pressures.

THE AFRO-ASIAN PRESENCE IN WORLD AFFAIRS

Into an uncertain world. Seeking to protect their newly found freedom, most of the new nations adopted a number of similar objectives. There was the universal desire to secure a voice in the councils of nations, especially the United Nations, and to have their sovereign status recognized. To support ambitious development projects, governments have sought loans and technical assistance, while at the same time attempting to avoid domination by the major industrialized nations. They are especially sensitive to the dangers of "neocolonialism," resulting from dependence upon imported military supplies and manufactured goods, upon trade patterns and commodity prices controlled by the developed countries, and upon outside sources of investment and ownership.

Closely tied in with fears of "neocolonialism" has been the determination of Third World nations to avoid involvement in superpower rivalry. Their diplomatic policy of nonalignment regarded the cold war as a frustrating facet of international affairs, obstructing the overriding task of consolidating fledgling regimes and their attack on economic backwardness, poverty, and disease. Confronted with similar hopes and fears, they have sought to cooperate with each other in various conferences and regional associations. These attempts have hardly fulfilled expectations. There has been little agreement on many important issues. The Arab League has been torn by dissension between socialist-republican regimes, such as Egypt, and traditionalist-monarchist states, such as Saudi Arabia. The Organization of African Unity has witnessed some gains in African cooperation, but its members have seemed primarily interested in pursuing their own national interests rather than those of continental significance.

Little else could be expected. After centuries of intense nationalism, western nations have only recently been moving towards regional interdependence in common markets, joint defence efforts, and monetary funds. It is unrealistic to expect the Third World nations, in little more than two decades, to proceed from colonial dependence to effective forms of international cooperation without first experiencing a substantial period of nationalism with its profound sense of cultural identity and political independence.

Afro-Asians in the United Nations. The most spectacular impact of the new nations has been in the United Nations, where they have been instrumental in transforming its membership and to some extent its tone and purpose. Initially with a roster of 51 members, the General Assembly had increased to 126 by 1970. The dominance of western members has decreased to 40 percent of the membership, with Afro-Asian states holding the balance of power. In 1961 about half the issues raised in the Assembly dealt with Africa; seldom has a UN bloc seized the limelight so quickly.

The overriding Afro-Asian preoccupation in the United Nations has been with anticolonialism and racial discrimination. While representatives of the Third World disagree on various issues, opposition to colonialism is an ideology they can all passionately support. Their constant pressure against the colonial powers, increasingly a minority in the Assembly, accelerated the rapid liquidation of colonies. Representatives of the new nations have also been vociferous in urging nuclear disarmament and supporting technical and economic assistance for underdeveloped areas.

Unfinished business in Africa. Meanwhile, southern Africa remains a potentially explosive area. The Zambesi has been called the frontier between black and white Africa. To the north lie the newly independent African states, but to the south are European-dominated Rhodesia, and white-ruled South Africa. Bordering these states are the Portuguese territories of Angola and Mozambique.

In the Union of South Africa the mounting strains are apparent in *apartheid*, the policy whereby the European minority has denied basic political and economic rights to the African majority. How long the white community could hold down the lid of this African boiler was problematical. It was felt that a new approach should be tried. The South African government inaugurated a program of territorial segregation. Eight distinct and partially self-governing African states known as Bantustans were planned, each to be aided by substantial economic grants. The first to be established was the Transkei, with a Bantu population of 3.5 million. This territory was given limited home rule in 1963. South Africa, however, still continued to depend upon a large African labor force domiciled and employed in European areas.

While revolt has been smoldering for several years in the Portuguese territories, the most acute situation has arisen in Rhodesia. In 1965 this British colony, controlled by a small white minority, declared its independence from Great Britain, which insisted that such action could not be countenanced without the prior grant of full political rights to the African majority. Despite a crippling trade embargo imposed by Britain and economic sanctions levied by the United Nations, Rhodesia refused to accept Britain's conditions, labeled as NIBMAR (no independence before majority rule).

If the European regime is ended in Rhodesia, Portuguese holdings would then likely succumb to the same pressure. White South Africa believes it would then be the ultimate objective. Rhodesia is thus regarded as a kind of bastion against black nationalism, and South African troops have actively joined local forces in seek-and-destroy missions against the guerrillas. In the fall of 1968 the British and Rhodesian prime ministers held a conference seeking some compromise solution perhaps on a promise of "unimpeded progress toward majority rule." No settlement was reached, however, and in the spring of 1970 the final ties with Britain were severed when Rhodesia assumed the status of a republic. In the following year, Britain worked out a new plan for reconciliation with Rhodesia. It called for new legal rights for Africans, some economic gains, and a slow advance toward black political power. This settlement, however, was overwhelmingly rejected by the African majority which numbers 5.2 million as compared with 250,000 Europeans.

Southern Africa will remain a troubled area in the forseeable future. It will pose difficult decisions for the West, especially for Britain and the United States, whose concern involves not only the stability of the area, access to important raw materials such as gold and chrome, but also South Africa's strategic importance now that the Suez Canal has been closed.

BIG-POWER INTRUSION IN THE THIRD WORLD

New nations' impact on world politics.   The emergence of some fifty new Third World nations inevitably has had a pervasive impact on the world community. Internal conflicts, political instability, and dependence on outside sources for aid have invited major power influence in the affairs of the emerging nations. The great powers in the West, as well as Russia and Communist China, have vied with each other in the Third World in obtaining access to raw materials and markets, in extending their influence by providing military aid, loans, and technical assistance. This is not to deny completely the element of some altruism in the policies of the major powers vis-a-vis the Third World. But given the competitive nature of great power relations it is not surprising that national interest should play a decisive role in international affairs. During his first state visit to independent Africa, Chou En-lai, premier of Communist China, announced that the "area was ripe for revolution." Several African states have complained of Chinese support of plots to overthrow their governments. In the Nigerian civil war over the secession of Biafra, both Russia and Britain supplied the central government with arms, while

France responded in kind for Biafra. All three powers were interested in strengthening their political and economic influence in Nigeria.

Big-power rivalry and intervention was also illustrated in the Congo following its independence from Belgium in 1960. The immediate aftermath was widespread chaos. This problem was referred to the United Nations, mainly on the initiative of the United States. The Soviet Union, however, sought to act independently by trying to circumvent the UN operation in the Congo. In effect this effort constituted a major cold war crisis. Supported by the great majority of its members, however, the United Nations successfully insulated the problem from big-power intervention.

Major-power rivalries have also been a factor in Indo-Pakistan relations. During the 1950's the United States supplied massive arms to Pakistan as a counterpose to potential Russian expansion. Such aid from any source was denounced and obdurately refused by India's prime minister, Nehru, who supported the neutralist policy of nonalignment. Following the Chinese invasion of north India in 1962, however, Nehru's government eagerly accepted American military aid. Simultaneously, Russia, increasingly disenchanted and fearful of China's growing power and mounting enmity, also sent arms to India. Nonalignment had obviously become bi-alignment. In 1963 Pakistan, miffed over American arms sent to India, modified its diplomatic posture as a strong partner of the West by turning to Communist China for a new friend and ally.

Bangla Desh born in revolt. This case study of major-power diplomacy in the Third World became increasingly complex when in 1971 Pakistan was confronted by a separatist movement in East Bengal. This eastern wing of Pakistan claimed, with much justification, that it was being economically exploited and denigrated by the central government in West Pakistan. In response the latter initiated a senseless campaign of brutality aimed at suppressing the revolt. Thousands of civilians were killed and literally millions of terrified refugees fled across the border into India. Saddled with the enormous expense of caring for the refugees, India prepared for a showdown with her traditional rival and foe, Pakistan. In August 1971 a strong ally for India and East Bengal was secured when a treaty of friendship and cooperation was signed with Soviet Russia. At the same time thousands of guerillas were given arms and trained in India. War broke out when Indian forces invaded East Bengal as an "army of liberation" and fighting ceased two weeks later with the surrender of an entire Pakistan army. With India's blessing, East Bengal became a new nation, Bangla Desh.

During these tragic events the United States, while remaining officially neutral, assumed a pro-Pakistan stance declaring that India was "the main aggressor." A factor in this diplomatic ploy was President Nixon's forthcoming trip to Peking and the hope of securing a détente with mainland China. Apparently the American administration did not wish to jeopardize this diplomatic gesture by exhibiting an unfriendly posture toward China's ally. At the same time by favoring Pakistan the United States hoped to block the consolidation of Soviet influence in India. In any event it was manifest that major-power rivalry could easily become part of the tensions of the Third World. And in this case study, whatever benefits may ultimately be derived by the United States in its relations with China, there could be no question that at the present time Russia had emerged as the winner in big-power rivalry compared to the United States and mainland China.

The Middle East: after a third round. Another area where the West, especially the United States, has been dangerously involved in the conflicts of the Third

World is in the Middle East. During the mid-1960's world peace was ominously threatened by the Arab-Israeli conflict. In 1948 and again in 1956 Israel and the Arab countries had gone to war over their respective claims, including Israel's right to survival and free access to the Suez Canal. Continuous Arab terrorist attacks along Israel's borders, Arab refusal to recognize the existence of the state of Israel, and the refusal of both nations to provide some meaningful solution to the problem of Arab refugees from the wars of 1948 and 1956 were constant threats to the status quo.

Throughout late 1966 and the first half of 1967 tension, never really below the surface, began to rise rapidly. Finally, the Arabs mobilized their troops, requested the withdrawal of the United Nations peace-keeping forces, and blockaded the Gulf of Aqaba. In this situation of rapidly increasing tension, war broke out on June 5. In seventy-two hours Israeli aircraft and tanks, with lightning speed,

All the horror of the Bangla Desh war for independence from Pakistan is graphic in this starving child, one of thousands who suffered a similar fate.

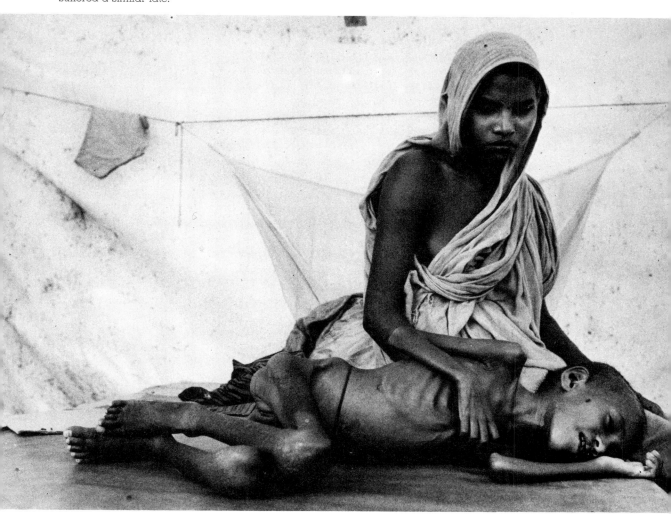

completely overwhelmed the combined Arab forces, and by the time a cease-fire was accepted on June 10, Israel occupied the entire Sinai peninsula, including the east bank of the Suez Canal, the whole west bank of the Jordan River, Old Jerusalem, and border areas inside Syria commanding tactically important heights. Nothing, however, had been settled by the conflict. For the moment Israel felt secure, but the Arab states refused to enter into any direct negotiations aimed at removing the causes of hostility.

The superpowers have been deeply involved in the course of events in the Middle East. This area not only has the world's largest reserves of oil but strategically is a land bridge connecting three continents. Until the summer of 1972 Russia was a major supplier of arms and technicians to the Arab states, especially Egypt. But in a surprise move President Sadat of Egypt ousted the Russians after their government had invested $3 billion in arms and provided 19,000 technicians and advisors to the Arab cause.

During 1971 President Sadat, Nasser's successor, repeatedly made threats of an Egyptian war to the death against Israel. At the same time the United States tried to engineer an interim agreement for reopening the Suez Canal and a token withdrawal of Israeli troops back from this waterway. The posture of both sides, however, remained inflexible. Egypt demanded the withdrawal of Israel from all occupied Arab territory before any treaty negotiations. Israel insisted on negotiations and settlement of secure, defensible boundaries before there could be any withdrawal from Arab territory. During this stalemate which continued into 1972, the United States continued to supply arms to Israel; and Arab guerillas carried on an intermittent campaign of terrorism. Israel, for its part, made retaliatory forays into Arab territory.

While big-power rivalry has exacerbated the situation, any solution to the problem depends on the Arabs and Israelis. The former have been deeply aroused by what they consider another alien and imperialistic intrusion into their midst, and they are reluctant to allow the humiliation of three defeats to remain unassuaged. On the other hand, the Israelis, after centuries of mistreatment of Jews in various lands and the recent memory of Hitler's unspeakable savagery, are determined to protect Israel. As one observer sees this confrontation:

> The essence of the tragedy is a struggle of right against right. Its catharsis is the cleansing pity of seeing how good men do evil despite themselves out of unavoidable circumstance and irresistible compulsion. When evil men do evil, their deeds belong to the realm of pathology. But when good men do evil, we confront the essence of human tragedy.[8]

WAR IN VIETNAM

The French war and the Geneva Conference. Following the end of hostilities in Indochina after World War II and the ejection of the Japanese forces, France sought to restore a semblance of its colonial authority. In 1946, however, it granted a measure of autonomy to Cambodia and Laos. The crucial problem was the status of Vietnam, where in 1945 a nationalist and pro-Communist movement led by Ho Chi Minh had established the independent Republic of Vietnam, usually referred to as the Vietminh regime. Negotiations led nowhere, and war broke out in December 1946. The struggle, at once anticolonial and ideological, lasted for nearly eight years and was characterized by cruel and violent tactics on both sides. The end came dramatically at Dien Bien Phu in 1954, when the French surrendered this massive stronghold along with 10,000 troops.

Later that year a conference was held at Geneva where agreements ended hostilities and established a truce line at the 17th parallel—the truce line being regarded as temporary, pending the holding of nationwide elections in July 1956 under international supervision. These elections were never held. Instead, a new political regime proclaimed the Republic of South Vietnam south of the truce line. Meanwhile, the split between the two geographical segments increased with the movement of refugees into South Vietnam and the progressive violation of the

A wounded child is carried from the battle area. After twenty years of protracted conflict, there is as yet little to show for the Vietnam War but a growing list of casualties and yet another generation of Vietnamese who know nothing of peace.

Geneva agreements by the introduction of military personnel and materials by the Communists on one hand and South Vietnam's allies on the other.

Washington had refused to sign the Geneva agreements; instead, it sponsored the establishment of the Southeast Asia Treaty Organization (SEATO) to combat the further spread of communism into Cambodia, Laos, and South Vietnam. In particular it sought to create a South Vietnamese regime capable of holding its own against the Vietminh and their fellow communists in South Vietnam.

America's involvement grows. At first the United States actively supported the regime of Ngo Dinh Diem, who had rejected Ho Chi Minh's requests for holding elections because he feared that the Saigon government would lose out to the Hanoi regime. Despite Washington's urgings, the Diem government refused to carry out comprehensive land reforms. Diem also suppressed opposition groups and dismantled the traditional village government system, substituting Saigon-appointed officials, most of whom were not even from the provinces whose villages they ruled. Meanwhile, thwarted in their aim to have North and South Vietnam united by elections, the Communists initiated guerrilla operations, thereby starting a Second Vietnamese War in 1957. In December 1960 the National Liberation Front (NLF), popularly known as the Viet Cong, was established in the south and thenceforth received support from Hanoi in its mounting operations. Diem, in the face of a growing crisis, became more autocratic and still less inclined to launch agrarian and other reforms. A coup and his assassination in 1963 did little to improve the situation as the NLF threatened to take over the entire country.

In 1960 there were only 800 American military advisers in the country; four years later this figure had risen to 23,000. In August 1964, North Vietnamese torpedo boats were accused of attacking United States destroyers in international waters in the Gulf of Tonkin. Following President Johnson's request, Congress adopted, by a Senate vote of 88-2 and a House vote of 416-0, a joint resolution which approved the taking of "all necessary measures . . . to prevent further aggression" and authorized the President, at his discretion, to assist South Vietnam in its defense—using armed force if required. Thereafter the war became increasingly Americanized, until by 1968 there were more than 500,000 American troops in the country. During these years the United States assumed a progressively larger share of the burden of actual combat and in 1965 initiated an intensive air war against North Vietnam. This air war failed to produce the desired results and became a subject of bitter controversy on the American domestic front.

The American dilemma in Vietnam. Washington's actions had been largely motivated by the "domino theory," which held that the fall of South Vietnam would only whet the communists' ambitions to take over much more of Southeast Asia and would trigger guerrilla explosions throughout the Third World. Whatever the motives, by the latter half of 1968 they had cost the United States more casualties than the Korean War and expenditures exceeding $100 billion. During the final months of President Johnson's administration, nonpartisan efforts were made to find an honorable solution to the conflict. All bombing of North Vietnam was ended, and peace talks between the interested parties commenced in Paris.

When he assumed office, President Nixon had an unmistakable mandate to end the conflict as speedily as national commitments permitted. In the summer of 1969 he initiated a policy of progressive withdrawal of American troops, coupled with Vietnamization of the fighting. This program saw no change in the enemy's hard line at Paris, which insisted that there could be no peace settlement or return of American war prisoners until Washington had withdrawn all its forces and ceased to support the South Vietnam government.

In the spring of 1972 North Vietnam launched a massive multi-pronged attack on key sectors of South Vietnam and scored substantial initial successes. When the situation looked critical for the Saigon regime, Mr. Nixon ordered the mining of all North Vietnamese ports and an unprecedented escalation of bombing to prevent the entry of war matériel into North Vietnam from its communist allies, and to blunt its attack in the south. The president coupled his decision with an offer to accept an internationally supervised truce throughout Vietnam and to withdraw all American forces within ninety days after the truce went into effect.

At the end of June 1972 evidence indicated that the American counterattack was in fact hurting the North Vietnamese war capability, but no one could be sure whether Hanoi was yet ready to negotiate an ending to the war. Meanwhile, Mr. Nixon remained committed to his Vietnamization policy and to reducing the number of American troops to 49,000. As of the summer of 1972 more than 500,000 men had been withdrawn, and all American ground forces had been removed. The United States, however, maintained in Southeast Asia substantial numbers of air and naval forces, the former mainly in Thailand. In the November 1972 elections both presidential candidates were committed to ending with all possible speed what was undoubtedly the most unpopular and divisive war in American history. Moreover, the aftermath was bound to be traumatic. "Peace when it comes may be no less bloody than the war, and our crisis of conscience will persist long after the last American soldier has left South Vietnam."[9]

CHAPTER 24

TOWARD A NEW
LIFE STYLE

Intellectual and Cultural Ferment
in the Twentieth Century

In one sense human history is a continuum. On any given day occur innumer-
able births and deaths throughout the world, each birth a quantum of new life that
merges into the pattern of the present like a thread woven into a tapestry or a dot
of light on a television screen. In this sense, there are no breaks in history but only
a gradual process of change in the planetary human pattern. And yet, if we are to
try to understand this changing pattern, we must look for points of reference to
which we can attach more than usual significance.

Bearing in mind that even during periods of massive innovation and rapid
change, everyday life often proceeds with little disturbance for great masses of
the population and that the effects of change may not become fully apparent for
many years, it is nevertheless obvious that our own century has witnessed
profound changes in the historical pattern. In particular, two global wars have
provided significant watersheds in the course of events. As a consequence, after
each holocaust men have acquired new perspectives in viewing both the world
which they inhabit and their own role and status as individuals. Those who grew
up after the First World War were bound to have a different outlook on life than
those whose values and attitudes had been shaped before 1914. Similarly, today
we are seeing the differences—and feeling the tensions—between those who grew
up in the interwar years and those whose life styles have been shaped by the
decades following World War I. Although these differences are commonly
referred to as "generation gaps," it should be recognized that they are not based
simply on the tensions that have always arisen between parents and their children
in the family unit. The divisions are more deeply rooted. Our century has spawned
different sets of values and life styles, and the resulting conflicts might be more
accurately described as "culture gaps."

The First World War brought to an end a century of relative stability in world
affairs. The previous hundred years had been characterized by an orderly if
mechanistic view of the universe, coupled with a general belief in man's ability to
master his environment. The prevailing mood was one of optimism that science
and representative government together would usher in a new age when, in

Tennyson's words, "the war drum throbbed no longer, and the battleflags were furled / In the Parliament of man, the Federation of the world." This comfortable assumption that progress was an almost inevitable process was shattered by a war intercontinental in its dimensions and unprecedented in its carnage. After 1918, politics, art, and social attitudes reflected widespread disillusionment with the old ways. A world-wide economic depression and a second global conflict even more destructive than its predecessor not only shaped the values of those who had grown up during this period but also bequeathed a legacy—including the atomic bomb—to the billions who have been born since 1945 in the greatest population explosion in history. The postwar years brought new possibilities for constructive and destructive purposes alike. Consequently, if this chapter places a special emphasis upon developments during the past quarter of a century, it is because these years have set the stage for the convulsions that are presently rocking contemporary society to its innermost foundations. And always the search goes on: for new values, new modes of expression, and new insights into the nature of man himself.

THE INTERWAR YEARS: 1919-1939

Science points the way. As we saw in Chapter 15, at the beginning of this century certain major scientific achievements occurred which were to lay the basis for a new interpretation of the universe. At this juncture we wish to recall certain of these developments because of their collective impact upon the course of thought for succeeding decades.

In 1900 Max Planck discovered new properties of atomic matter and the behavior of energy, thereby laying the basis of what is now called the quantum theory (see p. 312). Since he found that energy is transmitted in discontinuous "packages," or *quanta*, Planck strengthened the view that the atom itself was not a solid piece of matter but a unit of energy. Moreover, the quantum theory "indicates that precise location of small objects, such as electrons, is no longer possible, at least not by methods now at hand."[1] The physicist has to be content with mathematical probabilities; there is a factor of unpredictability in the phenomenal world. This aspect of quantum mechanics was further advanced by Werner Heisenberg with his "uncertainty principle" (1927); he showed that in atomic physics, while the behavior of groups of particles can be confidently predicted, no such prediction can be made for any one particle. This factor of indeterminacy has given rise to philosophical speculation beyond the bounds of physics. The universe seems to be governed by statistical regularities, yet it does not preclude elements of freedom of movement or choice for the individual.

The second revolutionary scientific development occurred in 1905 when Einstein published his Special Theory of Relativity which showed the interrelationships existing between mass, energy, and velocity (see p. 313). Of particular interest to us at this point, it represented a new way of thinking about the world of moving objects, involving the use of non-Euclidean geometry. While Newton's mechanics still continue to be of satisfactory use in everyday science and engineering, Einstein's more advanced concepts have completely reoriented men's attitudes toward the structure and mechanics of the universe. Moreover, as in the case of the quantum theory, these new concepts have had an important "spillover" effect. Not only was the Newtonian model of the cosmos, based upon *absolute* space, time, and gravitation, replaced by a relativistic space-time continuum, but henceforth other thinkers began to ask whether absolutes necessarily existed in their own disciplines. Consequently, religion, philosophy, morals, and ethics have been subjected to relativism. In addition, Einstein's conceptual approach helped shape our century's intellectual concern to search for "relationships," to stress "interdependence," and to analyze phenomena in terms of "systems."

Atomic structure and energy. The achievements of Planck and Einstein were especially important for atomic physics, probably the most revolutionary area of scientific development during the first half of this century. In 1897 Sir J. J. Thomson had disclosed that atoms contain particles carrying a negative electric charge—particles which he named electrons. In 1911 Ernest Rutherford discovered that the atom had a positively charged nucleus. His pupil, Niels Bohr, developed the theory that the atom is like a miniature solar system: most of the weight is concentrated in the nucleus around which the electrons revolve. Einstein's Special Theory suggested that the atomic nucleus must contain enormous energy, because mass and energy are convertible and the amount of energy is equal to the mass multiplied by the square of the velocity of light. (This means that one pound of coal, if converted entirely into energy, would release as much energy as the combustion of one and a third million tons of coal.) However, this knowledge seemed to promise no practical application because the atoms of radioactive elements, such as radium and uranium, disintegrated at their own speed, and scientists did not know how to speed up this process in order to release enough energy capable of being harnessed.

The interwar years changed the situation. In 1919 Rutherford succeeded in transmuting one element into another by bombarding its nucleus with positively charged particles, but to do so he had to use more energy than was thereby released. During the next two decades physicists constructed atom-smashing machines (such as the cyclotron and, later, the synchrotron) for bombarding the atomic nucleus. In 1932 the neutron in the nucleus was discovered, and this proved ideal for the purpose since it carried no electric charge and was not repulsed by the positive charge. Enrico Fermi and other physicists were now able to produce nuclear reactions; however, more energy still had to be expended than was thereby released from the bombarded nuclei. They realized that just as a fire can continue to burn only because the combustion of each portion of fuel raises adjoining portions to the temperature of combustion, so an atomic "chain reaction" was required to split atoms in such a way as to produce more neutrons, which might then hit other atoms and cause them in turn to split and emit neutrons—and so on in a continuous fashion. In January 1939, eight months before the outbreak of World War II, two German physicists found that the splitting of a uranium atom caused its nucleus to produce barium and also emit large amounts of energy. Subsequent studies in the United States and elsewhere confirmed that the neutrons released during such fission made a chain reaction possible. Thus was born the Atomic Age, with all its promise and peril implanted in the positively charged nucleus.

Biological advances. Meanwhile, by 1900 the experimental work upon heredity in plants as pioneered by Gregor Mendel (see p. 310) had been rediscovered, and its implications began to be vigorously pursued. As a result, the earlier concept that chance variations in the forms and processes of living creatures are alone responsible for evolution was supplanted by an understanding of ordered systems of genes and chromosomes. The life process itself was thus found to act in obedience to fundamental laws, and this conceptual breakthrough was dramatically corroborated by subsequent discoveries. Between World Wars I and II scientists isolated the enzyme (an organic catalyst, usually a protein, which controls a cell's chemical reactions) and discovered its relationship to genes. The next step was to find out the exact chemical nature of the gene itself, which proved to be composed of deoxyribonucleic acid, or DNA for short. Then, in 1953, James D. Watson and Francis H. C. Crick provided a model of the structure of the DNA molecule. It is built "like a spiral staircase" in a double helix—and is mathematically "programmed" so that "one molecule of DNA in a human cell contains as much information as several encyclopedia sets."[2] Since DNA is the fundamental genetic material, analysis of its structure is expected to provide us with far-reaching insights into the processes of heredity—and with knowledge capable of shaping mankind's future as a species. Consequently, biology and related disciplines may well become the most revolutionary area of scientific development during the second half of our century.

A new scientific world view. By 1940 the physical and biological sciences had largely restructured the fundamental bases of the phenomenal world. They pointed the way toward a unified concept of the structure and processes of the universe in which matter, energy, space, and time may be found to be different manifestations of a single, universal field. Scientific reasoning coupled with technology enabled men to reach new levels of understanding about atomic entities, the nonvisible but universally permeating force fields of gravitation and electromagnetism, and to construct meaningful models of both the macrocosmic universe and the microcosmic cell.

The significance of the new scientific world view would become progressively apparent in the postwar years as men realized how interrelated are all phenomenal systems, including man himself. He not only is part of a planetary ecology but possesses the intellectual capacity and tools to explore an extraterrestrial environment which is in turn regulated by laws that can be mathematically formulated and utilized. Thanks to quantum mechanics and the uncertainty principle, moreover, science has abandoned the clockwork determinism of previous centuries for a view of the universe that describes phenomena in terms of mass behavior, utilizing statistics and the laws of probability. In doing so, it has also recognized the subjective nature of human perception and understanding and has lent new credence to the argument that the evolutionary process remains open-ended.

The "Wasteland Era" in literature. Literature, no less than science, was transformed after 1919 by new techniques and subject matter. Until the First World War men of letters for the most part had contented themselves with themes and values familiar to the previous century. The majority continued to write as though theirs was the best of all possible worlds, because it was one in which "progress" seemed assured. This complacency was shattered by the holocaust of 1914-1918. The standards of western society, which had been guilty of the worst bloodbath in history, were inevitably challenged. The youths who had been promised that the war was to save the world for democracy emerged from the trenches bitterly disillusioned—as attested by the verse of Wilfred Owen and

Erich Maria Remarque's *All Quiet on the Western Front*, one of many novels inveighing against mass slaughter and the apparent futility of modern war.

The latest theories of physics and psychology were seized upon as starting points for literary vogues. Since according to the Relativity Theory nothing was "fixed" in the universe and the once "indivisible" atom could have its nucleus transformed, why should not all customs, laws, and moral standards be considered equally relative? Meanwhile, man's dignity as a rational being had been dealt a rude shock by the psychologists. The behaviorists pictured him as a set of conditioned reflexes, while the psychoanalysts explained his conduct in terms of emotional drives and subconscious urgings, not of reason and free will. Man now appeared as an irrational, puny bundle of viscera governed by forces outside his control, and whose society was a thinly veneered savagery.

The postwar social milieu did little to counteract such views. The 1920's in the United States have been described as an era of "tremendous trivia"—flagpole sitting, "red-hot mamas," speakeasies, Broadway tickertape parades for celebrities, the Charleston, and a national craze for speculating in stocks and Florida real estate. In parts of western Europe the era was marked by "tremendous"—but scarcely "trivial"—developments. In Italy, Mussolini and his Fascist followers had overthrown democratic government and instituted a totalitarian society, while in Germany, Hitler and his Nazi associates were bending every effort to destroy the Weimar Republic (see Chapter 21).

In 1922 the Anglo-American poet T. S. Eliot published *The Waste Land*, a long poem which expressed weariness with the ugliness and sterility of industrialized civilization. It began:

> April is the cruellest month, breeding
> Lilacs out of the dead land, mixing
> Memory and desire, stirring
> Dull roots with spring rain.
>
> . . . .
> What are the roots that clutch, what branches grow
> Out of this stony rubbish? Son of man,
> You cannot say, or guess, for you know only
> A heap of broken images, where the sun beats,
> And the dead tree gives no shelter, the cricket no relief,
> And the dry stone no sound of water.[3]

This work epitomized the atmosphere of skepticism and negation which largely pervaded the intellectual world in both England and the United States. Thus Aldous Huxley in verse, essays, and novels displayed a deep-seated skepticism regarding society's ability to act rationally, while Sinclair Lewis in a series of novels satirized the materialism and shallowness that he saw in much of American life during the twenties. In Germany, Oswald Spengler evinced a brooding pessimism in his massive historical work, *The Decline of the West*.

The era also saw the appearance of a number of psychological studies. For his part, the English novelist D. H. Lawrence emphasized the significance of the sexual drive. In the multivolumed *Remembrance of Things Past* the French writer Marcel Proust explored psychological time, human relationships, and his own perceptions and mental processes by means of the stream-of-consciousness technique. This influential work recognized no lasting significance in the external world; one's own consciousness alone remains real. Also employing stream-of-consciousness, the Irish-born James Joyce underscored the complexity and disorder of contemporary civilization in *Ulysses*, a report on the experiences of a group of people during a single day in Dublin.

Impact of the depression. In the 1930's, marked by the depression and the triumph of totalitarianism in Germany and Italy, literature reflected a new emphasis upon social problems and the plight of the individual. Europe produced a number of eloquent spokesmen in this field. The Hungarian-born Arthur Koestler, a one-time member of the Communist party who also fought in the Spanish Civil War, found himself increasingly disillusioned with the intellectual enslavement inherent in totalitarian ideologies and became a champion of political freedom, as his *Darkness at Noon* and other works attest. In France, André Malraux emphasized the heroic qualities which revolutionary struggle can arouse in men—a theme found in his novel *Man's Fate*—and in Italy, Ignazio Silone analyzed the problems of his poor compatriots with a mixture of compassion and democratic socialism.

One of the most trenchant critics of social injustice was the English writer George Orwell, who in the thirties directed his attack against capitalistic exploitation and subsequently against totalitarianism of both the right and left, as shown in *Animal Farm* (1945) as well as in his postwar novel *1984*. In the United States the poverty, ignorance, and decadence of some parts of the South were portrayed by William Faulkner, while the plight of the "Okies" who trekked to California in the depression in search of economic survival was recounted by John Steinbeck in his moving novel, *Grapes of Wrath*.

Developments in painting. As we saw in Chapter 15, the decades prior to World War I had witnessed both a reaction against academic painting and experimentation with new concepts and forms. Among the most prominent Expressionists were the Frenchman Matisse and the Russian Wassily Kandinsky (1866-1944), who by 1913 devoted his talents entirely to abstract art, allowing each viewer to derive his own interpretation and significance from the artist's arrangement of colors and form. Meanwhile, Cézanne's explorations in geometrizing nature had been further developed by the Cubists, notably Georges Braque (1882-1963) and Picasso. In their experiments with depicting an object from more than one vantage point, the Cubists were making use of concepts that were just becoming understood by science. Thus Braque's representation of a violin from several points of view, thereby emphasizing the concept of simultaneity, has been described as an esthetic counterpart to Einstein's Special Theory of Relativity, which appeared about the same time as the painting.

The interwar years saw Picasso modify his Cubist approach. One of his claims to permanent recognition, like that of the poet Eliot, lies in his continuous search after new standards and new forms of expression. He became the greatest artistic experimenter in an age full of experiments. Thus the 1920's found Picasso developing a neoclassical style, as seen in his "Woman in White," while in the following decade he painted his famous "Guernica"mural, vividly depicting the destruction of a small Spanish town by Fascist air forces in that country's civil war. Acknowledged a masterpiece, this painting combines artistic autonomy with a direct relationship to contemporary world events (see illustration, p. 520).

The Surrealists. Freud's emphasis upon the unconscious and irrational states of the human mind made a strong impact upon writers and artists alike. In the1920's there emerged in Europe the Surrealists, who saw the subconscious mind as the vehicle which could free man from the shackles of modern society and lead him to freedom. They felt an affinity with "primitive" art and its close associations with magical and mythological themes, and they exalted the irrational and violent in human experience. The Surrealists found much of their inspiration in the imagery of dreams, as illustrated so vividly in the paintings of one of the movement's most brilliant exponents, Salvador Dali.

Photography comes of age. The revolt against traditional ways of thinking could also be discerned in the photographic arts. Still photography and motion pictures, whose basic principles had been developed in the last century, became major vehicles of expression in the years following World War One. Photographers and film producers began to explore the unique qualities of their media, in pursuit of new and vivid ways of *seeing*. In photography the classic rules of composition which had guided painters were cast aside in a deliberate attempt to avoid sentimentality and flattery. The brilliant use of film editing by the Russian director Sergei Eisenstein helped point the way to motion pictures that were more than just recorded theater plays. Stylistically, the break with old values and the growth of a new social consciousness produced trends both to abstract expressionism and to documentary realism.

The documentary became an important way of arousing public opinion. True photoreportage began in the mid-twenties, by which time improved equipment and technical facilities had made it possible to catch fleeting expressions and movements under varying lighting conditions. As books and mass-circulation magazines replaced art exhibits in acting as galleries for talented photographers, they also helped spur a preoccupation with everyday people and situations.

Movies were also used for social commentary in many countries. The Russian film makers, who had been inspired to social consciousness by the revolution, were forced to curtail their experimentation and channel their social commentary to the demands of "socialist realism" under Stalin, who insisted that art be subordinated to the interests of the state. In Germany a greater perversion of the

Picasso's "Guernica," named for a city destroyed in the Spanish civil war, expresses not only the agony and brutality of that conflict but the horror of war itself. As shocking as a scream of pain, it is one of his most famous works.

The twentieth century saw the photographic arts attain not only popularity but full stature among the arts. Although early photographers used the traditional rules of painting as their standard, the realization that photography had a vitality of its own forced them to discover new modes of expression. Dorothea Lange, who helped stir public opinion during the depression era, was one of the leading proponents of photojournalism. Viewing her subjects unflinchingly, she was a master of photographic social commentary, as is evident in "White Angel Breadline."

cinema was accomplished under Hitler, as the power of film was harnessed to the purposes of Nazi propaganda.

Architecture and sculpture. In Chapter 15 we saw how Louis Sullivan helped revolutionize architectural concepts and techniques alike by his functional approach. In the interwar years functionalism developed into an internationally accepted style, with its most influential center located in Germany in the Bauhaus school, founded in 1918 by Walter Gropius. The center's teaching staff included architects such as Ludwig Mies van der Rohe (1886-1969) and artists Paul Klee (1879-1940) and Kandinsky. Teachers and students worked together in programs that aimed at joining artistic expression and industry in order to reconcile contemporary man with his technologically altered environment. From architecture to pottery, from typography to home furnishings, the Bauhaus design for living reflected its members' belief that art and function should be synthesized. After Hitler closed down the school in 1933, many of its prominent members fled to other countries to carry on their work and spread the Bauhaus philosophy. The period also produced other major architects espousing the functional approach. These included the Swiss-born Le Corbusier (1887-1965), whose creative employment of geometric forms has influenced architectural design not only in Europe and Brazil but later in India, where he designed Chandigarh, the new provincial capital of the Punjab.

In keeping with the functionalist approach, the interwar years saw architecture and sculpture being integrated in terms of larger environmental planning. Consequently sculpture ceased to be bound by the academic tradition of mere realistic depiction of the model, becoming instead more abstract, geometrical, and symbolic than heretofore. This fundamental change is seen clearly in the monumental figures of the British sculptor Henry Moore (1898-   ) which are largely abstract and show affinity with "primitive" forms.

Developments in music. During the interwar years Stravinsky and other composers continued to experiment in terms of polytonality, dissonant harmonies, and percussive rhythms. This period was also marked by a rediscovery of folk music, with the rhythms of Balkan folk songs finding their way into the music of the Hungarian composer Béla Bartók (1881-1945). The major development in popular music during the 1920's was jazz, an American form that originated with black musicians in New Orleans and which after the war spread over the continent. Radio and the phonograph helped popularize jazz and indeed became important media for propagating all kinds of music, both "classical" and "popular."

Growing out of a new technological culture which made new forms and new functions possible through the use of such materials as steel, concrete, and glass, contemporary architecture may eventually be remembered as the most revolutionary of the visual arts in the twentieth century. Massive sculptural grace enhances the entrance portico of the Assembly Building at Chandigarh, one of three major government buildings Le Corbusier designed for the new capital of the Punjab in India.

The temper of the times. The power discovered by physics in the atom had been unlocked under the pressure of war. The atomic bomb not only came to symbolize the strength of the postwar giants—the United States and the Soviet Union—but also brought home to men everywhere the precarious nature of existence upon this planet. Power realities found the United States and the Soviet Union dominating the global scene in a state of ideological, military, and geographical confrontation. The term "cold war" described this postwar state of international relations and also an attendant intellectual climate which tended to abort the ideals for which the "Grand Alliance" had fought and defeated the Axis.

As cold war tensions increased, anti-Communist feelings in the United States took on aspects of a crusade in the late 1940's and reached unexpected proportions. A widespread view that the government, labor unions, and universities were infested with Communists and their sympathizers was reinforced by the attacks of Senator Joseph McCarthy and his followers.

"The Silent Generation." The cold war spirit could not fail to make its impact upon the students of the fifties who, by the standards of the next decade, seemed to conform to the prevailing social philosophy. In the United States, for example, what dissatisfaction there was tended to manifest itself in cynicism and the kind of personal retreat typified in the writings of J. D. Salinger. The "cool" jazz of Dave Brubeck found much appeal among this generation of students, who became known as "The Silent Generation." Their basically apolitical attitude has been interpreted as reflecting a nation preponderantly intent upon personal interests and goals.

The most visible expression of dissent found form in the Beat movement, whose members believed that man's alienation from his world was the root cause of a contemporary social malaise. However, the Beats—or beatniks, as they were popularly known—lacked the direction or anger to be activists. Their subculture was artistic rather than political, their principal spokesmen being writers like the novelist Jack Kerouac and the poet Allen Ginsberg. Despite their retreat from involvement, the beatniks provided a refuge for alternative values and a portent of the more widespread rejection of the dominant value system which was to mark the next decade.

Affluence and the seeds of change. In many ways the fifties resembled the twenties, but with an added dash of paranoia to make up what they lacked in gaiety. In both decades the western nations were preoccupied with economic rebuilding and expansion, and their people with trying to return to the "good life" after the hardships of war. After World War II western Europe and North America were busy building the consumer society: automobiles, highways, supermarkets, television sets. Mass production brought new levels of economic prosperity but also raised new questions about the quality of life in industrial society. For many, suburbia came to symbolize conformity and homogenization of taste. On the other hand, many Americans today recall the "Eisenhower years" as an interlude of peace and prosperity between years of war and confusion.

Yet despite surface appearances, even the material affluence of the postwar West had become a vehicle for change. Mass prosperity was breaking up old status structures and enabling more people from all strata of society to pursue pastimes from stock-car racing to ballet. Television and universal education were giving children new horizons on the world. Young people could afford to buy records and attend concerts featuring new forms of popular music. One such innovation was rock and roll, a mixture of black rhythm-and-blues and white country-and-western music. Elvis Presley turned white youth on to the new sounds, thereby helping destroy the segregation in musical taste which had existed between the races.

Portents of change. Meanwhile, certain profound changes in American life were in the making. The Supreme Court's ruling in 1954 on school integration marked the beginning of the end of legal segregation in this country. A bus boycott in Montgomery, Alabama, brought to prominence a young Baptist minister named Martin Luther King, Jr. (1929-1968), and demonstrated the effectiveness of mass action as a tactic in the civil rights struggle. In 1956 C. Wright Mills published *The Power Elite*, a harsh analysis of contemporary American society which implied a pessimistic assessment of the prospects for democracy. In spite of the cold war atmosphere—the "better dead than Red" philosophy, the air-raid drills and shelters—a reaction was emerging in the latter years of the decade that set the stage for the widespread questioning of national priorities and the antimilitarism of the sixties.

In *The Affluent Society* (1958) John Kenneth Galbraith attacked the concept that production was the central economic problem of the times. He contended that the value system which emphasizes the ability of a society to produce invariably evaluates persons by the products they possess and artificially stimulates consumer demand. Galbraith questioned the kind of thinking that makes public expenditure for educational and other social needs seem an intrusion into the private accumulation of goods, and he called for a reassessment of society's goals. In the criticisms he raised, Galbraith anticipated the principal issues of the 1960's and 1970's, for it was above all the implications and assumptions of affluence that were to occupy the national spotlight in the succeeding years.

THE KNOWLEDGE AND CULTURE EXPLOSION: 1960's-1970's

A critical mass. The 1960's were something different. A decade that began with the Twist and "The New Frontier" in the United States ended with men on the moon and riots in the streets. In the process many governments, values, and whole cultures in various parts of the world were thrown into turmoil; none seemed to escape completely unscathed. It was as if all the fissionable elements of twentieth-century society had reached critical mass and exploded, bombarding the world with unexpected forces and mutant ideas. The sixties seemed to be dominated by the young—and their cultural and spiritual "mentors," such as the philosopher Herbert Marcuse, the psychoanalyst Erich Fromm, and the communications specialist Marshall McLuhan. Fashion, politics, and art felt the impact of the postwar baby boom. The excesses of the young horrified many of their elders.

The communications revolution. A transformation in communications has provided a new perspective of the world. Air travel and the automobile have given great masses of people unprecedented mobility. Whole nations have become economically interdependent as a result of technological advances and the multinational corporations. In such a world the values that were sustained by parochial uniqueness are rapidly disintegrating. Little wonder that children raised from birth in this new world often surprise their parents.

Marshall McLuhan, the much publicized Canadian prophet of the communications revolution, argues that there is an inherent relationship between technology and the way in which man perceives the world. Consequently the nature of any medium through which he is made aware of his environment becomes more important in determining the nature of that awareness than the content of the medium—hence the catchphrase "The medium is the message." According to McLuhan, the communications revolution occurring today signals a profound change in man's relation to his environment. The dominant western cultures which rose to prominence during the Renaissance, and which stressed specialized roles and the visual bias inherent in the printed word, are giving way to a world-wide "tribal echo chamber" that stresses empathy with the electronic environment and the interdependence of peoples. The transition from one type of culture to another is a time of great upheaval and pain as men strive desperately after roles that will enable them to regain a sense of identity. Whatever may be the merits of McLuhan's thesis—and they are hotly debated—his is an example of the self-analysis of an era that has been undergoing profound changes and trying to make sense of them.

"After affluence, what?" Economic security and the prolongation of the individual's education have enabled him as seldom before to examine himself and his society. In so doing, a substantial number among the young have accused modern industrial society of being deficient on two major counts. First, it has failed to distribute the economic product equitably among all sectors of the population. Second, it has failed to improve significantly the quality of life even in the midst of material abundance. Societal values which measure success in terms of material achievement no longer seem to provide meaningful direction for the life of the individual, and he feels alienated from the consumer society. It would appear that the traditional work ethic is losing much of its moral imperative in societies like that of the United States, which are being forced increasingly to concern themselves with leisure in its broadest sense, as the pursuit of quality replaces the pursuit of quantity. A corollary is the refusal of many to accept a life of postponed gratification in which the realization of dreams is subordinated to the necessity of functioning as a productive unit of the economy.

The counterculture. Instead, there developed what has been called a "counterculture." The individual is urged to develop his unique potential through an increased awareness of experiences afforded by the present. Imagination, spontaneity, and a heightened sense of feeling are stressed. Above all, the counterculture appeals for freer, more sensitive human relationships to replace a social structure which many think has alienated man both from his fellow man and from the world he inhabits.

The counterculture calls for a "new morality" whose fundamental tenets reject the concept of original sin. Instead, it sees human nature as basically good but thwarted by oppressive institutions. In its emphasis on liberating the human spirit, it recalls in different degrees both Rousseau's "noble savage" and nineteenth-century Marxism, as well as the "life, liberty, and pursuit of happiness" of the Declaration of Independence. There is thus a strong tendency to reject authority and what is regarded as institutional manipulation. This rejection is accompanied by an insistence on personal modes of conduct, as expressed in the cliché "Do your own thing."

The skeptics reply.   Critics have accused exponents of the counterculture of psychological and intellectual deficiencies. It has been suggested that because the postwar environment in which they were raised tended to be bland, uniform, and monotonous "like a modern housing development," they were conditioned to think in broad generalizations and to be preoccupied with collectivities and abstractions—rather than getting down to the specifics of surviving as individuals, in contrast to their parents who had personally to overcome the crises of the depression and World War II. Confrontation against the "system" with its large, impersonal government and corporate structures provides a substitute that enables these dissidents to release their frustrations and to mount their own crusade against new villains.

Finally, critics charge that the emphasis which the activists place upon mass action runs counter to the achievement of their professed humanistic goals. They have been accused of displaying the very technocratic philosophy which they claim to oppose. And in continually talking of such collectivities as "establishment" and "power structures," they may be displaying an inability to think of the realities that comprise today's complex institutions.

The Movement.   The Civil Rights Acts of the sixties represented a victory for the nonviolent civil rights movement under Martin Luther King's leadership and for the liberal forces which had responded to it. At the same time, American society witnessed the rise to prominence of the radical student politics which had been nurtured by the civil rights movement—and also of the more traditional forces of conservatism which had always represented a substantial segment of the nation. In short, the stage was being set for what has been described as "politics of confrontation."

In the United States the sense of social outrage that had affected so many during the civil rights movement became focused on problems of poverty and other ills. In eastern Europe there was a growing revolt against the stifling bureaucracies which had subverted the promise of Marxist revolution. Throughout the industrialized world a generation coming to maturity was taking seriously the old ideals on which their nations had been founded.

From Tokyo to Chicago, university students challenged the right to rule of those in power. Demonstrations sometimes met with violent reaction from authorities, with each side accusing the other of provoking the confrontation. The colonial status of much of eastern Europe was confirmed when a widespread reform movement in Czechoslovakia was crushed by the Russian-led invasion of August 1968. Although there was no international conspiracy of radicals, the world-wide communications network which had permitted youth to develop a supranational world outlook encouraged a feedback of ideas. Thus an uprising at Columbia University in April 1968 could be followed the next month by a worker-student rebellion in Paris which almost toppled the French government, both revolts sparked by local issues but involving certain shared assumptions about the nature of the political order.

The very nature of New Left radicalism makes it hard to define with accuracy. In its passion for "participatory democracy," it is marked by factionalism and lack of any stable organizational structure on a large scale. Socialism, pacifism, and anarchism exist together in varying degrees. The heterogeneous conglomeration of groups and individuals which propounds these philosophies is known collectively as "The Movement"—a term which aptly suggests the amorphous quality of the new radicalism. With its emphasis on decentralization, humanism, and cultural diversity, it differs from the more purely economic bias of the traditional Left. Today's radicals tend to feel that an individual can play a part in changing the world he lives in and therefore must assume the responsibility of striving to see his ideals realized. For many, participation in The Movement provides a sense of identity and direction that they fail to find in the "straight" world.

Liberals versus radicals. With the great expansion of higher education and with so many of those seeking change attending universities, it was inevitable that college campuses should become arenas of confrontation between liberals and radicals. Liberals and university administrators have accused the New Left of using fascist tactics in disrupting the traditional democratic procedures of free speech and compromise. At the same time, radicals have accused liberals of fascism in maintaining authoritarian and oppressive institutions. These charges and countercharges stem from fundamentally different assumptions about the nature of political institutions in "democracies."

Liberals believe that the institutions which order the political processes of these nations are in fact democratic—responsive to public demand—and can act as vehicles for effecting social changes desired by the public. From this it follows that those who refuse to be bound by the established political processes endanger the rights of all citizens and threaten to replace them with anarchy or totalitarianism. The radicals, on the other hand, through an analysis of society which is claimed to be basically Marxist, have come to the conclusion that present institutions are inherently authoritarian and deny the opportunity for fundamental social change. They argue that in order to establish a truly democratic society in which the hierarchical nature of human relations is abolished, one cannot be bound by procedures which permit only a semblance of change while in reality perpetuating the status quo.

Beyond the legal. A growing number of people are questioning traditional assumptions about man and his institutions. Social scientists today are less interested than heretofore in describing the formal structures by which societies regulate themselves and more interested in exploring the behavior patterns that explain man's interaction with his fellow man and physical environment. Going further, the psychoanalyst R. D. Laing, whose work has attracted widespread interest, has laid emphasis on the *experience* of the individual in the social context, and has stressed the interrelatedness of experience and behavior.

Affirmation of the validity of individual experience is extended by various social groups, who proclaim the validity of their unique collective experiences and seek to fulfill their respective potentials on their own terms. In the United States, for example, blacks, Indians and Chicanos have become more militant in their demands for attack on the root causes of injustice, while seeking to develop "authentic" ethnic identities. In many western countries a growing number of women are protesting that the acquisition of the ballot has ended neither social nor economic discrimination, and a growing body of literature, like *The Female Eunuch* by Germaine Greer, argues that women—and men too—have been denied the chance to develop their full human potential. Today the necessity of distinct male and female roles in a division of labor based on physical characteristics is breaking down because of a technology that increasingly enables brain to replace brawn. Such a development leads inevitably to the attempt to redefine the roles of the sexes based on an understanding of how much of an individual's makeup is biologically determined and how much is culturally conditioned. The very name of the Women's Liberation Movement, for example, suggests the abandonment of a purely legalistic analysis of social relations.

A new concept of art. Each age develops its own esthetic philosophy and relevant art forms. Today's world is marked by a breakdown of the traditional barrier separating "formal" and "popular" art. As we increasingly perceive our lives as part of an all-enveloping social and ecological system, we come to see the art through which we express our inner selves as inseparable from our environment. The elements of our technology are woven into our art forms, from pop art to electronic music. Total environment experiments have aimed at immersing their audiences in the media of their milieu and obliterating the distinction between spectator and performer.

For the theater it has been a time for experimenting with new ideas and techniques—including theaters-in-the-round and the emergence of street companies, bringing the theater to the people and involving them in dialogues about the issues of the day. Writers like Norman Mailer and Tom Wolfe have spearheaded the New Journalism, a type of reporting in which the author dispenses with any attempt to remain an aloof observer and instead plunges in to convey the color and emotional atmosphere of the event he is recording. "Involvement" is the key word.

The desire to experience and comprehend all facets of our civilization has spurred new interest in all the tools which mankind employs in coming to terms with nature. The boundaries of art expand accordingly. Pop artists like Andy Warhol help give us a new awareness of everyday objects and the media which permeate our lives. Understandably, both academics and laymen are fascinated by the implications of television, movies, and comic books.

Rock: a contemporary folk art. "Forms and rhythms in music are never changed without producing changes in the most important political forms and ways. . . . The new style quietly insinuates itself into manners and customs and from there it . . . goes on to attack laws and constitutions, displaying the utmost impudence, until it ends by overthrowing everything, both in public and in private."[4] Thus Plato recognized the relation between music and society. No one would suggest that rock music is the root cause of changes taking place in all walks of life. But as a major force in the matrix of the counterculture, rock both reflects the modern world and acts as a pervasive medium through which youth perceives and interprets that world.

The folk music revival of the early sixties was inextricably tied to the civil rights movement. Pete Seeger, Joan Baez, and others appeared regularly at civil rights rallies, none of which was complete without its quota of inspirational songs. In particular, Bob Dylan brought a new freedom to lyrics, whether his songs dealt with social problems or with personal visions. More than anyone else, he is credited with making the influence of poetry felt in modern popular song.

The Beatles and other British groups led the rock and roll resurgence. The dynamic "Mersey beat" struck an internationally responsive chord in young people discovering the possibilities open to their generation and restless to initiate change. In the mid-sixties the fusion of these revitalized forms of folk music and rock and roll produced an eclectic form of rock music assimilating and transmuting elements of other fields of popular and "serious" music, from country-and-western and jazz to baroque and Indian classical, and even to opera. Rock is a genuinely popular art in the sense that it is music by and for the people, stressing both audience involvement and encouraging free-form dancing that reflects the individuality and participation idealized by the counterculture. That rock acts as a focus for a sense of community was illustrated in the pop festivals which became a marked phenomenon in 1969.

African "black culture." Just as white America has its cultural roots in Europe, so black America traces its cultural antecedents to Africa. The rediscovery and reassertion of African values are epitomized in the term *Négritude*. It constitutes a rejection of western history and cultural standards and seeks to describe a uniquely African personality and culture on which new African societies can develop. The poetry of this cultural revolution was largely stimulated by two West Indians, Léon Damas and Aimé Césaire, and has perhaps reached its richest expression in the verse of the African Leopold Senghor. This mixture of rejected western technological standards and rediscovered African values is found in Césaire's lines:

> Listen to the white world
> how it resents its great efforts
> how their protest is broken under the rigid stars
> how their steel blue is paralysed in the mystery of the flesh.
> Listen how their defeats sound from their victories.
> Listen to the lamentable stumbling in the great alibis.
> Mercy! mercy for our omniscient naïve conquerors.
> Hurrah for those who never invented anything
> hurrah for those who never explored anything
> hurrah for those who never conquered anything
> hurrah for joy
> hurrah for love
> hurrah for the pain of incarnate tears.[5]

As a part of this search for a sense of identity and viable culture, the African novel discloses an emphasis upon the following themes: reactions to the initial stages of colonization (such as Chinua Achebe's *Things Fall Apart* and *Arrow of God*); education and, in particular, the difficulties of adjusting to western education; the movement of Africans from rural areas to the cities; problems of nation-building both before and after independence (such as Peter Abrahams' *A Wreath for Udomo* or Achebe's *A Man of the People*); and problems of a more universal nature, including those of personality and psychology (examined in Ezekiel Mphahlele's *The Wanderers*).

Of course it can be argued—even as the critics of the western counterculture contend—that the poets, novelists, and painters of the Third World are only a small, though highly articulate, minority and cannot claim to represent entire populations. This is obviously true, but the writers and artists reply that they seek both to rediscover long-buried indigenous values and to interpret the contemporary scene in order to give their people at once a sense of new identity and a direction for future social development.

In short, an intellectual and artistic ferment is occurring everywhere. According to the English historian, Geoffrey Barraclough, "the literary and artistic evidence is unequivocal. The European age—the age which extended from 1498 to 1947—is over, and with it the predominance of the old European scale of values.

Literature, like politics, has broken through its European bonds, and the civilization of the future . . . is taking shape as a world civilization in which all the continents will play their part."[6]

The new romanticism. Every age has had its dreamers as well as its "realists." Just as the elements of our environment are assimilated to the uses of art, so our inner visions are projected onto our environment. The last few years have seen the growth of a distinctly romantic conception of life that is world-wide in its sweep. We have just noted how this romantic perception of their social milieu has gripped the "dreamers" of the Third World—in terms of their national struggles, their rediscovery of the past, and the aspirations which they hold for their people. Among the artists and youth of western societies, in turn, passion, involvement, and idealism have replaced the cool and cynical detachment so typical of the immediate postwar years. In the midst of a society built by the rationale of science and dominated by "technocrats," the young once more see a universe filled with mystery and wonder.

Their behavior has assumed many forms. Some have plunged into astrology and the occult, while the young political radicals have been fascinated by revolutionary guerrilla leaders like Che Guevara and Ho Chi Minh. Psychedelic art abounds. In everything the imagination is exalted. The prevalent use of drugs reflects a wish not only to escape reality but also to find new ways of viewing the world and for experiences that lie beyond the boundaries of the ordinary and the rational.

The emphasis on experience and feeling today is undoubtedly accentuated by the threat of nuclear annihilation which has hung over the world since the end of World War II. The realization that the human race may be wiped out at any time—coupled with the accelerating pace of change in most facets of modern life—has undermined the traditional sense of biological and cultural continuity in history and intensified anxiety about life and death. Existential philosophers like Jean-Paul Sartre (1905-   ) and Albert Camus (1913-1960) have been moved to seek the means by which the individual might come to terms with his precarious existence and proceed to act in an intelligent manner. Again, in seeking to restore to their lives a sense of continuity, many have turned to the religious philosophies of the East.

The importance of self-determination is stressed, whether for individuals or nations. "All power to the people" is the cry of the militants and radicals. Cultural and ethnic groups all over the world demand the right to determine their own futures. The romantic seeks the independence which is a necessary precondition for a planetary interdependence that combines unity with diversity. In his life style he seeks to join inner fantasy and outer appearance into a new reality which transcends mere affectation.

Contemporary ferment and the historian. When change occurs gradually, so that new concepts, inventions, or values modify rather than destroy existing social institutions, it can be described as "evolutionary" in character. When, on the other hand, change occurs so rapidly or radically that the conceptual or institutional framework is destroyed, the historian may describe that phenomenon as "revolutionary." In the text we have examined a number of "revolutions," such as the Neolithic, Urban, Glorious, American, French, Russian, and Industrial. Whether these "revolutions" have been "good" or "bad" involves a value judgment: the first term is applied by their beneficiaries, the second by those who lost out in terms of ideology, fortune, or freedom. Therefore, if in fact we live in "revolutionary" times today, we cannot predict at this juncture—if indeed ever—whether the consequences will prove simply good or bad. As in most human affairs, the results may well turn out to be a mixed bag.

Instead, our interest assumes a different viewpoint. It does not call for value judgments but rather for perspective. We included in our above list of revolutions the "Industrial." Actually, economic historians disagree among themselves whether any such upheaval occurred to overturn the existing economic and social order and thereby create "overnight" a modern urban-industrial Britain. There is little doubt that the massive use of steam and iron supplanted existing production techniques and created a large-scale factory system. Yet a machine technology and incipient factory system had emerged as far back as the Middle Ages, while inventions in the past hundred years have created what is sometimes termed the "Second Industrial Revolution." In other words, we are suggesting that what may appear to be "sudden" and "revolutionary" in a brief time span becomes part of a larger, ongoing evolutionary process when viewed from a broader historical perspective. For example, when the civil rights legislation enacted in the United States during the past two decades is viewed from a limited perspective, it acquires a dimension of suddenness and innovation which can be described as "revolutionary." But when we consider these reforms within a historical continuum some rather "evolutionary" trends become evident: the reforms took place within an institutional structure that was sufficiently malleable to adjust to them; overall societal continuity was not only left intact but undoubtedly strengthened; and these changes represented an implementation, however belatedly, of the philosophical premises upon which American society had been founded.

Thus, while youth has *always* called for immediate, i.e., revolutionary, social reforms to end existing abuses, societal transformations are likely to be most enduring when they involve a synthesis of the new with the old. This calls not only for the abandonment of the obsolescent and spurious but for the retention of what is still relevant and worthwhile. To effect such syntheses has always been the historical challenge and creative opportunity for each succeeding generation.

EPILOGUE

THE CHALLENGES AHEAD

Historians are understandably reluctant about predicting the future because of all the unknown variables involved. For example, a third world war—employing thermonuclear weapons—could conceivably destroy life on this planet. Assuming, however, that mankind can avoid this holocaust, it is possible, on the basis of available data, to make meaningful projections about feasible developments in man's physical and societal environments for the year 2000, and even beyond.

Our attempts to extrapolate from today to tomorrow are based upon a fundamental guideline—man's perennial search for meaning and order in his relationship to the planet and his fellow beings. That relationship is dynamic because his technology continually alters the landscape and man's capacity to control the environment; it is also open-ended because the process evolves from simple to more complex stages of organization and interaction, thereby challenging man at every step with new problems but also holding out the promise of discovering new levels of meaning and order. Our Paleolithic ancestors sought both to discover purpose in their existence and to set their mark upon the firmament. In tomorrow's world we can expect man to continue with unflagging zeal the quest initiated some two million years ago.

Man is not only a tool-maker; he is also a problem-solver. If the solution of problems provides man with excitement and a sense of accomplishment, we need not fear that the decades ahead will find him bored, because they promise to confront him with some of the most massive problems in his variegated planetary existence. He will be challenged simultaneously in four interlocking environments: the physical, the political, the social, and the cultural—all of them global in their dimensions.

OUR PLANET

The population explosion. It is the application of technology to physical resources that sustains human life and ultimately sets the limits on the number of people who can be fed. But technology also provides the tools and techniques for lengthening life spans and reducing mortality rates. As a result, high birth rates are no longer closely matched by high death rates as they were until modern times; epidemics are much less frequent in most parts of the world, due largely to public health measures; and physical vitality has been increased by improved nutrition. These changes have brought about what is today familiarly called the "population explosion"—which, unless checked, could conceivably become the most catastrophic problem of the next half century.

In 1000 A.D. the estimated population of the world was 275 million, a figure which had approximately doubled by 1650. But whereas it took some 650 years for this increase to occur, the following 300 years brought a sixfold increase to over three billion people in 1962. In those three centuries some 23 billion people had been born—or more than half as many as in the preceding 76 centuries. And the factor of acceleration continues: for example, the estimated increase in the population of Asia during the second half of this century will roughly equal the population of the entire world as of 1958, while Latin America will triple its numbers.

Also, it would appear that the western percentage of world population probably reached its zenith around 1900 or shortly thereafter. Subsequently, Asia, Africa, and Latin America have been growing more rapidly than Europe, Russia, and North America. In other words, the regions possessing the most advanced technology and highest living standards are likely to be a progressively diminishing portion of the global population. Since economic production is outstripping biological reproduction in the advanced countries of the West while the reverse situation threatens to occur in the rest of the world during the decades ahead, the resulting demographic-economic disequilibrium is almost certain to generate massive political and social tensions.

Natural resources: plenty or penury ahead?   Can the planet's natural resources be allocated and developed to meet the growing needs of our accelerating population while still being conserved in amounts adequate for the unborn generations? Or are we exploiting them so quickly and wastefully that the decades ahead will find mankind impoverished? Earlier predictions of the inevitable total depletion of physical resources have proved premature. We have been able to discover new mineral deposits and mine others once considered inaccessible and to process ores and related sources hitherto discarded as being too low-grade to be economical. Also, synthetic substitutes for such raw materials as rubber have been developed, while in agriculture, land once considered lost to erosion has in many cases been reclaimed, and new techniques in plant breeding have raised crop yields spectacularly.

Yet a fundamental problem confronts us: the planet and its resources are finite, and demands on those resources are multiplying even faster than the population increase. The United States itself has become a resource-deficit country. In March 1970 the Assistant Secretary of the Interior for mineral resources warned that the outlook for the country to obtain the mineral and energy resources required over the next three decades was bleak. At a time when international competition for these resources would increase enormously, the richer domestic deposits had already been skimmed off, and the country's environment had deteriorated so far that the rising costs of preserving it must be added to the costs of resource exploitation. People everywhere are caught up in the "revolution of rising expectations." But will the earth's resources last long enough to enable the entire world—a world not of 3 billion but say 6 billion people—to approach the living standards of some 200 million Americans?

Americans comprise only 6 percent of the world's population, yet their advanced technology and unparalleled living standards consume upwards of fifty percent of current exploitation of global resources. It should be cause for sober reflection that they are also responsible for contributing about half of all planetary pollution. In 1970 President Nixon called for spending $10 billion over a five-year period to improve the quality of the national environment. While this initiative was commended, numerous scientists warned that three to five times that amount might have to be spent annually in order to save the environment and restore the quality of life known to earlier generations. Their concern has been reinforced by student demonstrations across the country. Environmental improvement and resource conservation will make heavy demands, calling as they must for a drastic reallocation of political, military, and social priorities, accompanied by large-scale financial expenditures in the civilian sector of the economy. In October 1972, Congress authorized $24.6 billion—over President Nixon's veto—for a massive water-cleaning program.

In June 1972 occurred an unprecedented development in mankind's awareness of the vulnerable state of its global ecology. Representatives of 114 nations met at Stockholm to attend the United Nations Conference on the Human Environment. There they agreed that a worldwide emergency exists; and that nations, despite their sovereignty, share responsibility for such common resources as the atmosphere and the oceans. The population explosion, a politically sensitive issue, was dealt with only indirectly, since it will be the subject of a UN conference in 1974. However, growing concern was voiced over the present accelerating depletion of the earth's nonreplenishable resources. The developing nations blamed the advanced industrial countries for the planet's environmental deterioration. But at the same time the Third World refused to accept any technological cutoff in the name of ecological protection, if they were thereby to be prevented from industrializing and raising their own living standards.

The broad ecological principles enacted at the conference are not legally binding on the participating nations; and they are certain to be opposed by powerful national and corporate interests, which seek immediate profits in plundering or polluting the earth and its life-support system. But for the first time machinery has been created through which world public opinion can apply pressure on governments to solve problems that threaten our common survival. In so doing, they can probably count on an invaluable innovation sponsored by the conference: an "earth-watch" network of monitoring stations by which conditions such as atmospheric and oceanic pollution can be continuously assessed as the basis for corrective actions.

Our environment—pleasant or polluted?   Not only is man the only creature capable of significantly altering the physical environment; he is also unique in his capacity to pollute and destroy it. As a litterbug he throws beer cans into the Grand Canyon while his children festoon the highways with discarded candy wrappers. His coal-fed generating plants fill the skies over metropolitan areas with hundreds of thousands of tons of soot and other impurities every year. His factories discharge a never-ending stream of industrial waste and toxicants into the Ohio and Mississippi and are presently creating patches of "dead water" in Lake Erie and elsewhere. Automobiles are the chief culprits in creating smog in Los Angeles and virtually every other North American city, while offshore oil drilling and oil-tanker sinkings have been guilty of spillage which has polluted shorelines in California, the Gulf of Mexico, Nova Scotia, England, and France and has destroyed untold wildlife.

Some ecologists warn that the wastes being released by our technology into the atomsphere in the form of carbon dioxide could raise temperatures to the point where, unless checked, a "hothouse" effect could completely alter the biosphere, that is, the zone in which all organic life exists. Meanwhile, how shall we get rid of millions of tons of garbage which annually pile up in the United States? By burning or burying it, or by dumping it into already polluted lakes and oceans? Most hazardous of all potential dangers to health, how and where shall our nuclear age dispose of radioactive materials without destroying the air, earth, or water resources of this planet?

OUR POLITICAL ENVIRONMENT

War or peace, or war and peace? Men have always sought to control their environment, including their fellow human beings, often by use of physical force. Recourse to violence, whether on American city streets or along disputed frontiers of newly created states in Africa or Asia, is not likely to end in the foreseeable future. But the fundamental nature of conflict has been altered in our century. Twice warfare has escalated from its original locus of conflict to engulf the world, and now several nations are armed with nuclear, and even thermonuclear, weapons, coupled with an intercontinental delivery capability. For the first time in two million years man has acquired the dubious distinction of being able to destroy his own species and perhaps even immolate the planet.

What are the options available in the years ahead? The first accepts the continuation of the most lethal, and expensive, arms race in history—on the "realistic" basis that the dynamics of technological invention require a continuous updating of national armaments because to lag behind could be fatal. Such weapons as the "Safeguard" anti-ballistic-missile system (ABM) and MIRV's (multiple independently targeted reentry vehicles) with thermonuclear warheads cost the American public many billions of dollars. Continuation with this unprecedentedly sophisticated weapons system would of course carry the arms race to a new plateau of potential mass destruction, with the prospect of still further escalation ahead.

Confronted with the grisly prospect of an unchecked arms race, many people have canvassed other options. Some advocate total disarmament. Unfortunately, more than a general consensus to outlaw war is required because the presence of even one dissenter in the international community can abort the entire process. Moreover, total disarmament among nations logically calls for a supranational agency entrusted with the authority and physical power to keep the peace, and states have not yet demonstrated their willingness to accept any such international authority.

A third option advocates a more limited objective, namely, to reduce armaments and prohibit the proliferation of nuclear weapons. In the 1960's the capacity of each superpower to destroy the other had resulted in a "balance of terror." Partial disarmament would at least reverse the continuing trend toward further arms escalation, with all the risks that such a race entails. But to deescalate also requires a rigorous maintenance of balance, since any unilateral act of reduction by one superpower would upset the balance in favor of the other camp.

The United States and the Soviet Union, however, have agreed on the folly of permitting an unchecked proliferation of nuclear-armed states. In 1968 they presented a draft treaty on nonproliferation which the United Nations adopted. While generally hailed as a sign of progress, this treaty has been rejected by Communist China, which contends that it is designed to ensure an atomic monopoly for the treaty's authors. Other nations, including France, have also objected to its provisions. Meanwhile, the United States and the Soviet Union have engaged in bilateral discussions at Helsinki and Vienna on limiting the use of strategic weapons. The SALT agreement to limit the number of ABM sites in Russia and the United States is a hopeful beginning. Similarly, the "hot line" linking Washington and Moscow is a tangible expression of sophisticated understanding between the superpowers on the war-and-peace equation.

The danger of uncontrollable violence exists rather at the other end of the power spectrum, among newly created states which all too often are both politically unstable and economically unviable yet share a common infection of nationalistic ambitions. Furthermore, a number of these small nations are linked by treaty with one or other of the superpowers so that, as client states, they are in a position to force the superpower into taking action that may go beyond the point which the latter's own interests or global commitments would counsel. This postwar proliferation of newly emergent countries and of client states could present the greatest risk of international tension and conflict in the years ahead.

International peacekeeping. To cope with this area of political instability requires a new technique in conflict-control. This has been developing in the form of international peacekeeping, in which "middle powers"—such as Canada, the Scandinavian countries, Brazil, and India—provide the United Nations with forces to cope with brush-fire conflicts before they get out of hand. United Nations peacekeeping has been able to contain conflicts in Indonesia, Kashmir, the Congo, Gaza, and Cyprus. That many of these crises remain localized rather than being resolved underscores a phenomenon with which we must learn to live in the years ahead: when ideological or national differences are too great to permit the pacific settlement of a dispute, the world community must act to quarantine it. Tomorrow's world is likely to be too complex to exist in terms of either war or peace; it is more likely to have to cope with war *and* peace together.

The United Nations role. The authority of the chief international organization is severely limited by the fact that the United Nations is composed of member governments, each of which possesses sovereign status. Consequently the organization is primarily the agent of its sovereign masters, who have been responsible in the last analysis for the successes and failures of this world body since its inception in 1945.

The organization's future role will depend largely upon the attitude that prevails regarding its character and purpose and the resulting support of peoples and governments. According to the late secretary-general, Dag Hammarskjöld, the member states can choose between two basic concepts. The first regards the United Nations as a static conference machinery for resolving conflicts of interests and accommodating ideologies with a view to peaceful coexistence, and served by a Secretariat which represents in its ranks those same interests and ideologies. The second concept regards the organization rather as a dynamic instrument through which governments should seek both to reconcile differences and to develop forms of executive action in order to further the purposes of the Charter, and served by a truly international Secretariat.

Notwithstanding valuable activities in nonpolitical areas, such as economic development, there was a general consensus that the United Nations on its twenty-fifth anniversary had reached a critical stage. Reflecting on the organization's inability to cope with such ominous problems as the Arab-Israeli confrontation and the war between India and Pakistan over the breakaway of East Pakistan (Bangla Desh), Secretary-General U Thant declared that the United Nations "has ten years to become effective or disappear."

OUR SOCIAL ENVIRONMENT

Technology in a space age. We can be certain that technology will continue to alter both our physical environment and many of our social values and goals. Space exploration promises to be among the most spectacular of these environment- and mind-expanding experiences. It is a measure of the accelerating pace of technological change that astronauts Armstrong and Aldrin set foot on the moon only two thirds of a century after the Wright brothers' first twelve-second flight at Kitty Hawk. Yet the exploration of space is more than simply an extension of air flight; it represents a new dimension in man's control of his environment. Physically and intellectually, it has created a new frontier. When the crew of Apollo 8 looked homeward to "that good earth," they saw a blue-green oasis of life in the barren wilderness of space. It has long been a fond hope that this view of the planet would enable mankind to see itself in a truer perspective and speed the end of the rivalries which divide men from one another. Moreover, in the challenge it provides, space exploration may help provide a meaningful alternative to war, as men pit their courage and energies against destructive forces that lie beyond the earth's atmosphere. And ultimately, the space age offers the hope of establishing contact with extraterrestrial intelligence elsewhere in the universe, and in all that such contact implies, even though this event may not be realized for centuries, if ever.

Technology's impact on our lives. On earth, meanwhile, technology promises to alter our lives progressively. Tomorrow's world will be much more automated than today's. Its mechanized and computerized economy will require much less physical effort, as well as fewer man-hours on the assembly line. Automation offers the opportunity to free man from drudgery and, by creating more leisure time, enables him to engage in creative, satisfying activity. In that sense, the new technology can assist people to develop their emotional and intellectual natures and thus come to more meaningful terms with their world. Such, at least, is the apparent promise of technology for the economically advanced countries, if not for the underdeveloped regions with their exploding populations having to compete for available resources and developmental capital.

Is the promise accompanied by a price tag? In the Industrial Revolution the means of production were mechanized, thus encouraging unrestricted production and the development of an economy that encouraged large-scale organization.

Capital formation, machines, production schedules, and distribution outlets have called for operations on a scale possible only for huge corporations; and in today's world we now find not only conglomerates that own and operate a variety of enterprises, ranging from, say, making soap to publishing books, but also multinational corporations which operate throughout the western world. Big business is matched in turn by big trade unions, and big government. But in such a world of gigantism, decisions all too often tend to be based on economies of scale rather than on social needs and values.

An economic structure based upon economies of scale can also exert massive pressures in the direction of societal conformity. In a mass society decisions affecting the life of each individual are often made by a small number of public or business administrators. Their choices may be dictated by what they hope to be the greatest amount of good for the greatest number of people, but they feel that their decisions, to be "scientific," first require that John Smith and Mary Jones be "processed" as digits in a computer system. Already each of us has become aware of the extent to which our daily lives are being subjected to the computer, in terms of social security numbers, bank checks, bills, credit cards, and zip codes. Yet what happens to the individual in this complex process of data-processing and decision-making—since presumably he or she is the ultimate subject of all this effort? Some economists, including John Galbraith, argue that the citizen, as a consumer, is today treated less as a subject than as the object of big business and big government. Not only do they largely decide the priorities and prices for the citizen-consumer, but they can also employ advertising and make use of the mass media to help create the desired demand.

Tomorrow's urban society. The exploding urban complexes of today will—in their future form—almost certainly dominate the physical environment of twenty-first-century man. Time and space, rather than production, will become the critical economic values in what has been described as a "postindustrial" society. Retaining the sense of spatial freedom which is so important to an individual's mental well-being is already a problem for substantial segments of humanity today, and the problem will assume even greater proportions in an urbanized world community unless effective countermeasures are taken. Today leading architects and urban planners are grappling with this problem of shaping the space man inhabits in order to make his environment livable. There is growing recognition of the need to think in terms of the totality of the environment and the interrelatedness of forms in space. "Today all development moves in the direction of making the aspect of major cities more rural and smaller rural agglomerations more urban. We now see the way before us, though it still has to be implemented: the reconquering of intimate life, the human scale, the planning for growth."[1]

Automation and cybernation can give man a new relationship with his environment. The centralization of the means of production that has hitherto been required by industry may no longer be necessary. It should prove possible to separate man and machine in space, thus alleviating much of the pollution and noise that afflicts the urban dweller today. Advances in electronic communication—such as the three-dimensional television foreshadowed by holography and personal transceivers that provide instantaneous person-to-person contact anywhere on earth—will permit greater physical mobility while at the same time shrinking the world to what Marshall McLuhan has called a "global village."

Unity and diversity. Science in our century has moved steadily in the direction of the integration of concepts and disciplines. In the political world we find a more complicated, and indeed paradoxical, situation. On the one hand, the process of decolonization has resulted in the creation of scores of new nation-states, each jealously maintaining its sovereign rights. At the same time, the technologically advanced countries have been progressively integrating their resources and placing less importance upon traditional political boundaries in order to create new forms of regional defence and economic development. The concept of the nation-state as the most important unit of the international political order no longer seems to satisfy the requirements of the new age. Technological developments and societal complexities are bringing men closer together and altering their consciousness of the world. Evidence of this new consciousness can be seen most clearly in the attitudes of today's youth, who tend to reject the idea of "my country right or wrong" and instead seek to confront the issues which are common to all men.

Barring a nuclear holocaust, the way ahead seems to lie in the direction of some kind of international community. The question then arises: what is to become of the individual in such a world, and what is to become of individual thought and life styles? Even in the small city-states of ancient Greece, men worried about the "tyranny of the majority," the subjugation of the individual to the mass. Are we to abolish war and poverty, only to replace them with mind-numbing uniformity? Will every African village have its piped-in musak, every polar community the same neon-lit supermarkets to be found in Dallas or Bangkok? Will the great masses of mankind, freed at last from backbreaking toil, spend their endless vacations in front of wall-to-wall television screens, popping down pep—or tranquilizing—pills like candy? If we are to avoid an Orwellian world order with its self-perpetuating equilibrium based upon a warfare totalitarianism, can we avoid in turn the pleasant meaninglessness of a *Brave New World*?

It would appear that despite unprecedented affluence, many people today suffer from anxiety and a sense of alienation. Failure to resolve conflict between international value systems (as demonstrated by the continuation of the most costly arms race in history) adds to the individual's inner tensions, as does the agglomeration of impersonal forces over which he feels unable to exercise any real control. Hence we find a paradox of physical security mated to psychological insecurity in those societies with the world's highest standards of living.

How efficacious is science? Looking ahead, some thinkers—including scientists themselves—have raised questions regarding the contributions which science and technology can make. Expenditures on national space programs can become so heavy as to delay the solution of domestic problems requiring massive investments. Again, as we saw earlier, medical triumphs have contributed to soaring population growth in underdeveloped countries, but when the economy does not keep pace, the net result can be an actual decline in living standards—paving the way in turn for domestic violence.

Another dilemma is the close relationship between science and war. Only a hair's-breadth divides the constructive from the destructive capacities of science—as the unleashing of atomic energy attests. After World War II physicists progressively came to realize that the optimistic concept of a "value-free" science was no longer valid. No longer is it possible for the scientist to pursue the "truth" in his laboratory unencumbered by the social and moral implications of his work. Henceforth, scientists will have to confront ethical considerations in determining the course of their work in the same way that policy-makers must confront them in determining political, social, and economic change.

Epilogue:
Challenges Ahead

This is the dawning of the Age of Aquarius . . .
Harmony and understanding
Sympathy and trust abounding
No more falsehoods or derisions
Golden living dreams of visions
Mystic crystal revelation
And the mind's true liberation.

From "Aquarius" by James Rado, Gerome Ragni, Galt McDermott and Nat Shapiro. Copyright © 1966, 1967, 1968 by James Rado, Gerome Ragni, Galt McDermott, Nat Shapiro, and United Artists Music Co., Inc. All rights controlled and administered by United Artists Music Co., Inc. 729 Seventh Ave., New York, N.Y. 10019. Used by permission.

The debate over progress. These lines from *Hair* speak of a belief in the possibility of a more perfect society emerging in the future. Is this optimism justified? Or does it indicate an unwillingness, or inability, to face the hard facts of life? Progress means many things to many people, and one man's crosstown freeway is another man's shattered neighborhood. To some, the Woodstock Music and Art Fair can symbolize everything that is wrong with the postwar generation; to others, the world's best hope for the future.

It is only in relatively recent times that man has become obsessed with the idea of progress. The Industrial Revolution accelerated the pace of change and made economic productivity seem a natural yardstick by which to measure progress. Capitalism's spectacular industrial growth in the nineteenth century contributed to the predominant belief that progress in human affairs was inevitable. And Marxist theory, while forecasting the obsolescence of capitalist society, raised the concept of progress to the status of a historical law in the minds of its followers.

In the twentieth century, as we have seen in the preceding chapters, war and scientific concepts of relativity and uncertainty did much to shatter the idea of inevitable progress, especially in the West. Communist nations have tended to retain the Marxist ideas of evolution and progress in society, ideas which help explain Marxism's appeal among many of the world's destitute and oppressed peoples. As we would expect, the debate over progress has also affected the contemporary cultural environment.

This debate is nowhere better illustrated than in science fiction, a branch of literature that has tended to concern itself with the societal implications of science. Western writers have exhibited a marked ambivalence toward the notion that science and the intellect can lead the way to a more civilized existence. The fear that science can, like fire, be a splendid servant but a terrible master, is evidenced in such "anti-utopias" as Orwell's *1984*. In marked contrast, Soviet authors tend to reflect the official view that technological change never poses a threat to man. Consequently they have criticized their western counterparts for preaching "relativism, the helplessness of the mind against the mysterious and unknowable universe, and the illusory nature of social progress."[2]

Changing moral and ethical standards. In the past, when societies had to endure "times that try men's souls," they were sustained by traditional religious, ethical, and moral values. But tomorrow's world will have to evolve new values to give meaning and direction to the challenges posed by science and technology. In

1968, for example, a biological breakthrough provided evidence of man's capability to create in a test tube what has been described as a primitive form of life. What are the implications here—or in transplanting the heart from a dead person to prolong the life of its recipient—for man's relationship to the overarching question of life and death: is he now attempting to play God? The same question applies to such issues as abortion and birth control. If to take human life can be murder, what shall we deem the act that denies life in the first place—as meritorious when viewed in a planetary context with its specter of an uncontrollable population explosion, or as reprehensible when a personal decision? Furthermore, who or what shall decide how much life would be good for the planet, and have we succeeded in resolving the important question of the inherent worth, or sanctity, of the individual? The present generation is confronted with fundamental moral issues for which there is often no historical precedent and will have to search for new answers to new as well as to old questions.

Religious faith in transition. Coming to terms with the new forces that have been unleashed in the contemporary world means seeking new identities—new views of man's relationship to his universe. Today the search for meaning and direction is evident in the changes that are taking place in religious life. On the one hand the Christian churches have been suffering from a general apathy. Many persons, especially among the young, feel that the church has lost its relevance; it seems unable to confront the issues of the times.

And yet there is also occurring a reawakening of religious sensitivity that goes beyond any institutional structure to express itself in a commitment to personal integrity and the quest for greater empathy with all other humans. It is marked by a reverence for life and the joys that may be found therein: "Life is holy—celebrate it!"

Many today find it difficult to accept the idea of a stern God remote from the joys and sorrows of the world or that either Judaism or Christianity has a monopoly on truth or can claim to be the exclusive vehicle for human salvation. In turning to mysticism and eastern religious philosophies, many westerners, especially among the young, are affirming their concept of a God who manifests Himself in all life, while their search for a relevant religious philosophy has encouraged the comparative study of all major religions. Just as the science of ecology has made us conscious as never before of our planetary interdependence, and that as earthlings we must survive or perish together, so an ecumenical spirit permeates the religious sphere.

This ecumenical movement seeks not only to cut across the centuries-old barriers that schismatized the Christian community into rival denominations but also to create a new relationship between Christian institutions and the secular world. More and more clergy are committing themselves to living their beliefs by espousing far-reaching social reform and taking their renewed faith among the people.

A towering figure in the ecumenical movement was Pope John XXIII. During his brief pontificate (1958-1963) he sought to heal ancient divisions within Christendom and to find ethical, moral, and spiritual denominators common to all the world's major religions. And in his mission, John XXIII emphasized the "dignity of the human person" whose "rights and obligations are universal and inviolable so they cannot in any way be surrendered." From such portents, it is possible to infer that the decades ahead will see the world's religions playing a more vital role in daily life, but in forms that may well differ from today's.

Education in tomorrow's world. What should be the role of education in preparing young people to cope with the fast-changing final third of this century? Tomorrow's society will be much more learning-oriented, and education will come increasingly to be regarded as a lifelong process of adjustment, self-understanding, and growth.

A problem arises in determining the appropriate curriculum to meet the changing needs of both society and the individual. The accelerative process quickens the tendency for data to become obsolete. As a result, the accumulation of facts can become self-defeating—unless the educational process can stimulate in the student what has been termed purposeful self-direction. In other words, there must be greater emphasis upon the recognition of problems and relationships arising from the corpus of factual information, a process that activates meaningful problem-solving responses. Consequently both the curriculum and the teaching process must be more strongly oriented toward the student himself as an active participant in the continuous reshaping of our social environment. Here data-retrieval banks and visual aid devices can be of service, by assisting the student to embark upon problems and lines of inquiry of specific concern to his own needs and objectives—with the teacher providing guidance and engaging in what could become a mutually rewarding intellectual dialogue.

Another problem at the center of our contemporary educational system is the lack of integration between our natural and social sciences and between theory and behavior. Today's students attend "multiversities," whose disciplines tend to be highly specialized and compartmentalized, lacking comparable terminologies and employing different methodological techniques. Perhaps this is the inevitable price which we must pay for the bewildering amounts of knowledge obtained in modern times, which in some disciplines doubles every ten to twenty years. To some critics of the contemporary academic environment, however, interdisciplinary activities disclose that important integrative principles do underlie the physical, mathematical, and social sciences and that they should be analyzed and applied. If such an analysis proves valid, we can expect a concerted effort to find and utilize conceptual principles and methods common to all the main branches of human learning.

Toward a new Renaissance? Times of great change are often times of great creativity. Upheavals in the social order, ferment in the arts, new ideas in science—all are bound together. Today is such a time of great change. Perhaps not since the Renaissance has there been such far-reaching change in society, and future centuries may well rank the transitional age in which we live as one of the principal watersheds in human history. Even today we are aware that we live in an exceptional age, and some would argue that what we are witnessing is in fact the beginning of a new Renaissance.

Men have often looked back longingly to an imagined Golden Age, especially in times when the idea of progress lacked credibility. Today, with the limitations of unrestricted technological advance becoming increasingly obvious, many long for a simpler life. If a new Renaissance is to eventuate, it would seem clear that we must strive to recapture the human scale in all things. Otherwise, the alternatives would appear to be ecological destruction, war, and totalitarianism. There must be a new set of priorities on the societal level. In particular, the enormous wealth that nations waste in war preparations must be diverted to alleviating social ills. Only in this way can technology's true promise be realized, and enable us to build a society that combines the gifts of science with a new social sanity. The dangers ahead are many, but with the decline of the old parochialisms and the rigid ideologies which accompanied them, a new wealth of ideas is becoming available with which to build the future.

Fundamental change will only become possible when there is a new scale of values permeating society, so that people refuse to tolerate the brutality and ugliness that has been an inherent part of human activity in past and present ages. In this there may lie an admonition to those in whom recent years have instilled a romantic idealism. A romanticism that looks only to the past must lead inevitably to a blind alley, but one that is intelligently rooted in the possibilities of the future can open the way to a new Renaissance in human creativity. Who knows—we might even succeed in establishing the world's first *humane* civilization.

SUGGESTIONS FOR READING

CHAPTER 1: ALONG THE BANKS OF RIVERS

The Cambridge Ancient History, Vols. I–II, 3rd ed. (Cambridge, 1971–1972) incorporates the latest research on prehistory and the ancient Near East. R. Braidwood, **Prehistoric Men,*** 7th ed. (Scott, Foresman, 1967) is the best short survey. Also recommended are J. Hawkes, **Prehistory*** (Mentor); Grahame Clark, **World Prehistory: An Outline,*** 2nd ed. (Cambridge, 1969); and H. Bandi, **The Art of the Stone Age** (Crown, 1961).

L. Cottrell, **Digs and Diggers: A Book of World Archaeology** (World, 1964) and C. W. Ceram, **Gods, Graves, and Scholars,** rev. ed. (Knopf, 1967) are popular surveys. M. Wheeler, **Archaeology from the Earth*** (Penguin) describes the techniques of the archaeologist.

W. Hallo and W. Simpson, **The Ancient Near East*** (Harcourt Brace Jovanovich, Inc., 1971) is brief, comprehensive, and up to date. Other short surveys are M. Covensky, **The Ancient Near Eastern Tradition*** (Harper & Row, 1966); Gordon Childe, **What Happened in History*** (Penguin); H. Frankfort, **The Birth of Civilization in the Near East*** (Anchor); and S. Moscati, **The Face of the Ancient Orient*** (Anchor).

G. Roux, **Ancient Iraq*** (Penguin) is an excellent, detailed history of ancient Mesopotamia. See also S. N. Kramer, **The Sumerians** (Univ. of Chicago, 1963) and the same author's popular **History Begins at Sumer*** (Anchor).

C. Aldred, **The Egyptians*** (Praeger) and L. Casson, **Ancient Egypt** (Time Inc., 1965) are two brief topical surveys. Alan Gardiner, **Egypt of the Pharaohs*** (Galaxy) is a detailed political history. On the Empire period see G. Steindorff and K. Seele, **When Egypt Ruled the East*** (Phoenix); L. Cottrell, **Life Under the Pharaohs*** (Grosset & Dunlap); and C. Aldred, **Akhenaton: Pharaoh of Egypt** (McGraw-Hill, 1969).

H. Frankfort *et al.,* **Before Philosophy*** (Penguin) is a notable interpretation of Mesopotamian and Egyptian thought. John A. Wilson, **The Culture of Ancient Egypt*** (Phoenix) is highly recommended. O. Neugebauer, **The Exact Sciences in Antiquity*** (Torchbooks) is the authoritative work on Mesopotamian and Egyptian mathematics and science. Also recommended are S. Hooke, **Middle Eastern Mythology*** (Penguin) and **Babylonian and Assyrian Religion** (Oklahoma, 1963).

O. R. Gurney, **The Hittites*** (Penguin) and D. Harden, **The Phoenicians*** (Praeger) are authoritative surveys.

J. A. Hexter, **The Judaeo-Christian Tradition*** (Harper & Row, 1966) is a succinct overview of Hebrew history and religion. Excellent longer surveys are H. M. Orlinsky, **Ancient Israel*** (Cornell); John Bright, **A History of Israel** (Westminster Press, 1959); Bernhard W. Anderson, **Understanding the Old Testament** (Prentice-Hall, 1957); and O. Eissfeldt, **The Old Testament: An Introduction** (Harper & Row, 1965).

A. Olmstead, **History of Assyria** (Scribner, 1923) and **History of the Persian Empire*** (Phoenix) are the standard accounts. See also R. N. Frye, **The Heritage of Persia*** (Mentor) and R. Zaehner, **The Dawn and Twilight of Zoroastrianism** (Putnam, 1961).

See also Seton Lloyd, **Art of the Ancient Near East*** (Praeger); H. Frankfort, **The Art and Architecture of the Ancient Orient** (Penguin, 1954); and I. E. S. Edwards, **The Pyramids of Egypt*** (Penguin).

CHAPTER 2: THE GLORY THAT WAS GREECE

P. MacKendrick, **The Greek Stones Speak*** (Mentor) and L. Cottrell, **The Bull of Minos*** (Universal) are popular accounts of the great archaeological discoveries in the Aegean area. See also R. W. Hutchinson, **Prehistoric Crete*** (Penguin); C. W. Blegen, **Troy and the Trojans** (Praeger, 1963); Alan E. Samuel, **The Mycenaeans in History*** (Prentice-Hall, 1966); and John Chadwick, **The Decipherment of Linear B*** (Vintage).

A. R. Burn, **The Pelican History of Greece*** (Penguin); M. I. Finley, **The Ancient Greeks*** (Compass); and A. Andrewes, **The Greeks** (Knopf, 1967) are valuable, fresh analyses. Other good surveys include M. Bowra, **The Greek Experience*** (Mentor); H. Kitto, **The Greeks*** (Penguin); and H. Lloyd-Jones, ed., **The Greek World*** (Penguin). N. G. L. Hammond, **A History of Greece to 322 B.C.,** 2nd ed. (Oxford, 1967) is a standard detailed history.

Chester G. Starr, **The Origins of Greek Civilization, 1100–650 B.C.** (Knopf, 1961) is an illuminating survey of the formative centuries of Greek civilization. See also T. B. L. Webster, **From Mycenae to Homer*** (Norton) and M. I. Finley, **The World of Odysseus*** (Compass). A. R. Burn, **The World of Hesiod** (Dutton, 1937) and **The Lyric Age of Greece** (Arnold, 1960) treat in detail the Greek renaissance of the seventh and sixth centuries B.C. On Greek colonization see John Boardman, **The Greeks Overseas*** (Penguin). On the transition from oligarchy to democracy see A. Andrewes, **The Greek Tyrants*** (Torchbooks) and W. G. Forrest, **The Emergence of Greek Democracy, 800–400 B.C.*** (McGraw-Hill, 1967).

Valuable special studies on politics, economics, and society include A. R. Burn, **Persia and the Greeks: The Defense of the West, 546–478 B.C.** (St. Martin, 1962); A. de Selincourt, **The World of Herodotus*** (Little, Brown); H. Mitchell, **Sparta*** (Cambridge); A. E. Zimmern, **The Greek Commonwealth: Politics and Economics in Fifth-Century Athens*** (Galaxy); G. Glotz, **Ancient Greece at Work*** (Norton); Victor Ehrenberg, **The Greek State*** (Norton); A. H. M. Jones, **Athenian Democracy** (Barnes and Noble, 1964); T. B. L. Webster, **Everyday Life in Classical Athens** (Putnam, 1969); and M. I. Finley, ed., **Slavery in Classical Antiquity** (Barnes and Noble, 1968).

Edith Hamilton, **The Greek Way*** (Norton) is a popular and enthusiastic appreciation of the beauty and values of Hellenic literature. A. Lesky, **A History of Greek Literature** (Crowell, 1966) is an outstanding detailed treatment. See also H. D. F. Kitto, **Greek Tragedy*** (Anchor) and John B. Bury, **Ancient Greek Historians*** (Dover).

*Indicates an inexpensive paperbound edition.

C. Seltman, **The Twelve Olympians*** (Apollo) recounts the myths and gay stories about the Olympian gods and goddesses. See also Michael Grant, **Myths of the Greeks and Romans*** (Mentor) and W. K. C. Guthrie, **The Greeks and Their Gods*** (Beacon).

Good introductions to Greek philosophy and science include W. K. C. Guthrie, **Greek Philosophers from Thales to Aristotle*** (Torchbooks); F. M. Cornford, **Before and After Socrates*** (Cambridge); and M. Clagett, **Greek Science in Antiquity*** (Collier). See also A. E. Taylor, **Socrates: The Man and His Thought*** (Anchor) and **The Mind of Plato*** (Univ. of Michigan); and W. D. Ross, **Aristotle*** (Barnes and Noble).

Recommended for the fine arts student are J. Pollitt, **Art and Experience in Classical Greece*** (Cambridge, 1972); J. Boardman, **Greek Art*** (Praeger); G. Richter, **A Handbook of Greek Art*** (Phaedon); A. W. Lawrence, **Greek Architecture** (Penguin, 1957); and M. Robertson, **Greek Painting** (Skira, 1959).

W. W. Tarn, **Hellenistic Civilisation,*** 3rd ed. (Meridian) is a detailed survey. On the career and motives of Alexander the Great see W. W. Tarn, **Alexander the Great*** (Beacon); and W. Wilcken, **Alexander the Great*** (Norton); A. R. Burn, **Alexander the Great and the Hellenistic World*** (Collier); G. T. Griffith, ed., **Alexander the Great: The Main Problems** (Barnes and Noble, 1966).

CHAPTER 3: THE GRANDEUR THAT WAS ROME

D. R. Dudley, **The Civilization of Rome*** (Mentor); R. Barrow, **The Romans*** (Penguin); M. Grant, **The World of Rome*** (Praeger, 1970); and P. Arnott, **The Romans and Their World*** (St. Martin, 1970) are brief, excellent surveys of Roman history and culture.

D. H. Lawrence, **Etruscan Places*** (Compass) is an enthusiastic appraisal of the Etruscan way of life. See also H. Pallotino, **The Etruscans*** (Penguin); and Emeline Richardson, **The Etruscans: Their Art and Civilization** (Univ. of Chicago, 1964). On archaeological discovery in Italy see P. MacKendrick, **The Mute Stones Speak*** (Mentor).

See also Alexander H. McDonald, **Republican Rome** (Praeger, 1966); C. G. Starr, **The Emergence of Rome as Ruler of the Western World,*** 2nd ed. (Cornell); E. Badian, **Roman Imperialism in the Late Republic,*** 2nd ed. (Cornell); Lily R. Taylor, **Party Politics in the Age of Caesar*** (University of California).

H. Scullard, **From the Gracchi to Nero,*** 3rd ed. (Barnes and Noble) and R. Syme, **The Roman Revolution*** (Oxford) describe the transition from the late Republic to the early Empire.

J. Balsdon, **Rome: The Story of an Empire*** (McGraw-Hill, 1971) is brief and well illustrated. Also interesting are T. Africa, **Rome of the Caesars*** (Wiley); H. Mattingly, **Roman Imperial Civilization*** (Norton); J. Balsdon, **Roman Women*** (Day); J. Carcopino, **Daily Life in Ancient Rome*** (Bantam); A. Sherwin-White, **Racial Prejudice in Imperial Rome** (Cambridge, 1967); and R. MacMullen, **Enemies of the Roman Order: Treason, Unrest and Alienation in the Empire** (Harvard, 1967).

See also Martin L. Clarke, **The Roman Mind: Studies in the History of Thought from Cicero to Marcus Aurelius*** (Harvard); M. Grant, **Roman Literature*** (Penguin); Edith Hamilton, **The Roman Way*** (Norton); M. Wheeler, **Roman Art and Architecture*** (Praeger); and H. J. Rose, **Religion in Greece and Rome*** (Torchbooks). J. A. Hexter, **The Judaeo-Christian Tradition*** (Harper & Row, 1966) is a brief but valuable survey of the evolution of ancient Judaism and Christianity. On the late ancient history of the Jews see also E. Bickermann, **From Ezra to the Last of the Maccabees: Foundations of Post-Biblical Judaism*** (Schocken, 1962); D. S. Russell, **The Jews from Alexander to Herod** (Oxford, 1967); and M. Burrows, **The Dead Sea Scrolls*** (Compass).

Albert Schweitzer, **The Quest of the Historical Jesus*** (Macmillan) surveys the attempts of scholars to discover the Jesus of history. See also E. J. Goodspeed, **A Life of Jesus*** (Torchbooks); M. Enslin, **Christian Beginnings*** (Torchbooks); and H. Kee and F. Young, **Understanding the New Testament** (Prentice-Hall, 1957).

H. Chadwick, **The Early Church*** (Penguin) is an excellent survey of the first five centuries of Church history. See also H. Mattingly, **Christianity in the Roman Empire*** (Norton); E. R. Dodds, **Pagan and Christian in an Age of Anxiety** (Cambridge, 1965); W. Frend, **Martyrdom and Persecution in the Early Church** (New York University, 1967); C. N. Cochrane, **Christianity and Classical Culture: A Study of Thought and Action from Augustus to Augustine*** (Galaxy); A. H. M. Jones, **Constantine and the Conversion of Europe*** (Collier).

S. Katz, **The Decline of Rome and the Rise of Medieval Europe*** (Cornell) is a concise, clear account. A. H. M. Jones, **The Decline of the Ancient World*** (Holt, Rinehart and Winston) is a recent detailed survey. See also F. Lot, **The End of the Ancient World and the Beginning of the Middle Ages*** (Torchbooks); and H. Dörries, **Constantine the Great*** (Torchbooks, 1972). For scholarly opinion on Rome's decline see D. Kagan, ed., **Decline and Fall of the Roman Empire: Why Did It Collapse?*** (Heath).

J. B. Bury, **The Invasion of Europe by the Barbarians*** (Norton) is the best general work on the nature and effect of the Germanic invasions. See also E. A. Thompson, **The Early Germans** (Oxford, 1965).

CHAPTER 4: CITADEL AND CONQUEROR

Charles Diehl, **Byzantium: Greatness and Decline*** (Rutgers) is highly recommended as a brief introduction. Also brief is R. Guerdan, **Byzantium: Its Triumphs and Tragedy*** (Capricorn).

D. A. Miller, **The Byzantine Tradition*** (Harper & Row, 1966) is a brief perceptive survey of Byzantine civilization. See also J. Hussey, **The Byzantine World*** (Torchbooks); and S. Runciman, **Byzantine Civilization*** (Meridian).

John W. Barker, **Justinian and the Later Roman Empire** (Wisconsin, 1966) is clear, lively, and recent. See also G. Downey, **Constantinople in the Age of Justinian** (Oklahoma, 1960); and Dean A. Miller, **Imperial Constantinople*** (Wiley, 1969).

Charles M. Brand, **Byzantium Confronts the West, 1184–1204** (Harvard, 1968) and D. Queller, ed., **The Latin Conquest of Constantinople*** (Wiley, 1970) describe the events marking the beginning of the disintegration of the Byzantine empire.

H. Magoulias, **Byzantine Christianity: Emperor, Church and the West*** (Rand McNally, 1970) and T. Ware, **The Orthodox Church*** (Penguin) are two good surveys. S. Runciman, **The Eastern Schism** (Oxford, 1955) disentangles fact from legend.

For descriptions of art see D. Talbot Rice, **Byzantine Art*** (Penguin) and A. Grabar, **Art of the Byzantine Empire** (Crown, 1966). For superb color reproductions of Byzantine mosaics, see H. Newmayer, **Byzantine Mosaics*** (Crown) and A. Grabar, **Byzantine Painting** (Skira, 1953).

F. Dvornik, **The Slavs in European History and Civilization** (Rutgers, 1962) emphasizes Byzantine influences. G. Vernadsky, **Kievan Russia** (Yale, 1948) is detailed and authoritative. M. Florinsky, **Russia: A History and an Interpretation,** Vol. I (Macmillan, 1954) is excellent on early Russia. See also G. Fedotov, **The Russian Religious Mind: Kievan Christianity, the Tenth to the Thirteenth Centuries*** (Torchbooks).

P. K. Hitti, **The Arabs: A Short History*** (Gateway) is an abridgment of a scholarly general history of the Arabs. See also C. Brockelmann, **History of the Islamic Peoples*** (Capricorn).

W. Montgomery Watt, **Muhammad: Prophet and Statesman*** (Oxford) is short and excellent. See also T. Andrae, **Mohammed: The Man and His Faith*** (Torchbooks). For an interpretation and translation of the Koran, see M. Pickthall, **The Meaning of the Glorious Koran*** (Mentor). H. A. R. Gibb, **Mohammedanism: An Historical Survey*** (Galaxy) is outstanding.

H. Pirenne, **Mohammed and Charlemagne*** (Barnes and Noble) propounds the thesis that the expansion of Islam, and not the Germanic invasions, brought about the economic disintegration of the western Roman world. See also A. Havighurst, ed., **The Pirenne Thesis: Analysis, Criticism, Revision*** (Heath).

P. Coles, **The Ottoman Impact on Europe*** (Harcourt Brace Jovanovich, Inc., 1968) is a lucid, profusely illustrated survey. See also S. Runciman, **The Fall of Constantinople, 1453*** (Cambridge).

R. A. Nicholson, **A Literary History of the Arabs*** (Cambridge, 1969) traces the growth of Arab thought and culture through its literature. See also P. Hitti, **Makers of Arab History*** (Torchbooks); G. von Grunebaum, **Medieval Islam*** (Phoenix); and D. Talbot Rice, **Islamic Art*** (Praeger).

CHAPTER 5: EUROPE'S SEARCH FOR STABILITY

J. Dahmus, **The Middle Ages: A Popular Survey*** (Image); D. Hay, **The Medieval Centuries*** (Torchbooks); and H. Trevor-Roper, **The Rise of Christian Europe*** (Harcourt Brace Jovanovich, Inc.) are valuable inexpensive surveys of the entire Middle Ages. Robert Lopez, **The Birth of Europe** (Evans-Lippincott, 1967) is original and stimulating.

J. Wallace-Hadrill, **The Barbarian West, 400–1000*** (Torchbooks); Richard E. Sullivan, **Heirs of the Roman Empire*** (Cornell); and A. R. Lewis, **Emerging Medieval Europe, A.D. 400–1000*** (Knopf) are excellent brief surveys of the Early Middle Ages. For greater detail see F. Lot, **The End of the Ancient World and the Beginnings of the Middle Ages*** (Torchbooks); H. Moss, **The Birth of the Middle Ages, 395–814*** (Oxford); and C. Dawson, **The Making of Europe*** (Meridian).

H. Fichtenau, **The Carolingian Empire: The Age of Charlemagne*** (Torchbooks) is the best work on the subject. See also R. Winston, **Charlemagne: From the Hammer to the Cross*** (Vintage). On the Carolingian Renaissance see E. Duckett, **Alcuin, Friend of Charlemagne: His World and His Work** (Macmillan, 1951) and M. Laistner, **Thought and Letters in Western Europe, A.D. 500 to 900*** (Cornell).

J. Brondsted, **The Vikings*** (Penguin) and Gwyn Jones, **A History of the Vikings** (Oxford, 1968) are outstanding on Viking activities.

Carl Stephenson, **Mediaeval Feudalism*** (Cornell) is a clear introduction. See also F. Ganshof, **Feudalism*** (Torchbooks); and H. S. Bennett, **Life on the English Manor*** (Cambridge). S. Painter, **French Chivalry*** (Cornell) is a delightful essay on the feudal, religious, and courtly aspects of chivalry.

R. Latourche, **The Birth of Western Economy: Economic Aspects of the Dark Ages*** (Torchbooks) and Robert Lopez, **The Commercial Revolution of the Middle Ages*** (Prentice-Hall, 1971) throw new light on economic history. For greater detail see **The Cambridge Economic History of Europe,** Vols. I, II (Cambridge, 1952, 1966).

H. Pirenne, **Economic and Social History of Medieval Europe*** (Harvest) and **Medieval Cities*** (Princeton) are two small classics on the revival of trade and growth of cities. See also F. Rörig, **The Medieval Town*** (California); P. Boissonade, **Life and Work in Medieval Europe*** (Torchbooks); E. Power, **Medieval People*** (Barnes and Noble); P. Ziegler, **The Black Death*** (Torchbooks); A. Sapori, **The Italian Merchant in the Middle Ages*** (Norton); and S. Thrupp, **The Merchant Class of Medieval London*** (Ann Arbor).

CHAPTER 6: FEUDALISM AND MANORIALISM

F. Heer, **The Medieval World: Europe, 1100–1350*** (Mentor); S. Painter, **The Rise of the Feudal Monarchies*** (Cornell); and R. H. C. Davis, **A History of Medieval Europe from Constantine to Saint Louis** (McKay, 1957) are excellent syntheses.

W. K. Ferguson, **Europe in Transition, 1300 to 1520** (Houghton Mifflin, 1963) is a comprehensive work of synthesis. See also D. Hay, **Europe in the Fourteenth and Fifteenth Centuries** (Harcourt Brace Jovanovich, Inc., 1967); E. Cheyney, **The Dawn of a New Era, 1250–1453*** (Torchbooks); R. E. Lerner, **The Age of Adversity: The Fourteenth Century*** (Cornell); Jerah Johnson and W. Percy, **The Age of Recovery: The Fifteenth Century*** (Cornell); and M. Aston, **The Fifteenth Century: The Prospect of Europe*** (Harcourt Brace Jovanovich, Inc.)

See also H. Cam, **England before Elizabeth*** (Torchbooks); G. Sayles, **The Medieval Foundations of England*** (Perpetua); H. Loyn, **The Norman Conquest*** (Torchbooks); D. Whitelock et al., **The Norman Conquest: Its Setting and Impact** (Scribner, 1966); Amy Kelly, **Eleanor of Aquitaine and the Four Kings*** (Vintage); Thomas M. Jones, ed., **The Becket Controversy*** (Wiley, 1970); A. R. Myers, **England in the Late Middle Ages*** (Penguin); and George Holmes, **The Later Middle Ages, 1272–1485*** (Norton).

For French history see R. Fawtier, **The Capetian Kings of France, 987–1328*** (St. Martin); C. Petit-Dutaillis, **The Feudal Monarchy in France and England: From the Tenth to the Thirteenth Centuries*** (Torchbooks); P. S. Lewis, **Later Medieval France** (St. Martin, 1967); E. Perroy, **The Hundred Years' War*** (Capricorn); and J. Michelet, **Joan of Arc*** (Ann Arbor).

J. Bryce, **The Holy Roman Empire*** (Schocken) is an old masterpiece; it should be supplemented by G. Barraclough, **The Origins of Modern Germany*** (Capricorn) and R. Herzstein, ed., **The Holy Roman Empire in the Middle Ages: Universal State or German Catastrophe?*** (Heath).

D. Waley, **The Italian City-Republics*** (McGraw-Hill, 1969) is an excellent social and political account, profusely illustrated. See also P. Laven, **A Comprehensive History of Renaissance Italy, 1464–1534*** (Capricorn).

Gabriel Jackson, **The Making of Medieval Spain*** (Harcourt Brace Jovanovich, Inc., 1972) is brief and highly readable with many illustrations. See also W. C. Atkinson, **A History of Spain and Portugal*** (Penguin) and J. H. Elliott, **Imperial Spain, 1469–1716*** (Mentor).

N. Riasanovsky, **History of Russia,*** 2nd ed. (Oxford, 1969) and G. Vernadsky, **History of Russia,*** rev. ed. (Yale, 1961) are excellent surveys. See also I. Grey, **Ivan III and the Unification of Russia*** (Collier) and S. Graham, **Ivan the Terrible** (Shoe String, 1968).

CHAPTER 7: TO THE GLORY OF GOD

M. W. Baldwin, **The Mediaeval Church*** (Cornell) is a perceptive essay on Church development through the pontificate of Innocent III. See also Jeffrey Russell, **A History of Medieval Christianity: Prophecy and Order*** (Crowell, 1968); M. Deanesly, **A History of the Medieval Church, 590–1500,*** 9th ed. (Barnes and Noble, 1969); and H. Daniel-Rops, **The Church in the Dark Ages, 406–1050** (Dutton, 1959).

G. Barraclough, **The Medieval Papacy*** (Harcourt Brace Jovanovich, Inc., 1968) is brief and lavishly illustrated. S. R. Packard, **Europe and the Church Under Innocent III** (Russell, 1927) is short and admirable. For greater detail see W. Ullmann, **The Growth of Papal Government in the Middle Ages,** 3rd ed. (Barnes and Noble, 1970). On Church-state political theory see K. Morrison, **Tradition and Authority in the Western Church, 300–1140** (Princeton, 1969); W. Ullmann, **A History of Political Thought: The Middle Ages*** (Penguin); C. McIlwain, **The Growth of Political Thought in the West** (Macmillan, 1932).

S. Runciman, **A History of the Crusades,*** 3 vols. (Cambridge) is highly recommended for both its literary and historical merit. R. A. Newhall, **The Crusades*** (Holt [Berkshire Studies]) is a brief, lucid introduction to the subject. Also recommended is Zoé Oldenbourg, **The Crusades*** (Ballantine).

D. Knowles, **The Monastic Order in England,** 2nd ed. (Cambridge, 1963) is considered to be the best introduction to medieval monasticism. See also H. Workman, **The Evolution of the Monastic Ideal*** (Beacon) and E. Duckett, **The Wandering Saints of the Early Middle Ages*** (Norton).

H. C. Lea, **The Inquisition of the Middle Ages*** (Torchbooks) and A. Turberville, **Medieval Heresy and the Inquisition,** (Shoe String, 1964) are standard accounts. Religious radicalism, particularly that inspired by the love ethic, is treated in N. Cohn, **The Pursuit of the Millennium*** (Torchbooks). On the Albigensian heresy see S. Runciman, **The Medieval Manichee** (Cambridge, 1947).

C. H. Haskins, **The Renaissance of the Twelfth Century*** (Meridian) is the basic study of the medieval intellectual revival. C. Brooke, **The Twelfth Century Renaissance*** (Harcourt Brace Jovanovich, Inc., 1969) surveys all aspects of culture and is copiously illustrated. R. W. Southern, **The Making of the Middle Ages*** (Yale) is a brilliant treatment of society, government, the Church, and intellectual and spiritual growth from the late tenth to the early thirteenth centuries.

D. Knowles, **The Evolution of Medieval Thought*** (Vintage) is an excellent introduction. Recommended for greater detail are G. Leff, **Medieval Thought: St. Augustine to Ockham*** (Penguin); R. Bolgar, **The Classical Heritage and Its Beneficiaries*** (Cambridge); F. Artz, **The Mind of the Middle Ages,** 3rd ed. (Knopf, 1958); J. Sikes, **Peter Abailard** (Russell, 1965); and A. C. Crombie, **Medieval and Early Modern Science,*** 2 vols. (Anchor).

C. H. Haskins, **The Rise of the Universities*** (Cornell) is a brief survey. See also G. Leff, **Paris and Oxford Universities in the Thirteenth and Fourteenth Centuries*** (Wiley, 1968).

William T. Jackson, **The Literature of the Middle Ages** (Columbia, 1960) and **Medieval Literature: A History and a Guide*** (Collier) are recommended surveys. Outstanding also are Helen Waddell, **Mediaeval Latin Lyrics*** (Penguin) and C. S. Lewis, **The Allegory of Love*** (Galaxy) on the literature of romantic love.

H. Focillon, **The Art of the West in the Middle Ages,*** 2 vols. (Phaidon) is excellent on Romanesque and Gothic art. Also recommended are C. Morey, **Christian Art*** (Norton); O. von Simson, **The Gothic Cathedral*** (Torchbooks); and A. Temko, **Notre-Dame of Paris*** (Compass).

Stimulating interpretations of the interrelationship of medieval art, thought, and spirit are Henry Adams, **Mont-Saint-Michel and Chartres*** (Anchor); E. Mâle, **The Gothic Image*** (Torchbooks); and E. Panofsky, **Gothic Architecture and Scholasticism*** (Meridian).

CHAPTER 8: MAN IS THE MEASURE

J. Russell Major, **The Age of the Renaissance and Reformation*** (Lippincott, 1970) is a brief interpretive synthesis. W. K. Ferguson, **The Renaissance*** (Holt, Rinehart & Winston) is an excellent brief survey of the Italian and Northern Renaissances. G. Sellery, **The Renaissance: Its Nature and Origins*** (Wisconsin) concentrates on leading personalities and movements. J. Huizinga, **The Waning of the Middle Ages*** (Anchor) is an influential study of "fading and decay" in the culture of northern Europe during the fourteenth and fifteenth centuries.

J. C. Burckhardt, **The Civilization of the Renaissance in Italy*** (Mentor) is the classic study; it should be read in conjunction with W. K. Ferguson, **The Renaissance in Historical Thought: Five Centuries of Interpretation** (Houghton Mifflin, 1948) and T. Helton, ed., **The Renaissance: A Reconsideration of the Theories and Interpretations of the Age*** (Wisconsin, 1961).

F. B. Artz, **Renaissance Humanism, 1300–1550*** (Kent State) is a very brief introduction to humanism. P. O. Kristeller, **Renaissance Thought: The Classic, Scholastic, and Humanist Strains*** (Torchbooks) is an excellent analysis of Italian humanism. See also J. H. Whitfield, **Petrarch and the Renascence** (Haskell, 1943).

G. Brucker, **Renaissance Florence** (Wiley, 1969) contains much information in a short space. See also C. Ady, **Lorenzo de' Medici and Renaissance Italy*** (Collier) and Eric R. Chamberlain, **Everyday Life in Renaissance Times*** (Capricorn).

Margaret M. Phillips, **Erasmus and the Northern Renaissance*** (Collier) is a valuable introduction. Outstanding studies of other Northern Renaissance figures include R. W. Chambers, **Thomas More*** (Ann Arbor); J. H. Hexter, **More's Utopia: The Biography of an Idea*** (Torchbooks); D. B. Lewis, **Doctor Rabelais** (Greenwood, 1969); and M. Chute, **Shakespeare of London*** (Everyman).

On printing and its effect on culture see P. Butler, **The Origin of Printing in Europe** (Univ. of Chicago, 1940).

F. B. Artz, **From the Renaissance to Romanticism: Trends in Style in Art, Literature, and Music, 1300–1830*** (Phoenix) is a valuable overall view of the arts through six centuries, with a comprehensive bibliography.

E. Newton, **European Painting and Sculpture*** (Penguin) is brief and particularly valuable on the Renaissance. Also recommended are Creighton Gilbert, ed., **Renaissance Art*** (Torchbooks, 1970) and A. Hauser, **A Social History of Art,** Vol. II, **Renaissance to Baroque*** (Vintage).

B. Berenson, **Italian Painters of the Renaissance*** (Meridian) and H. Wölfflin, **The Art of the Italian Renaissance*** (Schocken) are two classics of art history. On northern painting see O. Benesch, **The Art of the Renaissance in Northern Europe** (Phaidon, 1965) and F. M. Simpson, **History of Architectural Development,** Vol. IV, **Renaissance Architecture** (McKay, 1961).

On music see Alfred Einstein, **A Short History of Music*** (Vintage) and G. Reese, **Music in the Renaissance** (Norton, 1959).

CHAPTER 9: HERE I TAKE MY STAND

Good accounts of Church history during the fourteenth and fifteenth centuries are L. Elliott-Binns, **History of the Decline and Fall of the Medieval Papacy** (Shoe String, 1967) and L. von Pastor, **The History of the Popes from the Close of the Middle Ages,** Vol. I (Herder, 1923). See also G. Mollat, **The Popes at Avignon*** (Torchbooks); G. Leff, **Heresy in the Later Middle Ages,** 2 vols. (Barnes and Noble, 1967); K. McFarlane, **John Wycliffe and the Beginnings of English Nonconformity** (Verry, 1952); M. Spinka, **John Hus: A Biography** (Princeton, 1968); and R. Ridolfi, **The Life of Girolamo Savonarola** (Knopf, 1959).

G. L. Mosse, **The Reformation,*** 3rd ed. (Holt, Rinehart & Winston); E. H. Harbison, **The Age of Reformation*** (Cornell); Philip Hughes, **A Popular History of the Reformation*** (Image); R. H. Bainton, **The Reformation of the Sixteenth Century*** (Beacon); and A. G. Dickens, **Reformation and Society in Sixteenth-Century Europe*** (Harcourt Brace Jovanovich, Inc.) are all good brief surveys; the last volume cited contains many illustrations. J. Hurstfield, ed., **The Reformation Crisis*** (Torchbooks) contains brief, perceptive essays by noted scholars on major aspects of the Reformation era. See also John P. Dolan, **A History of the Reformation: A Conciliatory Assessment of Opposite Views*** (Mentor).

J. Huizinga, **Erasmus and the Age of the Reformation*** (Torchbooks) and E. H. Harbison, **The Christian Scholar in the Age of the Reformation*** (Scribner) are excellent on the northern humanists' criticisms of the Church.

R. H. Bainton, **Here I Stand: A Life of Martin Luther*** (Mentor) is the most readable account. See also E. Erikson, **Luther: A Study in Psychoanalysis and History*** (Norton); F. Lau, **Luther** (Westminster, 1963) and E. Schwiebert, **Luther and His Times** (Concordia, 1950).

Williston Walker, **John Calvin: The Organiser of Reformed Protestantism*** (Schocken) is probably the best introduction. G. Harkness, **John Calvin: The Man and His Ethics*** (Abingdon) and J. T. McNeill, **The History and Character of Calvinism*** (Scribner) are standard works. See also W. Monter, **Calvin's Geneva*** (Wiley, 1967) and J. Ridley, **John Knox** (Oxford, 1968).

A. G. Dickens, **The English Reformation*** (Schocken) and T. M. Parker, **The English Reformation to 1558,*** 2nd ed. (Oxford) are excellent surveys.

On the "left wing" of Protestantism, see F. Littell, **The Anabaptist View of the Church** (Beacon, 1958) and George H. Williams, **The Radical Reformation** (Westminster, 1962).

A. G. Dickens, **The Counter Reformation*** (Harcourt Brace Jovanovich, Inc., 1969) is brief and richly illustrated. Sympathetic Catholic accounts are H. Daniel-Rops, **The Catholic Reformation,** 2 vols. (Image) and P. Janelle, **The Catholic Reformation** (Bruce, 1949).

On the effects of the religious upheaval see W. Pauck, **The Heritage of the Reformation,*** rev. ed. (Galaxy, 1968); R. H. Tawney, **Religion and the Rise of Capitalism*** (Mentor); R. Kingdon and R. Linder, eds., **Calvin and Calvinism; Sources of Democracy?*** (Heath, 1970); H. Kamen, **The Rise of Toleration*** (McGraw-Hill, 1967); E. Troeltsch, **Protestantism and Progress: A Historical Study of the Relation of Protestantism to the Modern World*** (Beacon) and E. W. Monter, **European Witchcraft*** (Wiley, 1969).

CHAPTER 10: THE STRIFE OF STATES AND KINGS

The following are crisp, purposeful, and readable political surveys of all or part of the century and a half following the beginning of the Protestant Reformation:

M. L. Bush, **Renaissance, Reformation and the Outer World, 1450–1660*** (Torchbooks); H. Koenigsberger and G. Mosse, **Europe in the Sixteenth Century** (Holt, Rinehart & Winston, 1969); J. H. Elliott, **Europe Divided, 1559–1598*** (Torchbooks); T. Aston, ed., **Crisis in Europe: 1560–1660*** (Anchor); C. J. Friedrich, **The Age of the Baroque, 1610–1660*** (Torchbooks); A. Moote, **The Seventeenth Century: Europe in Ferment*** (Heath, 1970); P. Coles, **The Ottoman Impact on Europe*** (Harcourt Brace Jovanovich, Inc., 1968); Joseph R. Strayer, **On the Medieval Origins of the Modern State** (Princeton, 1970); K. H. D. Haley, **The Dutch in the Seventeenth Century** (Harcourt Brace Jovanovich, Inc., 1972); A. D. Ortiz, **The Golden Age of Spain, 1516–1659** (Basic Books, 1971); and G. Pages, **The Thirty Years War*** (Harper and Row, 1972).

J. H. Whitfield, **Machiavelli** (Russell, 1947) is a sympathetic account. The older, unfavorable view is well presented in H. Butterfield, **The Statecraft of Machiavelli*** (Collier). S. Anglo, **Machiavelli: A Dissection** (Harcourt Brace Jovanovich, Inc., 1970) is a perceptive study with new insights. See also the brilliant studies by G. Mattingly, **Renaissance Diplomacy*** (Penguin) and John W. Allen, **A History of Political Thought in the Sixteenth Century*** (Barnes and Noble).

J. Lynch, **Spain Under the Hapsburgs,** Vol. I, **Empire and Absolutism, 1516–1598** (Oxford, 1964) is the latest authoritative treatment. Also recommended are J. H. Elliott, **Imperial Spain, 1469–1716*** (Mentor); R. Trevor Davies, **The Golden Century of Spain, 1501–1621*** (Torchbooks); K. Brandi, **Emperor Charles V: The Growth and Destiny of a Man and a World*** (Humanities, 1965); R. B. Merriman, **Suleiman the Magnificent** (Cooper Square, 1944).

P. Geyl, **The Revolt of the Netherlands, 1555–1609*** (Barnes and Noble) is the best short account. C. Wedgwood, **William the Silent*** (Norton) is a beautifully written biography.

G. Mattingly, **The Armada*** (Sentry) is the classic account. Popular and profusely illustrated is Jay Williams, **The Spanish Armada** (Harper & Row, 1966).

Elizabeth Jenkins, **Elizabeth the Great*** (Capricorn) is short and lively. J. Neale, **Queen Elizabeth I*** (Anchor) is the most authoritative biography. Antonia Fraser, **Mary Queen of Scots** (Delacorte, 1969) is a best seller. See also J. Hurstfield, **Elizabeth I and the Unity of England*** (Torchbooks); W. C. Richardson, **Mary Tudor, the White Queen** (University Washington Press); A. L. Rowse, **The England of Elizabeth*** (Collier); S. Bindoff, **Tudor England*** (Penguin); R. Wernham, **Before the Armada: The Emergence of the English Nation, 1485–1588** (Harcourt Brace Jovanovich, Inc., 1966).

J. Neale, **The Age of Catharine de' Medici*** (Torchbooks) describes the religious and political troubles of sixteenth-century France.

C. V. Wedgwood, **The Thirty Years' War*** (Anchor) is a vigorous account. See also H. Holborn, **A History of Modern Germany,** Vol. I, **The Reformation** (Knopf, 1959), which is the standard survey of Hapsburg Germany to 1648.

CHAPTER 11: SEEK OUT, DISCOVER, AND FIND

C. Nowell, **The Great Discoveries and the First Colonial Empires*** (Cornell); J. H. Parry, **The Establishment of the European Hegemony: 1415–1715*** (Torchbooks); and **The Age of Reconnaissance: Discovery, Exploration and Settlement,** (Praeger, 1970) encompass excellent brief coverage. D. Lach, **Asia in the Making of Europe,** Vol. I: **The**

Century of Discovery (Univ. of Chicago, 1965) describes what Europe had learned about Asia by 1600.

S. E. Morison, **The European Discovery of America: The Northern Voyages** (Oxford, 1971) is an engrossing up-to-date survey. The best book on Columbus is S. E. Morison, **Admiral of the Ocean Sea** (Little, Brown, 1942), condensed as **Christopher Columbus, Mariner*** (Mentor). See also H. Holand, **Norse Discoveries and Explorations in North America*** (Dover) and Carl Sauer, **Northern Mists*** (California).

E. Prestage, **The Portuguese Pioneers** (Barnes and Noble, 1967) is the standard work. See also Jean Anderson, **Henry the Navigator, Prince of Portugal** (Westminster, 1969); and A. Toussaint, **History of the Indian Ocean** (Univ. of Chicago, 1966).

F. A. Kirkpatrick, **The Spanish Conquistadores*** (Meridian) is a colorful treatment. See also J. Bannon, ed., **The Spanish Conquistadores: Men or Devils?*** (Holt, Rinehart & Winston) and Carl Sauer, **The Early Spanish Main*** (California). W. H. Prescott, **History of the Conquest of Mexico*** (Phoenix) and **The Conquest of Peru*** (Mentor), both abridged, are historical classics. See also S. de Madariaga, **Hernán Cortés: Conqueror of Mexico** (University of Miami, 1967) and C. M. Parr, **Ferdinand Magellan: Circumnavigator** (Crowell, 1964).

M. Dobb, **Studies in the Development of Capitalism,*** 2nd ed. (New World) describes the meaning, origin, and development of capitalism. See also Robert L. Reynolds, **Europe Emerges: Transition Toward an Industrial World-Wide Society, 600–1750*** (Wisconsin), **The Cambridge Economic History of Europe,** Vol. IV: **The Economy of Expanding Europe in the Sixteenth and Seventeenth Centuries** (Cambridge, 1967). The following are excellent special studies: R. De Roover, **The Rise and Decline of the Medici Bank, 1397–1494*** (Norton); R. Ehrenberg, **Capitalism and Finance in the Age of the Renaissance: A Study of the Fuggers and Their Connections** (Kelley, 1928); and V. Barbour, **Capitalism in Amsterdam in the Seventeenth Century*** (Michigan). K. Haley, **The Dutch in the Seventeenth Century*** (Harcourt Brace Jovanovich, Inc., 1972) is a lively portrait of Dutch society with many contemporary illustrations.

A. P. Thornton, **Doctrines of Imperialism*** (Wiley, 1965); and Raymond Betts, **Europe Overseas: Phases of Imperialism** (Basic Books, 1968) contain good short accounts of early modern imperialism and mercantilism. See also C. Boxer, **Four Centuries of Portuguese Expansion, 1415–1825*** (California); **The Dutch Seaborne Empire, 1600–1800** (Knopf, 1965); and C. H. Haring, **The Spanish Empire in America*** (Harbinger).

On the African slave trade see D. Mannix and M. Cowley, **Black Cargoes*** (Compass) and J. Pope-Hennessy, **Sins of the Fathers: A Study of the Atlantic Slave Traders, 1441–1807** (Knopf, 1968). David B. Davis, **The Problem of Slavery in Western Culture*** (Cornell) is a historical review of the ideas advanced in justification of slavery.

On other aspects of the Commercial Revolution see Earl J. Hamilton, **American Treasure and the Price Revolution in Spain, 1501–1650** (Octagon, 1965); R. H. Tawney, **The Agrarian Problem in the Sixteenth Century*** (Torchbooks); and B. H. van Bath, **Agrarian History of Western Europe, A.D. 500–1850** (St. Martin, 1963).

CHAPTER 12: NEW DIMENSIONS OF THE MIND

R. W. Southern, **The Making of the Middle Ages*** (Yale) is a brilliant topical treatment of the eleventh and twelfth centuries. F. Heer, **The Medieval World*** (Mentor) vivid-ly pictures the society of the twelfth and thirteenth centuries.

M. W. Baldwin, **The Mediaeval Church*** (Cornell) is a perceptive essay on Church development through the pontificate of Innocent III. See also Jeffrey Russell, **A History of Medieval Christianity: Prophecy and Order** (Crowell, 1968); M. Deanesly, **A History of the Medieval Church, 590–1500,*** 9th ed. (Barnes and Noble, 1969); H. Daniel-Rops, **The Church in the Dark Ages, 406–1050** (Dutton, 1959).

G. Barraclough, **The Medieval Papacy*** (Harcourt Brace Jovanovich, Inc., 1968) is brief and lavishly illustrated. S. R. Packard, **Europe and the Church Under Innocent III** (Russell, 1927) is short and admirable. For greater detail see W. Ullmann, **The Growth of Papal Government in the Middle Ages,** 3rd ed. (Barnes and Noble, 1970). On Church-state political theory see K. Morrison, **Tradition and Authority in the Western Church, 300–1140** (Princeton, 1969); W. Ullmann, **A History of Political Thought: The Middle Ages*** (Penguin); and C. McIlwain, **The Growth of Political Thought in the West** (Macmillan, 1932).

D. Knowles, **The Monastic Order in England,** 2nd ed. (Cambridge, 1963) is considered to be the best introduction to medieval monasticism. See also H. Workman, **The Evolution of the Monastic Ideal*** (Beacon) and E. Duckett, **The Wandering Saints of the Early Middle Ages*** (Norton).

H. C. Lea, **The Inquisition of the Middle Ages*** (Torchbooks) and A. Turberville, **Medieval Heresy and the Inquisition** (Shoe String, 1964) are standard accounts. Religious radicalism, particularly that inspired by the love ethic, is treated in N. Cohn, **The Pursuit of the Millennium*** (Torchbooks). On the Albigensian heresy see S. Runciman, **The Medieval Manichee** (Cambridge, 1947).

C. Brooke, **The Twelfth Century Renaissance*** (Harcourt Brace Jovanovich, Inc., 1969) is a brief introduction, copiously illustrated. The basic study is C. H. Haskins, **The Renaissance of the Twelfth Century*** (Meridian).

D. Knowles, **The Evolution of Medieval Thought*** (Vintage) is an excellent introduction. Recommended for greater detail are G. Leff, **Medieval Thought: St. Augustine to Ockham*** (Penguin); R. Bolgar, **The Classical Heritage and Its Beneficiaries*** (Cambridge); F. Artz, **The Mind of the Middle Ages,** 3rd ed. (Knopf, 1958); J. Sikes, **Peter Abailard,** (Russell, 1965); F. Copleston, **Aquinas*** (Penguin) and A. C. Crombie, **Medieval and Early Modern Science,*** 2 vols. (Anchor).

C. H. Haskins, **The Rise of the Universities*** (Cornell) is a brief survey. See also G. Leff, **Paris and Oxford Universities in the Thirteenth and Fourteenth Centuries*** (Wiley, 1968).

William T. Jackson, **The Literature of the Middle Ages** (Columbia, 1960) and **Medieval Literature: A History and a Guide*** (Collier) are recommended surveys. Outstanding are Helen Waddell, **Mediaeval Latin Lyrics*** (Penguin); C. S. Lewis, **The Allegory of Love*** (Galaxy) on the literature of romantic love; and E. Curtius, **European Literature and the Latin Middle Ages*** (Torchbooks).

H. Focillon, **The Art of the West in the Middle Ages,** 2 vols. (Phaidon, 1963) is excellent on Romanesque and Gothic art. Also recommended are C. Morey, **Christian Art** (Norton, 1942); O. von Simson, **The Gothic Cathedral*** (Torchbooks); and A. Temko, **Notre-Dame of Paris*** (Compass).

Stimulating interpretations of the interrelationship of medieval art, thought, and spirit are Henry Adams, **Mont-Saint-Michel and Chartres*** (Anchor); E. Mâle,

The Gothic Image* (Torchbooks); and E. Panofsky, Gothic Architecture and Scholasticism* (Meridian).

CHAPTER 13: L'ETAT, C'EST MOI

Brief general introductions to the history of this period include J. M. Thompson, European History, 1494–1789* (Torchbooks); John B. Wolf, Toward a European Balance of Power, 1620–1715 (Rand McNally, 1970); M. Beloff, The Age of Absolutism, 1660–1815* (Torchbooks); C. J. Friedrich and C. Blitzer, The Age of Power* (Cornell); F. Manuel, The Age of Reason* (Cornell); M. S. Anderson, Eighteenth-Century Europe, 1713–1789* (Galaxy); and Orest and Patricia Ranum, eds., The Century of Louis XIV* (Harper & Row). Another introductory book, A. Cobban et al., The Eighteenth Century: Europe in the Age of Enlightenment (McGraw-Hill, 1969) contains almost six hundred illustrations.

The following are more detailed surveys: D. Maland, Europe in the Seventeenth Century (St. Martin's, 1966); A. Moote, The Seventeenth Century: Europe in Ferment (Heath, 1970); David Ogg, Europe in the Seventeenth Century* (Collier); J. Stoye, Europe Unfolding, 1648–1688* (Torchbooks); Matthew S. Anderson, Europe in the Eighteenth Century (Holt, Rinehart & Winston, 1961); and David Ogg, Europe of the Ancien Régime, 1715–1783* (Torchbooks). Also valuable are the pertinent volumes in the Rise of Modern Europe series* (Torchbooks).

On the eighteenth-century power struggle see L. Dehio, The Precarious Balance: Four Centuries of the European Power Struggle* (Vintage) and A. Sorel, Europe Under the Old Régime* (Torchbooks).

L. B. Packard, The Age of Louis XIV* (Holt, Rinehart & Winston); M. Ashley, Louis XIV and the Greatness of France* (Free Press); David Ogg, Louis XIV (Norton, 1968) is the latest detailed study. See also William F. Church, ed., The Impact of Absolutism in France: National Experience Under Richelieu, Mazarin, and Louis XIV* (Wiley, 1969); C. V. Wedgwood, Richelieu and the French Monarchy* (Collier); and J. C. Rule, Louis XIV and the Craft of Kingship (Ohio State).

W. H. Lewis, The Splendid Century: Life in the France of Louis XIV* (Anchor) is a popular account, beautifully written. P. Erlanger, The Age of Courts and Kings: Manners and Morals, 1558–1715* (Anchor) is witty and charming. R. Hatton, Europe in the Age of Louis XIV* (Harcourt Brace Jovanovich, Inc., 1969) is a profusely illustrated social history. See also O. Ranum, Paris in the Age of Absolutism* (Wiley, 1968).

R. Lockyer, Tudor and Stuart Britain, 1471–1714 (St. Martin's, 1964); Dorothy Marshall, Eighteenth Century England (McKay, 1962) are excellent general surveys. M. Ashley, England in the Seventeenth Century, 1603–1714* (Penguin) and G. Aylmer, A Short History of Seventeenth-Century England* (Mentor) are brief and first rate. The classic survey of the Stuart period is G. M. Trevelyan. England Under the Stuarts* (Barnes and Noble).

On the English constitutional crises see Philip Taylor, ed., The Origins of the English Civil War: Conspiracy, Crusade, or Class Conflict?* (Heath); Christopher Hill, The Century of Revolution, 1603–1714* (Norton); M. Ashley, The Greatness of Oliver Cromwell* (Collier); C. V. Wedgwood, Oliver Cromwell* (Collier); G. M. Trevelyan, The English Revolution, 1688–1689* (Galaxy). On the Levellers and Diggers see M. Walzer, The Revolution of the Saints: A Study of the Origins of Radical Politics* (Atheneum).

B. Sumner, Peter the Great and the Emergence of Russia* (Collier); L. J. Oliva, Russia in the Era of Peter the Great* (Spectrum); and G. S. Thomson, Catherine the Great and the Expansion of Russia* (Collier) are good brief accounts. Good reading also are K. Waliszewski, The Romance of an Empress: Catherine II of Russia (Shoe String, 1968); I. Grey, Catherine the Great (Lippincott, 1962); Otto Hoetzsch, The Evolution of Russia* (Harcourt Brace Jovanovich, Inc., 1966); and Marc Raeff, Peter the Great* (Heath, 1963).

S. B. Fay, The Rise of Brandenburg-Prussia to 1786,* rev. ed. (Holt, Rinehart & Winston) is an admirable introduction. See also H. Holborn, A History of Modern Germany, 1648–1840 (Knopf, 1963); Walter H. Wilson, The Soldier Kings: The House of Hohenzollern (Putnam, 1969); H. Rosenburg, Bureaucracy, Aristocracy, and Authority: The Prussian Experience, 1660–1815* (Beacon); G. A. Craig, The Politics of the Prussian Army: 1640–1945* (Galaxy); and D. B. Horn, Frederick the Great and the Rise of Russia* (Verry).

CHAPTER 14: THE RIGHTS OF MAN

Peter Gay, The Enlightenment: The Rise of Modern Paganism* (Vintage) is an eloquent treatment of the thinkers who greatly influenced the shape of modern society. R. Anchor, The Enlightenment Tradition* (Harper & Row) is a very brief overview. See also K. Martin, The Rise of French Liberal Thought* (Torchbooks) and W. H. Coates and H. V. White, The Emergence of Liberal Humanism, Vol. I of An Intellectual History of Western Europe (McGraw-Hill, 1966). J. Talmon, The Origins of Totalitarian Democracy* (Norton) stresses the influence of Rousseau.

G. Bruun, The Enlightened Despots,* 2nd ed. (Holt, Rinehart & Winston) is good reading and brief. See also J. Gagliardo, Enlightened Despotism* (Crowell); Paul Bernard, Joseph II (Twayne, 1968); and the biographies of Frederick the Great and Catherine the Great cited in Chapter 13.

C. Brinton, The Anatomy of Revolution,* rev. ed. (Vintage) is a comparative study of the English, American, French, and Russian revolutions. See also the detailed study by R. R. Palmer, The Age of the Democratic Revolution: A Political History of Europe and America, 1760–1800, 2 vols. (Princeton, 1959–1964).

Edmund S. Morgan, The Birth of the Republic, 1763–1789* (Univ. of Chicago) is an excellent brief history of the American Revolution. Also recommended are L. H. Gipson, The Coming of the Revolution, 1763–1775* (Torchbooks); Gordon S. Wood, The Creation of the American Republic, 1776–1787 (North Carolina, 1969); and Merrill Jensen, The Founding of a Nation (Oxford, 1968).

R. R. Palmer, The World of the French Revolution (Harper & Row, 1970) examines Europe before 1789, the Revolution, and its impact on European society. Other excellent syntheses are G. Rudé, Revolutionary Europe, 1783–1815* (Torchbooks); E. Hobsbawm, The Age of Revolution: Europe 1789–1848* (Mentor); and N. Hampson, The First European Revolution: 1776–1815* (Harcourt Brace Jovanovich, Inc., 1969), which is profusely illustrated.

G. Lefebvre, The Coming of the French Revolution* (Vintage) stresses the role of the reactionary nobility in precipitating the Revolution. C. Behrens, The Ancien Régime* (Harcourt Brace Jovanovich, Inc., 1969) is brief and richly illustrated.

L. Gershoy, The French Revolution, 1789–1799* (Holt, Rinehart & Winston) is a brief survey. Longer perceptive surveys are C. Brinton, A Decade of Revolution, 1789–1799* (Torchbooks); M. Sydenham, The French Revolution* (Capricorn); and James M. Thompson, The

French Revolution* (Galaxy). F. Kafker and L. Laux, eds., **The French Revolution: Conflicting Interpretations*** (Random House, 1968) samples the opinions of leading historians.

R. R. Palmer, **Twelve Who Ruled*** (Atheneum) is good reading on the Reign of Terror. James M. Thompson, **Robespierre and the French Revolution*** (Collier) is a sympathetic brief biography. G. Bruun, **Saint-Just: Apostle of the Terror** (Shoe String, 1966) describes a precursor of today's revolutionary student leaders. The importance of the class struggle is stressed in G. Rudé, **The Crowd in the French Revolution*** (Galaxy).

F. Markham, **Napoleon and the Awakening of Europe*** (Collier) is a good popular introduction to the Napoleonic period. G. Bruun, **Europe and the French Imperium, 1799–1814*** (Torchbooks) is a notable survey. See also J. Godechot, B. Hyslop, and D. Dowd, **The Napoleonic Era in Europe*** (Holt, Rinehart & Winston, 1970) and R. B. Holtman, **The Napoleonic Revolution*** (Lippincott, 1967).

F. Markham, **Napoleon*** (Mentor) is the best brief biography. G. Lefebvre, **Napoleon,** 2 vols. (Columbia, 1969) is a renowned study. P. Geyl, **Napoleon: For and Against*** (Yale) presents divergent evaluations by historians since 1815.

Irene Nicholson, **The Liberators: A Study of Independence Movements in Spanish America** (Praeger, 1969) is readable.

CHAPTER 15: ROMANTICS AND REALISTS

For an introduction to European scientific, intellectual, and esthetic developments during this period, see C. J. H. Hayes, **A Generation of Materialism: 1871–1900*** (Torchbooks); W. W. Wagar, ed., **European Intellectual History Since Darwin and Marx*** (Harper & Row); and R. N. Stromberg, **An Intellectual History of Modern Europe*** (Appleton).

For English literature see G. B. Woods, ed., **English Poetry and Prose of the Romantic Movement** (Scott, Foresman, 1950) and J. H. Buckley and G. B. Woods, eds., **Poetry of the Victorian Period,** 3rd ed. (Scott, Foresman, 1965). Other relevant works are G. L. Mosse, **The Culture of Western Europe, The Nineteenth and Twentieth Centuries: An Introduction** (Rand McNally, 1961); L. A. Willoughby, **The Romantic Movement in Germany** (Oxford, 1930); and B. Willey, **Nineteenth Century Studies*** (Torchbooks).

M. Raynal, **The Nineteenth Century: New Sources of Emotion from Goya to Gaugin** (Skira, 1952) is a first-rate introduction to nineteenth-century painting. See also M. Brion, **The Art of the Romantic Era*** (Praeger), as well as relevant chapters in E. H. Gombrich, **The Story of Art*** (Phaidon); H. W. and D. J. Janson, **Picture History of Painting*** (Washington Square); and F. B. Artz, **From the Renaissance to Romanticism: Trends in Style in Art, Literature, and Music, 1330–1830*** (Phoenix).

For a better understanding of major developments in what has been described as music's "golden century," see M. Brion, **Schumann and the Romantic Age** (Macmillan, 1956); A. Einstein, **Music in the Romantic Era** (Norton, 1947); P. A. Scholes, **Romantic and Nationist Schools of the Nineteenth Century,** Vol. II of **The Listener's History of Music,** 3rd. (Oxford, 1942); and H. C. Colles, **Ideals of the Nineteenth Century, the Twentieth Century,** Pt. III of **The Growth of Music** (Oxford, 1956). Well-written biographies of two titans in the world of music are M. M. Scott, **Beethoven** (Farrar, Straus, 1949); E. Valentin, **Beethoven: A Pictorial Biography** (Viking, 1958); and P. Latham, **Brahms** (Farrar, Straus, 1949).

In **The Voyage of the Beagle*** (Anchor) Darwin has left a journal of his experiences and observations about natural history and geology that led to the revolutionary **The Origin of Species*** (Collier). See also J. Huxley, ed., **The Living Thoughts of Darwin*** (Premier). Making use of unpublished documents, G. Himmelfarb in **Darwin and the Darwinian Revolution** (Norton, 1968) sheds valuable light on both the scientist's character and the age in which he lived. See also G. De Beer, **Charles Darwin*** (Anchor).

C. C. Gillispie, **Genesis and Geology*** (Torchbooks) is a review of the controversy between religion and science which preceded the publication of *The Origin of Species.* The involvement of Darwin and Thomas Huxley in the intellectual furor is dealt with in W. Irvine, **Apes, Angels, and Victorians*** (World).

S. Tax, ed., **Issues in Evolution,** Vol. III of **Evolution After Darwin** (Univ. of Chicago, 1960) is an assessment of the effects of Darwin's theories on modern-day science, philosophy, and religion. Excellent accounts of modern evolution are found in J. Huxley, **Evolution: the Modern Synthesis** (Allen and Unwin, 1958); T. Dobzhansky, **Genetics and the Origin of Species** (Oxford, 1951); and G. G. Simpson, **The Meaning of Evolution*** (Mentor). In his admirable **Social Darwinism in American Thought*** (Beacon) R. Hofstadter details the cult of force, struggle, and militarism in the United States during this period.

Excellent biographies of important scientists include W. W. Cheyne, **Lister and His Achievements** (Longmans, 1925); E. Curie, **Madame Curie*** (Pocket Books); H. Iltis, **The Life of Mendel** (Hafner, 1932); and R. Dubos, **Louis Pasteur, Free Lance of Science** (Little, Brown, 1950).

A. Maurois, **The Life of Balzac** (Harper & Row, 1966); and H. Troyat, **Tolstoy** (Doubleday, 1967) are outstanding studies of notable literary figures.

For significant developments in esthetic theory and painting in the decades preceding World War One, see C. Edward Gauss, **The Aesthetic Theories of French Artists: From Realism to Surrealism*** (Johns Hopkins) and E. F. Fry, **Cubism (World of Art Series)*** (Thames and Hudson). For an overall survey of developments during the past two centuries see H. L. C. Jaffe, **The Nineteenth and Twentieth Centuries,** Vol. 5 of the **Dolphin History of Painting*** (Thames and Hudson). A number of outstanding painters and their works are treated in individual publications; Fontana has issued a series of **Paintings*** in its **Art Books,** separately for Manet, Matisse, and Picasso. M. De Micheli has written **Cezanne*** and **Picasso*** for Thames and Hudson.

CHAPTER 16: THE INDUSTRIAL REVOLUTION AND ITS INFLUENCE

C. Singer *et al.,* eds., **The Late Nineteenth Century, 1850–1900,** Vol. V of **A History of Technology** (Oxford, 1958) is lavishly illustrated and clearly written, perhaps the best single work on technological accomplishments during this period. For a survey covering a longer time space, see D. W. Landes, **The Unbound Prometheus: Technological Change and Industrial Development in Western Europe from 1750 to the Present*** (Cambridge). On economic and industrial developments during the nineteenth century, see H. Heaton, **Economic History of Europe,** rev. ed. (Harper, 1948). Also recommended are T. Ashton, **The Industrial Revolution: 1760–1830*** (Galaxy); W. O. Henderson, **The Industrialization of Europe: 1780–1914*** (Harcourt Brace Jovanovich, Inc.); and J. C. Chambers and G. E. Mingay, **The Agricultural Revolution** (Schocken, 1966).

H. D. Aiken, ed., **The Age of Ideology: the Nineteenth Century Philosophers*** (Mentor) includes selections from the works of Hegel, Mill, and others. For a brief study of

Marx and his ideas, see I. Berlin, **Karl Marx; His Life and Environment*** (Galaxy). R. Payne provides a portrait of his personal life in **Marx** (Simon & Schuster, 1968).

K. Marx and F. Engels, **Basic Writings on Politics and Philosophy*** (Anchor) comprises a sizable selection from the writings of Marx and his chief associate, including the **Manifesto** in full, chosen to point up aspects of their thought that are having an impact on the world today, particularly in the underdeveloped countries. See also G. Hegel, **Selections,*** J. Loewenberg, ed. (Scribner) and K. Marx, **Das Kapital,*** S. Levitsky, ed. (Gateway).

Vivid insights into the life and prevailing attitudes of the period are provided by contemporary fiction and by biographical studies of leading personalities. Recommended, for example, are the novels of Stendhal, such as **The Charterhouse of Parma*** (Penguin), which portrays post-Napoleonic Italy and life at a reactionary court. The novels of Charles Dickens depict not only the more attractive—albeit often sentimentalized—aspects of traditional English country society but also the social injustices and urban degradation which all too often accompanied the advent of the Industrial Revolution. G. L. Strachey, **Queen Victoria** (Harbrace Modern Classics, 1949) is an example of modern biographical analysis.

CHAPTER 17: NATIONALISM AND AUTHORITARIAN REGIMES

The following are excellent on the general background of the period 1815–1850: J. McManners, **European History, 1789–1914*** (Torchbooks); A. J. May, **The Age of Metternich, 1814–1848,*** rev. ed. (Holt, Rinehart & Winston); E. Hobsbawm, **The Age of Revolution: Europe, 1789–1848*** (Mentor); J. Droz, **Europe Between Revolutions, 1815–1848*** (Torchbooks); F. Artz, **Reaction and Revolution, 1814–1832*** (Torchbooks); W. L. Langer, **Political and Social Upheaval, 1832–1852*** (Torchbooks); J. Talmon, **Romanticism and Revolt: Europe, 1815–1848*** (Harcourt Brace Jovanovich, Inc., 1967); Peter Stearns, **European Society in Upheaval: Social History Since 1800*** (Macmillan, 1967) and Jacques Barzun, **Romanticism and the Modern Ego*** (Little, Brown).

H. Nicolson, **The Congress of Vienna: A Study in Allied Unity, 1812–1822*** (Compass) is good reading. See also Henry A. Kissinger, **A World Restored: Metternich, Castlereagh and the Problems of Peace, 1812–1822*** (Sentry) and Henry F. Schwartz, ed., **Metternich, the "Coachman of Europe": Statesman or Evil Genius?*** (Heath).

G. Fasel, **Europe in Upheaval: The Revolutions of 1848*** (Rand McNally, 1970) is a valuable short synthesis of recent scholarship. Priscilla Robertson, **The Revolutions of 1848: A Social History*** (Princeton) is colorful and entertaining. A scholarly reassessment is F. Fejto, ed., **The Opening of an Era, 1848: An Historical Symposium** (Fertig, 1966). G. Rudé, **The Crowd in History, 1730–1848*** (Wiley) describes how crowds were turned into bellicose mobs.

John B. Wolf, **France, 1814–1919: The Rise of a Liberal-Democratic Society*** (Torchbooks) and A. Cobban, **A History of Modern France,*** Vol. II (Penguin) are notable surveys. For greater detail see F. Artz, **France Under the Bourbon Restoration, 1814–1830** (Russell, 1963); T. Howarth, **Citizen King: The Life of Louis-Philippe, King of the French** (Verry, 1961); G. Duveau, **1848: The Making of a Revolution*** (Vintage, 1968); and F. A. Simpson, **The Rise of Louis Napoleon** (Longmans, 1950).

Asa Briggs, **The Making of Modern England, 1783–1867: The Age of Improvement*** (Torchbooks) and E. L. Woodward, **The Age of Reform, 1815–1870,** 2nd ed. (Oxford, 1962) are valuable surveys. On social and economic change from 1815 to 1885 see S. Checkland, **The Rise of Industrial Society in England** (St. Martin's, 1964). See also Jasper Ridley, **Lord Palmerston** (Dutton, 1970) and Herman Ausubel, **John Bright*** (Wiley, 1966).

A. J. P. Taylor, **The Course of German History*** (Capricorn) is a short, pithy essay on German national history since the French Revolution. T. Hamerow, **Restoration, Revolution, Reaction: Economics and Politics in Germany, 1815–1871*** (Princeton) is highly praised. L. Namier, **1848: The Revolution of the Intellectuals*** (Anchor) is critical of the German liberals in the Frankfurt Assembly. See also R. W. Reichard, **Crippled From Birth: A German Social Democracy, 1844–1870** (Iowa State University Press).

Barbara Jelavich, **The Habsburg Empire in European Affairs, 1814–1918*** (Rand McNally, 1969) is an excellent brief history of the empire. A. J. P. Taylor, **The Habsburg Monarchy, 1809–1918*** (Torchbooks) is chatty and spirited. See also V. L. Tapie, **The Rise and Fall of the Hapsburg Monarchy** (Praeger, 1971).

A. J. Whyte, **The Evolution of Modern Italy, 1715–1920*** (Norton) is a sound survey. G. Salvemini, **Mazzini*** (Collier) is an authoritative biography.

R. C. Binkley, **Realism and Nationalism: 1852–1871*** (Torchbooks); C. J. H. Hayes, **A Generation of Materialism: 1871–1900*** (Torchbooks); and J. Munholland, **Origins of Contemporary Europe, 1890–1914*** (Harcourt Brace Jovanovich, Inc., 1970) are outstanding syntheses. A. J. P. Taylor, **The Struggle for Mastery in Europe, 1848–1918** (Oxford, 1954) and L. Seaman, **From Vienna to Versailles*** (Colophon) are well-written surveys of international relations.

K. Minogue, **Nationalism** (Basic, 1970) is a brief and stimulating historical survey. B. C. Shafer, **Nationalism: Myth and Reality*** (Harcourt Brace Jovanovich, Inc.) is an outstanding fuller account. See also H. Kohn, **The Idea of Nationalism*** (Collier) and **Prophets and Peoples: Studies in Nineteenth Century Nationalism*** (Collier).

C. Delzell, ed., **The Unification of Italy, 1859–1861: Cavour, Mazzini, or Garibaldi?*** (Holt, Rinehart & Winston) is part of the series on European Problem Studies.

W. Medicott, **Bismarck and Modern Germany*** (Torchbooks) is an excellent introduction to the era. Also recommended are E. Eyck, **Bismarck and the German Empire*** (Norton) and A. J. P. Taylor, **Bismarck: The Man and the Statesman*** (Vintage) which is generally hostile. Notable scholarly surveys are H. Holborn, **A History of Modern Germany, 1840–1945** (Knopf, 1969) and A. Rosenberg, **Imperial Germany: The Birth of the German Republic, 1871–1918*** (Oxford, 1970). See also Otto Pflanze, **Bismarck and the Development of Germany** (Princeton).

C. Macartney, **The Habsburg Empire, 1790–1918** (Macmillan, 1969) is a scholarly survey.

M. Karpovich, **Imperial Russia, 1801–1917*** (Holt, Rinehart & Winston) is brief and valuable. H. Seton-Watson, **The Russian Empire, 1801–1917** (Oxford, 1967) and **The Decline of Imperial Russia, 1855–1914*** (Praeger) are excellent longer surveys. W. E. Mosse, **Alexander II and the Modernization of Russia,*** 2nd ed. (Collier) is a brief biography. R. Charques, **The Twilight of Imperial Russia*** (Oxford, 1965) surveys the reign of the last tsar, Nicholas II. See also R. Massie, **Nicholas and Alexandra*** (Dell); Geroid Robinson, **Rural Russia Under the Old Regime*** (California); A. Yarmolinsky, **The Road to Revolution: A Century of Russian Radicalism*** (Collier, 1968); and J. Joll, **The Anarchists*** (Universal).

William Miller, **The Ottoman Empire and Its Successors, 1801–1927** (Octagon, 1966) is the standard work. L. Stavrianos, **The Balkans, 1815–1914*** (Holt, Rinehart & Winston) is a brief examination. R. H. Davison, **Turkey***

(Prentice-Hall, 1968) is a brief, well-written general history. See also Bernard Lewis, **The Emergence of Modern Turkey,*** 2nd ed. (Oxford) and F. Ahmad, **The Young Turks** (Oxford, 1970).

Matthew S. Anderson, **The Eastern Question, 1774–1923** (St. Martin's, 1966) is a new clarification. See also H. Kohn, **Pan-Slavism: Its History and Ideology*** (Vintage).

CHAPTER 18: HOPE AND HOLOCAUST

J. Munholland, **Origins of Contemporary Europe: 1890–1914*** (Harcourt Brace Jovanovich, Inc., 1970) is a brief, highly recommended synthesis. Barbara Tuchman, **The Proud Tower: A Portrait of the World Before the War, 1890–1914** (Macmillan, 1966) is very readable. D. Thomson, **England in the Nineteenth Century (1815–1914)*** (Penguin); J. Conacher, ed., **The Emergence of Parliamentary Democracy in Britain in the Nineteenth Century*** (Wiley, 1970) are valuable brief accounts. See also G. Kitson Clark, **The Making of Victorian England*** (Atheneum); George M. Young, **Victorian England: Portrait of an Age*** (Galaxy); P. Magnus, **Gladstone*** (Dutton); and Robert Blake, **Disraeli*** (Anchor). G. Dangerfield, **The Strange Death of Liberal England, 1910–1914*** (Capricorn) describes the inability of the Liberals to deal with major problems. See also G. M. Trevelyan, **British History in the Nineteenth Century and After*** (Torchbooks) and H. Ausubel, **The Late Victorians*** (Princeton).

Donald J. Harvey, **France Since the Revolution*** (Free Press, 1968); D. W. Brogan, **The French Nation: From Napoleon to Pétain*** (Colophon) are short perceptive surveys. See also B. Gooch, **The Reign of Napoleon III*** (Rand McNally, 1970); D. Thomson, **Democracy in France Since 1870,*** 5th ed. (Oxford); Roger L. Williams, ed., **The Commune of Paris, 1871*** (Wiley, 1970); and N. Halasz, **Captain Dreyfus: The Story of a Mass Hysteria*** (Simon & Schuster, 1968); Roger Soltau, **French Parties and Politics, 1871–1921** (Russell, 1965); and L. Derfler, ed., **The Dreyfus Affair*** (Heath, 1963).

S. B. Fay, **The Origins of the World War,*** 2 vols., 2nd ed. (Free Press) is sympathetic to Germany and Austria and long considered the standard guide, but see now F. Fischer, **Germany's Aims in the First World War*** (Norton) and W. Laqueur and G. Mosse, eds., **1914: The Coming of the First World War*** (Torchbooks). See also L. Lafore, **The Long Fuse: An Interpretation of the Origins of World War I*** (Lippincott, 1965); Oron J. Hale, **The Great Illusion, 1900–1919** (Harper & Row, 1971); D, Lee, ed., **The Outbreak of the First World War*** (Heath); and V. Dedijer, **The Road to Sarajevo** (Simon and Schuster, 1966).

A. J. P. Taylor, **History of the First World War*** (Berkley); H. Baldwin, **World War I*** (Grove); C. Falls, **The Great War*** (Capricorn) are good short accounts. Excellent special works include Barbara Tuchman, **The Guns of August*** (Dell); A. Moorehead, **Gallipoli*** (Harper & Row); A. Horne, **The Price of Glory: Verdun, 1916*** (Colophon); and E. Coffman, **The War to End All Wars: The American Military Experience in World War I** (Oxford, 1968).

CHAPTER 19: EXPANSION AND IMPERIALISM

O. Handlin *et al.*, eds., **The Harvard Guide to American History** (Harvard, 1954) is the indispensable bibliography. R. B. Morris, ed., **Encyclopedia of American History** (Harper, 1953) is the most convenient reference work. Recommended general surveys are S. E. Morison, **The Oxford History of the American People** (Harper & Row, 1965), a graphic survey by a distinguished histori-

an; and R. Hofstadter, **The American Political Tradition*** (Vintage), a brilliant and unorthodox interpretation of men and ideas from the Founding Fathers to F. D. R. See also O Handlin, **The Uprooted*** (Grosset and Dunlap, 1957).

R. W. Logan, **The Negro in the United States*** (Anvil) traces the progress of the American Negro. See also C. Vann Woodward, **The Strange Career of Jim Crow*** (Oxford); Lerone Bennett, Jr., **Before the Mayflower*** (Penguin); Winthrop D. Jordan, **White Over Black*** (Penguin); L. H. Fishel and B. Quarles, **The Black American*** (Scott, Foresman), a comprehensive anthology; Philip D. Curtin, **The Atlantic Slave Trade** (Wisconsin, 1969); and Benjamin Quarles, **The Negro in the Making of America*** (Macmillan, 1969).

For Canadian background, see J. Bartlet Brebner, **Canada, A Modern History** (University of Michigan, 1960).

John Harre and Keith Jackson, **New Zealand** (Walker, 1969) is a study of a multiracial society: Europeans and Maori. For provocative studies of history and society see O. H. K. Spate, **Australia** (Praeger, 1968) and Douglas Pike, **Australia** (Cambridge, 1969). On the rise of the gold and diamond industries and the background of the Boer War see C. W. De Kiewiet, **A History of South Africa, Social and Economic** (Oxford, 1941). For a comparative cultural study of the new Europes see Louis Hartz, **The Founding of New Societies** (Harcourt Brace Jovanovich, Inc., 1964) and C. Hartley Grattan, **The Southwest Pacific Since 1900** (Univ. of Michigan, 1963).

Provocative studies on nineteenth-century imperialism are G. H. Nadel and P. Curtis, eds., **Imperialism and Colonialism*** (Macmillan); H. M. Wright, ed., **The "New Imperialism"*** (Heath Problems); and A. P. Thornton, **Doctrines of Imperialism*** (Wiley). See also R. Koebner and H. Schmidt, **Imperialism** (Cambridge Univ., 1964) which deals mainly with British imperialism; James Morris, **Pax Britannica** (Harcourt Brace Jovanovich, Inc., 1968); and Donald C. Gordon, **The Moment of Power*** (Prentice-Hall) on the historical significance of the British empire in the nineteenth and twentieth centuries; and H. Gollwitzer, **Europe in the Age of Imperialism*** (Harcourt Brace Jovanovich, Inc., 1969).

Alan Burns, **In Defence of Colonies** (Verry, 1957) is a vigorous defense of the motives and positive results of British imperialism. Two famous attacks on imperialism are J. A. Hobson, **Imperialism,*** rev. ed. (Univ. of Mich.) and V. I. Lenin, **Imperialism, the Highest Stage of Capitalism*** (China Books).

Z. Marsh and G. W. Kingsnorth, **An Introduction to the History of East Africa*** (Cambridge Univ.); and J. D. Fage, **An Introduction to the History of West Africa*** (Cambridge Univ.) are two brief, useful studies. See also Ronald Robinson and J. Gallagher, **Africa and the Victorians** (St. Martin's, 1961) and Peter Duignan and L. H. Gann, eds., **Colonialism in Africa** 2 vols. (Cambridge Univ., 1969–1970), perceptive essays on the motivation of imperialism. English historian Reginald Coupland gives a vivid picture of the horrors of the slave trade and of the long campaign against it in **The British Anti-Slavery Movement**, 2nd ed. (Barnes and Noble, 1964). The challenge of Britain's imperial mission in Africa is mirrored in the lives of three men: F. Gross, **Rhodes of Africa** (Praeger, 1957); Lord Elton, **Gordon of Khartoum** (Knopf, 1955); and M. Perham, **Lugard, The Years of Adventure** (Archon, 1968). See also A. Moorehead, **The White Nile*** (Dell) and **The Blue Nile*** (Dell), fascinating accounts of exploration in central Africa; and R. and C. Oliver, eds., **Africa in the Days of Exploration*** (Spectrum).

For valuable insight into British rule and its consequences see M. Edwardes, **British India** (Taplinger,

1968); and S. Gopal, **British Policy in India** (Cambridge Univ., 1966).

Useful studies of China include Immanuel Hsu, **The Rise of Modern China** (Oxford, 1970); A. Feuerwerker, ed., **Modern China** (Prentice-Hall, 1964); and F. Wolfgang, **China and the West**, R. A. Wilson, trans. (Harper & Row, 1967).

W. G. Beasley, **The Modern History of Japan*** (Praeger) is a useful study. O. Statler, **Japanese Inn** (Random House, 1961) gives a colorful and dependable overview of Japanese history in the last three centuries.

Recommended for the coverage of events in Southeast Asia are D. G. E. Hall, **A History of South-East Asia** (St. Martin's, 1968); H. J. Benda and J. A. Larkin, **The World of Southeast Asia** (Harper & Row, 1967).

CHAPTER 20: THE WAGES OF WAR

R. Aron, **The Century of Total War*** (Beacon) is a thoughtful analysis of the happenings in the world since 1914. See also H. S. Hughes, **Contemporary Europe** (Prentice-Hall, 1961); G. M. Gathorne-Hardy, **A Short History of International Affairs, 1920–1939** (Oxford, 1950); J. M. Keynes, **The Economic Consequences of the Peace** (Harcourt Brace Jovanovich, Inc., 1920); U. Faulkner, **From Versailles to the New Deal** (Yale, 1951); and E. Leuchtenburg, **The Perils of Prosperity** (Univ. of Chicago, 1958).

E. Golob, **The Isms** (Harper, 1954) is a useful introduction to modern political and economic ideologies. See also J. H. Hallowell, **Main Currents of Modern Political Thought** (Holt, 1950); C. J. Friedrich and Z. Brzezinski, **Totalitarian Dictatorship and Autocracy*** (Praeger); and H. Arendt, **The Origins of Totalitarianism*** (Meridian).

H. Seton-Watson, **From Lenin to Khrushchev*** (Praeger) is a history of the Communist movement in the twentieth century. The most useful single volume on Russian history in this century is D. Treadgold, **Twentieth Century Russia** (Rand McNally, 1964). For the standard balanced history of the subject see W. H. Chamberlain, **The Russian Revolution, 1917–1921**, 2 vols. (Macmillan, 1952). See also J. Reshetar, Jr., **A Concise History of the Communist Party of the Soviet Union*** (Praeger) and G. F. Kennan, **Russia and the West** (Little, Brown, 1960).

S. W. Halperin, **Germany Tried Democracy*** (Norton) is the best short history of the Weimar Republic. For an insightful look at Versailles and the birth pangs of the Weimar Republic see Richard M. Watt, **The Kings Depart: The Tragedy of Germany*** (Simon & Schuster). Should be supplemented by F. L. Schuman, **Germany Since 1918** (Holt, 1937); W. L. Shirer, **The Rise and Fall of the Third Reich*** (Simon & Schuster); and G. Hilger and A. G. Meyer, **The Incompatible Allies: German-Soviet Relations** (Macmillan, 1953).

Three excellent critiques of Italian Fascism are A. Rossi, **The Rise of Italian Fascism** (Methuen, 1938); L. Fermi, **Mussolini*** (Phoenix); and E. Wiskemann, **Fascism and Italy*** (St. Martin's).

C. L. Mowat, **Britain Between the Wars** (Univ. of Chicago, 1955) is an excellent treatment of the period. For a disquieting analysis of Britain's foreign policy up to the eve of Munich see R. W. Seton-Watson, **Britain and the Dictators** (Fertig, 1968).

H. Wish, **Contemporary America**, 4th ed. (Harper & Row, 1966) is a standard survey. Two sound economic surveys are B. Mitchell, **Depression Decade** (Holt, Rinehart & Winston, 1947); and J. K. Galbraith, **The Great Crash*** (Houghton Mifflin). See also A. M. Schlesinger, Jr., **The Crisis of the Old Order, 1919–1933*** (Sentry).

Important works on individual states in the international scene are M. MacDonald, **The Republic of Austria, 1918–1934** (Oxford, 1946); C. Macartney, **Hungary and Her Successors** (Oxford, 1937); M. Childs, **Sweden*** (Yale); S. H. Thomson, **Czechoslovakia in European History** (Princeton, 1953); O. Halecki, **History of Poland** (Roy, 1956); R. West, **Black Lamb and Grey Falcon: A Journey Through Jugoslavia,*** 2 vols. (Compass); and L. Hanke, **Modern Latin America,*** 2 vols. (Anvil).

CHAPTER 21: THE TRAGIC DECADE AND GLOBAL CONFLICT

J. K. Galbraith, **The Great Crash, 1929*** (Sentry) is a dramatic account of the onset of the depression in the United States. F. L. Allen, **Only Yesterday*** (Bantam) is a lively social history of the 1930's. See also S. Adler, **The Isolationist Impulse*** (Collier) and D. Perkins, **The New Age of Franklin Roosevelt: 1932–1945*** (Univ. of Chicago).

W. L. Shirer, **The Rise and Fall of the Third Reich*** (Fawcett) is a full account by a jouranlist. Also notable are T. L. Jarman, **The Rise and Fall of Nazi Germany*** (Signet) and H. R. Trevor-Roper, **The Last Days of Hitler*** (Collier).

On the crisis in the west European democracies on the even of World War II, the following are recommended: A. Werth, **The Twilight of France, 1933–1940** (Harper, 1942); J. F. Kennedy, **Why England Slept*** (Dolphin); and H. Thomas, **The Spanish Civil War*** (Colophon).

For various viewpoints on its origin see J. L. Snell, ed., **The Outbreak of the Second World War*** (Heath); A. J. P. Taylor, **The Origins of the Second World War*** (Premier); and L. Lafore, **The End of Glory** (Lippincott, 1970).

E. McInnis, **The War**, 6 vols. (Oxford, 1940–1946) is one of the best accounts of World War II. W. Churchill, **The Second World War,*** 6 vols. (Bantam) is a brilliant panoramic survey. Good single-volume histories are P. Young, **A Short History of World War II*** (Apollo) and L. L. Snyder, **The War: A Concise History*** (Dell). See also A. Werth, **Russia at War, 1941–1945*** (Avon); C. Wilmot, **The Struggle for Europe*** (Colophon); D. D. Eisenhower, **Crusade in Europe*** (Dolphin); H. Feis, **Japan Subdued** (Princeton, 1961); and G. Wright, **The Ordeal of Total War*** (Torchbooks). Good discussions of wartime diplomacy are J. L. Snell, **Illusion and Necessity*** (Houghton Mifflin, 1963) and H. Feis, **Churchill, Roosevelt, Stalin*** (Princeton).

T. Taylor, **The March of Conquest*** (Simon & Schuster, 1958) recounts the amazing story of the initial German military triumphs. P. Fleming, **Operation Sea Lion*** (Ace) is an absorbing account of Hitler's plans to invade Britain. Excellent works on other highlights of the war include H. E. Salisbury, **The Nine Hundred Days: The Siege of Leningrad** (Harper & Row, 1969); C. Ryan, **The Longest Day: June 6, 1944*** (Crest); **The Last Battle** (Simon & Schuster, 1966); C. Fitzgibbon, **Officers' Plot to Kill Hitler*** (Avon); J. Toland, **Battle: The Story of the Bulge*** (Mentor); L. Collins and D. Lapierre, **Is Paris Burning?*** (Pocket Books); R. W. Thompson, **The Battle for the Rhine*** (Ballantine); and J. Hersey, **Hiroshima*** (Bantam).

Four studies documenting the enormity of the crimes perpetrated by the Nazis are L. Poliakov, **Harvest of Hate** (Syracuse, 1954); P. Tillare and C. Levy, **Betrayal at the Vel d'Hiv** (Hill and Wang, 1969); Lord Russell, **The Scourge of the Swastika** (Philosophical Lib., 1954); W. R. Harris, **Tyranny on Trial** (Southern Methodist Univ., 1954).

Important World War II novels include the triology by T. Plievier, **Stalingrad*** (Berkley); **Moscow*** (Ace); and

Berlin, A Novel* (Ace). Other excellent works are I. Shaw, **The Young Lions*** (Signet); N. Mailer, **The Naked and the Dead*** (Signet); N. Monsarrat, **The Cruel Sea*** (Pocket Books); and J. Hersey, **The War Lover*** (Bantam).

CHAPTER 22: THE QUEST FOR WORLD ORDER

J. Lukacs, **A New History of the Cold War*** (Anchor); D. Rees, **The Age of Containment*** (St. Martin's); and N. Graebner, **Cold War Diplomacy*** (Anvil) are broad treatments of postwar international tensions. Appraisals of the United Nations are found in N. Padelford and L. Goodrich, eds., **United Nations in the Balance*** (Praeger); A. Boyd, **United Nations: Piety, Myth and Truth*** (Penguin); and H. G. Nicholas, **The United Nations as a Political Institution*** (Galaxy).

Dean Acheson, **Present at the Creation** (Norton, 1969); H. Cleveland, **The Obligations of Power** (Harper & Row, 1966); D. Brandon, **American Foreign Policy: Beyond Utopianism and Realism*** (Appleton) analyze U.S. foreign policy.

The resurgence of western Europe is dealt with in M. Salvadori, **NATO: A Twentieth-Century Community of Nations*** (Anvil); J. Freymond, **Western Europe Since the War** (Praeger, 1964); and W. Feld, **The European Common Market and the World*** (Prentice-Hall). For specific countries see F. Boyd **British Politics in Transition, 1945–1963*** (Praeger); R. C. Macridis, ed., **De Gaulle: Implacable Ally*** (Harper & Row); A. Grosser, **The Federal Republic of Germany*** (Praeger); and N. Kogan, **A Political History of Postwar Italy*** (Praeger). For Latin America see A. P. Whitaker and D. C. Jordan, **Nationalism in Contemporary Latin America** (Free Press, 1966); K. H. Silvert, **The Conflict Society*** (Harper & Row); and D. B. Jackson, **Castro: The Kremlin and Communism in Latin America*** (Johns Hopkins). H. Feis, **Contest Over Japan*** (Norton) examines the situation resulting from Japan's defeat and occupation, while D. and E. T. Riesman, **Conversations in Japan** (Basic Books, 1967) analyzes contemporary Japanese society.

I. Deutscher, **The Unfinished Revolution** (Oxford, 1967) assesses the first fifty years of Soviet history. For postwar developments see E. Crankshaw, **Khrushchev's Russia*** (Penguin); A. Dallin and T. B. Larson, **Soviet Politics Since Khrushchev*** (Spectrum); and H. Swartz, **The Soviet Economy Since Stalin*** (Lippincott). The fragmentation of the Communist world is discussed in A. Dallin, ed., **Diversity in International Communism, A Documentary Record, 1961–1963*** (Columbia); A. Gyorgy, ed., **Issues of World Communism*** (Van Nostrand); and E. Crankshaw, **New Cold War: Moscow Versus Peking*** (Penguin). On the Communist bloc in eastern Europe see Z. Brzezinski, **The Soviet Bloc: Unity and Conflict**, rev. ed. (Harvard, 1967); and G. H. Skilling, **Communism, National and International*** (Oxford).

A. D. Barnett, **Communist China: The Early Years, 1949–1955*** (Praeger); J. Ch'en, **Mao and the Chinese Revolution*** (Galaxy); and Claude A. Buss, **People's Republic of China*** (Van Nostrand) examine the rise of Mao's regime. **The Great Cultural Revolution in China** (Tuttle, 1968) is a compilation of reference materials assembled by the Asia Research Center of Hong Kong.

On the prospects for improved relations between the western and Communist worlds see K. E. Boulding, **Conflict and Defense*** (Harper & Row); T. C. Schelling, **Arms and Influence*** (Yale); L. Bloomfield, ed., **Outer Space: Prospects for Man and Society*** (Praeger); and A. M. Taylor *et al.*, **Peacekeeping: International Challenge and Canadian Response*** (Canadian Institute of International Affairs).

CHAPTER 23: THE WEST AND THE THIRD WORLD

P. Welty, **The Asians*** (Preceptor) and H. G. Matthew, ed., **Asia in the Modern World*** (Mentor) are handy introductions. For valuable comparative studies see R. Emerson, **From Empire to Nation: The Rise of the Asian and African Peoples*** (Beacon) and J. Romein, **The Asian Century: A History of Modern Nationalism in Asia** (California, 1962).

H. Kohn and W. Sokolsky, **African Nationalism in the Twentieth Century*** (Anvil) summarizes twentieth-century developments. Two astute observers survey Africa as it was before the Second World War in J. Huxley, **Africa View** (Harper, 1931) and W. M. Macmillan, **Africa Emergent, A Survey of Social, Political, and Economic Trends in British Africa*** (Penguin).

G. Lenczowski, **The Middle East in World Affairs** (Cornell, 1956) is a first-rate survey. See also S. N. Fisher, **The Middle East** (Knopf, 1959); Howard M. Sachar, **The Emergence of the Middle East** (Knopf, 1939); and W. C. Smith, **Islam in Modern History*** (Mentor). A good short history of the Jewish people is Abba Eban, **My People** (Random House, 1969). See also B. Halperin, **The Idea of the Jewish State** (Harvard, 1961). The Arab view of the political control of Palestine is presented eloquently in G. Antonius, **The Arab Awakening: The Story of the Arab National Movement*** (Capricorn). On the impact of westernization on Turkey see N. Berkes, **The Development of Secularism in Turkey** (McGill Univ., 1964). Other special studies are S. H. Longrigg, **Syria and Lebanon Under French Mandate** (Oxford, 1958) and **Iraq, 1900 to 1950** (Oxford, 1953).

T. W. Wallbank, **A Short History of India and Pakistan** (Mentor) and **India in the New Era** (Scott, Foresman, 1951) are two useful authoritative surveys.

J. Cady, **Southeast Asia** (McGraw-Hill, 1964) is an interesting study. See also the perceptive appraisal by D. Dubois, **Social Forces in Southeast Asia** (Harvard, 1959). G. M. Beckmann, **The Modernization of China and Japan** (Harper & Row, 1962) interrelates the process of modernization in these two nations. K. S. Latourette, **A History of Modern China*** (Penguin) is an excellent resume. See also O. E. Clubb, **20th Century China** (Columbia, 1964). E. O. Reischauer, **Japan, Past and Present** (Knopf, 1964) emphasizes the modern period. For a detailed description of how the military extremists undermined parliamentary government in Japan see R. Storry, **The Double Patriots** (Houghton Mifflin, 1957).

The political transformation of Asia is treated in T. W. Wallbank, **The Partition of India** (Heath); M. Brecher, **The New States of Asia*** (Oxford); A. M. Taylor, **Indonesian Independence and the United Nations** (Cornell, 1952); and G. McT. Kahin, ed., **Major Governments of Asia**, 2nd ed. (Cornell, 1963). R. B. Morris, **The Emerging Nations and the American Revolution** (Harper & Row, 1970) appraises the influence of the first successful war of decolonization. See also David C. Gordon, **Self-Determination and History in the Third World** (Princeton, 1970).

P. J. Griffiths, **Modern India** (Praeger, 1965) describes postindependence India. See also G. Patterson, **Peking Versus Delhi** (Praeger, 1964); D. Wilbur, **Pakistan: Yesterday and Today*** (Holt, Rinehart & Winston); and Ved Mehta, **Portrait of India** (Farrar, Straus, 1969).

For studies of Southeast Asia see R. C. Bone's concise **Contemporary Southeast Asia*** (Random House); R. Butwell, **Southeast Asia Today and Tomorrow*** (Praeger); and B. Crozier, **Southeast Asia in Turmoil*** (Penguin). For specific countries see B. H. M. Vlekke, **Musantara: A History of Indonesia** (Quadrangle, 1959) and Richard

Allen, **A Short Introduction to the History and Politics of Southeast Asia*** (Oxford, 1970).

E. Hammer, **Vietnam Yesterday and Today** (Holt, Rinehart & Winston, 1966) and B. Newman, **Background to Viet Nam*** (Signet) are concise treatments of Vietnamese history. On the Vietnam War see M. E. Gettleman, ed., **Viet Nam: History, Documents, and Opinions on a Major World Crisis*** (Crest). For an official American view see Department of State, **Aggression from the North** (Publication 7839, Washington, D.C.). For personal assessments see C. Bain, **Vietnam: The Roots of Conflict*** (Spectrum); B. Fall, **The Two Vietnams**, 2nd rev. ed. (Praeger, 1967); A. M. Schlesinger, Jr., **The Bitter Heritage** (Houghton Mifflin, 1965); and Chester Cooper, **The Lost Crusade: America in Vietnam** (Dodd, Mead, 1970).

M. Halpern, **The Politics of Social Change in the Middle East and North Africa*** (Princeton) surveys the problems involved. Nasser's role is discussed in P. Mansfield, **Nasser's Egypt*** (Penguin). J. Morris, **Islam Inflamed** (Pantheon, 1957) and H. Finer, **Dulles Over Suez** (Quadrangle, 1964) analyze the Suez Canal problem. Arab-Israeli conflict is studied in W. Laquer, **The Road to Jerusalem** (Macmillan, 1968) and R. and W. Churchill, **The Six Day War** (Houghton Mifflin, 1967). W. Laquer, **The Struggle for the Middle East*** (Penguin, 1972) is the story of Soviet intrusion.

L. H. Gann and P. Duignan, **Burden of Empire** (Praeger, 1967) reevaluates African history and colonialism. The difficulties facing the newly emergent nations are analyzed in B. Crozier, **The Morning After** (Oxford, 1963); J. Hatch, **A History of Postwar Africa*** (Praeger); L. Gray Cowan, **The Dilemmas of African Independence** (Walker, 1964); and A. Rivkin, **Nation Building in Africa** (Rutgers, 1969). Ideological problems are the subject of Z. Brzezinski, ed., **Africa and the Communist World*** (Stanford). See also T. W. Wallbank, **Contemporary Africa*** (Anvil). On specific regions or countries see K. Post, **New States of West Africa*** (Penguin); D. Austin, **Politics in Ghana** (Oxford, 1964); C. Young, **Politics in the Congo*** (Princeton); J. A. Davis and J. K. Baker, eds., **Southern Africa in Transition** (Praeger, 1966); Okoi Arikpo, **The Development of Modern Nigeria*** (Penguin); and Rupert Emerson and Martin Kilson, **The Political Awakening of Africa** (Prentice-Hall, 1965).

V. McKay, **Africa in World Politics** (Harper & Row, 1963) is especially useful for Pan-Africanism and United States policy in Africa. Also recommended are W. Goldschmidt, **The United States and Africa,*** rev. ed. (Praeger) and H. R. Isaacs, **The New World of Negro Americans** (John Day, 1963).

CHAPTER 24: TOWARD A NEW LIFE STYLE

W. W. Wagar, ed., **Science, Faith and Man in the Twentieth Century*** (Torchbooks); C. R. Walker, **Modern Technology and Civilization*** (McGraw-Hill); and L. V. Berkner, **The Scientific Age: the Impact of Science on Society** (Yale, 1964) are useful overviews of scientific and intellectual developments since 1914.

For the contributions of some of the outstanding architects, see W. Gropius, **New Architecture and the Bauhaus*** (M.I.T.) and P. Blake's two studies, **Frank Lloyd Wright: Architecture and Space*** and **Mies van der Rohe: Architecture and Structure*** (Penguin). On the experimentation in art see A. Neumeyer, **Search for Meaning in Modern Art*** (Premier); and B. Rose, **American Art Since 1900*** (Praeger). See also P. Klee, **On Modern Art*** (Heinman) and P. Waldberg, **Surrealism***

(McGraw-Hill). The contributions of one of the century's most influential sculptors, Henry Moore, are found in his **Works*** (Fontana). On photography's rapid advance as an art form, see H. and A. Gernsheim, **Concise History of Photography*** (Grosset and Dunlap).

On the innovations in music see R. H. Myers, **Twentieth Century Music*** (Orion) and H. Hartog, ed., **European Music in the Twentieth Century*** (Pelican). The influence of jazz in the first half of the century is the subject of W. Sargeant, **Jazz: A History*** (McGraw-Hill); while the impact of rock and electronic forms in recent decades is discussed in Nik Cohn, **Rock from the Beginning** (Stein and Day, 1969) and J. Marks, **Rock and Other Four Letter Words: Music of the Electric Generation*** (Bantam).

A. Schlesinger, Jr., **Violence: America in the Sixties*** (Signet) analyzes the social upheavals of the last decade. Racial tensions in the United States are examined in G. Osofsky, **The Burden of Race: A Documentary History of Negro-White Relations in America*** (Harper & Row); M. L. King, Jr., **Where Do We Go From Here: Chaos or Community?*** (Beacon); J. Baldwin, **Nobody Knows My Name*** (Dell); L. E. Lomax, **The Negro Revolt*** (Signet); and R. L. Scott and W. E. Brockreide, eds., **The Rhetoric of Black Power** (Harper & Row). The problems of the "ghetto" in American cities are examined in **Report of the National Advisory Commission on Civil Disorders*** (Bantam); while problems of educational opportunity and discrimination are analyzed in the United States Civil Rights Commission, **Racial Isolation in the Public Schools** (Washington, D.C., 1967). Youth's criticism of contemporary technocratic society is the subject of T. Roszak, **The Making of a Counter Culture*** (Anchor). World-wide campus unrest is assessed in H. Bourges, ed., **The French Student Revolt: The Leaders Speak** (Hill and Wang, 1968) and J. H. Califano, Jr., **The Student Revolution*** (Norton).

The "population explosion" is examined in P. M. Hauser, ed., **The Population Dilemma*** (Spectrum). See also S. Mudd, ed., **The Population and the Use of World Resources** (Humanities, 1964) and W. S. Thompson, **Population and Progress in the Far East** (Univ. of Chicago, 1959). The demographic factor is closely related to the availability and use of natural resources. See H. Boyko, ed., **Science and the Future of Mankind** (Indiana, 1964) and H. H. Landsberg, **Natural Resources for U.S. Growth: A Look Ahead to the Year 2000*** (Johns Hopkins). Our traditional cities are in transition—and trouble. What are the processes responsible, and what should be our goals for change? These are questions asked in L. Mumford, **The City in History*** (Harbinger); J. Gottman, **Megalopolis*** (M.I.T.); E. Saarinen, **The City: Its Growth, Its Decay, Its Future*** (M.I.T.); and F. L. Wright, **The Living City*** (Mentor).

To encourage informed discussion by the American public, President Eisenhower's Commission on National Goals issued a report, **Goals for Americans** (Spectrum) dealing with objectives attainable both at home and abroad. Such goals will have to take account of the impact of technology upon traditional social behavior and values, such as are discussed in J. T. Dunlop, ed., **Automation and Technological Change*** (Spectrum) and N. Wiener, **The Human Use of Human Beings: Cybernetics and Society*** (Discus). Science's impact upon western humanistic values must also be considered thoughtfully, as found in F. W. Matson, **The Broken Image: Man, Science and Society*** (Anchor); M. Polanyi, **Science, Faith and Society*** (Phoenix); and Z. Brzezinski, **Between Two Ages: America's Role in the Technetronic Era** (Viking, 1970).

FOOTNOTES

PROLOGUE: PERSPECTIVE ON MAN

1. P. Gardiner, *The Nature of Historical Explanation* (London: Oxford University Press, 1952), p. 98.
2. H. Butterfield, *Christianity and History* (London: G. Bell & Sons, Ltd., 1949), p. 132.
3. See A. J. Toynbee, *Civilization on Trial* (New York: Oxford University Press, 1948).
4. From *A History of Europe,* Vol. I, by H. A. L. Fisher. Reprinted by permission of Curtis Brown Ltd.
5. Toynbee, p. 11.

PART ONE: THE ANCIENT WORLD

1. From *The Burden of Egypt,* translated by John A. Wilson. Copyright 1951 by The University of Chicago. All rights reserved. Published 1951. Composed and printed by The University of Chicago Press, Chicago, Illinois, U.S.A. Reprinted by permission of The University of Chicago Press.
2. I Corinthians 13:11-13. From *Today's English Version of the New Testament.* Copyright © American Bible Society 1966, 1971. Used by permission of the American Bible Society and William Collins Sons & Co. Ltd.

CHAPTER 1: ALONG THE BANKS OF RIVERS

1. Melville J. Herskovits, *The Human Factor in Changing Africa* (New York: Alfred A. Knopf, Inc., 1962), p. 38.
2. Tom B. Jones, *Ancient Civilization* (Chicago: Rand McNally & Co., 1960), p. 10.
3. H. Frankfort, *The Birth of Civilization in the Near East* (London: Williams and Norgate, Ltd., 1951), p. 60.
4. "Les reformes d'Urukagina," trans. by M. Lambert in *Revue d'Assyriologie,* L (Paris, 1956), p. 183.
5. James B. Pritchard, ed., *Ancient Near Eastern Texts Relating to the Old Testament,* 2nd ed., trans. by E. A. Speiser (Princeton: Princeton University Press, 1955), p. 119.
6. *Sumerische und Akkadische Hymnen und Gebete,* trans. by A. Falkenstein and W. von Soden (Zurich: Artemis-Verlag, 1953), p. 188. For a partial translation and full discussion of this text, see S. N. Kramer, *From the Tablets of Sumer* (Indian Hills, Col.: The Falcon's Wing Press, 1956), pp. 267–271.
7. H. de Genouillac, trans., in *Revue de'Assyriologie,* XXV (Paris, 1928), p. 148.
8. Quoted in Kramer, p. 50.
9. From *The Code of Hammurabi* by R. F. Harper, p. 3. Reprinted by permission of The University of Chicago Press. Copyright 1904. The University of Chicago.
10. Ibid., p. 49.
11. Ibid., p. 101.
12. From "Akkadian Myths and Epics," trans. E. A. Speiser in James B. Pritchard *Ancient Near Eastern Texts Relating to the Old Testament,* 3rd rev. edn., with Supplement (copyright © 1969 by Princeton University Press), p. 90. Reprinted by permission of Princeton University Press.
13. From *The Face of the Ancient Orient* by Sabatino Moscati. Reprinted by permission of Routledge & Kegan Paul Ltd.
14. From *The Burden of Egypt,* translated by John A. Wilson. Copyright 1951 by The University of Chicago. All rights reserved. Published 1951. Composed and printed by The University of Chicago Press, Chicago, Illinois, U.S.A. Reprinted by permission of The University of Chicago Press.
15. Adolf Erman, *The Literature of the Ancient Egyptians,* trans. by Aylward M. Blackman (London: Methuen & Co., Ltd., 1927), pp. 190, 196, 197.
16. Wilson, p. 120.
17. Ibid., p. 119.
18. Quoted in George Steindorff and George Hoyningen-Huene, *Egypt* (Locust Valley, N.Y.: J. J. Augustin Inc., 1943), p. 23.
19. From *When Egypt Ruled The East,* translated by George Steindorff and Keith E. Steele. Copyright 1942 by The University of Chicago. All rights reserved. Published January 1942. Composed and printed by The University of Chicago Press, Chicago, Illinois, U.S.A. Reprinted by permission of The University of Chicago Press.
20. From Akhenaton's "Hymn to the Sun" from *The Dawn of Conscience* by J. H. Breasted. Charles Scribner's Sons, 1939. Reprinted by permission of Charles Scribner's Sons.
21. Ezekiel 27:33–34. Revised Standard Version of the Bible.
22. B. W. Anderson, *Understanding the Old Testament* (Englewood Cliffs, N.J.: Prentice-Hall, Inc., 1957), p. 537.
23. I Samuel 8:6, 20. Revised Standard Version of the Bible.
24. I Kings 10:14 ff. Revised Standard Version of the Bible.
25. II Kings 25:14. Revised Standard Version of the Bible.

558

26. Micah 6:8. Revised Standard Version of the Bible.
27. D. D. Luckenbill, *Ancient Records of Assyria and Babylonia,* I (Chicago: University of Chicago Press, 1926), p. 147.
28. Quoted in Georges Roux, *Ancient Iraq* (Baltimore: Penguin Books, Inc., 1966), p. 278.
29. Nahum 3:8. Revised Standard Version of the Bible.
30. Herodotus, IX, 122; trans. by A. R. Burn, *Persia and the West* (New York: St. Martin's Press, 1962), p. 61.
31. Herodotus, *History,* VIII, 98; trans. by George Rawlinson.

CHAPTER 2: THE GLORY THAT WAS GREECE

1. Plutarch's *Lives,* II, trans. by Sir T. North (London: J. M. Dent & Sons Ltd., 1898), p. 144.
2. Quoted in Werner Jaeger, *Paideia: The Ideals of Greek Culture,* I (New York: Oxford University Press, 1939), p. 70.
3. "Laws," V, 735; in *The Dialogues of Plato,* II, trans. by B. Jowett (New York: Random House, 1937), p. 503.
4. Trans. by A. R. Burn, *The Pelican History of Greece* (Baltimore: Penguin Books, Inc., 1966), p. 186.
5. C. E. Robinson, *Hellas: A Short History of Ancient Greece* (New York: Pantheon Books, 1948), p. 68.
6. From Thucydides: *The History of the Peloponnesian War,* translated by Sir. R. W. Livingstone. Copyright © 1963 by the Oxford University Press. Reprinted by permission.
7. Thucydides, II, 40–41, trans. by Sir R. W. Livingstone.
8. Ibid., II, 65, p. 130.
9. Thucydides, I, 22, trans. by Sir R. W. Livingstone, pp. 44–45.
10. From *The Lyric Age of Greece* by A. R. Burn, p. 166. Reprinted by permission of Edward Arnold (Publishers) Ltd.
11. Ibid., p. 236.
12. From "Agamemnon" by Aeschylus, trans. Gilbert Murray, from *Ten Greek Plays,* ed. Lane Cooper. Reprinted by permission of George Allen & Unwin Ltd.
13. Quoted in *The Cambridge Ancient History,* XI (Cambridge: The University Press, 1936), p. 696.
14. G. Murray, *Hellenism and the Modern World* (Boston: Beacon Press, 1953), pp. 56–57.

CHAPTER 3: THE GRANDEUR THAT WAS ROME

1. Livy, *Roman History,* XXXIII, 33, trans. by E. T. Sage in The Loeb Classical Library (Cambridge: Harvard University Press, 1945), Vol. IX, p. 367.
2. Plutarch's *Lives,* "Tiberius Gracchus," IX, 5, trans. by Bernadotte Perrin in The Loeb Classical Library (Cambridge: Harvard University Press, 1945), Vol. X, pp. 165, 167.

3. Aelius Aristides, *To Rome* (Oration XXVI), trans. by S. Levin (Glencoe, Ill.: The Free Press, 1950), p. 126.
4. Virgil, *Aeneid,* VI, 847–853, in *Roman Civilization: Selected Readings,* II, ed. by Naphtali Lewis and Meyer Reinhold (New York: Columbia University Press, 1955), p. 23.
5. Lucretius, *On the Nature of the Universe,* Book III, line 70, trans. by Ronald Latham (Baltimore: Penguin Books, Inc., 1951), p. 98.
6. Horace, *Odes,* III, 29 (in part), trans. by John Dryden.
7. From *Roman Readings,* edited by Michael Grant. Copyright © 1958 by Michael Grant. Reprinted by permission of Penguin Books Ltd.
8. E. Wilson, *The Scrolls from the Dead Sea* (New York: Oxford University Press, 1955), p. 60.
9. Acts 22:6–8. From *Today's English Version of the New Testament.* Copyright © American Bible Society 1966, 1971. Used by permission of the American Bible Society and William Collins Sons & Co. Ltd.
10. Quoted in Henry Bettenson, ed., *Documents of the Christian Church* (London: Oxford University Press, 1943), p. 9.
11. Tacitus, *Germania,* Ch. 14, trans. by H. Mattingly, *Tacitus on Britain and Germany* (Harmondsworth: Penguin Books, Ltd., 1948), p. 112.
12. S. Katz, *The Decline of Rome and the Rise of Medieval Europe* (Ithaca, N.Y.: Cornell University Press, 1955), p. 7.

PART TWO: THE MIDDLE AGES

1. S. Katz, *The Decline of Rome and the Rise of Medieval Europe* (Ithaca, N.Y.: Cornell University Press, 1955), p. 98.
2. Quoted in Peter Arnott, *The Romans and Their World* (New York: St. Martin's Press, 1970), pp. 311–312.

CHAPTER 4: CITADEL AND CONQUEROR

1. Procopius, *History of the Wars,* Book I, trans. by H. B. Dewing (London: William Heinemann, Ltd., 1914), p. 231, 233.
2. D. Talbot Rice, *Byzantine Art* (Harmondsworth: Penguin Books, Ltd., 1954), pp. 150–151.
3. From Alfred Guillaume, *Islam* (Baltimore: Penguin Books, 1956). Copyright © the Estate of Alfred Guillaume, 1954, 1956. Reprinted by permission of Penguin Books Ltd.
4. *Rubáiyát of Omar Khayyám,* trans. by Edward Fitzgerald, Stanzas 12, 71.

CHAPTER 5: EUROPE'S SEARCH FOR STABILITY

1. Quoted in Sidney Painter, *French Chivalry: Chivalric Ideas and Practices in Medieval France* (Baltimore: Johns Hopkins Press, 1940), p. 169.

2. From *History of the British People* by M. Hulme. Copyright 1929 by Appleton-Century-Crofts.
3. E. P. Cheney, *The Dawn of a New Era, 1250–1453* (New York: Harper & Bros., 1936), p. 132.

CHAPTER 6: NATIONS IN THE MAKING

1. D. C. Douglas and G. Greenaway, *English Historical Documents, 1042–1189* (New York: Oxford University Press, 1953), p. 200.
2. W. S. Churchill, *The Birth of Britain,* Vol. I of *A History of the English-Speaking Peoples* (New York: Dodd, Mead & Co., 1965), p. 210.
3. Quoted in M. Cherniavsky, "'Holy Russia': A Study in the History of an Idea," *The American Historical Review,* LXIII, No. 3 (April 1958), p. 625.

CHAPTER 7: TO THE GLORY OF GOD

1. Quoted in R. H. C. Davis, *A History of Medieval Europe: From Constantine to Saint Louis* (London: Longmans, Green & Co., Ltd., 1957), p. 80.
2. Henry Bettenson, ed., *Documents of the Christian Church* (London: Oxford University Press, 1943), p. 144.
3. Summerfield Baldwin, *The Organization of Medieval Christianity* (New York: Henry Holt & Co., 1929), p. 35.
4. Quoted in J. Evans, *Life in Medieval France* (New York: Oxford University Press, 1925), p. 87.
5. From *Today's English Version of the New Testament.* Copyright © American Bible Society 1966, 1971. Used by permission of the American Bible Society and William Collins Sons & Co. Ltd.
6. Robert S. Lopez, *The Tenth Century: How Dark the Dark Ages?* (New York: Rinehart and Co., 1959), p. 1.
7. Quoted in Urban T. Holmes, Jr., "Transitions in European Education," in *Twelfth-Century Europe and the Foundations of Modern Society,* ed. by Marshall Clagett, Gaines Post, and Robert Reynolds (Madison: University of Wisconsin Press, 1961), p. 17.
8. Quoted in *Introduction to Contemporary Civilization in the West: A Source Book,* I (New York: Columbia University Press, 1946), p. 85.
9. *An Encyclopedist of the Dark Ages: Isidore of Seville,* trans. by E. Brehaut (New York: Columbia University Press, 1912), pp. 218–219.
10. *The Art of Falconry . . . of Frederick II of Hohenstaufen,* trans. by Casey A. Wood and F. Marjorie Fyfe (Boston: Charles T. Branford Co., 1943), pp. 3–4.
11. Quoted in H. O. Taylor, *The Mediaeval Mind,* II (London: Macmillan & Co. Ltd., 1938), p. 524.
12. "Golliardic Verse" from *Wine, Women and Song* by J. A. Symonds.
13. Amy Kelly, *Eleanor of Aquitaine and the Four Kings* (Cambridge: Harvard University Press, 1952), p. 86.
14. From "L'Inferno" from *The Divine Comedy* by Dante, translated by Dorothy L. Sayers. Reprinted by permission of David Higham Associates, Ltd. and A. Watkins, Inc.
15. From "Paradise" from *The Divine Comedy* by Dante, translated by J. B. Fletcher. Published 1931 by Columbia University Press. Reprinted by permission.
16. Geoffrey Chaucer, *Canterbury Tales,* trans. by J. U. Nicolson (New York: Crown Publishers, Inc., 1936), pp. 3–5.

CHAPTER 8: MAN IS THE MEASURE

1. William Shakespeare, *The Tempest,* Act V, Scene i.
2. Quoted in J. H. Randall, Jr., *The Making of the Modern Mind* (Boston: Houghton Mifflin Co., 1940), p. 213.
3. Quoted in F. B. Artz, *The Mind of the Middle Ages A.D. 200–1500,* 2nd ed. (New York: Alfred A. Knopf, Inc., 1954), p. 307.
4. *The Decameron of Giovanni Boccacio,* trans. Richard Aldington. Published by Garden City Publishing Co.
5. F. B. Artz, *From the Renaissance to Romanticism: Trends in Style in Art, Literature, and Music, 1300–1830* (Chicago: University of Chicago Press, 1962), p. 102.
6. Quoted in Randall, p. 118.
7. From the 1684 translation by Gilbert Burnet, in *Introduction to Contemporary Civilization in the West: A Source Book,* I (New York: Columbia University Press, 1946), p. 461.
8. Quoted in H. O. Taylor, *Thought and Expression in the Sixteenth Century,* I (New York: The Macmillan Company, 1920), pp. 328–329.
9. Montaigne, "Of the Education of Children," in *The Complete Works of Montaigne,* trans. by D. M. Frame (Stanford: Stanford University Press, 1957), p. 112.
10. Ibid., p. 110.
11. J. van der Elst, *The Last Flowering of the Middle Ages* (New York: Doubleday & Co., Inc., 1946), p. 59.

CHAPTER 9: HERE I TAKE MY STAND

1. From *Here I Stand: A Life of Martin Luther* by R. H. Bainton, Abingdon Press, 1950. Reprinted with permission of Abingdon Press.
2. Quoted in R. H. Bainton, *The Reformation of the Sixteenth Century* (Boston: Beacon Press, 1952), p. 27.
3. Quoted in C. Hayes, *A Political and Cultural History of Modern Europe,* I (New York: The Macmillan Company, 1933), p. 154.
4. Quoted in H. Bettenson, ed., *Documents of the Christian Church* (London: Oxford University Press, 1943), p. 261 ff.
5. Quoted in P. Smith, *The Age of the Reformation* (New York: Henry Holt & Co., 1920), p. 69.

6. Quoted in George L. Mosse, *The Reformation*, 3rd ed. (New York: Holt, Rinehart and Winston, Inc., 1963), p. 31.
7. Quoted in Bainton, *The Reformation of the Sixteenth Century*, p. 58.
8. Quoted in Bettenson, pp. 282–283.
9. From *The Twelve Articles* in A. Schrier *et al.*, *Modern European Civilization: A Documentary History of Politics, Society, and Thought from the Renaissance to the Present* (Chicago: Scott, Foresman and Co., 1963), pp. 105–106.
10. Quoted in H. J. Grimm, *The Reformation Era, 1500–1650* (New York: The Macmillan Company, 1956), p. 175.
11. Bainton, *The Reformation of the Sixteenth Century*, p. 114.
12. Bettenson, p. 365.
13. Quoted in F. Eby and C. F. Arrowood, *The Development of Modern Education* (New York: Prentice-Hall, Inc., 1936), p. 91.
14. *Concerning Heretics . . . An anonymous work attributed to Sebastian Castellio*, ed. by R. H. Bainton (New York: Columbia University Press, 1935), pp. 122–123.
15. Ibid., pp. 134–135.
16. Quoted in V. H. H. Green, *Luther and the Reformation* (New York: Capricorn Books, 1964), p. 141.
17. Ibid., p. 142.
18. R. H. Tawney, *Religion and the Rise of Capitalism* (Baltimore: Penguin Books, Inc., 1947), p. 99.

CHAPTER 10: THE STRIFE OF STATES AND KINGS

1. Quoted in B. Reynolds, *Proponents of Limited Monarchy in Sixteenth Century France: Francis Holman and Jean Bodin* (New York: Columbia University Press, 1931), p. 182.
2. Quoted in M. Guizot, *The History of France from the Earliest Times to 1848*, II (New York: Thomas Y. Crowell & Co., n. d.), p. 428.
3. *Machiavelli: The Prince and Other Works*, trans. by A. H. Gilbert (Chicago: Packard and Co., 1941), p. 177 (Ch. 26).
4. Ibid., p. 148 (Ch. 18).
5. Ibid., p. 150 (Ch. 18).
6. Ibid., p. 177 (Ch. 26).
7. Quoted in Carl L. Becker, *Modern History* (Chicago: Silver Burdett Co., 1942), pp. 204, 205.
8. Carl J. Friedrich, *The Age of Baroque, 1610–1660* (New York: Harper & Bros., 1952), p. 129.
9. See "Grotius: *Law of War and Peace, Prolegomena*," in *The American Journal of International Law*, XXXV, No. 2 (April 1941), pp. 206, 217.

CHAPTER 11: SEEK OUT, DISCOVER, AND FIND

1. "The letters patents of King Henry the seuenth granted vnto Iohn Cabot and his three sonnes, Lewis, Sebastian, and Sancius for the discouerie of new and vnknowen lands," from *The Voyages of the English Nation to America Before the Year 1600, from Hakluyt's Collection of Voyages*, I (Edinburgh: E. and G. Goldsmid, 1889), p. 21.
2. See H. Ingstad, "Vinland Ruins Prove Vikings Found the New World," *National Geographic Magazine*, Vol. 126, No. 5 (November 1964), pp. 708–734.
3. Quoted in Sir Percy Sykes, *A History of Exploration*, Harper Torchbooks (New York: Harper & Row, 1961), p. 108.
4. Quoted in H. H. Gowen, *An Outline History of Japan* (New York: D. Appleton Co., 1927), p. 255.
5. Quoted in Sir George Clark, *The Seventeenth Century* (New York: Oxford University Press, 1961), p. 24.
6. Quoted in H. Heaton, *Economic History of Europe* (New York: Harper & Bros., 1948), p. 238.
7. Heaton, p. 239.

CHAPTER 12: NEW DIMENSIONS OF THE MIND

1. Quoted in *Introduction to Contemporary Civilization in the West*, I (New York: Columbia University Press, 1946), pp. 845–859.
2. F. Bacon, *The Works of Francis Bacon*, III, ed. by J. Spedding (London: Longman and Co., 1861), p. 156.
3. Quoted in *Introduction to Contemporary Civilization in the West*, I, p. 557.
4. Quoted in *Sir Isaac Newton's Mathematical Principles of Natural Philosphy and His System of the World*, ed. and trans. by F. Cajori (Berkeley: University of California Press, 1946).
5. H. Butterfield, *The Origins of Modern Science* (London: G. Bell and Sons, Ltd., 1949), p. 104.
6. See P. Hazard, *The European Mind: The Critical Years* (New Haven: Yale University Press, 1953).
7. A. Pope, "The Universal Prayer," in *The Poetical Works of Alexander Pope* (London: John James Chidley, 1846), p. 145.
8. W. L. Dorn, *Competition for Empire, 1740–1763* (New York: Harper and Bros., 1940), p. 181.
9. Quoted in F. E. Manuel, *The Age of Reason* (Ithaca, N.Y.: Cornell University Press, 1951), p. 39.
10. G. M. Trevelyan, *History of England* (London: Longmans, Green & Co., Ltd., 1937), p. 514.
11. Preserved Smith, *Origins of Modern Culture, 1543–1687* (New York: P. F. Collier, Inc., 1962), p. 484.
12. A. Pope, "An Essay on Man," in *The Literature of England*, I, 5th ed., ed. by G. K. Anderson and W. E. Buckler (Glenview, Ill.: Scott, Foresman and Co., 1968), p. 1568.

CHAPTER 13: L'ETAT, C'EST MOI

1. Quoted in W. G. Crane *et al.*, *Twelve Hundred Years: The Literature of England*, I (New York: Stackpole and Heck, Inc., 1948), p. 572.

2. Sir Ernest Barker *et al., The European Inheritance,* II (London: Clarendon Press, 1954), p. 144.
3. Quoted in E. P. Cheyney, *Readings in English History Drawn from the Original Sources* (Boston: Ginn and Co., 1908), p. 503.
4. Quoted in P. Smith, *A History of Modern Culture,* I (London: George Routledge and Sons, Ltd., 1930), p. 226.
5. John Milton, "Areopagitica," in *The Literature of England,* I, 5th ed., ed. by G. K. Anderson and W. E. Buckler (Glenview, Ill.: Scott, Foresman and Co., 1968), p. 1182.
6. Quoted in G. B. Adams, *Constitutional History of England* (New York: Henry Holt & Co., 1934), p. 406.
7. Quoted in R. Ergang, *The Potsdam Führer, Frederick William I* (New York: Columbia University Press, 1941), p. 7.
8. W. L. Dorn, *Competition for Empire, 1740–1763* (New York: Harper & Bros., 1940), p. 9.
9. Quoted in Ibid., p. 314.

CHAPTER 14: THE RIGHTS OF MAN

1. Thomas Mun, "England's Treasure by Foreign Trade" (1664), in *Introduction to Contemporary Civilization in the West: A Source Book,* I (New York: Columbia University Press, 1946), p. 641.
2. Adam Smith, *An Inquiry into the Nature and Causes of the Wealth of Nations,* Modern Library Edition (New York: The Macmillan Company, 1937), pp. 14, 421.
3. Quoted in J. E. Gillespie, *A History of Geographical Discovery, 1400–1800* (New York: Henry Holt & Co., 1933), p. 99.
4. Quoted in G. P. Gooch, *Frederick the Great: the Ruler, the Writer, the Man* (New York: Alfred A. Knopf, Inc., 1947), p. 109.
5. Quoted in C. Rossiter, *The First American Revolution* (New York: Harcourt Brace Jovanovich, Inc., 1956), prefatory note.
6. C. J. H. Hayes, *A Political and Cultural History of Modern Europe,* I (New York: The Macmillan Company, 1932), p. 614.
7. "The Declaration of the Rights of Man," in *The World in Literature,* III, rev. ed., ed. by R. Warnock and G. K. Anderson (Glenview, Ill.: Scott, Foresman and Co., 1967), pp. 288–289.
8. Quoted in J. E. Gillespie, *A History of Europe, 1500–1815* (New York: Alfred A. Knopf, Inc., 1928), p. 529.
9. Quoted in L. Madelin, *The French Revolution* (London: William Heinemann, Ltd., 1916), p. 323.
10. Quoted in Gillespie, p. 537.
11. From *A History of Europe,* Vol. III, by H. A. L. Fisher. Reprinted by permission of Curtis Brown Ltd.
12. George Rudé, *Revolutionary Europe, 1783–1815* (New York: Harper Torchbooks, 1966), p. 290.

CHAPTER 15: ROMANTICS AND REALISTS

1. R. Browning, "Song from 'Pippa Passes,'" in *The Literature of England,* II, 5th ed., ed. by G. K. Anderson and W. E. Buckler (Glenview, Ill.: Scott, Foresman and Co., 1968), p. 657.
2. C. Darwin, "The Origin of Species," in *Introduction to Contemporary Civilization in the West,* II (New York: Columbia University Press, 1955), pp. 453–454.
3. Charles Darwin, "The Origin of Species," in *Introduction to Contemporary Civilization in the West,* II (New York: Columbia University Press, 1955), pp. 453–454.
4. Charles Darwin, *The Origin of Species* (New York: P. F. Collier & Son Company, 1909), pp. 527–528.
5. T. Veblen, *The Theory of the Leisure Class* (New York: The Macmillan Company, 1902), p. 188.

CHAPTER 16: THE INDUSTRIAL REVOLUTION AND ITS INFLUENCE

1. T. R. Malthus, "An Essay on Population," in *Introduction to Contemporary Civilization in the West,* II (New York: Columbia University Press, 1955), p. 196.
2. David Thomson, *England in the Nineteenth Century, 1815–1914* (Harmondsworth: Penguin Books, Ltd., 1950), p. 101.
3. Quoted in B. Willey, *Nineteenth Century Studies* (London: Chatto and Windus, 1949), p. 262.
4. The Earl of Beaconsfield, K. G., *Sybil; or, The Two Nations* (London: Longmans, Green & Co., Ltd., 1926), pp. 76–77.
5. W. Godwin, "Political Justice," in S. Hook, *Marx and the Marxists: The Ambiguous Legacy* (Princeton: D. Van Nostrand Co., Inc., 1955), p. 28.
6. Quoted in H. J. Laski, *Communist Manifesto: Socialist Landmark* (London: George Allen & Unwin, Ltd., 1948), p. 168.
7. Quoted in ibid., p. 141.

CHAPTER 17: NATIONALISM AND AUTHORITARIAN REGIMES

1. From *A History of Europe,* Vol. III, by H. A. L. Fisher. Reprinted by permission of Curtis Brown Ltd.
2. Quoted in J. S. Schapiro, *Modern and Contemporary European History, 1815–1940* (Boston: Houghton Mifflin Co., 1940), p. 222.
3. Quoted in Schapiro, p. 237.
4. Sir J. A. R. Marriott, *A Short History of France* (New York: Oxford University Press, 1944), p. 233.
5. Quoted in C. G. Robertson, *Bismarck* (London: Constable and Co., Ltd., 1918), p. 472.
6. I. Turgenev, *Fathers and Children,* trans. by C. Garnett (New York: The Macmillan Company, 1924), p. 36.

CHAPTER 18: HOPE AND HOLOCAUST

1. Quoted in F. Owen, *Tempestuous Journey: Lloyd George, His Life and Times* (London: Hutchinson & Co., Ltd., 1954), p. 186.
2. Quoted in J. V. Ducattillon, "The Church in

the Third Republic," in *The Making of Modern Europe,* II, ed. by H. Ausubel (New York: Dryden Press, 1951), p. 861.

3. Quoted by C. J. H. Hayes, *A Political and Cultural History of Modern Europe,* II (New York: The Macmillan Company, 1939), p. 572.

4. Viscount Grey of Fallodon, *Twenty-Five Years,* II (New York: Frederick A. Stokes Co., 1925), p. 20.

CHAPTER 19: EXPANSION AND IMPERIALISM

1. W. L. Langer, "A Critique of Imperialism," in *The Making of Modern Europe,* II, ed. by H. Ausubel (New York: Dryden Press, 1951), p. 928.

2. From "The White Man's Burden" from *Rudyard Kipling's Verse: Definitive Edition* (British title: *The Five Nations).* Reprinted by permission of Doubleday & Company, Inc., Mrs. George Bambridge, Methuen & Co. Ltd. and the Macmillan Company of Canada Ltd.

3. P. D. Curtin, *African History* (New York: The Macmillan Company, for the American Historical Association, 1964), p. 40.

4. L. M. Thompson in Louis Hartz, *The Founding of New Societies* (New York: Harcourt Brace Jovanovich, Inc., 1964), p. 207.

5. R. N. Rosecrance in ibid., p. 285.

6. J. Gallagher and R. Robinson, "The Imperialism of Free Trade," *The Economic Review,* Vol. VI, No. I, 1953, pp. 1–15.

7. M. Israel, "Great Britain, Europe and Empire," in *Pax Britannica,* ed., by M. Israel (Edinburgh and London: Oliver and Boyd, 1968), p. 7.

8. See especially R. Robinson and J. Gallagher, *Africa and the Victorians* (New York: St. Martin's Press, 1961).

9. See Hannah Arendt, *The Origins of Totalitarianism* (New York: Meridian Books, 1958), esp. Ch. 5.

10. J. Schumpter, *Imperialism: Its Sociology* (New York: Meridian Books, 1955), p. 65.

11. Curtin, p. 48.

12. K. S. Latourette, *A Short History of the Far East* (New York: The Macmillan Company, 1947), p. 184.

13. Li Chien-nung, *The Political History of China, 1840–1928,* trans. by Sau-Yu-Teng and J. Ingalls (Princeton: D. Van Nostrand Co., Inc., 1956), p. 29.

14. Quoted in N. D. Harris, *Europe and the East* (Boston: Houghton Mifflin Co., 1926), p. 285.

15. B. Davidson, *Africa: History of a Continent* (New York: The Macmillan Company, 1966), p. 293.

16. J. A. Hobson, *Imperialism: A Study* (London: Constable and Co., Ltd., 1905), p. 324.

CHAPTER 20: THE WAGES OF WAR

1. Quoted in L. M. Hacker and B. B. Kendrick, *The United States Since 1865* (New York: F. S. Crofts and Co., 1939), p. 520.

2. Quoted in F. P. Walters, *A History of the*

League of Nations, I (London: Oxford University Press, 1952), p. 48.

3. Quoted in R. J. Sontag, *European Diplomatic History, 1871–1932* (New York: The Century Co., 1933), p. 275.

4. Quoted by E. Achorn, *European Civilization and Politics Since 1815* (New York: Harcourt Brace Jovanovich, Inc., 1938), p. 470.

5. Quoted in Sontag, p. 392.

6. J. M. Keynes, *The Economic Consequences of the Peace* (London: Macmillan and Co. Ltd., 1924), p. 211.

7. G. F. Kennan, *The Decision to Intervene* (Princeton: Princeton University Press, 1958), p. 471.

8. Quoted in W. C. Langsam, *The World Since 1914* (New York: The Macmillan Company, 1943), p. 685.

9. W. H. Chamberlain, *The Russian Revolution, 1917–1921,* I (New York: The Macmillan Company, 1952), p. 73.

10. *The New Cambridge Modern History,* XII, 1960, p. 9.

11. E. Crankshaw, cited in "The Coup That Changed the World," *New York Times Magazine,* February 19, 1967, p. 96.

12. Karl Lowenstein, in *Governments of Continetal Europe,* ed. by J. T. Shotwell (New York: The Macmillan Company, 1940), p. 473.

CHAPTER 21: THE TRAGIC DECADE AND GLOBAL CONFLICT

1. Quoted in F. P. Chambers, C. P. Grant, C. C. Bayley, *This Age of Conflict* (New York: Harcourt Brace Jovanovich, Inc., 1943), p. 495.

2. J. K. Galbraith, *The Great Crash, 1929* (Boston: Houghton Mifflin Co., 1955), p. 104.

3. Ibid., Chapter X.

4. John H. Williams, "Economic Lessons of Two World Wars," in *An Age of Controversy,* ed. by G. Wright and A. Mejia, Jr. (New York: Dodd, Mead and Company, 1966), p. 239.

5. Quoted in A. Bullock, *Hitler: A Study in Tyranny* (London: Odhams Press, Ltd., 1952), pp. 642–643.

6. R. G. L. Waite, ed., *Hitler and Nazi Germany* (New York: Holt, Rinehart & Winston, Inc., 1965), p. 4.

7. Quoted in W. C. Langsam, *Major European and Asiatic Developments Since 1935* (New York: The Macmillan Company, 1938), p. 15.

8. Quoted in W. L. Langer and S. E. Gleason, *The Challenge to Isolation* (New York: Harper & Bros., 1952), p. 181.

9. S. E. Ayling, *Portraits of Power* (New York: Barnes & Noble, Inc., 1963), p. 159.

10. W. S. Churchill, *Blood, Sweat and Tears* (New York: G. P. Putnam's Sons, 1941), p. 297.

PART SEVEN: TOWARD A NEW WORLD

1. A. Toffler, *Future Shock* (New York: Bantam Books, Inc., 1971), p. 35.

CHAPTER 22: THE QUEST FOR WORLD ORDER

1. Hugh Seton-Watson, *From Lenin to Khrushchev: The History of World Communism* (New York: Frederick A. Praeger, Inc., 1960), p. 246.

CHAPTER 23: THE WEST AND THE THIRD WORLD

1. Quoted in H. Kohn, *Nationalism and Imperialism in the Hither East* (London: G. Routledge and Sons, Ltd., 1932), pp. 132–133.
2. J. Nehru, *Toward Freedom* (New York: John Day Co., 1942), p. 353.
3. Quoted in T. Walter Wallbank, "The Future of Colonies," *World Affairs Interpreter* (Los Angeles, Winter 1945), p. 375.
4. Quoted in James S. Coleman, *Nigeria: Background to Nationalism* (Berkeley: University of California Press, 1958), p. 240.
5. Quoted in Wallbank, "The Future of Colonies," p. 379.
6. From Prime Minister Harold Macmillan's speech, February 3, 1960, *Vital Speeches* (March 1, 1960).
7. Quoted in Earl Louis Mountbatten, *Time Only to Look Forward* (London: Nicholas Kaye, 1949), p. 74.
8. I. F. Stone, "Holy War," *The New York Review of Books*, IX, (Aug. 3, 1967), pp. 12–13.
9. Denis Warner, "Vietnam," *Atlantic* (August 1969), p. 22.

CHAPTER 24: TOWARD A NEW LIFE STYLE

1. Henry Margenau, *The Nature of Physical Reality: A Philosophy of Modern Physics* (New York: McGraw-Hill, 1950), p. 39.
2. John Pfeiffer, *The Cell* (New York: Life Science Library, 1964), p. 61.
3. From "The Waste Land" from *Collected Poems, 1909–1962* by T. S. Eliot. Reprinted by permission of Harcourt Brace Jovanovich, Inc. and Faber and Faber Ltd.
4. *The Republic,* Book IV.
5. Poem "Cahier d'un retour au pays natal" by Aime Cesaire from *Pan-Africanism* by Colin Legum. Reprinted by permission of Praeger Publishers and Pall Mall Press Ltd.
6. Geoffrey Barraclough, *An Introduction to Contemporary History* (Baltimore: Penguin Books, Inc., 1964) p. 268.

EPILOGUE: THE CHALLENGES AHEAD

1. Siegfried Giedion, *Space, Time and Architecture* (Cambridge: Harvard University Press, 1967), p. 36.
2. E. Brandis and V. Dmitrevskiy, "The Future: Its Promoters and False Prophets," *The Magazine of Fantasy and Science Fiction* (October 1965), pp. 62–63.

LIST OF ILLUSTRATIONS

LIST OF MAPS

PRONOUNCING INDEX

Suggested pronunciations for difficult or unusual words are respelled according to the table below.

a	hat, cap	f	fat, if	o	hot, rock	u	cup, son
ā	age, face	g	go, bag	ō	open, go	u̇	put, book
ã	care, air	h	he, how	ô	order, all	ü	rule, move
ä	father, far			oi	oil, toy	ū	use, music
		i	it, pin	ou	out, now		
b	bad, rob	ī	ice, five			v	very, save
ch	child, much			p	pet, cup	w	will, woman
d	did, red	j	jam, enjoy	r	run, try	y	you, yet
		k	kind, seek	s	say, yes	z	zero, breeze
		l	land, coal	sh	she, rush	zh	measure, seizure
e	let, best	m	me, am	t	tell, it		
ē	equal, see	n	no, in	th	thin, both	ə	represents:
ėr	term, learn	ng	long, bring	₮н	then, smooth	*a*	in *a*bout
						e	in tak*e*n
						i	in penc*i*l
						o	in lem*o*n
						u	in circ*u*s

FOREIGN SOUNDS

Y
as in French *lune.* Pronounce ē with the lips rounded as for English u̇ in *rule.*

H
as in German *ach.* Pronounce k without closing the breath passage.

N
as in French *bon.* The N is not pronounced, showing rather that the vowel before it is nasal.

Œ
as in French *deux.* Pronounce ā with the lips rounded as for ō.

A

Abbasid (a bas′id)
Abélard (ab′ə lärd), Pierre
Abu Bakr (ə bü′ bak′ər)
Aeneas (i nē′əs)
Aeschylus (es′kə ləs)
Agincourt (aj′in kōrt′)
Aix-la-Chapelle (āks′ lä sha pel′)
Akhenaton (ä′ke nä′tən)
Akkad (äk′äd)
Albigensians (al′bə jen′si ənz)
Albuquerque (al′bü kərk), Afonso de
Alcuin (al′kwin)
Amenhotep (äm′ən hō′tep) III
Antigonus (an tig′ə nəs) the One-Eyed
Anjou (an′jü)
Arianism (ār′i ən izm)
Aristarchus (ar′is tär′kəs)
Aton (ä′ton)
Avars (ä′värz)
Averroës (ə ver′ō ēz′)
Avicenna (av′ə sen′ə)
Avignon (ä vē nyôn′)

B

Bakunin (bä kü nyēn), Michael
Beccaria (bek′ä rē′ä), Cesare
Bede (bēd), Venerable
Berchtold (berk′tōlt), Leopold von
Boccaccio, Giovanni (bō kä′chi ō, jô vän′nē)
Bodin (bō daN′), Jean (zhäN
Boethius (bō ē′thi əs)
Boleyn (bul′in), Anne
Bolívar, Simón (bō lē′vär, sē mōn′)
Bologna (bə lōn′yə)
Bramante (brä män′te), Donato
Brueghel (broe′gəl), Pieter, the Elder
Brunelleschi, Filippo (brü′nel les′kē, fē lēp′pô)

C

Calais (kal ā′)
Cambyses (kam bī′sēz)
Canaan (kā′nən)
Capetian (kə pē′shən) kings
Capuchins (kap′yù chinz)
Cassiodorus (kash ō dō′rəs)
Cézanne, Paul (sā zän′, pôl)
Charlemagne (shär′lə man)
Château-Thierry (sha tō′tyär′i)
Chiang Kai-shek (chyäng′ kī′shek′)
Cistercian (sis tėr′shən) order
Colbert, Jean Baptiste (kôl bār′, zhäN ba tēst′)
Comitatus (kom′i tā′təs)
Comte, Auguste (kôNt, ō gyst′)
Condorcet (kōN dôr sā′), Marquis de
Conquistadores (kông kes′tä dô′res)
Cortés (kôr tez′), Hernando
Courbet, Gustave (kür bā′, gys täv′)
Crecy (kres′i)
Croesus (krē′səs)
Cuneiform (kū nē′ə fôrm′)
Curie (kū rē), Marie and Pierre

D

Daladier (dä lä dyā′), Edouard
Dante Alighieri (dän′te, ä′lē gyär′ē)
Danton (däN tōN′ or dan′tən), Georges Jacques

Darius (də rī′əs)
Daumier, Honoré (dō myā′, ô nô rē′)
Da Vinci, Leonardo (dä vēn′chē, le′ô när′dô)
Debussy, Claude (də by sē′, klōd)
Delacroix (də lä krwä′), Eugene
Delian (dē′li ən) League
Democritus (di mok′rə təs)
Descartes (dā kärt′), René
Diaspora (dī as′pə ra)
Diderot, Denis (dēd rō′, de nē′)
Diocletian (di′ə klē′shən)
Dionysus (dī ə ni′səs)
Don Quixote (don kē hō′tē) *de la Mancha*
Dostoevsky (dos′to yef′ski), Feodor
Dreyfus (drā fYS′)
Du Bois (dü bois′), W. E. B.
Duns Scotus (dunz skō′təs)
Dürer, Albrecht, (dY′rər, al′breHt)

E

Ecbatana (ek bat′ə nə)
Eratosthenes (er′ə tos′thə nēz′)

F

Faisal (fī′səl), Emir
Ficino, Marsilio (fē chē′nō, mär sē′lyō)
Flaubert (flō bār′), Gustave
Foch (fôsh), Marshal
Fugger (fug′ər) family

G

Galilei, Galileo (gal ə lā′ē, gal ə lē′o)
Garibaldi, Giuseppe (gar′i bôl′di, jü sep′ā)
Genghis Khan (jeng′gis kän′)
Ghiberti (gē ber′tē), Lorenzo
Giorgione (jôr jô′ne)
Giotto (jot′ō)
Goa (gō′a)
Goethe (goe′t ə), Johann Wolfgang von
Gracchus (grak′əs)
Grotius (grō′shi əs), Hugo
Guise (gēz) family

H

Hagia Sophia (hä′jə sō fē′ə)
Haydn (hī′dən), Franz Joseph
Hegel (hā′gəl), Georg Wilhelm Friedrich
Hejaz (hē jaz′)
Héloïse (e lô ēz′)
Herod (her′əd) the Great
Herodotus (hi rod′ə təs)
Herzegovina (her′tsə gō vē′nə)
Hippocrates (hi pok′rə tēz)
Ho Chi Minh (hō′chē′min′)
Holbein (hōl′bīn), Hans
Homo sapiens (hō′mō sā′pi enz′)
Hyksos (hik′sōs)

I

Ibn-Khaldun (ib′ən käl dün′)
Ibn-Saud, Abdul-Aziz (ib′ən sä üd′, ab dúl′ a zēz′)
Ile de France (ēl da fräNs′)
Isis (ī′sis)
Iturbide (ē túr bē′dä), Agustín de

K

Khufu (kü′fü)
Kiaochow (kyou′chou′) Bay
Kiev (kē′ef)
Knossos (nos′əs)

L

Laos (lä′ōs)
Latifundia (Lat ə fun′di ə)
Leibnitz (līp′nits), Gottfried

M

Macao (mə kä′o)
Mao Tse-tung (mäü′ dzé′ dung′)
Marat (mä rä′), Jean Paul
Montaigne (mon tān′), Michel de
Montesquieu (mon′tes kū′)
Mozart (mō′zärt), Wolfgang
Mozambique (mō′zəm bēk′)
Mycenae (mī sē′nē)

N

Napier (nā′pi ər), John
Navarre (nə vär′)
Nebuchadnezzar (neb′yù kəd nez′ər)
Nefertete (nef′ər tē′tē)
Nehru (nā′rü), Jawaharlal
Neuilly (nœ yē′)
Nicaea (nï sē′ə)
Nice (nēs)
Nietzsche (nē′chə), Friedrich
Nike (nī′kē) rebellion
Nkrumah (eng′krü′mä), Kwame
Novgorod (nôv′go rot)

O

Odovacar (ō′dō vä′kər)
Omar Khayyám (ō′mär kī äm′)
Orestes (ō res′tēz)

P

Paracelsus (par′ə sel′səs)
Parlement (pärl ə män′)
Pergamum (pėr′gə məm)
Pétain (pā tən′), Marshal
Petrarch (pē′trärk)
Petrine (pē′trin) theory
Punic (pū′nik) Wars
Pylos (pī′los)
Pyrrhus (pir′əs)
Pythagoras (pi thag′ə rəs)

Q

Quattrocento (kwät′trô chen′tô)

R

Rabelais, Francois (rab′ə lā′, fräɴ swä′)
Ramses (ram′sēz)
Raphael (raf′i əl)
Rembrandt van Rijn (rem′bränt vän rīn)
Renoir (rə nwär′), Pierre Auguste (ō gʏst′)
Richelieu (rē shə lyœ′), Cardinal
Risorgimento (ri sôr′ji men′tō)
Rodin, Auguste (rō daɴ′, ō gʏst′)
Rousseau, Jean Jacques (rü sō′, zhäɴ zhäk)
Rurik (rùr′ik)

S

Salian (sā′li ən) House
San Martín (san mär tēn′), José de
Sappho (saf′ō)
Saudi (sä ü′di) Arabia
Savonarola (sav′ə nə rō′lə)
Schmalkaldic (shmäl käl′dik)
Seleucid (si lü′sid) empire
Seljuk (sel jük′) Turks
Servetus (sər vē′təs)
Solon (sō′län)
Stolypin (sto lē′pin), Piotr Arkadevich
Suleiman (sʏ′lä män′) the Magnificent
Sulla (sul′ə), Cornelius
Sumer (sü′mər)

T

Thailand (tī′land)
Thales (thā′lēz)
Theodosius (thē′ə dō′shi əs)
Thermopylae (thər mop′ə lē′)
Thucydides (thü sid′ə dēz′)
Thutmose (thut′mōz)
Titian (tish′ən)
Tojo (tō′jō), General
Tordesillas (tôr′de sē′lyäs), Treaty of
Tours (tür)
Treitschke (trīch′kə), Heinrich von
Turgenev (tür gen′yef), Ivan
Tyre (tīr)
Tzu Hsi (tsü′ shē′)

U

Uganda (ū gan′də)
Ulfilas (ul′fi ləs)
Umayyad (ù mī′yəd)
Ur (ėr)

V

Valois (vä lwä′) dynasty
Van Eyck (vän īk′), Jan
Van Gogh (van gôʜ′), Vincent
Varangians (ve ran′ji ənz)
Vesalius (vi sä′lē əs), Andreas
Vespasian (ves pā′zhi ən)
Vico (vē′kō), Giovanni Battista
Vietnam (vē et′näm′)

W

Wagner (väg′ner), Richard
Weimar (vī′mär)
Weismann (vīs′män), August
Witan (wit′ən)

X

Xavier (zā′vi ər), St. Francis
Xerxes (zerk′sēz)

Y

Yahweh (yä′we)
Yaroslav (yä ro släv′) the Wise

Z

Zoroaster (zō′rō as′tər)
Swingli (tsving′lē), Ulrich

INDEX